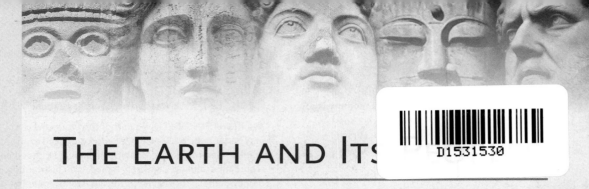

THE EARTH AND ITS

A GLOBAL HISTORY

VOLUME II:
Since 1500

FIFTH EDITION

Richard W. Bulliet
Columbia University

Pamela Kyle Crossley
Dartmouth College

Daniel R. Headrick
Roosevelt University

Steven W. Hirsch
Tufts University

Lyman L. Johnson
University of North Carolina—Charlotte

David Northrup
Boston College

WADSWORTH
CENGAGE Learning™

Australia • Brazil • Japan • Korea • Mexico • Singapore • Spain • United Kingdom • United States

WADSWORTH
CENGAGE Learning

The Earth and Its Peoples, 5e, Volume II
Richard W. Bulliet, Pamela Kyle Crossley,
Daniel R. Headrick, Steven W. Hirsch,
Lyman L. Johnson, David Northrup

Senior Publisher: Suzanne Jeans

Senior Acquisitions Editor: Nancy Blaine

Development Manager: Jeff Greene

Senior Development Editor: Tonya Lobato

Assistant Editor: Lauren Floyd

Editorial Assistant: Emma Goehring

Senior Media Editor: Lisa Ciccolo

Senior Marketing Manager: Katherine Bates

Marketing Coordinator: Lorreen Pelletier

Marketing Communications Manager:
    Christine Dobberpuhl

Senior Content Project Manager:
    Carol Newman

Senior Art Director: Cate Rickard Barr

Senior Print Buyer: Karen Hunt

Senior Rights Acquisition Account Manager:
    Katie Huha

Text Permissions Editor: Maria Maimone

Senior Photo Editor: Jennifer Meyer Dare

Photo Researcher: Carole Frohlich

Production Service: Lachina Publishing Services

Text Designer: Henry Rachlin

Cover Designer: Dutton & Sherman Design

Cover Image: Diego Rivera (1866–1957). "Rin
    del Corrido," detail of children learning.
    Mural, Court of Fiestas, Corridor of the
    Agrarian Revolution, West Wall, c. 1922–
    1928/Secretaria de Educaion Publica,
    Mexico City, D. F., Mexico/Schalkwijk/
    Art Resource, NY © 2011 Banco de Mexico
    Diego Rivera Frida Kahlo Museum Trust,
    Mexico, D. F./Artists Rights Society (ARS)

Compositor: Lachina Publishing Services

For product information and technology assistance, contact us at
Cengage Learning Customer & Sales Support, 1-800-354-9706
For permission to use material from this text or product,
submit all requests online at **www.cengage.com/permissions**
Further permissions questions can be emailed to
permissionrequest@cengage.com

Library of Congress Control Number: 2009931072

Student Edition:

ISBN-13: 978-1-4390-8475-5

ISBN-10: 1-4390-8475-0

Wadsworth
20 Channel Center Street
Boston, MA 02210
USA

Cengage Learning is a leading provider of customized learning solutions with
office locations around the globe, including Singapore, the United Kingdom,
Australia, Mexico, Brazil, and Japan. Locate your local office at:
international.cengage.com/region

Cengage Learning products are represented in Canada by Nelson Education, Ltd.

For your course and learning solutions, visit **www.cengage.com**

Purchase any of our products at your local college store or at our preferred
online store **www.ichapters.com**

Printed in the United States of America
1 2 3 4 5 6 7 13 12 11 10 09

BRIEF CONTENTS

CONTENTS

MAPS

FEATURES

 ENVIRONMENT + TECHNOLOGY

 DIVERSITY + DOMINANCE

 MATERIAL CULTURE

 ISSUES IN WORLD HISTORY

PREFACE

When this textbook reached its fourth edition, the authors felt justified in deeming their work a success. The first edition contained a basic concept. The second used the myriad valuable comments made by teachers and reviewers to make major adjustments in the presentation of that concept. The third edition incorporated a further round of comments and suggestions aimed at filling lacunae and improving the flow of the exposition. In the fourth edition the authors focused on refining their work, updating bibliographies, and incorporating the most recent scholarship. As in each prior edition, expanded features and improved pedagogical aids played important roles in the revision process.

In the fifth edition it is the look and feel of the book that we have rethought in the interest of making the text more inviting and accessible to today's students of world history. The transition from a two-column to a one-column page layout was not easy. It entailed trimming words from the main narrative of the text without sacrificing significant content. Each author approached this task with a sigh, but with a realization that all written works, whether nonfiction or fiction, can benefit from yet one more revision concentrating on fluency and precision of expression. They also recognized that the resulting pages would be not only easier to read, but also graced with ample margins for auxiliary references, glossary definitions, and other pedagogical aids. Adding substantially to the book's new look is a completely redrawn set of maps that are both more vivid and more informative than the maps they replace.

Yet the overall goal of *The Earth and Its Peoples* remains unchanged: a textbook that speaks not only for the past but also to today's student and teacher. Students and instructors alike should take away from this text a broad vision of human societies beginning as sparse and disconnected communities reacting creatively to local circumstances; experiencing ever more intensive stages of contact, interpenetration, and cultural expansion and amalgamation; and arriving at a twenty-first-century world in which people increasingly visualize a single global community.

Process, not progress, is the keynote of this book: a steady process of change over time, at first differently experienced in various regions, but eventually connecting peoples and traditions from all parts of the globe. Students should come away from this book with a sense that the problems and promises of their world are rooted in a past in which people of every sort, in every part of the world, confronted problems of a similar character and coped with them as best they could. We believe that our efforts will help students see where their world has come from and learn thereby something useful for their own lives.

CENTRAL THEMES AND GOALS

We subtitled *The Earth and Its Peoples* "A Global History" because the book explores the common challenges and experiences that unite the human past. Although the dispersal of early humans to every livable environment resulted in a myriad of different economic, social, political, and cultural systems, all societies displayed analogous patterns in meeting their needs and exploiting their environments. Our challenge was to select the particular data and episodes that would best illuminate these global patterns of human experience.

To meet this challenge, we adopted two themes for our history: "technology and the environment" and "diversity and dominance." The first theme represents the commonplace material bases of all human societies at all times. It grants no special favor to any cultural group even as it embraces subjects of the broadest topical, chronological, and geographical range. The second theme expresses the reality that every human society has constructed or inherited structures of domination. We examine practices and institutions of many sorts: military, economic, social, political, religious, and cultural, as well as those based on kinship, gender, and literacy. Simultaneously we recognize that alternative ways of life and visions of societal organization continually manifest themselves both within and in dialogue with every structure of domination.

With respect to the first theme, it is vital for students to understand that technology, in the broad sense of experience-based knowledge of the physical world, underlies all human activity. Writing is a technology, but so is oral transmission from generation to generation of lore about medicinal or poisonous plants. The magnetic compass is a navigational technology, but so is Polynesian mariners' hard-won knowledge of winds, currents, and tides that made possible the settlement of the Pacific islands.

All technological development has come about in interaction with environments, both physical and human, and has, in turn, affected those environments. The story of how humanity has changed the face of the globe is an integral part of our first theme. Yet technology and the environment do not explain or underlie all important episodes of human experience. The theme of "diversity and dominance" informs all our discussions of politics, culture, and society. Thus when narrating the histories of empires, we describe a range of human experiences within and beyond the imperial frontiers without assuming that imperial institutions are a more fit topic for discussion than the economic and social organization of pastoral nomads or the lives of peasant women. When religion and culture occupy our narrative, we focus not only on the dominant tradition but also on the diversity of alternative beliefs and practices.

ORGANIZATION

The Earth and Its Peoples uses eight broad chronological divisions to define its conceptual scheme of global historical development.

In **Part One: The Emergence of Human Communities, to 500 B.C.E.**, we examine important patterns of human communal organization in both the Eastern and Western Hemispheres. Small, dispersed human communities living by foraging spread to most parts of the world over tens of thousands of years. They responded to enormously diverse environmental conditions, at different times in different ways, discovering how to cultivate plants and utilize the products of domestic animals. On the basis of these new modes of sustenance, population grew, permanent towns appeared, and political and religious authority, based on collection and control of agricultural surpluses, spread over extensive areas.

Part Two: The Formation of New Cultural Communities, 1000 B.C.E.–400 C.E., introduces the concept of a "cultural community," in the sense of a coherent pattern of activities and symbols pertaining to a specific human community. While all human communities develop distinctive cultures, including those discussed in Part One, historical development in this stage of global history prolonged and magnified the impact of some cultures more than others. In the geographically contiguous African-Eurasian landmass, the cultures that proved to have the most enduring influence traced their roots to the second and first millennia B.C.E.

Part Three: Growth and Interaction of Cultural Communities, 300 B.C.E.–1200 C.E., deals with early episodes of technological, social, and cultural exchange and interaction on a continental scale both within and beyond the framework of imperial expansion. These are so different from earlier interactions arising from more limited conquests or extensions of political boundaries that they constitute a distinct era in world history, an era that set the world on the path of increasing global interaction and interdependence that it has been following ever since.

In **Part Four: Interregional Patterns of Culture and Contact, 1200–1550**, we look at the world during the three and a half centuries that saw both intensified cultural and commercial contact and increasingly confident self-definition of cultural communities in Europe, Asia, and Africa. The Mongol conquest of a vast empire extending from the Pacific Ocean to eastern Europe greatly stimulated trade and interaction. In the West, strengthened European kingdoms began maritime expansion in the Atlantic, forging direct ties with sub-Saharan Africa and beginning the conquest of the civilizations of the Western Hemisphere.

Part Five: The Globe Encompassed, 1500–1750, treats a period dominated by the global effects of European expansion and continued economic growth. European ships took over, expanded, and extended the maritime trade of the Indian Ocean, coastal Africa, and the Asian rim of the Pacific Ocean. This maritime commercial enterprise had its counterpart in European colonial empires in the Americas and a new Atlantic trading system. The contrasting capacities and fortunes of traditional land empires and new maritime empires, along with the exchange of domestic plants and animals between the hemispheres, underline the technological and environmental dimensions of this first era of complete global interaction.

In **Part Six: Revolutions Reshape the World, 1750–1870**, the word *revolution* is used in several senses: in the political sense of governmental overthrow, as in France and the Americas; in the metaphorical sense of radical transformative change, as in the Industrial Revolution; and in the broadest sense of a perception of a profound change in circumstances and world-view. Technology and environment lie at the core of these developments. With the rapid ascendancy of the Western belief that science and technology could overcome all challenges—environmental or otherwise—technology became an instrument not only of transformation but also of domination, to the point of threatening the integrity and autonomy of cultural traditions in nonindustrial lands.

Part Seven: Global Diversity and Dominance, 1850–1945, examines the development of a world arena in which people conceived of events on a global scale. Imperialism, world war, international economic connections, and world-encompassing ideological tendencies, such as nationalism and socialism, present the picture of a globe becoming increasingly interconnected. European dominance took on a worldwide dimension, seeming at times to threaten the diversity of human cultural experience with permanent subordination to European values and philosophies, while at other times triggering strong political or cultural resistance.

For **Part Eight: Perils and Promises of a Global Community, 1945 to the Present**, we divided the period since World War II into three time periods: 1945–1975, 1975–1991, and 1991 to the present. The challenges of the Cold War and postcolonial nation building dominated most of the period and unleashed global economic, technological, and political forces that became increasingly important in all aspects of human life. Technology is a key topic in Part Eight because of its integral role in the growth of a global community and because its many benefits in improving the quality of life seem clouded by real and potential negative impacts on the environment. Also highlighted are the harsh realities of war and economic disruption that have marked the first decade of the twenty-first century.

FEATURES AND NEW PEDAGOGICAL AIDS

As with previous editions, the fifth edition offers a number of valuable features and pedagogical aids designed to pique student interest in specific world history topics and help them process and retain key information. Historical essays for each of the eight parts called *Issues in World History* were added in the previous edition and were specifically designed to alert students to broad and recurring conceptual issues that are of great interest to contemporary historians; this feature has proved to be an instructor and student favorite. Four in-chapter essays on *Material Culture*, also new in the previous edition, call particular attention to the many ways in which objects and processes of everyday life can play a role in understanding human history on a broad scale. Thus essays like "Wine and Beer in the Ancient World" and "Fast Food" are not only interesting in and of themselves but also suggestive of how today's world historians find meaning in the ordinary dimensions of human life. The *Environment and Technology* feature, which has been a valuable resource in all prior editions of *The Earth and its Peoples*, serves to illuminate the major theme of the text by demonstrating the shared material bases of all human societies across time. Finally, *Diversity and Dominance*, also core to the theme of the text, is the primary source feature that brings a myriad of real historical voices to life in a common struggle for power and autonomy.

Pedagogical aids include the following:

Chapter Opening Focus Questions   These questions are keyed to every major subdivision of the chapter and serve to help students focus on the core chapter concepts.

New Section Reviews   Short bullet-point reviews have been added in this edition to summarize each major section in every chapter and remind students of key information.

New Chapter Conclusions   Every chapter now ends with a comparative conclusion that replaces the old summaries and helps students better synthesize chapter material and understand how it fits into the larger picture.

New Section Headings   Additional section headings have been added in every chapter to help organize the material into smaller digestible units and to help students and instructors locate key parts of the discussion.

New Marginal Key Term with Definitions   Students will no longer have to flip to the back of the textbook to look up unfamiliar terms.

New Icons   Throughout each chapter, icons direct students to corresponding online tools including interactive maps and primary sources.

New Web Resource Boxes   A complete list of website assets is provided at the end of every chapter.

CHANGES IN THIS EDITION

In addition to the many new pedagogical aids outlined above, numerous minor chapter-by-chapter changes have been made, including new illustrations, new maps, streamlining of the textual discussion, and updates to many of the boxed feature essays. Here are a few highlights:

- Chapter 1 has been updated to include chronological dates based on the most current thinking and a new discussion of how modern tools including genetic evidence have led to insights about the origin of the human species.
- An expanded discussion of external influences on early Southeast Asian civilizations appears in Chapter 7.
- Chapter 10 updates include a revised discussion of the beleaguered Byzantine Empire and factors that contributed to its demise, including Arab invasions and religious schisms.
- A new section heading in Chapter 10 called "The Time of Insecurity" discusses Muslim invasions and the rise of the Carolingian Empire in Medieval Europe.
- A revised discussion of Social Rebellion after the Black Death now appears in Chapter 15.
- A new heading in Chapter 17 called "The Counter Reformation and the Politics of Religion" includes a discussion of religion and the ambition of kings.
- The introduction to Chapter 22 has been revised.
- Chapter 32 includes an updated discussion about the Cold War confrontation between West and East plus a revised discussion of apartheid and South Africa's struggle for independence.
- The Environment and Technology feature in Chapter 33 has been thoroughly updated to include discussion and pictures of the latest technology.
- Chapter 34 features new material on the 2008 presidential election and the economic crisis. In addition, a new Diversity and Dominance feature called "Conflict and Civilization" now appears in this chapter.

FORMATS

To accommodate different academic calendars and approaches to the course, *The Earth and Its Peoples* is available in three formats. There is a one-volume hardcover version containing all 34 chapters, along with a two-volume paperback edition: Volume I: To 1550 (Chapters 1–16) and Volume II: Since 1500 (Chapters 16–34). For readers at institutions with the quarter system, we offer a three-volume paperback version: Volume A: To 1200 (Chapters 1–12), Volume B: From 1200 to 1870 (Chapters 12–26), and Volume C: Since 1750 (Chapters 22–34). Volume II includes an Introduction that surveys the main developments set out in Volume I and provides a groundwork for students studying only the period since 1500.

ANCILLARIES

A wide array of supplements accompany this text to assist students with different learning needs and to help instructors master today's various classroom challenges.

Instructor Resources

PowerLecture CD-ROM with ExamView® and JoinIn® This dual platform, all-in-one multimedia resource includes the Instructor's Resource Manual; Test Bank (content developed by Kathleen Addison of California State University, Northridge, and includes key term identification, multiple-choice, short answer/essay, and map questions); Microsoft® PowerPoint® slides of both lecture outlines and images and maps from the text that can be used as offered, or customized by importing personal lecture slides or other material; and JoinIn® PowerPoint® slides with clicker content. Also included is ExamView, an easy-to-use assessment and tutorial system that allows instructors to create, deliver, and customize tests in minutes. Instructors can build tests with as many as 250 questions using up to 12 question types, and using ExamView's complete word-processing capabilities, they can enter an unlimited number of new questions or edit existing ones.

HistoryFinder This searchable online database allows instructors to quickly and easily download thousands of assets, including art, photographs, maps, primary sources, and audio/video clips. Each asset downloads directly into a Microsoft® PowerPoint® slide, allowing instructors to easily create exciting PowerPoint presentations for their classrooms.

eInstructor's Resource Manual Prepared by Sheila Phipps of Appalachian State University. This manual has many features, including instructional objectives, chapter outlines, lecture suggestions, suggested debate and research topics, cooperative learning activities, and suggested online resources. Available on the instructor's companion website.

WebTutor™ on Blackboard® With WebTutor's text-specific, pre-formatted content and total flexibility, instructors can easily create and manage their own custom course website. WebTutor's course management tool gives instructors the ability to provide virtual office hours, post syllabi, set up threaded discussions, track student progress with the quizzing material, and much more. For students, WebTutor offers real-time access to a full array of study tools, including animations and videos that bring the book's topics to life, plus chapter outlines, summaries, learning objectives, glossary flashcards (with audio), practice quizzes, and weblinks.

WebTutor™ on WebCT® With WebTutor's text-specific, pre-formatted content and total flexibility, instructors can easily create and manage their own custom course website. WebTutor's course management tool gives instructors the ability to provide virtual office hours, post syllabi, set up threaded discussions, track student progress with the quizzing material, and much more. For students, WebTutor offers real-time access to a full array of study tools, including animations and videos that bring the book's topics to life, plus chapter outlines, summaries, learning objectives, glossary flashcards (with audio), practice quizzes, and weblinks.

WebTutor™ on Angel® With WebTutor's text-specific, pre-formatted content and total flexibility, instructors can easily create and manage their own custom course website.

WebTutor's course management tool gives instructors the ability to provide virtual office hours, post syllabi, set up threaded discussions, track student progress with the quizzing material, and much more. For students, WebTutor offers real-time access to a full array of study tools, including animations and videos that bring the book's topics to life, plus chapter outlines, summaries, learning objectives, glossary flashcards (with audio), practice quizzes, and weblinks.

Student Resources

Book Companion Site A website for students that features a wide assortment of resources to help students master the subject matter. The website includes a glossary, flashcards, crossword puzzles, learning objectives, pre-class quizzes, essay questions, critical thinking exercises, and weblinks. Throughout the text, icons direct students to relevant exercises and self-testing material located on the student companion website.

CL eBook This interactive multimedia ebook links out to rich media assets such as video and MP3 chapter summaries. Through this ebook, students can also access self-test quizzes, chapter outlines, focus questions, fill-in-the-blank exercises, chronology puzzles, essay questions (for which the answers can be emailed to their instructors), primary source documents with critical thinking questions, and interactive (zoomable) maps. Available on iChapters.

iChapters Save your students time and money. Tell them about www.iChapters.com for choice in formats and savings and a better chance to succeed in your class. iChapters.com, Cengage Learning's online store, is a single destination for more than 10,000 new textbooks, eTextbooks, eChapters, study tools, and audio supplements. Students have the freedom to purchase a-la-carte exactly what they need when they need it. Students can save 50 percent on the electronic textbook, and can pay as little as $1.99 for an individual eChapter.

Wadsworth World History Resource Center Wadsworth's World History Resource Center gives your students access to a "virtual reader" with hundreds of primary sources including speeches, letters, legal documents and transcripts, poems, maps, simulations, timelines, and additional images that bring history to life, along with interactive assignable exercises. A map feature including Google Earth™ coordinates and exercises will aid in student comprehension of geography and use of maps. Students can compare the traditional textbook map with an aerial view of the location today. It's an ideal resource for study, review, and research. In addition to this map feature, the resource center also provides blank maps for student review and testing.

Writing for College History, 1e Prepared by Robert M. Frakes, Clarion University. This brief handbook for survey courses in American history, Western Civilization/European history, and world civilization guides students through the various types of writing assignments they encounter in a history class. Providing examples of student writing and candid assessments of student work, this text focuses on the rules and conventions of writing for the college history course.

The History Handbook, 1e Prepared by Carol Berkin of Baruch College, City University of New York and Betty Anderson of Boston University. This book teaches students both basic and history-specific study skills such as how to read primary sources, research historical topics, and correctly cite sources. Substantially less expensive than comparable skill-building texts, *The History Handbook* also offers tips for Internet research and evaluating online sources.

Doing History: Research and Writing in the Digital Age, 1e Prepared by Michael J. Galgano, J. Chris Arndt, and Raymond M. Hyser of James Madison University. Whether you're starting down the path as a history major, or simply looking for a straightforward and systematic guide to writing a successful paper, you'll find this text to be an indispensible handbook to historical research. This text's "soup to nuts" approach to researching and writing about history addresses every step of the process, from locating your sources and gathering information, to writing clearly and making proper use of various citation styles to avoid plagiarism. You'll also learn how to make the most of every tool available to you—especially the technology that helps you conduct the process efficiently and effectively.

The Modern Researcher, 6e Prepared by Jacques Barzun and Henry F. Graff of Columbia University. This classic introduction to the techniques of research and the art of expression is used widely in history courses, but is also appropriate for writing and research methods courses in other departments. Barzun and Graff thoroughly cover every aspect of research, from the selection of a topic through the gathering, analysis, writing, revision, and publication of findings, presenting the process not as a set of rules but through actual cases that put the subtleties of research in a useful context. Part One covers the principles and methods of research; Part Two covers writing, speaking, and getting one's work published.

Reader Program Cengage Learning publishes a number of readers, some containing exclusively primary sources, others a combination of primary and secondary sources, and some designed to guide students through the process of historical inquiry. Visit Cengage.com/history for a complete list of readers.

Custom Options Nobody knows your students like you, so why not give them a text that is tailor-fit to their needs? Cengage Learning offers custom solutions for your course—whether it's making a small modification to *The Earth and Its Peoples* to match your syllabus or combining multiple sources to create something truly unique. You can pick and choose chapters, include your own material, and add additional map exercises along with the Rand McNally Atlas to create a text that fits the way you teach. Ensure that your students get the most out of their textbook dollar by giving them exactly what they need. Contact your Cengage Learning representative to explore custom solutions for your course.

Rand McNally Historical Atlas of the World, 2e This valuable resource features over 70 maps that portray the rich panoply of the world's history from preliterate times to the present. They show how cultures and civilization were linked and how they interacted. The maps make it clear that history is not static. Rather, it is about change and movement across time. The maps show change by presenting the dynamics of expansion, cooperation, and conflict. This atlas includes maps that display the world from the beginning of civilization; the political development of all major areas of the world; expanded coverage of Africa, Latin America, and the Middle East; the current Islamic World; and the world population change in 1900 and 2000.

Document Exercise Workbook Prepared by Donna Van Raaphorst, Cuyahoga Community College. A collection of exercises based around primary sources. Available in two volumes.

ACKNOWLEDGMENTS

In preparing the fifth edition, we benefited from the critical readings of many colleagues. Our sincere thanks go in particular to the following instructors: Susan Autry, Central Piedmont Community College; Anna Collins, Arkansas Tech University; William Connell, Christopher Newport University; Gregory Crider, Winthrop University; Shawn Dry, Oakland Community College; Nancy Fitch, California State University, Fullerton; Christine Haynes, University of North Carolina at Charlotte; Mark Herman, Edison College; Ellen J. Jenkins, Arkansas Tech University; Frank Karpiel, The Citadel; Ken Koons, Virginia Military Institute; David Longfellow, Baylor University; Heather Lucas, Georgia Perimeter College; Jeff Pardue, Gainesville State College; Craig Patton, Alabama A & M University; Linda Scherr, Mercer County Community College; Robert Sherwood, Georgia Military College; Brett Shufelt, Copiah-Lincoln Community College; Kristen Walton, Salisbury University; Christopher Ward, Clayton State University; William Wood, Point Loma Nazarene University.

When textbook authors set out on a project, they are inclined to believe that 90 percent of the effort will be theirs and 10 percent that of various editors and production specialists employed by their publisher. How very naïve. This book would never have seen the light of day had it not been for the unstinting labors of the great team of professionals who turned the authors' words into beautifully presented print. Our debt to the staff of Wadsworth, Cengage Learning remains undiminished in the fifth edition. Nancy Blaine, senior acquisitions editor, has offered us firm but sympathetic guidance throughout the revision process. Tonya

Lobato, senior development editor, offered astute and sympathetic assistance as the authors worked to incorporate many new ideas and subjects into the text. Carol Newman, senior content project manager, moved the work through the production stages to meet a challenging schedule. Carole Frohlich did an outstanding job of photo research. And Susan Zorn again lent her considerable copyediting skills to the text.

We thank also the many students whose questions and concerns, expressed directly or through their instructors, shaped much of this revision. We continue to welcome all readers' suggestions, queries, and criticisms. Please contact us at our respective institutions.

ABOUT THE AUTHORS

RICHARD W. BULLIET Professor of Middle Eastern History at Columbia University, Richard W. Bulliet received his Ph.D. from Harvard University. He has written scholarly works on a number of topics: the social and economic history of medieval Iran (*The Patricians of Nishapur* and *Cotton, Climate, and Camels in Early Islamic Iran*), the history of human-animal relations (*The Camel and the Wheel* and *Hunters, Herders, and Hamburgers*), the process of conversion to Islam (*Conversion to Islam in the Medieval Period*), and the overall course of Islamic social history (*Islam: The View from the Edge* and *The Case for Islamo-Christian Civilization*). He is the editor of the *Columbia History of the Twentieth Century*. He has published four novels, coedited *The Encyclopedia of the Modern Middle East*, and hosted an educational television series on the Middle East. He was awarded a fellowship by the John Simon Guggenheim Memorial Foundation and was named a Carnegie Corporation Scholar.

PAMELA KYLE CROSSLEY Pamela Kyle Crossley received her Ph.D. in Modern Chinese History from Yale University. She is Professor of History and Rosenwald Research Professor in the Arts and Sciences at Dartmouth College. Her books include *A Translucent Mirror: History and Identity in Qing Imperial Ideology*; *The Manchus*; *Orphan Warriors: Three Manchu Generations and the End of the Qing World*; and (with Lynn Hollen Lees and John W. Servos) *Global Society: The World Since 1900*. Her research, which concentrates on the cultural history of China, Inner Asia, and Central Asia, has been supported by the John Simon Guggenheim Memorial Foundation and the National Endowment for the Humanities.

DANIEL R. HEADRICK Daniel R. Headrick received his Ph.D. in History from Princeton University. Professor of History and Social Science, Emeritus, at Roosevelt University in Chicago, he is the author of several books on the history of technology, imperialism, and international relations, including *The Tools of Empire: Technology and European Imperialism in the Nineteenth Century*; *The Tentacles of Progress: Technology Transfer in the Age of Imperialism*; *The Invisible Weapon: Telecommunications and International Politics*; *Technology: A World History*; *Power Over Peoples: Technology, Environments and Western Imperialism, 1400 to the Present*; and *When Information Came of Age: Technologies of Knowledge in the Age of Reason and Revolution, 1700–1850*. His articles have appeared in the *Journal of World History* and the *Journal of Modern History*, and he has been awarded fellowships by the National Endowment for the Humanities, the John Simon Guggenheim Memorial Foundation, and the Alfred P. Sloan Foundation.

STEVEN W. HIRSCH Steven W. Hirsch holds a Ph.D. in Classics from Stanford University and is currently Associate Professor of Classics and History at Tufts University. He has received grants from the National Endowment for the Humanities and the Massachusetts Foundation for Humanities and Public Policy. His research and publications include *The Friendship of the Barbarians: Xenophon and the Persian Empire*, as well as articles and reviews in the *Classical Journal*, the *American Journal of Philology*, and the *Journal of Interdisciplinary History*. He is currently working on a comparative study of ancient Mediterranean and Chinese civilizations.

LYMAN L. JOHNSON Professor of History at the University of North Carolina at Charlotte, Lyman L. Johnson earned his Ph.D. in Latin American History from the University of Connecticut. A two-time Senior Fulbright-Hays Lecturer, he also has received fellowships from the Tinker Foundation, the Social Science Research Council, the National Endowment for the Humanities, and the American Philosophical Society. His recent books include *Death, Dismemberment, and Memory*; *The Faces of Honor* (with Sonya Lipsett-Rivera); *The Problem of Order in Changing Societies*; *Essays on the Price History of Eighteenth-Century Latin America* (with Enrique Tandeter); and *Colonial Latin America* (with Mark A. Burkholder). He also has published in journals, including the *Hispanic American Historical Review*, the *Journal of Latin American Studies*, the *International Review of Social History*, *Social History*, and *Desarrollo Económico*. He recently served as president of the Conference on Latin American History.

DAVID NORTHRUP Professor of History at Boston College, David Northrup earned his Ph.D. in African and European History from the University of California at Los Angeles. He earlier taught in Nigeria with the Peace Corps and at Tuskegee Institute. Research supported by the Fulbright-Hays Commission, the National Endowment for the Humanities, and the Social Science Research Council led to publications concerning pre-colonial Nigeria, the Congo (1870–1940), the Atlantic slave trade, and Asian, African, and Pacific islander indentured labor in the nineteenth century. A contributor to the *Oxford History of the British Empire* and *Blacks in the British Empire*, his latest book is *Africa's Discovery of Europe, 1450–1850*. In 2004 and 2005 he served as president of the World History Association.

NOTE ON SPELLING AND USAGE

Where necessary for clarity, dates are followed by the letters C.E. or B.C.E. The abbreviation C.E. stands for "Common Era" and is equivalent to A.D. (*anno Domini*, Latin for "in the year of the Lord"). The abbreviation B.C.E. stands for "before the Common Era" and means the same as B.C. ("before Christ"). In keeping with our goal of approaching world history without special concentration on one culture or another, we chose these neutral abbreviations as appropriate to our enterprise. Because many readers will be more familiar with English than with metric measurements, however, units of measure are generally given in the English system, with metric equivalents following in parentheses.

In general, Chinese has been Romanized according to the *pinyin* method. Exceptions include proper names well established in English (e.g., *Canton, Chiang Kaishek*) and a few English words borrowed from Chinese (e.g., *kowtow*). Spellings of Arabic, Ottoman Turkish, Persian, Mongolian, Manchu, Japanese, and Korean names and terms avoid special diacritical marks for letters that are pronounced only slightly differently in English. An apostrophe is used to indicate when two Chinese syllables are pronounced separately (e.g., *Chang'an*).

For words transliterated from languages that use the Arabic script—Arabic, Ottoman Turkish, Persian, Urdu—the apostrophe indicating separately pronounced syllables may represent either of two special consonants, the *hamza* or the *ain*. Because most English-speakers do not hear the distinction between these two, they have not been distinguished in transliteration and are not indicated when they occur at the beginning or end of a word. As with Chinese, some words and commonly used place-names from these languages are given familiar English spellings (e.g., *Quran* instead of *Qur'an, Cairo* instead of *al-Qahira*). Arabic romanization has normally been used for terms relating to Islam, even where the context justifies slightly different Turkish or Persian forms, again for ease of comprehension.

Before 1492 the inhabitants of the Western Hemisphere had no single name for themselves. They had neither a racial consciousness nor a racial identity. Identity was derived from kin groups, language, cultural practices, and political structures. There was no sense that physical similarities created a shared identity. America's original inhabitants had racial consciousness and racial identity imposed on them by conquest and the occupation of their lands by Europeans after 1492. All of the collective terms for these first American peoples are tainted by this history. *Indians, Native Americans, Amerindians, First Peoples,* and *Indigenous Peoples* are among the terms in common usage. In this book the names of individual cultures and states are used wherever possible. *Amerindian* and other terms that suggest transcultural identity and experience are used most commonly for the period after 1492.

There is an ongoing debate about how best to render Amerindian words in English. It has been common for authors writing in English to follow Mexican usage for Nahuatl and Yucatec Maya words and place-names. In this style, for example, the capital of the Aztec state is spelled Tenochtitlán, and the important late Maya city-state is spelled Chichén Itzá. Although these forms are still common even in the specialist literature, we have chosen to follow the scholarship that sees these accents as unnecessary. The exceptions are modern place-names, such as Mérida and Yucatán, which are accented. A similar problem exists for the spelling of Quechua and Aymara words from the Andean region of South America. Although there is significant disagreement among scholars, we follow the emerging consensus and use the spellings *khipu* (not *quipu*), *Tiwanaku* (not *Tiahuanaco*), and *Wari* (not *Huari*). However, we keep *Inca* (not *Inka*) and *Cuzco* (not *Cusco*), since these spellings are expected by most of our potential readers and we hope to avoid confusion.

The World Before 1500

- Antiquity: Humans, Cultures, and Conquests, to 400 c.e.
- Growth and Interaction, 400-1200
- Interregional Conquests and Exchanges, 1200-1500

History occurs in a continuous stream. Because new events are the products of their past, each historical period is intimately linked to what preceded it. As a Roman historian put it, "History doesn't make leaps." Nevertheless, modern historians find it useful to divide the past into eras or ages to make sense of the sweep of history. The longest historical eras are antiquity, the Middle Ages, and modern times. Volume II of *The Earth and Its Peoples* is devoted to the third of these—modern world history, the five centuries since about 1500.

World historians largely agree that the intensity of interaction around the world during the modern period distinguishes it from all earlier times. European maritime exploration opened up or intensified these contacts. The modern era is also characterized by the steady expansion of European political, economic, and cultural leadership in every part of the world.

How and when different parts of the world felt the impact of the West varied. By 1500 parts of the Americas were already reeling under the impact of their first contacts with Europeans, but in most other parts of the world the West did not make a big difference until the century after 1750 or even later. Thus, while in hindsight Western ascendancy seems to be a defining theme of modern history, for the people of Asia, Africa, and elsewhere the modern era was a time in which the internal patterns of historical change only gradually became altered by the growing influence of Westerners and by their own reactions to these influences.

In order to explain how the modern era came into being, the first chapter of Volume II of *The Earth and Its Peoples* (Chapter 16) begins in about 1450. To help the reader understand the broader sweep of history, this Introduction provides an overview of earlier eras. The Introduction reviews three periods of decreasing temporal length. The first is the very long period from human origins until the end of ancient history in about 400 c.e. Next comes the early medieval period down to about 1200; and, finally, the three hundred years immediately preceding 1500. Because the centuries after 1200 were most important for shaping the transition to the modern era, they receive the most detailed treatment.

ANTIQUITY: HUMANS, CULTURES, AND CONQUESTS, TO 400 C.E.

All historical periods were shaped by natural environment and human technology (whether simple tools, techniques, or complex machines). The paramount role played by environmental forces is apparent when historians seek to explain how human beings—and thus history—began. Like all other living creatures, early humans were products of biological adjustments to changing environments. Over millions of years, our ancestors in eastern and southern Africa evolved biologically to enhance their chances for survival. The evolution of an upright posture enabled early people to walk and run on two legs, thereby freeing their hands for tool making. The evolution of larger brains gave them the capacity to learn and understand all sorts of new things and devise techniques for putting them to use. Finally, evolutionary changes in the throat gave humans the capacity for speech, which, as language developed, had the dual effect of making complex social relations easier and fostering the development of intellectual culture.

With these physical traits in place, humans were able to develop in a direction taken by no other creature. Instead of relying on the glacially slow process of biological evolution to adapt their bodies to new environments, our ancestors used their minds to devise technologies for transforming nature to suit their needs. By the standards of today, these early technologies may seem crude—stone tools for cutting and chopping, clothing made from plants and animal skins, shelters in caves and huts—but they were sufficient to enable humans to survive environmental changes in their homelands. They also enabled bands of humans to migrate to new environments in every part of the world. Through trial and error Stone Age people learned what could safely be eaten in new environments. Other primates acted primarily by instinct; humans acted according to the dictates of culture. The capacity to create and change material and intellectual culture marked the beginning of human history.

Agricultural Civilizations

Beginning about 10,000 years ago, the transition from food gathering to food production marked a major turning point in history. Human communities in many different parts of the world learned to alter the natural food supply. Some people promoted the growth of foods they liked by scattering seeds on good soils and restricting the growth of competing plants. In time some people became full-time farmers. Other communities tamed wild animals whose meat, milk, fur, and hides they desired, and they controlled their breeding to produce animals with the most desired characteristics. Promoted by a warmer world climate, these agricultural revolutions slowly spread from the Middle East around the Mediterranean. People in South and East Asia, Africa, and the Americas domesticated other wild plants and animals for their use. Just as humans had ceased to rely on evolution to enable them to adjust to new surroundings, so too they had bypassed evolution in bringing new species of plants and animals into existence (see Map I.1).

The agricultural revolutions greatly enhanced people's chances for survival in two ways. One was a rapid increase in population fostered by the ability to grow and store more food (see Issues in World History: Climate and Population, to 1500). A second change was taking place in the composition of human communities. The earliest communities consisted of small bands of biologically related people and their spouses from other bands. However, more complex societies made their first appearances as more and more unrelated people concentrated in lush river valleys, where the soils, temperatures, and potential to irrigate with river water produced conditions suitable for farming.

In the Fertile Crescent of the Middle East, Egypt, India, and China the existence of a regular food surplus enabled a few people to develop highly specialized talents and tools that were not tied to food production. Some talented military leaders became rulers of large areas and headed government with specialized administrators. Specialists constructed elaborate irrigation systems, monumental palaces, and temples. Others made special metal tools and weapons, first of bronze, then of iron. Because of the value of their talents these specialists acquired privileges. It was grandest to be a king, queen, or head priest. For the average person, life was harder in complex societies than in parts of the world where such specialization had not yet occurred.

Scene from the Egyptian Book of the Dead, ca. 1300 B.C.E. The mummy of a royal scribe named Hunefar is approached by members of his household before being placed in the tomb. Behind Hunefar is jackel-headed Anubis, the god who will conduct the spirit of the deceased to the afterlife. The Book of the Dead provided Egyptians with the instructions they needed to complete this arduous journey and gain a blessed existence in the afterlife.

Culture and Civilization

Complex and populous agricultural societies developed specialists who dealt with abstract and unseen forces. This development was not entirely new. For tens of thousands of years before the first settled societies, humans had used their minds to think about the meaning of life. The remains of elaborate burials and sites of worship suggest that some early societies had clear beliefs in an afterlife and in spiritual forces that controlled their lives. Many cultures believed the sun, moon, and nature had supernatural powers.

Another form of intellectual activity was the collection of technical knowledge about the environment. Cultural communities learned what plants were best for food, clothing, or building materials and passed this knowledge along to later generations. Most specialized was the knowledge of how to make medicines and poisons. Assigning names for all these facilitated the transmission of this knowledge. In the absence of written records, very little specific information about these early treasuries of knowledge exists, but the elaborate and beautiful paintings in caves dating to tens of thousands of years before the emergence of early agricultural societies provide the clearest evidence of the cultural sophistication of early humans.

Cultural change surged as settled agricultural com- munities became more specialized. Temple priests devised elaborate rituals and prayers for the gods who protected the community, and they studied the movements of stars, planets, and the moon for signs of the progress of the seasons or the will of the gods. In Mesopotamia, Egypt, and elsewhere a new class of scribes used written symbols to preserve administrative and commercial records, laws, and bodies of specialized knowledge. Thoughtful people recorded the myths and legends passed down orally from earlier days, systematizing them and often adapting them to new social conditions, as well as creating new literary forms. Communications could now be sent unchanged over long distances. Some of these works were lost for millennia only to be rediscovered in recent times, allowing us to know much more about the lives, thoughts, and values of ancient peoples.

Empires and Regional

In time governments weakened or fell victim to conquest. Egypt, for example, fell to Nubians from up the Nile then to the Assyrians from Mesopotamia. Some conquerors created vast new empires. Late in the fourth century B.C.E., Alexander the Great brought everything from the eastern Mediterranean to India and Egypt under his sway, spreading Greek culture and language. After the collapse of Alexander's empire, the first of a series of Indian empires arose. In the second and first centuries B.C.E., Latin-speakers spread their rule, language, and culture throughout the Roman Empire, which encompassed the Mediterranean and reached across the Alps into Gaul (France) and Britain. At much the same time, the Han consolidated control over the densely populated lands of China, and successive rulers extended the sway of imperial China over much of East Asia. In the isolated continents of the Americas, advanced agricultural societies were also building larger states in late antiquity.

Essential to empire formation was the significant enhancement of old technologies and the development of new ones. In many parts of the world iron replaced bronze as the preferred metal

MAP I.1 **Early Centers of Plant and Animal Domestication** Many different parts of the world made original contributions to domestication during the Agricultural Revolutions that began about 10,000 years ago. Later interactions helped spread these domesticated animals and plants to new locations. In lands less suitable for crop cultivation, pastoralism and hunting remained more important for supplying food.

for tools and weapons. In the Middle East and China soldiers on horseback played important military roles. In most places there were advances in the fighting techniques and in defensive strategies and fortifications.

Empires encouraged the growth of cities to serve as administrative, economic, and cultural centers. Temples, palaces, monuments, markets, and public amenities advertised the glory of these imperial centers. Large states regularly mobilized large pools of labor for massive construction projects. By late antiquity, a few cities had populations in the hundreds of thousands—Alexandria in Egypt, Rome in Italy, Chang'an in China, Pataliputra in India—though such large numbers strained cities' capacities to supply food and water and dispose of waste. Such architectural monuments established "classical" styles that were frequently imitated and affected wide areas even after the empires were gone.

Other imperial building projects were more practical. The Roman and Chinese governments built thousands of miles of paved roads for moving troops and communication; long barrier walls and strings of forts defended frontier areas from invasion. Trade often flourished on these political frontiers, and good roads further encouraged trade. Improvements in shipping also encouraged the movement of goods over long distances and allowed transport of bulkier goods. Much long-distance trade in antiquity was in luxury goods for the privileged classes in urban civilizations. The search for exotic items tied remote parts of the world together and gave rise to new specialists both within the urban civilizations and in less stratified parts of the world. Gold, ivory, animal pelts, and exotic feathers from inner Africa reached Egypt. Phoenician mariners marketed lumber, papyrus (for paper), wine, and fish around the Mediterranean Sea. Other merchants carried silk from China across arid Central Asia to the Middle East and lands to the west. The advent of coinage in the first millennium B.C.E. stimulated local and regional economies.

The routes that carried goods also helped spread religions, inventions, and ideas. The Zoroastrian religion of the Persians became one of the great ethical creeds of antiquity. The diaspora of Jews from Palestine after their southern kingdom was destroyed by the Neo-Babylonian Empire in the seventh century B.C.E. also helped spread monotheistic beliefs. The beliefs and culture of the Greeks and Romans spread throughout their empires, largely because many of their subjects saw the advantages in adopting the ways of the ruling elite. Similarly, Indian traders introduced Hinduism and Buddhism to Southeast Asia.

GROWTH AND INTERACTION, 400-1200

During the Early Middle Ages expanding political and commercial links drew regions closer together. In addition, the growth of interregional trade and the spread of new world religions helped unite and redefine the boundaries of cultural regions, though divisions within religions undercut some of this cultural unity. All of these factors were interrelated, but let's begin with the one that left the most enduring impression on the course of history: the spread of world religions.

World Religions

The first religious tradition to experience widespread growth in this period was Buddhism, which spread from the Indian homeland where it had arisen around 500 B.C.E. One direction of growth was eastward into Southeast Asia. After 500 C.E. there were particular strongholds of the faith on the large islands of Ceylon, Sumatra, and Java, whose kings supported the growth of schools and monasteries and constructed temple complexes. Traders also carried Buddhism to China and from there to Korea, Japan, and Tibet. In some places Buddhism's growing strength led to political reactions. In China the Tang emperors reduced the influence of the monasteries in 840 by taking away their tax exemption and by promoting traditional Confucian values. A similar effort by the Tibetan royal family to curtail Buddhism failed, and Buddhist monks established their political dominance in mountainous Tibet. In India, however, Buddhism gradually lost support during this period and by 1200 had practically disappeared from the land of its origin.

Meanwhile, people in western Eurasia were embracing two newer religious systems. In the fourth century, Christianity became the official religion of the Roman Empire, adding new

Pierpont Morgan Library/ Art Resource, NY

Armored Knights in Battle   This painting from around 1135 shows the armament of knights at the time of the Crusades. Chain mail, a helmet, and a shield carried on the left side protect the rider. The lance carried underarm and the sword are the primary weapons. Notice that riders about to make contact with lances have their legs straight and braced in the stirrups, while riders with swords and in flight have bent legs.

followers all around the Mediterranean to this once persecuted faith. But when the western half of the empire collapsed under the onslaught of "barbarian" invasions in the late fifth century, the Latin Church had to shoulder alone the tasks of converting these peoples to Christianity and preserving the intellectual, political, and cultural heritage of Roman antiquity. In its religious mission the Latin Church was quite successful. One by one Frankish, German, English, Irish, Hungarian, and other leaders were converted, and their subjects gradually followed suit. Preserving other Roman achievements was more difficult. The church continued to use the Latin language and Roman law, and Christian monasteries preserved manuscripts of many ancient works. But the trading economy and urban life that had been the heart blood of ancient Rome became only a memory in most of the Latin West.

In the eastern Mediterranean, Byzantine Roman emperors continued to rule, and the Greek-speaking Christian church continued to enjoy political protection. Greek monks were also active Christian missionaries among the Slavic peoples of eastern Europe. The conversion of the Russian rulers in the tenth century was a notable achievement. However, by the middle of the next century, cultural, linguistic, and theological differences led to a deep rift between Greek and Rus sian Christians in the east and Latin Christians in the west.

Meanwhile, prophetic religion founded by Muhammad in the seventh century was spreading like a whirlwind out of its Arabian homeland. With great fervor Arab armies introduced Islam and an accompanying state system into the Middle East, across North Africa, and into the Iberian Peninsula. Over time most Middle Eastern and African Christians and members of other religions chose to adopt the new faith. Muslim merchants helped spread the faith along trade routes into sub-Saharan Africa and across southern Asia. Like Christianity, Islam eventually split along cultural, theological, and political lines as it expanded. Beginning in 1095, Latin Christians launched military Crusades against Muslim dominance of Christian holy places in Palestine. In later Crusades, political and commercial ends became more important than religious goals, and the boundaries between Christianity and Islam changed little.

Commercial and Political Contacts

In many other parts of the world empires played a fundamental role in defining and unifying cultural areas. Under the Tang and Song dynasties (618-1279) China continued to have stability and exhibited periods of remarkable economic growth and technological creativity. Ghana, the first notable empire in sub-Saharan Africa, emerged to control one end of the trans-Saharan trade. In the isolated continents of the Americas a series of cultural complexes formed in the Andes, among the Maya of the Yucatán, along the Mississippi, and in the arid North American southwest. But despite efforts by Christian northern Europeans to create a loosely centralized "Holy Roman Empire," a very decentralized political system prevailed in most of western Europe. In Japan development was moving in a similar direction.

Political and religious expansion helped stimulate regional and long-distance trade. The challenge of moving growing quantities of goods over long distances produced some important innovations in land and sea travel. Two of the most important land-based, long-distance routes in this period depended on pack animals, especially the camel. One was the Silk Road, a caravan route across Central Asia. On the other trade route, between sub-Saharan Africa and North Africa, camels carried goods across the Sahara, the world's largest desert.

The Silk Road took its name from the silk textiles that were carried from eastern China to the Mediterranean Sea. In return, the Chinese received horses and other goods from the West. In existence since about 250 B.C.E., this series of roads nearly 6,000-miles (9,000-kilometers) in length passed through arid lands whose pastoral populations provided guides, food, and fresh camels (specially bred for caravan work).

After 900 C.E. the Silk Road declined for a time. By coincidence, the trans-Saharan caravan routes were growing more important during the period from 700 to 1200. Here, too, horses were an important trade purchased by African rulers to the south in return for gold, slaves, and other goods. The pastoralists who controlled the Saharan oases became essential guides for the camel caravans.

Since ancient times sea travel had been important in moving goods over relatively short distances, usually within sight of land, as around the Mediterranean Sea, the Red Sea, the Persian Gulf, and among the islands of the East Indies. During this period the water links around and through the Indian Ocean were increasing enough to make it an alternative to moving goods from China to the Middle East. Shipments went from port to port and were exchanged many times. Special ships known as dhows made use of the seasonal shifts in the winds across the Indian Ocean to plan their voyages in each direction. These centuries also saw remarkable maritime voyages in the Pacific (see Chapter 16).

INTERREGIONAL CONQUESTS AND EXCHANGES, 1200-1500

Between 1200 and 1500, cultural and commercial contacts grew rapidly across wide expanses of Eur asia, Africa, the Americas, and the Indian Ocean. In part, the increased contacts were the product of an unprecedented era of empire building around the world. The Mongols conquered a vast empire spanning Eurasia from the Pacific to eastern Europe. Muslim peoples created new empires in India, the Middle East, and sub- Saharan Africa. Amerindian empires united extensive regions of the Americas. Most of Europe continued to lack political unity, but unusually powerful European kingdoms were expanding their frontiers.

Empires stimulated commercial exchanges. The Mongol conquests revived the Silk Road across Central Asia, while a complex maritime network centered on the Indian Ocean stretched around southern Eurasia from the South China Sea to the North Atlantic, with overland connections in all directions (see Map I.2). Trade in the Americas and Africa also expanded. In the fifteenth century, Portuguese and Spanish explorers began an expansion southward along the Atlantic coast of Africa that by 1500 had opened a new all-water route to the riches of the Indian Ocean and set the stage for transoceanic routes that for the first time were to span the globe.

Mongol, Muslim, and European expansion promoted the spread of technologies. Printing, compasses, crossbows, gunpowder, and firearms—all East Asian inventions found broader applications and new uses in western Eurasia. Both the Ottomans and the kingdoms of western Europe made extensive use of gunpowder technologies. However, the highly competitive and increasingly literate peoples of the Latin West surpassed all others of this period in their use of technologies that they borrowed from elsewhere or devised themselves. Europeans mined and refined more metals, produced more books, built more kinds of ships, and made more weapons than did people in any other comparable place on earth.

Why was so much change taking place all at once? Historians attribute many of the changes in South and Central Asia directly or indirectly to the empire building of the Mongols. But other changes took place far from that area. The role of simple coincidence, of course, should never be overlooked in history. And some historians believe that larger environmental factors were also at work—changes in climate that promoted population growth, trade, and empire building.

MAP 1.2 **Arteries of Trade and Travel in the Islamic World, to 1500** Ibn Battuta's journeys across Africa and Asia made use of land and sea routes along which Muslim traders and the Islamic faith had long traveled.

 Interactive Map

Mongols and Turks

The earliest and largest of the new empires was the work of the Mongols of northeastern Asia. Using their extraordinary command of horses and refinements in traditional forms of military and social organization, Mongols and allied groups united under Genghis Khan overran northern China in the early thirteenth century and spread their control westward across Central Asia to eastern Europe. By the later part of the century, the Mongol Empire stretched from Korea to Poland. It was ruled initially in four separate khanates: one in Russia, one in Iran, one in Central Asia, and one in China.

By ensuring traders protection from robbers and excessive tolls, the Mongol Empire revitalized the Silk Road. Never before had there been such a volume of commercial exchanges between eastern and western Eurasia. Easier travel also helped Islam and Buddhism spread to new parts of Central Asia.

The strains of holding such vast territories together caused the Mongol Empire to disintegrate over the course of the fourteenth and early fifteenth centuries. The Ming rulers of China overthrew Mongol rule in 1368 and began an expansionist foreign policy to reestablish China's predominance and prestige. Their armies repeatedly invaded Mongolia, reestablished dominion over Korea, and occupied northern Vietnam (Annam). One by one the other khanates collapsed.

The Mongols left a formidable legacy, but it was not Mongolian. Instead, Mongol rulers tended to adopt and promote the political systems, agricultural practices, and local customs of the peoples they ruled. Their encouragement of local languages helped later literary movements

National Palace Museum, Taipai, Taiwan, Republic of China

Silk Painting Depicting Khitan Hunters Resting Their Horses
The artist shows the Khitans' soft riding boots, leggings, and robes (much like those used by the Mongols) and the Khitans' patterned hairstyle, with part of the skull shaved and some of the hair worn long. Men in Central and North Asia (including Japan) used patterned hairstyles to indicate their political allegiance. The custom was documented in the 400s (but is certainly much older) and continued up to the twentieth century.

to flower. The political influence of the administrations the Mongols established in China, Iran, and Russia lingered even after locals had overthrown their rule, creating the basis for new national regimes.

At about the same time as the early Mongol expansion, Turkic war leaders from what is now Afghanistan were surging through the Khyber Pass and established a Muslim empire centered at Delhi. In short order, they overwhelmed the several Hindu states of north and central India and established a large empire ruled from the city of Delhi. The subsequent migration of large numbers of Muslims into India and the prestige and power of the Muslim ruling class brought India into the Islamic world. After their conquests in the Middle East, Mongols had recruited other Turkic-speaking Muslims from Central Asia to serve as their agents. In the decades after 1250, a large Turkic community in Anatolia (now Turkey) known as Ottomans took advantage of the weakness of the Byzantine Empire to extend their base in Anatolia. They then crossed into the Balkan Peninsula of southeastern Europe.

In the late 1300s, the Central Asian conqueror Timur (Tamerlane) shattered the Delhi Sultanate and stopped the expansion of the Ottoman Empire. The conquest and pillage of Timur's armies left the Delhi Sultanate a shadow of its former self, but the Ottoman Turks were able to reconstitute their empire in the fifteenth century. Ottoman conquerors swept deep into southeastern Europe (taking Constantinople, the last surviving remnant of the Byzantine Empire, in 1453) and southward into the Middle East, establishing a stable presence that was to endure into the twentieth century.

Indian Ocean Exchanges

In the wake of the Mongol Empire's collapse, the Indian Ocean assumed greater importance in the movement of goods across Eurasia. Alliances among Muslim merchants of many nationalities made these routes the world's richest trading area. Merchant dhows sailed among the trading ports, carrying cotton textiles, leather goods, grains, pepper, jewelry, carpets, horses, ivory, and many other goods. Chinese silk and porcelain and Indonesian spices entered from the east, meeting Middle Eastern and European goods from the west. It is important to note that Muslim merchant networks were almost completely independent of the giant Muslim land empires.

As a consequence of the Islamic world's political and commercial expansion, the number of adherents to the Muslim faith also grew. By 1500 Islam had replaced Buddhism as the second most important faith in India and was on its way to displacing Hinduism and Buddhism in Southeast Asia. The faith was also spreading in the Balkans. Meanwhile, raids by Arab pastoralists undermined ancient Christian states along Africa's upper Nile, leaving Ethiopia as the only Christian-ruled state in Africa. In the trading cities below the Sahara and along the Indian Ocean coast where Islam had established itself well before 1200, the strength and sophistication of Islamic religious practice was growing.

Mediterranean Exchanges

The Mediterranean Sea, which since antiquity had been a focus of commerce and cultural exchange for the peoples of Europe, the Middle East, and Africa, saw increased activity in the later Middle Ages. Part of the Mediterranean's importance derived from its trading links to the

Indian Ocean by land and water routes. Another area that contributed to expanded trade was northern Africa. Camel caravans brought great quantities of gold and large numbers of slaves to the Mediterranean from the lands below the Sahara. This trade facilitated the growth of the powerful empire of Mali, which controlled some of the main gold-producing regions of West Africa. The rulers of Mali became rich and Muslim. Their wars and those of other states produced the captives that were sold north. In the fourteenth century the disruption of supplies of slaves from the eastern Mediterranean led to more slaves being purchased in southern Europe.

Another part of the expansion of Mediterranean trade was tied to the revival of western Europe. In 1204 the Italian city-state of Venice had shown its determination to be a dominant player in the eastern Mediterranean by attacking the Greek city of Constantinople and ensuring access to the Black Sea. Trade routes from the Mediterranean spread northward to the Netherlands and connected by sea to the British Isles, the Baltic Sea, and the Atlantic. The growth of trade in Europe accompanied a revival of urban life and culture. Both the cities and the countryside saw increased use of energy, minerals, and technologies from printing to gunpowder. Despite a high level of warfare among European states and devastating population losses in the fourteenth century, much of Europe was exhibiting cultural and economic vitality that was to have great consequences for the entire world in the centuries that followed.

The Aztecs and Inca

In the continents of the Western Hemisphere, American peoples were also creating important empires in the period from 1200 to 1500, although they had more limited resources with which to do so. For thous- ands of years their cultures had developed in isolation from the rest of humanity and thus had been unable to borrow any plants, animals, or technologies. Amerindian conquests were made without the aid of riding animals like the Mongols' horses, without the iron weapons all Old World empire builders had been using for many centuries, and without the new gunpowder weaponry that some Eurasians were employing in their conquests in this period.

In the wake of the collapse of the Toltec Empire, a martial people known as the Aztecs pushed southward into the rich agricultural lands of central Mexico. At first the Aztecs placed them-

The Mesoamerican Ball Game From Guatemala to Arizona, archaeologists have found evidence of an ancient ball game played with a solid rubber ball on slope-sided courts shaped like a capital T. Among the Maya the game was associated with a creation myth and thus had deep religious meaning. There is evidence that some players were sacrificed. In this scene from a ceramic jar, players wearing elaborate ritual clothing—which includes heavy, protective pads around the chest and waist— play with a ball much larger than the ball actually used in such games. Some representations show balls drawn to suggest a human head.

Chrysler Museum of Art/Justin Kerr

selves at the service of strong indigenous residents, but after 1300 they began to build their own empire. Relying on their military skills, members of the Aztec warrior elite were able to conquer territories and reduce peasants to their service. The growth of a servile class at the bottom of society was paralleled by the growth of a powerful ruling class housed in well-constructed two-story dwellings in the Aztec capital cities. The servile laborers supplied the food needs of the growing cities and were impressed into building elaborate canals and land reclamation projects. Underpinning the power of the Aztec rulers were religious rituals that emphasized human sacrifice, mostly captives of the armies. By 1500 the Aztecs ruled a densely populated empire of subject and allied peoples.

Meanwhile, in the Andean highlands of western South America another powerful Amerindian empire was forming. Like central Mexico this region already had a rich agricultural base and a dense population when, in the fifteenth century, the Inca began using military skills to expand from a chiefdom into an empire. The Inca rulers, like the Aztecs, built impressive cities, promoted irrigation projects, and relied on religious rituals to bolster their authority. Tribute in goods and labor from their subject peoples supported their projects, and a network of mountain roads tied together the pieces of an empire that stretched for more than 3,000 miles (nearly 5,000 kilometers) north to south.

Both empires were cultural and commercial centers as well as political ones. In the Aztec Empire, well-armed private merchants controlled a long-distance trade in luxuries for the elites, including gold, jewels, feathered garments, and animal skins. There was also a network of local markets, large and small, that supplied the needs of more ordinary folks. State direction featured more prominently in Inca-ruled areas and promoted a vast exchange of specialized goods and a huge variety of foodstuffs grown at different altitudes.

SUGGESTED READING

A fuller treatment of all these topics can be found in the first volume of *The Earth and Its Peoples.* Richard Bulliet provides a brief overview of world history both before and after 1500 in "Themes, Conquerors, and Commerce," in Heidi Roupp, ed., *World History: A Resource Book* (1997).

For summaries of the latest scholarship on some select topics see these pamphlets in the American Historical Association's series "Essays in Global and Comparative History": John A. Mears, *Agricultural Origins in Global Perspective* (2003); Christopher Ehret, *Sudanic Civilization* (2003); Stanley M. Burstein, *The Hellenistic Period in World History* (1996); Richard M. Eaton, *Islamic History as World History* (1990); John E. Kicza, *The Peoples and Civilizations of the Americas Before Contact* (1998); Xinru Liu, *The Silk Road: Overland Trade and Cultural Interactions in Eurasia* (1998); Sarah Shaver Hughes and Brady Hughes, *Women in Ancient Civilizations* (1998); Jonathan S. Walters, *Finding Buddhists in Global History* (1998); Peter B. Golden, *Nomads and Sedentary Societies in Medieval Eurasia* (1998); and Janet Lippman Abu-Lughod, *The World System in the Thirteenth Century: Dead-End or Precursor?* (1993). Sarah Hughes and Brady Hughes have also edited a useful work correcting the dominance of patriarchal themes: *Women in World History,* vol. 1 (1995).

THE EARTH AND ITS PEOPLES

CHAPTER

16

CHAPTER OUTLINE

The Granger Collection, New York

Ferdinand Magellan Navigating the Straits Connecting the Atlantic and Pacific Oceans   This late-sixteenth-century print uses fanciful representations of native peoples and creatures to embellish Magellan's circumnavigation of the globe.

 Visit the website and ebook for additional study materials and interactive tools: www.cengage.com/history/bullietearthpeople5e

The Maritime Revolution, to 1550

I n 1511 young Ferdinand Magellan sailed from Europe around the southern tip of Africa and eastward across the Indian Ocean as a member of the first Portuguese expedition to explore the East Indies (maritime Southeast Asia). Eight years later, this time in the service of Spain, he led an expedition that sought to reach the East Indies by sailing westward. By the middle of 1521 Magellan's expedition had achieved its goal by sailing across the Atlantic, rounding the southern tip of South America, and crossing the Pacific Ocean—but at a high price.

- What were the objectives and major accomplishments of the voyages of exploration undertaken by Chinese, Polynesians, and other non-Western peoples?
- In this era of long-distance exploration, did Europeans have any special advantages over other cultural regions?
- What explains the different nature of Europe's interactions with Africa, India, and the Americas?

Of the five ships that had set out from Spain in 1519, only three made the long passage across the vast Pacific. Dozens of sailors died from starvation and disease during the voyage. In the Philippines, Magellan, having survived numerous mutinies during the voyage, died in battle on April 27, 1521, while aiding a local ruler who had promised to become a Christian.

To consolidate their dwindling resources, the expedition's survivors burned the least seaworthy of their remaining three ships and consolidated men and supplies. In the end only the *Victoria* made it home across the Indian Ocean and back to Europe. Nevertheless, the *Victoria*'s return to Spain on September 8, 1522, was a crowning example of Europeans' determination to make themselves masters of the oceans. A century of daring and dangerous voyages backed by the Portuguese crown had opened new routes through the South Atlantic to Africa, Brazil, and the rich trade of the Indian Ocean. Rival voyages sponsored by Spain since 1492 opened new contacts with the American continents. A maritime revolution was under way that would change the course of history.

This new maritime era marked the end of a long period when Asia had initiated most overland and maritime expansion. Asia had been the source of the most useful technologies and the most influential systems of belief. It was also home to the most powerful states and the richest trading networks. The success of Iberian voyages of exploration in the following century would redirect the world's center of power, wealth, and innovation to the West.

This maritime revolution broadened and deepened contacts, alliances, and conflicts across ancient cultural boundaries. Some of these contacts ended tragically for individuals like Magellan. Some proved disastrous for entire populations: Amerindians, for instance, suffered conquest, colonization, and a rapid decline in numbers. And sometimes the results were mixed: Asians and Africans found both risks and opportunities in their new relations with Europe.

GLOBAL MARITIME EXPANSION BEFORE 1450

Since ancient times travel across the world's seas and oceans had been one of the great challenges to technological ingenuity. Ships had to be sturdy enough to survive heavy winds and seas, and pilots had to learn how to cross featureless expanses of water to reach their destinations. In time ships, sails, and navigational techniques perfected in the more protected seas were adapted to open oceans.

However complex the solutions and dangerous the voyages, the rewards of sea travel made them worthwhile. Ships could move goods and people more profitably than any form of overland travel then possible. Crossing unknown waters, finding new lands, developing new markets, and establishing new settlements attracted adventurers from every continent. By 1450 daring mariners had discovered and settled most of the islands of the Pacific, the Atlantic, and the Indian Ocean, but no one had yet crossed the Pacific in either direction. Even the smaller Atlantic remained a barrier to contact between the Americas, Europe, and Africa. The inhabitants of Australia were also cut off from contact with the rest of humanity. All this was about to change.

The Pacific Ocean

Polynesian Voyages

The ancestors of the Polynesians originated in Asia. After centuries of island-hopping migrations that led from Melanesia (mel-uh-NEE-zhuh) to Fiji and Tonga, Polynesians had developed larger, more sea-worthy canoes, some 120 feet long (37 meters), and improved navigational skills that allowed them to extend their voyages over ever-greater distances (see Map 16.1). Between 100 and 300 B.C.E. they colonized the Marquesas (mar-KAY-suhs). No later than 500 C.E. Polynesians had settled the Hawaiian Islands 2,200 miles (3,541 kilometers) away. Around the same time Polynesian voyagers established settlements on Easter Island and New Zealand, both more

Polynesian Canoes   Pacific Ocean mariners sailing canoes such as these, shown in an eighteenth-century painting, made epic voyages of exploration and settlement. A large platform connects two canoes at the left, providing more room for the members of the expedition, and a sail supplements the paddlers.

CHRONOLOGY

	Pacific Ocean	Atlantic Ocean	Indian Ocean
	100 B.C.E.–800 C.E. Polynesian settlement of Pacific islands	770–1200 Viking voyages	
	1200–1300 Polynesian societies in Hawaii develop clear class structures with hereditary chiefs	1300s Settlement of Madeira, Azores, Canaries	
		Early 1300s Mali voyages	
1400			1405–1433 Voyages of Zheng He
		1418–1460 Voyages of Henry the Navigator	
		1440s First slaves from West Africa sent to Europe	
		1482 Portuguese at Gold Coast and Kongo	
		1486 Portuguese at Benin	
		1488 Bartolomeu Dias reaches Indian Ocean	
		1492 Columbus reaches Caribbean	
		1492–1500 Spanish conquer Hispaniola	
		1493 Columbus returns to Caribbean (second voyage)	
		1498 Columbus reaches mainland of South America (third voyage)	1497–1498 Vasco da Gama reaches India
1500		1500 Cabral reaches Brazil	
			1505 Portuguese bombard Swahili Coast cities
			1510 Portuguese take Goa
			1511 Portuguese take Malacca
			1515 Portuguese take Hormuz
	1519–1522 Magellan expedition	1519–1521 Cortés conquers Aztec Empire	
		1531–1533 Pizarro conquers Inca Empire	
		1536 Rebellion of Maco Inca in Peru	1535 Portuguese take Diu
			1538 Portuguese defeat Ottoman fleet
			1539 Portuguese aid Ethiopia

than 2,300 miles (3,702 kilometers) distant. These voyagers eventually reached the mainland of the Americas where they gained access to the sweet potato, domesticated first in South America. Long-distance voyages then spread this nutritious plant to Polynesian settlements as far away as New Zealand and beyond.

Both DNA evidence and linguistic similarities indicate that the Polynesian settlement of the islands of the eastern Pacific was planned and not the result of accident. Following voyages of reconnaissance, Polynesian mariners carried colonizing expeditions in fleets of large double-hulled canoes that relied on scores of paddlers as well as sails. A wide platform connected the two hulls of these crafts and permitted the transportation of passengers, domesticated animals, and plants crucial to the success of distant and isolated settlements. Success depended upon reliably navigating across thousands of miles of ocean using careful observation of the currents

MAP 16.1 **Exploration and Settlement in the Indian and Pacific Oceans Before 1500** Over many centuries, mariners originating in Southeast Asia gradually colonized the islands of the Pacific and Indian Oceans. The Chinese voyages led by Zheng He in the fifteenth century were lavish official expeditions.

e Interactive Map

and stars as the crews searched for evidence of land. Once established, each satellite settlement developed distinctive cultural attributes, since ongoing contact was very difficult. With population growth after 1200 C.E. these societies became more hierarchical and violent.

The Indian Ocean

While Polynesian mariners were settling Pacific islands, other Malayo-Indonesians were sailing westward across the Indian Ocean and colonizing the large island of Madagascar off the southeastern coast of Africa. These voyages continued through the fifteenth century, and today the inhabitants of Madagascar still speak Malayo-Polynesian languages. However, part of the island's population is descended from Africans who had crossed the 300 miles (500 kilometers) from the mainland to Madagascar, most likely in the centuries before 1500.

Other peoples had been using the Indian Ocean for trade since ancient times. Southeast Asia and eastern Africa as well as the Indian subcontinent provided coasts that seafarers might safely follow and coves for protection. Moreover, seasonal winds known as monsoons are so predictable and steady that navigation in these waters using sailing vessels called dhows (dow) was less difficult and dangerous than elsewhere.

The rise of medieval Islam gave Indian Ocean trade an important boost. The great Muslim cities of the Middle East provided a demand for valuable commodities, and networks of Muslim traders were active across the region. These traders shared a common language, ethic, and law and actively spread their religion to distant trading cities. By 1400 there were Muslim trading communities all around the Indian Ocean.

Chinese Voyages

These Indian Ocean traders largely operated outside the control of the empires and states they served, but in East Asia imperial China's rulers were growing more and more interested in these wealthy ports of trade. In 1368 the Ming dynasty overthrew Mongol rule and began to reestablish China's predominance and prestige abroad.

Having restored Chinese dominance in East Asia, the Ming moved to establish direct contacts with the peoples around the Indian Ocean, sending out seven imperial fleets between 1405 and 1433 (see Chapter 13). The enormous size of these expeditions, far larger than needed for exploration or promoting trade, indicates that the Ming sought to inspire awe of their power and

Dugald Sterner

Chinese Junk   This modern drawing shows how much larger one of Zheng He's ships was than one of Vasco da Gama's vessels. Watertight interior bulkheads made junks the most seaworthy large ships of the fifteenth century. Sails made of pleated bamboo matting hung from the junk's masts, and a stern rudder provided steering. European ships of exploration, though smaller, were faster and more maneuverable.

achievements. While curiosity about this prosperous region may have also been a motive, the fact that the ports visited by the fleets were major commercial centers suggests that expanding China's trade was an objective as well.

The scale of the Ming expeditions to the Indian Ocean Basin reflects imperial China's resources and importance. The first consisted of sixty-two specially built "treasure ships," large Chinese junks each about 300 feet long by 150 feet wide (90 by 45 meters). There were also at least a hundred smaller vessels. Each treasure ship had nine masts, twelve sails, many decks, and a carrying capacity of 3,000 tons (six times the capacity of Columbus's entire fleet). One expedition carried over 27,000 individuals, including infantry and cavalry troops. The ships were armed with small cannon, but in most Chinese sea battles arrows from highly accurate crossbows dominated the fighting.

Zheng He An imperial eunuch and Muslim, entrusted by the Ming emperor Yongle with a series of state voyages that took his gigantic ships through the Indian Ocean, from Southeast Asia to Africa.

Admiral **Zheng He** (jung huh) (1371–1435) commanded the expeditions. A Chinese Muslim with ancestral connections to the Persian Gulf, Zheng was a fitting emissary to the increasingly Muslim-dominated Indian Ocean Basin. The expeditions carried other Arabic-speaking Chinese as interpreters. One interpreter kept a journal that recorded local customs and beliefs. He observed new flora and fauna, noting exotic animals such as the black panther of Malaya and the tapir of Sumatra. In India he described the division of the coastal population into five classes, which correspond to the four Hindu varna and a separate Muslim class. He also recorded that traders in the rich Indian trading port of Calicut (KAL-ih-kut) could perform error-free calculations by counting on their fingers and toes rather than using the Chinese abacus. After his return, the interpreter went on tour in China, telling of these exotic places and "how far the majestic virtue of [China's] imperial dynasty extended."[1]

The Chinese "treasure ships" carried rich silks, precious metals, and other valuable goods intended as gifts for distant rulers. In return those rulers sent back gifts of equal or greater value to the Chinese emperor. Although the main purpose of these exchanges was diplomatic, they also stimulated trade between China and its southern neighbors. Interest in new contacts was not limited to the Chinese.

At least three trading cities on the Swahili (swah-HEE-lee) Coast of East Africa sent delegations to China between 1415 and 1416. The delegates from one of them, Malindi, presented the emperor of China with a giraffe, creating quite a stir among normally reserved imperial officials. These African delegations may have encouraged more contacts because the next three of Zheng's voyages reached the African coast. Unfortunately, no documents record how Africans and Chinese reacted to each other during these historic meetings between 1417 and 1433, but it appears that China's lavish gifts stimulated the Swahili market for silk and porcelain. An increase in Chinese imports of pepper from southern Asian lands also resulted from these expeditions.

Had the Ming court wished to promote trade for the profit of its merchants, Chinese fleets might have continued to play a dominant role in Indian Ocean trade. But some high Chinese officials opposed increased contact with peoples whom they regarded as barbarians incapable of making contributions to China. Such opposition caused a suspension in the voyages from 1424 to 1431. The final Chinese expedition sailed between 1432 and 1433. Later Ming emperors would focus their attention on internal matters, leaving a power vacuum in the Indian Ocean.

The Atlantic Ocean

Early European Maritime Expansion

The Vikings were the greatest mariners of the Atlantic in the early Middle Ages. These northern European raiders used their small, open ships to attack Europe's coastal settlements for several centuries. They also discovered and settled one island after another in the North Atlantic during these centuries of warmer temperatures. Like the Polynesians, the Vikings used their knowledge of the heavens and the seas rather than maps and other navigational devices to find their way over long distances.

The Vikings first settled Iceland in 770 and established a colony on Greenland in 982. By accident one group sighted North America in 986. Fifteen years later Leif Ericsson established a short-lived Viking settlement on the island of Newfoundland, which he called Vinland. When a colder climate returned after 1200, the northern settlements in Greenland went into decline and the Vikings abandoned Vinland.

Some southern Europeans applied maritime skills acquired in the Mediterranean and along the North Atlantic coast to explore to the south. Genoese and Portuguese expeditions pushed into the Atlantic in the fourteenth century, eventually exploring and settling the islands of Madeira (muh-DEER-uh), the Azores (A-zorz), and the Canaries.

African Voyages of Discovery

There is some evidence of African voyages of exploration in this period. The celebrated Syrian geographer al-Umari (1301–1349) relates that when Mansa Kankan Musa (MAHN-suh KAHN-kahn MOO-suh), the ruler of the West African empire of Mali, passed through Egypt on his lavish pilgrimage to Mecca in 1324, he told of voyages into the Atlantic undertaken by his predecessor, Mansa Muhammad. According to this source, Muhammad had sent out four hundred vessels with men and supplies, telling them, "Do not return until you have reached the other side of the ocean or if you have exhausted your food or water." After a long time one canoe returned, reporting that the others were lost in a "violent current in the middle of the sea." Muhammad himself then set out at the head of a second, even larger, expedition, from which no one returned.

Arawak Amerindian peoples who inhabited the Greater Antilles of the Caribbean at the time of Columbus.

Amerindian Voyages

In the Americas, early Amerindian voyagers from South America colonized the West Indies, and there were limited maritime contacts between Pacific coast populations in South America and Central America. By the year 1000 Amerindians known as the **Arawak** (AR-uh-wahk) (also called Taino) had followed the small islands of the Lesser Antilles (Barbados, Martinique, and Guadeloupe) to the Greater Antilles (Cuba, Hispaniola, Jamaica, and Puerto Rico) as well as to the Bahamas (see Map 16.2). The Carib followed the same route in later centuries, and by the late fifteenth century they had overrun most Arawak settlements in the Lesser Antilles and were raiding parts of the Greater Antilles. Both Arawak and Carib peoples also made contact with the North American mainland.

SECTION REVIEW

- Polynesians explored and settled the eastern Pacific from the Marquesas to Hawaii and Easter Island.
- The Indian Ocean became a center of commerce and cultural exchange. Between 1405 and 1433 Chinese Admiral Zheng He's seven expeditions established contacts with south Asian and African peoples.
- Vikings, Amerindians, and Africans also pursued long-distance explorations and settlements.

EUROPEAN EXPANSION, 1400–1550

The preceding survey shows that maritime expansion occurred in many parts of the world before 1450. Nevertheless, the epic sea voyages sponsored by the Iberian kingdoms of Portugal and Spain are of special interest because they began a maritime revolution that profoundly altered the course of world history. The Portuguese and Spanish expeditions ended the isolation of the Americas and increased the volume of global interaction.

Iberian overseas expansion was the product of two related phenomena. First, Iberian rulers had strong economic, religious, and political motives to expand their influence. And second, improvements in maritime and military technologies gave Iberians the means to master treacherous and unfamiliar ocean environments, seize control of existing maritime trade routes, and conquer new lands.

Motives for Exploration

The ambitions and adventurous personalities of the rulers of Portugal and Spain led them to sponsor voyages of exploration in the fifteenth century, but these voyages built upon four trends evident in the Latin West since about the year 1000: (1) the revival of urban life and trade, (2) the

e Interactive Map

MAP 16.2 **Middle America to 1533** Early Amerindian voyages from South America brought new settlers to the West Indies and western Mexico. The arrival of Europeans in 1492 soon led to the conquest and depopulation of Amerindians.

© Cengage Learning

unique alliance between merchants and rulers in Europe, (3) a struggle with Islamic powers for dominance of the Mediterranean that mixed religious motives with the desire for trade, and (4) growing intellectual curiosity about the outside world.

By 1450 the city-states of northern Italy had well-established trade links to northern Europe, the Indian Ocean, and the Black Sea, and their merchant princes had also sponsored an intellectual and artistic Renaissance. The Italian trading states of Venice and Genoa also maintained profitable commercial ties in the Mediterranean that depended on alliances with Muslims and gave their merchants privileged access to lucrative trade from the East. Even after the expansion of the Ottoman Empire disrupted their trade to the East, these cities did not take the lead in exploring the Atlantic. However, many individual Italians played leading roles in the Atlantic explorations.

The Iberian Background

In contrast, the special history and geography of the Iberian kingdoms led them in a different direction. Muslim invaders from North Africa had conquered most of Iberia in the eighth century. Centuries of warfare between Christians and Muslims followed, and by 1250 the Iberian kingdoms of Portugal, Castile, and Aragon had reconquered all of Iberia except the southern Muslim kingdom of Granada (see Chapter 15). The dynastic marriage of Isabel of Castile and Ferdinand of Aragon in 1469 facilitated the conquest of Granada in 1492 and the creation of Spain, sixteenth-century Europe's most powerful state.

Christian militancy continued to be an important motive for both Portugal and Spain in their overseas ventures. But the Iberian rulers and their adventurous subjects also sought material returns. With only a modest share of the Mediterranean trade, they were much more willing than the Italians to seek new routes to the rich trade of Africa and Asia via the Atlantic. Both kingdoms participated in the shipbuilding and the gunpowder revolutions that were under way in Atlantic Europe. Though not centers of Renaissance learning, both were especially open to new geographical knowledge.

Portuguese Voyages

Portugal's decision to invest significant resources in new exploration rested on a well-established Atlantic fishing industry and a history of anti-Muslim warfare. When the Muslim government of Morocco in northwestern Africa showed weakness in the fifteenth century, the Portuguese attacked, conquering the city of Ceuta (say-OO-tuh) in 1415. The capture of this rich North African city gave the Portuguese better intelligence of the caravans bringing gold and slaves to Ceuta from African states south of the Sahara. Militarily unable to push inland and gain direct access to the gold trade, the Portuguese sought more direct contact with the gold producers by sailing down the African coast.

Prince Henry of Portugal

Henry the Navigator Portuguese prince who promoted the study of navigation and directed voyages of exploration down the western coast of Africa in the fifteenth century.

Prince Henry (1394–1460), third son of the king of Portugal, had led the attack on Ceuta. Because he devoted the rest of his life to promoting exploration, he is known as **Henry the Navigator.** His official biographer emphasized Henry's mixed motives for exploration—converting Africans to Christianity, making contact with Christian rulers in Africa, and launching joint crusades with them against the Ottomans. Prince Henry also wished to discover new places and hoped that such new contacts would be profitable. Early explorations were concerned with Africa, but eventually reaching India became an explicit goal of Portuguese explorers. While called "the Navigator," Henry himself never ventured far from home. Instead, he founded a center of research at Sagres (SAH-gresh) to study navigation that built on the pioneering efforts of Italian merchants and fourteenth-century Jewish cartographers. This center collected geographical information from sailors and travelers and sponsored new expeditions to explore the Atlantic. Henry's ships established permanent contact with the islands of Madeira in 1418 and the Azores in 1439.

Henry's staff also improved navigational instruments that had come into Europe from China and the Islamic world. These instruments included the magnetic compass, first developed in China, and the astrolabe, an instrument of Arab or Greek invention that enabled mariners to determine their location at sea by measuring the position of the sun or the stars in the night sky. Even with such instruments, however, voyages still depended on the skill and experience of navigators.

European Sailing Technologies

Portuguese mariners also developed vessels appropriate for voyages of long-distance exploration. Neither the galleys in use in the Mediterranean, powered by large numbers of oarsmen, nor the three-masted ships of northern Europe with their square sails proved adequate for the

Portuguese Map of Western Africa, 1502   This map shows in great detail a section of African coastline that Portuguese explorers charted and named in the fifteenth century. The cartographer illustrated the African interior, which was almost completely unknown to Europeans, with drawings of birds and views of coastal sights: Sierra Leone (Serra lioa), named for a mountain shaped like a lion, and the Portuguese Castle of the Mine (Castello damina) on the Gold Coast.

caravel A small, highly maneuverable three-masted ship used by the Portuguese and Spanish in the exploration of the Atlantic.

Atlantic. The large crews of the galleys could not carry enough supplies for long voyages and the square-rigged northern vessels had trouble sailing at an angle to the wind. Instead, the voyages of exploration made use of a new vessel, the **caravel** (KAR-uh-vel), that was much smaller than the largest European ships and the Chinese junks Zheng used to explore the Indian Ocean. Their size permitted them to enter shallow coastal waters and explore upriver, but they were strong enough to weather ocean storms. They could be equipped with triangular lateen sails that could take the wind on either side for enhanced maneuverability or fitted with square Atlantic sails for greater speed in a following wind. The addition of small cannon made them good fighting ships as well. The caravels' economy, speed, agility, and power justified a contemporary's claim that they were "the best ships that sailed the seas."[2]

Pioneering captains had to overcome the common fear that South Atlantic waters were boiling hot or contained ocean currents that would prevent any ship entering them from ever returning home. It took Prince Henry fourteen years—from 1420 to 1434—to coax an expedition to venture beyond southern Morocco (see Map 16.3). These fears proved unfounded, but the next stretch of coast, 800 miles (1,300 kilometers) of desert, offered little to induce explorers south. It would take the Portuguese four decades to cover the 1,500 miles (2,400 kilometers) from Lisbon to Sierra Leone (see-ER-uh lee-OWN); it then took only three decades to explore the remaining 4,000 miles (6,400 kilometers) to the southern tip of the African continent.

In the years that followed, Portuguese explorers learned how to return to home speedily. Instead of battling the prevailing northeast trade winds and currents back up the coast, they discovered that by sailing northwest into the Atlantic to the latitude of the Azores, ships could pick up prevailing westerly winds that would blow them back to Portugal. The knowledge that ocean winds tend to form large circular patterns helped explorers discover many other ocean routes.

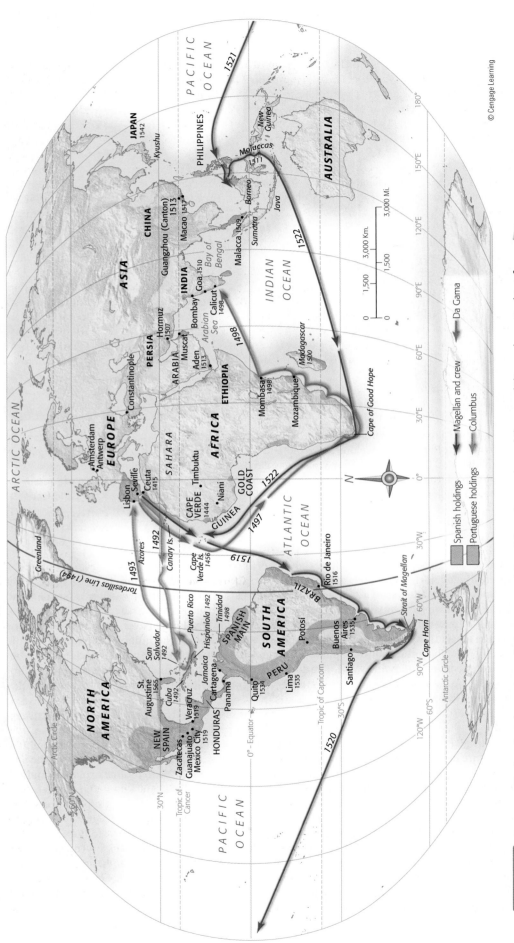

MAP 16.3 European Exploration, 1420–1542 Portuguese and Spanish explorers showed the possibility and practicality of intercontinental maritime trade. Before 1540 European trade with Africa and Asia was much more important than that with the Americas, but after the Spanish conquest of the Aztec and Inca Empires transatlantic trade began to increase. Notice the Tordesillas line, which in theory separated the Spanish and Portuguese spheres of activity.

© Cengage Learning

Interactive Map

Gold Coast Region of the
Atlantic coast of West Africa
occupied by modern Ghana;
named for its gold exports
to Europe from the 1470s
onward.

Bartolomeu Dias Portuguese explorer who in 1488
led the first expedition to sail
around the southern tip of
Africa from the Atlantic and
sight the Indian Ocean.

Vasco da Gama Portuguese
explorer. In 1497–1498 he
led the first naval expedition
from Europe to sail to India,
opening an important com-
mercial sea route.

Portuguese raids on the northwest coast of Africa and the Canary Islands during the 1440s initiated a profitable slave trade. The total number of Africans captured or purchased on voyages exceeded eighty thousand by the end of the century and rose steadily thereafter. However, the gold trade quickly became more important once the Portuguese contacted the trading networks that flourished in West Africa and reached across the Sahara. By 1457 enough African gold was coming back to Portugal for the kingdom to issue a new gold coin called the *cruzado* (crusader), another reminder of how deeply the Portuguese entwined religious and secular motives.

While the Portuguese crown continued to sponsor voyages of exploration, speedier progress resulted from the growing participation of private commercial interests. In 1469 a prominent Lisbon merchant named Fernão Gomes purchased from the Crown the privilege of exploring 350 miles (550 kilometers) of African coast in return for a trade monopoly. He discovered the unin-habited island of São Tomé (sow toh-MAY) located on the equator and converted it to a major producer of sugar dependent on slaves imported from the African mainland. In the next century the island served as a model for the sugar plantations of Brazil and the Caribbean. Gomes also explored the **Gold Coast**, which became the headquarters of Portugal's West African trade.

The expectation of finding a passage around Africa to the rich trade of the Indian Ocean spurred the final thrust down the African coast. In 1488 **Bartolomeu Dias** became the first Portuguese explorer to round the southern tip of Africa and enter the Indian Ocean. Then in 1497–1498 **Vasco da Gama** sailed around Africa and reached India (see Environment and Tech-nology: Vasco da Gama's Fleet). In 1500 ships on the way to India under the command of Pedro Alvares Cabral (kah-BRAHL) sailed too far west and reached the South American mainland. This discovery established Portugal's claim to Brazil, which would become one of the Western Hemisphere's richest colonies. The gamble that Prince Henry had begun eight decades earlier was about to pay off handsomely.

Spanish Voyages

In contrast to the persistence and planning behind Portugal's century-long exploration of the South Atlantic, haste and blind luck lay behind Spain's early discoveries. Throughout most of the fifteenth century, the Spanish kingdoms were preoccupied with internal affairs: completion of the reconquest of southern Iberia from the Muslims; amalgamation of the various dynasties; and the conversion or expulsion of religious minorities. The Portuguese had already found a new route to the Indian Ocean by the time the Spanish monarchs were ready to turn to overseas exploration.

Christopher Columbus
Genoese mariner who in the
service of Spain led expeditions across the Atlantic,
reestablishing contact
between the peoples of
the Americas and the Old
World and opening the way
to Spanish conquest and
colonization.

The leader of the Spanish overseas mission was **Christopher Columbus** (1451–1506), a Geno-ese mariner. His four voyages between 1492 and 1504 established the existence of a vast new world across the Atlantic, whose existence few in "old world" Eurasia and Africa had ever sus-pected. But Columbus refused to accept that he had found unknown new continents and peo-ples, insisting that he had succeeded in finding a shorter route to the Indian Ocean.

As a young man Columbus gained considerable experience of the South Atlantic while par-ticipating in Portuguese explorations along the African coast, but he had become convinced there was a shorter way to reach the riches of the East than the route around Africa. By his reck-oning (based on a serious misreading of a ninth-century Arab authority), the Canaries were a mere 2,400 nautical miles (4,450 kilometers) from Japan. The actual distance was five times as far.

It was not easy for Columbus to find a sponsor willing to underwrite the costs of testing his theory that one could reach Asia by sailing west. Portuguese authorities twice rejected his plan. Columbus received a more sympathetic hearing in 1486 from Castile's able ruler, Queen Isabel, but no commitment of support. After a four-year study a Castilian commission concluded that a westward sea route to the Indies rested on many questionable geographical assumptions, but Columbus's persistence finally won over the queen and her husband, King Ferdinand of Aragon. In 1492 they agreed to fund a modest expedition.

Columbus recorded in his log that he and his crew of ninety men "departed Friday the third day of August of the year 1492" toward "the regions of India." Their mission, the royal contract stated, was "to discover and acquire certain islands and mainland in the Ocean Sea." He car-ried letters of introduction from the Spanish sovereigns to Eastern rulers, including one to the "Grand Khan" (meaning the Chinese emperor), and brought an Arabic interpreter to facilitate

ENVIRONMENT + TECHNOLOGY

Vasco da Gama's Fleet

The four small ships that sailed for India from Lisbon in June 1497 may seem a puny fleet compared to the sixty-two Chinese vessels that Zheng He had led into the Indian Ocean ninety-five years earlier. But given the fact that China had a hundred times as many people as Portugal, Vasco da Gama's fleet represented at least as great a commitment of resources. In any event, the Portuguese expedition had a far greater impact on the course of history. Having achieved its aim of inspiring awe at China's greatness, the Chinese throne sent out no more expeditions after 1433. Although da Gama's ships seemed more odd than awesome to Indian Ocean observers, that modest fleet began a revolution in global relations.

Portugal spared no expense in ensuring that the fleet would make it to India and back. Craftsmen built extra strength into the hulls to withstand the powerful storms that Dias had encountered in 1488 at the tip of Africa. Small enough to be able to navigate any shallow harbors and rivers they might encounter, the ships were crammed with specially strengthened casks and barrels of water, wine, oil, flour, meat, and vegetables far in excess of what was required even on a voyage that would take the better part of a year. Arms and ammunition were also in abundance.

Three of da Gama's ships were rigged with square sails on two masts for speed and a lateen sail on the third mast. The fourth vessel was a caravel with lateen sails. Each ship carried three sets of sails and plenty of extra rigging so as to be able to repair any damages due to storms. The crusaders' red crosses on the sails signaled one of the expedition's motives.

The captains and crew—Portugal's most talented and experienced—received extra pay and other rewards for their service. Yet there was no expectation that the unprecedented sums spent on this expedition would bring any immediate return. According to a contemporary chronicle, the only immediate return the Portuguese monarch received was "the

Vasco da Gama's Flagship This vessel carried the Portuguese captain on his second expedition to India in 1505.

The Pierpont Morgan Library/Art Resource, New York

knowledge that some part of Ethiopia and the beginning of Lower India had been discovered." However, the scale and care of the preparations suggest that the Portuguese expected the expedition to open up profitable trade to the Indian Ocean. And so it did.

e PRIMARY SOURCE: The Agreement with Columbus on April 17 and April 30, 1492 Read the contract signed by Columbus and his royal patrons, and see what riches he hoped to gain from his expedition.

communication with the peoples of eastern Asia. The expedition traveled in three small ships, the *Santa María*, the *Niña*, and the *Pinta*. The *Niña* and the *Pinta* were caravels.

Unfavorable headwinds had impeded other attempts to explore the Atlantic west of the Azores, but Columbus chose a southern route because he had learned in his service with the Portuguese of west-blowing winds in the latitudes of the Canaries. In October 1492 the expedition reached the islands of the Caribbean. Columbus insisted on calling the inhabitants "Indians" because he believed that the islands were part of the East Indies. A second voyage to the Caribbean in 1493 did nothing to change his mind. Even when, two months after Vasco da Gama reached India in 1498, Columbus first sighted the mainland of South America on his third voyage, he stubbornly insisted it was part of Asia. But by then other Europeans were convinced that he had discovered islands and continents previously unknown to the Old World. Amerigo Vespucci's explorations, first on behalf of Spain and then for Portugal, led mapmakers to name the new continents "America" after him, rather than "Columbia" after Columbus.

To prevent disputes arising from their efforts to exploit their new discoveries and spread Christianity, Spain and Portugal agreed to split the world between them. The Treaty of Tordesillas (tor-duh-SEE-yuhs), negotiated by the pope in 1494, drew an imaginary line down the middle of the North Atlantic Ocean. The treaty allocated lands east of the line in Africa and southern Asia to Portugal; lands to the west in the Americas were reserved for Spain. Cabral's discovery of Brazil, however, gave Portugal a valid claim to the part of South America located east of the line.

Where would Spain's and Portugal's spheres of influence divide in the East? Given Europeans' ignorance of the earth's true size in 1494, it was not clear whether the Moluccas (muh-LOO-kuhz), whose valuable spices had been a goal of the Iberian voyages, were on Portugal's or Spain's side of the Tordesillas line. The size of the Pacific Ocean would determine the boundary. By chance, in 1513 a Spanish adventurer named Vasco Núñez de Balboa (bal-BOH-uh) crossed the Isthmus (a narrow neck of land) of Panama from the east and sighted the Pacific Ocean. Then in 1519 **Ferdinand Magellan** (ca. 1480–1521) began his expedition to complete Columbus's interrupted westward voyage by sailing around the Americas and across the Pacific. The Moluccas turned out to lie well within Portugal's sphere, as Spain formally acknowledged in 1529.

Despite Magellan's death during his voyage for the king of Spain, he was considered the first person to encircle the globe because a decade earlier he had sailed from Europe to the East Indies as part of an expedition sponsored by his native Portugal. His two voyages took him across the Tordesillas line, through the separate spheres claimed by Portugal and Spain, establishing the basis for Spanish colonization of the Philippines after 1564. Of course, in 1500 these European claims were largely theoretical.

Ferdinand Magellan Portuguese navigator who led the Spanish expedition of 1519–1522 that was the first to sail around the world.

Although Columbus failed to find a new route to the East, the consequences of his voyages for European expansion were momentous. Those who followed in his wake laid the basis for Spain's large colonial empire in the Americas and for the empires of other European nations. In turn, these empires promoted the growth of a major new trading network whose importance rivaled and eventually surpassed the Indian Ocean network. Both the eastward and the westward voyages of exploration marked a tremendous expansion of Europe's role in world history.

SECTION REVIEW

- Portugal and Spain initiated oversees explorations to expand Christianity and gain new markets.

- Portugal, aided by Prince Henry the Navigator, created a trading empire in Africa and the Indian Ocean.

- Columbus first revealed the Americas to Europe, and other Spanish explorers reached Asia by crossing the Pacific.

ENCOUNTERS WITH EUROPE, 1450–1550

European actions alone did not determine the global consequences of these new contacts. The ways in which Africans, Asians, and Amerindians perceived these visitors and interacted with them influenced developments as well. Everywhere indigenous peoples evaluated the Europeans as potential allies or enemies, and everywhere Europeans attempted to insert themselves into existing commercial and geopolitical arrangements. In general, Europeans made slow progress in establishing colonies and asserting political influence in Africa and Asia, even while profiting from new commercial ties. In the Americas, however, Spain, Portugal, and later other European powers moved rapidly to create colonial empires. In this case the long isolation of the Amerindians from the rest of the world made them more vulnerable to the diseases that these outsiders introduced, limiting their potential for resistance and facilitating European settlement.

Western Africa

The Portuguese in Africa

Many along the West African coast were eager for trade with the Portuguese, since it offered new markets for exports and access to imports cheaper than those transported overland from the Mediterranean. This was evident along the Gold Coast of West Africa, first visited by the Portuguese in 1471. Miners in the hinterland had long sold their gold to traders, who took it to trading cities along the southern edge of the Sahara, where it was sold to traders who had crossed the

Bronze Figure of Benin Ruler   Both this prince and his horse are protected by chain mail introduced in the fifteenth century to Benin by Portuguese merchants.

Antenna Gallery Dakar Senegal/ G.Dagli Orti/The Art Archive

desert from North Africa. Recognizing that they might get more favorable terms from the new visitors from the sea, coastal Africans were ready to negotiate with the royal representative of Portugal who arrived in 1482 to seek permission to erect a trading fort.

This Portuguese noble and his officers (likely including the young Christopher Columbus, who had entered Portuguese service in 1476) were eager to make a proper impression. They dressed in their best clothes, erected and decorated a reception platform, celebrated a Catholic Mass, and signaled the start of negotiations with trumpets, tambourines, and drums. The African king, Caramansa, staged his entrance with equal ceremony, arriving with a large retinue of attendants and musicians. Through an African interpreter, the two leaders exchanged flowery speeches pledging goodwill and mutual benefit. Caramansa then gave permission for a small trading fort, assured, he said, by the appearance of the Portuguese that they were honorable persons, unlike the "few, foul, and vile" Portuguese visitors of the previous decade.

Neither side made a show of force, but the Africans' upper hand was evident in Caramansa's warning that he and his people would move away, depriving their fort of food and trade, if the Portuguese acted aggressively. Trade at the post of Saint George of the Mine (later called Elmina) enriched both sides. The Portuguese crown had soon purchased gold equal to one-tenth of the world's production at the time. In return, Africans received large quantities of goods that Portuguese ships brought from Asia, Europe, and other parts of Africa.

After a century of aggressive expansion, the kingdom of Benin in the Niger Delta was near the peak of its power when it first encountered the Portuguese. Its oba (king) presided over an elaborate bureaucracy from a spacious palace in his large capital city, also known as Benin. In response to a Portuguese visit in 1486, the oba sent an ambassador to Portugal to learn more about these strangers. He then established a royal monopoly on trade with the Portuguese, selling pepper and ivory tusks (for export to Portugal) as well as stone beads, textiles, and prisoners of war (for resale at Elmina). In return, Portuguese merchants provided Benin with copper and brass, fine textiles, glass beads, and a horse for the king's royal procession. In the early sixteenth century, as the demand for slaves for the Portuguese sugar plantations on the nearby island of São Tomé grew, the oba first raised the price of slaves and then imposed restrictions that limited their sale.

Early contacts generally involved a mix of commercial, military, and religious exchanges. Some African rulers appreciated the advantage of European firearms over spears and arrows in conflicts with their enemies and actively sought them in trade. Because African religions were generally not exclusive, coastal rulers were also willing to test the value of the Christian practices promoted by the Portuguese. The rulers of Benin and Kongo, the two largest coastal kingdoms, accepted both Portuguese missionaries and soldiers as allies in battle to test the efficacy of the Christian religion and European weaponry.

However, Portuguese efforts to persuade the king and nobles of Benin to accept the Catholic faith ultimately failed. Early kings showed some interest, but after 1538 rulers declined to receive more missionaries. They also closed the market in male slaves for the rest of the sixteenth century. We do not know why Benin chose to limit its contacts with the Portuguese, but the result makes clear that these rulers had the power to control their contacts with Europeans.

The Kingdom of the Kongo

Farther south, on the lower Congo River, relations between the kingdom of Kongo and the Portuguese began similarly but had a very different outcome. Like the oba of Benin, the manikongo (mah-NEE-KONG-goh) (king of Kongo) sent delegates to Portugal, established a royal monopoly on trade with the Portuguese, and expressed interest in Christian teachings. Deeply impressed with the new religion, the royal family made Catholicism the kingdom's official faith. But Kongo, lacking ivory and pepper, had less to trade than Benin. To acquire the goods brought by Portugal and to pay the costs of the missionaries, it had to sell more and more slaves.

Soon the manikongo began to lose his royal monopoly over the slave trade. In 1526 the Christian manikongo, Afonso I (r. 1506–ca. 1540), wrote to his royal "brother," the king of Portugal, begging for his help in stopping the trade because unauthorized Kongolese were kidnapping and selling people, even members of good families (see Diversity and Dominance: Kongo's Christian King). Alfonso's appeals for help received no reply from Portugal, whose interests were now concentrated in the Indian Ocean. Soon rebellion and the relocation of the slave trade from his kingdom to the south weakened the manikongo's authority.

Eastern Africa

Different still were the reactions of the Muslim rulers of the coastal trading states of eastern Africa. As Vasco da Gama's fleet sailed up the coast in 1498, most rulers gave the Portuguese a cool reception, suspicious of the intentions of visitors who painted crusaders' crosses on their sails. But the ruler of one of the ports, Malindi, seeing the Portuguese as potential allies who could help him expand the city's trading position, provided da Gama with a pilot to guide him to India. The initial suspicions of the other rulers were proven correct seven years later when a Portuguese war fleet bombarded and looted most of the coastal cities of eastern Africa in the name of Christianity and commerce, while sparing Malindi.

The Portuguese and Ethiopia

Christian Ethiopia was another eastern African state that saw potential benefit in an alliance with the Portuguese. In the fourteenth and early fifteenth centuries, Ethiopia faced increasing conflict with Muslim states along the Red Sea. Emboldened by the rise of the Ottoman Turks, who had conquered Egypt in 1517 and launched a major fleet in the Indian Ocean to counter the Portuguese, the talented warlord of the Muslim state of Adal launched a furious assault on Ethiopia. Adal's decisive victory in 1529 reduced the Christian kingdom to a precarious state. At that point Ethiopia's contacts with the Portuguese became crucial.

For decades, delegations from Portugal and Ethiopia had explored a possible alliance based on their mutual adherence to Christianity. A key figure was Queen Helena of Ethiopia, who acted as regent for her young sons after her husband's death in 1478. In 1509 Helena sent a letter to "our very dear and well-beloved brother," the king of Portugal, along with a gift of two tiny crucifixes said to be made of wood from the cross on which Christ had died in Jerusalem. In her letter she proposed an alliance between her army and Portugal's fleet against the Turks; however, Helena's death in 1522 occurred before the alliance could be arranged. Ethiopia's situation then grew more desperate.

Finally, in 1539 when another woman ruler was holding what was left of the empire together, a small Portuguese force commanded by Vasco da Gama's son Christopher arrived to aid Ethiopia. With Portuguese help the Ethiopians renewed their struggle. While Muslim forces captured and tortured to death Christopher da Gama, their attack failed when their own leader was mortally wounded in battle. Portuguese aid helped the Ethiopian kingdom save itself from extinction, but a permanent alliance faltered because Ethiopian rulers refused to transfer their Christian affiliation from the patriarch of Alexandria to the Latin patriarch of Rome (the pope) as the Portuguese insisted.

As these examples illustrate, African encounters with the Portuguese before 1550 varied considerably, as much because of the strategies and leadership of particular African states as because of Portuguese policies. Africans and Portuguese might become royal brothers, bitter opponents, or partners in a mutually profitable trade, but Europeans remained a minor presence in most of Africa in 1550. By then the Portuguese had become far more interested in the Indian Ocean trade.

Kongo's Christian King

The new overseas voyages brought conquest to some and opportunities for fruitful borrowings and exchanges to others. The decision of the ruler of the kingdom of Kongo to adopt Christianity in 1491 added cultural diversity to Kongolese society and in some ways strengthened the hand of the king. From then on Kongolese rulers sought to introduce Christian beliefs and rituals while at the same time Africanizing Christianity to make it more intelligible to their subjects. In addition, the kings of Kongo sought a variety of more secular aid from Portugal, including schools and medicine. Trade with the Portuguese introduced new social and political tensions, especially in the case of the export trade in slaves for the Portuguese sugar plantations on the island of São Tomé to the north.

Two letters sent to King João (zhwao) III of Portugal in 1526 illustrate how King Afonso of Kongo saw his kingdom's new relationship with Portugal and the problems that resulted from it. (Afonso adopted that name when baptized as a young prince.) After the death of his father in 1506, Afonso successfully claimed the throne and ruled until 1542. His son Henrique became the first Catholic bishop of the Kongo in 1521.

These letters were written in Portuguese and penned by the king's secretary João Teixera (tay-SHER-uh), a Kongo Christian, who, like Afonso, had been educated by Portuguese missionaries.

6 July 1526

To the very powerful and excellent prince Dom João, our brother:

On the 20th of June just past, we received word that a trading ship from your highness had just come to our port of Sonyo. We were greatly pleased by that arrival for it had been many days since a ship had come to our kingdom, for by it we would get news of your highness, which many times we had desired to know, . . . and likewise as there was a great and dire need for wine and flour for the holy sacrament; and of this we had had no great hope for we have the same need frequently. And that, sir, arises from the great negligence of your highness's officials toward us and toward shipping us those things. . . .

Sir, your highness should know how our kingdom is being lost in so many ways that we will need to provide the needed cure, since this is caused by the excessive license given by your agents and officials to the men and merchants who come to this kingdom to set up shops with goods and many things which have been prohibited by us, and which they spread throughout our kingdoms and domains in such abundance that many of our vassals, whose submission we could once rely on, now act independently so as to get the things in greater abundance than we ourselves; whom we had formerly held content and submissive and under our vassalage and jurisdiction, so it is doing a great harm not only to the service of God, but also to the security and peace of our kingdoms and state.

And we cannot reckon how great the damage is, since every day the mentioned merchants are taking our people, sons of the land and the sons of our noblemen and vassals and our relatives, because the thieves and men of bad conscience grab them so as to have the things and wares of this kingdom that they crave; they grab them and bring them to be sold. In such a manner, sir, has been the corruption and deprivation that our land is becoming completely depopulated, and your highness should not deem this good nor in your service. And to avoid this we need from these kingdoms [of yours] no more than priests and a few people to teach in schools, and no other goods except wine and flour for the holy sacrament, which is why we beg of your highness to help and assist us in this matter. Order your agents to send here neither merchants nor wares, because it is our will that in these kingdoms there should not be any dealing in slaves nor outlet for them, for the reasons stated above. Again we beg your highness's agreement, since otherwise we cannot cure such manifest harm. May Our Lord in His mercy have your highness always under His protection and may you always do the things of His holy service. I kiss your hands many times.

From our city of Kongo. . . .

The King, Dom Afonso

Indian Ocean States

Vasco da Gama did not make a great impression on the citizens of Calicut when he arrived on the Malabar Coast of India in May 1498. Da Gama's four small ships were far less imposing than the Chinese fleets that had called at Calicut sixty-five years earlier and no larger than many of the dhows that filled the harbor of this rich and important trading city. The samorin (ruler) of Calicut and his Muslim officials showed only mild interest in the Portuguese as new trading partners, since the gifts brought by da Gama had provoked derisive laughter. Twelve pieces of fairly ordinary striped cloth, four scarlet hoods, six hats, and six wash basins seemed inferior goods to those accustomed to the luxuries of the Indian Ocean trade. When da Gama tried to defend his gifts as those of an explorer, not a rich merchant, the samorin cut him short, asking

18 October 1526

Very high and very powerful prince King of Portugal, our brother,

Sir, your highness has been so good as to promise us that anything we need we should ask for in our letters, and that everything will be provided. And so that there may be peace and health of our kingdoms, by God's will, in our lifetime. And as there are among us old folks and people who have lived for many days, many and different diseases happen so often that we are pushed to the ultimate extremes. And the same happens to our children, relatives, and people, because this country lacks physicians and surgeons who might know the proper cures for such diseases, as well as pharmacies and drugs to make them better. And for this reason many of those who had been already confirmed and instructed in the things of the holy faith of Our Lord Jesus Christ perish and die. And the rest of the people for the most part cure themselves with herbs and sticks and other ancient methods, so that they live putting all their faith in these herbs and ceremonies, and die believing that they are saved; and this serves God poorly.

And to avoid such a great error, I think, and inconvenience, since it is from God and from your highness that all the good and the drugs and medicines have come to us for our salvation, we ask your merciful highness to send us two physicians and two pharmacists and one surgeon, so that they may come with their pharmacies and necessary things to be in our kingdoms, for we have extreme need of each and every one of them. We will be very good and merciful to them, since sent by your highness, their work and coming should be for good. We ask your highness as a great favor to do this for us, because besides being good in itself it is in the service of God as we have said above.

Moreover, sir, in our kingdoms there is another great inconvenience which is of little service to God, and this is that many of our people, out of great desire for the wares and things of your kingdoms, which are brought here by your people, and in order to satisfy their disordered appetite, seize many of our people, freed and exempt men. And many times noblemen and the sons of noblemen, and our relatives are stolen, and they take them to be sold to the white men who are in our kingdoms and take them hidden or by night, so that they are not recognized. And as soon as they are taken by the white men, they are immediately ironed and branded with fire. And when they are carried off to be embarked, if they are caught by our guards, the whites allege that they have bought them and cannot say from whom, so that it is our duty to do justice and to restore to the free their freedom. And so they went away offended.

And to avoid such a great evil we passed a law so that every white man living in our kingdoms and wanting to purchase slaves by whatever means should first inform three of our noblemen and officials of our court on whom we rely in this matter, namely Dom Pedro Manipunzo and Dom Manuel Manissaba, our head bailiff, and Gonçalo Pires, our chief supplier, who should investigate if the said slaves are captives or free men, and, if cleared with them, there will be no further doubt nor embargo and they can be taken and embarked. And if they reach the opposite conclusion, they will lose the aforementioned slaves. Whatever favor and license we give them [the white men] for the sake of your highness in this case is because we know that it is in your service too that these slaves are taken from our kingdom; otherwise we should not consent to this for the reasons stated above that we make known completely to your highness so that no one could say the contrary, as they said in many other cases to your highness, so that the care and remembrance that we and this kingdom have should not be withdrawn. . . .

We kiss your hands of your highness many times.

From our city of Kongo, the 18th day of October,

The King, Dom Afonso

QUESTIONS FOR ANALYSIS

1. What sorts of things does King Afonso desire from the Portuguese?

2. What is he willing and unwilling to do in return?

3. What problem with his own people has the slave trade created, and what has King Afonso done about it?

4. Does King Afonso see himself as an equal to King João or his subordinate? Do you agree with that analysis?

Source: From António Brásio, ed., *Monumenta Missionaria Africana: Africa Ocidental (1471-1531)* (Lisbon: Agência Geral do Ultramar, 1952), I: 468, 470–471, 488–491. Translated by David Northrup.

whether he had come to discover men or stones: "If he had come to discover men, as he said, why had he brought nothing?"

Indian Ocean Trade and the Portuguese

Coastal rulers soon discovered that the Portuguese had no intention of remaining poor competitors in the rich trade of the Indian Ocean. Upon da Gama's return to Portugal in 1499, the jubilant King Manuel styled himself "Lord of the Conquest, Navigation, and Commerce of Ethiopia, Arabia, Persia, and India," setting forth the ambitious scope of his plans. Previously the Indian Ocean had been an open sea, used by merchants (and pirates) of all the surrounding coasts. Now the Portuguese crown intended to make it a Portuguese sea, the private property of Portugal alone.

The ability of little Portugal to assert control over the Indian Ocean stemmed from the superiority of its ships and weapons over those of the regional powers, especially the lightly armed

Ms. 1889, c. 97, Biblioteca Casanateunse Rome. Photo: Humberto Nicoletti Serra

Portuguese in India   In the sixteenth century Portuguese men moved to the Indian Ocean Basin to work as administrators and traders. This Indo-Portuguese drawing from about 1540 shows a Portuguese man speaking to an Indian woman, perhaps making a proposal of marriage.

merchant dhows. In 1505 a Portuguese fleet of eighty-one ships and some seven thousand men bombarded Swahili Coast cities. Next on the list were Indian ports. Goa, on the west coast of India, fell to a well-armed fleet in 1510, becoming the base from which the Portuguese menaced the trading cities of Gujarat (goo-juh-RAHT) to the north and Calicut and other Malabar Coast cities to the south. The Portuguese took the port of Hormuz, controlling entry to the Persian Gulf, in 1515, but Aden, at the entrance to the Red Sea, successfully resisted. The addition of the Gujarati port of Diu in 1535 consolidated Portuguese dominance of the western Indian Ocean.

Meanwhile, Portuguese explorers had been reconnoitering the Bay of Bengal and the waters farther east. The city of Malacca (muh-LAH-kuh) on the strait between the Malay Peninsula and Sumatra became the focus of their attention. During the fifteenth century Malacca had become the main entrepôt (ON-truh-poh) (a place where goods are stored or deposited and from which they are distributed) for the trade from China, Japan, India, the Southeast Asian mainland, and the Moluccas. Among the city's more than 100,000 residents an early Portuguese visitor counted eighty-four different languages, including those of merchants from as far west as Cairo, Ethiopia, and the Swahili Coast of East Africa. Many non-Muslim residents of the city supported letting the Portuguese join its cosmopolitan trading community, perhaps hoping to offset the growing solidarity of Muslim traders. In 1511, however, the Portuguese seized this strategic trading center outright with a force of a thousand fighting men, including three hundred recruited in southern India.

Force was not always necessary. On the China coast, local officials and merchants interested in profitable new trade with the Portuguese persuaded the imperial government to allow the Portuguese to establish a trading post at Macao (muh-COW) in 1557. Operating from Macao, Portuguese ships came to nearly monopolize trade between China and Japan.

In the Indian Ocean, the Portuguese used their control of major port cities to enforce an even larger trading monopoly. As their power grew, they required all spices, as well as goods carried between major ports like Goa and Macao, to be carried in Portuguese ships. In addition, the Portuguese tried to control and tax other Indian Ocean trade by requiring all merchant ships entering and leaving one of their ports to carry a Portuguese passport and pay customs duties. Portuguese patrols seized vessels that attempted to avoid these monopolies, confiscated their cargoes, and either killed the captain and crew or sentenced them to forced labor.

Reactions to this power grab varied. Like the emperors of China, the Mughal (MOO-gahl) emperors of India largely ignored Portugal's maritime intrusions, seeing their interests as maintaining control over their vast land possessions. The Ottomans responded more aggressively, supporting Egypt against the Christian intruders with a large fleet and fifteen thousand men between 1501 and 1509. Then, having absorbed Egypt into their empire, the Ottomans sent another large expedition against the Portuguese in 1538. Both expeditions failed because Ottoman galleys were no match for the faster, better-armed Portuguese vessels in the open ocean. However, the Ottomans continued to exercise control over the Red Sea and Persian Gulf.

The smaller trading states of the region were less capable of challenging Portuguese domination head-on, since rivalries among them impeded the formation of a common front. Some chose to cooperate with the Portuguese to maintain their prosperity and security. Others engaged in evasion and resistance. Two examples illustrate the range of responses among Indian Ocean peoples.

The merchants of Calicut put up some of the most sustained resistance. In retaliation, the Portuguese embargoed all trade with Aden, Calicut's principal trading partner, and centered their trade on the port of Cochin, which had once been a dependency of Calicut. Some Calicut merchants became adept at evading Portuguese naval patrols, but the price of resistance was the shrinking of Calicut's commercial importance as Cochin gradually became the major pepper-exporting port on the Malabar Coast.

The traders and rulers of the state of Gujarat farther north had less success in keeping the Portuguese at bay. At first they resisted Portuguese attempts at monopoly and in 1509 joined Egypt's failed effort to sweep the Portuguese from the Arabian Sea. But in 1535, finding his state at a military disadvantage due to Mughal attacks, the ruler of Gujarat made the fateful decision to allow the Portuguese to build a fort at Diu in return for their support. Once established, the Portuguese gradually extended their control, so that by midcentury they were licensing and taxing all Gujarati ships. Even after the Mughals (who were Muslims) took control of Gujarat in 1572, the Mughal emperor Akbar permitted the Portuguese to continue their maritime monopoly in return for allowing one ship a year to carry pilgrims to Mecca without paying the Portuguese any fee.

The Portuguese never gained complete control of the Indian Ocean trade, but their naval supremacy allowed them to dominate key ports and trade routes during the sixteenth century. The resulting profits from spices and other luxury goods had a dramatic effect. The Portuguese were now able to break the pepper monopoly long held by Venice and Genoa, who both depended on Egyptian middlemen, by selling at much lower prices. They were also able to fund a more aggressive colonization of Brazil.

In both Asia and Africa the consequences flowing from these events were startling. Asian and East African traders were now at the mercy of Portuguese warships, but their individual responses affected their fates. Some were devastated. Others prospered by meeting Portuguese demands or evading their patrols. Because the Portuguese sought to control trade routes, not occupy large territories, Portugal had little impact on the Asian and African mainlands, in sharp contrast to what was occurring in the Americas.

The Americas

The Spanish established a vast territorial empire in the Americas in contrast to the trading empires the Portuguese created in Africa and Asia. This outcome had little to do with differences between the two kingdoms, even though Spain had a much larger population and greater resources. The Spanish and Portuguese monarchies had similar motives for expansion and used identical ships and weapons. Rather, the isolation of the Amerindian peoples made their responses to outside contacts different from those of African and Indian Ocean peoples. Isolation slowed the development of metallurgy and other militarily useful technologies in the Americas and also made these large populations more susceptible to new diseases. It was the spread of deadly new diseases, especially smallpox, among Amerindians after 1518 that weakened their ability to resist and facilitated Spanish and Portuguese occupation.

The first Amerindians to encounter Columbus were the Arawak of Hispaniola (modern Haiti and the Dominican Republic) in the Greater Antilles and the Bahamas to the north (see Map 16.2). They cultivated maize (corn), cassava (a tuber), sweet potatoes, and hot peppers, as well as cotton and tobacco. Although the islands did not have large gold deposits, and, unlike West Africans, the Arawak did not trade gold over long distances, the natives were skilled at working gold. While the Arawak at first extended a cautious welcome to the Spanish, they learned to tell exaggerated stories about gold in other places to persuade them to move on.

When Columbus made his second trip to Hispaniola in 1493, he brought several hundred settlers who hoped to make their fortune, as well as missionaries who were eager to persuade the Amerindians to accept Christianity. The settlers demanded indigenous labor to look for gold, stole gold ornaments, confiscated food, and sexually assaulted native women, provoking the Arawak to rebel in 1495. In this and later conflicts, steel swords, horses, and body armor led to Spanish victories and the slaughter of thousands. Thousands more were forced to labor for the Spanish. Meanwhile, cattle, pigs, and goats introduced by the settlers devoured the Arawak's food crops, causing deaths from famine and disease. A governor appointed by the Spanish crown in 1502 institutionalized these demands by dividing the surviving Arawak on Hispaniola among his allies as laborers.

The actions of the Spanish in the Antilles imitated Spanish actions and motives during the wars against the Muslims in Spain in the previous centuries: they sought to serve God by defeating nonbelievers and placing them under Christian control—and to become rich in the process. Individual **conquistadors** (kon-KEY-stuh-dor) (conquerors) extended that pattern around the Caribbean as gold and indigenous labor became scarce on Hispaniola. New expeditions searched for gold and Amerindian labor across the Caribbean region, capturing Amerindians and relocating them to Hispaniola as slaves. The island of Borinquen (Puerto Rico) was conquered in 1508 and Cuba between 1510 and 1511.

Following two failed expeditions to Mexico, Governor Velázquez of Cuba appointed an ambitious and ruthless nobleman, **Hernán Cortés** (kor-TEZ) (1485–1547) to undertake a new effort. Cortés left Cuba in 1519 with six hundred fighting men, including many who had sailed with the earlier expeditions, and most of the island's stock of weapons and horses. After demonstrating his military skills in a series of battles with the Maya, Cortés learned of the rich Aztec Empire in central Mexico.

The Aztecs had conquered their vast empire only during the previous century, and many subject peoples were ready to embrace the Spanish as allies. They resented the tribute payments, forced labor, and large-scale human sacrifices demanded by the Aztecs. The Aztecs also had powerful native enemies, including the Tlaxcalans (thlash-KAH-lans), who became crucial supporters of Cortés. Like the peoples of Africa and Asia when confronted by Europeans, Amerindian peoples, like the Tlaxcalans of Mexico, calculated as best they could the potential benefit or threat represented by these strange visitors. Individual Amerindians also made these calculations. Malintzin (mah-LEENT-zeen) (also called Malinche), a native woman given to Cortés shortly after his arrival in the Maya region, became his translator, key source of intelligence, and mistress. As peoples and as individuals, native allies were crucial to the Spanish campaign.

While the emperor **Moctezuma II** (mock-teh-ZOO-ma) (r. 1502–1520) hesitated to use force and attempted diplomacy instead, Cortés pushed toward the Aztec capital of Tenochtitlan (teh-noch-TIT-lan). Spanish forces used firearms, cavalry tactics, and steel swords to great advantage in battles along their route. In the end Moctezuma agreed to welcome the Spaniards. As they approached his island capital, the emperor went out in a great procession, dressed in his finery, to welcome Cortés.

Despite Cortés's initial pledge that he came in friendship, Moctezuma was quickly imprisoned. The Spanish looted his treasury, interfered with the city's religious rituals, and eventually massacred hundreds during a festival. These actions provoked a mass rebellion directed against both the Spanish and Moctezuma. During the Spaniards' desperate escape, the Aztecs killed

The Spanish in the Caribbean

e PRIMARY SOURCE: A Dominican Voice in the Wilderness: Preaching Against Tyranny in Hispaniola A Dominican friar, and former landholder, expresses his outrage at the injustices committed against the native people.

conquistadors Early-sixteenth-century Spanish adventurers who conquered Mexico, Central America, and Peru.

The Conquest of the Aztecs

Hernán Cortés Spanish explorer and conquistador who led the conquest of Aztec Mexico in 1519–1521 for Spain.

Moctezuma II Aztec emperor who died while in custody of the Spanish conquistador Hernán Cortés.

Oronoz

Coronation of Emperor Moctezuma   This painting by an unnamed Aztec artist depicts the Aztec ruler's coronation. Moctezuma, his nose pierced by a bone, receives the crown from a prince in the palace at Tenochtitlan.

half the Spanish force and four thousand of Cortés's native allies. In the confusion Moctezuma also lost his life, either killed by the Spanish or in the Aztec attack.

The survivors, strengthened by Spanish reinforcements and aided by the Tlaxcalans, renewed their attack and captured Tenochtitlan in 1521. Their victory was aided by a smallpox epidemic that killed more of the city's defenders than did the fighting. One source remembered that the disease "spread over the people as a great destruction." Many Amerindians as well as Europeans blamed the devastating spread of this disease on supernatural forces. Cortés and other Spanish leaders then led expeditions to the north and south accompanied by the Tlaxcalans and other indigenous allies. Everywhere epidemic disease, especially smallpox, helped crush indigenous resistance.

The Conquest of the Inca

Spanish settlers in Panama had heard tales of rich and powerful civilizations to the south even before the conquest of the Aztecs. During the previous century the Inca had built a vast empire along the Pacific coast of South America (see Chapter 12). As the empire expanded through conquest, the Inca enforced new labor demands and taxes and even exiled rebellious populations from their lands.

About 1525 the Inca ruler Huayna Capac (WHY-nah KAH-pak) died in Quito, where he had led a successful military campaign. Two of his sons then fought for the throne. In the end **Atahualpa** (ah-tuh-WAHL-puh) (r. 1531–1533), the candidate of the northern army, defeated Huascar, the candidate of the royal court at Cuzco. As a result, the Inca military was decimated and the empire's political leadership weakened by the violence; at this critical time **Francisco Pizarro** (pih-ZAHR-oh) (ca. 1478–1541) and his force of 180 men, 37 horses, and two cannon entered the region.

Pizarro had come to the Americas in 1502 at the age of twenty-five to seek his fortune and had participated in the conquest of Hispaniola and in Balboa's expedition across the Isthmus of

Atahualpa Last ruling Inca emperor of Peru. He was executed by the Spanish.

Francisco Pizarro Spanish explorer who led the conquest of the Inca Empire of Peru in 1531–1533.

The Execution of Inca Ruler Atahualpa Felipe Guaman Poma de Ayala, a native Andean from the area of Huamanga in Peru, drew this representation of the execution. While Pizarro sentenced Atahualpa to death by strangulation, not beheading, Guaman Poma's illustration forcefully made the point that Spain had imposed an arbitrary and violent government on the Andean people.

Musée du Quai Branley/Scala Picture Library

Panama. In the 1520s he gambled his fortune to finance the exploration of the Pacific south of the equator, where he learned of the riches of the Inca. With a license from the king of Spain, he set out from Panama in 1531 to conquer them.

Having seen signs of the civil war after landing, Pizarro arranged to meet the Inca emperor, Atahualpa, near the Andean city of Cajamarca (kah-hah-MAHR-kah) in November 1532. With supreme boldness and brutality, Pizarro's small band of armed men attacked Atahualpa and his followers as they entered an enclosed courtyard. Though surrounded by an Inca army of at least forty thousand, the Spaniards were able to use their cannon to create confusion while their swords brought down thousands of the emperor's lightly armed retainers and servants. Pizarro now replicated in Peru Cortés's strategy by capturing the Inca ruler.

Atahualpa, seeking to guard his authority, quickly ordered the execution of his imprisoned brother Huascar. He also attempted to purchase his freedom. Having noted the glee with which the

SECTION REVIEW

- African kingdoms reacted in various ways to the opportunities and threats created by the arrival of the Portuguese, but only Kongo embraced Christianity and accepted a large Portuguese military presence in the sixteenth century.

- However, the Portuguese used military force to consolidate a trade empire in the Indian Ocean.

- After the Spanish occupied the Caribbean, Cortés led an expedition that conquered the Aztecs, weakened by epidemic.

- The Spanish under Pizarro conquered the Inca Empire, already suffering from civil war, and then fell on each other, but surviving conquistadors continued to explore the Americas.

Spaniards seized gold and silver, Atahualpa offered a ransom he thought would satisfy even the greediest among them: rooms filled to shoulder height with gold and silver. The Inca paid the ransom of 13,400 pounds (6,000 kilograms) of gold and 26,000 pounds (12,000 kilograms) of silver, but the Spaniards still executed Atahualpa. With the unity of the Inca Empire already battered by the civil war and the deaths of Atahualpa and his brother Huascar, the Spanish occupied Cuzco, the capital city.

Nevertheless, Manco Inca, whom the Spanish had placed on the throne following the execution of his brother Atahualpa, led a massive native rebellion in 1536. Although defeated by the Spanish, Manco Inca and his followers retreated to the interior and created a much-reduced independent kingdom that survived until 1572. The victorious Spaniards, now determined to settle their own rivalries, initiated a bloody civil war fueled by greed and jealousy. Before peace was established, this struggle took the lives of Francisco Pizarro and most of the other prominent conquistadors. Incited by the fabulous wealth of the Aztecs and Inca, conquistadors now extended their exploration and conquest of South and North America, dreaming of new treasures to loot.

CONCLUSION

The voyages of exploration undertaken by the Chinese and Polynesians pursued diverse objectives. The great voyages of the Chinese in the early fifteenth century were motivated by an interest in trade, curiosity, and the desire to project imperial power. For the Polynesians, exploration opened the opportunity to both project power and demonstrate expertise while at the same time settling satellite populations that would relieve population pressures. The Vikings, Africans, and Amerindians all undertook long-distance explorations as well, although with fewer lasting consequences. The projection of European influence between 1450 and 1550 was in some ways similar to that of other cultural regions in that it expanded commercial linkages, increased cross-cultural contacts, and served the ambitions of political leaders. But the result of their voyages proved to be a major turning point in world history. During those years European explorers opened new long-distance trade routes across the world's three major oceans, for the first time establishing regular contact among all the continents. As a result, a new balance of power arose in parts of Atlantic Africa, the Indian Ocean, and the Americas.

The rapid expansion of European empires and the projection of European military power around the world would have seemed unlikely in 1492. No European power matched the military and economic strength of China, and few could rival the Ottomans. Spain lacked strong national institutions, and Portugal had a small population; both had limited economic resources. Because of these limitations, the monarchs of Spain and Portugal allowed their subjects greater initiative as they engaged distant cultures.

The pace and character of European expansion in Africa and Asia were different than in the Americas. In Africa local rulers were generally able to limit European military power to coastal outposts and to control European trade. Only in the Kongo were the Portuguese able to project their power inland. In the Indian Ocean there were mature markets and specialized production for distant consumers when Europeans arrived. Here Portuguese (and later Dutch and British) naval power allowed Europeans to harvest large profits and influence regional commercial patterns, but most native populations continued to enjoy effective autonomy for centuries.

In the Americas, however, the terrible effects of epidemic disease and the destructiveness of the conquest led to the rapid creation of European settlements and the subordination of the surviving indigenous population. The Spanish and Portuguese found few long-distance markets and little large-scale production of goods that they could export profitably to Europe. The Americas would eventually produce great amounts of wealth, but this production of gold, silver, and sugar resulted from the introduction of new technologies, the imposition of oppressive new forms of labor, such as slavery, and the development of new roads and ports.

KEY TERMS

Zheng He p. 423
Arawak p. 424
Henry the Navigator p. 426
caravel p. 427

Gold Coast p. 429
Bartolomeu Dias p. 429
Vasco da Gama p. 429
Christopher Columbus p. 429

Ferdinand Magellan p. 431
conquistadors p. 438
Hernán Cortés p. 438
Moctezuma II p. 438

Atahualpa p. 439
Francisco Pizarro p. 439

EBOOK AND WEBSITE RESOURCES

Primary Sources

The Agreement with Columbus on April 17 and April 30, 1492

A Dominican Voice in the Wilderness: Preaching Against Tyranny in Hispaniola

Interactive Maps

Map 16.1 Exploration and Settlement in the Indian and Pacific Oceans Before 1500

Map 16.2 Middle America to 1533

Map 16.3 European Exploration, 1420–1542

Plus flashcards, practice quizzes, and more. Go to:
www.cengage.com/history/bullietearthpeople5e

SUGGESTED READING

Abu-Lughod, Janet. *Before European Hegemony: The World System, A.D. 1250–1350.* 1989. A speculative reassessment of the Mongols and the Indian Ocean trade in the creation of an economic world system.

Cipolla, Carlo M. *Guns, Sails, and Empires: Technological Innovation and the Early Phases of European Expansion, 1400–1700.* 1965. A simple introduction to the technologies of European expansion.

Cuyvers, Luc. *Into the Rising Sun: The Journey of Vasco da Gama and the Discovery of the Modern World.* 1998. Examines the impact of finding a sea route to India.

Fernandez-Armesto, Felipe. *Before Columbus: Exploration and Colonization from the Mediterranean to the Atlantic, 1229–1492.* 1987. Examines the medieval background to European intercontinental voyages.

Jennings, Jesse D., ed. *The Prehistory of Polynesia.* 1979. A reliable guide to Polynesian expansion.

Kamen, Henry. *Spain, 1469–1714: A Society of Conflict,* 2nd ed. 1991. A reliable guide to Spain in the age of maritime empire.

Levenson, Joseph R., ed. *European Expansion and the Counter Example of Asia, 1300–1600.* 1967. A collection of essays on the different expansions covered by this chapter.

McNeil, William F. *Visitors to Ancient America: The Evidence for European and Asian Presence in America Prior to Columbus.* 2004. Examines evidence of early voyages and contacts across both the Atlantic and Pacific.

Northrup, David. *Africa's Discovery of Europe, 1450–1850.* 2002. Looks at the perceptions of the peoples European explorers encountered.

Parry, J. H. *The Age of Reconnaissance: Discovery, Exploration, and Settlement, 1450–1650.* 1963. A general history with an emphasis on maritime techniques.

Phillips, William D., and Carla Rhan Phillips. *The Worlds of Christopher Columbus.* 1992. Examines the mariner and his times in terms of modern concerns.

Reid, Anthony. *Southeast Asia in the Age of Commerce, 1450–1680,* 2 vols. 1988, 1993. Deals with what were known as the East Indies.

Restall, Matthew. *Seven Myths of the Spanish Conquest.* 2003. Concentrates on continuities of Amerindian life in the face of European onslaught.

Russell-Wood, A. J. R. *The Portuguese Empire: A World on the Move.* 1998. The earliest European maritime empire.

Scammell, G. V. *The World Encompassed: The First European Maritime Empires, c. 800–1650.* 1981. A good general introduction to European expansion.

Severin, Tim. *The Brendan Voyage.* 2000. Vividly recounts a modern retracing of pre-Columbian Irish voyages.

Thornton, John. *Africa and Africans in the Making of the Atlantic World, 1400–1800,* 2nd ed. 1998. Examines Africans' encounters with Europeans and their involvement in the Atlantic economy.

Todorov, Tzvetan. *The Conquest of America.* 1985. Focuses on the shortcomings of Columbus and his Spanish peers.

NOTES

1. Ma Huan, *Ying-yai Sheng-lan: "The Overall Survey of the Ocean's Shores,"* ed. Feng Ch'eng-Chün, trans. J. V. G. Mills (Cambridge, England: Cambridge University Press, 1970), 180.

2. Alvise da Cadamosto in *The Voyages of Cadamosto and Other Documents*, ed. and trans. G. R. Crone (London: Hakluyt Society, 1937), 2.

CLIMATE AND POPULATION TO 1500

During the millennia before 1500, human populations expanded in three momentous surges. The first occurred after 50,000 B.C.E. when humans emigrated from their African homeland to all of the inhabitable continents. After that, the global population remained steady for several millennia. During the second expansion, between about 5000 and 500 B.C.E., population rose from about 5 million to 100 million as agricultural societies spread around the world (see Figure 1). Again population growth then slowed for several centuries before a third surge took world population to over 350 million by 1200 C.E. (Figure 2 shows population in China and Europe).

For a long time historians tended to attribute these population surges to cultural and technological advances. Indeed, a great many changes in culture and technology are associated with adaptation to different climates and food supplies in the first surge and with the domestication of plants and animals in the second. However, historians have not found a cultural or technological change to explain the third surge, nor can they explain why creativity would have stagnated for long periods between the surges. Something else must have been at work.

Recently historians have begun to pay more attention to the impact of long-term variations in global climate. By examining ice cores drilled out of glaciers, scientists have been able to compile records of thousands of years of climate change. The comparative width of tree rings from ancient forests has provided additional data on periods of favorable and unfavorable growth. Such evidence shows that cycles of population growth and stagnation followed changes in global climate.

Historians now believe that global temperatures were above normal for extended periods from the late 1100s to the late 1200s C.E. In the temperate lands where most of the

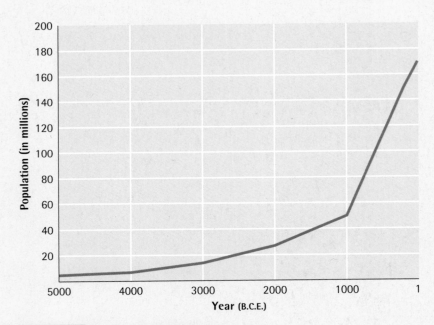

FIGURE 1 World Population, 5000–1 B.C.E.

world's people lived, above-normal temperatures meant a longer growing season, more bountiful harvests, and thus a more adequate and reliable food supply. The ways in which societies responded to the medieval warm period are as important as the climate change, but it is unlikely that human agency alone would have produced the medieval surge. One notable response was that of the Vikings, who increased the size and range of their settlements in the North Atlantic, although their raids also caused death and destruction.

Some of the complexities involved in the interaction of human agency, climate, and other natural factors are also evident in the demographic changes that followed the medieval warm period. During the 1200s the Mongol invasions caused death and disruption of agriculture across Eurasia. China's population, which had been over 100 million in 1200, declined by a third or more by 1300. The Mongol invasions did not cause harm west of Russia, but climate changes in the 1300s resulted in population losses in Europe. Unusually heavy rains caused crop failures and a prolonged famine in northern Europe from 1315 to 1319.

The freer movement of merchants within the Mongol Empire also facilitated the spread of disease across Eurasia, culminating in the great pandemic known as the Black Death in Europe. The demographic recovery under way in China was reversed. The even larger population losses in Europe may have been affected by the decrease in global temperatures to their lowest point in many millennia between 1350 and 1375. After 1400 improving economic conditions enabled population to recover more rapidly in Europe than in China, where the conditions of rural life remained harsh.

Because many other historical circumstances interact with changing weather patterns, historians have a long way to go in deciphering the role of climate in history. Nevertheless, it is a factor that can no longer be ignored.

FIGURE 2 Population in China and Europe, 1–1500 C.E.

PART V

Library of Congress

Map of the World, ca. 1595 After Ferdinand Magellan, the next explorer to circumnavigate the world was Sir Francis Drake (ca. 1540–1596). Departing with five ships in 1577, Drake nonetheless completed the majority of his voyage in a single ship, the *Golden Hind*, returning to England in 1580. This hand-colored engraving by Jodocus Hondius shows his route. Supported by Queen Elizabeth and other investors, Drake raided Spanish ships and ports and returned with great riches. Unlike Magellan, he traveled far northward before crossing the Pacific, harboring for several weeks near San Francisco Bay and making friendly contact with the native peoples there. Drake played a decisive role in England's victory against the Spanish Armada in 1588.

446

The Globe Encompassed, 1500–1750

The decades between 1500 and 1750 witnessed a tremendous expansion of commercial, cultural, and biological exchanges around the world. New long-distance sea routes linked Europe with sub-Saharan Africa and the existing maritime networks of the Indian Ocean and East Asia. Spanish and Portuguese voyages ended the isolation of the Americas and created new webs of exchange in the Atlantic and Pacific. Overland expansion of Muslim, Russian, and Chinese empires also increased global interaction.

These expanding contacts had major demographic and cultural consequences. Domesticated animals and crops from the Old World transformed agriculture in the Americas, while Amerindian foods such as the potato became staples of the diet of the Old World. European diseases, meanwhile, devastated the Amerindian population, facilitating the establishment of large Spanish, Portuguese, French, and British empires. Europeans introduced enslaved Africans to relieve the labor shortage. Immigrant Africans and Europeans brought new languages, religious practices, music, and forms of personal adornment.

In Asia and Africa, by contrast, the most important changes owed more to internal forces than to European actions. The Portuguese seized control of some important trading ports and networks in the Indian Ocean and pioneered new contacts with China and Japan. In time, the Dutch, French, and English expanded these profitable connections, but in 1750 Europeans were still primarily a maritime force. Asians and Africans generally retained control of their lands and participated freely in overseas trade.

The Islamic world saw the dramatic expansion of the Ottoman Empire in the Middle East and the establishment of the Safavid Empire in Iran and the Mughal Empire in South Asia. In northern Eurasia, Russia and China acquired vast new territories and populations, while a new national government in Japan promoted economic development and stemmed foreign influence.

CHAPTER
17

CHAPTER OUTLINE

Kunsthistorisches Museum, Vienna/ The Bridgeman Art Library

Hunters in the Snow, 1565   This January scene, by the Flemish artist Pieter Bruegel the Elder, shows many everyday activities.

 Visit the website and ebook for additional study materials and interactive tools: www.cengage.com/history/bullietearthpeople5e

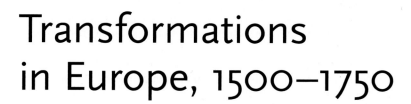

Transformations in Europe, 1500–1750

F our years before his death, the Flemish artist Pieter Bruegel the Elder (ca. 1525–1569) painted *Hunters in the Snow*, a masterpiece of the cultural revival that later ages would call the European **Renaissance**. After a period of apprenticeship, in 1551 Bruegel became a master painter in the Antwerp Painters Guild. Though he also painted biblical and allegorical subjects, Bruegel is remembered best for his technical skill and powers of observation, which were demonstrated in his depictions of the everyday life that surrounded him. Other forms of culture flourished as well in early modern Europe, as exemplified by the musical compositions of Johann Sebastian Bach (1685–1750) in Germany and Antonio Vivaldi (ca. 1675–1741) in Italy, and by the literature of William Shakespeare (1564–1616) in England and Miguel de Cervantes (1547–1616) in Spain.

In this period Europe also developed powerful and efficient armies, economies, and governments, which larger states elsewhere in the world feared, envied, and sometimes imitated. The balance of power was shifting slowly in Europe's favor. At the beginning of this era, the Ottomans threatened Europe, but by 1750, as the remaining chapters of Part Five detail, Europeans had brought much of the world under their control. No single nation was responsible for this success. The Dutch eclipsed the pioneering Portuguese and Spanish; then the English and French bested the Dutch. This was also a period of dynamic cultural change. At the beginning of this era a single Christian tradition dominated western Europe. By its end secular political institutions and economic interests had grown stronger, while Catholic and Protestant churches were weakened by religious wars. Equally influential was the challenge to Christianity's long domination of European intellectual life posed by the Scientific Revolution and the Enlightenment.

The years from 1500 to 1750 were not simply an age of progress for Europe. For many, the ferocious competition of European armies, merchants, and ideas was a wrenching experience. The growth of powerful states extracted a terrible price in death and destruction. The Reformation brought widespread religious persecution and religious warfare as well as greater individual choice in religion. Women's fortunes remained closely tied to their social class, and few gained equality with men. The expanding economy benefited members of the emerging merchant elite and their political allies, but in an era of rising prices Europe's urban and rural poor struggled to survive.

- How did the interplay of traditional beliefs and revolutionary ideas influence the cultural history of early modern Europe?
- What factors contributed to the wealth of some Europeans and the great poverty of others in this period?
- How did differing policies in the areas of religion, foreign relations, and economics determine the very different experiences of early modern European states?

Renaissance (European) A period of intense artistic and intellectual activity, said to be a "rebirth" of Greco-Roman culture. Usually divided into an Italian Renaissance, from roughly the mid-fourteenth to mid-fifteenth century, and a Northern (trans-Alpine) Renaissance, from roughly the early fifteenth to early seventeenth century.

CULTURE AND IDEAS

During the Reformation, theological controversies broke the religious unity of the Latin Church and contributed to long and violent wars. A huge witch scare demonstrated the endurance of traditional folklore and popular beliefs. While the influence of classical ideas from Greco-Roman antiquity increased among better-educated Europeans, some bold thinkers challenged the authority of the ancients. They introduced new ideas about the motion of the planets and encouraged others to challenge traditional social and political systems; these new ideas would help promote revolutionary changes in the period after 1750. Each of these events had its own causes, but the technology of the printing press broadened the impact of all.

Early Reformation

papacy The central administration of the Roman Catholic Church, of which the pope is the head.

In 1500 the **papacy**, the central government of Latin Christianity, simultaneously gained stature and suffered from corruption and dissent. Recovered from a period when competing popes supported by rival rulers disputed control of the church, popes now exercised greater power funded by larger donations and tax receipts. The construction of fifty-four new churches and other buildings in Rome served to demonstrate the church's power and showcase the artistic Renaissance then under way. The church leadership intended the size and splendor of the magnificent new Saint Peter's Basilica in Rome to glorify God, display the skill of Renaissance artists and builders, and enhance the standing of the papacy, but the vast expense of its construction and rich decoration also caused scandal.

indulgence The forgiveness of the punishment due for past sins, granted by the Catholic Church authorities as a reward for a pious act. Martin Luther's protest against the sale of indulgences is often seen as touching off the Protestant Reformation.

The skillful overseer of the design and financing of the Saint Peter's Basilica was Pope Leo X (r. 1513–1521), a member of the wealthy Medici (MED-ih-chee) family of Florence, famous for its patronage of the arts. Pope Leo's artistic taste was superb and his personal life free from scandal, but he was more a man of action than a spiritual leader. During his papacy the church aggressively raised funds for the basilica and other ambitious projects. The sale of **indulgences**—a forgiveness of the punishment due for past sins, was seen by many as abusive and scandalous.

Private Collection/The Bridgeman Art Library

Luther and the Reformation   This sixteenth-century woodcut of Martin Luther shows him writing his demands for religious reform with a symbolically oversized quill pen on the door of All Saints Church in Wittenberg, Germany.

CHRONOLOGY

	Politics and Culture	Environment and Technology	Warfare
1500	1500s Spain's golden century		
	1519 Protestant Reformation begins		1526–1571 Ottoman attack on Hapsburg Empire
	1540s Scientific Revolution begins		
	1545 Catholic Reformation begins		1546–1555 German Wars of Religion
			1562–1598 French Wars of Religion
			1566–1648 Netherlands Revolt
	Late 1500s Witch-hunts increase		
		1590s Dutch develop flyboats; Little Ice Age begins	
1600	1600s Holland's golden century	1600s Depletion of forests growing	
		1609 Galileo's astronomical telescope	
			1618–1648 Thirty Years War
			1642–1648 English Civil War
			1652–1678 Anglo-Dutch Wars
			1667–1697 Wars of Louis XIV
		1682 Canal du Midi completed	1683–1697 Ottoman wars
			1701–1714 War of the Spanish Succession
1700	1700s The Enlightenment begins		
		1750 English mine nearly 5 million tons of coal a year	
		1755 Lisbon earthquake	

Martin Luther

e PRIMARY SOURCE: Table Talk Read Martin Luther in his own words, speaking out forcefully and candidly—and sometimes with humor—against Catholic institutions.

Protestant Reformation Religious reform movement within the Latin Christian Church beginning in 1519. It resulted in the "protesters" forming several new Christian denominations, including the Lutheran and Reformed Churches and the Church of England.

A young professor of sacred scripture, Martin Luther (1483–1546), objected to this practice and to other excesses. As the result of a powerful religious experience, Luther had forsaken money and marriage for a monastic life of prayer, self-denial, and study. In his religious quest, he found personal consolation in a passage in Saint Paul's Epistle stating that salvation resulted from religious faith, not from "doing certain things." That passage led Luther to object to the way preachers emphasized giving money to the church more than they emphasized faith. He wrote to Pope Leo to complain of this abuse and challenged the preachers to a debate on the theology of indulgences.

This theological dispute was also a contest between two strong-willed men. Largely ignoring the theological objections, Pope Leo regarded Luther's letter as a challenge to papal power and moved to silence him. During a debate in 1519, a papal representative led Luther into open disagreement with church doctrines, for which the papacy condemned him. Blocked in his effort to reform the church from within, Luther burned the papal bull (document) of condemnation, rejected the pope's authority, and began the movement known as the **Protestant Reformation**.

Accusing those whom he called "Romanists" (Roman Catholics) of relying on "good works," Luther insisted that the only way to salvation was through faith in Jesus Christ. He further declared that Christian belief should be based on the word of God in the Bible and on Christian tradition, not on the authority of the pope. Luther's use of the printing press to spread his ideas won him the support of powerful Germans, who responded to his nationalist portrayal of an Italian pope seeking to beautify Rome with German funds.

The Reformation Spreads

Luther's denunciation of the ostentation and corruption of the church led others to call for a return to authentic Christian practices and beliefs. John Calvin (1509–1564), a well-educated Frenchman who left the study of law for theology after experiencing a religious conversion, became an influential Protestant leader. As a young man, Calvin published a synthesis of Christian teachings in 1535, *The Institutes of the Christian Religion*. Although Calvin agreed with Luther's emphasis on faith over works, he denied that human faith alone could merit salvation. Salvation, Calvin believed, was a gift God gave to those He "predestined." Calvin also went farther than Luther in curtailing the power of the clerical hierarchy and in simplifying religious rituals. Calvinist congregations elected their own governing committees and created regional and national synods (councils) to regulate doctrinal issues. Calvinists also displayed simplicity in dress, life, and worship, avoiding ostentatious living and stripping churches of statues, most musical instruments, stained-glass windows, incense, and vestments.

The Reformers appealed to genuine religious sentiments, but their successes and failures were also due to local political and economic conditions. It was no coincidence that German-born Luther had his greatest success among German speakers and linguistically related Scandinavians and not surprising that peasants and urban laborers sometimes defied their masters by adopting a different faith. Protestants were no more inclined than Roman Catholics to question male dominance in the church and the family, but most Protestants rejected the medieval tradition of celibate priests and nuns and advocated Christian marriage for all adults.

The Counter Reformation and the Politics of Religion

Catholic Reformation
Religious reform movement within the Latin Christian Church, begun in response to the Protestant Reformation. It clarified Catholic theology and reformed clerical training and discipline.

Shaken by the intensity of the Protestant attack, the Catholic Church undertook its own reforms. A council that met at the city of Trent in northern Italy between 1545 and 1563 sought to distinguish Catholic doctrines from Protestant "errors" and reaffirmed the supremacy of the pope. The council also called for bishops to reside in their dioceses and dioceses to maintain a theological seminary to train priests. The creation in 1540 of a new religious order, the Society of Jesus, or "Jesuits," by a Spanish nobleman, Ignatius of Loyola (1491–1556), was among the most important events of the **Catholic Reformation**. Well-educated Jesuits helped stem the Protestant tide by their teaching and preaching (see Map 17.1), and they gained converts through overseas missions (see Chapters 18 and 21).

Religion and the Ambitions of Kings

Given the complexity and intensity stirred by the Protestant Reformation, it is not surprising that both sides persecuted and sometimes executed those of differing views. Bitter "wars of religion" would continue in parts of western Europe until 1648. The rulers of Spain and France actively defended the Catholic tradition against Protestant challenges. Following the pattern used by his predecessors to suppress Jewish and Muslim practices, King Philip II of Spain used the Inquisition to enforce religious orthodoxy. Suspected Protestants, as well as critics of the king, were accused of heresy, some were punished by death, and even those acquitted learned not to challenge the church or the king again.

In France the Calvinist opponents of the Valois dynasty gained the military advantage in the French Wars of Religion (1562–1598). In the interest of national unity, their leader Prince Henry of Navarre ultimately embraced the Catholic faith of the majority of his subjects when he ruled as Henry IV of France. In their embrace of a union of church and state, Henry IV, his son King Louis XIII, and his grandson King Louis XIV supported the Catholic Church. Ultimately, Louis XIV revoked the Edict of Nantes (nahnt) by which his grandfather had granted religious freedom to his Protestant supporters in 1598.

In England King Henry VIII had initially been a strong defender of the papacy against Lutheran criticism. But when Henry failed to obtain a papal annulment of his marriage to Catherine of Aragon, who had not furnished him with a male heir, he challenged the papacy's authority over the English church. First the English archbishop of Canterbury annulled Henry's marriage in 1533 and then Parliament made the king head of an autonomous Church of England.

Like many Protestant rulers, Henry used his authority to disband monasteries and convents and seize their lands. He gave some land to his powerful allies and sold other land to pay for his new navy. While the king's power had grown at the expense of the Catholic Church, religious belief and practice were changing also. The new Anglican Church distanced itself from Catholic ritual and theology, but English Puritans (Calvinists who wanted to "purify" the church of all

Catholic practices and beliefs) sought more. When Puritans petitioned to eliminate bishops in 1603, the first Stuart king, James I, reminded them of the traditional role of religion in supporting royal power: "No bishops, no king."

Local Religion, Traditional Culture, and Witch-Hunts

Both in the Protestant north and the Catholic south the institutions of religious orthodoxy were weakest in villages and small towns. In these settings, local religion commonly blended the rituals and beliefs of the established churches with local folk customs, pre-Christian beliefs, ancient curing practices, love magic, and the casting of spells. The vigor and power of these local religious traditions ebbed and flowed in response to the strength of national and regional religious institutions everywhere in Europe. The widespread **witch-hunts** that Protestants and Catholics undertook in early modern Europe were one manifestation of the ongoing contest between formal religious institutions and local beliefs and cultural heritage.

Prevailing European ideas about the natural world blended two distinct traditions. One was the folklore about magic and forest spirits passed down orally from pre-Christian times. The second was the biblical teachings of the Christian and Jewish scriptures, heard by all in church and read by growing numbers in vernacular translations. In the minds of most people, Christian teachings about miracles, saints, and devils mixed easily with folklore.

witch-hunt The pursuit of people suspected of witchcraft, especially in northern Europe in the late sixteenth and seventeenth centuries.

The World of Magic and Spirits

Zentralbibliothek Zürich, Ms. F. 23, p. 56

Death to Witches   This woodcut from 1574 depicts three women convicted of witchcraft being burned alive in Baden, Switzerland. The well-dressed townsmen look on stolidly.

MAP 17.1 **Religious Reformation in Europe** The Reformation brought greater religious freedom but also led to religious conflict and persecution. In many places the Reformation accelerated the trend toward state control of religion and added religious differences to the motives for wars among Europeans.

e Interactive Map

© Cengage Learning

Predominant religion in 1555

- Lutheran
- Calvinist (Reformed)
- Church of England
- Roman Catholic
- Orthodox
- Muslim
- ▲ Spread of Calvinism
- ▲ Huguenot center
- ◯ Ottoman Empire, 1566

ATLANTIC OCEAN

North Sea

Baltic Sea

Black Sea

Mediterranean Sea

Adriatic Sea

IRELAND
Dublin

SCOTLAND 1560
Edinburgh
John Knox, 1505–1572

ENGLAND 1536
London
Oxford
John Wyclif, 1320–1384
Plymouth

Penetration of Calvinism to England after 1558

NORWAY 1536/1607
Bergen

SWEDEN
Stockholm
Helsinki
Riga

DENMARK
Copenhagen
Hamburg

NETHERLANDS
Amsterdam
Antwerp
Brussels
Münster

LITHUANIA
Warsaw

PRUSSIA
BRANDENBURG

SAXONY
Wittenberg
Birthplace of Martin Luther, 1483–1546
Eisleben
Erfurt
Leipzig

POLAND

HOLY ROMAN EMPIRE
Nuremberg
Marburg
Worms
Edict of Worms, 1521
Speyer
Augsburg
Munich
Stuttgart
Strasbourg

BOHEMIA
Prague
Jan Hus, 1369–1415

MORAVIA

AUSTRIA
Vienna

HUNGARY
Buda
Pest
Belgrade

TRANSYLVANIA
MOLDAVIA
WALLACHIA
Danube R.
BESSARABIA

SERBIA
BULGARIA
OTTOMAN EMPIRE
GREECE

FRANCE
Paris
Noyon
Birthplace of John Calvin, 1509–1564
Rennes
Orleans
Nantes
Edict of Nantes, 1598
La Rochelle
Bordeaux
Toulouse
Avignon
Marseilles

Basel
Zurich
Ulrich Zwingli, 1484–1531
Geneva
John Calvin
Council of Trent, 1545–1563
Trent
Milan
Pavia
Genoa
Venice

ITALY
Pisa
Florence
Rome
Roman Inquisition established, 1542
Naples
Bari

Corsica
Sardinia
Sicily

Balearic Is.

SPAIN
Madrid
Toledo
Barcelona
Valencia
Granada
Seville
Loyola
Birthplace of Ignatius Loyola, 1491–1556

PORTUGAL
Lisbon

MOROCCO

ALGIERS
OTTOMAN EMPIRE

TUNIS

Like people in other parts of the world, most early modern Europeans believed that natural events could have supernatural causes. When crops failed or domestic animals died unexpectedly, many people blamed unseen spirits and sought the help of men and women seen to have special powers. Many believed these same intermediaries had the power to solve romantic problems, fix disputes with masters or employers, or satisfy a desire for revenge.

Europeans continued to attribute human triumphs and tragedies to supernatural causes as well. When an earthquake destroyed much of Lisbon, Portugal's capital city, in November 1755, for example, both educated and uneducated people saw the event as a punishment sent by God. A Jesuit charged it "scandalous to pretend that the earthquake was just a natural event." An English Protestant leader agreed, comparing Lisbon's fate with that of Sodom, the city that God destroyed because of the sinfulness of its citizens, according to the Hebrew Bible.

The Witch-Hunts

The extraordinary fear of the power of witches that swept across northern Europe in the late sixteenth and seventeenth centuries was powerful testimony to belief in the spiritual causes of natural events. Historians estimate that secular and church authorities tried over a hundred thousand people—some three-fourths of them women—for practicing witchcraft. Trial records make it clear that both the accusers and the accused believed that it was possible for angry and jealous individuals to use evil magic and the power of the Devil to cause people and domestic animals to sicken and die or to cause crops to wither in the fields. Researchers think that at least some of those accused in early modern Europe may really have tried to use witchcraft to harm their enemies. However, it was the Reformation's focus on the Devil—the enemy of God—as the source of evil and the Counter Reformation Catholic Church's enforcement of orthodoxy that promoted and justified these efforts to identify and punish witchcraft.

No single reason can explain the rise in witchcraft accusations and fears in early modern Europe, but, for both the accusers and the accused, there are plausible connections between the witch-hunts and rising social tensions, rural poverty, and environmental strains. Far from being a bizarre aberration, witch-hunts reflected the tension between popular beliefs and practices and the ambitions of aggressive new religious and political institutions.

The Scientific Revolution

Among the educated, the writings of Greco-Roman antiquity and the Bible were the most trusted guides to the natural world. The Renaissance had recovered many manuscripts of ancient writers, some of which were printed and widely circulated. The greatest authority on physics was Aristotle, a Greek philosopher who taught that everything on earth was reducible to four elements. The surface of the earth was composed of the two heavy elements, earth and water. The atmosphere was made up of two lighter elements, air and fire, which floated above the ground. Higher still were the sun, moon, planets, and stars, which, according to Aristotelian physics, were so light and pure that they floated in crystalline spheres. This division between the ponderous, heavy earth and the airy, celestial bodies accorded perfectly with the commonsense perception that all heavenly bodies revolved around the earth.

Scientific Revolution The intellectual movement in Europe, initially associated with planetary motion and other aspects of physics, that by the seventeenth century had laid the groundwork for modern science.

The prevailing conception of the universe was also influenced by the ancient Greek mathematician Pythagoras, who proved the famous theorem that still bears his name: in a right triangle, the square of the hypotenuse is equal to the sum of the squares of the other two sides ($a^2 + b^2 = c^2$). Pythagoreans attributed the ability of simple mathematical equations to describe physical objects to mystical properties. They attached special significance to the simplest (to them perfect) geometrical shapes: the circle (a point rotated around another point) and the sphere (a circle rotated on its axis). They believed that celestial objects were perfect spheres orbiting the earth in circular orbits.

In the sixteenth century, however, the careful observations and mathematical calculations of some daring and imaginative European investigators began to challenge these prevailing conceptions of the physical world. These pioneers of the **Scientific Revolution** demonstrated that natural causes could explain the workings of the universe.

New Questions and Methods

Over the centuries, observers of the nighttime skies had plotted the movements of the heavenly bodies, and mathematicians had worked to fit these observations into the prevailing theories of circular orbits. To make all the evidence fit, they had come up with eighty different spheres and some ingenious theories to explain the many seemingly irregular movements. Pondering these complications, a Polish monk and mathematician named Nicholas Copernicus

Maritime Museum Kronberg Castle Denmark/ G.Dagli Orti/The Art Archive

Tycho Brahe at Work Between 1576 and 1597, on the island of Ven between Denmark and Sweden, Tycho built the best observatory in Europe and set a new standard for accurate celestial observations before the invention of the telescope. This contemporary hand-colored engraving shows the Danish astronomer at work.

e **PRIMARY SOURCE:**
Letter to the Grand
Duchess Christina Read Galileo's passionate defense of his scientific research against those who would condemn it as un-Christian.

(1473–1543) came up with a simpler solution: switching the center of the different orbits from the earth to the sun.

Copernicus did not challenge the idea that the sun, moon, and planets were light, perfect spheres or that they moved in circular orbits. But his placement of the sun, not the earth, at the center began a revolution in understanding the structure of the heavens and the central place of humans in the universe. To escape anticipated controversies, Copernicus delayed the publication of his heliocentric (sun-centered) theory until the end of his life.

Other astronomers, including the Danish Tycho Brahe (1546–1601) and his German assistant Johannes Kepler (1571–1630), strengthened and improved on Copernicus's model, showing that planets actually move in elliptical, not circular, orbits. The most brilliant of the Copernicans was the Italian Galileo Galilei (gal-uh-LAY-oh gal-uh-LAY-ee) (1564–1642). In 1609 Galileo built a telescope through which he could look more closely at the heavens. Able to magnify distant objects thirty times beyond the power of the naked eye, Galileo saw that heavenly bodies were not the perfectly smooth spheres of the Aristotelians. The moon, he reported in *The Starry Messenger* (1610), had mountains and valleys; the sun had spots; other planets had their own moons. In other words, the earth was not alone in being heavy and changeable.

At first, the Copernican universe found more critics than supporters because it so directly challenged not just popular ideas but also the intellectual synthesis of classical and biblical authorities. Is the Bible wrong, asked the theologians, when the Book of Joshua says that, by God's command, "the sun [not the earth] stood still . . . for about a whole day" to give the ancient Israelites victory in their conquest of Palestine? If Aristotle's physics was wrong, worried other traditionalists, would not the theological synthesis built on other parts of his philosophy be open to question?

Intellectual and religious leaders encouraged political authorities to suppress the new ideas. Most Protestant leaders, following the lead of Martin Luther, condemned the heliocentric universe as contrary to the Bible. Catholic authorities waited longer to act. After all, both Copernicus and Galileo were Roman Catholics. Copernicus had dedicated his book to the pope, and in 1582 another pope, Gregory XIII, had used the latest astronomical findings to issue a new and more accurate calendar (still used today). Galileo ingeniously argued that the conflict between scripture and science was only apparent because the word of God was expressed in the language of ordinary people, but in nature God's truth was revealed more perfectly in a language that could be learned by careful observation and scientific reasoning. Galileo also ridiculed those who were slow to accept his findings. Smarting under Galileo's stinging sarcasm, his enemies complained to the Inquisition, which prohibited him from publishing further on the subject.

Scientific Knowledge Expands

Despite official opposition, printed books spread the new scientific ideas among scholars across Europe. In England, Robert Boyle (1627–1691) demonstrated the usefulness of the experimental method and along with others became an enthusiastic missionary of mechanical science, using the Royal Society, chartered in London in 1662, to promote knowledge of the natural world. Another Englishman, the mathematician Isaac Newton (1642–1727), carried Galileo's demonstration that the heavens and earth share a common physics to its logical conclusion by formulating mathematical laws that governed all physical objects. His Law of Gravity and his role in developing calculus made him the most famous and influential man of his era, serving as president of the Royal Society from 1703 until his death.

As late as 1700 most religious and intellectual leaders viewed the new science with suspicion or outright hostility because of the unwanted challenge it posed to established ways of thought. Yet most of the principal pioneers of the Scientific Revolution were convinced that scientific discoveries and revealed religion were not in conflict. However, by showing that the Aristotelians and biblical writers held ideas about the natural world that were untrue, these pioneers opened the door to others who used reason to challenge a broader range of unquestioned traditions and superstitions. The world of ideas was forever changed.

The Early Enlightenment

Advances in scientific thought inspired some to question the reasonableness of everything from agricultural methods to laws, religion, and social hierarchies. They believed that they could apply the scientific method to analyze economics, politics, and social organization and devise the best policies. This enthusiasm for an open and critical examination of human society energized a movement known as the **Enlightenment**. Like the Scientific Revolution, this movement was the work of a few "enlightened" individuals, who often faced bitter opposition from the political and religious establishments. Leading Enlightenment thinkers became accustomed to having their books burned or banned, and many spent long periods in exile to escape persecution.

Influences besides the Scientific Revolution affected the Enlightenment. The religious warfare and intolerance associated with the struggle between Catholicism and Protestantism undermined the moral authority of religion for many, and the efforts of church authorities to impugn the breakthroughs of science pushed European intellectual life in a secular direction. The popular bigotry manifested in the brutal treatment of suspected witches also shocked many thoughtful people. The leading French thinker Voltaire (1694–1778) declared: "No opinion is worth burning your neighbor for."

Although many circumstances shaped "enlightened" thinking, the new scientific methods and discoveries provided the clearest model for changing European society. Voltaire posed the issues in these terms: "It would be very peculiar that all nature, all the planets, should obey eternal laws" but a human being, "in contempt of these laws, could act as he pleased solely according to his caprice." The English poet Alexander Pope (1688–1774) made a similar point in verse: "Nature and Nature's laws lay hidden in night; / God said, 'Let Newton be' and all was light."

The Enlightenment was more a frame of mind than a coherent movement. Individuals who embraced it drew inspiration from different sources and promoted different agendas. Its proponents were clearer about what they disliked than about what changes were necessary. Some thought an "enlightened" society could function with the mechanical orderliness of planets spinning in their orbits. Nearly all were optimistic that—at least in the long run—their discoveries would improve human beliefs and institutions. This faith in progress would help foster political and social revolutions after 1750, as Chapter 22 recounts.

While the Catholic Church and many Protestant clergymen opposed the Enlightenment, European monarchs selectively endorsed new ideas. Monarchs, ambitious to increase their power, found anticlerical intellectuals useful allies against church power and wealth. More predictably, monarchs and their reforming advisers discovered in the Enlightenment's demand for more rational and predictable policies justification for the expansion of royal authority and modern tax systems. Europe in 1750 was a place where political and religious divisions, growing literacy, and the printing press made it possible for these controversial and exciting new ideas to thrive in the face of opposition from ancient and powerful institutions.

Enlightenment A philosophical movement in eighteenth-century Europe that fostered the belief that one could reform society by discovering rational laws that governed social behavior and were just as scientific as the laws of physics.

The Enlightenment and Cultural Change

 PRIMARY SOURCE: Treatise on Toleration Voltaire makes a powerful argument for cultural and religious tolerance.

SECTION REVIEW

- Outraged by corrupt church practices, reformers like Luther and Calvin challenged papal authority and traditional Catholic theology.

- In response to the Protestant reformers, the Catholic Church launched a Counter Reformation.

- Both Protestants and Catholics, seeking to enforce orthodoxy, sanctioned widespread witch-hunts.

- The thinkers of the Scientific Revolution challenged traditional biblical and Greco-Roman conceptions of the cosmos.

- The advances in science prompted Enlightenment thinkers to question many conventional ideas and practices.

SOCIAL AND ECONOMIC LIFE

European society was dominated by a small number of noble families who enjoyed privileged access to high offices in the church, government, and military and, in most cases, exemption from taxation. Below them was a much larger class of prosperous commoners that included many clergy, bureaucrats, professionals, and military officers as well as merchants, some artisans, and rural landowners. The vast majority of men and women were very poor. Laborers, journeymen, apprentices, and rural laborers struggled to earn their daily bread but often faced unemployment and privation. The poorest members of society lived truly desperate lives, surviving only through guile, begging, or crime. Women remained subordinated to men.

Some social mobility did occur, however, particularly in the middle. The principal engine of social change was the economy, and the locations where social change occurred most readily were the cities. A secondary means of change was education—for those who could get it.

The Bourgeoisie

Europe's cities grew in response to expanding trade. In 1500 Paris was the only northern European city with over 100,000 inhabitants. By 1700 both Paris and London had populations over 500,000, and twenty other European cities contained over 60,000 people.

Cities as Engines of Change

bourgeoisie In early modern Europe, the class of well-off town dwellers whose wealth came from manufacturing, finance, commerce, and allied professions.

The Netherlands

Urban wealth came from manufacturing and finance, but especially from trade, both within Europe and overseas. The French called the urban class that dominated these activities the **bourgeoisie** (boor-zwah-ZEE) (burghers, town dwellers). Members of the bourgeoisie devoted long hours to their businesses and poured much of their profits back into them or into new ventures. Even so, most had enough money to live comfortably in large houses, and some had servants. In the seventeenth and eighteenth centuries wealthier consumers could buy exotic luxuries imported from the far corners of the earth—Caribbean and Brazilian sugar and rum, Mexican chocolate, Virginia tobacco, North American furs, East Indian cotton textiles and spices, and Chinese tea.

The Netherlands provides a good example of bourgeois enterprise. Dutch manufacturers and craftsmen turned out a variety of goods in their factories and workshops. The highly successful textile industry concentrated on the profitable weaving, finishing, and printing of cloth, leaving the spinning to low-paid workers elsewhere. Along with fine woolens and linens, the Dutch made cheaper textiles for mass markets. Other factories in Holland refined West Indian sugar, brewed beer from Baltic grain, cut Virginia tobacco, and made imitations of Chinese ceramics (see Environment and Technology: East Asian Porcelain in Chapter 21). Free from the censorship imposed by political and religious authorities in neighboring countries, Holland's printers published books in many languages, including manuals with the latest advances in machinery, metallurgy, agriculture, and other technical areas. For a small nation that lacked timber and other natural resources, this was a remarkable achievement.

With a population of 200,000 in 1700, Amsterdam was Holland's largest city and Europe's major port. The Dutch developed huge commercial fleets that dominated sea trade in Europe and overseas. They introduced new ship designs, including the *fluit*, or "flyboat," a large-capacity cargo ship that was inexpensive to build and required only a small crew. Another successful type of merchant ship, the heavily armed "East Indiaman," helped the Dutch establish their supremacy in the Indian Ocean. By one estimate, the Dutch conducted more than half of all the oceangoing commercial shipping in the world in the seventeenth century (for details see Chapters 20 and 21). Dutch mapmaking supported these distant commercial connections (see Environment and Technology: Mapping the World). Amsterdam also served as Europe's financial center. Seventeenth-century Dutch banks had such a reputation for security that wealthy individuals and governments from all over western Europe entrusted them with their money. The banks in turn invested these funds in real estate, loaned money to factory owners and governments, and provided capital for big business operations overseas.

Like merchants in the Islamic world, Europe's merchants relied on family and ethnic networks. In addition to families of local origin, the most dynamic northern European cities were culturally diverse, hosting merchant colonies from Venice, Florence, Genoa, and other Italian cities as well

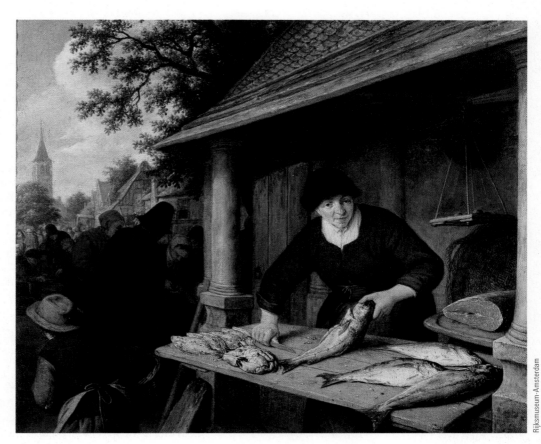

The Fishwife, 1572   Women were essential partners in most Dutch family businesses. This scene by the Dutch artist Adriaen van Ostade shows a woman preparing fish for retail sale.

as Jewish merchants who had fled religious persecution in Iberia. Other Jewish communities emigrated from eastern Europe to the German states, especially after the Thirty Years War.

The bourgeoisie sought mutually beneficial alliances with European monarchs, who welcomed economic growth as a means of increasing state revenues. The Dutch government pioneered chartering **joint-stock companies** like the Dutch East and West India Companies, which were granted monopolies for trade with the East and West Indies. France and England chartered companies of their own. These companies then sold shares to individuals to raise large sums for overseas enterprises while spreading the risks (and profits) among many investors (see Chapter 19). Investors could buy and sell shares in specialized financial markets called **stock exchanges**, an Italian innovation transferred to the cities of northwestern Europe in the sixteenth century. The greatest stock market in the seventeenth and eighteenth centuries was the Amsterdam Exchange, founded in 1530. Large insurance companies also emerged in this period, and insuring long voyages against loss became a standard practice after 1700.

Governments also sought to promote trade by investing in infrastructure. The Dutch built numerous canals to improve transport and drain the lowlands for agriculture. Other governments financed canals as well, including systems of locks to raise barges up over hills. One of the most important was the 150-mile (240-kilometer) Canal du Midi built by the French government between 1661 and 1682 to link the Atlantic and the Mediterranean.

After 1650 the Dutch faced growing competition from the English, who were developing their own close association between business and government. With government support, the English merchant fleet doubled between 1660 and 1700, and foreign trade rose by 50 percent. As a result, state revenue from customs duties tripled. In a series of wars (1652–1678) the English

joint-stock company
A business, often backed by a government charter, that sold shares to individuals to raise money for its trading enterprises and to spread the risks (and profits) among many investors.

stock exchange   A place where shares in a company or business enterprise are bought and sold.

England and France

Mapping the World

In 1602 in China the Jesuit missionary Matteo Ricci printed an elaborate map of the world. Working from maps produced in Europe and incorporating the latest knowledge gathered by European maritime explorers, Ricci introduced two changes to make the map more appealing to his Chinese hosts. He labeled it in Chinese characters, and he split his map down the middle of the Atlantic so that China lay in the center. This version pleased the Chinese elite, who considered China the "Middle Kingdom" surrounded by lesser states. A copy of Ricci's map in six large panels adorned the emperor's Beijing palace.

The stunningly beautiful maps and globes of sixteenth-century Europe were the most complete, detailed, and useful representations of the earth that any society had ever produced. The best mapmaker of the century was Gerhard Kremer, who is remembered as Mercator (the merchant) because his maps were so useful to European ocean traders. By incorporating the latest discoveries and scientific measurements, Mercator could depict the outlines of the major continents in painstaking detail, even if their interiors were still largely unknown to outsiders.

To represent the spherical globe on a flat map, Mercator drew the lines of longitude as parallel lines. Because such lines actually meet at the poles, Mercator's projection greatly exaggerated the size of every landmass and body of water distant from the equator. However, Mercator's rendering offered a very practical advantage: sailors could plot their course by drawing a straight line between their point of departure and their destination. Because of this useful feature, the Mercator projection of the world remained in common use until quite recently. To some extent, its popularity came from the exaggerated size this projection gave to Europe. Like the Chinese, Europeans liked to think of themselves as at the center of things. Europeans also understood their true geographical position better than people in any other part of the world.

British Library Board, MAPS.C.4.6.1

Dutch World Map, 1641   It is easy to see why the Chinese would not have liked to see their empire at the far right edge of this widely printed map. Besides the distortions caused by the Mercator projection, geographical ignorance exaggerates the size of North America and Antarctica.

government used its new naval might to break Dutch dominance in overseas trade and to extend England's colonial empire.

Some successful members of the bourgeoisie in England and France chose to use their wealth to raise their social status. By retiring from their businesses and buying country estates, they could become members of the **gentry**. They loaned money to impoverished peasants and to

gentry The class of land-holding families in England below the aristocracy.

Port of Amsterdam Ships, barges, and boats of all types are visible in this busy seventeenth-century scene. The large building in the center is the Admiralty House, the headquarters of the Dutch East India Company.

members of the nobility and in time increased their land ownership. Some sought aristocratic husbands for their daughters. The old nobility found such alliances attractive because of the large dowries that the bourgeoisie provided. In France a family could gain the exemption from taxation by living in gentility for three generations or, more quickly, by purchasing a title from the king.

Peasants and Laborers

Serfdom, which bound men and women to land owned by a local lord, had begun to decline after the great plague of the mid-fourteenth century. As population recovered in western Europe, the competition for work exerted a downward pressure on wages, reducing the usefulness of serf-dom to landowners. In eastern Europe, on the other hand, large-scale landowners producing grain for cities found the bound labor of serfs crucial for profits. There had been a brief expansion of slavery in southern Europe with the introduction of African slaves around 1500, but after 1600 Europeans shipped nearly all African slaves to the Americas.

The Rural Poor

There is much truth in the argument that western Europe continued to depend on unfree labor but kept it at a distance in its colonies rather than at home. In any event, legal freedom did little to make a peasant's life safer and more secure. The efficiency of European agriculture had improved little since 1300. As a result, bad years brought famine; good ones provided only small surpluses. Indeed, the material conditions experienced by the poor in western Europe may have worsened between 1500 and 1750 as the result of warfare, environmental degradation, and economic contractions. Europeans also felt the adverse effects of a century of relatively cool climate that began in the 1590s. During this **Little Ice Age** average temperatures fell only a few degrees, but the effects were startling (see Issues in World History: The Little Ice Age on page 576).

Little Ice Age A century-long period of cool climate that began in the 1590s. Its ill effects on agriculture in northern Europe were notable.

By 1700 high-yielding new crops from the Americas were helping the rural poor avoid starvation. Once grown only as famine foods, potatoes and maize (corn) became staples for the rural poor in the eighteenth century. Potatoes sustained life in northeastern and central Europe and in Ireland, while poor peasants in Italy subsisted on maize. The irony is that all of these lands were major exporters of wheat, but most of those who planted and harvested it could not afford to eat it.

Deforestation

Other rural residents made their living as miners, lumber-jacks, and charcoal makers. The expanding iron industry in England provided work for all three, but the high consumption of

deforestation The removal of trees faster than forests can replace themselves.

wood fuel caused serious **deforestation**. One early-seventeenth-century observer lamented: "Within man's memory, it was held impossible to have any want of wood in England. But . . . at present, through the great consuming of wood . . . and the neglect of planting of woods, there is a great scarcity of wood throughout the whole kingdom."[1] Eventually, the high price of wood and charcoal encouraged smelters to use coal as an alternative fuel. England's coal mining increased twelvefold, from 210,000 tons in 1550 to 2,500,000 tons in 1700 and nearly 5 million tons by 1750.

France was more heavily forested than England, but increasing deforestation prompted Jean Baptiste Colbert, France's minister of finance, to predict that "France will perish for lack of wood." By the late eighteenth century deforestation had become an issue even in Sweden and Russia, where iron production had become a major industry.

Poverty and Violence

Even in the prosperous Dutch towns, half of the population lived in acute poverty. Authorities estimated that permanent city residents who were too poor to tax, the "deserving poor," made up 10 to 20 percent of the population. That calculation did not include the large numbers of "unworthy poor"—recent migrants from impoverished rural areas, peddlers traveling from place to place, and beggars (many with horrible deformities and sores) who tried to survive on charity. The pervasive poverty of rural and urban Europe shocked those who were not hardened to it. In about 1580 the mayor of the French city of Bordeaux (bor-DOH) asked a group of visiting Amerindian chiefs what impressed them most about European cities. The chiefs are said to have expressed astonishment at the disparity between the fat, well-fed people and the poor, half-starved men and women in rags. Why, the visitors wondered, did the poor not grab the rich by the throat or set fire to their homes?[2]

In fact, misery provoked many rebellions in early modern Europe. For example, in 1525 peasant rebels in the Alps attacked both nobles and the clergy as representatives of the privileged and landowning classes. They had no love for merchants either, whom they denounced for lending at interest and charging high prices. Rebellions multiplied as rural conditions worsened. In southwestern France alone some 450 uprisings occurred between 1590 and 1715, many of them set off by food shortages and tax increases. A rebellion in southern France in 1670 began when a mob of townswomen attacked the tax collector. It quickly spread to the country, where peasant leaders cried, "Death to the people's oppressors!" Authorities dealt severely with such revolts and executed or maimed their leaders.

Women and the Family

Women's social and economic status was closely tied to that of their husbands. In some nations a woman could inherit a throne (see Table 17.1 on page 468 for examples)—in the absence of a male heir. These rare exceptions do not negate the rule that women everywhere ranked below men, but one should also not forget that class and wealth defined a woman's position in life more than her sex. The wife or daughter of a rich man, for example, though often closely confined, had a materially better life than any poor man. Sometimes a single woman might secure a position of responsibility, as in the case of women from good families who headed convents in Catholic countries. But while unmarried women were routinely controlled by fathers and married women controlled by husbands, some widows independently controlled substantial properties and other assets.

Marriage and the Family

In contrast to the arranged marriages that prevailed in much of the rest of the world, young men and women in early modern Europe often chose their own spouses, but privileged families were much more likely to arrange marriages than poor ones. Royal and noble families carefully plotted the suitability of their children's marriages in furthering family interests. Bourgeois parents were less likely to force their children into arranged marriages, but the fact that nearly all found spouses within their own social class strongly suggests that the bourgeoisie promoted marriages that furthered their business alliances.

Europeans also married later than people in other cultural regions. Sons often put off marriage until they could live on their own. Many young women also had to work—helping their parents, as domestic servants, or in some other capacity—to save money for the dowry expected by potential husbands. A dowry was the money and household goods—the amount varied by social class—that enabled a young couple to begin marriage independent of their parents. The typical groom in western and central Europe could not hope to marry before his late twenties, and his bride would be a few years younger—in contrast to the rest of the world, where people usually married in their teens.

Besides enabling young people to be independent of their parents, the late age of marriage in early modern Europe also held down the birthrate and thus limited family size. Even so, about one-tenth of urban births were to unmarried women, often servants. Many mothers, unable to provide for these infants, left them on the doorsteps of churches, convents, or rich households. Many perished. Delayed marriage and poverty helped force unfortunate young women newly arrived from the countryside into brothels.

Education

Bourgeois parents were very concerned that their children have the education and training necessary for success. They promoted the establishment of municipal schools to provide a solid education, including Latin and perhaps Greek, for their sons, who were then sent abroad to learn modern languages or to a university to earn a law degree. Legal training was useful for conducting business and was a prerequisite for obtaining judicial or treasury positions. Daughters were less likely to be formally educated, but women with basic education often helped their husbands as bookkeepers, and some inherited businesses.

The fact that most schools barred female students, as did most guilds and professions, explains why women were not prominent in the cultural Renaissance, the Reformation, the Scientific Revolution, and the Enlightenment. Yet from a global perspective, women in early modern Europe were more prominent in the creation of culture than were women in most other parts of the world. Recent research has discovered numerous successful women who were painters, musicians, and writers. Indeed, the spread of learning, the stress on religious reading, and the growth of business likely meant that Europe led the world in female literacy. In the late 1600s some wealthy French women began organizing intellectual gatherings, and many were prominent letter writers. Galileo's daughter, Maria Celeste Galilei, carried on a detailed correspondence with her father from the confinement of the convent she had vowed never to leave. Nevertheless, in a period when most men were illiterate, the number of literate women was small, and only women in wealthier families might have a good education.

SECTION REVIEW

- Early modern European society was more fluid than it appeared, with an expanding economy and improved education promoting some mobility.

- The urban bourgeoisie created much of Europe's wealth through trade, manufacture, finance, and technological innovation.

- Monarchs sought alliances with the bourgeoisie, whose wealth afforded them political and social advancement as well as revenue.

- Oppressed by economic and environmental trends, peasants and laborers generally lived in poverty, and their misery often provoked rebellion.

- Although women remained subordinate to men, class and wealth were the main determinants of their positions in life.

POLITICAL INNOVATIONS

The monarchs of early modern Europe occupied the apex of the social order, were arbitrators of the intellectual and religious conflicts of their day, and exercised important influence on the economies of their realms. Many European monarchs introduced reforms in this era that achieved a higher degree of political centralization and order, but their ambitions and rivalries could also provoke destructive and costly conflicts. In some cases, civil and international conflicts forced monarchs to find common ground with potential enemies or introduce political innovations that strengthened their nations. During this period, political leadership in Europe passed from Spain to the Netherlands and then to England and France.

Holy Roman Empire Loose federation of mostly German states and principalities, headed by an emperor elected by the princes. It lasted from 962 to 1806.

State Development

There was a great deal of political diversity in early modern Europe. City-states and principalities abounded, either independently or bound together in federations, of which the **Holy Roman Empire** of the German heartland was the most notable example. There were also a small number

MAP 17.2 **The European Empire of Charles V** Charles was Europe's most powerful monarch, ruling Spain from 1516 and the Holy Roman Empire from 1519 to his abdication in 1556. The map does not show his extensive holdings in the Americas and Asia.

e Interactive Map

© Cengage Learning

NORTH AND SOUTH AMERICA

ATLANTIC OCEAN

PACIFIC OCEAN

Caribbean Sea

Gulf of Mexico

Rio Grande

FLORIDA

CUBA
Havana
Santiago

ESPAÑOLA
PUERTO RICO

Guadalajara
Mexico City
Veracruz
Oaxaca
Guatemala

TRINIDAD
Caracas

Cartagena
Panama
Bogotá
Quito

Lima
Cuzco
Potosí

Santiago

Buenos Aires

São Paulo

Rio de Janeiro
Salvador (Bahia)
Recife (Pernambuco)

Amazon R.

Tropic of Cancer
Equator
Tropic of Capricorn

Cape Horn
Strait of Magellan

Spanish holdings, 1550

0   1,000 Km.
0   1,000 Mi.

ATLANTIC OCEAN

North Sea

Baltic Sea

Mediterranean Sea

Adriatic Sea

IRELAND
SCOTLAND
ENGLAND
London

NETHERLANDS
Amsterdam
Antwerp

DENMARK
Hamburg

POLAND

BRANDENBURG
ANHALT
LUSATIA
SILESIA
MORAVIA
BOHEMIA
UPPER PALATINATE
HESSE-KASSEL
RHINE PALATINATE
WÜRTEMBERG
BAVARIA
AUSTRIA
SALZBURG
TYROL
VIENNA
HUNGARY

SWISS CONFED.
LORRAINE
FRANCHE-COMTÉ
CHAROLAIS
SAVOY
MILAN
GENOA
REP. OF VENICE
MODENA

Paris
FRANCE

NAVARRE
ARAGON
ANDORRA

CASTILE
Madrid
Seville
GRANADA
PORTUGAL
Lisbon

BALEARIC IS.
CORSICA (to Genoa)
SARDINIA

PAPAL STATES
Rome
NAPLES
Naples
SICILY
Malta

OTTOMAN EMPIRE
Otranto

Crete

Danube R.

Tangiers
MOROCCO
Melilla
Oran
Algiers
Bougie
Bona
Tunis
TUNIS

ALGIERS
NORTH AFRICA
TRIPOLI
Misurata
Benghazi
CYRENAICA

OTTOMAN EMPIRE
EGYPT
Alexandria

Lands inherited by Charles V
Lands gained by Charles V, 1519–1556
States favorable to Charles V
Enemies of Charles V
Boundary of the Holy Roman Empire

0   150   300 Km.
0   150   300 Mi.

of republics. At the same time a number of strong monarchies emerged and developed national identities.

Dynastic ambitions and historical circumstances combined to favor and then block the creation of a single, integrated empire in the early sixteenth century. In 1519 electors of the Holy Roman Empire chose Charles V (r. 1519–1556) to be the new emperor. Like his predecessors for three generations, Charles belonged to the powerful **Habsburg** (HABZ-berg) family of Austria, but he had also inherited the Spanish thrones of Castile and Aragon in 1516. With these vast resources (see Map 17.2), Charles hoped lead a Christian coalition to halt the advance into southeastern Europe of the Ottoman Empire, whose Muslim rulers already controlled most of the Middle East and North Africa.

Charles and his Christian allies did stop the Ottomans at the gates of Vienna in 1529, although Ottoman attacks continued until 1697. But Charles's efforts to forge his several possessions into Europe's strongest state failed. Francis I of France, who had also sought election as Holy Roman Emperor, openly supported the Muslim Turks to weaken his rival. In addition, many German princes, swayed by Luther's appeals to German nationalism, opposed Charles's defense of Catholic doctrine in the imperial Diet (assembly).

After these disputes turned to open warfare in 1546 (the German Wars of Religion), Charles V gave up his efforts at unification, abdicated control of his various possessions to different heirs, and retired to a monastery in 1556. By the Peace of Augsburg (1555), he had already recognized the princes' right to choose whether Catholicism or Lutheranism would prevail in their particular states, and permitted them to keep the church lands they had seized. The triumph of religious diversity ended Charles's political ambitions and put off German political unification for three centuries.

The rulers of Spain, France, and England were more successful in promoting national political unification and religious unity. The most successful rulers reduced the autonomy of the church and the nobility by making them part of a unified national structure with the monarch at its head (see Diversity and Dominance: Political Craft and Craftiness). The imposition of royal power over the church in the sixteenth century was stormy, but the outcome was clear. Bringing the nobles and other powerful interests into a centralized political system took longer and led to more diverse outcomes.

The Monarchies of England and France

Over the course of the seventeenth century, the monarchs of England and France faced intense conflict with powerful rivals. Religion was never absent as an issue in these struggles, but the different constitutional outcomes they produced were of more significance in the long run.

To evade any check on his power, King Charles I of England (see Table 17.1) ruled for eleven years without summoning Parliament, his kingdom's representative body. Lacking Parliament's consent to new taxes, he raised funds by coercing "loans" from wealthy subjects and applying existing tax laws more broadly. In 1640 a rebellion in Scotland forced him to summon Parliament to approve new taxes to pay for an army. Noblemen and churchmen sat in the House of Lords while representatives from towns and counties sat in the House of Commons. Before it would authorize new taxes, Parliament insisted on strict guarantees that the king would never again ignore the body's traditional rights. King Charles refused and attempted to arrest of his critics in the House of Commons in 1642, plunging the kingdom into the **English Civil War**.

Militarily defeated in 1648, Charles refused to compromise. A year later a "Rump" Parliament purged of his supporters ordered his execution. Parliament then replaced the monarchy with a republic led by the Puritan general Oliver Cromwell who ruled until his death in 1658. Cromwell expanded England's presence overseas and imposed firm control over Ireland and Scotland, but was also unwilling to share power with Parliament. Parliament restored the Stuart line in the person of Charles II (r. 1660–1685). James II, his brother, inherited the throne, but provoked new conflict by refusing to respect Parliament's rights and by baptizing his heir as a Roman Catholic. The leaders of Parliament forced him into exile in the bloodless Glorious Revolution of 1688. The Bill of Rights of 1689 formalized this new constitutional order by requiring the king to call Parliament frequently to consent to changes in laws or to raise an army in peacetime. Another law reaffirmed the official status of the Church of England but extended religious toleration to dissenting Puritans.

Charles V

Habsburg A powerful European family that provided many Holy Roman Emperors, founded the Austrian (later Austro-Hungarian) Empire, and ruled sixteenth- and seventeenth-century Spain.

The Growing Power of Kings

England

English Civil War (1642–1649) A conflict over royal versus parliamentary rights, caused by King Charles I's arrest of his parliamentary critics and ending with his execution. Its outcome checked the growth of royal absolutism and, with the Glorious Revolution of 1688 and the English Bill of Rights of 1689, ensured that England would be a constitutional monarchy.

Political Craft and Craftiness

Political power was becoming more highly concentrated in early modern Europe, but absolute dominance was more a goal than a reality. Whether subject to constitutional checks or not, rulers were very concerned with creating and maintaining good relations with their more powerful subjects. Their efforts to manipulate public opinion and perceptions have much in common with the efforts of modern politicians to manage their "image."

A diplomat and civil servant in the rich and powerful Italian city-state of Florence, Niccolò Machiavelli, is best known for his book The Prince (1532). This influential essay on the proper exercise of political power has been interpreted as cynical by some and as supremely practical and realistic by others. Because Machiavelli did not have a high opinion of the intelligence and character of most people, he urged rulers to achieve obedience by fear and deception. But he also suggested that genuine mercy, honesty, and piety may be superior to feigned virtue.

In What Manner Princes Should Keep Their Faith

It must be evident to every one that it is more praiseworthy for a prince always to maintain good faith, and practice integrity rather than craft and deceit. And yet the experience of our own times has shown those princes have achieved great things who made small account of good faith, and who understood by cunning to circumvent the intelligence of others; and that in the end they got the better of those whose actions were dictated by loyalty and good faith. You must know, therefore, that there are two ways of carrying on a struggle; one by law and the other by force. The first is practiced by men, and the other by animals; and as the first is often insufficient, it becomes necessary to resort to the second.

. . . If men were altogether good, this advice would be wrong; but since they are bad and will not keep faith with you, you need not keep faith with them. Nor will a prince ever be short of legitimate excuses to give color to his breaches of faith. Innumerable modern examples could be given of this; and it could easily be shown how many treaties of peace, and

how many engagements, have been made null and void by the faithlessness of princes; and he who has best known how to play the fox has ever been the most successful.

But it is necessary that the prince should know how to color this nature well, and how to be a great hypocrite and dissembler. For men are so simple, and yield so much to immediate necessity, that the deceiver will never lack dupes. I will mention one of the most recent examples. [Pope] Alexander VI never did nor ever thought of anything but to deceive, and always found a reason for doing so . . . and yet he was always successful in his deceits, because he knew the weakness of men in that particular.

It is not necessary, however, for a prince to possess all the above-mentioned qualities; but it is essential that he should at least seem to have them. I will even venture to say, that to have and practice them constantly is pernicious, but to seem to have them is useful. For instance, a prince should seem to be merciful, faithful, humane, religious, and upright, and should even be so in reality; but he should have his mind so trained that, when occasion requires it, he may know how to change to the opposite. And it must be understood that a prince, and especially one who has but recently acquired his state, cannot perform all those things which cause men to be esteemed as good; he being obligated, for the sake of maintaining his state, to act contrary to humanity, charity, and religion. And therefore, it is necessary that he should have a versatile mind, capable of changing readily, according as the winds and changes of fortune bid him; and, as has been said above, not to swerve from the good if possible, but to know how to resort to evil if necessity demands it.

A prince then should be very careful never to allow anything to escape his lips that does not abound in the abovementioned five qualities, so that to see and to hear him he may seem all charity, integrity, and humanity, all uprightness and all piety. And more than all else is it necessary for a prince to seem to possess the last quality; for mankind in general judge more by what they see than by what they feel, every one being capable of the former, and few of the latter. Everybody sees what you seem to be, but few really feel what you are; and those few dare

---

France

Versailles The huge palace built for French king Louis XVI south of Paris. The palace symbolized both French power and the triumph of royal authority over the French nobility.

In France the Estates General, like the English Parliament, represented the traditional rights of the clergy, the nobility, and the towns (that is, the bourgeoisie). The Estates General was able to assert its rights during the sixteenth-century French Wars of Religion, when the monarchy was weak. Thereafter Bourbon monarchs generally ruled without calling it into session. They avoided financial crises by more efficient tax collection and by selling appointments to high government offices. In justification they claimed that the monarch had absolute authority to rule in God's name on earth.

Louis XIV moved his court to a gigantic new palace at **Versailles** (vuhr-SIGH) in 1682. The palace helped the French monarch triumph over the traditional rights of the nobility, clergy, and not oppose the opinion of the many, who are protected by the majority of the state; for the actions of all men, and especially those of princes, are judged by the result, where there is no other judge to whom to appeal.

A prince should look mainly to the successful maintenance of his state. For the means which he employs for this will always be counted honorable, and will be praised by everybody; for the common people are always taken in by appearances and by results, and it is the vulgar mass that constitutes the world.

Because, as Machiavelli argued, appearances count for as much in the public arena as realities, it is difficult to judge whether rulers' statements expressed their real feelings and beliefs or what may have been the most expedient to say at the moment. An example is this speech Queen Elizabeth of England made at the end of November 1601 to Parliament after a particularly difficult year. One senior noble had led a rebellion and was subsequently executed. Parliament was pressing for extended privileges. Having gained the throne in 1558 after many difficulties (including a time in prison), the sixty-eight-year-old queen had much experience in the language and wiles of politics and was well aware of the importance of public opinion. Reprinted many times, the speech became famous as "The Golden Speech of Queen Elizabeth."

I do assure you, there is no prince that loveth his subjects better, or whose love can countervail our love. There is no jewel, be it of never so rich a price, which I set before this jewel: I mean your love. For I do esteem it more than any treasure or riches; for that we know how to prize, but love and thanks I count invaluable.

And, though God has raised me high, yet this I count the glory of my crown, that I have reigned with your loves. This makes me that I do not so much rejoice that God hath made me to be a Queen, as to be Queen over so thankful a people.

Therefore, I have cause to wish nothing more than to content the subjects; and that is the duty I owe. Neither do I desire to live longer days than I may see your prosperity; and that is my only desire.

And as I am that person that still (yet under God) has delivered you, so I trust, by the almighty power of God, that I shall be His instrument to preserve you from every peril, dishonour, shame, tyranny, and oppression. . . .

Of myself I must say this: I was never any greedy scraping grasper, nor a straight, fast-holding prince, nor yet a waster. My heart was never set on worldly goods, but only for my subjects' good. What you bestow on me, I will not hoard it up, but receive it to bestow on you again. Yea, mine own properties I count yours, and to be expended for your good. . . .

To be a king and wear a crown is a thing more glorious to them that see it, than it is pleasing to them that bear it. For myself, I was never so much enticed with the glorious name of king, or royal authority of a queen, as delighted that God made me his instrument to maintain his truth and glory, and to defend this Kingdom (as I said) from peril, dishonour, tyranny and oppression.

There will never Queen sit in my seat with more zeal to my country, care for my subjects, and that sooner with willingness will venture her life for your good and safety than myself. For it is not my desire to live nor reign longer than my life and reign shall be for your good. And though you have had and may have many more princes more mighty and wise sitting in this state, yet you never had or shall have any that will be more careful and loving. Shall I ascribe anything to myself and my sexly weakness? I were not worthy to live then; and of all, most unworthy of the great mercies I have had from God, who has even yet given me a heart, which never feared foreign or home enemy. I speak to give God the praise . . . That I should speak for any glory, God forbid.

QUESTIONS FOR ANALYSIS

1. **Do you find Machiavelli's advice to be cynical or realistic?**

2. **Describe how a member of Parliament might have responded to Queen Elizabeth's declarations of her concern for the welfare of her people above all else.**

3. **Can a ruler be sincere and manipulative at the same time?**

Source: From *The Historical, Political, and Diplomatic Writings of Niccolo Machiavelli*, trans. Christian E. Detmold (Boston: Houghton Mifflin and Company, 1891), II: 54–59; and Heywood Townshend, *Historical Collections, or an Exact Account of the Proceedings of the Last Four Parliaments of Q. Elizabeth* (London: Basset, Crooke, and Cademan, 1680), 263–266.

towns, since the elaborate ceremonies and banquets at the royal court served to keep nobles away from their estates where they might plot rebellion. Capable of housing ten thousand people and surrounded by elaborately landscaped grounds and parks, the palace became an effective symbol of royal absolutism.

While the balance of powers in the English model would be widely admired in later times, most European rulers admired and imitated the centralized powers and absolutist claims of the French. The checks and balances of the English model gained a favorable press with the beginnings of the Enlightenment. In his influential *Second Treatise of Civil Government* (1690), the English political philosopher John Locke (1632–1704) disputed monarchial claims to absolute

TABLE 17.1	Rulers in Early Modern Western Europe	
Spain	*France*	*England/Great Britain*
Habsburg Dynasty	**Valois Dynasty**	**Tudor Dynasty**
Charles I (King of Spain 1516–1556), also known as Charles V (Holy Roman Emperor 1519–1556)	Francis I (1515–1547)	Henry VIII (1509–1547)
	Henry II (1547–1559)	Edward VI (1547–1553)
	Francis II (1559–1560)	Mary I (1553–1558)
Philip II (1556–1598)	Charles IX (1560–1574)	Elizabeth I (1558–1603)
	Henry III (1574–1589)	
Philip III (1598–1621)	**Bourbon Dynasty**	**Stuart Dynasty**
Philip IV (1621–1665)	Henry IV (1589–1610)[a]	James I (1603–1625)
Charles II (1665–1700)	Louis XIII (1610–1643)	Charles I (1625–1649)[a,b]
	Louis XIV (1643–1715)	(Puritan Republic, 1649–1660)
		Charles II (1660–1685)
		James II (1685–1688)[b]
		William III (1689–1702) and Mary II (1689–1694)
		Anne (1702–1714)
Bourbon Dynasty		**Hanoverian Dynasty**
Philip V (1700–1746)		
Ferdinand VI (1746–1759)		George I (1714–1727)
	Louis XV (1715–1774)	George II (1727–1760)

[a]Died a violent death. [b]Was overthrown.

authority by divine right. He argued that rulers derived their authority from the consent of the governed and were subject to the law. If monarchs overstepped the law, Locke asserted, citizens had the right and the duty to rebel. The consequences of this idea are considered in Chapter 22.

Warfare and Diplomacy

In addition to the civil wars that afflicted the Holy Roman Empire, France, and England, European states fought numerous international conflicts. Warfare was almost constant in early modern Europe (see the Chronology at the beginning of the chapter). In their pursuit of power monarchs expended vast sums of money and caused widespread devastation and death. The worst of the international conflicts, the Thirty Years War (1618–1648), caused long-lasting depopulation and economic decline in much of the Holy Roman Empire.

European Militaries

These wars also led to dramatic improvements in the skill and weaponry of European armed forces, making them among the most powerful in the world. The numbers of men in arms increased steadily throughout the early modern period. French forces, for example, grew from about 150,000 in 1630 to 400,000 by the early eighteenth century. Even smaller European states built up impressive armies. Sweden, with under a million people, had one of the finest and best-armed military forces in the seventeenth century. Though the country had fewer than 2 million inhabitants in 1700, Prussia's army made it one of Europe's major powers.

Larger armies required more effective command structures. In the words of a modern historian, European armies "evolved . . . the equivalent of a central nervous system, capable of activating technologically differentiated claws and teeth."[3] New signaling techniques improved control of battlefield maneuvers. Frequent drills for professional troops and militias trained

Versailles   Constructed during the reign of Louis XVI of France, the palace of Versailles could house ten thousand people. Surrounded by elaborately landscaped grounds and parks, the palace became an effective symbol of royal absolutism.

troops to obey orders instantly and improved morale. New fortifications able to withstand cannon bombardments were constructed to protect major urban centers. While each state tried to outdo its rivals by improvements in military hardware, battles between evenly matched armies often ended in stalemates that prolonged the wars. Victory increasingly depended on naval superiority.

England was the only major nation that did not maintain an army. Its power depended on its navy. England's rise as a sea power had begun under King Henry VIII, who spent heavily on ships and promoted a domestic iron industry to supply cannon. The crushing defeat of the Spanish Armada in 1588 by Henry's daughter, Elizabeth I, demonstrated the usefulness of these decisions. The Royal Navy also copied innovative ship designs from the Dutch in the second half of the seventeenth century. By the early eighteenth century, the Royal Navy had surpassed the rival French fleet in numbers. Now more secure, England merged with Scotland to become Great Britain. It then annexed Ireland and built a North American empire.

Although France was Europe's most powerful state, coalitions of the other great powers frustrated Louis XIV's efforts to expand its borders. In a series of eighteenth-century wars beginning with the War of the Spanish Succession (1701–1714), the combination of Britain's naval strength and the land armies of Austria and Prussia blocked French expansionist efforts and prevented the Bourbons from uniting the thrones of France and Spain.

This defeat of the French monarchy's empire-building efforts illustrated the principle of **balance of power** in international relations: the major European states formed temporary

balance of power The policy in international relations by which, beginning in the eighteenth century, the major European states acted together to prevent any one of them from becoming too powerful.

Balance of Power

MAP 17.3 **Europe in 1740** By the middle of the eighteenth century the great powers of Europe were France, the Austrian Empire, Great Britain, Prussia, and Russia. Spain, the Holy Roman Empire, and the Ottoman Empire were far weaker in 1740 than they had been two centuries earlier.

Legend:
- French Bourbon lands
- Spanish Bourbon lands
- Austrian Habsburg lands
- Prussian lands
- Great Britain
- Boundary of the Holy Roman Empire
- Russian Empire
- Russian gains, by 1725
- Ottoman Empire, 1722

© Cengage Learning

Interactive Map

ATLANTIC OCEAN

GREAT BRITAIN
SCOTLAND
Edinburgh
ENGLAND
London
Thames R.
IRELAND • Dublin

North Sea

NORWAY
Oslo •
KINGDOM OF DENMARK
DENMARK
SWEDEN
Baltic Sea

RUSSIAN EMPIRE
Moscow •
St. Petersburg •
INGRIA
ESTONIA
LIVONIA
Riga •
LITHUANIA
Smolensk •
Kiev •
UKRAINE
Don R.
Dnieper R.
Dniester R.

POLAND
Warsaw •
Vistula R.
EAST PRUSSIA

UNITED NETHERLANDS
Utrecht •
HANOVER
BRANDENBURG-PRUSSIA
Berlin •
Elbe R.
SAXONY
Oder R.
SILESIA
BOHEMIA
HOLY ROMAN EMPIRE
PALATINATE
Rhine R.
LORRAINE
Strasbourg •
BAVARIA
Danube R.
AUSTRIA
Vienna •

FRANCE
Paris •
Seine R.
Loire R.
Garonne R.
Toulouse •
Marseilles •
Rhône R.
SWITZERLAND
SAVOY
MILAN
GENOA
MODENA
TUSCANY
PAPAL STATES
Rome •
Po R.

Corsica (Genoa)
Sardinia (Austria)
Minorca (Gr. Br.)
Balearic Is.

PORTUGAL
Lisbon •
SPAIN
Madrid •
Duero R.
Tagus R.
Ebro R.
CATALONIA
GIBRALTAR (Gr. Br.)

Mediterranean Sea

KINGDOM OF NAPLES
Naples •
Sicily (Savoy)

REPUBLIC OF VENICE
Adriatic Sea
CROATIA
SLAVONIA
BOSNIA
HERZEGOVINA
SERBIA
Belgrade •
MONTENEGRO
ALBANIA
HUNGARY
Buda •
Pest •
TRANSYLVANIA
WALLACHIA
MOLDAVIA
BULGARIA
Danube R.

GREECE
OTTOMAN EMPIRE
Constantinople •
Aegean Sea
Black Sea
CRIMEA

N

300 Mi.
0   150   300 Km.
0   150

The Spanish Armada King Phillip II of Spain sent a massive fleet against England in 1588. England's defeat of the Spanish fleet weakened Spain and began England's rise to naval dominance.

alliances to prevent any one state from becoming too powerful. During the next two centuries, though adhering to four different branches of Christianity, the great powers of Europe—Catholic France, Anglican Britain, Catholic Austria, Lutheran Prussia, and Orthodox Russia (see Map 17.3)—maintained an effective balance of power in Europe by shifting their alliances for geopolitical rather than religious reasons. These pragmatic alliances were the first successful efforts at international peacekeeping.

Paying the Piper

To pay these extremely heavy military costs, European rulers had to increase their revenues. The most successful of them after 1600 promoted mutually beneficial, if often uneasy, alliances with commercial elites. Merchants and bankers sought to limit taxation and regulation and enhance the enforcement of contracts and the collection of debts without accepting insupportable tax burdens. Both sides believed that military power capable of protecting overseas expansion was crucial to economic growth, but they also knew that the cost of defending distant colonies could be overwhelming.

Spain and the Balance Sheet of Empire

Spain, sixteenth-century Europe's mightiest state, illustrates the costs of an aggressive military policy when coupled with a failure to promote economic development. Expensive wars against the Ottomans, northern European Protestants, and rebellious Dutch subjects led Spain to default and bankruptcy four times during the reign of King Philip II. The Spanish rulers' concerns for religious uniformity and traditional aristocratic privilege further undermined the country's economy. In the name of religious uniformity they expelled Jewish merchants, persecuted Protestant dissenters, and forced tens of thousands of Muslim farmers and artisans into exile. In the name of aristocratic privilege the 3 percent of the population that controlled 97 percent of the land in 1600 was exempt from taxation, while high sales taxes discouraged manufacturing.

For a time, vast imports of silver and gold from Spain's American colonies filled the treasury. These bullion shipments led to inflation (rising prices) across Europe, but prices rose fastest in Spain, making goods imported from France or other European nations cheaper than local goods. As a result, by 1700 most goods imported into Spain's colonies were of foreign origin. A Spanish saying captured the problem: American silver was like rain on the roof—it poured down and washed away.

Commerce and the Rise of the Netherlands

The rise of the Netherlands as an economic power stemmed from very different policies. The Spanish crown had acquired these resource-poor but commercially successful provinces as part of Charles V's inheritance. The decision of his son, King Philip II, to impose Spain's ruinous sales tax and to enforce Catholic orthodoxy drove the Dutch to revolt in 1566 and again in 1572. If successful, those measures would have discouraged business and driven away the Calvinists, Jews, and others who were essential to Dutch prosperity. The Dutch fought with skill and ingenuity, raising and training an army and a navy that were among the most effective in Europe. Unable to bear the military costs any longer, Spain accepted a truce that recognized autonomy in the northern Netherlands in 1609. Finally, in 1648, the independence of the seven United Provinces of the Free Netherlands (their full name) became final.

Rather than being ruined by the long war, the Netherlands emerged as the world's greatest trading nation. This economic success owed much to a decentralized government. During the long struggle against Spain, the provinces united around the prince of Orange, their sovereign, who served as commander-in-chief of the armed forces. But in economic matters each province was free to pursue its own interests. The maritime province of Holland grew rich by favoring commercial interests.

International Competition

After 1650 the Dutch faced growing competition from the English, who were developing their own close association of business and government. In a series of wars (1652–1678) England used its naval might to break Dutch dominance in overseas trade and extend its own colonial empire. With government support, the English merchant fleet doubled between 1660 and 1700, and foreign trade rose by 50 percent. As a result, state revenue from customs duties tripled. During the eighteenth century Britain's trading position strengthened still more.

The debts run up by the Anglo-Dutch Wars helped persuade the English monarchy to greatly enlarge the government's role in managing the economy. The government increased revenues by taxing the formerly exempt landed estates of the aristocrats and by collecting taxes directly. Previously, private individuals known as tax farmers had advanced the government a fixed sum of money; in return they could keep whatever money they were able to collect from taxpayers. To secure cash quickly for warfare and other emergencies and to reduce the burden of debts from earlier wars, England imitated the Dutch by creating a central bank that could issue long-term loans at low rates.

The French government also developed its national economy, especially under the royal advisor Jean Baptiste Colbert. He streamlined tax collection, promoted French manufacturing and shipping by imposing taxes on foreign goods, and improved transportation within France itself. Yet the power of the wealthy aristocrats kept the French government from following England's lead in taxing wealthy landowners, collecting taxes directly, and securing low-cost loans. Nor did France succeed in managing its debt as efficiently as England. (The role of governments in promoting overseas trade is also discussed in Chapter 19.)

SECTION REVIEW

- Greater political centralization enabled early modern monarchs to exert increased influence on economic, religious, and social life.

- While the Holy Roman Empire fragmented along religious and political lines, Spain, France, and England achieved greater centralization and religious unity.

- Spain enforced Catholic unity through the Inquisition and France through Bourbon policy, while in England the church became an arm of royal power.

- In both England and France, monarchs struggled with rivals over the limits of royal authority.

- Armies grew larger and more sophisticated while European powers strove to maintain a balance of power.

- High military costs drove the European powers to attempt a variety of tax and financial policies, the most successful being those of England and the Netherlands.

CONCLUSION

Early modern Europe witnessed the weakening of the Catholic Church and the Protestant Reformation. Rejecting the authority of the pope and criticizing the institution of indulgences, Luther insisted on the moral primacy of faith over deeds; Calvin went further, holding that salvation was predestined by God. The pioneers of the Scientific Revolution such as Copernicus and Newton showed that they could explain the workings of the physical universe in natural terms. These scientists did not see any conflict between science and religion, but they paved the way for more secular thinkers of the Enlightenment, who believed that human reason was capable of—and responsible for—discovering the laws that govern social behavior.

Thanks to foreign and domestic trade, European cities in this period experienced rapid growth and the rise of a wealthy commercial class. The Netherlands in particular prospered from expanded manufacturing and trade: with the formation of joint-stock companies and a powerful stock market, Amsterdam became Europe's major port and financial center. For peasants and laborers, however, life did not improve much: serfdom had all but ended in western Europe, only to rise in eastern Europe. Agricultural techniques had not improved substantially since medieval times, and environmental hardships such as the Little Ice Age and deforestation caused by mining and logging brought great difficulties to the poor. Rural poverty, coupled with the exemption from taxation enjoyed by wealthy landowners, sparked numerous armed rebellions. Women were dependent on their families' and husbands' wealth or lack of it, and were barred from attending schools or joining guilds and professions.

Differing policies in the areas of religion, foreign relations, and economics explain the different histories of Europe's early modern states. Charles V, unable to reconcile the diverse interests of his Catholic and Protestant territories and their powerful local rulers, failed to create a unified Holy Roman Empire. Henry VIII, having failed to win an annulment of his marriage to Catherine of Aragon, severed all ties with the pope and led Parliament to accept him as head of the Church of England. Power struggles in England during this period led to a stronger Parliament, while in France a stronger monarchy emerged, symbolized by Louis XIV's construction of the palace at Versailles. Spain was Europe's mightiest state in the sixteenth century, but its failure to suppress the Netherlands Revolt and the costs of other wars led to bankruptcy. In the seventeenth century the United Netherlands had become the dominant commercial power on the continent.

The growth of English naval power led to the defeat of the Dutch in the Anglo-Dutch Wars and of France in the early eighteenth century when it attempted to expand its own empire through a union with Spain. Unlike Spain and France, which maintained aristocrats' traditional exemption from taxation, England began to tax their estates, and this policy—together with the establishment of direct taxation and the creation of a central bank from which it could secure low-cost loans—gave England a stronger financial foundation than its rivals enjoyed.

KEY TERMS

EBOOK AND WEBSITE RESOURCES

e Primary Sources

Table Talk

Letter to the Grand Duchess Christina

Treatise on Toleration

e Interactive Maps

Map 17.1 Religious Reformation in Europe

Map 17.2 The European Empire of Charles V

Map 17.3 Europe in 1740

Plus flashcards, practice quizzes, and more. Go to:
www.cengage.com/history/bullietearthpeople5e

SUGGESTED READING

Bergin, Joseph. *The Short Oxford History of Europe: The Seventeenth Century*. 2001. A general overview.

Braudel, Fernand. *Civilization and Capitalism, 15th–18th Century*. Trans. Siân Reynolds. 3 vols. 1992. A sweeping interpretation by an eminent historian.

Casey, James. *Early Modern Spain: A Social History*. 1999. A general look at an important country.

Cipolla, Carlo M. *Before the Industrial Revolution: European Society and Economy, 1000–1700*, 3rd ed. 1993. An excellent introduction to social and economic life.

Fagan, Brian. *The Little Ice Age: How Climate Made History, 1300–1850*. 2000. An important episode in climate history.

Hall, A. R. *The Scientific Revolution, 1500–1800: The Formation of the Modern Scientific Attitude*, 2nd ed. 1962. A basic introduction to the intellectual ferment of the era.

Huppert, George. *After the Black Death: A Social History of Early Modern Europe*, 2nd ed. 1998. An excellent introduction to this period's social and economic history.

Israel, Jonathan. *The Dutch Republic: Its Rise, Greatness and Fall, 1477–1806*. 1995. Study of a key country.

Jütte, Robert. *Poverty and Deviance in Early Modern Europe*. 1994. Looks at non-elite perspectives.

Le Roy Ladurie, Emmanuel. *The Royal French State, 1460–1610*. Trans. Juliet Vale. 1994. *The Ancien Régime: A History of France, 1610–1774*. Trans. Mark Greengrass. 1996. A two-volume look at a key country by an eminent historian.

Levack, Brian P. *The Witch-Hunt in Early Modern Europe*, 2nd ed. 1995. A good starting point for studying Europe's obsession with witchcraft.

Outram, Dorinda. *The Enlightenment*, 2nd ed. 2005. Provides a recent summary of research.

Parker, Geoffrey. *Military Revolution: Military Innovation and the Rise of the West, 1500–1800*, 2nd ed. 1996. Technological development in a violent era.

Shapin, Steven. *The Scientific Revolution*. 1996. An accessible introduction.

Sharpe, J. A. *Early Modern England: A Social History, 1550–1760*, 2nd ed. 1997. A good single-country survey.

Wallerstein, Immanuel. *The Modern World-System*, vol. 2, *Mercantilism and the Consolidation of the European World-Economy, 1600–1750*. 1980. Presents an influential economic theory of Europe's relation to the world.

Wiesner, Merry E. *Women and Gender in Early Modern Europe*, 2nd ed. 2000. Examines topics in women's history.

NOTES

1. Quoted by Carlo M. Cipolla, "Introduction," *The Fontana Economic History of Europe*, vol. 2, *The Sixteenth and Seventeenth Centuries* (Glasgow: Collins/Fontana Books, 1976), 11–12.

2. Michel de Montaigne, *Essais* (1588), ch. 31, "Des Cannibales."

3. William H. McNeill, *The Pursuit of Power: Technology, Armed Force, and Society Since A.D. 1000* (Chicago: University of Chicago Press, 1982), 124.

CHAPTER OUTLINE

ENVIRONMENT + TECHNOLOGY   *A Silver Refinery at Potosí, Bolivia, 1700*

DIVERSITY + DOMINANCE   *Race and Ethnicity in the Spanish Colonies: Negotiating Hierarchy*

© President and Fellows of Harvard College, Peabody Museum of Archaeology and Ethnology, 41-72-10/20

Choctaw Village in Louisiana at Time of French Colonial Rule   This scene of village life illustrates the integration of the Choctaw in the colonial economy. The painting places a young African slave and European trade goods in a scene where the Choctaw pursue traditional tasks.

Visit the website and ebook for additional study materials and interactive tools: www.cengage.com/history/bullietearthpeople5e

The Diversity of American Colonial Societies, 1530–1770

Shulush Homa—an eighteenth-century Choctaw leader called "Red Shoes" by the English—faced a dilemma. For years he had befriended the French who had moved into the lower Mississippi Valley, protecting their outlying settlements from other indigenous groups and producing a steady flow of deerskins for trade. In return he received guns and gifts as well as honors previously given only to chiefs. Though born a commoner, he had parlayed his skillful politicking with the French—and the shrewd distribution of the gifts he received—to enhance his position in Choctaw society. Then his fortunes turned. In the course of yet another war between England and France, the English cut off French shipping. Faced with followers unhappy over his sudden inability to supply French guns, Red Shoes forged a dangerous new arrangement with the English that led his former allies, the French, to put a price on his head. His murder in 1747 launched a civil war among the Choctaw. By the end of this conflict both the French colonial population and the Choctaw people had suffered greatly.

- How did the Columbian Exchange alter the natural environment of the Americas?
- What role did forced labor play in the main industries of Spanish America and Brazil?
- What were the main similarities and differences among colonies of Spain, Portugal, England, and France?
- What were the effects of the colonial reforms and wars among imperial powers that dominated the Americas during the eighteenth century?

The story of Red Shoes reveals a number of themes from the period of European colonization of the Americas. First, although the wars, epidemics, and territorial loss associated with European settlement threatened Amerindians, many adapted the new technologies and new political possibilities to their own purposes and thrived—at least for a time. In the end, though, the best that they could achieve was a holding action. The people of the Old World were coming to dominate the people of the New World.

Second, after centuries of isolation, the political and economic demands of European empires forced the Americas onto the global stage. The influx of Europeans and Africans resulted in a vast biological and cultural transformation, as new plants, animals, diseases, peoples, and technologies fundamentally altered the natural environment. This was not a one-way transfer, however. The technologies and resources of the New World also contributed to profound changes in the Old. Among them, American staple crops helped fuel a population spurt in Europe, Asia, and Africa while American riches altered European economic, social, and political relations.

Third, the story of Red Shoes and the Choctaw illustrates the complexity of colonial society, in which Amerindians, Europeans, and Africans all contributed to the creation of new cultures. Although similar processes took place throughout the Americas, the particulars varied from place to place, creating a diverse range of cultures. The society that arose in each colony reflected the colony's mix of native peoples, its connections to the slave trade, and the characteristics of the European society establishing the colony. As the colonies matured, new concepts of identity developed, and those living in the Americas began to see themselves as distinct.

THE COLUMBIAN EXCHANGE

Columbian Exchange The exchange of plants, animals, diseases, and technologies between the Americas and the rest of the world following Columbus's voyages.

The term **Columbian Exchange** refers to the transfer of peoples, animals, plants, and diseases between the New and Old Worlds. The European invasion and settlement of the Western Hemisphere opened a long era of biological and technological transfers that altered American environments. Within a century of first settlement, the domesticated livestock and major agricultural crops of the Old World (the known world before Columbus's voyage) had spread over much of the Americas, and the New World's useful staple crops had enriched the agricultures of Europe, Asia, and Africa. Old World diseases that entered the Americas with European immigrants and African slaves devastated indigenous populations. These dramatic population changes weakened native peoples' capacity for resistance and accelerated the transfer of plants, animals, and related technologies. As a result, the colonies of Spain, Portugal, England, and France became vast arenas of cultural and social experimentation.

Demographic Changes

Because of their long isolation from other continents (see Chapter 16), the peoples of the New World lacked immunity to diseases introduced from the Old World. As a result, death rates among Amerindian peoples during the epidemics of the early colonial period were very high. The lack of reliable estimates of the Amerindian population at the moment of contact has frustrated efforts to measure the deadly impact of these diseases, but scholars agree that Old World diseases had a terrible effect on native peoples. According to one estimate, the population of central Mexico fell from more than 13 million to approximately 700,000 in the century that followed 1521. In this same period the populations of the Maya and Inca regions declined by nearly 75 percent or more. Brazil's native population fell by more than 50 percent within a century of the arrival of the Portuguese.

Early Epidemics

Smallpox, which arrived in the Caribbean in 1518, was the most deadly of the early epidemics. In Mexico and Central America, 50 percent or more of the Amerindian population died during the first wave of smallpox epidemics. The disease then spread to South America with equally devastating effects. Measles arrived in the New World in the 1530s and was followed by diphtheria, typhus, influenza, and pulmonary plague. Mortality was often greatest when two or more diseases struck at the same time. Between 1520 and 1521 influenza and other ailments attacked the Cakchiquel of Guatemala. Their chronicle recalls:

> *Great was the stench of the dead. After our fathers and grandfathers succumbed, half the people fled to the fields. The dogs and vultures devoured the bodies. . . . So it was that we became orphans, oh my sons! . . . We were born to die!*[1]

By the mid-seventeenth century malaria and yellow fever were also present in tropical regions of the Americas. The deadliest form of malaria arrived with the African slave trade, ravaging the already reduced native populations and afflicting Europeans as well.

The development of English and French colonies in North America in the seventeenth century led to similar patterns of contagion and mortality. In 1616 and 1617 epidemics nearly exterminated New England's indigenous groups. Epidemics also followed French fur traders as far as Hudson Bay and the Great Lakes. Although there is very little evidence that Europeans con-

CHRONOLOGY

	Spanish America	Brazil	British America	French America
1500	1518 Smallpox arrives in Caribbean	1520 Appointment of first Viceroy of Brazil		
	1535 Creation of Viceroyalty of New Spain			1534–1542 Jacques Cartier's voyages to explore Newfoundland and Gulf of St. Lawrence
	1540s Creation of Viceroyalty of Peru	1540–1600 Era of Amerindian slavery		
	1542 New Laws attempt to improve treatment of Amerindians	After 1540 Sugar begins to dominate the economy		
	1545 Silver discovered at Potosí, Bolivia			
1600			1607 Jamestown founded	1608 Quebec founded
	1625 Population of Potosí reaches 120,000	By 1620 African slave trade provides majority of plantation workers	1620 Plymouth founded	
		1630s Quilombo of Palmares founded		
			1660 Slave population in Virginia begins period of rapid growth	
			1664 English take New York from Dutch	
				1699 Louisiana founded
1700	1700 Last Habsburg ruler of Spain dies			
	1713 First Bourbon ruler of Spain crowned			
		1750–1777 Reforms of marquis de Pombal	1754–1763 French and Indian War	1760 English take Canada
	1770s and 1780s Amerindian revolts in Andean region			

sciously used disease as a tool of empire, the deadly results of contact clearly undermined the ability of native peoples to resist settlement.

Transfer of Plants and Animals

Even as epidemics swept through the indigenous population, the New and the Old Worlds were participating in a vast exchange of plants and animals that radically altered diet and lifestyles in both regions. Settlers brought all the staples of southern European agriculture—such as wheat, olives, grapes, and garden vegetables—to the Americas soon after contact. Colonization also introduced African and Asian crops such as rice, bananas, coconuts, breadfruit, and sugar. While natives remained loyal to their traditional staples, they added many foods like citrus fruits, melons, figs, and sugar as well as onions, radishes, and salad greens to their cuisines.

Diffusion of Plants and Animals

In return the Americas offered the Old World an abundance of useful plants. Maize, potatoes, and manioc revolutionized agriculture and diet in parts of Europe, Africa, and Asia (see

Oronoz

The Columbian Exchange In this painting an Amerindian woman milks a cow, suggesting how the Columbian Exchange altered native culture and environment. While livestock sometimes destroyed the fields of native peoples, cattle, sheep, pigs, and goats also provided food, leather, and wool.

Environment and Technology: Amerindian Foods in Africa, in Chapter 19). Many experts assert that the growth of world population after 1700 resulted from the spread of these useful crops, which provided more calories per acre than did most Old World staples. Beans, squash, tomatoes, sweet potatoes, peanuts, chilies, and chocolate also gained widespread acceptance in the Old World. In addition, the New World provided the Old with plants that provided dyes, medicine, varieties of cotton, and tobacco.

The introduction of European livestock had a dramatic impact on New World environments and cultures. Faced with few natural predators, cattle, pigs, horses, and sheep, as well as pests like rats and rabbits, multiplied rapidly in the Americas. On the vast plains of southern Brazil, Uruguay, and Argentina, for example, herds of wild cattle and horses exceeded 50 million by 1700.

Where Old World livestock spread most rapidly, environmental changes were dramatic. Many priests and colonial officials noted the destructive impact of marauding livestock on Amerindian agriculturists. The first viceroy of Mexico, Antonio de Mendoza, wrote to the Spanish king: "May your Lordship realize that if cattle are allowed, the Indians will be destroyed." Sheep, which grazed grasses close to the ground, were also an environmental threat.

Yet the viceroy's stark choice misrepresented the complex response of indigenous peoples to these new animals. Wild cattle on the plains of South America, northern Mexico, and Texas provided indigenous peoples with abundant supplies of meat and hides, for example. In the present-day southwestern United States, the Navajo became sheepherders and expert weavers. Even in the centers of European settlement, Amerindians turned European animals to their own advantage by becoming muleteers, cowboys, and sheepherders.

No animal had a more striking effect on the cultures of native peoples than the horse, which increased the efficiency of hunters and the military capacity of warriors on the plains. The horse permitted the Apache, Sioux, Blackfoot, Comanche, Assiniboine, and others to more efficiently hunt the vast herds of buffalo in North America. The horse also revolutionized the cultures of the Mapuche and Pampas peoples in South America.

SECTION REVIEW

- The creation of Spanish and Portuguese empires in America accelerated global exchanges of peoples, plants, animals, diseases, and technologies.

- Old World diseases decimated New World peoples and made them vulnerable to European expansion, and Old World animals overran the landscape and changed New World practices.

- Both the Old and New Worlds also profited from the introduction of new plants and animals.

SPANISH AMERICA AND BRAZIL

Forging Colonial Society

The frontiers of conquest and settlement expanded rapidly. Within one hundred years of Columbus's first voyage to the Western Hemisphere, the Spanish Empire in America included most of the islands of the Caribbean and a vast area that stretched from northern Mexico to the plains of the Rio de la Plata region (a region that includes the modern nations of Argentina, Uruguay, and Paraguay). Portuguese settlement developed more slowly, but before the end of the sixteenth century, Portugal had occupied most of the Brazilian coast.

Early settlers from Spain and Portugal sought to create colonial societies based on the institutions and customs of their homelands. They viewed society as a vertical hierarchy of estates (classes of society), as uniformly Catholic, and as an arrangement of patriarchal extended-family networks. They quickly moved to establish the religious, social, and administrative institutions that were familiar to them.

Despite the imposition of foreign institutions and loss of life caused by epidemics, indigenous peoples exercised a powerful influence on the development of colonial societies. Aztec and Inca elite families sought to protect their traditional privileges and rights through marriage or less formal alliances with Spanish settlers. They also used colonial courts to defend their claims to land. In Spanish and Portuguese colonies, indigenous military allies and laborers proved crucial to the development of European settlements. Nearly everywhere, Amerindian religious beliefs and practices survived beneath the surface of an imposed Christianity. Amerindian languages, cuisines, medical practices, and agricultural techniques also survived the conquest and influenced the development of Latin American culture.

PRIMARY SOURCE: General History of the Things in New Spain Read an account of the Spanish conquest of the Aztec Empire, compiled from eyewitness testimony by the Aztecs themselves.

The African slave trade added a third cultural stream to colonial Latin American society. At first, African slaves were concentrated in plantation regions of Brazil and the Caribbean (see Chapter 19), but by the end of the colonial era, Africans and their descendants were living throughout Spanish and Portuguese America, introducing elements of their agricultural practices, music, religious beliefs, cuisine, and social customs to colonial societies.

State and Church

The Spanish crown moved quickly to curb the independent power of the conquistadors and to establish royal authority over both defeated native populations and European settlers, but geography and technology thwarted this ambition. European officials could not control the distant colonies too closely because it took a ship more than two hundred days to make a roundtrip voyage from Spain to Veracruz, Mexico. Additional months of travel were required to reach Lima, Peru.

Spanish and Portuguese Colonial Governments

As a result, the highest-ranking Spanish officials in the colonies, the viceroys of New Spain and Peru, enjoyed broad power, but they also faced obstacles to their authority in the vast territories they sought to control. Created in 1535, the Viceroyalty of New Spain, with its capital in Mexico City, included Mexico, the southwest of what is now the United States, Central America, and the islands of the Caribbean. Created five years later, the Viceroyalty of Peru, with its capital in Lima, governed Spanish South America (see Map 18.1).

Until the seventeenth century, most colonial officials were born in Spain, but fiscal mismanagement eventually forced the Crown to sell appointments. As a result, local-born members of the colonial elite gained many offices.

In the sixteenth century Portugal concentrated its resources and energies on Asia and Africa. Because early settlers found neither mineral wealth nor rich native empires in Brazil, the Portuguese king was slow to create expensive mechanisms of colonial government in the New World, but mismanagement forced the king to appoint a governor-general in 1549 and make Salvador Brazil's capital. In 1720 the king named the first viceroy of Brazil.

The government institutions of the Spanish and Portuguese colonies had a more uniform character and were much more extensive and costly than those later established in North America by France and Great Britain. The enormous wealth produced in Spanish America by silver and gold mines and in Brazil by sugar plantations and, after 1690, gold mines financed these large and intrusive colonial bureaucracies. These institutions made the colonies more responsive to the initiatives of Spanish and Portuguese monarchs, but they also thwarted local

NEW
FRANCE
(Conquered by
England,1760)

Effective frontier
of Spanish settlement

ENGLISH COLONIES
(Independence declared, 1776)

40°W

40°N

ATLANTIC
OCEAN

Colorado R.

Mississippi R.

Rio Grande

Silver
Silver
COAHUILA

Gulf of Mexico

FLORIDA
(Ceded to England, 1763–1783)

VICEROYALTY OF NEW SPAIN
BAJIO LEÓN (1535)

Zacatecas
Guanajuato
Guadalajara

Havana

Sugar cane
Beef
Tobacco

HAITI [SAINT-DOMINGUE]
(Ceded to France, 1697)

20°N

Mexico City
Silver
Veracruz

Sugar cane
Indigo

Cacao

Sugar cane

Beef

Sugar cane

PUERTO RICO

Sugar
cane
Cochineal

BRITISH
HONDURAS

Guatemala

JAMAICA
(Conquered by England, 1655)

SANTO DOMINGO

Sugar cane

Cochineal
Cacao
Indigo

Silver

Caribbean Sea

Sugar cane

Pearls
Cacao

Caracas

Orinoco R.

Gold

Magdalena R.

GUIANA

Bogotá

VICEROYALTY OF
NEW GRANADA
(Separated from
Viceroyalty of Peru,
1717, 1739)

Equator 0°

Quito

Amazon R.

Forest
products

PACIFIC
OCEAN

VICEROYALTY
OF PERU
(1590s)

Sugar cane

VICEROYALTY
OF BRAZIL
(1720)

Sugar
cane

Pernambuco

Lima

Cuzco

Sugar
cane
Salvador

Sugar
cane

La Paz

Cacao

Chuquisaca
(La Plata; Sucre)

ANDES

Potosí

Paraná R.

Diamonds
Gold

20°S

Yerba
Tobacco

São Paulo

Rio de Janeiro
(Capital, 1763)

VICEROYALTY OF
LA PLATA
(Separated from
Viceroyalty of Peru,
1776)

Wheat

Beef and
hides

Montevideo

AUDIENCIA
OF CHILE
(Retained by
Viceroyalty of Peru,
1776)

Santiago

Buenos Aires
Beef and
hides

0   500   1,000 Km.

0   500   1,000 Mi.

Claimed but not
settled by Spain

Territories claimed by Spain

Viceroyalty of New Spain

Viceroyalty of New Granada

Viceroyalty of Peru and Audiencia of Chile

Viceroyalty of Rio de la Plata

Islas Malvinas
(Falkland Islands)

Territories claimed by Portugal

Viceroyalty of Brazil

Silver mine

Cape Horn

80°W   60°W

© Cengage Learning

MAP 18.1 **Colonial Latin America in the Eighteenth Century** Spain and Portugal controlled most of the Western Hemisphere in the eighteenth century. In the sixteenth century they had created new administrative jurisdictions—viceroyalties—to defend their respective colonies against European rivals. Taxes assessed on colonial products helped pay for this extension of governmental authority.

e Interactive Map

Private Collection

Saint Martín de Porres (1579–1639) Martín de Porres was the illegitimate son of a Spanish nobleman and a black servant. He entered the Dominican Order in Lima, Peru, where he was known for his generosity, his religious visions, and his ability to heal the sick. In this painting the artist celebrates Martín de Porres's spirituality while representing him doing the type of work presumed to be suitable for a person of mixed descent.

economic initiative and political experimentation. More importantly, the heavy tax burden imposed by these colonial states drained capital from the colonies, slowing investment and retarding economic growth.

The Catholic Church

In both Spanish America and Brazil, the Catholic Church became the primary agent for the introduction and transmission of Christian belief as well as European language and culture. The church undertook the conversion of Amerindians, ministered to the spiritual needs of European settlers, and promoted intellectual life through the introduction of the printing press and the founding of schools and universities.

Spain and Portugal justified their American conquests by assuming an obligation to convert native populations to Christianity. This effort to convert America's native peoples expanded Christianity on a scale similar to its earlier expansion in Europe at the time of Constantine in the fourth century. In New Spain alone hundreds of thousands of conversions and baptisms were achieved within a few years of the conquest. However, the small numbers of missionaries limited quality of indoctrination. One Dominican claimed to the king that the Franciscans "have taken and occupied three fourths of the country, though they do not have enough friars for it. . . . In most places they are content to say a mass once a year; consider what sort of indoctrination they give them!"[2]

The Catholic clergy sought to achieve their evangelical ends by first converting members of the Amerindian elites, in the hope that they could persuade others to follow their example. To pursue this objective, Franciscan missionaries in Mexico created a seminary to train members of the indigenous elite to become priests, but they curtailed these idealistic efforts when church authorities discovered that many converts were secretly observing old beliefs and rituals. The trial and punishment of two converted Aztec nobles for heresy in the 1530s and the torture of hundreds of Maya in the 1560s repelled the church hierarchy, ending both the violent repression of native religious practice and the effort to recruit an Amerindian clergy.

Despite its failures, the Catholic clergy did provide native peoples with some protections against the abuse and exploitation of Spanish settlers. The priest **Bartolomé de Las Casas** (1474–1566) was the most influential defender of the Amerindians in the early colonial period. He arrived in Hispaniola in 1502 as a settler and initially lived off the forced labor of Amerindians. Deeply moved by the deaths of so many Amerindians and by the misdeeds of the Spanish, Las Casas entered the Dominican Order and later became the first bishop of Chiapas, in southern Mexico. For the remainder of his long life Las Casas served as the most important advocate for native peoples. His most important achievement was the enactment of the New Laws of 1542—reform legislation that outlawed the enslavement of Amerindians and limited other forms of forced labor.

European clergy had arrived in the Americas with the intention of transmitting Catholic Christian belief and ritual without alteration. The linguistic diversity of Amerindian populations and their geographic dispersal over a vast landscape defeated this ambition. The resulting slow progress and limited success of evangelization led to the appearance of a unique Amerindian Christianity that blended European Christian beliefs with important elements of traditional native cosmology and ritual. The Catholic clergy and most European settlers viewed this evolving mixture as the work of the Devil or as evidence of Amerindian inferiority. Instead, it was one component of the process of cultural borrowing and innovation that contributed to a distinct and original Latin American culture.

After 1600 the terrible loss of Amerindian population caused by epidemics and growing signs of resistance to conversion led the Catholic Church to redirect most of its resources from native regions in the countryside to growing colonial cities and towns with large European populations. One important outcome of this altered mission was the founding of universities and secondary schools and the stimulation of urban intellectual life. Over time, the church became the richest institution in the Spanish colonies, controlling ranches, plantations, and vineyards as well as serving as the society's banker.

Colonial Economies

The silver mines of Peru and Mexico and the sugar plantations of Brazil dominated the economic development of colonial Latin America. The mineral wealth of the New World fueled the early development of European capitalism and funded Europe's greatly expanded trade with Asia. Profits produced in these economic centers also promoted the growth of colonial cities, concentrated scarce investment capital and labor resources, and stimulated the development of livestock raising and agriculture in neighboring rural areas (see Map 18.1). Once established, this colonial dependence on mineral and agricultural exports left an enduring social and economic legacy in Latin America.

The Spanish and later the Portuguese produced gold worth millions of pesos, but silver mines in the Spanish colonies generated the most wealth and therefore exercised the greatest economic influence. The first important silver strikes occurred in Mexico in the 1530s and 1540s. In 1545 the Spanish discovered the single richest silver deposit in the Americas at **Potosí** (poh-toh-SEE) in Alto Peru (what is now Bolivia). The silver of Alto Peru and Peru dominated the Spanish colonial economy until 1680, when it was surpassed by Mexican silver production. At first, miners extracted silver ore by smelting: crushed ore, packed with charcoal, was fired in a furnace, but this wasteful use of forest resources destroyed forests near the mining centers. Faced with rising fuel costs, Mexican miners developed an efficient method of chemical extraction that relied on mixing mercury with the silver ore (see Environment and Technology:

Bartolomé de Las Casas

Bartolomé de Las Casas First bishop of Chiapas, in southern Mexico. He devoted most of his life to protecting Amerindian peoples from exploitation. His major achievement was the New Laws of 1542, which limited the ability of Spanish settlers to compel Amerindians to labor for them.

Colonial Mining

Potosí Located in Bolivia, one of the richest silver mining centers and most populous cities in colonial Spanish America.

ENVIRONMENT + TECHNOLOGY

A Silver Refinery at Potosí, Bolivia, 1700

The silver refineries of Spanish America were among the largest and most heavily capitalized industrial enterprises in the Western Hemisphere during the colonial period. By the middle of the seventeenth century the mines of Potosí, Bolivia, had attracted a population of more than 120,000.

The accompanying illustration shows a typical refinery (*ingenio*). Aqueducts carried water from large reservoirs on nearby mountainsides to the refineries. The water wheel shown on the right drove two sets of vertical stamps that crushed ore. Each iron-shod stamp was about the size and weight of a telephone pole. Amerindian laborers then sorted, dried, and mixed the crushed ore with mercury and other catalysts to extract the silver. Miners then separated the amalgam using a combination of washing and heating. The end result was a nearly pure ingot of silver that was later assayed and taxed at the mint.

Silver production carried a high environmental cost. Forests were cut to provide fuel and the timbers needed to shore up mine shafts and construct stamping mills and other machinery. Unwanted base metals produced in the refining process poisoned the soil. In addition, the need for tens of thousands of horses, mules, and oxen to drive machinery and transport material led to overgrazing and widespread erosion.

A Bolivian Silver Refinery, 1700
The silver refineries of Spanish America were among the largest industrial establishments in the Western Hemisphere.

Legend
(A) Storage sheds for ore
(B) Two water-driven stamping mills to crush ore
(C) Additional stamping mill
(D) Screen to sort ore
(E) Ore packed in mixing box
(F) Mercury and catalysts added to ore
(G) Amalgamation occurs
(H) Ore dried in furnace
(I) Mercury removed
(J) Refined ore washed
(K) Ore assayed
(L) Poor-quality ore remixed with catalysts
(M) Housing
(N) Offices and sheds
(O) Aqueduct
(P) Chapel
(Q) Mill owner's house

Encomienda and Mita

encomienda A grant of authority over a population of Amerindians in the Spanish colonies. It provided the grant holder with a supply of cheap labor and periodic payments of goods by the Amerindians. It obliged the grant holder to Christianize the Amerindians.

Slavery and Slave Trade

A Silver Refinery at Potosí, Bolivia, 1700). Silver yields and profits increased with the use of mercury amalgamation, but this process, too, had severe environmental costs, since mercury is a poison that contaminated the environment and sickened the Amerindian work force.

From the time of Columbus, indigenous populations had been compelled to provide labor for European settlers in the Americas. Until the 1540s in Spanish colonies, Spanish authorities divided Amerindians among settlers, who forced them to provide labor or goods. This form of forced labor was called **encomienda** (in-co-mee-EN-dah). As epidemics and mistreatment led to the decline in Amerindian population, reforms such as the New Laws sought to eliminate the encomienda. The discovery of silver, however, led to new forms of compulsory labor. In the mining region of Mexico, where epidemics had reduced Amerindian populations, silver miners came to rely on wage laborers. Peru's Amerindian population survived in larger numbers, allowing the Spanish to impose a form of labor called the mita (MEE-tah). Under this system, one-seventh of adult male Amerindians were compelled to work for two to four months each year in mines, farms, or textile factories.

As the Amerindian population declined with new epidemics, villages were forced to shorten the period between mita obligations. Instead of serving every seven years, many men returned to mines after only a year or two. Unwilling to accept mita service and the other tax burdens imposed on Amerindian villages, thousands abandoned traditional agriculture and moved permanently to Spanish mines and farms as laborers. The long-term result of these individual decisions weakened Amerindian village life and promoted the assimilation of Amerindians into Spanish-speaking Catholic colonial society.

Before the settlement of Brazil, the Portuguese had already developed sugar plantations using African slave labor on the Atlantic islands of Madeira, the Azores, the Cape Verdes, and São Tomé. Because of the success of these early experiences, they were able to quickly transfer this profitable form of agriculture to Brazil. After 1540 sugar production expanded rapidly, and by the seventeenth century it dominated the Brazilian economy.

At first the Portuguese sugar planters enslaved Amerindians captured in war or seized from their villages. Thousands of Amerindian slaves died during the epidemics that raged across Brazil in the sixteenth and seventeenth centuries. This led to the development of an internal slave

Tobacco Factory Machinery in Colonial Mexico City   The tobacco factory in eighteenth-century Mexico City used a horse-driven mechanical shredder to produce snuff and cigarette tobacco.

Archivo General de Indias, Seville, Spain

trade by slave raiders who pushed into the interior, even attacking Amerindian populations in neighboring Spanish colonies.

Amerindian slaves remained an important source of labor and slave raiding a significant business in frontier regions into the eighteenth century. But sugar planters eventually came to rely more on African slaves. African slaves at first cost much more than Amerindian slaves, but planters found them more productive and more resistant to disease. As profits from the plantations increased, imports of African slaves rose from an average of two thousand per year in the late sixteenth century to approximately seven thousand per year a century later, outstripping the immigration of free Portuguese settlers. Between 1650 and 1750, for example, nearly five African slaves arrived in Brazil for every immigrant from Europe.

Colonial Networks of Trade

Within Spanish America, the mining centers of Mexico and Peru eventually exercised global economic influence. American silver increased the European money supply, promoting commercial expansion and, later, industrialization. Large amounts of silver also flowed across the Pacific to the Spanish colony of the Philippines, where it paid for Asian spices, silks, and pottery.

The rich mines of Peru, Bolivia, and Mexico stimulated urban population growth as well as commercial links with distant agricultural and textile producers. The population of the city of Potosí, high in the Andes, reached 120,000 inhabitants by 1625. This rich mining town became the center of a vast regional market that depended on Chilean wheat, Argentine livestock, and Ecuadorian textiles.

The sugar plantations of Brazil played a similar role in integrating the economy of the south Atlantic region. Brazil exchanged sugar, tobacco, and reexported slaves for yerba (Paraguayan tea), hides, livestock, and silver produced in neighboring Spanish colonies. Portugal's increasing openness to British trade also allowed Brazil to become a conduit for an illegal trade between Spanish colonies and Europe. At the end of the seventeenth century, the discovery of gold in Brazil promoted further regional and international economic integration.

Society in Colonial Latin America

creoles In colonial Spanish America, term used to describe someone of European descent born in the New World. Elsewhere in the Americas, the term is used to describe all nonnative peoples.

With the exception of some early viceroys, few members of Spain's nobility came to the New World. *Hidalgos* (ee-DAHL-goes)—lesser nobles—were well represented, as were Spanish merchants, artisans, miners, priests, and lawyers. Small numbers of criminals, beggars, and prostitutes also found their way to the colonies. This flow of immigrants from Spain was never large, and Spanish settlers were always a tiny minority in a colonial society numerically dominated by Amerindians and rapidly growing populations of Africans, **creoles** (whites born in America to European parents), and people of mixed ancestry (see Diversity and Dominance: Race and Ethnicity in the Spanish Colonies: Negotiating Hierarchy).

Colonial Elites

The most powerful conquistadors and early settlers sought to create a hereditary social and political class comparable to the European nobility. But their systematic abuse of Amerindian communities and the catastrophic effects of the epidemics of the sixteenth century undermined their economic position. Colonial officials, the clergy, and the richest merchants inherited their social position. Europeans dominated the highest levels of the church and government as well as commerce, while wealthy American-born creoles controlled colonial agriculture and mining. Although tensions between Spaniards and creoles were inevitable, most elite families included both groups.

Amerindian Adaptations

Before the Europeans arrived in the Americas, the native peoples were members of a large number of distinct cultural and linguistic groups. The effects of conquest and epidemics undermined this rich social and cultural complexity and the relocation of Amerindian peoples to promote conversion or provide labor further eroded ethnic boundaries among native peoples. Application of the racial label "Indian" by colonial administrators and settlers helped organize the tribute and labor demands imposed on native peoples, but it also registered the cultural costs of colonial rule.

Amerindian elites struggled to survive in the new political and economic environments created by military defeat and European settlement. Some sought to protect their positions by forging marriage or less formal relations with colonists. As a result, some indigenous and settler families were tied together by kinship in the decades after conquest, but these links weakened

Race and Ethnicity in the Spanish Colonies: Negotiating Hierarchy

Many European visitors to colonial Latin America were interested in the mixing of Europeans, Amerindians, and Africans in the colonies. Many also commented on the treatment of slaves. The passages that follow allow us to examine two colonial societies.

Two young Spanish naval officers and scientists, Jorge Juan and Antonio de Ulloa, arrived in the colonies in 1735 as members of a scientific expedition. They later wrote the first selection after visiting the major cities of the Pacific coast of South America and traveling across some of the most difficult terrain in the hemisphere. In addition to their scientific chores, they described architecture, local customs, and the social order. In this section they describe the ethnic mix in Quito, now the capital of Ecuador.

The second selection was published in Lima under the pseudonym Concolorcorvo around 1776. We now know that the author was Alonso Carrío de la Vandera. Born in Spain, he traveled to the colonies as a young man. He served in many minor bureaucratic positions, one of which was the inspection of the postal route between Buenos Aires and Lima. Carrío turned his long and often uncomfortable trip into an insightful, and sometimes highly critical, examination of colonial society. The selection that follows describes Córdoba, Argentina.

Juan and Ulloa and Carrío seem perplexed by colonial efforts to create and enforce a racial taxonomy that stipulated and named every possible mixture of European, Amerindian, and African, and they commented on the vanity and social presumptions of the dominant white population. We are fortunate to have these contemporary descriptions of the diversity of colonial society, but it is important to remember that these authors were clearly rooted in their time and confident in the superiority of Europe. Although they noted many of the abuses of Amerindian, mixed, and African populations and sometimes punctured the pretensions of colonial elites, they were also quick to assume the inferiority of the nonwhite population.

Quito

This city is very populous, and has, among its inhabitants, some families of high rank and distinction; though their number is but small considering its extent, the poorer class bearing here too great a proportion. The former are the descendants either of the original conquerors, or of presidents, auditors, or other persons of character [high rank], who at different times came over from Spain invested with some lucrative post, and have still preserved their luster, both of wealth and descent, by intermarriages, without intermixing with meaner families though famous for their riches. The commonalty may be divided into four classes; Spaniards or Whites, Mestizos, Indians or Natives, and Negroes, with their progeny. These last are not proportionally so numerous as in the other parts of the Indies; occasioned by it being something inconvenient to

bring Negroes to Quito, and the different kinds of agriculture being generally performed by Indians.

The name of Spaniard here has a different meaning from that of Chapitone [sic] or European, as properly signifying a person descended from a Spaniard without a mixture of blood. Many Mestizos, from the advantage of a fresh complexion, appear to be Spaniards more than those who are so in reality; and from only this fortuitous advantage are accounted as such. The Whites, according to this construction of the word, may be considered as one sixth part of the inhabitants.

The Mestizos are the descendants of Spaniards and Indians, and are to be considered here in the same different degrees between the Negroes and Whites, as before at Carthagena [sic]; but with this difference, that at Quito the degrees of Mestizos are not carried so far back; for, even in the second or third generations, when they acquire the European color, they are considered as Spaniards. The complexion of the Mestizos is swarthy and reddish, but not of that red common in the fair Mulattos. This is the first degree, or the immediate issue of a Spaniard and Indian. Some are, however, equally tawny with the Indians themselves, though they are distinguished from them by their beards: while others, on the contrary, have so fine a complexion that they might pass for Whites, were it not for some signs which betray them, when viewed attentively. Among these, the most remarkable is the lowness of the forehead, which often leaves but a small space between their hair and eye-brows; at the same time the hair grows remarkably forward on the temples, extending to the lower part of the ear. Besides, the hair itself is harsh, lank, coarse, and very black; their nose very small, thin, and has a little rising on the middle, from whence it forms a small curve, terminating in a point, bending towards the upper lip. These marks, besides some dark spots on the body, are so constant and invariable, as to make it very difficult to conceal the fallacy of their complexion. The Mestizos may be reckoned a third part of the inhabitants.

The next class is the Indians, who form about another third; and the others, who are about one sixth, are the Castes [mixed]. These four classes, according to the most authentic accounts taken from the parish register, amount to between 50 and 60,000 persons, of all ages, sexes, and ranks. If among these classes the Spaniards, as is natural to think, are the most eminent for riches, rank, and power, it must at the same time be owned, however melancholy the truth may appear, they are in proportion the most poor, miserable and distressed; for they refuse to apply themselves to any mechanic business, considering it as a disgrace to that quality they so highly value themselves upon, which consists in not being black, brown, or of a copper color. The Mestizos, whose pride is regulated by prudence, readily apply themselves to arts and trades, but chose those of the greatest repute, as painting, sculpture, and the like, leaving the meaner sort to the Indians.

Córdoba

There was not a person who would give me even an estimate of the number of residents comprising this city, because neither the secular nor the ecclesiastical council has a register, and I know not how these colonists prove the ancient and distinguished nobility of which they boast; it may be that each family has its genealogical history in reserve. In my computation, there must be within the city and its limited common lands around 500 to 600 residents, but in the principal houses there are a very large number of slaves, most of them Creoles [native born] of all conceivable classes, because in this city and in all of Tucumán there is no leniency about granting freedom to any of them. They are easily supported since the principal aliment, meat, is of such moderate price, and there is a custom of dressing them only in ordinary cloth which is made at home by the slaves themselves, shoes being very rare. They aid their masters in many profitable ways and under this system do not think of freedom, thus exposing themselves to a sorrowful end, as is happening in Lima.

As I was passing through Córdoba, they were selling 2,000 Negroes, all Creoles from Temporalidades [property confiscated from the Jesuit order in 1767], from just the two farms of the [Jesuit] colleges of this city. I have seen the lists, for each one has its own, and they proceed by families numbering from two to eleven, all pure Negroes and Creoles back to the fourth generation, because the priests used to sell all of those born with a mixture of Spanish, mulatto, or Indian blood. Among this multitude of Negroes were many musicians and many of other crafts; they proceeded with the sale by families. I was assured that the nuns of Santa Teresa alone had a group of 300 slaves of both sexes, to whom they give their just ration of meat and dress in the coarse cloth which they make, while these good nuns content themselves with what is left from other ministrations. The number attached to other religious establishments is much smaller, but there is a private home which has 30 or 40, the majority of whom are engaged in various gainful activities. The result is a large number of excellent washerwomen whose accomplishments are valued so highly that they never mend their outer skirts in order that the whiteness of their undergarments may be seen. They do the laundry in the river, in water up to the waist, saying vaingloriously that she who is not soaked cannot wash well. They make ponchos [hand-woven capes], rugs, sashes, and sundries, and especially decorated leather cases which the men sell for 8 reales each, because the hides have no outlet due to the great distance to the port; the same thing happens on the banks of the Tercero and Cuarto rivers, where they are sold at 2 reales and frequently for less.

The principal men of the city wear very expensive clothes, but this is not true of the women, who are an exception in both Americas and even in the entire world, because they dress decorously in clothing of little cost. They are very tenacious in preserving the customs of their ancestors. They do not permit slaves, or even freedmen who have a mixture of Negro blood, to wear any cloth other than that made in this country, which is quite coarse. I was told recently that a certain bedecked mulatto [woman] who appeared in Córdoba was sent word by the ladies of the city that she should dress according to her station, but since she paid no attention to this reproach, they endured her negligence until one of the ladies, summoning her to her home under some other pretext, had the servants undress her, whip her, burn her finery before her eyes, and dress her in the clothes befitting her class; despite the fact that the [victim] was not lacking in persons to defend her, she disappeared lest the tragedy be repeated.

QUESTIONS FOR ANALYSIS

1. What do the authors of these selections seem to think about the white elites of the colonies? Are there similarities in the ways that Juan and Ulloa and Carrío describe the mixed population of Quito and the slave population of Córdoba?

2. How do these depictions of mestizos and other mixtures compare with the image of the family represented in the painting of castas on page 490?

3. What does the humiliation of the mixed-race woman in Córdoba tell us about ideas of race and class in this Spanish colony?

Sources: Jorge Juan and Antonio de Ulloa, *A Voyage to South America*, The John Adams translation (abridged), Introduction by Irving A. Leonard (New York: Alfred A. Knopf, 1964), 135–137, copyright © 1964 by Alfred A. Knopf, Inc. Used by permission of Alfred A. Knopf, a division of Random House, Inc.; Concolorcorvo, *El Lazarillo, A Guide for Inexperienced Travelers Between Buenos Aires and Lima, 1773*, translated by Walter D. Kline (Bloomington: Indiana University Press, 1965), 78–80. Used with permission of Indiana University Press.

with the passage of time. Indigenous leaders also established political alliances with members of the colonial administrative classes. Hereditary native elites gained some security by becoming essential intermediaries between the indigenous masses and colonial administrators, collecting Spanish taxes and organizing the labor of their dependents for colonial enterprises.

Indigenous commoners suffered the heaviest burdens. Tribute payments, forced labor obligations, and the loss of traditional land rights were common. European domination dramatically changed the indigenous world by breaking the connections between peoples and places and transforming religious life, marriage practices, diet, and material culture. The survivors of these terrible shocks learned to adapt to the new colonial environment by embracing some elements of the dominant colonial culture or entering the market economies of the cities. They also learned new forms of resistance, like using colonial courts to protect community lands or to resist the abuses of corrupt officials.

Afro Latin American Experience

Thousands of blacks, many born in Iberia or long resident there, participated in the conquest and settlement of Spanish America. Most of these were slaves; more than four hundred slaves participated in the conquests of Peru and Chile alone. In the fluid social environment of the conquest era, many were able to gain their freedom. Juan Valiente escaped from his master in Mexico and then participated in Francisco Pizarro's conquest of the Inca Empire. He later became one of the most prominent early settlers of Chile.

With the opening of a direct slave trade with Africa (for details, see Chapter 19), the cultural character of the black population of colonial Latin America was altered dramatically. While Afro-Iberians spoke Spanish or Portuguese and were Catholic, African slaves arrived in the colonies with different languages, religious beliefs, and cultural practices. European settlers viewed these differences as signs of inferiority that served as a justification for prejudice and discrimination.

A large percentage of slaves imported in the sixteenth century came from West Central Africa where they had had exposure to elements of Iberian culture including religion, language, and technology. The legacy of these common cultural elements facilitated African influence on the emerging colonial cultures of Latin America. But significant differences were present as

Painting of Castas This is an example of a common genre of colonial Spanish American painting. In the eighteenth century there was increased interest in ethnic mixing, and wealthy colonials as well as some Europeans commissioned sets of paintings that showed mixed families. The artist typically placed the couples in what he believed was an appropriate setting. In this example, the artist depicted the Amerindian husband with his mestiza (European and Amerindian mixture) wife in an outdoor market where they sold fowl. Colonial usage assigned their child the dismissive racial label "coyote."

well and in regions with large slave majorities, especially the sugar-producing regions of Brazil, these cultural and linguistic barriers often divided slaves and made resistance more difficult. Over time, elements from many African traditions blended and mixed with European (and in some cases Amerindian) language and beliefs to forge distinct local cultures.

Slave resistance took many forms, including sabotage, malingering, running away, and rebellion. Although many slave rebellions occurred, colonial authorities were always able to reestablish control. Groups of runaway slaves, however, were sometimes able to defend themselves for years. In both Spanish America and Brazil, communities of runaways (called quilombos [key-LOM-bos] in Brazil and palenques [pah-LEN-kays] in Spanish colonies) were common. The largest quilombo was Palmares in Brazil.

Slaves served as skilled artisans, musicians, servants, artists, cowboys, and even soldiers. However, the vast majority worked in agriculture. Conditions for slaves were worst on the sugar plantations of Brazil and the Caribbean, where harsh discipline, brutal punishments, and back-breaking labor were common. Because planters preferred to buy male slaves, there was always a gender imbalance on plantations, proving a significant obstacle to the traditional marriage and family patterns of both Africa and Europe.

Brazil attracted smaller numbers of European immigrants than did Spanish America, and its native populations were smaller and less urbanized. It also came to depend on the African slave as a source of labor earlier than any other American colony. By the early seventeenth century, Africans and their American-born descendants were by far the largest racial group in Brazil. As a result, Brazilian colonial society (unlike Spanish Mexico and Peru) was more influenced by African culture than by Amerindian culture.

Both Spanish and Portuguese law provided for manumission, the granting of freedom to individual slaves, and colonial courts sometimes intervened to protect slaves from the worst physical abuse or to protect married couples from forced separation. The majority of those gaining their liberty had saved money and purchased their own freedom. This meant that manumission was more about the capacity of individual slaves and slave families to earn income and save than about the generosity of slave owners. Among the minority of slaves to be freed without compensation, household servants were the most likely beneficiaries. Slave women received the majority of manumissions, and because children born subsequently were considered free, the free black population grew rapidly.

Within a century of settlement, groups of mixed descent were in the majority in many regions. There were few marriages between Amerindian women and European men, but less formal relationships were common. Few European fathers recognized their mixed offspring, who were called **mestizos** (mess-TEE-zoh). Nevertheless, this rapidly expanding group came to occupy a middle position in colonial society, dominating urban artisan trades and small-scale agriculture and ranching. In frontier regions many members of the elite were mestizos, some proudly asserting their descent from the Amerindian elite. The African slave trade also led to the appearance of new American ethnicities. Individuals of mixed European and African descent—called **mulattos**—came to occupy an intermediate position in the tropics similar to the social position of mestizos in Mesoamerica and the Andean region. In Spanish Mexico and Peru and in Brazil, mixtures of Amerindians and Africans were also common. These mixed-descent groups were called castas (CAZ-tahs) in Spanish America.

The American colonies of Spain and Portugal grew rich from the export of silver, gold, and sugar, but depended on the forced labor of Amerindians and African slaves. The Catholic Church provided for the spiritual needs of settlers but also converted Amerindians and Africans to Christianity. As time passed, new peoples—the mixed offspring of Amerindians, Europeans, and Africans—and new blended American cultures developed.

mestizo The term used by Spanish authorities to describe someone of mixed Amerindian and European descent.

New Peoples and New Identities

mulatto The term used in Spanish and Portuguese colonies to describe someone of mixed African and European descent.

SECTION REVIEW

- Colonial governments were created to rule distant colonies.
- The Catholic Church led conversion of Amerindian peoples and spread European cultures and languages.
- Silver mining and sugar production dominated colonial Latin American economies.
- Spanish and Portuguese colonies relied on forced labor of Amerindians and African slaves.
- New peoples and new cultures resulted from colonial contacts among Amerindians, Europeans, and Africans.

ENGLISH AND FRENCH COLONIES IN NORTH AMERICA

The North American colonial empires of England and France and the colonies of Spain and Portugal had many characteristics in common (see Map 18.1). The governments of England and France hoped to find easily extracted forms of wealth or great indigenous empires like those of the Aztecs or Inca. Like the Spanish and Portuguese, English and French settlers responded to native peoples with a mixture of diplomacy and violence. African slaves proved crucial to the development of all four colonial economies.

Important differences, however, distinguished North American colonial development from the Latin American model. The English and French colonies were developed nearly a century after Cortés's conquest of Mexico and Portuguese settlement of Brazil. The intervening period witnessed significant economic and demographic growth in Europe. It also witnessed the Protestant Reformation, which helped propel English and French settlement in the Americas. By the time England and France secured a foothold in the Americas, increased trade had led to greater integration of world cultural regions. Distracted by ventures elsewhere and by increasing military confrontation in Europe, neither England nor France imitated the large and expensive colonial bureaucracies established by Spain and Portugal. As a result, private companies and individual proprietors played a much larger role in the development of English and French colonies.

Early English Experiments

England's effort to gain a foothold in the Americas in the late sixteenth century failed, but its effort to establish colonies in the seventeenth century proved more successful. The English relied on private capital to finance settlement and continued to hope that the colonies would become sources of high-value products such as silver, citrus, and wine. English experience in colonizing Ireland after 1566 also influenced these efforts. In Ireland land had been confiscated, cleared of its native population, and offered for sale to English investors. The city of London, English guilds, and wealthy private investors all purchased Irish "plantations" and then recruited "settlers." By 1650 investors had sent nearly 150,000 English and Scottish immigrants to Ireland. Indeed, Ireland attracted six times as many colonists in the early seventeenth century as did New England.

The South

In 1606 London investors organized as the Virginia Company took up the challenge of colonizing Virginia. A year later 144 settlers disembarked at Jamestown, an island 30 miles (48 kilometers) up the James River in the Chesapeake Bay region. Additional settlers arrived in 1609. The investors and settlers hoped for immediate profits, but the location was a swampy and unhealthy place where nearly 80 percent of the settlers died in the first fifteen years from disease or Amerindian attacks. There was no mineral wealth, no passage to Asia, and no docile and exploitable native population.

In 1624 the English crown dissolved the Virginia Company because of its mismanagement. Freed from the company's commitment to the original location, colonists pushed deeper into the interior and developed a sustainable economy based on furs, timber, and, increasingly, tobacco. The profits from tobacco soon attracted new immigrants. Along the shoreline of Chesapeake Bay and the rivers that fed it, settlers spread out, developing plantations and farms. Colonial Virginia's dispersed population contrasted with the greater urbanization of Spanish and Portuguese America, where large and powerful cities and networks of secondary towns flourished. No city of any significant size developed in colonial Virginia.

From the beginning, colonists in Latin America had relied on forced labor of Amerindians to develop the region's resources. The African slave trade compelled the migration of millions of additional forced laborers to the colonies of Spain and Portugal. The English settlement of the Chesapeake Bay region added a new system of forced labor to the American landscape: indentured servitude. **Indentured servants** were racially and religiously indistinguishable from free settlers and eventually accounted for approximately 80 percent of all English immigrants to Vir-

indentured servant
A migrant to British colonies in the Americas who paid for passage by agreeing to work for a set term ranging from four to seven years.

Indentured Servants and Slaves

ginia and the neighboring colony of Maryland. A young man or woman unable to pay for transportation to the New World accepted an indenture (contract) that bound him or her to a term ranging from four to seven years of labor in return for passage and, at the end of the contract, a small parcel of land, some tools, and clothes.

During the seventeenth century approximately fifteen hundred indentured servants, mostly male, arrived each year (see Chapter 19 for details on the indentured labor system). Planters were more likely to purchase the cheaper limited contracts of indentured servants rather than African slaves during the initial period of high mortality rates. As life expectancy improved, planters began to purchase more slaves because they believed they would earn greater profits from slaves owned for life than from indentured servants bound for short periods of time. As a result, Virginia's slave population grew rapidly from 950 in 1660 to 120,000 by 1756.

Virginia Government

House of Burgesses Elected assembly in colonial Virginia, created in 1618.

By the 1660s Virginia was administered by a Crown-appointed governor and by representatives of towns meeting together as the **House of Burgesses**. When elected representatives began to meet alone as a deliberative body, they initiated a form of democratic representation that distinguished the English colonies of North America from the colonies of other European powers. Ironically, this expansion in colonial liberties and political rights occurred along with the dramatic increase in the colony's slave population. The intertwined evolution of American freedom and American slavery gave England's southern colonies a unique and conflicted political character that endured after independence.

Carolina Fur Trade

English settlement of the Carolinas initially relied on profits from the fur trade. English fur traders pushed into the interior to compete with French trading networks based in New Orleans and Mobile. Native peoples eventually provided over 100,000 deerskins annually to this profitable commerce, but at a high environmental and cultural cost. As Amerindian peoples hunted more intensely, they disrupted the natural balance of animals and plants in southern forests. The profits of the fur trade altered Amerindian culture as well, leading villages to place less emphasis on subsistence hunting, fishing, and traditional agriculture. Amerindian life was profoundly altered by deepening dependencies on European products, including firearms, metal tools, textiles, and alcohol.

While being increasingly tied to the commerce and culture of the Carolina colony, indigenous peoples were simultaneously weakened by epidemics, alcoholism, and a rising tide of ethnic conflicts generated by competition for hunting grounds. Conflicts among indigenous peoples—who now had firearms—became more deadly, and many captured Amerindians were sold as slaves to local colonists, who used them as agricultural workers or exported to the sugar plantations of the Caribbean. Dissatisfied with the terms of trade imposed by fur traders and angered by this slave trade, Amerindians launched attacks on English settlements in the early 1700s. Their defeat by colonial military forces inevitably led to new seizures of Amerindian land by European settlers.

South Carolina, a Colony of Plantations and Slaves

The northern part of the Carolinas, settled from Virginia, followed that colony's mixed economy of tobacco and forest products. Slavery expanded slowly in this region. Charleston and the interior of South Carolina followed a different path. Settled first by planters from Barbados in 1670, this colony developed an economy based on plantations and slavery in imitation of the colonies of the Caribbean and Brazil. In 1729 North and South Carolina became separate colonies.

Despite an unhealthy climate, the prosperous rice and indigo plantations near Charleston attracted both free immigrants and increasing numbers of African slaves. African slaves were present from the founding of Charleston and were instrumental in introducing irrigated rice agriculture along the coastal lowlands. They were also crucial to developing plantations of indigo (a plant that produced a blue dye) at higher elevations away from the coast. Many slaves were given significant responsibilities. As one planter sending two slaves and their families to a frontier region put it: "[They] are likely young people, well acquainted with Rice & every kind of plantation business, and in short [are] capable of the management of a plantation themselves."[3]

As profits from rice and indigo rose, the importation of African slaves created a black majority in South Carolina. African languages, as well as African religious beliefs and diet, strongly influenced this unique colonial culture. Gullah, a dialect with African and English roots, evolved as the common idiom of the Carolina coast. Africans played a major role in South Carolina's largest slave uprising, the Stono Rebellion of 1739. After a group of about twenty slaves, many of them African Catholics who sought to flee south to Spanish Florida, seized firearms, about a hundred slaves from nearby plantations joined them. The colonial militia defeated the rebels and executed many of them, but the rebellion shocked slave owners throughout England's southern colonies and led to greater repression.

Colonial South Carolina was the most hierarchical society in British North America. Planters controlled the economy and political life. The richest families maintained impressive households in Charleston, the largest city in the southern colonies, as well as on their plantations in the countryside. Small farmers, cattlemen, artisans, merchants, and fur traders held an intermediate but clearly subordinate social position. Native peoples continued to participate in colonial society but lost ground from the effects of epidemic disease and warfare. As in colonial Latin America, a large mixed population blurred racial and cultural boundaries. On the frontier, the children of white men and Amerindian women held an important place in the fur trade. In the plantation regions and Charleston, the offspring of white men and black women often held preferred positions within the slave work force.

New England

The colonization of New England by two separate groups of Protestant dissenters, Pilgrims and Puritans, put the settlement of this region on a different course. The **Pilgrims**, who came first, wished to break completely with the Church of England, which they believed was still essentially Catholic. As a result, in 1620 approximately one hundred settlers—men, women, and children—established the colony of Plymouth on the coast of present-day Massachusetts. Although nearly half of the settlers died during the first winter, the colony survived until 1691, when the larger Massachusetts Bay Colony of the Puritans absorbed Plymouth.

The **Puritans** wished to "purify" the Church of England, not break with it. They wanted to abolish its hierarchy of bishops and priests, free it from governmental interference, and limit membership to people who shared their beliefs. Subjected to increased discrimination in England for their efforts to transform the church, large numbers of Puritans began emigrating from England in 1630.

The Puritan leaders of the Massachusetts Bay Company—the joint-stock company that had received a royal charter to finance the Massachusetts Bay Colony—carried the company charter with them from England to Massachusetts. By bringing the charter, which spelled out company rights and obligations as well as the direction of company government, they limited Crown efforts to control them. By 1643 more than twenty thousand Puritans had settled in the Bay Colony.

Immigration to Massachusetts differed from immigration to the Chesapeake and to South Carolina. Most newcomers to Massachusetts arrived with their families. Whereas 84 percent of Virginia's white population in 1625 was male, Massachusetts had a normal gender balance in its population almost from the beginning. It was also the healthiest of England's colonies. The result was a rapid natural increase in population. The population of Massachusetts quickly became more "American" than the population of southern or Caribbean colonies, whose survival depended on a steady flow of English immigrants and slaves to counter high mortality rates. Massachusetts also was more homogeneous and less hierarchical than the southern colonies.

Political institutions evolved from the terms of the company charter. Settlers elected a governor and a council of magistrates drawn from the board of directors of the Massachusetts Bay Company. By 1650, disagreements between this council and elected representatives of the towns led to the creation of a lower legislative house that selected its own speaker and developed procedures and rules similar to those of the House of Commons in England. The result was much greater autonomy and greater local political involvement than in the colonies of Latin America.

Economically, Massachusetts differed dramatically from the southern colonies. Agriculture met basic needs, but poor soils and harsh climate offered no opportunity to develop cash crops like tobacco or rice. To pay for imported tools, textiles, and other essentials, the colonists needed to discover some profit-making niche in the growing Atlantic market. Fur, timber, and fish provided the initial economic foundation, but New England's economic well-being soon depended on providing commercial and shipping services in a dynamic and far-flung commercial arena that included the southern colonies, the Caribbean islands, Africa, and Europe.

In Spanish and Portuguese America, heavily capitalized monopolies (companies or individuals given exclusive economic privileges) dominated international trade. In New England, by

Pilgrims Group of English Protestant dissenters who established Plymouth Colony in Massachusetts in 1620 to seek religious freedom after having lived briefly in the Netherlands.

Puritans English Protestant dissenters who believed that God predestined souls to heaven or hell before birth. They founded Massachusetts Bay Colony in 1629.

Dissenters and Merchants of Massachusetts

contrast, individual merchants survived by discovering smaller but more sustainable profits in diversified trade across the Atlantic. The colony's commercial success rested on market intelligence, flexibility, and streamlined organization. Urban population growth suggests the success of this development strategy. With sixteen thousand inhabitants in 1740, Boston, the capital of Massachusetts Bay Colony, was the largest city in British North America.

Lacking a profitable agricultural export like tobacco, New England did not develop the extreme social stratification of the southern plantation colonies. Slaves and indentured servants were present, but in very small numbers. While New England was ruled by the richest colonists and shared the racial attitudes of the southern colonies, it also was the colonial society with fewest differences in wealth and status and with the most uniformly British and Protestant population in the Americas.

The Middle Atlantic Region

Iroquois Confederacy An alliance of five northeastern Amerindian peoples (six after 1722) that made decisions on military and diplomatic issues through a council of representatives. Allied first with the Dutch and later with the English, the Confederacy dominated the area from western New England to the Great Lakes.

Diversity and Dynamism of New York and Pennsylvania

Much of the future success of English-speaking America was rooted in the rapid economic development and remarkable cultural diversity that appeared in the Middle Atlantic colonies. In 1624 the Dutch West India Company established the colony of New Netherland and located its capital on Manhattan Island. Although poorly managed and underfinanced from the start, the colony commanded the potentially profitable and strategically important Hudson River. Dutch merchants established trading relationships with the **Iroquois Confederacy**—an alliance among the Mohawk, Oneida, Onondaga, Cayuga, and Seneca peoples—and with other native peoples that gave them access to the rich fur trade of Canada. When confronted by an English military expedition in 1664, the Dutch surrendered without a fight. James, duke of York and later King James II of England, became proprietor of the colony, which was renamed New York.

Tumultuous politics and corrupt public administration characterized New York, but the development of New York City as a commercial and shipping center guaranteed the colony's success. Located at the mouth of the Hudson River, the city played an essential role in connecting the region's grain farmers to the booming markets of the Caribbean and southern Europe.

"Johnson Hall," by E. L. Henry. Courtesy, Albany Institute of History and Art

The Home of Sir William Johnson, British Superintendent for Indian Affairs, Northern District As the colonial era drew to a close, the British attempted to limit the cost of colonial defense by negotiating land settlements with native peoples, but the growing tide of western migration doomed these agreements. William Johnson (1715–1774) maintained a fragile peace along the northern frontier by building strong personal relations with influential leaders of the Mohawk and other members of the Iroquois Confederacy. His home in present-day Johnstown, New York, shows the mixed nature of the frontier—the relative opulence of the main house offset by the two defensive blockhouses built for protection.

By the early eighteenth century, New York Colony had a diverse population that included English colonists; Dutch, German, and Swedish settlers; and a large slave community.

Pennsylvania began as a proprietary colony and as a refuge for Quakers, a persecuted religious minority. Because the English king Charles II was indebted to his father, William Penn secured an enormous grant of territory (nearly the size of England) in 1682. As proprietor (owner) of the land, Penn had sole right to establish a government, subject only to the requirement that he provide for an assembly of freemen.

Penn quickly lost control of the colony's political life, but the colony enjoyed remarkable success. By 1700 Pennsylvania had a population of more than 21,000, and Philadelphia, its capital, soon passed Boston to become the largest city in the British colonies. Healthy climate, excellent land, relatively peaceful relations with native peoples (prompted by Penn's emphasis on negotiation rather than warfare), and access through Philadelphia to good markets led to rapid economic and demographic growth in the colony.

Both Pennsylvania and South Carolina were grain-exporting colonies, but they were very different societies. South Carolina's rice plantations required large numbers of slaves. In Pennsylvania free workers produced the bulk of the colony's grain crops on family farms. As a result, Pennsylvania's economic expansion in the late seventeenth century occurred without reproducing South Carolina's hierarchical and repressive social order. By the early eighteenth century, however, the prosperous city of Philadelphia did have a large population of black slaves and freedmen. Many were servants in the homes of wealthy merchants, but the fast-growing economy offered many opportunities in skilled trades as well.

French America

Patterns of French settlement more closely resembled those of Spain and Portugal than of England. The French were committed to missionary activity among Amerindian peoples and emphasized the extraction of natural resources—furs rather than minerals. Between 1534 and 1542 the navigator and promoter Jacques Cartier explored the region of Newfoundland and the Gulf of St. Lawrence in three voyages. A contemporary of Cortés and Pizarro, Cartier hoped to find mineral wealth, but the stones he brought back to France turned out to be quartz and iron pyrite, "fool's gold."

New France French colony in North America, with a capital in Quebec, founded 1608. New France fell to the British in 1763.

The French waited more than fifty years before establishing settlements in North America. Coming to Canada after spending years in the West Indies, Samuel de Champlain founded the colony of **New France** at Quebec (kwuh-BEC), on the banks of the St. Lawrence River, in 1608. This location provided ready access to Amerindian trade routes, but it also compelled French settlers to take sides in the region's ongoing warfare. Champlain allied New France with the Huron and Algonquin peoples, traditional enemies of the powerful Iroquois Confederacy. Although French firearms and armor at first tipped the balance of power to France's native allies, the Iroquois Confederacy proved to be a resourceful and persistent enemy.

The Fur Trade

coureurs de bois French fur traders, many of mixed Amerindian heritage, who lived among and often married with Amerindian peoples of North America.

The European market for fur, especially beaver, fueled French settlement. Young Frenchmen were sent to live among native peoples to master their languages and customs. These **coureurs de bois** (koo-RUHR day BWA), or runners of the woods, often began families with indigenous women. Their mixed children, called métis (may-TEES), helped direct the fur trade. Amerindians actively participated in the trade because they came to depend on the goods they received in exchange for furs—firearms, metal tools, textiles, and alcohol. This change in the material culture of native peoples led to overhunting, which rapidly transformed the environment and led to the depletion of beaver and deer populations. It also increased competition among native peoples for hunting grounds, thus promoting warfare.

The proliferation of firearms made indigenous warfare more deadly. The Iroquois Confederacy responded to the increased military strength of France's Algonquin allies by forging commercial and military links with Dutch and later English settlements along the Hudson River. Now well armed, the Iroquois Confederacy nearly eradicated the Huron in 1649 and inflicted a series of humiliating defeats on the French. At the high point of their power in the early 1680s, Iroquois hunters and military forces gained control of much of the Great Lakes region and the Ohio River Valley. A large French military expedition and a relentless attack focused on Iroquois villages and agriculture finally checked Iroquois power in 1701.

Frances Anne Hopkins, "Shooting the Rapids," Library and Archives Canada, Ref. # C-2774

Canadian Fur Traders   The fur trade provided the economic foundation of early Canadian settlement. Fur traders were cultural intermediaries. They brought European technologies and products like firearms and machine-made textiles to native peoples and native technologies and products like canoes and furs to European settlers. This canoe with sixteen paddlers was adapted from the native craft by fur traders to transport large cargoes.

The Catholic Church in Canada

In French Canada, the Jesuits led the effort to convert native peoples to Christianity as they had in Brazil and Paraguay. Missionaries mastered native languages, created boarding schools for young boys and girls, and set up model agricultural communities for converted Amerindians. The Jesuits' greatest successes coincided with a destructive wave of epidemics and renewed warfare among native peoples in the 1630s. Eventually, they established churches throughout Huron and Algonquin territories. Nevertheless, native culture persisted. In 1688 a French nun who had devoted her life to instructing Amerindian girls expressed her frustration with the resilience of indigenous culture:

> We have observed that of a hundred that have passed through our hands we have scarcely civilized one. . . . When we are least expecting it, they clamber over our wall and go off to run with their kinsmen in the woods, finding more to please them there than in all the amenities of our French house.[4]

Even though the fur trade flourished, population growth was slow. Founded at about the same time as French Canada, Virginia had twenty times more European residents by 1627. Canada's small settler population and the fur trade's dependence on the voluntary participation of Amerindians allowed indigenous peoples to retain greater independence and more control over their traditional lands than was possible in the colonies of Spain, Portugal, or England. Unlike these colonial regimes, which sought to transform ancient ways of life or force the transfer of native lands, the French were compelled to treat indigenous peoples as allies and trading partners.

© Cengage Learning

MAP 18.2 **European Claims in North America, 1755–1763** The results of the French and Indian War dramatically altered the map of North America. France's losses precipitated conflicts between Amerindian peoples and the rapidly expanding population of the British colonies.

e Interactive Map

French Colonial Expansion

Despite Canada's small population and limited resources, the French aggressively expanded to the west and south. They founded Louisiana in 1699, but by 1708 there were fewer than three hundred soldiers, settlers, and slaves in the territory. Like Canada, Louisiana depended on the fur trade and on alliances with Amerindian peoples who became dependent on European goods. In 1753 a French official reported a Choctaw leader as saying, "[The French] were the first . . . who made [us] subject to the different needs that [we] can no longer now do without."[5]

France's North American colonies were threatened by wars between France and England and by the population growth and increasing prosperity of neighboring English colonies. The "French and Indian War" that began in 1754 led to the wider conflict called the Seven Years War, 1756–1763, that determined the fate of French Canada (see Map 18.2). England committed a larger military force to the struggle and, despite early defeats, took the French capital of Quebec in 1759. The peace agreement forced France to yield Canada to the English and cede Louisiana to Spain. Amerindian populations soon recognized the difference between the

SECTION REVIEW

- Without Latin America's wealth in silver, gold, and sugar, British North American colonies developed strong regional characters and strong local political traditions.

- British colonies attracted large numbers of free immigrants, but indentured servitude and slavery were crucial to economic development.

- The southern colonies' dependence on forced labor and plantation agriculture led to a society that was more hierarchical and less democratic that those found in the colonies of New England and the Middle Atlantic region.

- With small population and limited resources, French colonies in North America depended on political and military alliances and commercial relations with native peoples.

- Eventually England defeated France and gained control of North America east of the Mississippi.

English and the French. One Canadian indigenous leader commented to a British officer after the French surrender: "We learn that our lands are to be given away not only to trade thereon but also . . . in full title to various [English] individuals. . . . We have always been a free nation, and now we will become slaves, which would be very difficult to accept after having enjoyed our liberty so long."[6] With the loss of Canada the French concentrated their efforts on their sugar-producing colonies in the Caribbean (see Chapter 19).

COLONIAL EXPANSION AND CONFLICT

Beginning in the last decades of the seventeenth century, nearly all the European colonies in the Americas experienced economic expansion and population growth. In the next century, the imperial powers responded by strengthening administrative and economic control of their colonies. They also sought to force colonial populations to pay a larger share of the costs of administration and defense. These efforts at reform and restructuring coincided with a series of imperial wars fought along Atlantic trade routes and in the Americas. France's loss of its North American colonies in 1763 was one of the most important results of these struggles. Equally significant, colonial populations throughout the Americas became more aware of separate national identities and more aggressive in asserting local interests against the will of distant monarchs.

Imperial Reform in Spanish America and Brazil

Spain's Habsburg dynasty ended when Charles II died without an heir in 1700 (see Table 17.1 on page 468). After thirteen years of conflict involving the major European powers, Philip of Bourbon, grandson of Louis XIV of France, gained the Spanish throne. Under Philip V and his heirs, Spain reorganized its administration and tax collection and liberalized colonial trade policies. Spain also created new commercial monopolies and strengthened its navy to protect colonial trade.

For most of the Spanish Empire, the eighteenth century was a period of remarkable economic expansion associated with population growth. Amerindian populations began to recover from the early epidemics; the flow of Spanish immigrants increased; and the slave trade to plantation colonies was expanded. Mining production increased, with silver production rising steadily into the 1780s. Agricultural exports also expanded, especially exports of tobacco, dyes, hides, chocolate, cotton, and sugar.

The Spanish and Portuguese kings also sought to reduce the power of the Catholic Church while at the same time transferring some church wealth to their treasuries. These efforts led to a succession of confrontations between colonial officials and the church hierarchy. To the kings of Portugal and Spain, the Jesuits symbolized the independent power of the church. This led the Portuguese king to expel this powerful order from his territories in 1759. The Spanish king followed this decision in 1767. In practice these actions forced many colonial-born Jesuits from their native lands and closed the schools that had educated many members of the colonial elite.

Colonial Grievances and Rebellion

Bourbon political and fiscal reforms also contributed to a growing sense of colonial grievance by limiting creoles' access to colonial offices and by imposing new taxes and monopolies that transferred more colonial wealth to Spain. Consumer and producer resentment in the colonies led to a series of violent confrontations with Spanish administrators. Colonial residents viewed the reforms as a more intrusive and expensive colonial government that overturned the informal constitution that had long governed the empire. However, the Spanish effort to recruit local elites as military officers to improve imperial defense offered some colonial residents a compensatory opportunity for higher social status and greater responsibility.

Tupac Amaru II Member of Inca aristocracy who led a rebellion against Spanish authorities in Peru in 1780–1781. He was captured and executed with his wife and other members of his family.

In addition to tax rebellions and urban riots, colonial reforms also provoked Amerindian uprisings. In 1780 the Peruvian Amerindian leader José Gabriel Condorcanqui began the largest rebellion. He assumed the name of his Inca ancestor Tupac Amaru (TOO-pack a-MAH-roo), whom the Spanish executed in 1572. Although a hereditary Quechua leader, **Tupac Amaru II** received his education from the Jesuits and had close ties to the local bishop and other powerful colonial authorities. He was also actively involved in colonial trade. Tupac Amaru II did not clearly state whether he sought to end local injustices or overthrow Spanish rule, but he clearly

Sir Henry Chamberlain, Views and Costumes of the City and Neighborhoods of Rio de Janeiro, London, 1822

Market in Rio de Janeiro   In many of the cities of colonial Latin America, female slaves and black free women dominated retail markets. In this scene from late colonial Brazil, Afro-Brazilian women sell a variety of foods and crafts.

sought to redress the grievances of Amerindian communities who suffered from the mita and from taxes. As his rebellion spread, he attracted creoles, mestizos, and slaves as well as Amerindians to his cause. After his capture in 1781, the Spanish brutally executed Tupac Amaru II along with his wife and fifteen other family members and allies. By the time Spanish authority was firmly reestablished, more than 100,000 lives had been lost and enormous amounts of property destroyed.

Brazil also experienced a similar period of expansion and reform after 1700. Portugal created new administrative positions and gave monopoly companies exclusive rights to little-developed regions. As in Spanish America, a more intrusive colonial government that imposed new taxes led to rebellions and plots, including open warfare in 1707 between local-born "sons of the soil" and "outsiders" in São Paulo. The most aggressive period of reform occurred during the ministry of the marquis of Pombal (1750–1777). The discovery in Brazil of gold in the 1690s and diamonds after 1720 financed the reforms. Brazil's exports of minerals as well as coffee and cotton deepened dependence on the slave trade, and nearly 2 million African slaves were imported in the eighteenth century.

Reform and Reorganization in British America

England's efforts to reform and reorganize its North American colonies began earlier than the Bourbon initiative in Spanish America. After the period of Cromwell's Puritan Republic (see Chapter 17), the restored Stuart king, Charles II, undertook an ambitious campaign to establish greater control over the colonies. Between 1651 and 1673 a series of Navigation Acts sought to severely limit colonial trading and colonial production that competed directly with English manufacturers. England also attempted to increase royal control over colonial political life by replacing colonial charters and proprietorships. Because the king viewed the New England colonies as centers of smuggling, he temporarily suspended their elected assemblies while appointing colonial governors and granting them new fiscal and legislative powers.

Settler Resistance in British North America

James II's overthrow in the Glorious Revolution of 1688 ended this confrontation, but not before colonists were provoked to resist and, in some cases, rebel. Colonials overthrew the governors of New York and Massachusetts and removed the Catholic proprietor of Maryland. William and Mary restored relative peace, but these conflicts alerted colonials to the potential aggression of the English government. Colonial politics would remain confrontational until the American Revolution.

During the eighteenth century the English colonies experienced renewed economic growth and attracted a new wave of European immigration, but social divisions were increasingly evident. The colonial population in 1770 was more urban, more clearly divided by class and race, and more vulnerable to economic downturns. Crises were provoked when imperial wars with France and Spain disrupted trade in the Atlantic, increased tax burdens, forced military mobilizations, and provoked frontier conflicts with the Amerindians. On the eve of the American Revolution, England defeated France and weakened Spain. The cost, however, was great. Administrative, military, and tax policies imposed to gain this empire-wide victory alienated much of the American colonial population.

SECTION REVIEW

- In the eighteenth century all European imperial powers attempted to impose reforms on their American colonies.
- Colonial reforms disrupted colonial economic and political accommodations and led to rebellion and resistance.

CONCLUSION

The New World colonial empires of Spain, Portugal, France, and England had many characteristics in common. All subjugated Amerindian peoples and introduced large numbers of enslaved Africans. Within all four empires European settlement and the introduction of Old World animals and plants altered the natural environment. Europeans also introduced Old World diseases, such as smallpox, that had a devastating effect on the native populations. Colonists in all four applied the technologies of the Old World to the resources of the New, producing mineral and agricultural wealth and exploiting the commercial possibilities of the emerging Atlantic market in ways that accelerated the integration of Europe, Asia, and America.

Each of the New World empires also reflected the distinctive cultural and institutional heritages of its colonizing power. Mineral wealth allowed Spain to develop the most centralized empire, with political and economic power concentrated in great cities like Mexico City and Lima. Portugal and France pursued objectives similar to Spain's, but neither Brazil's agricultural economy, based on sugar, nor France's Canadian fur trade produced the financial resources and levels of centralized control achieved by Spain. Nevertheless, unlike Britain, all three of these Catholic powers were able to impose and enforce significant levels of religious and cultural uniformity.

Greater cultural and religious diversity characterized British North America. Immigrants came to the colonies from the British Isles, including all of Britain's religious traditions, as well as from Germany, Sweden, the Netherlands, and France. British colonial government varied somewhat from colony to colony and was more responsive to local interests. Thus colonists in British North America were better able than those in the areas controlled by Spain, Portugal, and France to respond to changing economic and political circumstances and to influence government policies. Most importantly, the British colonies attracted many more European immigrants than did the other New World colonies. Between 1580 and 1760 French colonies received 60,000 European immigrants, Brazil 523,000, and the Spanish colonies 678,000. Within a shorter period—between 1600 and 1760—the British settlements welcomed 746,000. Population in British North America—free and slave combined—had reached an extraordinary 2.5 million by 1775.

KEY TERMS

Columbian Exchange p. 478
Bartolomé de Las Casas p. 484
Potosí p. 484
encomienda p. 486

creoles p. 487
mestizo p. 491
mulatto p. 491
indentured servant p. 492
House of Burgesses p. 493

Pilgrims p. 494
Puritans p. 494
Iroquois Confederacy p. 495

New France p. 496
coureurs de bois p. 496
Tupac Amaru II p. 499

EBOOK AND WEBSITE RESOURCES

e Primary Source

General History of the Things in New Spain

e Interactive Maps

Map 18.1 Colonial Latin America in the Eighteenth Century

Map 18.2 European Claims in North America, 1755–1763

Plus flashcards, practice quizzes, and more. Go to:
www.cengage.com/history/bullietearthpeople5e

SUGGESTED READING

Bailyn, Bernard. *The Origins of American Politics.* 1986. A helpful introduction to early American politics.

Blackburn, Carole. *Harvest of Souls: The Jesuit Missions and Colonialism in North America, 1632–1650.* 2000. An essential examination of the conversion efforts in French Canada.

Burkholder, Mark A., and Lyman L. Johnson. *Colonial Latin America,* 5th ed. 2005. Provides a good introduction to early Latin America.

Bushman, Richard. *King and People in Provincial Massachusetts.* 1985. A strong discussion of politics in late colonial New England.

Crosby, Alfred W., Jr. *The Columbian Exchange: Biological and Cultural Consequences of 1492.* 1972. *Ecological Imperialism.* 1986. Pioneering works in the study of cross-Atlantic history.

Curtin, Philip D. *The Rise and Fall of the Plantation Complex.* 1990. Excellent introduction to the Atlantic system.

Davis, David Brion. *The Problem of Slavery in Western Culture.* 1966. A classic study of this topic from a broad perspective.

Eccles, William J. *France in America,* rev. ed. 1990. An excellent overview of French colonialism in North America.

Elliott, J. H. *Empires of the Atlantic World.* 2006. A masterful comparative study of European New World empires.

Eltis, David. *The Rise of African Slavery in the Americas.* 2000.

Fischer, David Hackett. *Albion's Seed: Four British Folkways in America.* 1989. A general study of the British colonies.

Gallay, Alan. *The Indian Slave Trade: The Rise of the English Empire in the American South, 1670–1717.* 2002. An important examination of the Indian slave trade and its consequences.

Klein, Herbert S. *The Atlantic Slave Trade.* 1999.

McAlister, Lyle N. *Spain and Portugal in the New World, 1492–1700.* 1984. A useful introduction to the era of Iberian rule.

Melville, Elinor G. K. *A Plague of Sheep: Environmental Consequences of the Spanish Conquest of Mexico.* 1994. Looks at what happens when a new domestic species is introduced.

Miller, Shawn William. *An Environmental History of Latin America.* 2007. The first three chapters provide an excellent introduction to environmental change in the colonial period.

Nash, Gary B. *Red, White, and Black: The Peoples of Early America,* 5th ed. 2005. Studies the complexity of colonial society in North America.

Schwartz, Stuart B. *Sugar Plantations in the Formation of Brazilian Society: Bahia, 1550–1835.* 1985. This book remains the best analysis of the Brazilian sugar sector.

Serulnikov, Sergio. *Subverting Colonial Authority.* 2003. An excellent study of native rebellions in late colonial Spanish America.

Taylor, William. *Magistrates of the Sacred: Priests and Parishioners in Eighteenth-Century Mexico.* 1996. An essential study of the colonial church in Mexico.

Usner, Daniel H., Jr. *Indians, Settlers, and Slaves in a Frontier Exchange Economy: The Lower Mississippi Valley Before 1783.* 1992. One of the most useful examinations of the intersection of indigenous peoples and European empires.

NOTES

1. Quoted in Alfred W. Crosby, Jr., *The Columbian Exchange: Biological and Cultural Consequences of 1492* (Westport, CT: Greenwood, 1972), 58.
2. Fray Andés de Moguer, 1554, quoted in James Lockhart and Enrique Otte, eds., *Letters and People of the Spanish Indies Sixteenth Century* (1976), 216.
3. Crosby, *The Columbian Exchange*, 58.
4. Quoted in R. Douglas Francis, Richard Jones, and Donald B. Smith, *Origins: Canadian History to Confederation* (Toronto: Holt, Rinehart, and Winston of Canada, 1992), 52.
5. Quoted in Daniel H. Usner, Jr., *Indians, Settlers and Slaves in a Frontier Exchange Economy: The Lower Mississippi Valley Before 1783*, Institute of Early American History and Culture Series (Chapel Hill: University of North Carolina Press, 1992), 96.
6. Quoted in Cornelius J. Jaenen, "French and Native Peoples in New France," in *Interpreting Canada's Past*, ed. J. M. Bumsted, vol. 1, 2nd ed. (Toronto: Oxford University Press, 1993), 73.

CHAPTER
19

CHAPTER OUTLINE

From William Clark, *Ten Views in the Islands of Antigua*, 1823. British Library Board

Caribbean Sugar Mill   The windmill crushes sugar cane, whose juice is boiled down in the smoking building next door.

 Visit the website and ebook for additional study materials and interactive tools: www.cengage.com/history/bulliettearthpeople5e

The Atlantic System and Africa, 1550–1800

By the eighteenth century, Caribbean colonies had become the largest producers of sugar in the world. Slaves represented about 90 percent of the islands' population and provided nearly all the labor for harvesting and processing sugar cane. The profitable expansion of sugar agriculture in the seventeenth century opened a new era in the African slave trade. As larger and faster ships carried growing numbers of slaves from Africa, the human cost escalated, as the following example demonstrates.

In 1694 the English ship *Hannibal* called at the West African port of Whydah (WEE-duh) to purchase slaves. The king of Whydah invited the ship's captain and officers to his residence, where they negotiated an agreement on the prices for slaves. In all, the *Hannibal* purchased 692 slaves, of whom about a third were women and girls. The ship's doctor then carefully inspected the naked captives to be sure they were of sound body, young, and free of disease. After their purchase, the slaves were branded with an H (for *Hannibal*) to establish ownership. Once they were loaded on the ship, the crew put shackles on the men to prevent their escape.

To keep the slaves healthy, the captain had the crew feed them twice a day on boiled corn meal and beans brought from Europe and flavored with hot peppers and palm oil purchased in Africa. Each slave received a pint (half a liter) of water with every meal. In addition, the slaves were made to "jump and dance for an hour or two to our bagpipe, harp, and fiddle" every evening to keep them fit. Despite the incentives and precautions for keeping the cargo alive, deaths were common among the hundreds of people crammed into every corner of a slave ship. The *Hannibal*'s experience was worse than most; it lost 320 slaves and 14 crew members to smallpox and dysentery during the seven-week voyage to Barbados.

As the *Hannibal*'s experience suggests, the Atlantic slave trade took a devastating toll in African lives and was far from a sure-fire money maker for European investors, who in this case lost more than £3,000 on the voyage. Nevertheless, the slave trade and plantation slavery were crucial pieces of a booming new **Atlantic system** that moved goods and wealth, as well as peoples and cultures, around the Atlantic.

- How important was sugar production to the European colonies of the West Indies and to the expansion of the African slave trade?
- What effect did sugar plantations have on the natural environment and on living conditions?
- What was the relationship between private investors and European governments in the development of the Atlantic economy?
- How did sub-Saharan Africa's expanding contacts in the Atlantic compare with its contacts with the Islamic world?

Atlantic system The network of trading links after 1500 that moved goods, wealth, people, and cultures around the Atlantic Basin.

PLANTATIONS IN THE WEST INDIES

The West Indies was the first place in the Americas reached by Columbus, and it was also the first region in the Americas where native populations collapsed from epidemics. It took a long time to repopulate these islands and forge economic links with other parts of the Atlantic. But after 1650 sugar plantations, African slaves, and European capital made these islands a major center of the Atlantic economy.

Colonization Before 1650

Spanish settlers introduced sugar-cane cultivation into the West Indies shortly after 1500, but these colonies soon fell into neglect as attention shifted to colonizing the American mainland. After 1600 the West Indies revived as a focus of colonization, this time by northern Europeans interested in growing tobacco and other crops. In the 1620s and 1630s, English and French colonists settled many islands of the Antilles. With greater government support, the English colonies prospered first, largely by producing tobacco.

The Tobacco Era

Tobacco, a New World leaf long used by Amerindians for recreation and medicine, was finding a new market among seventeenth-century Europeans. Despite the opposition of individuals like King James I of England, who condemned tobacco smoke as "dangerous to the eye, hateful to the nose, harmful to the brain, and dangerous to the lungs," the habit spread. By 1614 seven thousand shops in and around London sold tobacco.

The first tobacco colonies suffered from diseases, hurricanes, and attacks by native Caribs and the Spanish. They also suffered from shortages of supplies from Europe and shortages of labor sufficient to clear land and plant tobacco. The governments of France and England controlled costs by allowing private investors organized as **chartered companies** to develop the colonies in exchange for monopoly control and annual fees. These companies provided passage to the colonies for poor Europeans who were obligated to work three or four years as indentured servants (see Chapter 18). As a result the French and English populations grew rapidly in the 1630s and 1640s. By the middle of the century, however, these Caribbean colonies were in crisis due to stiff competition from Virginia tobacco, also cultivated by indentured servants. Profits grew when the English, French, and Dutch colonies of the Caribbean switched from tobacco to sugar cane and from European indentured laborers to the labor of African slaves.

chartered companies
Groups of private investors who paid an annual fee to France and England in exchange for a monopoly over trade to the West Indies colonies.

The Portuguese and the Dutch and Sugar

The Portuguese first developed sugar plantations that relied on African slaves on islands along the African coast. They later introduced this complex in Brazil (see Chapter 18). By 1600 Brazil was the Atlantic world's greatest sugar producer. The Dutch were early participants in the Brazilian sugar business as investors, merchants, and processors. Dutch independence from Spain early in the seventeenth century threatened this profitable commerce because the Spanish crown ruled Portugal and Brazil. As part of its struggle with Spain, the Dutch government chartered the **Dutch West India Company** in 1621. This powerful private trading company captured a Spanish treasure fleet in 1628 and used some of the windfall to finance an assault on Brazil's valuable sugar-producing areas. By 1635 the Dutch company controlled much of Brazil's sugar region. Over the next fifteen years the Dutch improved the efficiency of the Brazilian sugar industry and also profited from supplying African slaves and European goods.

Dutch West India Company
Trading company chartered by the Dutch government to conduct its merchants' trade in the Americas and Africa.

Like its assault on Brazil, the Dutch West India Company's entry into the African slave trade combined economic and political motives. It seized the important West African trading station of Elmina from the Portuguese in 1638 and took their port of Luanda (loo-AHN-duh) on the Angolan coast in 1641. From these coasts the Dutch shipped slaves to Brazil and the West Indies. Although the Portuguese were able to drive the Dutch out of Angola after a few years, Elmina remained the Dutch West India Company's headquarters in West Africa.

Once free of Spanish rule in 1640, the Portuguese crown turned its attention to reconquering Brazil and by 1654 had driven the last of the Dutch from that country. Some of the expelled planters transplanted their capital and knowledge of sugar production to Dutch Caribbean colonies as well as to the English and French islands.

CHRONOLOGY

	West Indies	Atlantic	Africa
1500	ca. 1500 Spanish settlers introduce sugar-cane cultivation	1530 Amsterdam Exchange opens	1500–1700 Gold trade predominates
			1591 Morocco conquers Songhai
1600	1620s and 1630s English and French colonies in Caribbean	1621 Dutch West India Company chartered	1638 Dutch take Elmina
	1640s Dutch bring sugar plantation system from Brazil		
	1655 English take Jamaica	1654 Dutch expelled from Brazil	
		1660s English Navigation Acts	
	1670s French occupy western half of Hispaniola (modern Haiti)	1672 Royal African Company chartered	
			1680s Rise of Asante
1700	1700 West Indies surpass Brazil in sugar production	1698 French *Exclusif*	
		1700 to present Atlantic system flourishing	1700–1830 Slave trade predominates
		1713 English receive slave trade monopoly from Spanish Empire	1720s Rise of Dahomey
			1730 Oyo makes Dahomey pay tribute
	1760 Tacky's rebellion in Jamaica		

Sugar and Slaves

The infusion of Dutch expertise and money revived the French colonies of Guadeloupe and Martinique, but the English colony of Barbados best illustrates the dramatic transformation that sugar brought to the seventeenth-century Caribbean. In 1640 Barbados's economy depended largely on tobacco, mostly grown by European settlers, both free and indentured. By the 1680s sugar had become the principal crop and enslaved Africans were three times as numerous as Europeans. Exporting up to 15,000 tons of sugar a year, Barbados had become the wealthiest and most populous of England's American colonies. By 1700 Barbados and other West Indian colonies had collectively surpassed Brazil as the world's principal source of sugar.

The Slave Trade   The expansion of sugar plantations in the West Indies required a sharp increase in the volume of the slave trade from Africa (see Figure 19.1). During the first half of the seventeenth century about ten thousand slaves a year had arrived from Africa. Most were destined for Brazil and the mainland Spanish colonies. In the second half of the century the trade averaged twenty thousand slaves, and more than half landed in the English, French, and Dutch West Indies. A century later, as sugar production increased and the Spanish colony of Cuba became a major importer of slaves, the volume of the Atlantic slave trade tripled.

Indentured Servants   Cash-short tobacco planters in the seventeenth century preferred indentured Europeans to African slaves because they cost half as much. Poor European men and women were willing to work for little in order to get to the Americas, where they could acquire their own land cheaply at the end of their term of service. However, as the cultivation of sugar spread after 1750, speculators drove land prices in the West Indies so high that former indentured servants could no longer afford to buy land. As a result, poor Europeans chose to indenture themselves in Britain's North American colonies, where cheap land was still available. Rather than raise wages to attract European laborers, Caribbean sugar planters switched to slaves.

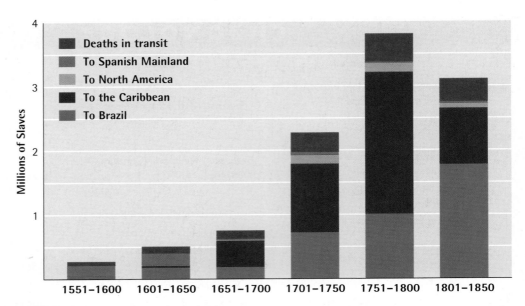

FIGURE 19.1 **Transatlantic Slave Trade from Africa, 1551–1850** *Source:* Data from David Eltis, "The Volume and Structure of the Transatlantic Slave Trade: A Reassessment," *William and Mary Quarterly*, 3rd Series, 58 (2001), tables II and III.

SECTION REVIEW

- England and France relied on private investors organized as chartered companies to develop their Caribbean colonies.

- European colonies in the Caribbean at first depended on tobacco exports but then concentrated on producing sugar, which was more profitable.

- The Dutch helped develop the sugar industry as investors, refiners, slave traders, and disseminators of technology.

- European indentured servants provided crucial labor for Caribbean plantations in the early years, but planters switched to African slaves when the flow of indentured laborers was redirected to North America.

Rising sugar prices helped the West Indian sugar planters afford the higher cost of African slaves. The fact that slaves lived seven years on average after their arrival, while the typical indentured labor contract was for only three or four years, also made slaves a better investment. Dutch and other traders responded to rising demand by increasing the flow of slaves to meet the needs of the expanding plantations (see Figure 19.1), but slave prices rose throughout the eighteenth century. These high labor costs were one more factor favoring large plantations over smaller operations.

PLANTATION LIFE IN THE EIGHTEENTH CENTURY

To find more land for sugar plantations, France and England expanded their Caribbean holdings by attacking older Spanish colonies. In 1655 the English seized Jamaica from the Spanish (see Map 18.1 on page 482). They also took Havana, Cuba, in 1762 and held the city for a year. By the time the occupation ended, English merchants had imported large numbers of slaves and Cuba had begun to switch from tobacco to sugar production. The French seized the western half of the Spanish island of Hispaniola in the 1670s. During the eighteenth century this new French colony of Saint Domingue (san doh-MANGH) (present-day Haiti) became the greatest producer of sugar in the Atlantic world, while Jamaica surpassed Barbados as England's most important sugar colony. The technological, environmental, and social transformation of these island colonies illustrates the power of the new Atlantic system.

Courtesy of the John Carter Brown Library at Brown University

Plantation Scene, Antigua, British West Indies   The sugar made at the mill in the background was sealed in barrels and loaded on carts that oxen and horses drew to the beach. By means of a succession of vessels the barrels were taken to the ship that hauled the cargo to Europe. The importance of African labor is evident from the fact that only one white person appears in the painting.

Technology and Environment

Sugar production had both an agricultural and an industrial character. On both small farms and large plantations, growing and harvesting sugar cane required only simple tools like spades, hoes, and machetes. Once the cane was cut, however, a more complex and expensive process was needed to produce sugar. Slaves rushed the cane to mills, where it was crushed and the juice extracted. Lead-lined wooden troughs carried cane juice to a series of large copper kettles where excess water was boiled off, leaving thick syrup. Placed in conical clay molds, the syrup turned to crystallized sugar as it dried. The small refiners used crushing mills driven by animals or even laborers, while the large plantations used larger and more efficient mills that relied on wind or water power. These economies of scale meant that over time large producers had lower costs and greater profits.

Large Plantations

To make the operation more efficient and profitable, investors sought to utilize the costly crushing and refining machinery intensively. As a result, West Indian plantations expanded from an average of around 100 acres (40 hectares) in the seventeenth century to at least twice that size in the eighteenth century. Some plantations were even larger. In 1774 Jamaica's 680 sugar plantations averaged 441 acres (178 hectares), with the largest over 2,000 acres (800 hectares). Jamaica specialized so heavily in sugar production that the island had to import most of its food. Saint Domingue had a comparable number of plantations of smaller average size but generally higher productivity. The French colony was also more diverse in its economy. Although sugar production was paramount, some planters raised provisions for local consumption and crops such as coffee and cacao for export.

Plantations and the Environment

Sugar agriculture had a mixed environmental record. Some practices were not destructive. Planters powered their mills by water, wind, or animals and fueled their boilers by burning crushed cane. They fertilized their fields using manure from their cattle. Yet high profits led planters to exploit nature ruthlessly in other ways. Repeated cultivation of a single crop removes more nutrients from the soil than animal fertilizer and fallow periods can restore. Instead of rotating sugar with other crops to restore the nutrients naturally, planters found it more profitable to clear new lands when yields declined in the old fields. When land was exhausted, planters often moved on to new islands. Many of the English who settled Jamaica had been planters on Barbados. Similarly, the pioneer planters on Saint Domingue came from older French sugar colonies. In the second half of the eighteenth century, Jamaican sugar production began to fall behind Saint Domingue, which still had virgin land.

In addition to soil exhaustion and deforestation, the introduction of nonnative animals and cultivated plants transformed the Caribbean region. The Spanish brought cattle, pigs, and horses, which multiplied rapidly. They also introduced new plants. Bananas and plantains from the Canary Islands were a valuable addition to the food supply, and sugar and rice formed the basis of plantation agriculture, along with native tobacco. Other food crops arrived with the slaves from Africa, including okra, black-eyed peas, yams, grains such as millet and sorghum, and mangoes. Many of these new animals and plants were useful additions to the islands, but they crowded out indigenous species. New World foods also found their way to Africa (see Environment and Technology: Amerindian Foods in Africa).

The most tragic and dramatic transformation of the West Indies was demographic. Chapter 16 detailed how disease and abuse nearly eliminated the indigenous peoples of the large islands within fifty years of Columbus's first voyage. Far earlier and more completely than in any mainland colony, the West Indies were repeopled from across the Atlantic—first from Europe and then from Africa.

Slaves' Lives

plantocracy In the West Indian colonies, the rich men who owned most of the slaves and most of the land, especially in the eighteenth century.

During the eighteenth century West Indian plantation colonies were the world's most polarized societies. On most islands 90 percent or more of the inhabitants were slaves. Power resided in the hands of a **plantocracy**, a small number of very rich men who owned most of the slaves and most of the land. Between the slaves and the masters was a small middle group of estate managers, government officials, artisans, and small farmers, nearly all white. Some free blacks owned property or entered commerce. It is only a slight simplification to describe eighteenth-century Caribbean society as being made up of a large, abject class of slaves and a small, powerful class of masters.

The Organization of Slave Labor

The profitability of a Caribbean plantation depended on extracting as much work as possible from the slaves, and plantations achieved exceptional productivity through the threat and use of force. The slaves' long workday might stretch to eighteen hours or more when the cane harvest and milling were in full swing. As Table 19.1 shows, on a typical Jamaican plantation about 80 percent of the slaves were actively engaged in productive tasks; the only exceptions were infants, the seriously ill, and the very old.

Table 19.1 also illustrates how planters organized slaves by age, sex, and ability. Only 2 or 3 percent of the slaves were house servants. About 70 percent of the able-bodied slaves worked in the fields, generally in one of three labor gangs. A "great gang," made up of the strongest slaves in the prime of life, did the heaviest work, such as breaking up the soil at the beginning of the planting season. A second gang of youths, elders, and less fit slaves did somewhat lighter work. A "grass gang," composed of children under the supervision of an elderly slave, was responsible for weeding and other simple work, such as collecting grass for the animals. Women often formed the majority of the field laborers, even in the great gang. Nursing mothers took their babies with them to the fields. Slaves too old for field labor tended the toddlers.

Because the slave trade imported twice as many males as females, men outnumbered women on Caribbean plantations. As Table 19.1 shows, a little over half of adult males did non-gang work. Some tended livestock, and others were skilled craftsmen, such as blacksmiths and carpenters. The most important artisan slave was the head boiler, who oversaw the delicate process of reducing the cane sap to crystallized sugar and molasses.

The Treatment of Slaves

driver A privileged male slave whose job was to ensure that a slave gang did its work on a plantation.

Planters often rewarded skilled slaves with better-quality food and clothing or time off, but most slaves were compelled to work hard by fear of the lash. Slave gangs were led by a privileged male slave, appropriately called the "**driver**," whose job was to ensure that the gang completed its work. Since production quotas were high, slaves toiled in the fields from sunup to sunset, except for meal breaks. Those who fell behind due to fatigue or illness soon felt the sting of the whip. Planters punished openly rebellious slaves who refused to work, disobeyed orders, or tried to

Amerindian Foods in Africa

The migration of European plants and animals across the Atlantic to the New World was one side of the Columbian Exchange (see Chapter 18). The Andean potato, for example, became a staple crop of the poor in Europe, and cassava (a Brazilian plant cultivated for its edible roots) and maize (corn) moved across the Atlantic to Africa.

Maize was a high-yielding grain that could produce much more food per acre than many grains indigenous to Africa. The varieties of maize that spread to Africa were not modern highbred "sweet corn" but starchier types found in white and yellow corn meal. Cassava—not well known to modern North Americans except perhaps in the form of tapioca—became the most important New World food in Africa. Truly a marvel, cassava had the highest yield of calories per acre of any staple food and thrived even in poor soils and during droughts. Both the leaves and the root could be eaten. Ground into meal, the root could be made into a bread that would keep for up to six months, or it could be fermented into a beverage.

Cassava and maize were probably accidentally introduced into Africa by Portuguese ships from Brazil that discarded leftover supplies after reaching Angola. It did not take long for local Africans to recognize the food value of these new crops, especially in drought-prone areas. As the principal farmers in Central Africa, women must have played an important role in learning how to cultivate, harvest, and prepare these foods. By the eighteenth century Lunda rulers hundreds of miles from the Angolan coast were actively promoting the cultivation of maize and cassava on their royal estates in order to provide a more secure food supply.

Some historians of Africa believe that in the inland areas these Amerindian food crops provided the nutritional base for a population increase that partially offset losses due to the Atlantic slave trade. By supplementing the range of food crops available and by enabling populations to increase in lightly

Engraving from André Thevet, *Les Singularitez de la France Antarctique*. Paris: Maurice de la Porte, 1557. Courtesy of the James Bell Library, University of Minnesota

Cassava Plant   Both the leaves and the starchy root of the cassava plant could be eaten.

settled or famine-prone areas, cassava and maize, along with peanuts and other New World legumes, permanently altered Africans' environmental prospects.

escape with floggings, confinement in irons, or mutilation. While slaves usually did not work in the fields on Sunday, they could not rest, but had to use this time to farm their own provisioning grounds to supplement meager rations, maintain their dwellings, and do other chores, such as washing and mending their rough clothes.

Except for occasional holidays—including the Christmas-week revels in the British West Indies—there was little time for recreation and relaxation. Slaves might sing in the fields, but singing was simply a way to distract themselves from fatigue and the monotony of the work. There was certainly no time for schooling, nor were masters willing to educate slaves beyond skills useful to the plantation.

Slave Health

Time for family life was also inadequate. Although the large proportion of young adults in plantation colonies ought to have led to a high rate of natural increase, despite the sex imbalance that resulted from the slave trade, the opposite occurred. Poor nutrition and overwork lowered fertility. The continuation of heavy fieldwork made it difficult for a pregnant woman to carry a child to term or a mother to ensure an infant's survival. As a result of these conditions, along with disease and accidents from dangerous mill equipment, deaths heavily outnumbered births on West Indian plantations (see Table 19.2). Life expectancy for slaves in nineteenth-century

| TABLE 19.1 | Slave Occupations on a Jamaican Sugar Plantation, 1788 |

Occupations and Conditions	Men	Women	Boys and Girls	Total
Field laborers	62	78		140
Tradesmen	29			29
Field drivers	4			4
Field cooks		4		4
Mule-, cattle-, and stablemen	12			12
Watchmen	18			18
Nurse		1		1
Midwife		1		1
Domestics and gardeners		5	3	8
Grass-gang			20	20
Total employed	125	89	23	237
Infants			23	23
Invalids (18 with yaws)				32
Absent on roads				5
Superannuated [elderly]				7
Overall total				304

Source: From Michael Craton, James Walvin, and David Wright, eds., *Slavery, Abolition and Emancipation*, p. 103. Copyright © 1976. Reprinted by permission of Pearson Education Limited.

| TABLE 19.2 | Birth and Death on a Jamaican Sugar Plantation, 1779–1785 |

Year	Born Males	Born Females	Purchased	Died Males	Died Females	Proportion of Deaths
1779	5	2	6	7	5	1 in 26
1780	4	3	—	3	2	1 in 62
1781	2	3	—	4	2	1 in 52
1782	1	3	9	4	5	1 in 35
1783	3	3	—	8	10	1 in 17
1784	2	1	12	9	10	1 in 17
1785	2	3	—	0	3	1 in 99
Total	19	18	27	35	37	
	Born 37			Died 72		

Source: From Michael Craton, James Walvin, and David Wright, eds., *Slavery, Abolition and Emancipation*, p. 105. Copyright © 1976. Reprinted by permission of Pearson Education Limited.

seasoning An often difficult period of adjustment to new climates, disease environments, and work routines, such as that experienced by slaves newly arrived in the Americas.

Brazil was only 23 years of age for males and 25.5 years for females. The figures were probably similar for the eighteenth-century Caribbean. A callous opinion, common among slave owners in the Caribbean and in parts of Brazil, held that it was cheaper to import a youthful new slave from Africa than to raise one to the same age on a plantation.

The harsh conditions of plantation life played a major role in shortening slaves' lives, but the greatest killer was disease. Dysentery caused by contaminated food and water was common. Slaves newly arrived from Africa went through the period of adjustment to a new environment known as **seasoning**, during which one-third, on average, died of unfamiliar diseases. Slaves

Fotomas/Topham/The Image Works

Punishment for Slaves In addition to whipping and other cruel punishments, slave owners devised other ways to shame and intimidate slaves into obedience. This metal face mask prevented the wearer from eating or drinking.

also suffered from diseases brought with them, including malaria. On the plantation profiled in Table 19.1, for example, more than half of the slaves incapacitated by illness had yaws, a painful and debilitating skin disease common in Africa. As a consequence, only slave populations in the healthier temperate zones of North America experienced natural increase.

Such high mortality greatly added to the volume of the Atlantic slave trade, since plantations had to continually purchase new slaves to replace those who died (see Table 19.2). The high mortality and low fertility of this cruel labor system meant that increased sugar production depended on an ever-expanding slave trade. As a result, the majority of slaves on most West Indian plantations were African-born, and African religious beliefs, patterns of speech, styles of dress and adornment, and music were prominent parts of West Indian life.

Given the harsh conditions of their lives, it is not surprising that slaves in the West Indies often sought to gain their freedom. Individual slaves often ran away. Sometimes large groups of plantation slaves rose in rebellion against their bondage and abuse. For example, a slave named Tacky, who had been a chief on the Gold Coast of Africa, led a large rebellion in Jamaica in 1760. After his followers broke into a fort and armed themselves, slaves from nearby plantations joined them. This force attacked several plantations, setting them on fire and killing the planter families. Tacky died in the fighting, and three of his lieutenants stoically endured cruel deaths by torture meant to deter others from rebellion.

Because European planters believed that slaves with the strongest African heritage led rebellions, they tried to curtail African cultural traditions. They required slaves to learn the colonial language and discouraged the use of African languages by deliberately mixing slaves from different parts of Africa. In French and Portuguese colonies, slaves were encouraged to adopt Catholic religious practices, though African deities, beliefs, and practices survived, serving as the foundation for modern African-derived religions like candomblé. In the British West Indies, where only Quaker slave owners encouraged Christianity among their slaves before 1800, African herbal medicine remained strong, as did African beliefs concerning nature spirits and witchcraft.

Slave Resistance

e **PRIMARY SOURCE: The Interesting Narrative of Olaudah Equiano and Written by Himself** Read selections from an ex-slave's autobiography, one of the most influential abolitionist books published in England.

Free Whites and Free Blacks

The lives of the free population were very different from the lives of slaves. In the French colony of Saint Domingue, which had nearly half of all slaves in the Caribbean in the eighteenth century, there were three categories of free people. At the top were wealthy owners of large sugar plantations (the *grands blancs* [grawn blawnk], or "great whites"), who dominated the economy and society of the island. Second came less-well-off Europeans (*petits blancs* [pay-TEE blawnk], or "little whites"). Most served as colonial officials, retail merchants, or small-scale agriculturalists. Most members of both groups owned slaves. Third came the free blacks. There were almost as many free blacks as free whites. While they ranked below whites socially, many free blacks owned property, and a surprising number also owned slaves.

The Planter Elite

The plantation elite was even more powerful in British colonies. Whereas sugar constituted about half of Saint Domingue's exports, in Jamaica the figure was over 80 percent. Such concentration on sugar crowded out small cultivators, white or black, and confined most landholding to

Courtesy of National Library, Institute of Jamaica

Cudjoe, Leader of the Jamaican Maroons, Negotiates a Peace Treaty In 1738, after decades of successful resistance to the British, the maroon Cudjoe negotiated a peace treaty that recognized the freedom of his runaway followers. Unable to defeat the maroons, the British also granted land and effective self-government to the maroons in exchange for an end to raids on plantations and the promise to return future slave runaways.

a few larger owners. At midcentury three-quarters of the farmland in Jamaica belonged to individuals who owned 1,000 acres (400 hectares) or more.

One source estimated that a planter had to invest nearly £20,000 ($100,000) to acquire a medium-size Jamaican plantation of 600 acres (240 hectares) in 1774. A third of this money went for land on which to grow sugar and food crops, pasture animals, and cut timber and firewood. A quarter of the expense was for the mill and refinery. The largest expense was the purchase of 200 slaves at £40 ($200) each. In comparison, the wage of an English rural laborer at this time was about £10 ($50) a year (one-fourth the price of a slave), and the annual incomes in 1760 of the ten wealthiest noble families in Britain averaged only £20,000 each.

Reputedly the richest Englishmen of this time, West Indian planters often translated their wealth into political power and social prestige. The richest planters put their plantations under the direction of managers and lived in Britain. Between 1730 and 1775 seventy absentee planters secured election to the British Parliament, where they formed an influential voting bloc. Those who resided in the West Indies exercised political power through the control of colonial assemblies.

In most European plantation colonies it was possible to grant freedom to an individual slave or group of slaves. **Manumission** (the legal grant of freedom by an owner) was more common in Brazil and the Spanish and French colonies than in English colonies. Among English colonies, manumissions were more common in the Caribbean than in North America. While some plantation owners in the Caribbean freed slave women with whom they had had sexual relationships or freed the children of their mistresses, the largest group of freed slaves across the Americas had purchased their freedom. Manumissions led to the development of a large free black population in many colonies. Since the legal condition of children followed that of the mother, slave families often struggled to free women in childbearing years first so that their children would be born free. By the late eighteenth

manumission A grant of legal freedom to an individual slave.

SECTION REVIEW

- Sugar production required larger investments in land, slaves, and machinery than other forms of colonial agriculture.

- Large-scale sugar plantations were more efficient and profitable than smaller plantations.

- Sugar plantations had high environmental costs due to deforestation and soil exhaustion.

- Slaves were closely organized and forced to be productive through the use of harsh punishments.

- Slave populations of the Caribbean experienced high mortality rates and low fertility rates.

- Slaves sought freedom through manumission or flight or rebellion; some groups of runaways, maroons, forced authorities to recognize their freedom.

century free blacks made up a large portion of the black populations of Brazil and the French colonies.

Runaway Communities

maroon A slave who ran away from his or her master. Often a member of a community of runaway slaves in the West Indies and South America.

As in Brazil and Spanish colonies (see Chapter 18), escaped slaves constituted another part of the free black population. Communities of runaways, called **maroons**, were numerous in Jamaica and Hispaniola as well as in the Guianas (guy-AHN-uhs). Jamaican maroons, after withstanding several attacks by the colony's militia, signed a treaty in 1738 that recognized their independence in return for their cooperation in stopping new runaways and suppressing slave revolts. Unable to win decisive victories, colonial authorities in Spanish, Dutch, and Portuguese colonies signed similar treaties with runaway leaders as well.

CREATING THE ATLANTIC ECONOMY

At once archaic in their cruel system of slavery and oddly modern in their specialization in a single product for export, the West Indian plantation colonies were the bittersweet fruits of a new Atlantic trading system. Changes in the character of Atlantic commerce illustrate the rise of this new system. In the sixteenth century Spanish treasure fleets laden with silver and gold bullion had dominated Atlantic trade. In the late seventeenth and eighteenth centuries the Atlantic trade was dominated by sugar ships returning to Europe from the West Indies and Brazil and by slave ships transporting an average of 250 African captives each to the Americas.

In addition to the plantation system, new economic institutions, new partnerships between private investors and governments in Europe, and new working relationships between European and African merchants created the Atlantic economy. This new trading system is a prime example of how European capitalist relationships were reshaping the world.

Capitalism and Mercantilism

Many of the Spanish and Portuguese voyages of exploration in the fifteenth and sixteenth centuries were government ventures, and both Spain and Portugal tried to restrict the overseas trade of their colonies using royal monopolies (see Chapters 16 and 18). Monopoly control, however, proved both expensive and inefficient. The success of the Atlantic economy in the seventeenth and eighteenth centuries depended much more on private enterprise, which made trade more efficient and profitable. European private investors were attracted to colonial trade by the rich profits generated by New World agriculture and mining, but their success depended on new institutions and the continuation of government protection to reduce the possibility of catastrophic loss.

Capitalism and the Atlantic World

capitalism The economic system of large financial institutions—banks, stock exchanges, investment companies—that first developed in early modern Europe. *Commercial capitalism*, the trading system of the early modern economy, is often distinguished from *industrial capitalism*, the system based on machine production.

The growth of the Atlantic economy was one part of the development of modern **capitalism**. The essence of this economic system was the expansion of credit and the development of large financial institutions—banks, stock exchanges, and chartered trading companies—that enabled merchants and investors to conduct business at great distances from their homes while reducing risks and increasing profits. Originally developed for business dealings within Europe, the capitalist system expanded overseas in the seventeenth century, when slow economic growth in Europe led many investors to seek profits in the production and export of colonial products like sugar and tobacco and in satisfying the colonial demand for European products.

Banks were crucial to this process. By the early seventeenth century Dutch banks had developed such a reputation for security that individuals and governments from all over western Europe entrusted them with large sums of money. To make a profit, Dutch and other European banks invested these funds in real estate, industries, loans to governments, and overseas trade.

Individuals seeking higher returns than those provided by banks could purchase shares in a joint-stock company, a sixteenth-century forerunner of the modern corporation. Individuals bought and sold shares in specialized financial markets called stock exchanges. The Amsterdam Exchange, founded in 1530, became the greatest stock market in the seventeenth and eighteenth centuries. To reduce risks in overseas trading, merchants and trading companies

Mercantilism

mercantilism European government policies of the sixteenth, seventeenth, and eighteenth centuries designed to promote overseas trade between a country and its colonies and accumulate precious metals by requiring colonies to trade only with their motherland country. The British system was defined by the Navigation Acts, the French system by laws known as the *Exclusif*.

Royal African Company A trading company chartered by the English government in 1672 to conduct its merchants' trade on the Atlantic coast of Africa.

bought insurance on their ships and cargoes to cover potential losses. Banks and stock markets appeared much later in the Iberian world, slowing the rate of economic growth.

European states sought to monopolize the profits produced in their colonial empires by controlling trade and accumulating capital in the form of gold and silver. This system was called **mercantilism**. Mercantilist policies strongly discouraged citizens from trading with foreign merchants and used armed force when necessary to secure exclusive relations.

Chartered companies were an important part of mercantilist capitalism. In 1602 the Netherlands gave the Dutch East India Company a monopoly over trade in the Indian Ocean. Private investors who bought shares in the company were amply rewarded when the Dutch East India Company captured control of long-distance trade in the Indian Ocean from the Portuguese (see Chapter 20). As we have seen, the Dutch West India Company, chartered in 1621, sought similar benefits in the Atlantic trade by seizing sugar-producing areas in Brazil and African slaving ports from the Portuguese.

These successes inspired other governments to set up their own chartered companies. In 1672 a royal charter placed all English trade with West Africa in the hands of the **Royal African Company (RAC)**, which established its headquarters at Cape Coast Castle, just east of Elmina on the Gold Coast. The French government also chartered companies and promoted overseas trade and colonization. Jean Baptiste Colbert (kohl-BEAR), King Louis XIV's minister of finance from 1661 to 1683, chartered the French East India and French West India Companies to expel Dutch and English traders from French colonies.

French and English governments also used military force to gain trade advantages in the Americas. Restrictions on Dutch access to French and English colonies provoked a series of wars with the Netherlands between 1652 and 1678 (see Chapter 17). The larger English and French navies defeated the Dutch and drove the Dutch West India Company into bankruptcy. Military and diplomatic pressure also forced Spain after 1713 to grant England and later France monopoly rights to supply slaves to its colonies.

With Dutch competition in the Atlantic reduced, the French and English limited the privileges of their chartered companies. Such new mercantilist policies fostered competition among a nation's own citizens, while using high tariffs and restrictions to exclude foreigners. In the 1660s England passed a series of Navigation Acts that confined trade with its colonies to English ships and cargoes; it later opened trade in Africa to any English subject, claiming that competition would cut the cost of slaves to West Indian planters. The French called their mercantilist legislation, codified in 1698, the *Exclusif* (ek-skloo-SEEF), highlighting its exclusionary intentions. Other mercantilist laws sought to protect national manufacturing and agricultural interests from the competition of colonies, imposing prohibitively high taxes on their manufactured goods and products like refined sugar.

As a result of these mercantilist measures, the Atlantic became Britain, France, and Portugal's most important overseas trading area. The value of imports from West Indian colonies alone accounted for over one-fifth the value of total British imports, while French West Indian colonies played an even larger role in France's overseas trade. Only the Dutch, closed out of much of the American trade, depended more heavily on Asian trade (see Chapter 20). Profits from the Atlantic economy, in turn, promoted further economic expansion and increased the revenues of European governments.

The Atlantic Circuit

Atlantic Circuit The network of trade routes connecting Europe, Africa, and the Americas that underlay the Atlantic system.

Middle Passage The part of the Atlantic Circuit involving the transportation of enslaved Africans across the Atlantic to the Americas.

At the heart of this trading system was a clockwise network of sea routes known as the **Atlantic Circuit** (see Map 19.1). The first leg, from Europe to Africa, carried European manufactures—notably metals, hardware, and guns—as well as great quantities of cotton textiles brought from India. While some of these goods were exchanged for West African gold, ivory, timber, and other products, most goods went to purchase slaves, who were transported across the Atlantic to the plantation colonies in what was known as the **Middle Passage**. On the third leg, plantation goods from the colonies returned to Europe. Each leg carried goods from where they were abundant and relatively cheap to where they were scarce and therefore valuable. Thus, in theory, each leg of the Atlantic Circuit could earn profits. In practice, shipwrecks, deaths, piracy, and other risks could turn profit into loss.

MAP 19.1 **The Atlantic Economy** By 1700 the volume of maritime exchanges among the Atlantic continents had begun to rival the trade of the Indian Ocean Basin. Notice the trade in consumer products, slave labor, precious metals, and other goods. Silver trade to East Asia laid the basis for a Pacific Ocean economy.

Plantation zone

NORTH AMERICA
Azores
Madeira Is.
Canary Is.
Mexico City
Cuba
Jamaica
Puerto Rico
Hispaniola
Cape Verde Is.
Trinidad
Panama
Quito
PERU
SOUTH AMERICA
Lima
BRAZIL
Potosi
Rio de Janeiro
PACIFIC OCEAN
Santiago
Buenos Aires
ATLANTIC OCEAN
Strait of Magellan
Cape Horn

0   2,000 Km.
0   2,000 Mi.

Great Britain
France
Portugal
Spain
Netherlands
Trade from Europe
Trade from Africa
Trade from Americas
Trade from Asia

ARCTIC OCEAN

NORTH AMERICA
MEXICO
LOUISIANA
Hudson Bay
RUPERT'S LAND
NEW FRANCE
QUEBEC
THIRTEEN COLONIES
Mississippi R.
Veracruz
Acapulco
Silver (to the Philippines)
Silks, spices, porcelain
FLORIDA
Havana
CUBA
JAMAICA
Porto Bello
SAINT-DOMINGUE (Fr.)
Hispaniola
SANTO DOMINGO (Sp.)
Silver
NEWFOUNDLAND (To Gr. Br., 1713)
NOVA SCOTIA (ACADIA) (To Gr. Br., 1713)
Tobacco
Furs
Silver
Sugar
Colonial products
GREAT BRITAIN
NETHERLANDS
FRANCE
SPAIN
PORTUGAL
EUROPE
ASIA
Manufactured goods
Guadeloupe (Fr.)
Martinique (Fr.)
Barbados (Gr. Br.)
NEW GRANADA
Lima
PERU
Amazon R.
Silver
DUTCH GUIANA
FRENCH GUIANA
Sugar
SOUTH AMERICA
BRAZIL
Silver
NORTH ATLANTIC OCEAN
Canary Is. (Spain)
Gold
Manufactured goods
Cape Verde Is. (Port.)
Cape Verde
AFRICA
Slave Coast
Gold Coast
Slaves
ANGOLA
SOUTH ATLANTIC OCEAN
Buenos Aires

© Cengage Learning

e Interactive Map

The three-sided Atlantic Circuit is only one of many commercial routes that serviced Atlantic trade. Ships making the long voyage from Europe to the Indian Ocean and Asia typically exchanged African gold and American silver for cotton textiles and spices. Merchants then sold these Asian goods in Africa and the Americas as well as in Europe. Many commercial routes were more direct, carrying manufactured goods from Europe or foodstuffs and lumber from New England to the Caribbean. Some Rhode Island and Massachusetts merchants participated in a "Triangular Trade" that carried rum to West Africa, slaves to the West Indies, and molasses and rum back to New England. There was also a considerable two-way trade between Brazil and Angola that exchanged Brazilian tobacco and liquor for slaves. Brazilian tobacco also found its way north as a staple of the Canadian fur trade.

European investment capital, manufactured goods, and shipping dominated the Atlantic system. Europe was also the principal market for American plantation products, products that transformed material culture. Before the seventeenth century, sugar was scarce and expensive in Europe and was mostly consumed by the rich. As colonial production increased, prices fell and consumption of sugar in England rose to about 4 pounds (nearly 2 kilograms) per person in 1700. Europeans of modest means spooned sugar into popular new beverages imported from overseas—tea, coffee, and chocolate—to overcome the beverages' natural bitterness. Consumption increased to about 18 pounds (8 kilograms) by the early nineteenth century (well below the American average of about 100 pounds [45 kilograms] a year in 1960).

The African Slave Trade

The flow of sugar to Europe depended on the flow of slaves from Africa (see Map 19.2). The rising volume of the Middle Passage is one measure of the expansion of the Atlantic system. During the 150 years following the arrival of Europeans in the Americas, the slave trade brought some 800,000 Africans across the Atlantic. Volume rose to nearly 7.5 million slaves during the boom in sugar production between 1650 and 1800. The West Indies, including Cuba, imported nearly 50 percent of this total, while Brazil received nearly a third and North America another 5 percent. The rest went to Spain's mainland colonies (see Figure 19.1).

Seventeenth-century mercantilist policies placed much of the Atlantic slave trade in the hands of chartered companies. During their existence the Dutch West India Company and the English Royal African Company each carried about 100,000 slaves across the Atlantic. In the eighteenth century private English traders from Liverpool and Bristol controlled about 40 percent of the slave trade. The French, operating out of Nantes and Bordeaux, handled about 20 percent and the Dutch only 6 percent. The Portuguese supplying Brazil and other places had nearly 30 percent of the Atlantic slave trade, in contrast to the 3 percent carried in North American ships.

Conditions in the Middle Passage

While the volume and duration of the slave trade indicate that it was profitable, the relative value of European goods and African slaves as well as slave prices in American ports determined the profit of individual voyages. Slave traders also had to deliver as many healthy slaves as possible for sale in the plantation colonies, but the terrible conditions on slave ships and a

Slave Ship This model of the English vessel *Brookes* shows the specially built section of the hold where enslaved Africans were packed together during the Middle Passage. Girls, boys, and women were confined separately.

MAP 19.2 **The African Slave Trade, 1500–1800** After 1500 a vast new trade in slaves from sub-Saharan Africa to the Americas joined the ongoing slave trade to the Islamic states of North Africa, the Middle East, and India. The West Indies were the major destination of the Atlantic slave trade, followed by Brazil.

e Interactive Map

long and treacherous voyage lasting from six to ten weeks led to high mortalities. Some ships arrived with all of their slaves alive, but large, even catastrophic, losses of life were common (see Figure 19.1). On average, however, slave traders succeeded in lowering mortality during the Middle Passage from about 23 percent on voyages before 1700 to half that in the last half of the eighteenth century.

Failed escapes and mutinies contributed to mortality. When opportunities presented themselves (nearness to land, illness among the crew), some enslaved Africans tried to overpower their captors and escape. Male slaves were routinely shackled together to prevent escapes while they were still in sight of land or when mutiny was feared while at sea. As a precaution, slave traders also commonly confined male slaves below deck during most of the voyage, except at mealtimes, when the crew brought them up in small groups under close supervision. In any event, "mutinies" were rarely successful and defeated mutineers were treated with brutality.

Mistreatment also contributed to the high mortality of the Middle Passage. Although it was in the interests of the captain and crew to deliver their slave cargo in good condition, slavers used whippings, beatings, and even executions to maintain order. Some slaves developed deep psychological depression, known to contemporaries as "fixed melancholy," and refused to eat. Crews attempted to force-feed these slaves, but some successfully

SECTION REVIEW

- Banks, stock markets, and insurance companies helped European nations to develop their colonial empires.

- European nations used mercantilism, a mix of fiscal and trade policies, to monopolize the economic benefits from colonial possessions.

- The Atlantic Circuit was a network of trade networks that connected Europe with Africa and the Western Hemisphere.

- Between 1650 and 1800, 7.5 million African slaves were brought to Europe's American colonies, nine times the number imported in the previous 150 years.

- Conditions on the slave ships were unhealthy and harsh, and mortality rates were high.

willed themselves to death. The dangers and brutalities of the slave trade were so notorious that many ordinary seamen shunned such work. As a consequence, cruel and brutal officers and crews abounded on slave ships.

Although examples of unspeakable cruelties are common in the records, most deaths in the Middle Passage were the result of disease. Dysentery spread by contaminated food and water caused many deaths. Others died of contagious diseases such as smallpox carried on board by infected slaves or crew members. These maladies spread quickly in the crowded and unsanitary confines of the ships, claiming the lives of slaves already physically weakened and mentally traumatized by their ordeals. Crew members were exposed to the same epidemics. It is a measure of the callousness of the age, as well as the cheapness of European labor, that over the course of a round-trip voyage from Europe the proportion of crew deaths could be as high as the slave deaths.

AFRICA, THE ATLANTIC, AND ISLAM

The Atlantic system took a terrible toll in African lives both during the Middle Passage and under the harsh conditions of plantation slavery. Many other Africans died while being marched to African ports for sale. The overall effects on Africa of these losses and of other aspects of the slave trade have been the subject of considerable historical debate. It is clear that the trade's impact depended on the intensity and terms of different African regions' involvement.

Any assessment of the Atlantic system's effects in Africa must also take into consideration the fact that some Africans profited from the trade by capturing and selling slaves. They chained the slaves together or bound them to forked sticks for the march to the coast, then bartered them to the European slavers for trade goods. The effects on the enslaver were different from the effects on the enslaved. Finally, a broader understanding of the Atlantic system's effects in sub-Saharan Africa comes from comparisons with the effects of Islamic contacts.

The Gold Coast and the Slave Coast

As Chapter 16 showed, early European visitors to Africa's Atlantic coast were interested more in trading than in colonizing the continent. As the Africa trade mushroomed after 1650, this pattern continued. African kings and merchants sold slaves and goods at many coastal sites, but the growing slave trade did not lead to substantial European colonization.

The transition to slave trading was not sudden. Even as slaves were becoming Atlantic Africa's most valuable export, goods such as gold, ivory, and timber remained important. For example, during its eight decades of operation from 1672 to 1752, the Royal African Company made 40 percent of its profits from gold, ivory, and forest products. In some parts of West Africa, such nonslave exports remained predominant even at the peak of the trade.

African Participation in the Slave Trade

African merchants were very discriminating about merchandise they took in exchange for slaves or goods. A ship that arrived with goods of low quality or not suited to local tastes found it hard to purchase a cargo at a profitable price. European guidebooks to the African trade carefully noted the color and shape of beads, the pattern of textiles, the type of guns, and the sort of metals that were in demand on each section of the coast (see Map 19.3). Although African preferences for merchandise varied, textiles, hardware, and guns were in high demand. Of the goods the Royal African Company traded in West Africa in the 1680s, over 60 percent were Indian and European textiles and 30 percent were hardware and weaponry. In the eighteenth century, tobacco and rum from the Americas became welcome imports.

PRIMARY SOURCE: A Voyage to New Calabar River in the Year 1699 Learn about the slave trade in West Africa, from a Frenchman on an English slave-trading expedition.

Both Europeans and Africans attempted to drive the best bargain for themselves and sometimes engaged in deceitful practices. The strength of the African bargaining position, however, may be inferred from the fact that as the demand for slaves rose, so too did their price in Africa. In the course of the eighteenth century the value of goods needed to purchase a slave on the Gold Coast doubled and in some places tripled or quadrupled.

African governments on the Gold and Slave Coasts forced Europeans to observe African trading customs and prevented them from taking control of African territory. Rivalry among

e Interactive Map

MAP 19.3 **West African States and Trade, 1500–1800** The Atlantic and the trans-Saharan trade brought West Africans new goods and promoted the rise of powerful states and trading communities. The Moroccan invasion of Songhai and Portuguese colonization of the Angolan ports of Luanda and Benguela showed the political dangers of such relations.

European nations, each of which established its own trading "castles" along the Gold Coast, also reduced bargaining strength because Africans could shop for better deals among these competitors. In 1700 the head of the Dutch East India Company in West Africa, Willem Bosman (VIL-uhm boos-MAHN), bemoaned the fact that, to stay competitive against other European traders, his company had to include large quantities of muskets and gunpowder in the goods it exchanged, thereby adding to Africans' military power.

Bosman also related that his agents had to first pay the local king a substantial customs duty before buying slaves at Whydah and then had to pay a premium price for the slaves. By African standards, Whydah was a rather small kingdom controlling only the port and its immediate hinterland. In 1727, Dahomey (dah-HOH-mee), strengthened militarily by firearms acquired in the slave trade, annexed Whydah.

Two other regional powers, the kingdoms of Oyo (aw-YOH) and Asante (uh-SHAN-tee), also participated in the Atlantic trade, but neither kingdom was as dependent on it as Dahomey. Overseas trade formed a relatively modest part of the economies of these large and populous states, which maintained extensive overland trade with their northern neighbors and with states across the Sahara. Like the great medieval empires of the western Sudan, Oyo and Asante grew more powerful from external trade but were not dependent on it. In 1730, the Oyo kingdom overran Dahomey, forcing it to pay an annual tribute to keep its independence.

How did African kings and merchants obtain slaves for sale? Bosman dismissed misconceptions prevailing in Europe in his day. "Not a few in our country," he wrote to a friend in 1700, "fondly imagine that parents here sell their children, men their wives, and one brother the other. But those who think so, do deceive themselves; for this never happens on any other account but that of necessity, or some great crime; but most of the slaves that are offered to us are prisoners of war, which are sold by the victors as their booty."[1] His statement confirms other accounts claiming that prisoners of war were the most common source of slaves, but it is harder to prove that capturing slaves for export was a main cause of wars. "Here and there," conclude two respected historians of Africa, "there are indications that captives taken in the later and more peripheral stages of these wars were exported overseas, but it would seem that the main impetus of conquest was only incidentally concerned with the slave-trade."[2]

An early-nineteenth-century king of Asante had a similar view: "I cannot make war to catch slaves in the bush, like a thief. My ancestors never did so. But if I fight a king, and kill him when he is insolent, then certainly I must have his gold, and his slaves, and his people are mine too. Do not the white kings act like this?"[3] English rulers had indeed sentenced seventeenth-century Scottish and Irish prisoners to forced labor in the West Indies. One may imagine that neither African nor European prisoners shared their kings' view that such actions were legitimate.

The Bight of Biafra and Angola

In the eighteenth century the slave trade expanded eastward to the Bight (bite) of Biafra. In contrast to the Gold and Slave Coasts, where strong kingdoms predominated, the densely populated interior of the Bight of Biafra contained no large states. Even so, powerful merchant princes of the coastal ports made European traders give them rich presents.

The Trade Expands

Using a network of markets and inland routes, regional merchants supplied European slave traders at the coast with debtors, victims of kidnapping, and convicted criminals. As the volume of the Atlantic trade along the Bight of Biafra expanded in the late eighteenth century, some inland markets evolved into giant fairs with different sections specializing in slaves and imported goods. In the 1780s an English ship's doctor reported that African merchants collected slaves at fairs in the interior and that groups of twelve hundred to fifteen hundred enslaved men and women were then sent to the coast from a single fair.[4]

The local context of the Atlantic trade was different south of the Congo estuary at Angola, the greatest source of slaves for the Atlantic trade (see Map 19.2). This was also the one place along

Luanda, Angola Luanda was founded by the Portuguese in 1575 and became the center of the slave trade to Brazil. In this eighteenth-century print the city's warehouses and commercial buildings line the city streets. In the foreground captives are dragged to the port for shipment to the Western Hemisphere.

New York Public Library/Art Resource, NY

the Atlantic coast where a single European nation, Portugal, controlled a significant amount of territory. Except for a brief period when the Dutch exercised control in the seventeenth century, Portuguese residents of the main ports of Luanda and Benguela (ben-GWAY-luh) served as middlemen between the caravans that arrived from the interior and the ships that crossed from Brazil. From these coastal cities Afro-Portuguese traders guided large caravans of trade goods inland to exchange for slaves at special markets.

Many of the slaves sold at these markets were prisoners of war captured by expanding African states. By the late eighteenth century prisoners captured in wars fought as far away as 600 to 800 miles (1,000 to 1,300 kilometers) were carried to the ports for transportation. Many were victims of wars of expansion fought by the giant federation of Lunda kingdoms. As elsewhere in Africa, prisoners sold as slaves seem to have been a byproduct of African wars, rather than the objective of the warring parties.

Research has identified a link between severe eighteenth-century droughts and the development of the Angolan slave trade. The environmental crisis in the hinterland drove famished refugees to better-watered areas.[5] Powerful African leaders gained control of these refugees in return for supplying them with food and water. These leaders valued refugee children, who would quickly assimilate, and adult women, who were valued as food producers and for reproduction. They often sold adult male refugees as slaves because they were more likely than women and children to escape or challenge the ruler's authority. They used the textiles, weapons, and alcohol they received in return for slaves as gifts to attract new followers and to cement the loyalty of their established allies. The most successful became heads of powerful new states, stabilizing areas devastated by war and drought and repopulating them with the refugees and prisoners.

Although the organization of Atlantic trade varied from African region to region, it expanded and prospered because both European merchants and African elites benefited. African rulers and merchants exported slaves and other products to obtain foreign goods that made them wealthier and more powerful. Most of the exported slaves were prisoners taken in wars associated with African state growth. But strong African states or powerful merchant communities also proved better able to defend African territory and limit European economic advantages. The Africans who gained from this trade were the rich and powerful few. Many more Africans were losers in the exchanges.

Africa's European and Islamic Contacts

The ways in which sub-Saharan Africans established new contacts with Europe paralleled their much older pattern of relations with the Islamic world. But there were striking similarities and differences in Africans' political, commercial, and cultural interactions with these two external influences between 1500 and 1800.

During the three and a half centuries of contact up to 1800, Africans ceded very little territory to Europeans. Local African rulers kept close tabs on the European trading posts they permitted along the Gold and Slave Coasts and collected lucrative rents and fees. Aside from some uninhabited islands off the Atlantic coast, Europeans established colonial beachheads in only two places, the Portuguese colony of Angola and the Dutch East India Company's Cape Colony at the southern tip of the continent. The Dutch colony was tied to Indian Ocean trade, not to the Atlantic trade, and, unlike Angola, did not export slaves. Most the Cape Colony's 25,750 slaves in 1793 were from Madagascar, South Asia, and the East Indies, not Africa.

North Africa had become a part of the Islamic world in the first century of Islamic expansion. Sub-Saharan Africans gradually learned of Muslim beliefs and practices from traders who crossed the Sahara from North Africa or who sailed from the Middle East to the Swahili trading cities of East Africa. In the sixteenth century the new Islamic Ottoman Empire annexed all of North Africa except Morocco, while Ethiopia lost extensive territory to other Muslim conquerors.

Until 1590 the Sahara remained an effective buttress against invasion from powerful northern states. The **Songhai** (song-GAH-ee) Empire of West Africa challenged the status quo when it pushed its frontier into the Sahara from the south. Ruled by an indigenous Muslim dynasty, Songhai drew its wealth from the trans-Saharan trade (see Map 19.3). This expansion led the kingdom of Morocco to challenge Songhai by sending a military expedition of four thousand

West Africa and Islam

Songhai A people, language, kingdom, and empire in western Sudan in West Africa. At its height in the sixteenth century, the Muslim Songhai Empire stretched from the Atlantic to the land of the Hausa and was a major player in the trans-Saharan trade.

Hausa An agricultural and trading people of central Sudan in West Africa. Aside from their brief incorporation into the Songhai Empire, the Hausa city-states remained autonomous until the Sokoto Caliphate conquered them in the early nineteenth century.

The Islamic Slave Trade

Bornu A powerful West African kingdom at the southern edge of the Sahara in the Central Sudan, which was important in trans-Saharan trade and in the spread of Islam. Also known as Kanem-Bornu, it endured from the ninth century to the end of the nineteenth.

men south across the desert. Although half the invading force perished, the survivors armed with firearms defeated Songhai's army of forty thousand in 1591. While Morocco was never able to annex the western Sudan, its forces extracted a massive tribute in slaves and goods from the local population and imposed tolls on trade for the next two centuries.

With Morocco's destruction of Songhai, the **Hausa** trading cities in the central Sudan attracted most of the caravans bringing textiles, hardware, and weapons across the Sahara. The goods the Hausa imported and distributed through their trading networks were similar to those that coastal African traders commanded from the Atlantic trade, except for the absence of alcohol, prohibited to Muslims. The goods they sent back in return also resembled the major African exports into the Atlantic: gold, textiles and leather goods, and slaves.

Few statistics of the slave trade to the Islamic north exist, but the size of the trade seems to have been substantial, if smaller than the transatlantic trade at its peak. Between 1600 and 1800 slave traders sent about 850,000 slaves to Muslim North Africa (see Map 19.2). A nearly equal number of slaves from sub-Saharan Africa entered the Islamic Middle East and India by way of the Red Sea and the Indian Ocean.

In contrast to the plantation slavery of the Americas, most African slaves in the Islamic world were soldiers and servants. In the late seventeenth and eighteenth centuries Morocco's rulers employed an army of 150,000 African slaves, trusting their loyalty more than that of recruits from their own lands. Moroccans also used slaves on sugar plantations, as servants, and as artisans. Unlike in the Americas, the majority of African slaves in the Islamic world were women who served wealthy households as concubines, servants, and entertainers. The trans-Saharan slave trade also included a much higher proportion of children than the Atlantic trade.

The central Sudanese kingdom of **Bornu** illustrates several aspects of trans-Saharan contacts. Ruled by the same dynasty since the ninth century, this Muslim state had grown and expanded in the sixteenth century as the result of guns imported from the Ottoman Empire. Bornu retained many captives from its wars or sold them as slaves to the north in return for the firearms and horses that underpinned the kingdom's military power. One Bornu king, Mai Ali, conspicuously displayed his kingdom's new power and wealth while on four pilgrimages to

Traders Approaching Timbuktu As they had done for centuries, traders brought their wares to this ancient desert-edge city. Timbuktu's mosques tower above the ordinary dwellings of the fabled city.

The Art Archive

Mecca between 1642 and 1667. On the last, an enormous entourage of slaves—said to number fifteen thousand—accompanied him.

Like Christians of this period, Muslims saw no moral impediment to owning or trading in slaves. Indeed, Islam considered enslaving "pagans" to be a meritorious act because it brought them into the faith. Although Islam forbade the enslavement of Muslims, Muslim rulers in Bornu, Hausaland, and elsewhere were not strict observers of that rule (see Diversity and Dominance: Slavery in West Africa and the Americas).

Sub-Saharan Africans had much longer exposure to Islamic cultural influences than to European cultural influences. Scholars and merchants learned to use the Arabic language to communicate with visiting North Africans and to read the Quran. Islamic beliefs and practices as well as Islamic legal and administrative systems were influential in African trading cities on the southern edge of the Sahara and on the Swahili coast. In some places Islam had extended its influence among rural people, but in 1750 it was still very much an urban religion.

European cultural influence in Africa was more limited. Some coastal Africans had shown an interest in Western Christianity after contacts with the Portuguese, but in the 1700s only Angola had a significant number of Christians. Coastal African traders found it useful to learn European languages, but African languages continued to dominate inland trade routes. A few African merchants sent their sons to Europe to learn European ways. One of these young men, Philip Quaque (KWAH-kay), who was educated in England, was ordained as a priest in the Church of England and became the official chaplain of the Cape Coast Castle from 1766 until his death in 1816.

Atlantic and Muslim Slave Trades Compared

Overall, how different and similar were the material effects of Islam and Europe in sub-Saharan Africa by 1800? While Muslims and Europeans obtained slaves from sub-Saharan Africa, the European trade was larger. The Atlantic trade carried about 8 million Africans to the Americas between 1550 and 1800. During this period the Islamic trade to North Africa and the Middle East transported perhaps 2 million African captives. What were the effects on Africa's population? Scholars generally agree on three points: (1) even at the peak of the trade in the 1700s, sub-Saharan Africa's overall population remained very large; (2) localities that contributed heavily to the slave trade, such as lands near the Slave Coast, suffered acute losses; (3) the ability of a population to recover from losses was related to the proportion of fertile women who were shipped away. The fact that Africans sold fewer women than men into the larger Atlantic trade somewhat reduced the long-term demographic effects of this larger trade.

The slave trade had a mixed impact on sub-Saharan economies. Africans were very particular about what they received in exchange for slaves, and their imports reflected their tastes and needs. The limited volume of manufactured imports could not overwhelm established African weavers, metalworkers, and other producers, and some imported products like textiles and metal bars stimulated the local production of tools and clothing. However, while African as well as European states benefited by taxing this trade, most of the economic benefits went to European nations and to their American colonies.

Profits from transporting and selling slaves mostly went to European merchants and ship owners. European manufacturers, like the producers of textiles and metal goods, profited as well. But Europe's American colonies were the major beneficiaries of the African slave trade. With Amerindian population diminished by epidemics and European immigration inadequate to develop American resources, it was the forced labor of African slaves that made possible the enormous wealth produced in a vast region that spread from the Chesapeake to the Río de la Plata. This wealth accelerated the rapid expansion of Western capitalism in the seventeenth and eighteenth centuries, a period that witnessed the political and economic decline of the Ottoman Empire, the dominant state of the Middle East, and other Muslim kingdoms (see Chapter 20).

SECTION REVIEW

- Powerful rulers and merchants protected African territory from Europeans and imposed control over trade terms.
- Most slaves exported to the Western Hemisphere were prisoners of war.
- African trade and cultural relations with European nations paralleled already-established relations with Muslim regions.
- The African slave trade with the Muslim world was smaller than the Atlantic slave trade but lasted longer.
- Most African slaves sent to the Islamic world served as soldiers or servants.

Slavery in West Africa and the Americas

Social diversity was common in Africa, and the domination of masters over slaves was a feature of many societies. Ahmad Baba (1556–1627) was an outstanding Islamic scholar in the city of Timbuktu. He came from an old Muslim family of the city. In about 1615 he replied to some questions that had been sent to him. His answers reveal a great deal about the official and unofficial condition of slavery in the Sudan of West Africa, especially in the Hausa states of Kano and Katsina (see Map 19.3).

You asked: What have you to say concerning the slaves imported from the lands of the Sudan whose people are acknowledged to be Muslims, such as Bornu, . . . Kano, Goa, Songhay, Katsina and others among whom Islam is widespread? Is it permissible to possess them [as slaves] or not?

Know—may God grant us and you success—that these lands, as you have stated are Muslim. . . . But close to each of them are lands in which are unbelievers whom the Muslim inhabitants of these lands raid. Some of these unbelievers are under the Muslims' protection and pay them [taxes]. . . . Sometimes there is war between the Muslim sultans of some of these lands and one attacks the other, taking as many prisoners as he can and selling the captive though he is a free-born Muslim. . . . This is a common practice among them in Hausaland; Katsina raids Kano, as do others, though their language is one and their situations parallel; the only difference they recognize among themselves is that so-and-so is a born Muslim and so-and-so is a born unbeliever. . . .

Whoever is taken prisoner in a state of unbelief may become someone's property, whoever he is, as opposed to those who have become Muslims of their own free will . . . and may not be possessed at all.

A little over a century later another African provided information about enslavement practices in the Western Sudan. Ayuba Suleiman Diallo (ah-YOO-bah SOO-lay-mahn JAH-loh) (1701–?) of the state of Bondu some 200 miles from the Gambia River was enslaved and transported to Maryland, where he was a slave from 1731 to 1733. When an Englishman learned of Ayuba's literacy in Arabic, he recorded his life story, anglicizing his name to Job Solomon. According to the account, slaves in Bondu did much of the hard work, while men of Ayuba's class were free to devote themselves to the study of Islamic texts.

In February, 1730, Job's father hearing of an English ship at Gambia River, sent him, with two servants to attend him, to sell two Negroes, and to buy paper, and some other necessaries; but desired him not to venture over the river, because the country of the Mandingoes, who are enemies to the people of Futa, lies on the other side. Job not agreeing with Captain Pike (who commanded the ship, lying then at Gambia, in the service of Captain Henry Hunt, brother to Mr. William Hunt, merchant, in Little Tower-street, London) sent back the two servants to acquaint his father with it, and to let him know that he intended to go no farther. Accordingly . . . he crossed the River Gambia, and disposed of his Negroes for some cows. As he was returning home, he stopped for some refreshment at the house of an old acquaintance; and the weather being hot, he hung up his arms in the house, while he refreshed himself. . . . It happened that a company of the Mandingoes, . . . passing by at that time, and observing him unarmed, rushed in, to the number of seven or eight at once, at a back door, and pinioned Job, before he could get his arms, together with his interpreter, who is a slave in Maryland still. They then shaved their heads and beards, which Job and his man resented as the highest indignity; tho' the Mandingoes meant no more by it, than to make them appear like slaves taken in war. On the 27th of February, 1730, they carried them to Captain Pike at Gambia, who purchased them; and on the first of March they were put on board. Soon after Job found means to acquaint Captain Pike that he was the same person that came to trade with him a few days before, and after what manner he had been taken. Upon this Captain Pike gave him free leave to redeem himself and his man; and Job sent to an acquaintance of his father's, near Gambia, who promised to send to Job's father, to inform him of what had happened, that he might take some course to have him set at liberty. But it being a fortnight's [two weeks'] journey between that friend's house and his father's, and the ship sailing in about a week after, Job was brought with the rest of the slaves to Annapolis in Maryland, and delivered to Mr. Vachell Denton. . . .

Mr. Vachell Denton sold Job to one Mr. Tolsey in Kent Island in Maryland, who put him to work in making tobacco; but he was soon convinced that Job had never been used to such labour. He every day showed more and more uneasiness under this exercise, and at last grew sick, being no way able to bear it; so his master was obliged to find easier work for him, and therefore put him to tend the cattle. Job would often leave the cattle, and withdraw into the woods to pray; but a white boy frequently watched him, and whilst he was at his devotion would mock him and throw dirt in his face. This very much disturbed Job, and added considerably to his other misfor-

CONCLUSION

European merchants and investors played a central role in the creation of the Atlantic system. European merchants had expanded trade in the century before Columbus, trading over longer distances and using new credit mechanisms to facilitate transactions. They had engaged the tunes; all which were increased by his ignorance of the English language, which prevented his complaining, or telling his case to any person about him. Grown in some measure desperate, by reason of his present hardships, he resolved to travel at a venture; thinking he might possibly be taken up by some master, who would use him better, or otherwise meet with some lucky accident, to divert or abate his grief. Accordingly, he travelled thro' the woods, till he came to the County of Kent, upon Delaware Bay. . . . There is a law in force, throughout the [mid-Atlantic] colonies . . . as far as Boston in New England, viz. that any Negroe, or white servant who is not known in the county, or has no pass, may be secured by any person, and kept in the common [jail], till the master of such servant shall fetch him. Therefore Job being able to give no account of himself, was put in prison there.

This happened about the beginning of June 1731, when I, who was attending the courts there, and heard of Job, went with several gentlemen to the [jailer's] house, being a tavern, and desired to see him. He was brought into the tavern to us, but could not speak one word of English. Upon our talking and making signs to him, he wrote a line to two before us, and when he read it, pronounced the words Allah and Mahommed; by which, and his refusing a glass of wine we offered him, we perceived he was a Mahometan [Muslim], but could not imagine of what country he was, or how he got thither; for by his affable carriage, and the easy composure of his countenance, we could perceive he was no common slave.

When Job had been some time confined, an old Negroe man, who lived in that neighborhood, and could speak the Jalloff [Wolof] language, which Job also understood, went to him, and conversed with him. By this Negroe the keeper was informed to whom Job belonged, and what was the cause of his leaving his master. The keeper thereupon wrote to his master, who soon after fetched him home, and was much kinder to him than before; allowing him place to pray in, and in some other conveniences, in order to make his slavery as easy as possible. Yet slavery and confinement was by no means agreeable to

JOB, SON OF SOLLIMAN DGIALLO, HIGH PRIEST OF BONDA IN THE COUNTRY OF FOOTA, AFRICA.

British Library Board

Job, who had never been used to it; he therefore wrote a letter in Arabick to his father, acquainting him with his misfortunes, hoping he might yet find means to redeem him. . . . It happened that this letter was seen by James Oglethorpe, Esq. [founder of the colony of Georgia and director of the Royal African Company]; who, according to his usual goodness and generosity, took compassion on Job, and [bought him from his master]; his master being very willing to part with him, as finding him no ways fit for his business.

In spring 1733 Job's benefactors took him to England, teaching him passable English during the voyage, and introduced him to the English gentry. Job attracted such attention that local men took up a collection to buy his freedom and pay his debts, and they also introduced him at the royal court. In 1735 Job returned to Gambia in a Royal African Company ship, richly clothed and accompanied by many gifts.

QUESTIONS FOR ANALYSIS

1. Since Ahmad Baba points out that Islamic law permitted a Muslim to raid and enslave non-Muslims, do you think that the non-Muslim Mandinka (Mandingoes) would have considered it justifiable to enslave Ayuba, since he was a Muslim?

2. Which aspects of Ayuba Suleiman's experiences of enslavement were normal, and which unusual?

3. How different might Ayuba's experiences of slavery have been had he been sold in Jamaica rather than Maryland?

4. How strictly was the ban against enslaving Muslims observed in Hausaland?

Source: Thomas Hodgkin, ed., *Nigerian Perspectives: An Historical Anthology*, 2nd ed. (London: Oxford University Press, 1975), 154–156; Thomas Bluett, *Some Memoirs of the Life of Job, the Son of Solomon the High Priest of Boonda in Africa* (London: Richard Ford, 1734), 16–24.

markets of Asia through Muslim middlemen and initiated the first tentative contacts with African markets. By the seventeenth century a more confident and adventurous European investor class was ready to promote colonial production and long-distance trade in a much more aggressive way. The development of banks, stock exchanges, and chartered companies supported these new ambitions.

The new Atlantic trading system had great importance in world history. In the first phase of their expansion Europeans conquered and colonized the Americas and captured major Indian Ocean trade routes. The development of the Atlantic system showed their ability to move beyond capturing the benefits of existing systems to create a major new trading network. Beginning in the seventeenth century, the English, Dutch, and French created new colonies in the Caribbean to compete with earlier colonies created by the Spanish and Portuguese (see Chapter 18). While these colonies remained fragile for decades, settlers found ways to profitably produce goods sought by European consumers. Tobacco was the first, but sugar soon supplanted it.

The establishment of plantation societies was not just a matter of replacing native vegetation with alien plants and native peoples with Europeans and Africans. More fundamentally, it made these once-isolated islands part of a dynamic trading system controlled from Europe. The West Indies was not the only place affected. Brazil, large parts of Spanish Central and South America, and the southern region of British North America developed similar linkages, producing sugar, cacao, cotton, coffee, and indigo and using slave labor.

Despite the central importance of their shared dependence on export markets and African slaves, there were important differences among Europe's American tropical colonies. Only the English experimented with indentured labor on a large scale. But like the colonies of the Portuguese, Dutch, and French, they soon depended on African slave labor. Joint-stock companies and individual investors were crucial to the English colonies. The French entered the process late, but the French state and French monopoly companies quickly produced a massive flow of slaves while securing a profitable home market for the sugar of Saint Domingue and other colonies. After the Dutch attacked but failed to hold Portugal's sugar-producing colony of Brazil and the slave-exporting colony of Angola, they became influential in the transfer of sugar technology and the expansion of the slave trade. While Spain had introduced sugar to the Caribbean and imported African slaves in the early sixteenth century, its most important Caribbean colony, Cuba, joined the sugar revolution late, becoming the major destination for the slave trade and the major producer of sugar by 1820.

While Africa played an essential role in the Atlantic system, importing trade goods and exporting slaves to the Americas, the Atlantic system dominated Europe's American colonies much more comprehensively. Africans remained in control of their continent and interacted culturally and politically more with the Islamic world than with the Atlantic.

Sub-Saharan Africa had long-established trade connections with the Islamic world that included the sale of slaves. These trade relationships facilitated the spread of Islam to sub-Saharan Africa and the creation of Islamic states like Mali and Songhai (see Chapter 14). The volume of the Atlantic trade was much larger than the Islamic slave trade, but the Islamic trade persisted after reformers ended the Atlantic trade (see Chapter 24). Between 1550 and 1800 four slaves crossed the Atlantic to European colonies for every slave carried across the Sahara. While more males were carried across the Atlantic, the Islamic trade took more women and children, and few slaves in the Islamic region were subjected to the brutal labor conditions of the West Indian plantations.

KEY TERMS

Atlantic system p. 505
chartered
　companies p. 506
Dutch West India
　Company p. 506

plantocracy p. 510
driver p. 510
seasoning p. 512
manumission p. 514
maroon p. 515

capitalism p. 515
mercantilism p. 516
Royal African
　Company p. 516
Atlantic Circuit p. 516

Middle Passage p. 516
Songhai p. 523
Hausa p. 524
Bornu p. 524

EBOOK AND WEBSITE RESOURCES

e Primary Sources

The Interesting Narrative of Olaudah Equiano and Written by Himself

A Voyage to New Calabar River in the Year 1699

e Interactive Maps

Map 19.1 The Atlantic Economy

Map 19.2 The African Slave Trade, 1500–1800

Map 19.3 West African States and Trade, 1500–1800

Plus flashcards, practice quizzes, and more. Go to: www.cengage.com/history/bullietearthpeople5e

SUGGESTED READING

Blackburn, Robin. *The Making of New World Slavery*. 1997. A reliable introduction to the topic.

Curtin, Philip D. *The Rise and Fall of the Plantation Complex*. 1990. Excellent introduction to the Atlantic system.

Davis, David Brion. *Inhuman Bondage. The Rise and Fall of Slavery in the New World*. 2006. While centered on the American South, Davis provides a challenging summary of the larger implications of slavery in the Americas.

Davis, David Brion. *The Problem of Slavery in Western Culture*. 1966. A classic study from a broad perspective.

Eltis, David. *The Rise of African Slavery in the Americas*. 2000.

Heywood, Linda M., and John K. Thornton. *Central Africans, Atlantic Creoles, and the Foundation of the Americas, 1585–1660*. Examines the cultural influences of Central Africans in the development of the Americas.

Klein, Herbert S. *African Slavery in Latin America and the Caribbean*. 1986. A fine synthesis of research on New World slavery, including North American slave systems.

Lovejoy, Paul. *Transformations in Slavery: A History of Slavery in Africa*, 2nd ed. 2000. Contains recent research on slavery and the African, Atlantic, and Muslim slave trades.

Manning, Patrick. *Slavery and African Life: Occidental, Oriental, and African Slave Trades*. 1990. A reliable comparison of the Atlantic and Muslim slave trades.

Northrup, David. *Africa's Discovery of Europe, 1450–1850*. 2002. An exploration of connections of African communities to the Atlantic world.

Northrup, David, ed. *The Atlantic Slave Trade*, 2nd ed. 2002. A collection of debates on the slave trade.

Ogot, B. A., ed. *UNESCO General History of Africa*, vol. 5. 1992. A good place for students to begin research on African topics.

Oliver, Roland, and Anthony Atmore. *The African Middle Ages, 1400–1800*, 2nd ed. 2003. A useful summary of African history in this period.

Price, Richard, ed. *Maroon Societies: Rebel Slave Communities in the Americas*, 2nd ed. 1979. The classic study of slave runaway communities in the Caribbean.

Thomas, Hugh. *The Slave Trade: The Story of the Atlantic Slave Trade, 1440–1870*. 1999. This is one of the best comprehensive treatments of the slave trade.

Thornton, John. *Africa and Africans in the Making of the Atlantic World, 1400–1800*, 2nd ed. 1998. Examines cultural connections among African communities on both sides of the Atlantic.

Trimingham, J. Spencer. *The Influence of Islam upon Africa*. 1968.

Wallerstein, Immanuel. *The Modern World-System*, 3 vols. (1974–1989). An examination of the global context of early modern capitalism.

Webb, James L. A., Jr. *Desert Frontier: Ecological and Economic Change Along the Western Sahel, 1600–1850*. 1995. A useful introduction to Islam's cultural and commercial contacts with sub-Saharan Africa.

NOTES

1. Willem Bosman, *A New and Accurate Description of Guinea, etc.* (London, 1705), quoted in David Northrup, ed., *The Atlantic Slave Trade* (Lexington, MA: D. C. Heath, 1994), 72.

2. Roland Oliver and Anthony Atmore, *The African Middle Ages, 1400–1800* (Cambridge, England: Cambridge University Press, 1981), 100.

3. King Osei Bonsu, quoted in Northrup, ed., *The Atlantic Slave Trade*, 93.

4. Alexander Falconbridge, *Account of the Slave Trade on the Coast of Africa* (London: J. Phillips, 1788), 12.

5. Joseph C. Miller, "The Significance of Drought, Disease, and Famine in the Agriculturally Marginal Zones of West-Central Africa," *Journal of African History*, 23 (1982): 17–61.

Funeral Procession of Suleiman the Magnificent   Each Ottoman sultan wore a distinctive turban, hence the visible turban representing the body in the hearse.

Visit the website and ebook for additional study materials and interactive tools: www.cengage.com/history/bullietearthpeople5e

Southwest Asia and the Indian Ocean, 1500–1750

I n 1541 a woman named Sabah appeared before an Ottoman judge in the town of Aintab in southern Turkey to answer several charges: that she had brought men and women together illegally and that she had fostered heresy. In her court testimony, she stated the following:

> I gather girls and brides and women in my home. I negotiated with Ibrahim b. Nazih and the two youths who are his apprentices, and in exchange for paying them a month's fee, I had them come every day to the girls and brides in my house and I had them preach and give instruction. There are no males at those sessions besides the said Ibrahim and his apprentices; there are only women and girls and young brides. This kind of thing is what I have always done for a living.[1]

Two male neighbors testified differently:

> She holds gatherings of girls and brides and women in her home. . . . While she says that she has [Ibrahim] preach, she actually has him speak evil things. She has him conduct spiritual conversations with these girls and brides. . . . [I]n the ceremonies, the girls and brides and women spin around waving their hands, and they bring themselves into a trancelike state by swaying and dancing. They perform the ceremonies according to Kizilbash teachings. We too have wives and families, and we are opposed to illegal activities like this.[2]

The judge made no finding on the charge of heresy, but he ordered Sabah to be publicly humiliated and banished from town for unlawfully mixing the sexes. Ibrahim was also banished.

This uncommon story taken from Ottoman religious court records sheds light on several aspects of daily life in a provincial town. It provides an example of a woman making her living by arranging religious instruction for other women. It also demonstrates the willingness of neighbors, in this case males, to complain in court about activities they considered immoral. And its suggestion that Sabah was promoting the qizilbash heresy, which at that time was considered a state threat because it was the ideology of the enemy Safavid Empire next door, shows that townspeople thought it plausible that women could act to promote religious doctrines.

Studies of everyday life through court records and other state and nonstate documents are a recent development in Ottoman and Safavid history. They produce an image of these societies that differs greatly from the pomp and formality conveyed by European travelers and official histories. As a consequence, accounts

- ■ How did the Ottoman Empire rise to power, and what factors contributed to its transformation?
- ■ How did the Safavid Empire both resemble and differ from its neighbors?
- ■ How did the Mughal Empire combine Muslim and Hindu elements into an effective state?
- ■ What role does maritime history play in the political and economic life of this period?

of capricious and despotic actions taken by shahs and sultans are increasingly being balanced by stories of common people, who were much more concerned with the maintenance of a sound legal and moral order than were some of the denizens of the imperial palaces. The doings of rulers remain an important historical focus, of course, but stories about ordinary folk perhaps give a better picture of the habits and mores of the majority of the population.

THE OTTOMAN EMPIRE, TO 1750

Ottoman Empire Islamic state founded by Osman in northwestern Anatolia ca. 1300. After the fall of the Byzantine Empire, the Ottoman Empire was based at Istanbul (formerly Constantinople) from 1453 to 1922. It encompassed lands in the Middle East, North Africa, the Caucasus, and eastern Europe.

The most long-lived of the post-Mongol Muslim empires was the **Ottoman Empire**, founded around 1300 (see Map 20.1). By extending Islamic conquests into eastern Europe, starting in the late fourteenth century, and by taking Syria and Egypt from the Mamluk rulers in the early sixteenth, the Ottomans seemed to recreate the might of the original Islamic caliphate, the empire established by the Muslim Arab conquests in the seventh century. However, the empire was actually more like the new centralized monarchies of France and Spain (see Chapter 17) than any medieval model.

Enduring more than five centuries, until 1922, the Ottoman Empire survived several periods of wrenching change, some caused by internal problems, others by the growing power of European adversaries. These periods of change reveal the problems faced by huge land-based empires around the world.

Expansion and Frontiers

Established around 1300, the Ottoman Empire grew from a tiny state in northwestern Anatolia because of three factors: (1) the shrewdness of its founder, Osman (from which the name *Ottoman* comes), and his descendants, (2) control of a strategic link between Europe and Asia on the Dardanelles strait, and (3) the creation of an army that took advantage of the traditional skills of the Turkish cavalryman and the new military possibilities presented by gunpowder.

The Battle of Kosovo

At first, Ottoman armies concentrated on Christian enemies in Greece and the Balkans, in 1389 conquering a strong Serbian kingdom at the Battle of Kosovo (KO-so-vo). Much of southeastern Europe and Anatolia was under the control of the sultans by 1402. In 1453, Sultan Mehmed II, "the Conqueror," laid siege to Constantinople. His forces used enormous cannon to bash in the city's walls, dragged warships over a high hill from the Bosporus strait to the city's inner harbor to get around its sea defenses, and finally penetrated the city's land walls through a series of direct infantry assaults. The fall of Constantinople—henceforth commonly known as Istanbul—brought to an end over eleven hundred years of Byzantine rule and made the Ottomans seem invincible.

Suleiman the Magnificent

Suleiman the Magnificent The most illustrious sultan of the Ottoman Empire (r. 1520–1566); also known as Suleiman Kanuni, "The Lawgiver." He significantly expanded the empire in the Balkans and eastern Mediterranean.

Selim (seh-LEEM) I, "the Grim," conquered Egypt and Syria in 1516 and 1517, making the Red Sea the Ottomans' southern frontier. His son Suleiman (SOO-lay-man) the Magnificent (r. 1520–1566), presided over the greatest Ottoman assault on Christian Europe. Suleiman seemed unstoppable: he conquered Belgrade in 1521, expelled the Knights of the Hospital of St. John from the island of Rhodes the following year, and laid siege to Vienna in 1529. Vienna was saved by the need to retreat before the onset of winter more than by military action. In later centuries, Ottoman historians looked back on the reign of Suleiman as the period when the imperial system worked to perfection, and they spoke of it as the golden age of Ottoman greatness.

While Ottoman armies pressed deeper and deeper into eastern Europe, the sultans also sought to control the Mediterranean. Between 1453 and 1502, the Ottomans fought the opening rounds of a two-century war with Venice, the most powerful of Italy's commercial city-states. The initial fighting left Venice in control of its lucrative islands for another century. But it also left Venice a reduced military power compelled to pay tribute to the Ottomans.

The Portuguese Threat

In the early sixteenth century, merchants from southern India and Sumatra sent emissaries to Istanbul requesting naval support against the Portuguese. The Ottomans responded vigorously to Portuguese threats close to their territories, such as at Aden at the southern entrance

CHRONOLOGY

	Ottoman Empire	Safavid Empire	Mughal Empire
1500		1502–1524 Shah Ismail establishes Safavid rule in Iran	
	1516–1517 Selim I conquers Egypt and Syria		
	1520–1566 Reign of Suleiman the Magnificent; peak of Ottoman Empire		1526 Babur defeats last sultan of Delhi
	1529 First Ottoman siege of Vienna		
			1556–1605 Akbar rules in Agra; peak of Mughal Empire
	1571 Ottoman naval defeat at Lepanto		
		1587–1629 Reign of Shah Abbas the Great; peak of Safavid Empire	
1600			
	1610 End of Anatolian revolts		
			1658–1707 Aurangzeb imposes conservative Islamic regime
1700			
		1722 Afghan invaders topple last Safavid shah	
	1730 Janissary revolt begins period of Ottoman conservatism	1736–1747 Nadir Shah temporarily reunites Iran; invades India (1739)	1739 Iranians under Nadir Shah sack Delhi

Robert Frerck/Woodfin Camp & Associates

Aya Sofya Mosque in Istanbul   Originally a Byzantine cathedral, Aya Sofya (in Greek, Hagia Sophia) was transformed into a mosque after 1453, and four minarets were added. It then became a model for subsequent Ottoman mosques. To the right behind it is the Bosporus strait dividing Europe and Asia, to the left the Golden Horn inlet separating the old city of Istanbul from the newer parts. The gate to the Ottoman sultan's palace is to the right of the mosque. The pointed tower to the left of the dome is part of the palace.

Ottoman Empire, 1520
Territory added, 1566
Safavid Empire, ca. 1600
Mughal Empire, 1530
Territory added, 1656
Major battle

© Cengage Learning

MAP 20.1 **Muslim Empires in the Sixteenth and Seventeenth Centuries** Iran, a Shi'ite state flanked by Sunni Ottomans on the west and Sunni Mughals on the east, had the least exposure to European influences. Ottoman expansion across the southern Mediterranean Sea intensified European fears of Islam. The areas of strongest Mughal control dictated that Islam's spread into Southeast Asia would be heavily influenced by merchants and religious figures from Gujarat instead of from eastern India.

Interactive Map

to the Red Sea, but their efforts farther afield were insufficient to stifle growing Portuguese domination.

Eastern luxury products still flowed to Ottoman markets. Portuguese power was territorially limited to fortified coastal points, such as Hormuz at the entrance to the Persian Gulf, Goa in western India, and Malacca in Malaya. It never occurred to the Ottomans that a sea empire held together by flimsy ships could truly rival a great land empire fielding an army of a hundred thousand men. Why commit major resources to subduing an enemy whose main threat was a demand that merchant vessels, mostly belonging to non-Ottoman Muslims, buy protection from Portuguese attack? The Ottomans did send a small naval force to Indonesia, but they never formulated a consistent or aggressive policy with regard to political and economic developments in the Indian Ocean.

Central Institutions

The Janissary Corps

By the 1520s, the Ottoman Empire was the most powerful and best-organized state in either Europe or the Islamic world. Its military was balanced between cavalry archers, primarily

Janissaries Infantry, originally of slave origin, armed with firearms and constituting the elite of the Ottoman army from the fifteenth century until the corps was abolished in 1826.

Turks, and **Janissaries** (JAN-nih-say-rees), Christian prisoners of war induced to serve as military slaves.

Slave soldiery had a long history in Islamic lands, but the conquest of Christian territories in the Balkans in the late fourteenth century gave the Ottomans access to a new military resource. Converted to Islam, these "new troops," called *yeni cheri* in Turkish and *Janissaries* in English, gave the Ottomans unusual military flexibility. Since horseback riding and bowmanship were not part of their cultural backgrounds, they readily accepted the idea of fighting on foot and learning to use guns, which at that time were still too heavy and awkward for a horseman to load and fire. The Janissaries lived in barracks and trained all year round.

Child Levy

The process of selection for Janissary training changed early in the fifteenth century. The new system, called the *devshirme*, imposed a regular levy of male children on Christian villages in the Balkans and occasionally elsewhere. Recruited children were placed with Turkish families to learn their language and then were sent to the sultan's palace in Istanbul for an education that included instruction in Islam, military training, and, for the most talented, what we might call liberal arts. This regime, sophisticated for its time, produced not only the Janissary soldiers but also, from among the chosen few who received special training, senior military commanders and heads of government departments up to the rank of grand vizier.

The cavalrymen were supported by land grants and administered most rural areas in Anatolia and the Balkans. They maintained order, collected taxes, and reported for each summer's campaign with their horses, retainers, and supplies, all paid for from the taxes they collected. When not campaigning, they stayed at home.

Naval Warfare

A galley-equipped navy was manned by Greek, Turkish, Algerian, and Tunisian sailors, usually under the command of an admiral from one of the North African ports. The balance of the Ottoman land forces brought success to Ottoman arms in recurrent wars with the Safavids, who were much slower to adopt firearms, and in the inexorable conquest of the Balkans. Expansion by sea was less dramatic. A major expedition against Malta in the western Mediterranean failed in 1565. Combined Christian forces also achieved a massive naval victory at the Battle of Lepanto, off Greece, in 1571. But the Ottomans' resources were so extensive that in a year's time they had replaced all of the galleys sunk in that battle.

The Military Class

The Ottoman Empire became cosmopolitan in character. The sophisticated court language, Osmanli (os-MAHN-lih) (the Turkish form of *Ottoman*), shared basic grammar and vocabulary with Turkish, but Arabic and Persian elements made it distinct from the language spoken by Anatolia's nomads and villagers. Everyone who served in the military or the bureaucracy and conversed in Osmanli was considered to belong to the *askeri* (AS-keh-ree), or "military," class. Members of this class were exempt from taxes and owed their well-being to the sultan.

The Ottomans saw the sultan as providing justice for his "flock of sheep" (*raya* [RAH-yah]) and the military protecting them. In return, the raya paid the taxes that supported both the sultan and the military. In reality, the sultan's government remained comparatively isolated from the lives of most subjects. As Islam gradually became the majority religion in Balkan regions, Islamic law (the Shari'a [sha-REE-ah]) conditioned urban institutions and social life (see Diversity and Dominance: Islamic Law and Ottoman Rule). Local customs prevailed among non-Muslims and in many rural areas, and non-Muslims looked to their own religious leaders for guidance in family and spiritual matters.

Crisis of the Military State, 1585–1650

As military technology evolved, cannon and lighter-weight firearms played an ever-larger role on the battlefield. Accordingly, the size of the Janissary corps—and its cost to the government—grew steadily, and the role of the Turkish cavalry diminished. To pay the Janissaries, the sultan started reducing the number of landholding cavalrymen. Revenues previously spent on their living expenses and military equipment went directly into the imperial treasury. Inflation caused by a flood of cheap silver from the New World bankrupted many of the remaining landholders, who were restricted by law to collecting a fixed amount of taxes. Their land was returned to the state. Displaced cavalrymen, armed and unhappy, became a restive element in rural Anatolia.

Crisis and Revolt

This complicated situation resulted in revolts that devastated Anatolia between 1590 and 1610. Former landholding cavalrymen, short-term soldiers released at the end of the campaign season, peasants overburdened by emergency taxes, and even impoverished students of reli-

Islamic Law and Ottoman Rule

Ebu's-Su'ud was the Mufti of Istanbul from 1545 to 1574, serving under the sultans Suleiman the Magnificent (1520–1566) and his son Selim II (1566–1574). Originally one of many city-based religious scholars giving opinions on matters of law, the mufti of Istanbul by Ebu's-Su'ud's time had become the top religious official in the empire and the personal adviser to the sultan on religious and legal matters. The position would later acquire the title Shaikh al-Islam.

Historians debate the degree of independence these muftis had. Since the ruler, as a Muslim, was subject to the Shari'a, the mufti could theoretically veto his policies. On important matters, however, the mufti more often seemed to come up with the answer that best suited the sultan who appointed him. This bias is not apparent in more mundane areas of the law.

The collection of Ebu's-Su'ud's fatwas, or legal opinions, from which the examples below are drawn shows the range of matters that came to his attention. They are also an excellent source for understanding the problems of his time, the relationship between Islamic law and imperial governance, and the means by which the state asserted its dominance over the common people. Some opinions respond directly to questions posed by the sultan. Others are hypothetical, using the names Zeyd, 'Amr, and Hind the way police today use John Doe and Jane Doe. While qadis, or Islamic judges, made findings of fact in specific cases on trial, muftis issued only opinions on matters of law. A qadi as well as a plaintiff or defendant might ask a question of a mufti. Later jurists consulted collections of fatwas for precedents, but the fatwas had no permanent binding power.

On the plan of Selim II to attack the Venetians in Crete in 1570

A land was previously in the realm of Islam. After a while, the abject infidels overran it, destroyed the colleges and mosques, and left them vacant. They filled the pulpits and the galleries with the tokens of infidelity and error, intending to insult the religion of Islam with all kinds of vile deeds, and by spreading their ugly acts to all corners of the earth.

His Excellency the Sultan, the Refuge of Religion, has, as zeal for Islam requires, determined to take the aforementioned land from the possession of the shameful infidels and to annex it to the realm of Islam.

When peace was previously concluded with the other lands in the possession of the said infidels, the aforenamed land was included. An explanation is sought as to whether, in accordance with the pure shari'a, this is an impediment to the Sultan's determining to break the treaty.

Answer: There is no possibility that it could ever be an impediment. For the Sultan of the People of Islam (may God glorify his victories) to make peace with the infidels is legal only when there is a benefit to all Muslims. When there is no benefit, peace is never legal. When a benefit has been seen, and it is then observed to be more beneficial to break it, then to break it becomes absolutely obligatory and binding.

His Excellency [Muhammad] the Apostle of God (may God bless him and give him peace) made a ten-year truce with the Meccan infidels in the sixth year of the Hegira. His Excellency 'Ali (may God ennoble his face) wrote a document that was corroborated and confirmed. Then, in the following year, it was considered more beneficial to break it and, in the eighth year of the Hegira, [the Prophet] attacked [the Meccans], and conquered Mecca the Mighty.

On war against the Shi'ite Muslim Safavids of Iran

Is it licit according to the shari'a to fight the followers of the Safavids? Is the person who kills them a holy warrior, and the person who dies at their hands a martyr?

Answer: Yes, it is a great holy war and a glorious martyrdom.

Assuming that it is licit to fight them, is this simply because of their rebellion and enmity against the [Ottoman] Sultan of the People of Islam, because they drew the sword against the troops of Islam, or what?

Answer: They are both rebels and, from many points of view, infidels.

Can the children of Safavid subjects captured in the Nakhichevan campaign be enslaved?

Answer: No.

The followers of the Safavids are killed by order of the Sultan. If it turns out that some of the prisoners, young and old, are [Christian] Armenian[s], are they set free?

Answer: Yes. So long as the Armenians have not joined the Safavid troops in attacking and fighting against the troops of Islam, it is illegal to take them prisoner.

On the Holy Land

Are all the Arab realms Holy Land, or does it have specific boundaries, and what is the difference between the Holy Land and other lands?

Answer: Syria is certainly called the Holy Land. Jerusalem, Aleppo and its surroundings, and Damascus belong to it.

On land-grants

What lands are private property, and what lands are held by feudal tenure [i.e., assignment in exchange for military service]?

Answer: Plots of land within towns are private property. Their owners may sell them, donate them or convert them to trust. When [the owner] dies, [the land] passes to all the heirs. Lands held by feudal tenure are cultivated lands around villages, whose occupants bear the burden of their services and pay a portion of their [produce in tax]. They cannot sell the land, donate it or convert it to trust. When they die, if they have sons, these have the use [of the land]. Otherwise, the cavalry-man gives [it to someone else] by *tapu* [title deed].

On the consumption of coffee

Zeyd drinks coffee to aid concentration or digestion. Is this licit?

Answer: How can anyone consume this reprehensible [substance], which dissolute men drink when engaged in games and debauchery?

The Sultan, the Refuge of Religion, has on many occasions banned coffee-houses. However, a group of ruffians take no notice, but keep coffee-houses for a living. In order to draw the crowds, they take on unbearded apprentices, and have ready instruments of entertainment and play, such as chess and backgammon. The city's rakes, rogues and vagabond boys gather there to consume opium and hashish. On top of this, they drink coffee and, when they are high, engage in games and false sciences, and neglect the prescribed prayers. In law, what should happen to a judge who is able to prevent the said coffee-sellers and drinkers, but does not do so?

Answer: Those who perpetrate these ugly deeds should be prevented and deterred by severe chastisement and long imprisonment. Judges who neglect to deter them should be dismissed.

On matters of theft

How are thieves to be "carefully examined"?

Answer: His Excellency 'Ali (may God ennoble his face) appointed Imam Shuraih as judge. It so happened that, at that time, several people took a Muslim's son to another district. The boy disappeared and, when the people came back, the missing boy's father brought them before Judge Shuraih. [When he brought] a claim [against them on account of the loss of his son], they denied it, saying: "No harm came to him from us." Judge Shuraih thought deeply and was perplexed.

When the man told his tale to His Excellency 'Ali, [the latter] summoned Judge Shuraih and questioned him. When Shuraih said; "Nothing came to light by the shari'a," ['Ali] summoned all the people who had taken the man's son, separated them from one another, and questioned them separately. For each of their stopping places, he asked: "What was the boy wearing in that place? What did you eat? And where did he disappear?" In short, he made each of them give a detailed account, and when their words contradicted each other, each of their statements was written down separately. Then he brought them all together, and when the contradictions became apparent, they were no longer able to deny [their guilt] and confessed to what had happened.

This kind of ingenuity is a requirement of the case. [This fatwa appears to justify investigation of crimes by the state instead of by the qadi. Judging from court records, which contain very few criminal cases, it seems likely that in practice, many criminal cases were dealt with outside the jurisdiction of the qadi's court.]

Zeyd takes 'Amr's donkey without his knowledge and sells it. Is he a thief?

Answer: His hand is not cut off.

Zeyd mounts 'Amr's horse as a courier and loses it. Is compensation necessary?

Answer: Yes.

In which case: What if Zeyd has a Sultanic decree [authorizing him] to take horses for courier service?

Answer: Compensation is required in any case. He was not commanded to lose [the horse]. Even if he were commanded, it is the person who loses it who is liable.

On homicides

Zeyd enters Hind's house and tries to have intercourse forcibly. Since Hind can repel him by no other means, she strikes and wounds him with an axe. If Zeyd dies of the wound, is Hind liable for anything?

Answer: She has performed an act of Holy War [*jihad*].

QUESTIONS FOR ANALYSIS

1. What do these fatwas indicate with regard to the balance between practical legal reasoning and religious dictates?

2. How much was the Ottoman government constrained by the Shari'a?

3. What can be learned about day-to-day life from materials of this sort?

Source: Excerpts from Colin Imber, *Ebu's-Su'ud: The Islamic Legal Tradition*. Copyright © Colin Imber, originating publisher Edinburgh University Press. All rights reserved. Used with permission of Stanford University Press: www.sup.org, and Edinburgh University Press, www.euppublishing.com.

Ottoman Glassmakers on Parade Celebrations of the circumcisions of the sultan's sons featured parades organized by the craft guilds of Istanbul. This float features glassmaking, a common craft in Islamic realms. The most elaborate glasswork included oil lamps for mosques and colored glass for the small stained-glass windows below mosque domes.

Topkapi Palace Museum

gion formed bands of marauders. Anatolia experienced the worst of the rebellions and suffered greatly from emigration and the loss of agricultural production. But an increase in banditry, made worse by the government's inability to stem the spread of muskets among the general public, beset other parts of the empire as well.

Janissary Privileges

In the meantime, the Janissaries took advantage of their growing influence to gain relief from prohibitions on their marrying and engaging in business. Janissaries who involved themselves in commerce lessened the burden on the state budget, and married Janissaries who enrolled sons or relatives in the corps made it possible in the seventeenth century for the government to save state funds by abolishing forced recruitment. These savings, however, were more than offset by the increase in the total number of Janissaries and in their steady deterioration as a military force, which necessitated the hiring of more and more supplemental troops.

Economic Change and Growing Weakness

A very different Ottoman Empire emerged from this crisis. The sultan once had led armies. Now he mostly resided in his palace and had little experience of the real world, and the affairs of government were overseen more and more by the chief administrators—the grand viziers.

Tax Farming

The Janissaries took advantage of their increased power to make membership in their corps hereditary. Their involvement in crafts and trading took a toll on their military skills, but they continued to be a powerful faction in urban politics. Land grants in return for military service also disappeared, and tax farming arose in their place. Tax farmers paid specific taxes, such as customs duties, in advance in return for the privilege of collecting a greater amount from the actual taxpayers.

Rural administration, already disrupted by the rebellions, suffered from the transition to tax farms. The former military landholders had kept order on their lands in order to maintain their incomes. Tax farmers were less likely to live on the land. The imperial government therefore faced greater administrative burdens and came to rely heavily on powerful provincial governors or on wealthy men who purchased lifelong tax collection rights and behaved more or less like private landowners.

The Port of Izmir

Rural disorder and decline in administrative control sometimes opened the way for new economic opportunities. The port of Izmir (IZ-meer), known to Europeans by the ancient name "Smyrna," had a population in 1580 of around two thousand, many of them Greek-speaking Christians. By 1650 the population had increased to between thirty thousand and forty thousand. Along with refugees from the Anatolian uprisings and from European pirate attacks along the coast came European merchants and large colonies of Armenians and Jews. A French traveler in 1621 wrote: "At present, Izmir has a great traffic in wool, beeswax, cotton, and silk, which the Armenians bring there instead of going to Aleppo . . . because they do not pay as many dues."[3]

Izmir transformed itself between 1580 and 1650 from a small town into a multiethnic, multireligious, multilinguistic entrepôt because of the Ottoman government's inability to control trade and the slowly growing dominance of European traders in the Indian Ocean. Spices from the East, though still traded in Aleppo and other long-established Ottoman centers, were not to be found in Izmir. Aside from Iranian silk brought in by caravan, European traders at Izmir purchased local agricultural products—dried fruits, sesame seeds, nuts, and olive oil. As a consequence, local farmers who previously had grown grain for subsistence shifted their plantings more and more to cotton and other cash crops, including, after its introduction in the 1590s, tobacco, which quickly became popular in the Ottoman Empire despite government prohibitions (see Environment and Technology: Tobacco and Waterpipes). In this way, the agricultural economy of western Anatolia, the Balkans, and the Mediterranean coast—the Ottoman lands most accessible to Europe (see Map 20.1)—became enmeshed in a growing European commercial network.

Second Siege of Vienna

At the same time, military power slowly ebbed. The ill-trained Janissaries sometimes resorted to hiring substitutes to go on campaign, and the sultans relied on partially trained seasonal recruits and on armies raised by the governors of frontier provinces. A second mighty siege on Vienna failed in 1683, and by the middle of the eighteenth century it was obvious to the Austrians and Russians that the Ottoman Empire was weakening. On the eastern front, however, Ottoman exhaustion after many wars was matched by the demise in 1722 of their perennial adversary, the Safavid state of Iran.

Trade Agreements

The Ottoman Empire lacked both the wealth and the inclination to match European economic advances. Overland trade from the East dwindled as political disorder in Safavid Iran cut deeply into Iranian silk production. Coffee, an Arabian product that rose from obscurity in the fifteenth century to become the rage first in the Ottoman Empire and then in Europe, was grown in the highlands of Yemen and exported by way of Egypt. By 1770, however, Muslim merchants trading in the Yemeni port of Mocha (MOH-kuh) (literally "the coffee place") were charged 15 percent in duties and fees. But European traders, benefiting from long-standing trade agreements with the Ottoman Empire, paid little more than 3 percent.

Such trade agreements, called capitulations, from Latin *capitula*, or chapter, were first granted as favors by powerful sultans, but they eventually led to European domination of Ottoman seaborne trade. Nevertheless, the Europeans did not control strategic ports in the Mediterranean comparable to Malacca in the Indian Ocean and Hormuz on the Persian Gulf, so their economic power stopped short of colonial settlement or direct control in Ottoman territories.

The Tulip Period

A few astute Ottoman statesmen observed the growing disarray of the empire and advised the sultans to reestablish the land-grant and devshirme systems of Suleiman's reign. Most people, however, could not perceive the downward course of imperial power, much less the reasons behind it. Far from seeing Europe as the enemy that would eventually dismantle the empire, the Istanbul elite experimented with European clothing and furniture styles and purchased printed books from the empire's first (and short-lived) press. Ottoman historians named the period between 1718 and 1730 when European fashions were in favor the **"Tulip Period"** because of the craze for high-priced tulip bulbs that swept Ottoman ruling circles. The craze echoed a Dutch tulip mania that had begun in the mid-sixteenth century, when the flower was introduced into Holland from Istanbul. The mania peaked in 1636 with particularly rare bulbs going for 2,500 florins apiece—the value of twenty-two oxen.

Tulip Period (1718–1730) Last years of the reign of Ottoman sultan Ahmed III, during which European styles and attitudes became briefly popular in Istanbul.

Patrona Halil Rebellion

In 1730, however, gala soirees at which guests watched turtles with candles on their backs wander in the dark through massive tulip beds gave way to a conservative Janissary revolt with strong religious overtones. Sultan Ahmed III abdicated, and the leader of the revolt, Patrona Halil (pa-TROH-nuh ha-LEEL), an Albanian former seaman and stoker of the public baths, swaggered around the capital for several months dictating government policies before he was seized and executed.

ENVIRONMENT + TECHNOLOGY

Tobacco and Waterpipes

Tobacco, a plant native to the Western Hemisphere, may have been introduced into Ottoman Syria as early as 1570 and was certainly known in Istanbul by 1600. In Iran, one historian noted that when an Uzbek ruler entered the northeast province of Khurasan in 1612 and called for tobacco, it was quickly provided for him, while a Spanish diplomat remarked just a few years later that Shah Abbas, who had banned smoking as a sinful practice, nevertheless permitted an envoy from the Mughal sultan to indulge. European traders initially brought tobacco by sea, but it quickly became a cultivated crop in Mughal India, whence it was exported to Iran. By the middle of the seventeenth century, however, it had also become a significant crop in Ottoman and Safavid territories.

The waterpipe became a distinctive means of smoking in the Islamic world, but when the device came into use is disputed. Iranian historians assert that it was invented in Iran, where one reference in poetry goes back to before 1550. This early date suggests that waterpipes may have been used for smoking some other substance before tobacco became known. Straight pipes of clay or wood were also used, especially in Turkish areas and among poorer people.

The Persian word for a waterpipe, *qalyan*, comes from an Arabic verb meaning "to boil, or bubble." Arabic has two common words: *nargila*, which derives ultimately from the Sanskrit word for "coconut," and *shisha*, which means "glass" in Persian. In India, where coconuts were often used to contain the water, the usual term was *hookah*, meaning "jar." The absence of a clear linguistic indication of the country of origin enhances the possibility that waterpipes evolved and spread before the introduction of tobacco.

All levels of society took to smoking, with women enjoying it as much as men. The leisurely ceremony of preparing and lighting the waterpipe made it an ideal pastime in coffeehouses, which became popular in both the Ottoman and Safavid Empires. In other settings, the size and fragility of the waterpipe could cause inconvenience. When traveling, wealthy Iranian men sometimes had a pipe carrier in their entourage who carried the *qalyan* in his hand and had a small pot containing hot coals dangling from his saddle in case his master should wish to light up on the road.

From Rudi Matthee, *The Pursuit of Pleasure: Drugs and Stimulants in Iranian History, 1500–1900* [Princeton: Princeton University Press] p. 125

Iranian Waterpipe Moistened tobacco is placed in cup A, and a glowing coal is put on top of it to make it smolder. When the smoker draws on the stem sticking out to the side, the smoke bubbles up from beneath the water, which cools and filters it. The sophisticated manufacture shown in this drawing, which was rendered in 1622, supports the theory that the waterpipe went through a lengthy period of development before the seventeenth century.

The Patrona Halil rebellion confirmed the perceptions of a few that the Ottoman Empire was facing severe difficulties. Yet decay at the center spelled benefit elsewhere. In the provinces, ambitious and competent governors, wealthy landholders, urban notables, and nomad chieftains took advantage of the central government's weakness. By the middle of the eighteenth century groups of Mamluks had regained a dominant position in Egypt. Though Selim I had defeated the Mamluk sultanate in the early sixteenth century, the practice of buying slaves in the Caucasus and training them as soldiers reappeared by the end of the century in several Arab cities. In Baghdad, Janissary commanders and Georgian mamluks competed for power, with the latter emerging triumphant by the mid-eighteenth century.

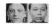

Muhammad ibn Abd al-Wahhab	In Aleppo and Damascus, however, the Janissaries came out on top. Meanwhile, in central Arabia, a puritanical Sunni movement inspired by Muhammad ibn Abd al-Wahhab began a remarkable rise beyond the reach of Ottoman power. Although no region declared full independence, the sultan's power was slipping away to the advantage of a broad array of lower officials and upstart chieftains in all parts of the empire while the Ottoman economy was reorienting itself toward Europe.

SECTION REVIEW

- The Ottoman Empire grew through the skill of its founding rulers, control of strategic territory, and military power.

- The empire expanded into southern and eastern Europe, the Middle East, and Africa, reaching its height under Suleiman the Magnificent.

- Unwilling to build a strong navy, the Ottomans never adapted to developments in the Indian Ocean.

- The empire rested on the military led by the sultan, and changes in military structure ultimately weakened the state.

- As the imperial economy reoriented toward Europe, the central government weakened, permitting the rise of local powers.

THE SAFAVID EMPIRE, 1502–1722

Safavid Empire Iranian kingdom (1502–1722) established by Ismail Safavi, who declared Iran a Shi'ite state.

The **Safavid Empire** of Iran (see Map 20.1) resembled its long-time Ottoman foe in many ways: it initially relied militarily on cavalry paid through land grants; its population spoke several different languages; and it was oriented inward away from the sea. It also had distinct qualities that to this day set Iran off from its neighbors: it derived part of its legitimacy from the pre-Islamic dynasties of ancient Iran, and it adopted the Shi'ite form of Islam.

Safavid Society and Religion

Iranian Shi'ism

Shi'ites Muslims belonging to the branch of Islam believing that God vests leadership of the community in a descendant of Muhammad's son-in-law Ali. Shi'ism is the state religion of Iran.

Persian Culture

The ultimate victor in a complicated struggle for power among Turkish chieftains west of the Ottoman Empire was Ismail (IS-ma-eel), a boy of Kurdish, Iranian, and Greek ancestry. In 1502, at the age of sixteen, Ismail proclaimed himself shah of Iran and declared that from that time forward his realm would be devoted to Shi'ite Islam, which revered the family of Muhammad's son-in-law Ali. Although Ismail's reasons for compelling Iran's conversion to Shi'ism are unknown, the effect of this radical act was to create a deep chasm between Iran and its neighbors, all of which were Sunni. Iran became a truly separate country for the first time since its incorporation into the Islamic caliphate in the seventh century.

The imposition of Shi'ite belief made the split permanent, but differences between Iran and its neighbors had long been in the making. Persian, written in the Arabic script from the tenth century onward, had emerged as the second language of Islam. Iranian scholars and writers normally read Arabic as well as Persian and sprinkled their writings with Arabic phrases, but their Arab counterparts were much less inclined to learn Persian. After the Mongols destroyed Baghdad, the capital of the Islamic caliphate, in 1258, Iran developed largely on its own, having more extensive contacts with India—where Muslim rulers favored the Persian language—than with the Arabs.

In the post-Mongol period, artistic styles in Iran, Afghanistan, and Central Asia also went their own way. Painted and molded tiles and tile mosaics, often in vivid turquoise blue, became the standard exterior decoration of mosques in Iran but never were used in Syria and Egypt. Persian poets raised verse to peaks of perfection that had no reflection in Arabic poetry, generally considered to be in a state of decline.

Freer Gallery of Art, Smithsonian Institution, Washington, D.C.: Purchase, F1945.9a

Mughal Emperor Jahangir Embracing the Safavid Shah Abbas Painted by the Mughal artist Abu al-Hasan around 1620, this miniature shows the artist's patron, Jahangir, on the right standing on a lion, dominating the diminutive Shah Abbas, standing on a sheep. Though this may accurately reflect Jahangir's view of their relationship, in fact Shah Abbas was a powerful rival for control of Afghanistan, the gateway to India and the meeting point of the lion and the sheep. The globe the monarchs stand on reflects the spread of accurate geographical ideas into the Muslim world.

To be sure, Islam itself provided a tradition of belief, learning, and law that crossed ethnic and linguistic borders, but Shah Ismail's imposition of Shi'ism set Iran significantly apart. Shi'ite doctrine says that all temporal rulers, regardless of title, are temporary stand-ins for the **"Hidden Imam"**: the twelfth descendant of Ali, the prophet Muhammad's cousin and son-in-law, who disappeared as a child in the ninth century. Some Shi'ite scholars concluded that the faithful should calmly accept the world as it was and wait quietly for the Hidden Imam's return. Others maintained that they themselves should play a stronger role in political affairs because they were best qualified to know the Hidden Imam's wishes. These two positions, which still play a role in Iranian Shi'ism, tended to enhance the self-image of religious scholars as independent of imperial authority and stood in the way of their becoming subordinate government functionaries, as happened in the Ottoman Empire.

Hidden Imam Last in a series of twelve descendants of Muhammad's son-in-law Ali, whom Shi'ites consider divinely appointed leaders of the Muslim community. In occlusion since ca. 873, he is expected to return as a messiah at the end of time.

Shi'ism also affected the psychological life of the people. Annual commemoration of the martyrdom of Imam Husayn (d. 680), Ali's son and the third Imam, regularized an emotional outpouring with no parallel in Sunni lands. Day after day for two weeks, preachers recited the woeful tale to crowds of weeping believers, and elaborate street processions, often organized by craft guilds, paraded chanting and self-flagellating men past crowds of reverent onlookers. Of course, Shi'ites elsewhere observed rites of mourning for Imam Husayn, but the impact of these rites was especially great in Iran, where 90 percent of the population was Shi'ite. Over time, the subjects of the Safavid shahs came to feel more than ever a people apart.

A Tale of Two Cities: Isfahan and Istanbul

Shah Abbas

Shah Abbas I The fifth and most renowned ruler of the Safavid dynasty in Iran (r. 1587–1629). Abbas moved the royal capital to Isfahan in 1598.

Differences and Similarities

Outwardly, the Ottoman capital of Istanbul looked quite different from Isfahan (is-fah-HAHN), which became Iran's capital in 1598 by decree of **Shah Abbas I** (r. 1587–1629). Built on seven hills on the south side of the narrow Golden Horn inlet, Istanbul boasted a skyline punctuated by the gray stone domes and thin, pointed minarets of the great imperial mosques. The mosques surrounding the royal plaza in Isfahan, in contrast, had unobtrusive minarets and brightly tiled domes that rose to gentle peaks. High walls surrounded the sultan's palace in Istanbul. Shah Abbas in Isfahan focused his capital on the giant royal plaza, which was large enough for his army to play polo, and he used an airy palace overlooking the plaza to receive dignitaries and review his troops.

The harbor of Istanbul, the primary Ottoman seaport, teemed with sailing ships and smaller craft, many of them belonging to a colony of European merchants perched on a hilltop on the north side of the Golden Horn. Isfahan, far from the sea, was only occasionally visited by Europeans. Most of its trade was in the hands of Jews, Hindus, and especially a colony of Armenian Christians brought in by Shah Abbas.

Royal Square in Isfahan Built by the order of Shah Abbas over a period of twenty years starting in 1598, the open space is as long as five football fields (555 by 172 yards). At the upper left end of the square in this drawing is the entrance to the covered bazaar, at the bottom the immense Royal Mosque. The left-hand side adjoins the shah's palace and state administrative office. A multistory pavilion for reviewing troops and receiving guests overlooks the square across from the smaller domed personal mosque of the shah.

Reproduced with permission from Klaus Herdeg, *Formal Structure in Islamic Architecture of Iran and Turkestan* [New York: Rizzoli, 1990]

Beneath these superficial differences, the two capitals had much in common. Wheeled vehicles were scarce in hilly Istanbul and nonexistent in Isfahan. Both cities were built for walking and, aside from the royal plaza in Isfahan, lacked the open spaces common in contemporary European cities. Streets were narrow and irregular. Houses crowded against each other in dead-end lanes. Residents enjoyed their privacy in interior courtyards. Artisans and merchants organized themselves into guilds that had strong social and religious as well as economic bonds. The shops of each guild adjoined each other in the markets.

Concealment of Women

Women were seldom seen in public, even in Istanbul's mazelike covered market or in Isfahan's long, serpentine bazaar. At home, the women's quarters—called *anderun* (an-deh-ROON), or "interior," in Iran and *harem*, or "forbidden area," in Istanbul—were separate from the public rooms where the men of the family received visitors. In both areas, low cushions, charcoal braziers for warmth, carpets, and small tables constituted most of the furnishings.

The private side of family life has left few traces, but it is apparent that women's society—consisting of wives, children, female servants, and sometimes one or more eunuchs—was not entirely cut off from the outside world. Ottoman court records reveal that women, using male agents, were very active in the urban real estate market. Often they were selling inherited shares of their father's estate, but some both bought and sold real estate on a regular basis and even established religious endowments for pious purposes.

Women and Islamic Law

The fact that Islamic law, unlike some European codes, permitted a wife to retain her property after marriage gave some women a stake in the general economy and a degree of independence from their spouses. Women also appeared in other types of court cases, where they often testified for themselves, for Islamic courts did not recognize the role of attorney. Although comparable Safavid court records do not survive, historians assume that a parallel situation prevailed in Iran.

Styles of Dress

European travelers commented on the veiling of women outside the home, but the norm for both sexes was complete coverage of arms, legs, and hair. Miniature paintings indicate that ordinary female garb consisted of a long, ample dress with a scarf or long shawl pulled tight over the forehead to conceal the hair. Lightweight trousers, either close-fitting or baggy, were often worn under the dress. This mode of dress was not far different from that of men. Poor men wore light trousers, a long shirt, a jacket, and a hat or turban. Wealthier men wore over their trousers ankle-length caftans, often closely fitted around the chest.

Public life was almost entirely the domain of men. Poetry and art, both somewhat more elegantly developed in Isfahan than in Istanbul, were as likely to extol the charms of beardless boys

Austrian National Library, picture archive

Cosmopolitan Istanbul

Istanbul Family on the Way to a Bath House Public baths, an important feature of Islamic cities, set different hours for men and women. Young boys, such as the lad in the turban shown here, went with their mothers and sisters. Notice that the children wear the same styles as the adults.

as pretty women. Despite religious disapproval of homosexuality, attachments to adolescent boys were neither unusual nor hidden. Women who appeared in public—aside from non-Muslims, the aged, and the very poor—were likely to be slaves. Miniature paintings frequently depict female dancers, musicians, and even acrobats in attitudes and costumes that range from decorous to decidedly erotic.

Despite social similarities, the overall flavors of Isfahan and Istanbul were not the same. Isfahan had its prosperous Armenian quarter across the river from the city's center, but it was not a truly cosmopolitan capital, just as the peoples of the Safavid realm were not remarkably diverse. Like other rulers of extensive land empires, Shah Abbas located his capital toward the center of his domain within comparatively easy reach of any threatened frontier. Istanbul, in contrast, was a great seaport and a crossroads located on the straits separating the sultan's European and Asian possessions.

People of all sorts lived or spent time in Istanbul: Venetians, Genoese, Arabs, Turks, Greeks, Armenians, Albanians, Serbs, Jews, Bulgarians, and more. In this respect, Istanbul conveyed the cosmopolitan character of major seaports from London to Canton (Guangzhou) and belied the fact that its prosperity rested on the vast reach of the sultan's territories rather than on the voyages of its merchants.

Economic Crisis and Political Collapse

The silk fabrics of northern Iran were the mainstay of the Safavid Empire's foreign trade. However, the manufacture that eventually became most powerfully associated with Iran was the deep-pile carpet made by knotting colored yarns around stretched warp threads. Different cities produced distinctive carpet designs. Women and girls did much of the actual knotting work. Overall, Iran's manufacturing sector was neither large nor notably productive. Most of the shah's subjects, whether Iranians, Turks, Kurds, or Arabs, lived by subsistence farming or herding. Neither area of activity recorded significant technological advances during the Safavid period.

Military Costs The Safavids, like the Ottomans, had difficulty finding the money to pay troops armed with firearms. This crisis occurred somewhat later in Iran because of its greater distance from Europe. By the end of the sixteenth century, it was evident that a more systematic adoption of cannon and firearms in the Safavid Empire would be needed to hold off the Ottomans and the Uzbeks (UHZ-bex) (Turkish rulers who had succeeded the Timurids on Iran's Central Asian frontier; see Map 20.1). Like the Ottoman cavalry a century earlier, the warriors furnished by the nomad leaders were not inclined to trade in their bows for firearms. Shah Abbas responded by establishing a slave corps of year-round soldiers and arming them with guns. The Christian converts to Islam who initially provided the manpower for the new corps were mostly captives taken in raids on Georgia in the Caucasus (CAW-kuh-suhs).

In the late sixteenth century, the inflation caused by cheap silver spread into Iran; then overland trade through Safavid territory declined because of mismanagement of the silk monopoly after Shah Abbas's death in 1629. As a result, the country faced the unsolvable problem of finding money to pay the army and bureaucracy. Trying to

Nomads and Inflation

unseat the nomads from their lands to regain control of taxes was more difficult and more disruptive militarily than the piecemeal dismantlement of the land-grant system in the Ottoman Empire. The nomads were still a cohesive military force, and pressure from the center simply caused them to withdraw to their mountain pastures until the pressure subsided. By 1722, the government had become so weak and commanded so little support from the nomadic groups that an army of marauding Afghans was able to capture Isfahan and effectively end Safavid rule.

THE MUGHAL EMPIRE, 1526–1761

What distinguished the Indian empire of the Mughal (MOH-guhl) sultans from the empires of the Ottomans and Safavids was the fact that India was a land of Hindus ruled by a Muslim minority. Muslim dominion in India was the result of repeated military campaigns from the early eleventh century onward, and the Mughals had to contend with the Hindus' long-standing resentment of the destruction of their culture by Muslims. Thus, the challenge facing the Mughals was not just conquering and organizing a large territorial state but also finding a formula for Hindu-Muslim coexistence.

Mughal Empire Muslim state (1526–1857) exercising dominion over most of India in the sixteenth and seventeenth centuries.

Political Foundations

Babur and Akbar

Babur (BAH-bur) (1483–1530), the founder of the **Mughal Empire**, was a Muslim descendant of both Timur and Genghis Khan (*Mughal* is Persian for "Mongol"). Invading from Central Asia, Babur defeated the last Muslim sultan of Delhi (DEL-ee) in 1526. Babur's grandson **Akbar** (r. 1556–1605), a brilliant but mercurial man, established the central administration of the expanding state. Under him and his three successors—the last of whom died in 1707—all but the southern tip of India fell under Mughal rule, administered first from Agra and then from Delhi.

Akbar Most illustrious sultan of the Mughal Empire in India (r. 1556–1605). He expanded the empire and pursued a policy of conciliation with Hindus.

Akbar granted land revenues to military officers and government officials in return for their service. Ranks, called *mansabs* (MAN-sabz), some high and some low, entitled their holders to revenue assignments. As in the other Islamic empires, revenue grants were not considered hereditary, and the central government kept careful track of their issuance.

mansabs In India, grants of land given in return for service by rulers of the Mughal Empire.

With a population of 100 million, a thriving trading economy based on cotton cloth, and a generally efficient administration, India under Akbar was probably the most prosperous empire of the sixteenth century. He and his successors faced few external threats and experienced generally peaceful conditions in their northern Indian heartland.

Akbar's Reign

Foreign trade boomed at the port of Surat in the northwest, which also served as an embarkation point for pilgrims on their way to Mecca. Like the Safavids, the Mughals had no navy or merchant ships. The government saw the Europeans—after Akbar's time, primarily Dutch and English, the Portuguese having lost most of their Indian ports—less as enemies than as shipmasters whose naval support could be procured as needed in return for trading privileges.

Hindus and Muslims

Rajputs

The Mughal state inherited traditions of unified imperial rule from both the Islamic caliphate and the more recent examples of Genghis Khan and Timur. Those traditions did not necessarily mean religious intolerance. Seventy percent of the *mansabdars* (man-sab-DAHRZ) (officials holding land revenues) appointed under Akbar were Muslim soldiers born outside India, but 15 percent were Hindus. Most of the Hindu appointees were warriors from the north called **Rajputs** (RAHJ-putz), one of whom rose to be a powerful revenue minister.

Rajputs Members of a mainly Hindu warrior caste from northwest India. The Mughal emperors drew most of their Hindu officials from this caste, and Akbar married a Rajput princess.

Akbar, the most illustrious ruler of his dynasty, differed from his Ottoman and Safavid counterparts—Suleiman the Magnificent and Shah Abbas the Great—in his striving for social harmony and not just for more territory and revenue. His marriage to a Rajput princess signaled his desire for reconciliation and even intermarriage between Muslims and Hindus. The birth of a son in 1569 ensured that future rulers would have both Muslim and Hindu ancestry.

Akbar ruled that in legal disputes between two Hindus, decisions would be made according to village custom or Hindu law as interpreted by local Hindu scholars. Shari'a law was in force for Muslims. Akbar made himself the legal court of last resort, creating an appeals process not usually present in Islamic jurisprudence.

Victoria and Albert Museum, London/The Bridgeman Art Library

Elephants Breaking Bridge of Boats   This illustration of an incident in the life of Akbar illustrates the ability of Mughal miniature painters to depict unconventional action scenes. Because the flow of rivers in India and the Middle East varied greatly from dry season to wet season, boat bridges were much more common than permanent constructions.

Akbar also made himself the center of a new "Divine Faith" incorporating Muslim, Hindu, Zoroastrian, Sikh (sick), and Christian beliefs. He was strongly attracted by Sufi ideas, which permeated the religious rituals he instituted at his court. To promote serious consideration of his religious principles, he oversaw, from a catwalk high above the audience, debates among scholars of all religions assembled in his octagonal private audience chamber. When courtiers uttered the Muslim exclamation "Allahu Akbar"—"God is great"—they also understood it in its second grammatical meaning: "God is Akbar."

Akbar's religious views did not survive him, but the court culture he fostered, reflecting a mixture of Muslim and Hindu traditions, flourished until his zealous great-grandson Aurangzeb (ow-rang-ZEB) (r. 1658–1707) reinstituted many restrictions on Hindus. Mughal and Rajput miniature paintings reveled in precise portraits of political figures and depictions of scantily clad women, even though they brought frowns to the faces of pious Muslims, who deplored the representation of human beings. Most of the leading painters were Hindus. In addition to the florid style of Persian verse favored at court, a new taste developed for poetry and prose in the popular language of the Delhi region. The modern descendant of this language is called *Urdu* in Pakistan and *Hindi* in India.

Central Decay and Regional Challenges

Nadir Shah's Sack of Delhi

Mughal power did not long survive Aurangzeb's death in 1707. Some historians consider the land-grant system a central element in the rapid decline of imperial authority, but other factors were at play as well. Aurangzeb's additions to Mughal territory in southern India were not all well integrated into the imperial structure, and strong regional powers arose to challenge Mughal military supremacy. A climax came in 1739 when Nadir Shah, a warlord who had seized power in Iran after the fall of the Safavids, invaded the Mughal capital and carried off to Iran the "peacock throne," the priceless jewel-encrusted symbol of Mughal grandeur. Another throne was found for the later Mughals to sit on; but their empire, which survived in name to 1857, was finished.

Increasing Fragmentation

In 1723, Nizam al-Mulk (nee-ZAHM al-MULK), the powerful vizier of the Mughal sultan, gave up on the central government and established his own nearly independent state at Hyderabad in the eastern Deccan. Other officials bearing the title *nawab* (nah-WAHB) became similarly independent in Bengal and Oudh (OW-ad) in the northeast, as did the Marathas in the center. In the northwest, simultaneous Iranian and Mughal weakness allowed the Afghans to establish an independent kingdom.

Some of these regional powers, and the smaller princely states that arose on former Mughal territory, were prosperous and benefited from the removal of the sultan's heavy hand. Linguistic and religious communities, freed from the religious intolerance instituted during the reign of Aurangzeb, similarly enjoyed greater opportunity for political expression. However, this disintegration of central power favored the intrusion of European adventurers.

French Traders

In 1741 Joseph François Dupleix (doo-PLAY) took over the presidency of the French stronghold of Pondicherry (pon-dih-CHER-ree) and began a new phase of European involvement in India. He captured the English trading center of Madras and used his small contingent of European and European-trained Indian troops to become a power broker in southern India. Though offered the title *nawab,* Dupleix preferred to operate behind the scenes, using Indian princes as puppets. His career ended in 1754 when he was called home. Deeply involved in wars in Europe, the French government was unwilling to pursue further adventures in India. Dupleix's departure opened the way for the British, whose ventures in India are described in Chapter 26.

THE MARITIME WORLDS OF ISLAM, 1500–1750

As land powers, the Mughal, Safavid, and Ottoman Empires faced similar problems in the seventeenth and eighteenth centuries. Complex changes in military technology and in the world economy, along with the increasing difficulty of basing an extensive land empire on military forces paid through land grants, affected them all adversely. These difficulties contributed to the often dynamic development of power centers away from the imperial capital.

Joint-Stock Companies

The new pressures faced by land powers were less important to seafaring countries intent on turning trade networks into maritime empires. Improvements in ship design, navigation accuracy, and the use of cannon gave an ever-increasing edge to European powers competing with local seafaring peoples. Moreover, the development of joint-stock companies, in which many merchants pooled their capital, provided a flexible and efficient financial instrument for exploiting new possibilities. The English East India Company was founded in 1600, the Dutch East India Company in 1602.

Although the Ottomans, Safavids, and Mughals did not effectively contest the growth of Portuguese and then Dutch, English, and French maritime power, the majority of non-European shipbuilders, captains, sailors, and traders were Muslim. Groups of Armenian, Jewish, and Hindu traders were also active, but they remained almost as aloof from the Europeans as the Muslims did. The presence in every port of Muslims following the same legal traditions and practicing their faith in similar ways cemented the Muslims' trading network. Islam, from its very outset in the life and preaching of Muhammad (570–632), had favored trade and traders. Unlike Hinduism, it was a proselytizing religion, a factor that encouraged the growth of coastal Muslim communities as local non-Muslims associated with Muslim commercial activities converted and intermarried with Muslims from abroad.

Jesuit Missionaries

Although European missionaries, particularly the Jesuits, tried to extend Christianity into Asia and Africa (see Chapters 16 and 21), most Europeans, the Portuguese excepted, did not treat local converts or the offspring of mixed marriages as full members of their communities. Islam was generally more welcoming. As a consequence, Islam spread extensively into East Africa and Southeast Asia during precisely the same time as rapid European commercial expansion. Even without the support of the Muslim land empires, Islam became a source of resistance to growing European domination.

Muslims in Southeast Asia

Indians in the East Indies

Historians disagree about the chronology and manner of Islam's spread in Southeast Asia. Arab traders appeared in southern China as early as the eighth century, so Muslims probably reached the East Indies (the island portions of Southeast Asia) at a similarly early date. Nevertheless, the dominance of Indian cultural influences in the area for several centuries thereafter indicates that early Muslim visitors had little impact on local beliefs. Clearer indications of conversion and the formation of Muslim communities date from roughly the fourteenth century, with the strongest overseas linkage being to the port of Cambay in India (see Map 20.2) rather than to the Arab world. Islam first took root in port cities and in some royal courts and spread inland only slowly, possibly transmitted by itinerant Sufis.

Although appeals to the Ottoman sultan for support against the Europeans ultimately proved futile, Islam strengthened resistance to Portuguese, Spanish, and Dutch intruders. When the Spaniards conquered the Philippines during the decades following the establishment of their first fort in 1565, they encountered Muslims on the southern island of Mindanao (min-duh-NOW) and the nearby Sulu archipelago. They called them "Moros," the Spanish term for their old enemies, the Muslims of North Africa. In the ensuing Moro wars, the Spaniards portrayed the Moros as greedy pirates who raided non-Muslim territories for slaves. In fact, they were political, religious, and commercial competitors whose perseverance enabled them to establish the Sulu Empire based in the southern Philippines, one of the strongest states in Southeast Asia from 1768 to 1848.

Other local kingdoms that looked on Islam as a force to counter the aggressive Christianity of the Europeans included the actively proselytizing Brunei (BROO-neye) Sultanate in northern Borneo and the **Acheh** (AH-cheh) **Sultanate** in northern Sumatra. At its peak in the early seventeenth century, Acheh succeeded Malacca as the main center of Islamic expansion in Southeast Asia. It prospered by trading pepper for cotton cloth from Gujarat in India. Acheh declined after the Dutch seized Malacca from Portugal in 1641.

How well Islam was understood in these Muslim kingdoms is open to question. In Acheh, for example, a series of women ruled between 1641 and 1699. This practice ended when local Muslim scholars obtained a ruling from scholars in Mecca and Medina that Islam did not approve of female rulers. After this ruling, scholarly understandings of Islam gained greater prominence in the East Indies.

Historians have looked at merchants, Sufi preachers, or both as the first propagators of Islam in Southeast Asia. The scholarly vision of Islam, however, took root in the sixteenth century by way of pilgrims returning from years of study in Mecca and Medina. Islam promoted the dissemination of writing in the region. Some of the returning pilgrims wrote in Arabic, others in Malay or Javanese. As Islam continued to spread, *adat* ("custom"), a form of Islam rooted in pre-Muslim religious and social practices, retained its preeminence in rural areas over practices centered on the Shari'a, the religious law. But the royal courts in the port cities began to heed the views of the pilgrim teachers. Though different in many ways, both varieties of Islam provided believers with a firm basis of identification in the face of the growing European presence. Christian missionaries gained most of their converts in regions that had not yet converted to Islam, such as the northern Philippines.

Muslims in Coastal Africa

Muslim rulers also governed the East African ports that the Portuguese began to visit in the fifteenth century, though they were not allied politically (see Map 20.2). People living in the millet and rice lands of the Swahili Coast—from the Arabic *sawahil* (suh-WAH-hil) meaning "coasts"—had little contact with those in the dry hinterlands. Throughout this period, the East African lakes region and the highlands of Kenya witnessed unprecedented migration and relocation of peoples because of drought conditions that persisted from the late sixteenth through most of the seventeenth century.

Cooperation among the trading ports of Kilwa, Mombasa, and Malindi was hindered by the thick bush country that separated the cultivated tracts of coastal land and by the fact that the ports competed with one another in the export of ivory; ambergris (AM-ber-grees) (a whale byproduct used in perfumes); and forest products such as beeswax, copal tree resin, and wood. Kilwa also exported gold. In the eighteenth century slave trading, primarily to Arabian ports but also to India, increased in importance. Because Europeans—the only peoples who kept consistent records of slave-trading activities—played a minor role in this slave trade, few records have survived to indicate its extent. Perhaps the best estimate is that 2.1 million slaves were exported between 1500 and 1890, a little over 12.5 percent of the total traffic in African slaves during that period (see Chapter 19).

Margin notes:

Acheh Sultanate Muslim kingdom in northern Sumatra. Main center of Islamic expansion in Southeast Asia in the early seventeenth century, it declined after the Dutch seized Malacca from Portugal in 1641.

The Dutch Capture Malacca

Islam and Literacy

Trading Ports

MAP 20.2 **European Colonization in the Indian Ocean, to 1750** Since Portuguese explorers were the first Europeans to reach India by rounding Africa, Portugal gained a strong foothold in both areas. Rival Spain was barred from colonizing the region by the Treaty of Tordesillas in 1494, which limited Spanish efforts to lands west of a line drawn through the mid-Atlantic Ocean. The line carried around the globe provided justification of Spanish colonization in the Philippines. French, British, and Dutch colonies date from after 1600, when joint-stock companies provided a new stimulus for overseas commerce.

e Interactive Map

Malindi

The Portuguese conquered all the coastal ports from Mozambique northward except Malindi, with whose ruler Portugal cooperated. A Portuguese description of the ruler names some of the cloth and metal goods that Malindi imported, as well as some local manufactures:

The King wore a robe of damask trimmed with green satin and a rich [cap]. He was seated on two cushioned chairs of bronze, beneath a rough sunshade of crimson satin attached to a pole. An old man, who attended him as a page, carried a short sword in a silver sheath. There were many players on [horns], and two trumpets of ivory richly carved and of the size of a man, which were blown through a hole in the side, and made sweet harmony with the [horns].[4]

Robert Harding World Imagery

Portuguese Fort Guarding Musqat Harbor   Musqat in Oman and Aden in Yemen, the best harbors in southern Arabia, were targets for imperial navies trying to establish dominance in the Indian Ocean. Musqat's harbor is small and circular, with one narrow entrance overlooked by this fortress. The palace of the sultan of Oman is still located at the opposite end of the harbor.

Oman Arab state based in Musqat, the main port in the southeast region of the Arabian peninsula. Oman succeeded Portugal as a power in the western Indian Ocean in the eighteenth century.

Initially, the Portuguese favored the port of Malindi, which caused the decline of Kilwa and Mombasa. Repeatedly plagued by local rebellion, Portuguese power suffered severe blows when the Arabs of **Oman** in southeastern Arabia captured their south Arabian stronghold at Musqat (1650) and then went on to seize Mombasa (1698), which had become the Portuguese capital in East Africa. The Portuguese briefly retook Mombasa but lost control permanently in 1729. From then on, the Portuguese had to content themselves with Mozambique in East Africa and a few remaining ports in India (Goa) and farther east (Macao and Timor).

Oman Builds an Empire

The Omanis created a maritime empire of their own, one that worked in greater cooperation with the African populations. The Bantu language of the coast, broadened by the absorption of Arabic, Persian, and Portuguese loanwords, developed into **Swahili** (swah-HEE-lee), which was spoken throughout the region. Arabs and other Muslims who settled in the region intermarried with local families, giving rise to a mixed population that played an important role in developing a distinctive Swahili culture.

Swahili Bantu language with Arabic loanwords spoken in coastal regions of East Africa.

Islam also spread in the southern Sudan in this period, particularly in the dry areas away from the Nile River. This growth coincided with a waning of Ethiopian power as a result of Portugal's stifling of trade in the Red Sea. Yet no significant contact developed between the emerging Muslim Swahili culture and that of the Muslims in the Sudan to the north.

Muslim Revival in Morocco

In Northwest Africa the seizure by Portugal and Spain of coastal strongholds in Morocco provoked a militant response. The Sa'adi family, which claimed descent from the Prophet Muhammad, led a resistance to Portuguese aggression that climaxed in victory at the battle of al-Qasr al-Kabir (Ksar el Kebir) in 1578. The triumphant Moroccan sultan, Ahmad al-Mansur, restored his country's strength and independence. By the early seventeenth century naval expeditions from the port of Salé, referred to in British records as "the Sally Rovers," raided European shipping as far as Britain itself.

Corsairs, or sea raiders, working out of Algerian, Tunisian, and Libyan ports brought the same sort of warfare to the Mediterranean. European governments called these Muslim raiders pirates and slave-takers, and they leveled the same charges against other Muslim mariners in the Persian Gulf and the Sulu Sea. But there was little distinction between the actions of the Muslims and of their European adversaries.

European Powers in Southern Seas

The Dutch in the East Indies

Through their well-organized Dutch East India Company, the Dutch played a major role in driving the Portuguese from their possessions in the East Indies. Just as the Portuguese had tried to dominate the trade in spices, so the Dutch concentrated at first on the spice-producing islands of Southeast Asia. The Portuguese had seized Malacca, a strategic town on the narrow strait at the end of the Malay Peninsula, from a local Malay ruler in 1511 (see Chapter 16). The Dutch took it away from them in 1641, leaving Portugal little foothold in the East Indies except the islands of Ambon (am-BOHN) and Timor (see Map 20.2).

Batavia, the Center of Dutch Trade

Although the United Netherlands was one of the least autocratic countries of Europe, the governors-general appointed by the Dutch East India Company deployed almost unlimited powers in their efforts to maintain their trade monopoly. They could even order the execution of their own employees for "smuggling"—that is, trading on their own. Under strong governors-general, the Dutch fought a series of wars against Acheh and other local kingdoms on Sumatra and Java. In 1628 and 1629 their new capital at **Batavia**, now the city of Jakarta on Java, was besieged by a fleet of fifty ships belonging to the sultan of Mataram (MAH-tah-ram), a Javanese kingdom. The Dutch held out with difficulty and eventually prevailed when the sultan was unable to get effective help from the English.

Batavia Fort established ca. 1619 as headquarters of Dutch East India Company operations in Indonesia; today the city of Jakarta.

Suppressing local rulers, however, was not enough to control the spice trade once other European countries adopted Dutch methods, learned more about where goods might be acquired, and started to send more ships to Southeast Asia. In the course of the eighteenth century, therefore, the Dutch gradually turned from being middlemen between Southeast Asian producers and European buyers to producing crops in areas they controlled, notably in Java. Javanese teak forests yielded high-quality lumber, and coffee, transplanted from Yemen, grew well in the western hilly regions. In this new phase of colonial export production, Batavia developed from being the headquarters town of a far-flung enterprise to being the administrative capital of a conquered land.

Beyond the East Indies, the Dutch utilized their discovery of a band of powerful eastward-blowing winds (called the "Roaring Forties" because they blow throughout the year between 40 and 50 degrees south latitude) to reach Australia in 1606. In 1642 and 1643 Abel Tasman became the first European to set foot on Tasmania and New Zealand and to sail around Australia, signaling European involvement in that region (see Chapter 26).

SECTION REVIEW

- From its inception in the time of Muhammad, Islam flowered in places of trade, and beginning around 1500, the majority of non-European shipbuilders, captains, sailors, and traders were Muslim.

- A number of local kingdoms in Southeast Asia took on Islam as a force to resist the aggressive Christianity of the Europeans.

- Many Muslims in coastal Africa intermarried with locals, creating a mixed population that played a key part in the development of a distinctive Swahili culture.

- Over time the successes of European trading companies changed the balance of power in the southern seas, but local merchants never completely disappeared from the commercial scene.

CONCLUSION

It is no coincidence that the Mughal, Safavid, and Ottoman Empires declined simultaneously in the seventeenth and eighteenth centuries. The complex changes in military technology and in the world economy that were under way in smaller European countries either passed them by or affected them adversely. Despite their efforts on conquering more and more land, these land-based empires faced increasing difficulty in maintaining traditional military forces paid through land grants.

The opposite was true for seafaring countries intent on turning trade networks into maritime empires. Improvements in ship design, navigation accuracy, and the use of cannon gave an ever-increasing edge to European powers competing with local seafaring peoples. In contrast to the age-old Asian tradition that imperial wealth came from control of broad expanses of agricultural land, European countries promoted joint-stock companies and luxuriated in the prosperity gained from their ever-increasing control of Indian Ocean commerce.

That a major shift in world economic and political alignments was well under way by the late seventeenth century was scarcely perceivable in those parts of Asia and Africa ruled by the Ottoman and Mughal sultans and the Safavid shahs. They relied mostly on land taxes, usually indirectly collected via holders of land grants or tax farmers, rather than on customs duties or control of markets to fill the government coffers. With ever-increasing military expenditures, these taxes fell short of the rulers' needs. Oblivious to the fundamental problem of the entire economic system, imperial courtiers pursued their luxurious ways, poetry and the arts continued to flourish, and the quality of manufacturing and craft production remained generally high. Eighteenth-century European observers marveled no less at the riches and industry of these eastern lands than at the fundamental weakness of their political and military systems.

KEY TERMS

Ottoman Empire p. 532
Suleiman the Magnificent p. 532
Janissaries p. 535
Tulip Period p. 539

Safavid Empire p. 541
Shi'ites p. 541
Hidden Imam p. 542
Shah Abbas I p. 542
Mughal Empire p. 545

Akbar p. 545
mansabs p. 545
Rajputs p. 545
Acheh Sultanate p. 548
Oman p. 550

Swahili p. 550
Batavia p. 551

EBOOK AND WEBSITE RESOURCES

 Interactive Maps

Map 20.1 Muslim Empires in the Sixteenth and Seventeenth Centuries

Map 20.2 European Colonization in the Indian Ocean, to 1750

Plus flashcards, practice quizzes, and more. Go to: www.cengage.com/history/bullietearthpeople5e

SUGGESTED READING

Arjomand, Said Amir. *The Shadow of God and the Hidden Imam: Religion, Political Order, and Societal Change in Shiite Iran from the Beginning to 1890.* 1984. Contains the best analysis of the complicated relationship between Shi'ism and monarchy.

Braude, Benjamin, and Bernard Lewis, eds. *Christians and Jews in the Ottoman Empire: The Functioning of a Plural Society.* 1982. Diverse studies dealing with religious minorities.

Goffman, Daniel. *The Ottoman Empire and Early Modern Europe.* 2002. Compares the Ottomans with contemporary European kingdoms.

Hattox, Ralph S. *Coffee and Coffeehouses: The Origins of a Social Beverage in the Medieval Near East.* 1988. An excellent contribution to Ottoman social history.

Ikram, S. M. *History of Muslim Civilization in India and Pakistan.* 1989. A broad treatment of the entire development of Islamic society in India with emphasis on the Mughal period.

Imber, Colin. *The Ottoman Empire, 1300–1650: The Structure of Power.* 2002. On the Ottoman Empire in its prime.

Inalcik, Halil, and Donald Quataert, eds. *An Economic and Social History of the Ottoman Empire, 1300–1914.* 1994. A valuable collection of articles on nonpolitical matters.

Lapidus, Ira. *A History of Islamic Societies*, 2nd ed. 2002. Offers the best comprehensive and comparative account of the post-Mongol Islamic land empires.

Marcus, Abraham. *The Middle East on the Eve of Modernity: Aleppo in the Eighteenth Century*. 1989. An outstanding study of an Arab city under Ottoman rule.

Martin, Esmond Bradley, and Chryssee Perry Martin. *Cargoes of the East: The Ports, Trade and Culture of the Arabian Seas and Western Indian Ocean*. 1978. A popular and well-illustrated work on the western Indian Ocean.

Matthee, Rudi. *The Pursuit of Pleasure: Drugs and Stimulants in Iranian History, 1500–1900*. 2005. Studies court life and popular culture through wine, tobacco, opium, coffee, and tea.

Newman, Andrew. *Safavid Iran: Rebirth of a Persian Empire*. 2006. A provocative reinterpretation of Safavid rule.

Ogot, B. A., ed. *UNESCO General History of Africa*, vol. 5, *Africa from the Sixteenth to the Eighteenth Century*. 1992. A useful collection of articles on an understudied field.

Peirce, Leslie. *The Imperial Harem: Women and Sovereignty in the Ottoman Empire*. 1993. Skillfully treats the role of women in the governance of the empire.

Richards, John F. *The Mughal Empire*. 1993. A comprehensive history.

NOTES

1. Leslie Peirce, *Morality Tales: Law and Gender in the Ottoman Court of Aintab* (Berkeley: University of California Press, 2003), 258.
2. Ibid., 262.
3. Daniel Goffman, *Izmir and the Levantine World, 1550–1650* (Seattle: University of Washington Press, 1990), 52.
4. Edmund Bradley Martin and Chryssee Perry Martin, *Cargoes of the East: The Ports, Trade and Culture of the Arabian Seas and Western Indian Ocean* (1978), 17.

CHAPTER
21

CHAPTER OUTLINE

Russian Ambassadors to Holland Display Their Furs, 1576   Representatives from Muscovy impressed the court of King Maximilian II of Bohemia with their sable coats and caps.

 Visit the website and ebook for additional study materials and interactive tools: www.cengage.com/history/bullietearthpeople5e

Northern Eurasia, 1500–1800

■ How did Japan respond to domestic social changes and the challenges posed by contact with foreign cultures?
■ How did China deal with military and political challenges both inside and outside its borders?
■ To what extent was Russia's expanding empire influenced by relations with western Europe in this period?

In the seventeenth century, the Ming dynasty in China was threatened by **Manchu** armies from Manchuria in the northeast. To pay the army defending Beijing (bay-JING), the emperor slashed the government payroll. Among those thrown out of his job as an apprentice ironworker was one Li Zicheng (lee ZUH-cheng). By 1630 Li Zicheng had found work as a soldier, but he and his fellow soldiers mutinied when the government failed to provide needed supplies. A natural leader, Li soon headed several thousand Chinese rebels. In 1635 he and other rebel leaders gained control over much of north central China.

Manchu Federation of Northeast Asian peoples who founded the Qing Empire.

Wedged between the Manchu armies to the north and the rebels to the southwest, the Ming government tottered. Li Zicheng's forces began to move toward Beijing, along the way conscripting young men from captured towns into their army. The rebels promised to end the abuses of the Ming and restore peace and prosperity. In April 1644 Li's forces took over Beijing without a fight. The last Ming emperor hanged himself in the palace garden, bringing to an end the dynasty that had ruled China since 1368.

Victory was short-lived, however. Fearful of uneducated, violent men like Li ruling the land, the Ming general Wu Sangui joined forces with the Manchus. Li had incidentally captured one of the general's favorite concubines and taken her for himself. Together Wu and the Manchus retook Beijing in June. Li's forces scattered, and a year later he was dead, either a suicide or beaten to death by peasants whose food he tried to steal.[1]

Meanwhile, the Manchus made it clear that they were the new masters of China. They installed their young sovereign as emperor and over the next two decades hunted down the last of the Ming loyalists and heirs to the throne.

China was not the only state in northern Eurasia facing foreign threats and uprisings from within. Between 1500 and 1800 Japan and Russia experienced similar turbulence as they underwent massive political and economic change. Besides challenges from nearby neighbors, the three also faced new contacts and challenges from the commercially and militarily powerful European states.

JAPANESE REUNIFICATION

Japan experienced three major changes between 1500 and 1800: internal and external military conflicts, political growth and strengthening, and expanded commercial and cultural contacts. Along with its culturally homogenous population and natural boundaries, Japan's smaller size made the process of political unification shorter than in the great empires of China and Russia. Japan also differed in its responses to new contacts with western Europeans.

Civil War and the Invasion of Korea, 1500–1603

Daimyo and Samurai

In the twelfth century different parts of Japan had fallen under the rule of warlords known as *daimyo* (DIE-mee-oh) (see Chapter 11). Each daimyo had a castle town, a small bureaucracy, and a band of warriors, the *samurai* (SAH-moo-rye). Daimyo pledged a loose allegiance to the Japanese emperor residing in the capital city of Kyoto (KYOH-toh) and to the shogun, the hereditary chief of the emperor's government and armies. But neither figure held significant political power.

Hideyoshi

Warfare among the different daimyo was common, and in the late 1500s it culminated in a prolonged civil war. The warlord to emerge from the war was Hideyoshi (HEE-duh-YOH-shee). In 1592, buoyed with his success in Japan, the supremely confident Hideyoshi invaded the Asian mainland with 160,000 men. He apparently intended to first conquer Korea and then make himself emperor of China.

daimyo Literally, great name(s). Japanese warlords and great landowners, whose armed samurai gave them control of the Japanese islands from the eighth to the later nineteenth century. Under the Tokugawa Shogunate they were subordinated to the imperial government.

samurai Literally "those who serve," the hereditary military elite of the Tokugawa Shogunate.

The Korean and Japanese languages are closely related, but the dominant influence on Korean culture had long been China, to which Korean rulers generally paid tribute. In many ways the Yi dynasty that ruled Korea from 1392 to 1910 was a model Confucian state. Although Korea had developed its own system of writing in 1443 and made extensive use of printing with movable type from the fifteenth century on, most printing continued to use Chinese characters.

Against Hideyoshi's invaders the Koreans employed all the technological and military skill for which the Yi period was renowned. Ingenious covered warships, or "turtle boats," intercepted a portion of the Japanese fleet. The mentally unstable Hideyoshi countered with brutal punitive measures as his armies advanced through the Korean peninsula and into the Chinese province of Manchuria. However, after Hideyoshi's death in 1598, the other Japanese military leaders withdrew their forces, and the Japanese government made peace in 1606.

The invasion devastated Korea. In the turmoil after the Japanese withdrawal, the Korean *yangban* (nobility) laid claim to so much taxpaying land that royal revenues may have fallen by two-thirds. China suffered even more dire consequences. The battles in Manchuria weakened Chinese garrisons there, permitting Manchu opposition to consolidate. Manchu forces invaded Korea in the 1620s and eventually compelled the Yi to become a tributary state. As already related, the Manchus would be in possession of Beijing, China's capital, by 1644.

The Tokugawa Shogunate, to 1800

Tokugawa Ieyasu

After Hideyoshi's demise, Tokugawa Ieyasu (TOH-koo-GAH-wah ee-ay-YAH-soo) (1543–1616) asserted his domination over other daimyo and in 1603 established a new military government known as the **Tokugawa Shogunate**. The shoguns created a new administrative capital at Edo (ED-oh) (now Tokyo). Trade along the well-maintained road between Edo and the imperial capital of Kyoto promoted the development of the Japanese economy and the formation of other trading centers (see Map 21.1 on page 562).

Tokugawa Shogunate The last of the three shogunates of Japan.

Economic Growth

Although the Tokugawa Shogunate gave Japan more political unity than the islands had seen in centuries, the regionally based daimyo retained a great deal of power and autonomy. Ieyasu and his successors struggled for political centralization, but economic integration proved to be a more important feature of Tokugawa Japan. Because shoguns required the daimyo to visit Edo frequently, good roads and maritime transport linked the city to the castle towns on three of Japan's four main islands. Commercial traffic developed along these routes. The shogun paid the lords in rice, and the lords paid their followers in rice. Recipients converted much of this rice into cash, a practice that led to the development of rice exchanges at Edo and at Osaka (OH-sah-kah), where merchants speculated in rice prices. By the late seventeenth century Edo was one of the largest cities in the world, with nearly a million inhabitants.

The domestic peace of the Tokugawa era forced the warrior class to adapt to the growing bureaucratic needs of the state. As the samurai became better educated and more attuned to

CHRONOLOGY

	Korea and Japan	China and Central Asia	Russia
1500			
		1517 Portuguese embassy to China	
	1543 First Portuguese contacts		1547 Ivan IV adopts title of tsar
			1582 Russians conquer Khanate of Sibir
	1592 Japanese invasion of Korea		
1600		1601 Matteo Ricci allowed to reside in Beijing	
	1603 Tokugawa Shogunate formed		1613–1645 Rule of Mikhail, the first Romanov tsar
	1633–1639 Edicts close down trade with Europe	1644 Qing conquest of Beijing	1649 Subordination of serfs complete
		1662–1722 Rule of Emperor Kangxi	
		1689 Treaty of Nerchinsk with Russia	1689–1725 Rule of Peter the Great
		1691 Qing control of Inner Mongolia	
1700	1702 Trial of the Forty-Seven Ronin		1712 St. Petersburg becomes Russia's capital
		1736–1796 Rule of Emperor Qianlong	
			1762–1796 Rule of Catherine the Great
	1792 Russian ships first spotted off the coast of Japan		1799 Alaska becomes a Russian colony

the tastes of the civil elite, they became important customers for merchants dealing in silks, *sake* (SAH-kay) (rice wine), fans, porcelain, lacquer ware, books, and moneylending. The state attempted—unsuccessfully—to curb the independence of the merchants when the economic well-being of the samurai was threatened by low rice prices or high interest rates.

The 1600s and 1700s were centuries of high achievement in artisanship. Japanese skills in steel making, pottery, and lacquer ware were joined by excellence in the production of porcelain (see Environment and Technology: East Asian Porcelain), thanks in no small part to Korean experts brought back to Japan after the invasion of 1592. In the early 1600s manufacturers and merchants amassed enormous family fortunes. Several of the most important industrial and financial enterprises—for instance, the Mitsui (MIT-soo-ee) companies—had their origins

Korean Turtle Boats This painting shows a fleet of Korean warships under the command of Admiral Yi SunShin, who repelled numerous attacks by the Japanese in the last decade of the sixteenth century. Yi SunShin is celebrated for his invention of the "turtle boat," the world's first ironclad warship.

National Museum of Seoul/photo: Dr. Yushin Yoo

East Asian Porcelain

By the 1400s artisans in China, Korea, and Japan were all producing high-quality pottery with lustrous surface glazes. The best quality, intended for the homes of the wealthy and powerful, was made of pure white clay and covered with a hard translucent glaze. Artisans often added intricate decorations in cobalt blue and other colors. Cheaper pottery found a huge market in East Asia.

Such pottery was also exported to Southeast Asia, the Indian Ocean, and the Middle East. Little found its way to Europe before 1600, but imports soared once the Dutch established trading bases in East Asia. Europeans called the high-quality ware "porcelain." Blue and white designs were especially popular.

One of the great centers of Chinese production was at the large artisan factory at Jingdezhen (JING-deh-JUHN). No sooner had the Dutch tapped into this source than the civil wars and Manchu conquests disrupted production in the middle 1600s. Desperate for a substitute source, the Dutch turned to porcelain from Japanese producers at Arita and Imari, near Nagasaki. Despite Japan's restriction of European trade, the Dutch East India Company transported some 190,000 pieces of Japanese ceramic ware to the Netherlands between 1653 and 1682.

In addition to a wide range of Asian designs, Chinese and Japanese artisans made all sorts of porcelain for the European market. These included purely decorative pottery birds, vases, and pots as well as utilitarian vessels and dishes intended for table use. The serving dish illustrated here came from dinnerware sets the Japanese made especially for the Dutch East India Company. The VOC logo at the center represents the first letters of the company's name in Dutch. It is surrounded by Asian design motifs.

After the return of peace in China, the VOC imported tens of thousands of Chinese porcelain pieces a year. The Chinese artisans sometimes produced imitations of Japanese designs that had become popular in Europe. Meanwhile, the Dutch were experimenting with making their own imitations of East Asian porcelain, right down to the Asian motifs and colors that had become so fashionable in Europe.

Photograph courtesy Peabody Essex Museum, #83830

Japanese Export Porcelain Part of a larger set made for the Dutch East India Company.

e **PRIMARY SOURCE: Some Observations on Merchants** Read more about business operations in Tokugawa Japan and learn the recipe for merchant success put forward by business owner Mitsui Takafusa.

in sake breweries of the early Tokugawa period and then branched out into manufacturing, finance, and transport.

Wealthy merchants weakened the Tokugawa policy of controlling commerce by cultivating close alliances with their regional daimyo and, if possible, with the shogun himself. By the end of the 1700s the merchant families of Tokugawa Japan held the key to future modernization and the development of heavy industry.

Japan and the Europeans

Direct contacts with Europeans presented Japan with new opportunities and problems. Within thirty years of the arrival of the first Portuguese in 1543, the daimyo were fighting with Western-style firearms, copied and improved upon by Japanese armorers.

The Japanese welcomed but closely regulated traders from Portugal, Spain, the Netherlands, and England. Aside from the brief boom in porcelain exports in the seventeenth century, few Japanese goods went to Europe, and not much from Europe found a market in Japan. The Japanese sold the Dutch copper and silver, which the Dutch exchanged in China for silks that they then resold in Japan. The Japanese, of course, had their own trade with China.

Jesuit Missionaries   Portuguese and Spanish merchant ships also brought Catholic missionaries. One of the first, Francis Xavier, went to India in the mid-sixteenth century looking for converts and later

The Fotomas Index/The Bridgeman Art Library

Comprehensive Map of the Myriad Nations   Thanks to the "Dutch studies" scholars and to overseas contacts, many Japanese were well informed about the cultures, technologies, and political systems of various parts of the world. This combination map and ethnographic text of 1671 enthusiastically explores the differences among the many peoples living or traveling in Asia. The map of the Pacific hemisphere has the north pole on the left and the south pole on the extreme right of the drawing.

traveled throughout Southeast and East Asia. He spent two years in Japan and died in 1552, hoping to gain entry to China.

Japanese responses to Xavier and other Jesuits (members of the Catholic religious order the Society of Jesus) were mixed. Many ordinary Japanese found the new faith deeply meaningful, but the Japanese elite more often opposed it as disruptive and foreign. By 1580 more than 100,000 Japanese had become Christians, and one daimyo gave Jesuit missionaries the port city of Nagasaki (NAH-guh-SAHK-kee). In 1613 Date Masamune (DAH-tay mah-suh-MOO-nay), the fierce and independent daimyo of northern Honshu (HOHN-shoo), sent his own embassy to the Vatican, by way of the Philippines (where there were significant communities of Japanese merchants and pirates) and Mexico City. Some daimyo converts ordered their subjects to become Christians as well.

Japanese Christianity

By the early seventeenth century there were some 300,000 Japanese Christians and even some Japanese priests. However, suspicions about the intentions of the Europeans turned the new shogunate in Edo into a center of hostility toward Christianity. A decree issued in 1614 banned Christianity and charged its adherents with seeking to overthrow true doctrine, change the government, and seize the country. Some missionaries left Japan; others worked underground. The government began persecutions in earnest in 1617, and the beheadings, crucifixions, and forced recantations over the next several decades destroyed almost the entire Christian community.

To keep Christianity from resurfacing, a series of decrees issued between 1633 and 1639 sharply curtailed trade with Europe. Europeans who entered illegally faced the death penalty. Japanese subjects were required to produce certificates from Buddhist temples attesting to their religious orthodoxy and loyalty to the regime.

Archives Charmet/The Bridgeman Art Library

Woodblock Print of the "Forty-Seven Ronin" Story The saga of the forty-seven ronin and the avenging of their fallen leader has fascinated the Japanese public since the event occurred in 1702. This colored woodcut from the Tokugawa period shows the leaders of the group pausing on the snowy banks of the Sumida River in Edo (Tokyo) before storming their enemy's residence.

The exclusion of Europe was not total. A few Dutch were permitted to reside on a small artificial island in Nagasaki's harbor, and a few Japanese were licensed to supply their needs. What these intermediaries learned about European weapons technology, shipbuilding, mathematics and astronomy, anatomy and medicine, and geography was termed "Dutch studies."

Tokugawa restrictions on the number of Chinese ships that could trade in Japan were harder to enforce. Regional lords in northern and southern Japan not only pursued overseas trade and piracy but also claimed dominion over islands between Japan and Korea and southward toward Taiwan, including present-day Okinawa. Despite such evasions, the new shogunate unquestionably achieved substantial success in exercising its authority.

Elite Decline and Social Crisis

During the 1700s population growth put a great strain on the well-developed lands of central Japan. In more remote provinces, where the lords promoted new settlements and agricultural expansion, the rate of economic growth was significantly greater.

A Rice Economy

Also troubling the Tokugawa government in the 1700s was the shogunate's inability to stabilize rice prices and halt the economic decline of the samurai. The Tokugawa government realized that the rice brokers could manipulate prices and interest rates to enrich themselves at the expense of the samurai, who had to convert their rice allotments into cash. Early Tokugawa laws designed to regulate interest and prices were later supplemented by laws requiring moneylenders to forgive samurai debts. But these laws were not always enforced. By the early 1700s many lords and samurai were dependent on the willingness of merchants to provide credit.

The legitimacy of the Tokugawa shoguns rested on their ability to reward and protect the interests of the lords and samurai who had supported their rise to power. Moreover, the Tokugawa government, like the governments of China, Korea, and Vietnam, accepted the Confucian idea that agriculture should be the basis of state wealth and that merchants, who were considered morally weak, should occupy lowly positions in society. Tokugawa decentralization, however, not only failed to hinder but actually stimulated the growth of commercial activities.

From the founding of the Tokugawa Shogunate in 1603 until 1800, the economy grew faster than the population. Household amenities and cultural resources that in China appeared only in the cities were common in the Japanese countryside. Despite official disapproval, merchants enjoyed relative freedom and influence in eighteenth-century Japan. They produced a vivid culture of their own, fostering the development of *kabuki* theater, colorful woodblock prints and silk-screened fabrics, and restaurants.

SECTION REVIEW

- From the civil war among the daimyo emerged Hideyoshi, who, as supreme warlord, invaded Korea and China.

- After Hideyoshi's death, Tokugawa Ieyasu established the Tokugawa Shogunate, with its capital at Edo.

- The Tokugawa provided political unity and fostered economic expansion but failed to control commerce.

- The Japanese engaged in regulated trade with Europeans, but rising suspicions caused the Tokugawa to restrict foreign contacts.

- Economic growth nourished a new merchant-class culture, but the position of the samurai deteriorated under economic and social pressures.

Ronin

The "Forty-Seven Ronin" (ROH-neen) incident of 1701–1703 exemplified the ideological and social crisis of Japan's transformation from a military to a civil society. A senior minister provoked a young daimyo into drawing his sword at the shogun's court. For this offense the young lord was sentenced to commit *seppuku* (SEP-poo-koo), the ritual suicide of the samurai. His own followers then became *ronin*, "masterless samurai," obliged by the traditional code of the warrior to avenge their deceased master. They broke into the house of the senior minister and killed him and others in his household. Then they withdrew to a temple in Edo and notified the shogun of what they had done out of loyalty to their lord and to avenge his death.

A legal debate ensued. To deny the righteousness of the ronin would be to deny samurai values. But to approve their actions would create social chaos, undermine laws against murder, and deny the shogunal government the right to try cases of samurai violence. The shogun ruled that the ronin had to die but would be permitted to die honorably by committing seppuku. Traditional samurai values had to surrender to the supremacy of law. The purity of purpose of the ronin is still celebrated in Japan, but since then Japanese writers, historians, and teachers have recognized that the self-sacrifice of the ronin for the sake of upholding civil law was necessary.

THE LATER MING AND EARLY QING EMPIRES

Like Japan, China after 1500 experienced civil and foreign wars, an important change in government, and new trading and cultural relations with Europe and its neighbors. The internal and external forces at work in China were different and operated on a much larger scale, but they led in similar directions. By 1800 China had a greatly enhanced empire, an expanding economy, and growing doubts about the importance of European trade and Christianity.

Ming Empire Empire based in China that Zhu Yuanzhang established after the overthrow of the Yuan Empire. The Ming emperor Yongle sponsored the building of the Forbidden City and the voyages of Zheng He. The later years of the Ming saw a slowdown in technological development and economic decline.

The Ming Empire, 1500–1644

The economic and cultural achievements of the early **Ming Empire** (see Chapter 13) continued during the 1500s. But this productive period was followed by many decades of political weakness, warfare, and rural woes until a new dynasty, the Qing (ching) from Manchuria, guided China back to peace and prosperity.

The Europeans whose ships began to seek out new contacts with China in the early sixteenth century left many accounts of their impressions. They were astonished at Ming China's imperial power, exquisite manufactures, and vast population. European merchants bought such large quantities of the high-grade blue-on-white porcelain commonly used by China's upper classes that in English all fine dishes became known simply as "china."

Economic Growth

The growing integration of China into the world economy stimulated rapid growth in the silk, cotton, and porcelain industries. Agricultural regions that supplied raw materials to these industries and food for the expanding urban populations also prospered. In exchange for Chinese exports, tens of thousands of tons of silver from Japan and Latin America flooded into China in the century before 1640. The influx of silver led many Chinese to substitute payments in silver for land taxes, labor obligations, and other kinds of dues.

Ming cities had long been culturally and commercially vibrant. Many large landowners and absentee landlords lived in town, as did officials, artists, and rich merchants who had purchased ranks or prepared their sons for the examinations. The elite classes had created a brilliant culture in which novels, operas, poetry, porcelain, and painting were all closely interwoven. Small businesses catering to the urban elites prospered through printing, tailoring, running restaurants, or selling paper, ink, ink-stones, and writing brushes. The imperial government operated factories for the production of ceramics and silks. Enormous government complexes at Jingdezhen and elsewhere invented assembly-line techniques and produced large quantities of high-quality ceramics for sale in China and abroad.

Despite these achievements, serious problems developed that left the Ming Empire economically and politically exhausted. There is evidence that the climate changes known as the Little Ice Age in seventeenth-century Europe affected the climate in China as well (see Issues in World History: The Little Ice Age on page 576). Annual temperatures dropped, reached a low point about 1645, and remained low until the early 1700s. The resulting agricultural distress and famine fueled large uprisings that speeded the end of the Ming Empire. The devastation caused by these uprisings and the spread of epidemic disease resulted in steep declines in local populations.

Problems of Adjustment

The rapid urban growth and business speculation that were part of the burgeoning of the trading economy also produced problems. Some provinces suffered from price inflation caused by the flood of silver. In contrast to the growing involvement of European governments in promoting economic growth, the Ming government pursued some policies that hindered growth. Despite the fact that earlier experiments with paper currency had failed, Ming governments persisted in issuing new paper money and copper coinage, even after abundant supplies of silver had won the approval of the markets. Corruption was also a serious government problem. By the end of the Ming period disorder and inefficiency plagued the imperial factories, touching off strikes in the late sixteenth and seventeenth centuries. During a labor protest at Jingdezhen in 1601, workers threw themselves into the kilns to protest working conditions.

Yet the urban and industrial sectors of later Ming society fared much better than the agricultural sector, which failed to maintain the strong growth of early Ming times. Despite knowledge of new African and American crops gained from European traders, farmers were slow to change their ways. Neither the rice-growing regions in southern China nor the wheat-growing regions in northern China experienced a meaningful increase in productivity under the later Ming. After 1500 economic depression in the countryside, combined with recurring epidemics in central and southern China, kept rural population growth in check.

Ming Collapse and the Rise of the Qing

e Interactive Map

Although these environmental, economic, and administrative problems existed, the primary reasons for the fall of the Ming Empire were internal rebellion and rising Manchu power. Inse-

MAP 21.1 **The Qing Empire, 1644–1783** The Qing Empire began in Manchuria and captured north China in 1644. Between 1644 and 1783 the Qing conquered all the former Ming territories and added Taiwan, the lower Amur River basin, Inner Mongolia, eastern Turkestan, and Tibet. The resulting state was more than twice the size of the Ming Empire.

© Cengage Learning

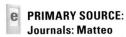

Mongols and Manchus

cure boundaries had been a recurrent peril. The Ming had long been under pressure from the powerful Mongol federations of the north and west. In the late 1500s large numbers of Mongols were unified by their devotion to the Dalai Lama (DAH-lie LAH-mah), or universal teacher of Tibetan Buddhism. Building on this spiritual unity, a brilliant leader named Galdan restored Mongolia as a regional military power around 1600. The Manchus, an agricultural people who controlled the region north of Korea, grew stronger in the northeast.

In the southwest, native peoples repeatedly resisted the immigration of Chinese farmers. Pirates based in Okinawa and Taiwan, many of them Japanese, frequently looted the southeast coast. Ming military resources, concentrated against the Mongols and the Manchus in the north, could not be deployed to defend the coasts. As a result, many southern Chinese migrated to Southeast Asia to profit from the sea-trading networks of the Indian Ocean.

The Japanese invasion of 1592 to 1598 (see section on Japan) prompted the Ming to seek the assistance of Manchu troops that they were then unable to restrain. With the rebel leader Li Zicheng in possession of Beijing (see the beginning of this chapter) and the emperor dead by his own hand, a Ming general joined forces with the Manchu leaders in the summer of 1644. Instead of restoring the Ming, however, the Manchus claimed China for their own and began a forty-year conquest of the rest of the Ming territories, as well as Taiwan and parts of Mongolia and Central Asia (see Map 21.1 and Diversity and Dominance: Gendered Violence: The Yangzhou Massacre).

Qing Empire Empire established in China by Manchus who overthrew the Ming Empire in 1644. At various times the Qing also controlled Manchuria, Mongolia, Turkestan, and Tibet. The last Qing emperor was overthrown in 1911.

A Manchu family headed the new **Qing Empire**, and Manchu generals commanded the military forces. But Manchus made up a very small portion of the population. The overwhelming majority of Qing officials, soldiers, merchants, and farmers were ethnic Chinese. Like other successful invaders of China, the Qing soon adopted Chinese institutions and policies.

Trading Companies and Missionaries

For European merchants, the China trade was second in importance only to the spice trade of southern Asia. China's vast population and manufacturing skills drew a steady stream of ships from western Europe, but enthusiasm for the trade developed only slowly at the imperial court.

A Portuguese ship reached China at the end of 1513 but was not permitted to trade. A formal Portuguese embassy in 1517 got bogged down in Chinese protocol and procrastination, and China expelled the Portuguese in 1522. Finally, in 1557 the Portuguese gained the right to trade from a base in Macao (muh-KOW) on the southern coast. Spain's Asian trade was conducted from Manila in the Philippines, which also linked with South America across the Pacific. For a time, the Spanish and the Dutch both maintained trading outposts on the island of Taiwan, but in 1662 they were forced to concede control to the Qing, who for the first time incorporated Taiwan into China.

The Dutch East India Company

By then, the Dutch East India Company (VOC) had displaced the Portuguese as the major European trader in the Indian Ocean and was establishing itself as the main European trader in East Asia. VOC representatives courted official favor in China by acknowledging the moral superiority of the emperor. They performed the ritual kowtow (in which the visitor knocked his head on the floor while crawling toward the throne) to the Ming emperor.

Jesuits in China

Catholic missionaries accompanied the Portuguese and Spanish merchants to China, just as they did to Japan. While the Franciscans and Dominicans pursued the conversion efforts at the bottom of society that had worked so well in Japan, the Jesuits focused on China's intellectual and political elite. In this they were far more successful than they had been in Japan—at least until the eighteenth century.

PRIMARY SOURCE: Journals: Matteo Ricci This story about Jesuit missionaries in China provides an interesting look at the nexus of religion and politics in the early seventeenth century.

The outstanding Jesuit of late Ming China, Matteo Ricci (mah-TAY-oh REE-chee) (1552–1610), became expert in the Chinese language and an accomplished scholar of the Confucian classics. Under Ricci's leadership, the Jesuits adapted Catholicism to Chinese cultural traditions while introducing the Chinese to the latest science and technology from Europe. From 1601 Ricci resided in Beijing on an imperial stipend as a Western scholar. Later Jesuits headed the office of astronomy that issued the official calendar.

Emperor Kangxi

Kangxi Qing emperor (r. 1662–1722). He oversaw the greatest expansion of the Qing Empire.

The seventeenth and eighteenth centuries—particularly the reigns of the **Kangxi** (KAHNG-shee) (r. 1662–1722) and Qianlong (chee-YEN-loong) (r. 1736–1796) emperors—were a period of economic, military, and cultural achievement in China. The early Qing emperors repaired the roads and waterworks, lowered transit taxes, cut rents and interest rates, and established incentives for resettling areas devastated by peasant rebellions. Foreign trade was encouraged.

Gendered Violence: The Yangzhou Massacre

The Qing were not eager for reminders of their brutal takeover to circulate. This rare eyewitness account smuggled out of China reveals not just the violence of the conquest but also the diversity of its impact on men and women.

The account begins in 1645 as rumors of approaching Manchu soldiers spread through Yangzhou, an important city near the juncture of the Yangzi River and the Grand Canal, and the soldiers charged with its defense begin to flee.

Crowds of barefoot and disheveled refugees were flocking into the city. When questioned, they were too distraught to reply. At that point dozens of mounted soldiers in confused waves came surging south looking as though they had given up all hope. Among them appeared a man who turned out to be the commandant himself. It seems he had intended to leave by the east gate but could not because the enemy soldiers outside the wall were drawing too near; he was therefore forced to cut across this part of town to reach the south gate. This is how we first learned for sure that the enemy troops would enter the city. . . .

My house backed against the city wall, and peeping through the chinks in my window, I saw the soldiers on the wall marching south then west, solemn and in step. Although the rain was beating down, it did not seem to disturb them. This reassured me because I gathered that they were well-disciplined units.

. . . For a long time no one came. I retreated again to the back window and found that the regiment on the wall had broken ranks; some soldiers were walking about, others standing still.

All of a sudden I saw some soldiers escorting a group of women dressed in Yangzhou fashion. This was my first real shock. Back in the house, I said to my wife, "Should things go badly when the soldiers enter the city, you may need to end your life."

"Yes," she replied, "Whatever silver we have you should keep. I think we women can stop thinking about life in this world." She gave me all the silver, unable to control her crying. . . .

Soon my younger brother arrived, then my two older brothers. We discussed the situation and I said, "The people who live in our neighborhood are all rich merchants. It will be disastrous if they think we are rich too." I then urged my brothers to brave the rain and quickly take the women by the

back route to my older brother's house. His home was situated behind Mr. He's graveyard and was surrounded by the huts of poor families. . . .

The cunning soldiers, suspecting that many people were still hidden, tried to entice them out by posting a placard promising clemency. About fifty to sixty people, half of them women, emerged. My elder brother said, "We four by ourselves will never survive if we run into these vicious soldiers, so we had better join the crowd. Since there are so many of them, escape will be easier. . . ."

The leaders were three Manchu soldiers. They searched my brothers and found all the silver they were carrying, but left me untouched. At that point some women appeared, two of whom called out to me. I recognized them as the concubines of my friend Mr. Zhu Shu and stopped them anxiously. They were disheveled and partly naked, their feet bare and covered with mud up to the ankles. One was holding a girl whom the soldiers hit with a whip and threw into the mud. Then we were immediately driven on. One soldier, sword in hand, took the lead; another drove us from behind with a long spear; and a third walked along on our right and left flanks alternately, making sure no one escaped. In groups of twenty or thirty we were herded along like sheep and cattle. If we faltered we were struck, and some people were even killed on the spot. The women were tied together with long chains around their necks, like a clumsy string of pearls. Stumbling at every step, they were soon covered with mud. Here and there on the ground lay babies, trampled by people or horses.

. . . We then entered the house of [a] merchant, . . . which had been taken over by the three soldiers. Another soldier was already there. He had seized several attractive women and was rifling their trunks for fancy silks, which he piled in a heap. Seeing the three soldiers arrive, he laughed and pushed several dozen of us into the back hall. The women he led into a side chamber. . . .

The three soldiers stripped the women of their wet clothing all the way to their underwear, then ordered the seamstress to measure them and give them new garments. The women, thus coerced, had to expose themselves and stand naked. What shame they endured! Once they had changed, the soldiers grabbed them and forced them to join them in eating and

Vietnam, Burma, and Nepal sent embassies to the Qing tribute court and carried the latest Chinese fashions back home. Overland routes from Korea to Central Asia revived.

The Manchu aristocrats who led the conquest of Beijing and north China dominated the first Qing emperor and served as regents for his young son, who was declared emperor in 1662. This child-emperor, Kangxi, sparred politically with the regents until 1669, when at age sixteen he executed the chief regent and thereby gained real control of the government. An intellectual prodigy who had mastered classical Chinese, Manchu, and Mongolian and memorized the Chinese classics, Kangxi guided imperial expansion and maintained stability until his death in 1722.

In the north, the Qing rulers feared an alliance between Galdan's Mongol state and the expanding Russian presence along the **Amur** (AH-moor) **River.** In the 1680s Qing forces attacked

Amur River This river valley was a contested frontier between northern China and eastern Russia until the settlement arranged in the Treaty of Nerchinsk (1689).

drinking, then did whatever they pleased with them, without any regard for decency.

[The narrator escapes and hides atop a wooden canopy over a bed.] Later on a soldier brought a woman in and wanted her to sleep with him in the bed below me. Despite her refusal he forced her to yield. "This is too near the street. It is not a good place to stay," the woman said. I was almost discovered, but after a time the soldier departed with the woman. . . . [The narrator flees again and is reunited with his wife and relatives.]

At length, however, there came a soldier of the "Wolf Men" tribe, a vicious-looking man with a head like a mouse and eyes like a hawk. He attempted to abduct my wife. She was obliged to creep forward on all fours, pleading as she had with the others, but to no avail. When he insisted that she stand up, she rolled on the ground and refused. He then beat her so savagely with the flat of his sword that the blood flowed out in streams, totally soaking her clothes. Because my wife had once admonished me, "If I am unlucky I will die no matter what; do not plead for me as a husband or you will get caught too," I acted as if I did not know she was being beaten and hid far away in the grass, convinced she was about to die. Yet the depraved soldier did not stop there; he grabbed her by the hair, cursed her, struck her cruelly, and then dragged her away by the leg. . . . Just then they ran into a body of mounted soldiers. One of them said a few words to the soldier in Manchu. At this he dropped my wife and departed with them. Barely able to crawl back, she let out a loud sob, every part of her body injured. . . .

Unexpectedly there appeared a handsome looking man of less than thirty, a double-edged sword hung by his side, dressed in Manchu-style hat, red coat, and a pair of black boots. His follower, in a yellow jacket, was also very gallant in appearance. Immediately behind them were several residents of Yangzhou. The young man in red, inspecting me closely, said, "I would judge from your appearance that you are not one of these people. Tell me honestly, what class of person are you?"

I remembered that some people had obtained pardons and others had lost their lives the moment they said that they were poor scholars. So I did not dare come out at once with the truth and instead concocted a story. He pointed to my wife and son and asked who they were, and I told him the truth. "Tomorrow the prince will order that all swords be sheathed and all of you will be spared," he said and then commanded his followers to give us some clothes and an ingot of silver. He also asked me, "How many days have you been without food?"

"Five days," I replied.

"Then come with me," he commanded. Although we only half trusted him, we were afraid to disobey. He led us to a well-stocked house, full of rice, fish, and other provisions. "Treat these four people well," he said to a woman in the house and then left. . . .

The next day was [April 30]. Killing and pillaging continued, although not on the previous scale. Still the mansions of the rich were thoroughly looted, and almost all the teenage girls were abducted. . . . every grain of rice, every inch of silk now entered these tigers' mouths. The resulting devastation is beyond description.

[May 2]. Civil administration was established in all the prefectures and counties; proclamations were issued aimed at calming the people, and monks from each temple were ordered to burn corpses. The temples themselves were clogged with women who had taken refuge, many of whom had died of fright or starvation. The "List of Corpses Burned" records more than eight hundred thousand, and this list does not include those who jumped into wells, threw themselves into the river, hanged themselves, were burned to death inside houses, or were carried away by the soldiers. . . .

When this calamity began there had been eight of us: my two elder brothers, my younger brother, my elder brother's wife, their son, my wife, my son, and myself. Now only three of us survived for sure, though the fate of my wife's brother and sister-in-law was not yet known. . . .

From the 25th of the fourth month to the 5th of the fifth month was a period of ten days. I have described here only what I actually experienced or saw with my own eyes; I have not recorded anything I picked up from rumor or hearsay.

QUESTIONS FOR ANALYSIS

1. **What accounts for the soldiers' brutal treatment of the women?**

2. **What did different women do to protect themselves?**

3. **Having conquered, what did the Manchu do to restore order?**

Source: Reprinted with permission of the Free Press, a division of Simon and Schuster Adult Publishing Group from *Chinese Civilization: A Sourcebook*, Second Edition, edited by Patricia Buckley Ebrey, pp. 272–279. Copyright © 1993 by Patricia Buckley Ebrey.

Contact with Russia   the wooden forts built by hardy Russian scouts on the river's northern bank. Neither empire sent large forces into the Amur territories, so the contest was partly a struggle for the goodwill of the local peoples. The Qing emperor emphasized the importance of treading lightly in the struggle:

> Upon reaching the lands of the Evenks and the Dagurs you will send to announce that you have come to hunt deer. Meanwhile, keep a careful record of the distance and go, while hunting, along the northern bank of the Amur until you come by the shortest route to the town of Russian settlement at Albazin. Thoroughly reconnoiter its location and situation. I don't think the Russians will take a chance on attacking you. If they offer you food, accept it and show your gratitude. If they do attack you, don't fight back. In that case, lead your people and withdraw into our own territories.[2]

Emperor Kangxi In a portrait from about 1690, the young Manchu ruler is portrayed as a refined scholar in the Confucian tradition. He was a scholar and had great intellectual curiosity, but this portrait would not suggest that he was also capable of leading troops in battle.

The Palace Museum, Beijing

Qing forces twice attacked Albazin. The Qing were worried about Russian alliances with other frontier peoples, while Russia wished to protect its access to the furs, timber, and metals concentrated in Siberia, Manchuria, and Yakutsk. The Qing and Russians were also rivals for control of northern Asia's Pacific coast. Seeing little benefit in continued conflict, in 1689 the two empires negotiated the Treaty of Nerchinsk, using Jesuit missionaries as interpreters. The treaty fixed the border along the Amur River and regulated trade across it. Although this was a thinly settled area, the treaty proved important, and the frontier it demarcated has long endured.

The next step was to settle the Mongolian frontier. Kangxi personally led troops in the great campaigns that defeated Galdan and brought Inner Mongolia under Qing control by 1691.

Unlike the rulers of Japan, who drove Christian missionaries out, Kangxi welcomed Jesuit advisers, discussed scientific and philosophical issues with them, and put them in important offices. Jesuits helped create maps in the European style as practical guides to newly conquered regions and as symbols of Qing dominance. Kangxi considered introducing the European calendar, but protests from the Confucian elite caused him to drop the plan. When he fell ill with malaria in the 1690s, Jesuit medical treatment (in this case, South American quinine) aided his recovery. Kangxi also ordered the creation of illustrated books in Manchu detailing European anatomical and pharmaceutical knowledge.

Christian Compromises To gain converts, the Jesuits made important compromises in their religious teaching. Most importantly, they tolerated Confucian ancestor worship. This aroused controversy between the Jesuits and their Catholic rivals in China, the Franciscans and Dominicans, and also between the Jesuits and the pope. In 1690 the disagreement reached a high pitch. Kangxi wrote to Rome supporting the Jesuit position and after further dispute ordered the expulsion of all missionaries who refused to sign a certificate accepting his position. The Jesuit presence in China declined in the eighteenth century, and later Qing emperors persecuted Christians rather than naming them to high offices.

Chinese Influences on Europe

The exchange of information that Kangxi had fostered was never one-way. While the Jesuits brought forward new knowledge of anatomy, for example, the Qing demonstrated an early form of inoculation, called "variolation," that had helped curtail smallpox after the conquest of Beijing. The technique inspired Europeans to develop other vaccines.

Similarly, Jesuit writings about China excited admiration in Europe. The wealthy and the aspiring middle classes demanded Chinese things—or things that looked to Europeans as if they could be Chinese. Silk, porcelain, and tea were avidly sought, along with cloisonné jewelry, jade, lacquered and jeweled room dividers, painted fans, and carved ivory (which originated in Africa and was finished in China). Wallpaper began as an adaptation of the Chinese practice of covering walls with enormous loose-hanging watercolors or calligraphy scrolls. By the mid-1700s special workshops throughout China were producing wallpaper and other consumer items according to the specifications of European merchants. The items were exported to Europe via Canton.

Qing Political Philosophy Qing political philosophy impressed Europeans, too. In the late 1770s poems supposedly written by Emperor Qianlong were translated into French and disseminated in intellectual circles. In them the Qing emperors rule as benevolent despots campaigning against superstition

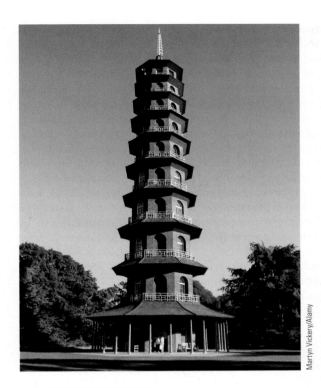

Great Pagoda at Kew Gardens A testament to Europeans' fascination with Chinese culture is the towering Pagoda at the Royal Botanic Gardens in London. Completed in 1762, it was designed by Sir William Chambers as the principal ornament in the pleasure grounds of the White House at Kew, residence of Augusta, the mother of King George III.

and ignorance, curbing aristocratic excesses, and patronizing science and the arts. This image of a practical, secular, compassionate ruler impressed the French thinker Voltaire, who proclaimed that Qing emperors were model philosopher-kings and advocated such rulership as a protection against the growth of aristocratic privilege.

Tea and Diplomacy

To maintain control over trade, facilitate tax collection, and suppress piracy, the Qing permitted only one market point for each foreign sector. Thus Europeans could trade only at Canton.

Britain and the Trade Deficit

This system worked well enough until the late 1700s, when Britain became worried about its massive trade deficit with China. From bases in India and Singapore, British traders moved eastward and by the early 1700s dominated European trading in Canton, displacing the Dutch. The directors of the East India Company (EIC) anticipated limitless profits from China's gigantic markets and advanced technologies.

Tea from China had spread overland to Russia, Central Asia, and the Middle East in medieval and early modern times to become a prized import. Consumers knew it by its northern Chinese name, *cha*—as did the Portuguese. Other western Europeans acquired tea from the sea routes and with it the name used in the Fujian province of coastal China and Taiwan: *te*. In much of Europe, tea competed with chocolate and coffee as a fashionable drink by the mid-1600s.

The Macartney Mission

British tea importers accumulated great fortunes. However, the Qing Empire took payment in silver and rarely bought anything from Britain. With domestic revenues declining in the later 1700s, the Qing government needed the silver and was disinclined to loosen import restrictions. To make matters worse, the East India Company had managed its worldwide holdings badly. As it teetered on bankruptcy, its attempts to manipulate Parliament became increasingly intrusive. In 1792 the British government dispatched Lord George Macartney, a well-connected peer with practical experience in Russia and India, to China. Staffed by scientists, artists, and translators as well as guards and diplomats, the **Macartney mission** showed Britain's great interest in the Qing Empire as well as the EIC's desire to revise the trade system.

Macartney mission The unsuccessful attempt by the British Empire to establish diplomatic relations with the Qing Empire.

To fit Chinese traditions, Macartney portrayed himself as a "tribute emissary" come to salute the Qianlong emperor's eightieth birthday. However, he refused to perform the kowtow, though he did agree to bow on one knee as he would to King George III. The Qianlong emperor received Macartney courteously in September 1793 but refused to alter the Canton trading system, open new ports of trade, or allow the British to establish a permanent mission in Beijing. The emperor sent a letter to King George explaining that China had no need to increase its foreign trade, had no use for Britain's ingenious devices and manufacturers, and set no value on closer diplomatic ties.

Dutch, French, and Russian missions to achieve what Macartney could not do also failed. European frustration mounted while admiration for China faded. The Qing court would not communicate with foreign envoys or observe the simplest rules of the European diplomatic system. In Macartney's view, China was like a venerable old warship, well maintained and splendid to look at, but obsolete and no longer up to the task.

Population and Social Stress

The Chinese who escorted Macartney and his entourage in 1792–1793 took them through China's prosperous cities and productive farmland. They did not see, however, the economic and environmental decline that had set in during the last decades of the 1700s.

Environmental Deterioration

 PRIMARY SOURCE: Edict on Trade with Great Britain Learn why elaborate gifts brought by a British delegation and bestowed personally by Lord Macartney on Emperor Qianlong failed to convince him to accept Britain's trade proposals.

Population growth—a tripling in size since 1500—had intensified demand for food and for more intensive agriculture. With an estimated 350 million people in the late 1700s, China had twice the population of all of Europe. Despite efficient farming and the gradual adoption of New World crops like corn and sweet potatoes, population pressure touched off social and environmental problems. Increased demand for building materials and firewood reduced woodlands. Deforestation, in turn, accelerated wind and water erosion and increased flooding. Dams and dikes were not maintained, and silted-up river channels were not dredged. By the end of the eighteenth century parts of the thousand-year-old Grand Canal linking the rivers of north and south China were nearly unusable, and the towns that bordered it were starved for commerce.

Some interior districts responded to this misery by increasing their output of export goods like tea, cotton, and silk. Some peasants sought seasonal jobs in better-off agricultural areas or worked in low-status jobs as barge pullers, charcoal burners, or night soil (human waste) carriers. Begging, prostitution, and theft increased in the cities. Rebellions broke out in flood-ravaged central and southwestern China. Indigenous peoples concentrated in the less fertile lands in the south and in the northern and western borderlands of the empire often joined in revolts (see Map 21.2).

The Qing government was not up to controlling its vast empire. It was twice the size of the Ming geographically, but it employed about the same number of officials. The government's dependence on working alliances with local elites had led to widespread corruption and shrinking government revenues. The Qing's spectacular rise had ended, and decline had set in.

 Interactive Map

MAP 21.2 **Climate and Diversity in the Qing Empire** The Qing Empire encompassed different environmental zones, and the climate differences corresponded to population density and cultural divisions. Wetter regions to the east of the 15-inch rainfall line also contained the most densely populated 20 percent of Qing land. The drier, less densely populated 80 percent of the empire was home to the greatest portion of peoples who spoke languages other than Chinese. Many were nomads, fishermen, hunters, and farmers who raised crops other than rice.

© Cengage Learning

Cultural groups, by predominant economic activity

Agricultural
- Han

Nomadic/Agricultural
- Tibetan
- Mongol
- Turkic

Hunting/Fishing/Agricultural
- Tungusic, Manchu

Fishing/Gathering/Agricultural
- Thai, Miao-Yao, Mon-Khmer
- Malayo-Polynesian

- Other

THE RUSSIAN EMPIRE

From modest beginnings in 1500, Russia expanded rapidly during the next three centuries to create an empire that stretched from eastern Europe across northern Asia and into North America. Russia also became one of the major powers of Europe by 1750.

The Drive Across Northern Asia

During the centuries just before 1500, the history of the Russians had been dominated by steppe nomads (see Chapter 13). The Mongol Khanate of the Golden Horde ruled the Russians and their neighbors from the 1240s until 1480.

Under the Golden Horde Moscow became the most important Russian city and the center of political power. Moscow lay in the forest zone that stretched across Eurasia north of the treeless steppe (grasslands) favored by Mongol horsemen. The princes of **Muscovy** (MUSS-koe-vee), the territory surrounding the city of Moscow, led the movement against the Golden Horde and ruthlessly annexed the territories of the neighboring Russian state of Novgorod in 1478.

Once free from Mongol domination, the princes of Moscovy set out on conquests that in time made them masters of all the Golden Horde territories and then of a far greater empire. Prince Ivan IV (r. 1533–1584) pushed the conquests south and east at the expense of the Khanates of Kazan and Astrakhan (see Map 21.3).

At the end of the sixteenth century, Russians ruled the largest state in Europe and large territories on the Asian side of the **Ural Mountains** as well. After 1547 the Russian ruler used the title **tsar** (zahr) (from the Roman imperial title *caesar*), the term Russians had used for the rulers of the Mongol Empire. The Russian church promoted the idea of Moscow as the "third Rome," successor to the Roman Empire's second capital, Constantinople, which had fallen to the Ottoman Turks in 1453.

Yet Russian claims to greatness were also exaggerated: in 1600 the empire was poor, backward, and landlocked. Only one seaport—often frozen Arkhangelsk in the north—connected to the world's oceans. The Crimean Turks to the south were powerful enough to sack Moscow in 1571. Beyond them, the Ottoman Empire controlled access to the Black Sea, while the Safavid rulers of Iran dominated the trade of southern Central Asia. The powerful kingdoms of Sweden and Poland-Lithuania to the west similarly blocked Russian access to the Baltic Sea.

The one route open to expansion, **Siberia**, had much to recommend it. Many Russians preferred the forested north to the open steppes; and the thinly inhabited region abounded in valuable resources, most notably the soft, dense fur that forest animals grew to survive the long

Muscovy Russian principality that emerged gradually during the era of Mongol domination. The Muscovite dynasty ruled without interruption from 1276 to 1598.

The Rise of Muscovy

Ural Mountains This north-south range separates Siberia from the rest of Russia. It is commonly considered the boundary between the continents of Europe and Asia.

tsar (czar) From Latin caesar, this Russian title for a monarch was first used in the sixteenth century.

The Problem of Seaports

Siberia The extreme northeastern sector of Asia, including the Kamchatka Peninsula and the present Russian coast of the Arctic Ocean, the Bering Strait, and the Sea of Okhotsk.

Strogonov Fur Traders

winters. Like their counterparts in Canada (see Chapter 18), Russian pioneers in Siberia made a living from animal pelts. The foreign merchants who came to buy these furs in Moscow provided the tsars with revenue and European contacts.

The Strogonovs, a wealthy Russian trading family, led the early Russian exploration of Siberia. The small indigenous bands of foragers had no way of resisting the armed adventurers the Strogonovs hired. Using rifles, their troops attacked and destroyed the only political power in the region, the Khanate of Sibir, in 1582. Moving through the dense forests by river, Russian fur trappers were able to reach the Pacific during the seventeenth century and soon crossed over into Alaska. Russian political control followed more slowly into what was more a frontier zone with widely scattered forts than a province under full control. Beginning in the early seventeenth century the tsar also used Siberia as a penal colony for criminals and political prisoners.

In the 1640s Russian settlers began to grow grain in the Amur River Valley east of Mongolia. As seen already, by the time the Qing reacted to the Russian presence, the worrisome threat of Galdan's Mongol military power had arisen. Equally concerned about the Mongols, the Russians were pleased to work out a frontier agreement. The 1689 Treaty of Nerchinsk recognized Russian claims west of Mongolia but required the Russians to withdraw their settlements farther east.

Russian Society and Politics to 1725

Russian expansion involved demographic changes as well as new relations between the tsar and the elite classes. A third transformation affected the freedom and mobility of the Russian peasantry.

As the empire expanded, it incorporated people with different languages, religious beliefs, and ethnic identities. Orthodox missionaries made great efforts to Christianize the peoples of Siberia in much the same way that Catholic missionaries did in Canada. But among the relatively more populous steppe peoples, Islam prevailed over Christianity as the dominant religion. Differences in how people made their living were equally fundamental. Russians tended to live as farmers, hunters, builders, scribes, or merchants, while those newly incorporated into the empire were mostly herders, caravan workers, and soldiers.

Cossacks

Cossacks Peoples of the Russian Empire who lived outside the farming villages, often as herders, mercenaries, or outlaws. Cossacks led the conquest of Siberia in the sixteenth and seventeenth centuries.

As people mixed, individual and group identities became complex. There was diversity even among Russian speakers who were Russian Orthodox in faith. The name ***Cossack***, which applied to bands of people living on the steppes between Moscovy and the Caspian and Black Seas, probably comes from a Turkic word for a warrior or mercenary soldier. Actually, Cossacks had diverse origins and beliefs, but they all belonged to close-knit bands, fought superbly from the saddle, and terrified both villagers and legal authorities. Cossack allegiances with rulers were temporary; loyalty to the chiefs of their bands was paramount.

Cossacks provided most of the soldiers and settlers employed by the Strogonovs, and they founded every major town in Russian Siberia. They also manned the Russian camps on the Amur River. West of the Urals the Cossacks defended Russia against Swedish and Ottoman incursions, but they also preserved their political autonomy. Those in the rich and populous lands of the Ukraine, for example, rebelled when the tsar agreed to a division of their lands with Poland-Lithuania in 1667.

The Romanovs

In the early seventeenth century Swedish and Polish forces briefly occupied Moscow on separate occasions. This "Time of Troubles" marked the end of the old line of Muscovite rulers. The Russian aristocracy—the boyars (BOY-ar)—allowed one of their own, Mikhail Romanov (ROH-man-off or roh-MAN-off) (r. 1613–1645), to inaugurate a dynasty that would soon consolidate its own authority while successfully competing with neighboring powers. The Romanovs often represented conflicts between Slavic Russians and Turkic steppe peoples as being between Christians and "infidels" or between the civilized and the "barbaric." Despite this rhetoric, it is important to understand that these cultural groups were defined less by blood ties than by the ways in which they lived.

Serfs

As centralized tsarist power rose, the freedom of the peasants who tilled the land in European Russia fell. The Moscovy rulers and early tsars rewarded their loyal nobles with grants of land that obliged the local peasants to work for the lords. Law and custom permitted peasants to change masters during a two-week period each year, which encouraged lords to treat their peasants well; but the rising commercialization of agriculture also raised the value of these labor obligations.

The Russian Empire
- Russia in 1533
- Added by 1598
- Added by 1721
- Added by 1796
- ✖ Fort

PACIFIC OCEAN

BRITISH NORTH AMERICA (CANADA)

Novo Arkhangelsk (Sitka)
TLINGIT
RUSSIAN AMERICA (ALASKA)
ALEUTS
INUIT
INUIT
Bering Strait
Bering Sea
INUIT

GREENLAND

ARCTIC OCEAN

Iceland

Arctic Circle

CHUKCHI
KORYAKS
Kolyma R.
Petropavlovsk
ALEUTS
Kamchatka Peninsula
Zashiversk
Yana R.
Okhotsk
Sea of Okhotsk
Sakhalin I.
Lena R.
Olenek R.
Zhigansk
Yakutsk
SIBERIA
Khatanga R.
EVENKI
Vilyuy R.
YAKUTS
LAMUTS
Amur R.
Lower Tunguska R.
EVENKI
TUNGUSY
Taz R.
MANCHURIA
Nerchinsk
Kara Sea
OSTYAKS
Yenisey R.
Obdorsk
SAMOYEDS
Bratsk
Ob R.
OSTYAKS
Kem R.
Krasnoyarsk
Irkutsk
Barents Sea
TARTARS
Surgut
SWEDEN
Verkhoturye
Tula R.
URAL MOUNTAINS
Kama R.
GREAT BRITAIN
NORWAY
Arkhangelsk
Tobol R.
Ishim R.
Omsk
Irtysh R.
MONGOLIA
FINLAND
St. Petersburg
Baltic Sea
Novgorod
Riga
HOLY ROMAN EMPIRE
Moscow
Nizhni Novgorod
Biysk
QING EMPIRE
PRUSSIA
Smolensk
Samara
POLAND
Ural R.
KAZAKS
AUSTRIA
Kiev
Saratov
COSSACKS
UKRAINIANS
Dnieper R.
Dniester R.
COSSACKS
Volga R.
Aral Sea
HUNGARY
Black Sea
Caspian Sea
TIBET
OTTOMAN EMPIRE
GEORGIA
BHUTAN
AFGHANISTAN
NEPAL
BURMA
IRAN
INDIA

Border set in 1826

50°N
60°N
70°N
80°N

120°W 100°W 80°W 60°W 40°W 20°W 0° 20°E 40°E 60°E 80°E 100°E 120°E 140°E 160°E 180° 160°E 140°E 120°E
140°W

70°N

© Cengage Learning

MAP 21.3 The Expansion of Russia, 1500–1800 Sweden and Poland initially blocked Russian expansion in Europe, while the Ottoman Empire blocked the southwest. In the sixteenth century, Russia began to expand east, toward Siberia and the Pacific Ocean. By the end of the rule of Catherine the Great in 1796, Russia encompassed all of northern and northeastern Eurasia.

e Interactive Map

Long periods of warfare in the late sixteenth and early seventeenth centuries disrupted peasant life and caused many to flee to the Cossacks or across the Urals. Some who couldn't flee sold themselves into slavery to keep from starving. When peace returned, landlords sought to recover the runaways and bind them more tightly to their land. A law change in 1649 finally transformed the peasants into **serfs** by eliminating the period when they could change masters and ordering runaways to return to their masters.

Like slavery, serfdom was hereditary. In theory the serf was tied to a piece of land, not owned by a master. In practice, strict laws narrowed the difference between serf and slave. In the Russian census of 1795, serfs made up over half the population. Landowners made up only 2 percent, or roughly the same as they did in the Caribbean.

serf In medieval Europe, an agricultural laborer legally bound to a lord's property and obligated to perform set services for the lord. In Russia some serfs worked as artisans and in factories; serfdom was not abolished there until 1861.

Peter the Great

The greatest of the Romanovs, Tsar **Peter the Great** (r. 1689–1725), reduced Russia's isolation and increased the empire's size and power. He turned Russia away from its Asian cultural connections and toward what he deemed the advanced civilization of the West. In fact, he accelerated trends under way for some time. When he ascended the throne, there were already hundreds of foreign merchants in Moscow. Military officers from western Europe had already trained a major part of the army in new weapons and techniques, and Italian builders were already influencing church and palace architecture. Peter accelerated these tendencies.

Peter matured quickly both physically and mentally. In his youth the government was in the hands of his half-sister Sophia, who was regent for him and her sickly brother Ivan. Living on an estate near the foreigners' quarter outside Moscow, Peter learned what he could of life outside Russia and busied himself gaining practical skills in blacksmithing, carpentry, shipbuilding, and the arts of war. He organized his own military drill unit among other young men. When Princess Sophia tried to take complete control of the government in 1689, Peter rallied enough support to send her to a monastery, secure the abdication of Ivan, and take charge of Russia. He was still in his teens.

Peter concerned himself with Russia's expansion and modernization. To secure a port on the Black Sea, he constructed a small but formidable navy. Describing his wars with the Ottoman Empire as a new crusade to liberate Constantinople from the Muslim sultans, Peter also fancied himself the legal protector of Orthodox Christians living under Ottoman rule. Peter's forces seized the port of Azov in 1696 but lost it again in 1713, thus calling a halt to southward expansion.

Peter the Great Russian tsar (r. 1689–1725). He enthusiastically introduced Western languages and technologies to the Russian elite, moving the capital from Moscow to the new city of St. Petersburg.

In the winter of 1697–1698, after his Black Sea campaign, Peter traveled in disguise across Europe to discover how western European societies were becoming so powerful and wealthy. He paid special attention to ships and weapons, even working for a time as a ship's carpenter in the Netherlands. With great insight, he perceived that western European success owed as much to trade and toleration as to technology. Trade generated the money to spend on weapons, while toleration attracted talented persons fleeing persecution. Upon his return to Russia, Peter resolved to expand and reform his vast and backward empire.

In the long and costly Great Northern War (1700–1721), his modernized armies broke Swedish control of the Baltic Sea, making possible more direct contacts between Russia and Europe. Peter's victory forced the European powers to recognize Russia as a major power for the first time.

On land captured from Sweden at the eastern end of the Baltic, Peter built St. Petersburg, his window on the West. In 1712 the city became Russia's capital. To demonstrate Russia's new sophis-

Collection, Countess Bobrinskoy / Michael Holford

Peter the Great This portrait from his time as a student in Holland in 1697 shows Peter as ruggedly masculine and practical, quite unlike most royal portraits of the day that posed rulers in foppish elegance and haughty majesty. Peter was a popular military leader as well as an autocratic ruler.

The Fontanka Canal in St. Petersburg in 1753 The Russian capital continued to grow as a commercial and administrative center. As in Amsterdam, canals were the city's major arteries. On the right is a new summer palace built by Peter's successor.

tication, Peter ordered architects to build St. Petersburg's houses and public buildings in the baroque style then fashionable in France.

Peter also pushed the Russian elite to imitate European fashions. He personally shaved off his noblemen's long beards to conform to Western styles. To end the traditional seclusion of upper-class Russian women, Peter required officials, military officers, and merchants to bring their wives to the social gatherings he organized in the capital. He also directed the nobles to educate their children.

Another strategy was to reorganize Russian government along the lines of the powerful German state of Prussia. He sharply reduced the traditional roles of the boyars in government and the army, replacing the old boyar council with a group of appointed advisers in St. Petersburg. Members of the traditional nobility continued to serve as generals and admirals, but officers in Peter's modern, professional army and navy were promoted according to merit, not birth.

A decree of 1716 proclaimed that the tsar "is not obliged to answer to anyone in the world for his doings, but possesses power and authority over his kingdom and land, to rule them at his will and pleasure as a Christian ruler." Under this expansive definition of his role, Peter brought the Russian Orthodox Church more firmly under state control, built factories and iron and copper foundries to provide munitions and supplies for the military, and increased the burdens of taxes and forced labor on the serfs. Peter was an absolutist ruler of the sort then common in western Europe, and he had no more intention of improving the conditions of the serfs than did the European slave owners of the Americas.

PRIMARY SOURCE: Edicts and Decrees
Read a selection of Peter the Great's decrees, and find out how he wished to modernize, and westernize, Russia.

SECTION REVIEW

- Muscovy became the center of Russian political power and led the movement against Mongol domination.

- Ivan IV expanded Muscovy, and the Strogonovs sponsored exploration of fur-rich Siberia.

- Russian society blended diverse ethnicities, religions, and cultural practices, a mixture embodied in the Cossacks.

- Emerging from the Time of Troubles, the Romanov tsars worked to centralize royal authority and to institutionalize serfdom.

- Peter the Great accelerated Russia's westernization, fought wars of expansion, and enlarged the power of the tsar.

- Expansion continued eastward and westward, and Catherine the Great continued Peter's westernizing policies.

Consolidation of the Empire

Russia's eastward expansion continued under Peter the Great and his successors. The frontier settlement with China and Kangxi's quashing of Inner Mongolia in 1689 freed Russians to concentrate on the northern Pacific. The Pacific northeast was colonized, and in 1741 an expedition led by Captain Vitus Bering crossed the strait (later named for him) into North America. In 1799 a Russian company of merchants received a monopoly over the Alaskan fur trade, and its agents were soon active along the entire northwestern coast of North America.

Far more important than these immense territories in the cold and thinly populated north were the populous agricultural lands to the west acquired during the reign of Catherine the Great (r. 1762–1796). A successful war with the Ottoman Empire gave Russia control of the north shore of the Black Sea by 1783, though not of the straits leading to the Mediterranean. Three successive partitions of the once powerful kingdom of Poland between 1772 and 1795 advanced Russia's frontiers 600 miles (nearly 1,000 kilometers) to the west (see Map 21.3). When Catherine died, the Russian Empire extended from Poland in the west to Alaska in the east, from the Barents Sea in the north to the Black Sea in the south.

Catherine also made important additions to Peter's policies of promoting industry and building a canal system to improve trade. Besides furs, the Russians had also become major exporters of gold, iron, and timber. Catherine implemented administrative reforms and showed a special talent for diplomacy. Through her promotion of the ideas of the Enlightenment, she expanded Peter's policies of westernizing the Russian elite.

CONCLUSION

China and Russia are examples of the phenomenal flourishing of empires in Eurasia between 1500 and 1800. Already a vast empire under the Ming, China doubled in size under the Qing, mostly through westward expansion into less densely populated areas. In expanding from a modestly sized principality into the world's largest land empire, Russia added rich and well-populated lands to the west and south and far larger but less populous lands to the east. Russia and China were land based, just like the Ottoman and Mughal Empires, with the strengths and problems of administrative control and tax collection that size entailed.

Japan was different. Though nominally headed by an emperor, Japan's size and ethnic homogeneity do not support calling it an empire in the same breath with China and Russia. Tokugawa Japan was similar in size and population to France, the most powerful state of western Europe, but its political system was much more decentralized. Japan's efforts to add colonies on the East Asian mainland had failed.

China had once led the world in military innovation (including the first uses of gunpowder), but the modern "gunpowder revolution" of the fifteenth and sixteenth centuries was centered in the Ottoman Empire and western European states. Although the centuries after 1500 were full of successful military operations, Chinese armies continued to depend on superior numbers and tactics for their success, rather than on new technology. As in the past, infantrymen armed with guns served alongside others armed with bows and arrows, swords, and spears.

The military forces of Japan and Russia underwent more innovative changes than those of China, in part through Western contacts. In the course of its sixteenth-century wars of unification, Japan produced its own gunpowder revolution but thereafter lacked the motivation and the means to stay abreast of the world's most advanced military technology. By the eighteenth century Russia had made greater progress in catching up with its European neighbors, but its armies still relied more on their size than on the sophistication of their weapons.

Naval power provides the greatest military contrast among China, Russia, and Japan. Eighteenth-century Russia constructed modern fleets of warships in the Baltic and Black Seas, but neither China nor Japan developed navies commensurate with their size and coastlines. China's defenses against pirates and other sea invaders were left to its maritime provinces, whose small war junks were armed with only a half-dozen cannon. Japan's naval capacity was similarly decentralized. In 1792, when Russian ships exploring the North Pacific turned toward the Japanese coast, the local daimyo used his own forces to chase them away. All Japanese daimyo understood that they would be on their own if foreign incursions increased.

The expansion of China and Russia incorporated not just new lands but also diverse new peoples. Chinese society had long been diverse, and its geographical, occupational, linguistic, and religious differences grew as the Qing expanded (see Map 21.1). China had also long used Confucian models, imperial customs, and a common system of writing to transcend such differences and to assimilate elites. Russia likewise approached its new peoples with a mixture of pragmatic tolerance and a propensity for seeing Russian ways and beliefs as superior. The Russian language was strongly promoted. Religion was a particular sore point, as Russian Orthodox missionaries, with the support of the tsars, encouraged conversion of Siberian peoples. Russia absorbed new ideas and styles from western Europe, although even among the elite these influences often overlay Russian traditions in a very superficial way. In contrast, Japan remained more culturally homogeneous, and the government reacted with great intolerance to the growing influence of converts to western Christianity.

Forced labor remained common in the Russian and Chinese Empires. Serfdom grew more brutal and widespread in Russia in the seventeenth and eighteenth centuries, although the expansion of the frontier eastward across Siberia also opened an escape route for many peasants and serfs. Some Chinese peasants also improved their lot by moving to new territories, but population growth increased overall misery in the eighteenth century. China was also notable for the size of its popular insurrections, especially the one that toppled the Ming.

KEY TERMS

Manchu p. 555

daimyo p. 556

samurai p. 556

Tokugawa
   Shogunate p. 556

Ming Empire p. 561

Qing Empire p. 563

Kangxi p. 563

Amur River p. 564

Macartney mission p. 567

Muscovy p. 569

Ural Mountains p. 569

tsar (czar) p. 569

Siberia p. 569

Cossacks p. 570

serf p. 572

Peter the Great p. 572

EBOOK AND WEBSITE RESOURCES

e **Primary Sources**

Some Observation on Merchants

Journals: Matteo Ricci

Edict on Trade with Great Britain

Edicts and Decrees

e **Interactive Maps**

Map 21.1 The Qing Empire, 1644–1783

Map 21.2 Climate and Diversity in the Qing Empire

Map 21.3 The Expansion of Russia, 1500–1800

Plus flashcards, practice quizzes, and more. Go to:
www.cengage.com/history/bullietearthpeople5e

SUGGESTED READING

Berry, Mary Elizabeth. *Hideyoshi*. 1982. An account of the reunification of Japan at the end of the sixteenth century.

Chie Nakane and Shinzaburo Oishi. *Tokugawa Japan: The Social and Economic Antecedents of Modern Japan*. Trans. Conrad Totman. 1990. Early modern Japan from a contemporary perspective.

Cooper, Michael, and Jonathan D. Spence. *The Memory Palace of Matteo Ricci*. 1984. An engrossing account of Jesuits in East Asia in the sixteenth and seventeenth centuries.

Crossley, Pamela Kyle. *The Manchus*. 2002. A history of the people who ruled China during the Qing dynasty.

Crummey, Robert O. *Aristocrats and Servitors: The Boyar Elite in Russia, 1613–1689*. 1983. Russia before Peter the Great.

Kappeler, Andreas. *The Russian Empire: A Multiethnic History*. 2001. Deals with all of the empire's peoples, not just the Russians.

Keay, John. *The Honourable Company: A History of the English East India Company*. 1994. A study of Indian Ocean trade and colonization.

Massie, Robert K. *Peter the Great: His Life and World*. 1980. A highly readable biography for a general audience.

Morris-Suzuki, Tessa. *The Technological Transformation of Japan from the Seventeenth to the Twenty-first Century*. 1994. Analyzes the roots of modern Japanese technological development.

Rawski, Evelyn Sakakida. *The Last Emperors: A Social History of Qing Imperial Institutions*. 1998. A reinterpretation of the success of the Manchus' Qing Empire.

Spence, Jonathan D. *The Search for Modern China*. 1990. China during the transition from the Ming to Qing periods.

Wills, John E. *Pepper, Guns, and Parleys: The Dutch East India Company and China, 1662–1681*. 2005. Describes China's relations with European traders.

Wills, John E., Jr. *1688: A Global History*. 2001. Part III, "Three Worlds Apart: Russia, China, and Japan," provides stimulating comparisons.

NOTES

1. Adapted from Jonathan D. Spence, *The Search for Modern China* (New York: W. W. Norton, 1990), 21–25.

2. Adapted from G. V. Melikhov, "Manzhou Penetration into the Basin of the Upper Amur in the 1680s," in *Manzhou Rule in China*, ed. S. L. Tikhvinshii (Moscow: Progress Publishers, 1983).

THE LITTLE ICE AGE

A giant volcanic eruption in the Peruvian Andes in 1600 affected the weather in many parts of the world for several years. When volcanic ash from the eruption of Mount Huanyaputina (hoo-AHN-yah-poo-TEE-nuh) shot into the upper atmosphere and spread around the world, it screened out sunlight. As a result, the summer of 1601 was the coldest in two hundred years in the Northern Hemisphere.

Archaeologist Brian Fagan has pointed out that Mount Huanyaputina's chilling effects were a spectacular event in a much longer pattern of climate change that has been called the Little Ice Age.[1] Although global climate had been cooling since the late 1200s, in the northern temperate regions the 1590s had been exceptionally cold. Temperatures remained cooler than normal throughout the seventeenth century.

The most detailed information on the Little Ice Age comes from Europe. Glaciers in the Alps grew much larger. Trade became difficult when rivers and canals that had once been navigable in winter froze solid from bank to bank. In the coldest years, the growing season in some places was as much as two months shorter than normal. Unexpectedly late frosts withered the tender shoots of newly planted crops in spring. Wheat and barley ripened more slowly during cooler summers and were often damaged by early fall frosts.

People could survive a smaller-than-average harvest in one year by drawing on food reserves, but when cold weather damaged crops in two or more successive years, the consequences were devastating. Deaths due to malnutrition and cold increased sharply when summer temperatures in northern Europe registered 2.7°F (1.5°C) lower than average in 1674 and 1675 and again in 1694 and 1695. The cold spell of 1694 and 1695 caused a famine in Finland that carried off a quarter to a third of the population.

At the time people had no idea what was causing the unusual cold of the Little Ice Age. Advances in climate history make it clear that the cause was not a single terrestrial event such as the eruption of Mount Huanyaputina. Nor was the Little Ice Age the product of human actions, unlike some climate changes such as today's global warming.

Ultimately, the earth's weather is governed by the sun. In the seventeenth century astronomers in Europe reported seeing fewer sunspots, dark spots on the sun's surface that are indicative of solar activity and thus the sun's warming power. Diminished activity in the sun was primarily responsible for the Little Ice Age.

If the sun was the root cause, the effects of global cooling should not have been confined to northern Europe. Although contemporary accounts are much scarcer in other parts of the world, there is evidence of climate changes around the world in this period. Observations of sunspots in China, Korea, and Japan drop to zero between 1639 and 1700. China experienced unusually cool weather in the seventeenth century, but the warfare and disruption accompanying the fall of the Ming and the rise of the Qing probably were much more to blame for the famines and rural distress of that period.

By itself, a relatively slight decrease in average annual temperature would not have a significant effect on human life outside the northern temperate areas. However, evidence suggests that there was also a significant rise in humidity in this period in other parts of the world. Ice cores drilled into ancient glaciers in the Arctic and Antarctic show increased snowfall. Information compiled by historian James L. A. Webb, Jr., shows that lands south of the Sahara received more rainfall between 1550 and 1750 than they had during the previous era.[2] Increased rainfall would have been favorable for pastoral people, whose herds found new pasture in what had once been desert, and for the farmers farther south whose crops got more rain.

In the eighteenth century the sun's activity began to return to normal. Rising temperatures led to milder winters and better harvests in northern Eurasia. Falling rainfall allowed the Sahara to advance southward, forcing the agricultural frontier to retreat.

NOTES

1. Brian Fagan, *The Littlest Ice Age: How Climate Made History, 1300–1850* (New York: Basic Books, 2000).

2. James L. A. Webb, Jr., *Desert Frontier: Ecological Change Along the Western Sahel, 1600–1850* (Madison: University of Wisconsin Press, 1995).

PART VI

Library of Congress

South America 1820s This map of South America from the 1820s records the comprehensive success of the independence movements. With the exception of the Guyanas, no colonial governments remain. As we examine this map, we are also reminded of the failure of two political experiments designed to hold together geographically and ethnically diverse regions in a single national government. In the northwest is Colombia (also called Gran Colombia) created by the era's greatest revolutionary leader, Simón Bolívar. It quickly broke apart to form the modern nations of Venezuela, Colombia, and Ecuador. The United Provinces of Río de la Plata, located in the southeast, also soon collapsed, giving birth to the nations of Argentina, Paraguay, and Uruguay.

Revolutions Reshape
the World, 1750–1870

Between 1750 and 1870, nearly every part of the world experienced dramatic political, economic, and social change. The beginnings of industrialization, the American, French, and Haitian revolutions, as well as the revolutions for independence in Latin America, transformed political and economic life. European nations expanded into Africa, Asia, and the Middle East while Russia and the United States acquired vast new territories.

The Industrial Revolution introduced new technologies and patterns of work that made these societies wealthier and militarily more powerful. Western intellectual life became more secular. The Atlantic slave trade and later slavery itself were abolished, and the first efforts to improve the status of women were initiated.

The Industrial Revolution led to a new wave of imperialism. France conquered Algeria, and Great Britain expanded its colonial rule in India and established colonies in Australia and New Zealand. European political and economic influence also expanded in Africa and Asia. The Ottoman Empire and the Qing Empire met this challenge by implementing reform programs that preserved traditional structures while adopting elements of Western technology and organization. Though lagging behind western Europe in transforming its economy and political institutions, Russia attempted modernization efforts, including the abolition of serfdom.

The economic, political, and social revolutions that began in the mideighteenth century shook the foundations of European culture and led to the expansion of Western power around the globe. Some of the nations of Asia, Africa, and Latin America reformed and strengthened their own institutions and economies, while others pushed for more radical change. After 1870 Western imperialism became more aggressive, and few parts of the world were able to resist it.

CHAPTER

22

CHAPTER OUTLINE

Burning of Cap Français, Saint Domingue, in 1793   In 1791, the slaves of Saint Domingue, France's richest colony, began a rebellion that, after years of struggle, ended slavery and created the Western Hemisphere's second independent nation, Haiti.

 Visit the website and ebook for additional study materials and interactive tools: www.cengage.com/history/bullietearthpeople5e

Revolutionary Changes in the Atlantic World, 1750–1850

I n August 1791 slaves and free blacks began an insurrection in the plantation district of northern Saint Domingue (san doe-MANG) (present-day Haiti). During the following decade and a half, Haitian revolutionaries abolished slavery; defeated military forces from Britain and France; and achieved independence.

News and rumors about revolutionary events in France had helped move the island's slave community to rebel. These same events had divided the island's white population into royalists (supporters of France's King Louis XVI) and republicans (who sought an end to monarchy). The large free mixed-race population secured some political rights from the French Assembly but then rose in rebellion when the slave-owning elite reacted violently.

A black freedman, François Dominique Toussaint, led the insurrection. Taking the name Toussaint L'Ouverture (too-SAN loo-ver-CHORE), he became one of the most remarkable representatives of the revolutionary era. He organized the rebels militarily, negotiated with the island's competing factions and with representatives of Britain and France, and wrote his nation's first constitution. Commonly portrayed as a fiend by slave owners, Toussaint became a towering symbol of resistance to oppression to slaves everywhere.

The Haitian slave rebellion was an important event in the political and cultural transformation of the Western world. Profound changes to the economy, politics, and intellectual life occurred as well. The Industrial Revolution (see Chapter 23) increased manufacturing productivity and led to greater global interdependence, new patterns of consumerism, and altered social structures. At the same time, intellectuals questioned the traditional place of monarchy and religion in society. Merchants, professionals, and manufacturers enriched by economic dynamism provided an audience for the new intellectual currents as they pressed for a larger political role.

This revolutionary era turned the Western world "upside down." The *ancien régime* (ahn-see-EN ray-ZHEEM), the French term for Europe's old order, rested on medieval principles: politics dominated by powerful monarchs, intellectual and cultural life dominated by religion, and economics dominated by hereditary agricultural elites. In the West's new order, commoners entered political life; science took the place of religion in intellectual life; and economies opened to competition.

- How did the costs of imperial wars and the Enlightenment challenge the established authority of monarchs and religion in Europe and the American colonies?
- What were the direct causes of the American Revolution?
- What were the origins and accomplishments of the French Revolution?
- How did revolution in one country help incite revolution elsewhere?

This radical transformation did not take place without false starts or setbacks. Imperial powers resisted the loss of colonies; monarchs and nobles struggled to retain their ancient privileges; and the church fought against the claims of science. While the liberal and nationalist ideals of the eighteenth-century revolutionary movements were sometimes thwarted in Europe and the Americas, belief in national self-determination and universal suffrage and a passion for social justice continued to animate reformers into the twentieth century.

PRELUDE TO REVOLUTION: THE EIGHTEENTH-CENTURY CRISIS

The cost of wars fought among Europe's major powers over colonies and trade helped precipitate the revolutionary era that began in 1775 with the American Revolution. Britain, France, and Spain were the central actors in these global struggles, but other imperial powers participated as well. While these nations had previously fought unpopular and costly wars and paid for them with new taxes, changes in Western intellectual and political environments now produced a much more critical response. Any effort to extend monarchical power or impose new taxes now raised questions about the rights of individuals and the authority of political institutions.

Colonial Wars and Fiscal Crises

In the seventeenth century competition among European powers became global in character. The newly independent Netherlands attacked the American and Asian colonies of Spain and Portugal, even seizing parts of Portugal's colonial empire in Brazil and Angola. Europe's other emerging sea power, Great Britain, attacked Spanish fleets and seaports in the Americas. These rivalries made the defense of trade routes and distant colonies more expensive and difficult.

The eighteenth century further tested the ability of European powers to pay for their imperial ambitions. As Dutch power ebbed, Britain and France began a long struggle for political preeminence in western Europe and for territory and trade outlets in the Americas and Asia as the older empires of Spain and Portugal struggled to hang on. Nearly all of Europe's great powers participated in the War of the Spanish Succession (1701–1714). A war between Britain and Spain over smuggling broadened into a generalized European conflict, the War of Austrian Succession (1740–1748). A frontier conflict between French and British forces and their Amerindian allies then led to a wider struggle, the Seven Years War (1756–1763). With peace Britain emerged with undisputed control of North America east of the Mississippi River and France had surrendered Canada and its holdings in India.

The Cost of War

The enormous cost of these conflicts distinguished them from earlier wars. Traditional taxes collected in traditional ways no longer covered the obligations of governments. While Britain's total budget before the Seven Years War had averaged only £8 million, in 1763 war debt had reached £137 million and interest payments alone exceeded £5 million. Even as European economies expanded, fiscal crises overtook one European government after another. In an intellectual environment transformed by the Enlightenment, the need for new revenues provoked debate and confrontation within a vastly expanded and more critical public.

The Enlightenment and the Old Order

Enlightenment A philosophical movement in eighteenth-century Europe that fostered the belief that one could reform society by discovering rational laws that governed social behavior and were just as scientific as the laws of physics.

The complex and diverse intellectual movement called the **Enlightenment** applied the methods and questions of the Scientific Revolution of the seventeenth century to the study of human society as well as to the natural world. But some European intellectuals sought to systematize knowledge and organize reference materials. For example, the Swedish botanist Carolus Linnaeus (kar-ROLL-uhs lin-NEE-uhs) sought to categorize all living organisms, and Samuel Johnson published a comprehensive English dictionary. In France Denis Diderot (duh-nee DEE-duh-roe) worked with other thinkers to create a compendium of human knowledge, the thirty-five-volume *Encyclopédie*.

CHRONOLOGY

	The Americas	Europe
1750	1754–1763 French and Indian War	1756–1763 Seven Years War
	1770 Boston Massacre	
1775	1776 American Declaration of Independence	
	1778 United States alliance with France	1778 Death of Voltaire and Rousseau
	1781 British surrender at Yorktown	
	1783 Treaty of Paris ends American Revolution	1789 Storming of Bastille begins French Revolution; Declaration of Rights of Man and Citizen in France
	1791 Slaves revolt in Saint Domingue (Haiti)	1793–1794 Reign of Terror in France
	1798 Toussaint L'Ouverture defeats British in Haiti	1795–1799 The Directory rules France
		1799 Napoleon overthrows the Directory
1800	1804 Haitians defeat French invasion and declare independence	1804 Napoleon crowns himself emperor
		1814 Napoleon abdicates; Congress of Vienna opens
		1815 Napoleon defeated at Waterloo
		1830 Greece gains independence; revolution in France overthrows Charles X
		1848 Revolutions in France, Austria, Germany, Hungary, and Italy

The Intellectual Challenge to Old Order

Other thinkers pursued lines of inquiry that challenged long-established religious and political institutions (see Chapter 17). Some argued that if scientists could understand the laws of nature, then surely similar forms of disciplined investigation might reveal laws of human nature. Others wondered whether society and government could be better regulated and more productive if guided by science rather than by hereditary rulers and the church. These new perspectives and the intellectual optimism that fed them helped guide the revolutionary movements of the late eighteenth century.

The English political philosopher John Locke (1632–1704) argued in 1690 that governments were created to protect life, liberty, and property and that the people had a right to rebel when a monarch violated these natural rights. Locke's closely reasoned theory began with the assumption that individual rights were the foundation of civil government. In *The Social Contract*, published in 1762, the French-Swiss intellectual Jean-Jacques Rousseau (zhan-zhock roo-SOE) (1712–1778) asserted that the will of the people was sacred and that the legitimacy of monarchs depended on the consent of the people. Although both men believed that government rested on the will of the people, Locke emphasized the importance of individual rights secured institutionally while Rousseau, much more distrustful of society and government, envisioned the people acting collectively as a result of shared historical experience.

e **PRIMARY SOURCE:**
Rousseau Espouses Popular Sovereignty and the General Will Modern democracies owe much to the political ideas of this French philosopher.

All Enlightenment thinkers were not radicals like Rousseau. There was never a uniform program for political and social reform, and the era's intellectuals often disagreed about principles and objectives. While the Enlightenment is commonly associated with hostility toward religion and monarchy, few intellectuals openly expressed republican or atheist sentiments. Even Voltaire, one of the Enlightenment's most critical intellects and great celebrities, believed that Europe's monarchs were likely agents of political and economic reform.

Monarchs and the Enlightenment

Indeed, sympathetic members of the nobility and reforming European monarchs such as Charles III of Spain (r. 1759–1788), Catherine the Great of Russia (r. 1762–1796), and Frederick the Great of Prussia (r. 1740–1786) actively sponsored and promoted the dissemination of new ideas, providing patronage for many intellectuals. They recognized that elements of the Enlightenment buttressed their own efforts to expand royal authority at the expense of religious institutions, the nobility, and regional autonomy. Goals such as the development of national bureaucracies staffed by civil servants selected on merit, the creation of national legal systems, and the modernization of tax systems united many of Europe's monarchs and intellectuals. Monarchs also understood that the era's passion for science and technology held the potential of fattening national treasuries and improving economic performance.

Though willing to embrace reform proposals when they served royal interests, Europe's monarchs moved quickly to suppress or ban radical ideas that promoted republicanism or directly attacked religion. However, too many channels of communication were open to permit a thoroughgoing suppression of ideas. In fact, censorship tended to enhance intellectual reputations, and persecuted intellectuals generally found patronage in the courts of foreign rivals.

The Community of Ideas

Many of the major intellectuals of the Enlightenment corresponded with each other as well as with political leaders. This communication led to numerous firsthand contacts among the intellectuals of different nations and helped create a more coherent assault on what they saw as ignorance—beliefs and values associated with the ancien régime. Rousseau met the Scottish philosopher David Hume in Paris. Later, when Rousseau feared arrest, Hume helped him seek refuge in Britain. Similarly, Voltaire sought patronage and protection in England and later in Prussia.

Women were instrumental in the dissemination of the new ideas. In England educated middle-class women purchased and discussed books and pamphlets. Some were important contributors to intellectual life as writers and commentators, raising by example and in argument the issue of the rights of women. In Paris wealthy women made their homes centers of debate, intellectual speculation, and free inquiry. Their salons brought together philosophers, social critics, artists, members of the aristocracy, and the commercial elite.

The intellectual ferment of the era deeply influenced the expanding middle class in Europe and the Western Hemisphere. Members of this class were eager consumers of books and inexpensive newspapers and journals that were widely available. This broadening of the intellectual audience overwhelmed traditional institutions of censorship. New public venues like the thousands of coffee-houses and teashops of cities and market towns also became locations to discuss scientific discoveries, new technologies, and controversial works on human nature and politics.

The Enlightenment and the New World

Many European intellectuals were interested in the Americas. Some Europeans continued to dismiss the region as barbaric and inferior, but others used idealized accounts of the New World to support their critiques of European society. Many looked to Britain's North American colonies for confirmation of their belief that human nature unconstrained by the corrupted practices of Europe's old order would quickly produce material abundance and social justice. More than any other American, the writer and inventor **Benjamin Franklin** came to symbolize the vast potential of America.

Benjamin Franklin American intellectual, inventor, and politician who helped negotiate French support for the American Revolution.

Born in Boston in 1706, the young Franklin trained as a printer. In Philadelphia he succeeded in business and became famous for his *Poor Richard's Almanac*. He retired at forty-two to pursue writing, science, and public affairs. Franklin was instrumental in the creation of the Philadelphia Free Library, the American Philosophical Society, and the University of Pennsylvania. His contributions were both practical and theoretical. He was the inventor of bifocal glasses, the lightning rod, and an efficient wood-burning stove. In 1751 he published the scientific paper, *Experiments and Observations on Electricity*, which won him acclaim from European intellectuals.

Franklin was also an important political figure. He served in many capacities in the colonies and was selected as a delegate to the Continental Congress that issued the Declaration of Independence in 1776. He later became ambassador to Paris, where his achievements, witty conversation, and careful self-promotion made him the symbol of the era. His life seemed to confirm the Enlightenment's most radical objective, the freeing of human potential from the effects of inherited privilege.

PRIMARY SOURCE: The United States Declaration of Independence Read a selection from Jefferson's famous text, which lays out the Enlightenment principles on which the United States was founded.

As Franklin demonstrates, the Western Hemisphere shared in Europe's intellectual ferment. As the Enlightenment penetrated the New World, intellectuals actively debated the legitimacy of colonialism itself. European efforts to reform colonial policies by unilaterally altering colonial institutions and overturning long-established political practices further radicalized colonial intellectuals. Among peoples compelled to accept the dependence and inferiority explicit in colonial rule, the idea that government authority rested on the consent of the governed proved explosive.

The Counter Enlightenment

Many intellectuals resisted the Enlightenment, seeing it as a dangerous assault on the authority of the church and monarchy. This Counter Enlightenment was most influential in

Beer Street (1751) William Hogarth's engraving shows an idealized London street scene where beer drinking is associated with manly strength, good humor, and prosperity. The self-satisfied corpulent figure in the left foreground reads a copy of the king's speech to Parliament. We can imagine him offering a running commentary to his drinking companions as he reads.

France and other Catholic nations. Its adherents emphasized the importance of faith to human happiness and social well-being. They also emphasized duty and obligation to the community of believers in opposition to the concern for individual rights and individual fulfillment common in the works of the Enlightenment. Most importantly for the politics of the era, they rejected their enemies' enthusiasm for change and utopianism, reminding their readers of human fallibility and the importance of history. While the central ideas of the Enlightenment gained strength across the nineteenth century, the Counter Enlightenment provided ideological support for the era's conservatism and later popular antidemocratic movements.

Folk Cultures and Popular Protest

While intellectuals and the reforming royal courts of Europe debated the rational and secular enthusiasms of the Enlightenment, most people in Western society remained loyal to competing cultural values grounded in the preindustrial past. Regional folk cultures were rooted in the memory of shared experience and nourished by religious practices that encouraged emotional release. These cultural traditions included coherent expressions of the rights and obligations that connected people with their rulers. Authorities who violated these understandings were likely to face violent opposition.

Reform and Popular Culture

In the eighteenth century, European monarchs sought to increase their authority and to centralize power by reforming tax collection, judicial practice, and public administration. Although monarchs viewed these changes as reforms, common people often saw them as violations of sacred customs and responded with bread riots, tax protests, and attacks on royal officials. These violent actions sought to preserve custom and precedent rather than overturn traditional authority. In Spain and the Spanish colonies protesting mobs often expressed love for the monarch while at the same time assaulting his officials and preventing the implementation of reforms, shouting "Long Live the King! Death to Bad Government!"

Enlightenment-era reformers sought to bring order and discipline to the citizenry by banning or altering numerous popular traditions—such as harvest festivals, religious holidays, and country fairs—that enlivened the drudgery of everyday life. These events were popular celebrations of sexuality and individuality as well as opportunities for masked and costumed celebrants to mock the greed, pretension, and foolishness of government officials, the wealthy, and the clergy. Hard drinking, gambling, and blood sports like cockfighting and bearbaiting were popular in preindustrial mass culture, but reformers viewed them as corrupt and decadent. Reforming governments undertook to substitute civic rituals, patriotic anniversaries, and institutions of self-improvement for older customs, often provoking protests and riots.

The efforts of ordinary men and women to resist the growth of government power and the imposition of new cultural forms provide an important political undercurrent to much of the revolutionary agitation and conflict between 1750 and 1850. Spontaneous popular uprisings and protests punctuated nearly every effort at reform in the eighteenth century. But popular protest gained revolutionary potential only when it coincided with ideological division and conflict within the governing class.

SECTION REVIEW

- Wars fought to protect colonies and trade routes overwhelmed the fiscal resources of European powers.

- European intellectuals applied the methods of scientific inquiry to political and cultural issues in the Enlightenment.

- In the Counter Enlightenment some intellectuals rejected attacks on tradition and religion.

- The effort to create uniform and rational administration provoked defense of folk culture and tradition.

THE AMERICAN REVOLUTION, 1775–1800

In British North America, clumsy efforts to increase colonial taxes to cover rising defense expenditures and to diminish the power of elected colonial legislatures outraged a populace accustomed to local autonomy. Once begun, the American Revolution ushered in a century-long process of political and cultural transformation in Europe and the Americas. By the end of this revolutionary century constitutions had limited or overturned the authority of monarchs, and religion had lost its dominance of Western intellectual life. At the same time revolutionary changes in manufacturing and commerce replaced the long-established social order determined by birth with a new social ideal emphasizing competition and social mobility.

Frontiers and Taxes

After defeating the French in 1763, the British government faced two related problems in its North American colonies. As settlers pushed west into Amerindian lands, Britain feared the likelihood of renewed conflict and rising military expenses. Already burdened with heavy debts, Britain tried to limit settler pressure on Amerindian lands and get colonists to shoulder more of the costs of colonial defense and administration.

British Frontier Policy

In the Great Lakes region the British tried to contain costs by reducing fur prices and by refusing to continue the French practice of giving gifts and paying rent for frontier forts to Amerindian peoples. But lower fur prices forced native peoples to hunt more aggressively, putting pressure on the environment and endangering some species. The situation got worse as settlers and white trappers pushed across the Appalachians to compete with indigenous hunters. The predictable result was renewed violence along the frontier led by Pontiac, an Ottawa chief. His broad alliance of native peoples drove the British military from some western outposts but was defeated within a year.

The British government's panicked reaction was the Proclamation of 1763, which established a western limit for settlement, undermining the claims of thousands of established farmers without effectively protecting Amerindian land. No one was satisfied. In 1774 Britain tried again to slow the movement of settlers onto Amerindian lands by annexing western territories to the province of Quebec. This provoked bitter resentment in the colonies.

New Colonial Tax and Commercial Policies

While frontier issues increased colonial hostility and suspicion, they did not lead to a breach. But British efforts to transfer the cost of imperial wars to the colonists through a campaign of fiscal reforms and new taxes sparked a political confrontation that ultimately led to rebellion. New British commercial regulations endangered New England's profitable trade with Spanish and French Caribbean sugar colonies. More disruptive still was Britain's outlawing of colonial issues of paper money, a custom made necessary by the colonies' chronic balance-of-payments deficits. Colonial legislatures responded by protesting these measures while angry colonists organized boycotts of British goods.

Colonial Protests

Colonists deeply resented the Stamp Act of 1765, a tax on all legal documents, newspapers, pamphlets, and nearly all printed material. Now propertied colonists, including holders of high office and members of the colonial elite, assumed leading roles in protests. Critics of these measures used fiery political language, identifying Britain's rulers as "parricides" and "tyrants," while women from prominent colonial families organized boycotts of British goods. Colonial women now viewed the production of homespun textiles as a patriotic obligation. Organizations such as the Sons of Liberty were more confrontational, holding public meetings, intimidating royal officials, and organizing committees to enforce the boycotts. Although this combination of protest and boycott forced the repeal of the Stamp Act, Britain soon imposed new taxes and duties. Parliament also sent British troops to quell colonial riots. One indignant woman expressed her anger to a British officer:

> [T]he most ignorant peasant knows . . . that no man has the right to take their money without their consent. The supposition is ridiculous and absurd, as none but highwaymen and robbers attempt it. Can you, my friend, reconcile it with your own good sense, that a body of men in Great Britain, who have little intercourse with America . . . shall invest themselves with a power to command our lives and properties [?][1]

British authorities reacted to boycotts and attacks on royal officials by threatening colonial liberties. They dissolved the colonial legislature of Massachusetts and sent two regiments of soldiers to reestablish control of Boston's streets. Popular support for a complete break with Britain grew after March 5, 1770, when British soldiers fired at an angry Boston crowd, killing five civilians. The "Boston Massacre" exposed the naked force on which colonial rule rested and radicalized public opinion throughout the colonies.

Parliament attempted to calm colonial opinion by repealing some taxes and duties, but it stumbled into another crisis when it granted the East India Company a monopoly to import tea to the colonies. This decision raised again the constitutional issue of Parliament's right to tax the colonies. The crisis came to a head when protesters dumped tea worth £10,000 into Boston harbor. Britain responded by appointing a military man, Thomas Gage, as governor of Massachusetts and by closing the port of Boston. British troops now enforced public order in Boston, and public administration was in the hands of a general. This militarization of colonial government undermined Britain's constitutional authority and made rebellion inevitable.

The Granger Collection, New York

The Tarring and Feathering of a British Official, 1774
British periodicals responded to the rising tide of colonial protest by focusing on mob violence and the breakdown of public order. This illustration portrayed the brutal treatment given John Malcomb, commissioner of customs at Boston. For many in Britain, colonial demands for liberty were little more than an excuse for mob violence.

The Course of Revolution, 1775–1783

When representatives elected to the Continental Congress met in Philadelphia in 1775, patriot militia had already fought British troops at Lexington and Concord, Massachusetts (see Map 22.1). Events were propelling the colonies toward revolution. Congress assumed the powers of government. They created a currency and organized an army led by **George Washington** (1732–1799), a Virginia planter who had served in the French and Indian War.

The angry rhetoric of thousands of street-corner speakers and the inflammatory pamphlet *Common Sense*, written by Thomas Paine, a recent immigrant from England, propelled popular support for independence. On July 4, 1776, Congress approved the Declaration of Independence, the document that proved to be the most enduring statement of the revolutionary era's ideology:

> *We hold these truths to be self evident: That all men are created equal; that they are endowed by their creator with certain unalienable rights; that among these are life, liberty and the pursuit of happiness; that, to secure these rights, governments are instituted among men, deriving their just powers from the consent of the governed.*

The Declaration's affirmation of popular sovereignty and individual rights would influence the language of revolution and popular protest around the world.

Great Britain reacted by sending additional military forces to pacify the colonies. By 1778 Britain had 50,000 British troops and 30,000 German mercenaries in the colonies. Despite the existence of a large loyalist community, the British army found it difficult to control the countryside. Although British forces won most of the battles, Washington slowly built a competent Continental army as well as civilian support networks that provided supplies and financial resources.

The British government also tried to find a political compromise that would satisfy colonial grievances. Half-hearted efforts to resolve the conflict over taxes failed, and an offer to roll back the clock and reestablish the administrative arrangements of 1763 made little headway. Overconfidence in its military and poor leadership kept the British from finding a political solution before revolutionary institutions were in place and the armies engaged. By allowing confrontation to occur, the British government lost the opportunity to mobilize and give direction to the large numbers of loyalists and pacifists in the colonies.

Along the Canadian border, both sides solicited Amerindians as allies and feared them as potential enemies. For over a hundred years, members of the powerful Iroquois Confederacy—Mohawk, Oneida, Onondaga, Cayuga, Seneca, and (after 1722) Tuscarora—had protected their traditional lands with a combination of diplomacy and warfare. Just as the American Revolution forced settler families to join the rebels or remain loyal, it divided the Iroquois, who fought on both sides.

The Mohawk proved to be valuable British allies. Their loyalist leader **Joseph Brant** (Thayendanegea [ta-YEHN-dah-NEY-geh-ah]) organized Britain's most potent fighting force along the Canadian border. His raids along the northern frontier earned him the title "Monster" Brant, but he was actually a man who moved easily between European and Amerindian cultures. Educated by missionaries, he was fluent in English and helped translate Protestant religious tracts into Mohawk. He was friendly with many loyalist families and British officials and had traveled to London for an audience with George III (r. 1760–1820).

The defeat in late 1777 of Britain's general John Burgoyne by General Horatio Gates at Saratoga, New York, put the future of the Mohawk at risk. American forces followed this victory with destructive attacks on Iroquois villages that reduced their political and military power. After Britain's defeat, Brant and the Mohawk joined the loyalist exodus to Canada.

The British defeat at Saratoga also convinced France to enter the war as an ally of the United States in 1778. French military help proved crucial, supplying American forces and forcing the British to defend their colonies in the Caribbean. The French contribution was most clear in the final battle, fought at Yorktown, Virginia, in 1781 (see Map 22.1). With the American army supported by French soldiers and a French fleet, General Charles Cornwallis surrendered to Washington as the British military band played "The World Turned Upside-Down."

This victory effectively ended the war, and the Continental Congress sent representatives to the peace conference with instructions to work in tandem with the French. Believing that France was more concerned with containing British power than with guaranteeing a strong

George Washington Military commander of the American Revolution. He was the first elected president of the United States (1789–1799).

Joseph Brant Mohawk leader who supported the British during the American Revolution.

MAP 22.1 **The American Revolutionary War** The British army won most of the major battles, and British troops held most of the major cities. Even so, the American revolutionaries eventually won a comprehensive military and political victory.

Labels on map:

BRITISH CANADA

General John Burgoyne surrenders at Saratoga, October 17, 1777.

British abandon Boston, March 17, 1776, after Bunker Hill battle.

British occupy New York, August 27, 1776, following American defeat in Brooklyn Heights battle.

Franco–American Treaty of Amity and Commerce and Treaty of Alliance signed in Paris, France, February 1778.

American Army winters at Valley Forge, 1777–1778.

Cornwallis surrenders at Yorktown, October 17, 1781.

Legend:
- Territorial claims of the Thirteen Colonies
- Other British territory
- British victory
- American victory

© Cengage Learning

e Interactive Map

United States, America's peace delegation chose to negotiate directly with Britain and gained a generous settlement. The Treaty of Paris (1783) granted unconditional independence and established generous boundaries for the former colonies. In return the United States promised to repay prewar debts due to British merchants and to allow loyalists to recover property confiscated by patriot forces. In the end, loyalists were badly treated, and thousands left for Canada.

The Construction of Republican Institutions, to 1800

Even before the Declaration of Independence, many colonies had created new governments. Leaders in the new states summoned constitutional conventions to draft formal charters. Europeans were fascinated by the drafting of written constitutions and by their ratification by popular vote. Many early state constitutions were translated and published in Europe. Remembering colonial conflicts with royal governors, state constitutions placed severe limits on executive authority and granted broad powers to legislatures. Many state constitutions included bills of rights to provide further protection against tyranny.

Creating a New Government

It proved more difficult to frame a national constitution. The Second Continental Congress sent the Articles of Confederation—the first constitution of the United States—to the states for approval in 1777, but it was not accepted until 1781. It created a one-house legislature in which each state had a single vote. While a simple majority of the thirteen states was sufficient to pass minor legislation, nine votes were necessary for declaring war, imposing taxes, and coining or borrowing money. A committee, not a president, exercised executive power. Given the intended weakness of this government, it is remarkable that it defeated Great Britain.

Many of the most powerful political figures in the United States recognized that the Confederation was unable to enforce unpopular requirements of the peace treaty such as the recognition of loyalist property claims, the payment of prewar debts, and even the payment of military salaries and pensions to veterans. As a result, Virginia invited the other states to discuss the government's failure to deal with trade issues in September 1786. This assembly called for a new convention to meet in Philadelphia. A rebellion led by Revolutionary War veterans in western Massachusetts gave the assembling delegates a sense of urgency.

Constitutional Convention
Meeting in 1787 of the elected representatives of the thirteen original states to write the Constitution of the United States.

The **Constitutional Convention**, which met in May 1787, achieved a nonviolent second American Revolution. The delegates pushed aside the announced purpose of the convention— "to render the constitution of the federal government adequate to the exigencies of the union"— and secretly undertook to write a new constitution with George Washington serving as presiding officer.

Debate focused on representation, electoral procedures, executive powers, and the relationship between the federal government and the states. The final compromise distributed political power among executive, legislative, and judicial branches and divided authority between the federal government and the states. The chief executive—the president—was to be elected indirectly by "electors" selected by ballot in the states.

The Limits of Democracy

Although this constitution created the most democratic government of the era, only a minority of the adult population had full political rights. While some northern states were hostile to slavery, southern leaders protected the institution. Slaves were denied participation in the political process, but slave states were permitted to count three-fifths of the slave population to allocate the number of congressional representatives, thus multiplying the political power of the slave-owning class. Southern delegates also gained a twenty-year continuation of the slave trade to 1808 and a fugitive slave clause that required all states to return runaway slaves to masters.

Women had led prewar boycotts and had organized relief and charitable organizations during the war. Some had served in the military as nurses, and a smaller number had joined the ranks disguised as men. Nevertheless, women were denied political rights in the new republic. Only New Jersey granted the vote to women and African Americans who met property requirements, and in 1807 state lawmakers eliminated this right.

> **SECTION REVIEW**
>
> - Britain tried to prevent new settlements on Amerindian lands and limit the expense of frontier defense.
> - New colonial tax and commercial policies provoked colonial protest and boycotts in North America.
> - Armed conflict between British troops and colonists led to the calling of the Continental Congress and the Declaration of Independence.
> - French support for the American Revolution proved crucial.
> - The American states supported the creation of a new constitution that divided the powers of government.

THE FRENCH REVOLUTION, 1789–1815

The French Revolution undermined traditional monarchy and hereditary aristocracy as well as the power of the Catholic Church but, unlike the American Revolution, did not create enduring representative institutions. The colonial revolution in North America, however, did not confront so directly the entrenched privileges of an established church, monarchy, and aristocracy. Among its achievements, the French Revolution expanded mass participation in political life and radicalized the democratic tradition inherited from the English and American experiences. The political passions unleashed by revolutionary events in France also ultimately led to rule by popular demagogues and the dictatorship of Napoleon.

French Society and Fiscal Crisis

French society was divided in three estates. The clergy, called the First Estate, numbered about 130,000 in a nation of 28 million. The Catholic clergy was organized hierarchically, and members of the hereditary nobility held almost all top positions in the church. The church owned about

10 percent of the nation's land and extracted substantial amounts of wealth from the economy in the form of tithes and ecclesiastical fees, but it paid few taxes.

The 300,000 members of the nobility, the Second Estate, controlled about 30 percent of the land and retained ancient rights on much of the rest. Nobles held most high administrative, judicial, military, and church positions. Though barred from some types of commercial activity, nobles were important participants in wholesale trade, banking, manufacturing, and mining. Like the clergy, this estate was hierarchical: important differences in wealth, power, and outlook separated the higher from the lower nobility. In the eighteenth century many wealthy commoners who purchased administrative and judicial offices claimed noble status.

The Third Estate

The Third Estate included everyone else, from wealthy financiers to beggars. The number of propertied and successful commoners grew rapidly in the eighteenth century. Commerce, finance, and manufacturing accounted for much of the wealth of the Third Estate. Wealthy commoners also owned nearly a third of the nation's land. This literate and socially ambitious group supported an expanding publishing industry, subsidized the fine arts, and purchased many of the extravagant new homes built in Paris and other cities.

Artisans, shopkeepers, and small landowners owned property and lived decently when crops were good and prices stable, but by 1780 poor harvests had increased their cost of living and led to a decline in consumer demand for their products. They were rich enough to fear the loss of their property and status and well educated enough to be aware of the growing criticism of the king, but they lacked the means to influence policy.

The Poor

Poverty was common. Peasants accounted for 80 percent of the French population. The poverty and vulnerability of peasant families forced young children to seek seasonal work and led many to crime and beggary. In Paris and other French cities the vile living conditions and unhealthy diet of the urban poor were startling to visitors from other European nations. City streets swarmed with beggars and prostitutes. The problem of child abandonment suggests the wretchedness of the French poor. On the eve of the French Revolution parents gave up at least 40,000 children per year. Their belief that these children would be adopted was no more than a convenient fiction; in reality the majority died of neglect.

Unable to afford decent housing, obtain steady employment, or protect their children, the poor periodically erupted in violent protest and rage. In the countryside the decisions of the nobility or clergy to increase taxes and other burdens often led to violence. In towns and cities any increase in the price of bread could spark a riot, since bread prices determined the quality of life of the poor. These explosive episodes, however, were not revolutionary in character; rioters sought immediate relief rather than structural change. That was to change when the Crown tried to solve its fiscal crisis.

The cost of the War of the Austrian Succession began the crisis. Louis XV (r. 1715–1774) tried to impose new taxes on the nobility and other privileged groups, but this led to widespread protests. New debt from the Seven Years War deepened the crisis and compelled the king to impose emergency fiscal measures. The Parlement of Paris, an appeal

Private Collection

Parisian Stocking Mender   The poor lived very difficult lives. This woman uses a discarded wine barrel as a shop where she mends socks.

The Politics of Debts and Taxes

court, resisted these measures. Frustrated by these actions, French authorities exiled members of the Parlement and pushed through a series of unpopular fiscal measures.

When the twenty-two-year-old Louis XVI assumed the throne in 1774, he faced a desperate fiscal situation compounded by the growing opposition of French courts. In 1774 his chief financial adviser warned that the government could barely afford to operate; as he put it, "the first gunshot [act of war] will drive the state to bankruptcy." Despite this warning, the king decided to support the American Revolution, delaying collapse by borrowing enormous sums and disguising the growing debt in misleading fiscal accounts. By the end of the war, more than half of France's national budget was required to pay the interest on its debt.

In 1787 the desperate king called an Assembly of Notables to approve a radical and comprehensive reform of the economy and fiscal policy. Despite the fact that the king's advisers selected this assembly from the high nobility, the judiciary, and the clergy, these representatives of privilege proved unwilling to support the proposed reforms and new taxes.

Protest Turns to Revolution, 1789–1792

Estates General France's traditional national assembly with representatives of the three estates, or classes, in French society: the clergy, nobility, and commoners. The calling of the Estates General in 1789 led to the French Revolution.

In frustration, the king dismissed the Notables and attempted to implement reforms on his own, but his effort was met by an increasingly hostile judiciary and by popular demonstrations. The refusal of the elite to grant needed tax concessions forced the king to call the **Estates General**, a customary consultative body representing the three estates that had not met since 1614. The narrow self-interest and greed of the rich—who would not tolerate an increase in their own taxes—rather than the grinding poverty of the common people had created the conditions for revolution.

The Third Estate Acts

In late 1788 and early 1789 members of the three estates came together throughout the nation to discuss grievances and elect representatives to meet at Versailles (vuhr-SIGH). The Third Estate's representatives were mostly men of substantial property, but some were angry with the king's ministers and inclined to move France toward constitutional monarchy with an elected legislature. Many nobles and members of the clergy sympathized with the reform agenda of the Third Estate, but deep internal divisions over procedural and policy issues limited the power of the First and the Second Estates. Nevertheless, some clergy, and eventually nobles, joined with the Third Estate.

After six weeks of deadlock, the Third Estate, with allies from the other estates, signaled its ambitions by calling itself the National Assembly. Fearful of the growing assertiveness of these representatives, the king locked them out of their meeting place. They moved to an indoor tennis court and pledged to write a constitution. The ascendant ideas of the era, that the people are sovereign and the legitimacy of rulers depends on their fulfilling the people's will, now swept away the king's narrow desire to solve the nation's fiscal crisis. Louis prepared for a confrontation with the National Assembly by moving military forces to Versailles. Before he could act, the people of Paris intervened.

A succession of bad harvests beginning in 1785 had propelled bread prices upward throughout France and provoked an economic depression as demand for nonessential goods collapsed. By the time the Estates General met, nearly a third of the Parisian work force was unemployed. Hunger and anger marched hand in hand through working-class neighborhoods.

The Bastille Falls

When the people of Paris heard that the king was massing troops in Versailles to arrest the representatives, crowds of common people began to seize arms and mobilize. On July 14, 1789, a crowd attacked the Bastille (bass-TEEL), a medieval fortress used as a prison. The futile defense of the Bastille cost ninety-eight lives before its garrison surrendered. Enraged, the attackers hacked the commander to death and then paraded through the city with his head and that of Paris's chief magistrate stuck on pikes.

These events coincided with uprisings by peasants in the country. Peasants sacked manor houses and destroyed documents that recorded their traditional obligations. They refused to pay taxes and dues to landowners and seized common lands. Forced to recognize the fury raging through rural areas, the National Assembly voted to end traditional obligations and the privileges of the nobility and church, essentially ending the feudal system. Having won this victory, peasants ceased their revolt.

Declaration of the Rights of Man and the Citizen Statement of fundamental political rights adopted by the French National Assembly at the beginning of the French Revolution.

These popular uprisings strengthened the hand of the National Assembly in its dealings with the king and led to passage of the **Declaration of the Rights of Man and the Citizen**, which stated the principles for a future constitution. There were similarities between the language

Declaration of the Rights of Man and the Citizen

Parisians Storm the Bastille An eyewitness to the storming of the Bastille on July 14, 1789, painted this representation of this epochal event, still celebrated by the French as a national holiday.

Photos12.com-ARJ

ⓔ PRIMARY SOURCE: The Declaration of the Rights of Man and the Citizen This document, drafted by the National Assembly of France, is an Enlightenment cousin of Jefferson's Declaration.

The Women of Paris Act

Revolutionary Changes Begin

of this declaration and the U.S. Declaration of Independence. Thomas Jefferson, author of the American document, was U.S. ambassador to Paris and offered his opinion to those drafting the French statement. The French declaration, however, was more sweeping in its language. Among the enumerated natural rights were "liberty, property, security, and resistance to oppression." The Declaration of the Rights of Man and the Citizen also guaranteed free expression of ideas, equality before the law, and representative government.

While delegates debated political issues in Versailles, the economic crisis worsened in Paris. Women employed in the garment industry and small shopkeepers were particularly hard hit. Because the working women of Paris faced high food prices every day as they struggled to feed their families, their anger had a hard edge. Public markets became political arenas where the urban poor met daily in angry assembly. Here the revolutionary link between the material deprivation of the French poor and the political aspirations of the French bourgeoisie was forged.

On October 5, thousands of market women marched the 12 miles (19 kilometers) to Versailles. They forced their way into the National Assembly to demand action: "the point is that we want bread," they shouted. The crowd then entered the royal apartments, killed some of the king's guards, and searched for Queen Marie Antoinette (ann-twah-NET), whom they hated as a symbol of extravagance. They then forced the royal family to relocate to Paris.

With the king's ability to resist democratic change overcome by the Paris crowd, the National Assembly achieved a radically restructured French society in the next two years. It passed a new constitution that dramatically limited monarchial power and abolished the nobility as a hereditary class. Economic reforms swept away monopolies and trade barriers within France. Renamed the Legislative Assembly, legislators took on the church, seizing its lands to use as collateral for a new paper currency, mandating the election of priests, and placing them on the public payroll. When the Assembly forced priests to take a loyalty oath, however, many Catholics joined a growing counterrevolutionary movement.

At first, many European monarchs welcomed the weakening of the French king, but by 1791 Austria and Prussia threatened to intervene in support of the monarchy. The Legislative Assembly responded by declaring war. Although the war went badly at first for French forces, people across France responded patriotically to foreign invasions, forming huge new volunteer armies and mobilizing national resources to meet the challenge.

The Terror, 1793–1794

In this period of national crisis and foreign threat, the French Revolution entered its most radical phase. A failed effort by the king and queen to escape from Paris cost the king his remaining popular support. On August 10, 1792, a crowd invaded his palace in Paris, forcing the king to seek protection in the Legislative Assembly, which suspended his authority and ordered his imprisonment. These actions helped lead to the creation of a new legislative and executive body, the National Convention.

Rumors of counterrevolutionary plots kept working-class neighborhoods in an uproar, and in September a mob surged through the city's prisons, killing nearly half the prisoners. Swept along by popular passion, the newly elected National Convention convicted Louis XVI of treason, sentenced him to death, and proclaimed France a republic. The guillotine ended the king's life in January 1793 (see Environment and Technology: The Guillotine). These events precipitated a wider war with nearly all of Europe's powers allied against France.

The Jacobins

Jacobins Radical republicans during the French Revolution. They were led by Maximilien Robespierre from 1793 to 1794.

Maximilien Robespierre Young provincial lawyer who led the most radical phases of the French Revolution. His execution ended the Reign of Terror.

The National Convention—the new legislature of the French Republic—convened in September. Almost all its members were from the middle class, and nearly all were **Jacobins** (JAK-uh-bin)—the most uncompromising democrats. Deep political differences, however, separated moderate Jacobins—called "Girondists (juh-RON-dist)," after a region in southern France—and radicals known as "the Mountain." Members of the Mountain—so named because their seats were on the highest level in the assembly hall—were more sympathetic than the Girondists to the demands of the Parisian working class and less patient with parliamentary procedure. **Maximilien Robespierre** (ROBES-pee-air), a young, little-known lawyer influenced by Rousseau's ideas, dominated the Mountain.

With the French economy in crisis and Paris suffering from inflation, high unemployment, and scarcity, Robespierre used the popular press and political clubs to forge an alliance with the volatile Parisian working class. His growing strength in the streets allowed him to purge and execute many of his enemies in the National Convention and to restructure the government. He placed executive power in the hands of the newly formed Committee of Public Safety, which created special courts to seek out and punish enemies of the Revolution.

Women and the Revolution

Among the groups that lost influence were the active feminists of the Parisian middle class and the working-class women who had sought the right to bear arms in defense of the Revolution. These women had provided decisive leadership at crucial times, helping propel the Revolution toward widened suffrage and a more democratic structure. Armed women had actively participated in every confrontation with conservative forces. It is ironic that the National Convention—the revolutionary era's most radical legislative body—chose to repress the militant feminist forces that had prepared the ground for its creation.

Faced with rebellion in the provinces and foreign invasion, Robespierre and his allies unleashed a period of repression called the Reign of Terror (1793–1794) (see Diversity and Dominance: Robespierre and Wollstonecraft Defend and Explain the Terror). During the Terror, executions and deaths in prison claimed 40,000 lives while another 300,000 suffered imprisonment. The revolutionary government took new actions against the clergy as well, including the provocative measure of forcing priests to marry. Even time was subject to revolutionary change. A new republican calendar created twelve 30-day months divided into 10-day weeks. Sunday, with its Christian meanings, disappeared from the calendar.

The End of Robespierre

By spring 1794 the Revolution was secure from foreign and domestic enemies, but repression continued. Among the victims were some of Robespierre's closest political collaborators during the Terror. The execution of these former allies prepared the way for Robespierre's own fall by undermining the sense of invulnerability that had secured the loyalty of his remaining

Playing Cards from the French Revolution Even playing cards could be used to attack the aristocracy and Catholic Church. In this pack of cards, "Equality" and "Liberty" replaced kings and queens.

The Guillotine

No machine more powerfully symbolizes the revolutionary era than the guillotine. The machine immortalizes Joseph Ignace Guillotin (1738–1814), a physician and member of the French Constituent Assembly. In 1789 Guillotin recommended that executions be made more humane by use of a beheading device. He sought to replace hangings, used for commoners, and beheadings by axe, used for the nobility. Both forms of execution were often conducted with little skill, leading to gruesome and painful deaths. Guillotin believed that a properly designed machine would produce predictable, nearly painless deaths and remove the social distinction between commoners and nobles, embarrassing in a more egalitarian age.

After 1791 execution by beheading became the common sentence for all capital crimes. Another physician, Antoine Louis, secretary of the College of Surgeons, designed the actual machine. Once directed to produce a suitable device, Louis, in many ways a typical technician of his time, systematically examined devices used elsewhere and experimented until satisfied with his results. Praised by contemporaries because it seemed to remove human agency, and therefore revenge, from the death penalty, the guillotine became the physical symbol of the Terror.

The Art Archive

The Guillotine The guillotine, introduced as a more humane and democratic alternative to traditional executions, came to symbolize the arbitrary violence of the French Revolution. In this contemporary cartoon Robespierre, the architect of the Terror, serves as executioner while surrounded by guillotines.

partisans. After French victories eliminated the immediate foreign threat in 1794, conservatives in the Convention voted to arrest Robespierre and then ordered his execution along with that of nearly a hundred of his allies in July 1794.

Reaction and the Rise of Napoleon, 1795–1815

Purged of Robespierre's collaborators, the Convention began to undo the radical reforms. It removed emergency economic controls that held down prices and protected the working class. Gone also was toleration for violent popular demonstrations. When the Paris working class rose in protest in 1795, the Convention reacted with overwhelming military force. It allowed the Catholic Church to regain much of its former influence, but it did not return the church's confiscated wealth. It also put in place a more conservative constitution that protected property, established a voting process that reduced the power of the masses, and created a new executive authority, the Directory.

After losing the election of 1797, the Directory refused to give up power, effectively ending the republican phase of the Revolution. Political authority now depended on coercive force rather than elections. Two years later, a brilliant young general in the French army, **Napoleon Bonaparte** (1769–1821), seized power. Just as the American and French Revolutions had been the start of the modern democratic tradition, the military intervention that brought Napoleon to power in 1799 marked the advent of another modern form of government: popular authoritarianism.

Napoleon Bonaparte
General who overthrew the French Directory in 1799 and became emperor of the French in 1804. Failed to defeat Great Britain and abdicated in 1814. Returned to power briefly in 1815 but was defeated and died in exile.

Napoleon

Robespierre and Wollstonecraft Defend and Explain the Terror

*Many Europeans who had been sympathetic to the French Revo-
lution were repelled by the Terror. In 1793 and 1794, while France
was at war with Austria, Prussia, Great Britain, Holland, and
Spain, revolutionaries in Paris executed about 2,600 people,
including the king and queen, members of the nobility, and
Catholic clergy. Critics of the Revolution asked if these excesses
were not worse than those committed by the French monarchy.
Others defended the violence as necessary, arguing that enemies
of the Revolution provoked the Terror.*

*The following two opinions date from 1794. Maximilien
Robespierre was the head of the Committee of Public Safety,
the effective head of the revolutionary government. He was a
provincial lawyer who rose to power in Paris as the Revolution
radicalized. In the statement that follows he argues that violence
is necessary in the defense of liberty, making this statement on
the eve of his own political demise. In 1794 the revolutionary
movement he had helped create removed him from power and
ordered his execution.*

*Mary Wollstonecraft, an English intellectual and advocate for
women's rights who was living in Paris at the time of the execution of Louis XVI, was troubled by the violence, and her discussion of these events is more an apology than a defense. She had
published her famous* A Vindication of the Rights of Woman
*in 1792, after which she left for Paris. Wollstonecraft left Paris
after war broke out between France and Britain. She remained
an important force in European intellectual life until her death
from complications of childbirth in 1797.*

Maximilien Robespierre, "On the Moral and Political Principles of Domestic Policy"

[L]et us deduce a great truth: the characteristic of popular
government is confidence in the people and severity towards
itself.

The whole development of our theory would end here if
you had only to pilot the vessel of the Republic through calm
waters; but the tempest roars, and the revolution imposes on
you another task.

This great purity of the French revolution's basis, the very
sublimity of its objective, is precisely what causes both our
strength and our weakness. Our strength, because it gives to us
truth's ascendancy over imposture, and the rights of the public

interest over private interests; our weakness, because it rallies
all vicious men against us, all those who in their hearts contemplated despoiling the people and all those who intend to
let it be despoiled with impunity, both those who have rejected
freedom as a personal calamity and those who have embraced
the revolution as a career and the Republic as prey. Hence the
defection of so many ambitious or greedy men who since the
point of departure have abandoned us along the way because
they did not begin the journey with the same destination in
view. The two opposing spirits that have been represented in a
struggle to rule nature might be said to be fighting in this great
period of human history to fix irrevocably the world's destinies, and France is the scene of this fearful combat. Without,
all the tyrants encircle you; within, all tyranny's friends conspire; they will conspire until hope is wrested from crime. We
must smother the internal and external enemies of the Republic or perish with it; now in this situation, the first maxim of
your policy ought to be to lead the people by reason and the
people's enemies by terror.

If the spring of popular government in time of peace is virtue, the springs of popular government in revolution are at
once virtue and terror: virtue, without which terror is fatal; terror, without which virtue is powerless. Terror is nothing other
than justice, prompt, severe, inflexible; it is therefore an ema-
nation of virtue; it is not so much a special principle as it is a
consequence of the general principle of democracy applied to
our country's most urgent needs.

It has been said that terror is the principle of despotic government. Does your government therefore resemble despotism? Yes, as the sword that gleams in the hands of the heroes
of liberty resembles that with which the henchmen of tyranny
are armed. Let the despot govern by terror his brutalized subjects; he is right, as a despot. Subdue by terror the enemies of
liberty, and you will be right, as founders of the Republic. The
government of the revolution is liberty's despotism against
tyranny. Is force made only to protect crime? And is the thun-
derbolt not destined to strike the heads of the proud?

. . . Society owes protection only to peaceable citizens; the
only citizens in the Republic are the republicans. For it, the
royalists, the conspirators are only strangers or, rather, enemies. This terrible war waged by liberty against tyranny is it
not indivisible? Are the enemies within not the allies of the
enemies without? The assassins who tear our country apart,
the intriguers who buy the consciences that hold the people's

The American and French Revolutions resulted in part from conflicts over representation.
If the people were sovereign, what institutions best expressed popular will? In the United States
the answer was the expansion of the right to vote and creation of representative institutions. The
French Revolution took a different direction with the Reign of Terror. Interventions on the floor
of the National Convention by market women and soldiers, the presence of common people at
revolutionary tribunals and at public executions, and the expansion of military service were all

mandate; the traitors who sell them; the mercenary pamphleteers hired to dishonor the people's cause, to kill public virtue, to stir up the fire of civil discord, and to prepare political counterrevolution by moral counterrevolution—are all those men less guilty or less dangerous than the tyrants whom they serve?

Mary Wollstonecraft, "An Historical and Moral View of the Origin and Progress of the French Revolution"

Weeping scarcely conscious that I weep, O France! Over the vestiges of thy former oppression, which, separating man from man with a fence of iron, sophisticated [complicated] all, and made many completely wretched; I tremble, lest I should meet some unfortunate being, fleeing from the despotism of licentious freedom, hearing the snap of the guillotine at his heels, merely because he was once noble, or has afforded an asylum to those whose only crime is their name—and, if my pen almost bound with eagerness to record the day that leveled the Bastille [an abbey used as a prison before the Revolution] with the dust, making the towers of despair tremble to their base, the recollection that still the abbey is appropriated to hold the victims of revenge and suspicion [she means that the Bastille remained a prison for those awaiting revolutionary justice]. . . .

Excuse for the Ferocity of the Parisians

The deprivation of natural, equal, civil, and political rights reduced the most cunning of the lower orders to practice fraud, and the rest to habits of stealing, audacious robberies, and murders. And why? Because the rich and poor were separated into bands of tyrants and slaves, and the retaliation of slaves is always terrible. In short, every sacred feeling, moral and divine, has been obliterated, and the dignity of man sullied, by a system of policy and jurisprudence as repugnant to reason as at variance with humanity.

The only excuse that can be made for the ferocity of the Parisians is then simply to observe that they had not any confidence in the laws, which they had always found to be merely cobwebs to catch small flies [the poor]. Accustomed to be punished themselves for every trifle, and often for only being in the way of the rich, or their parasites, when, in fact, had the Parisians seen the execution of a noble, or priest, though convicted of crimes beyond the daring of vulgar minds? When justice, or the law, is so partial, the day of retribution will come with the

red sky of vengeance, to confound the innocent with the guilty. The mob were barbarous beyond the tiger's cruelty. . . .

Let us cast our eyes over the history of man, and we shall scarcely find a page that is not tarnished by some foul deed or bloody transaction. Let us examine the catalogue of the vices of men in a savage state, and contrast them with those of men civilized; we shall find that a barbarian, considered as a moral being, is an angel, compared with the refined villain of artificial life. Let us investigate the causes which have produced this degeneracy, and we shall discover that they are those unjust plans of government which have been formed by peculiar circumstances in every part of the globe.

Then let us coolly and impartially contemplate the improvements which are gaining ground in the formation of principles of policy; and I flatter myself it will be allowed by every humane and considerate being that a political system more simple than has hitherto existed would effectually check those aspiring follies, which, by imitation, leading to vice, have banished from governments the very shadow of justice and magnanimity.

Thus had France grown up and sickened on the corruption of a state diseased. . . . it is only the philosophical eye, which looks into the nature and weighs the consequences of human actions, that will be able to discern the cause, which has produced so many dreadful effects.

QUESTIONS FOR ANALYSIS

1. Why does Robespierre believe that revolution cannot tolerate diversity of opinion? Are his reasons convincing?

2. How does Robespierre distinguish the terror of despots from the terror of liberty?

3. How does Wollstonecraft explain the "ferocity" of the Parisians?

4. What does Wollstonecraft believe will come from this period of violence?

Sources: Maximilien Robespierre, "On the Moral and Political Principles of Domestic Policy," February 5, 1794, *Modern History Sourcebook: Robespierre: Terror and Virtue, 1794, http://www.fordham.edu/halsall/mod/robespierre-terror.html*; Mary Wollstonecraft, "An Historical and Moral View of the Origin and Progress of the French Revolution," *A Mary Wollstonecraft Reader*, ed. Barbara H. Solomon and Paula S. Berggren (New York: New American Library, 1983), 374–375, 382–383.

forms of political communication that temporarily satisfied the French people's desire to influence their government. Napoleon tamed these forms of political expression to organize Europe's first popular dictatorship. He succeeded because his military reputation promised order to a society exhausted by a decade of crisis, turmoil, and bloodshed.

France Under Napoleon

Napoleon sought to realize France's dream of dominating Europe while providing effective protection for persons and property at home. Negotiations with the Catholic Church led to the

Concordat of 1801. This agreement gave French Catholics the right to freely practice their religion, but it also recognized the French government's authority to nominate bishops and retain priests on the state payroll. In his comprehensive rewriting of French law, the Civil Code of 1804, Napoleon won the support of the peasantry and the middle class by asserting two basic principles inherited from the moderate first stage of the French Revolution: equality in law and protection of property. Some members of the nobility were won over when Napoleon declared himself emperor and France an empire in 1804. Despite his willingness to make dramatic changes, he continued the denial of political rights for women begun during the Terror. The Civil Code denied women basic political rights and only allowed them to participate in the economy with the guidance and supervision of fathers and husbands.

While it reestablished order, the Napoleonic system denied or restricted many individual rights. Free speech was limited. Criticism of the government, viewed as subversive, was proscribed, and most opposition newspapers disappeared. Spies and informers directed by the minister of police enforced these draconian policies.

French Expansion and Defeat

Ultimately, the Napoleonic system depended on the success of French arms (see Map 22.2). From Napoleon's assumption of power until his fall, no single European state could defeat the French military. Austria and Prussia suffered humiliating defeats and became allies of France. Only Britain, protected by its powerful navy, remained able to thwart Napoleon's plans to dominate Europe.

Desiring to again extend French power to the Americas, Napoleon invaded Portugal in 1807 and Spain in 1808. Spanish and Portuguese patriots supported by Great Britain eventually tied French armies down in a costly conflict. Frustrated by events on the Iberian Peninsula and faced with a faltering economy, Napoleon made the fateful decision to invade Russia. In June 1812 he began his campaign with the largest army ever assembled in Europe, approximately 600,000 men. His army took Moscow but after five weeks abandoned the city. During the retreat, the brutal Russian winter and attacks by Russian forces destroyed Napoleon's army. A broken and battered remnant of 30,000 made it back to France.

After the debacle in Russia, Austria and Prussia deserted Napoleon and entered an alliance with England and Russia against France. Unable to defend Paris, Napoleon abdicated the throne in April 1814 and was exiled to the island of Elba off the coast of Italy. The victorious allies then restored the French monarchy. The following year Napoleon escaped from Elba and returned to France, but an allied army defeated his forces in 1815 at Waterloo, in Belgium. His final exile was on the distant island of St. Helena in the South Atlantic, where he died in 1821.

SECTION REVIEW

- The heavy burden of debt, caused in part by support of the American Revolution, forced Louis XVI to call the Estates General.
- When some members of the nobility and clergy joined the rebellious Third Estate they formed the National Assembly.
- The hungry Parisian masses radicalized the movement for reform by storming the Bastille and forcing the king to move to Paris.
- The Legislative Assembly, led by Robespierre, executed the king and initiated the Terror.
- Exhausted by the violence of the Terror and threatened by foreign enemies, France turned to Napoleon Bonaparte, who dominated Europe until he was defeated in 1814.

REVOLUTION SPREADS, CONSERVATIVES RESPOND, 1789–1850

Even as the dictatorship of Napoleon tamed the democratic legacy of the French Revolution, revolutionary ideology was spreading and taking hold in Europe and the Americas. In Europe the French Revolution promoted nationalism and republicanism. In the Americas the legacies of the American and French Revolutions led to a new round of struggles for independence. News of revolutionary events in France destabilized the colonial regime in Saint Domingue (present-day Haiti), a small French colony on the western half of the island of Hispaniola, and helped initiate the first successful slave rebellion. In Europe, however, the spread of revolutionary fervor was met by the concerted reaction of an alliance of conservative monarchs committed to extinguishing further revolutionary outbreaks.

The Haitian Revolution, 1789–1804

In 1789 the French colony of Saint Domingue was among the richest colonies in the Americas. Its production of sugar, cotton, indigo, and coffee accounted for two-thirds of France's tropical imports and generated nearly one-third of all French foreign trade. This wealth depended on a brutal slave regime. The harsh punishments and poor living conditions experienced by Saint Domingue's slaves were notorious throughout the Caribbean. The resulting high mortality and low fertility rates created an insatiable demand for African slaves. As a result, in 1790 the majority of the colony's 500,000 slaves were African-born.

When news of the meeting of the Estates General arrived on the island in 1789, wealthy planters sent a delegation to Paris to seek more home rule and greater economic freedom for Saint Domingue. The free mixed-race population, the **gens de couleur** (zhahn deh koo-LUHR), also sent representatives. Representing a large class of free black planters and urban merchants who owned slaves, they sought to limit race discrimination, not to end slavery. As the French Revolution became more radical, the gens de couleur forged an alliance with sympathetic French radicals, who saw the colony's wealthy planters as royalists and aristocrats.

The political turmoil in France weakened the authority of colonial administrators in Saint Domingue. In the vacuum that resulted, rich planters, poor whites, and the gens de couleur all pursued their narrow interests, engendering an increasingly bitter and confrontational struggle. Given the slaves' hatred of the brutal regime that oppressed them and the accumulated grievances of the free people of color, there was no way to limit the violence once the control of the slave owners slipped. When Vincent Ogé (oh-ZHAY), leader of the gens de couleur mission to France, returned to Saint Domingue in 1790, the planters captured him and ordered his torture and execution. The free black and slave populations soon repaid this cruelty in kind.

By 1791 whites, led by the planter elite, and the gens de couleur were engaged in open warfare. A slave rebellion begun on the plantations of the north transformed this conflict (see Map 22.3). Rebelling slaves destroyed plantations, killed masters and overseers, and burned crops. Their emerging leadership relied on elements of African political practice and revolutionary ideology from France to mobilize and direct the rebelling slaves.

The rebellious slaves gained the upper hand under the command of **François Dominique Toussaint L'Ouverture**, a former domestic slave, who created a disciplined military force. The 1794 decision of the radical National Convention in Paris to abolish slavery in all French possessions strengthened Toussaint politically. As leader he swept aside his local rivals, defeated a British expeditionary force in 1798, and then led an invasion of the neighboring Spanish colony

gens de couleur Free men and women of color in Haiti. They sought greater political rights and later supported the Haitian Revolution.

The Haitian Revolution Begins

François Dominique Toussaint L'Ouverture Leader of the Haitian Revolution. He freed the slaves and gained effective independence for Haiti despite military interventions by the British and French.

Toussaint L'Ouverture

Haiti's Former Slaves Defend Their Freedom
In this representation, a veteran army sent by Napoleon to reassert French control in Haiti battles with Haitian forces in a tropical forest. The combination of Haitian resistance and yellow fever defeated the French invasion.

Bettmann/Corbis

MAP 22.2 Napoleon's Europe, 1810 By 1810 Great Britain was the only remaining European power at war with Napoleon. Because of the loss of the French fleet at the Battle of Trafalgar in 1805, Napoleon was unable to threaten Britain with invasion, and Britain was able to actively assist the resistance movements in Spain and Portugal, thereby helping weaken French power.

e Interactive Map

© Cengage Learning

Legend:
- French empire
- Dependent states
- Allied with Napoleon
- At war with Napoleon
- ★ Major battle

0 200 400 Km.
0 400 Mi.

GREAT BRITAIN
London
ATLANTIC OCEAN
North Sea
KINGDOM OF NORWAY AND DENMARK
Stockholm
KINGDOM OF SWEDEN
St. Petersburg
Copenhagen
Baltic Sea
Lübeck
Hamburg
Bremen
SWEDISH POMERANIA
Königsberg
Danzig
Tilsit
Friedland 1807
Neman R.
Moscow
Borodino 1812
Smolensk
RUSSIAN EMPIRE
Kiev
Brussels
Waterloo 1815
Amiens
Paris
Lunéville
Berlin
Elbe R.
WESTPHALIA
Auerstädt 1806
SAXONY
Jena 1806
PRUSSIA
GRAND DUCHY OF WARSAW
CONFEDERATION OF THE RHINE
Rhine R.
WÜRTTEMBERG
BADEN
BAVARIA
Zurich
SWITZERLAND
Austerlitz 1805
Wagram 1809
Vienna
Pressburg
Buda
Pest
AUSTRIAN EMPIRE
Danube R.
Black Sea
Constantinople
OTTOMAN EMPIRE
FRANCE
Marseilles
Genoa
Marengo 1800
Milan
KINGDOM OF ITALY
ILLYRIAN PROVINCES
Corsica
Sardinia
Elba
Rome
Naples
KINGDOM OF NAPLES
Palermo
KINGDOM OF SICILY
Malta (Gr. Br.)
Mediterranean Sea
Ionian Is. (Gr. Br.)
Athens
SPAIN
Madrid
PORTUGAL
Lisbon
Trafalgar 1805
GIBRALTAR (Gr. Br.)

ATLANTIC OCEAN

Tortue

French forces commanded by Victor Emmanuel Leclerc, February 1802

Vincent Ogé executed, February 1791

FLORIDA
THE BAHAMAS
CUBA
PUERTO RICO
JAMAICA
SANTO DOMINGO
SAINT-DOMINGUE

Toussaint L'Ouverture captured and sent to prison in France, 1802

Santo Domingo invaded by forces of Toussaint L'Ouverture, 1801

Caribbean Sea

British invade, 1794

SAINT-DOMINGUE

SANTO DOMINGO

Controlled by forces of André Rigaud

Saint-Domingue
First phase of slave insurrection August 22–26, 1791

© Cengage Learning

MAP 22.3 **The Haitian Revolution** On their way to achieving an end to slavery and gaining national independence, the Haitian revolutionaries were forced to defeat British and French military interventions as well as the local authority of the slave masters.

 Interactive Map

of Santo Domingo, freeing slaves there. While Toussaint asserted his loyalty to France, he gave the French government no effective role in local affairs.

As reaction overtook revolution in France, both the abolition of slavery and Toussaint's political position were threatened. When the Directory contemplated the reestablishment of slavery, Toussaint protested:

> *Do they think that men who have been able to enjoy the blessing of liberty will calmly see it snatched away? They supported their chains only so long as they did not know any condition of life more happy than slavery. But today when they have left it, if they had a thousand lives they would sacrifice them all rather than be forced into slavery again.[2]*

In 1802 Napoleon sent a large military force to reestablish both French colonial authority and slavery in Saint Domingue (see Map 22.3). At first French forces were successful, capturing Toussaint and sending him to France, where he died in prison. Eventually, however, the loss of thousands of lives to yellow fever and the resistance of the revolutionaries turned the tide. In 1804 Toussaint's successors declared independence, and the free republic of Haiti joined the United States as the second independent nation in the Western Hemisphere.

Congress of Vienna Meeting of representatives of European monarchs called to reestablish the old order after the defeat of Napoleon I.

The Congress of Vienna and Conservative Retrenchment, 1815–1820

In 1814–1815 representatives of Britain, Russia, Austria, Prussia, and other European nations met as the **Congress of Vienna** to reestablish political order in Europe. The French Revolution and Napoleon's imperial ambitions had threatened the survival of Europe's old order. Ancient monarchies had been overturned and dynasties replaced with interlopers. Long-established political institutions were overturned and international borders ignored. The very existence of the nobility and church had seemed at risk. Under the leadership of the Austrian foreign minister, Prince Klemens von Metternich (MET-uhr-nik) (1773–1859), the victorious allies worked to create a comprehensive peace settlement that would safeguard the conservative order.

The Holy Alliance

The central objective of the Congress of Vienna was to create a strong and stable France as the best guarantee of future peace. It reestablished the French monarchy and recognized France's 1792 borders, although most of the allies received some territorial gains. Metternich believed that a strong and stable France had to be offset by a balance of power. Austria, Russia, and Prussia therefore formed a separate alliance to repress revolutionary and nationalist movements that sought to imitate the French Revolution. In 1820 this "Holy Alliance" used military force to defeat liberal revolutions in Spain and Italy. The Holy Alliance also attempted to blunt the force of revolutionary ideas by repressing republican and nationalist ideas in universities and the press. While Metternich's program of conservative retrenchment succeeded in the short term, the powerful ideas associated with liberalism and nationalism remained a vital part of European political life throughout the nineteenth century.

Nationalism, Reform, and Revolution, 1821–1850

Greek Independence

Despite the power of the conservative monarchs, popular support for national self-determination and democratic reform grew throughout Europe. Greece had been under Ottoman control since the fifteenth century. In 1821 Greek patriots launched an independence movement. Metternich and other conservatives opposed Greek independence, but European artists and writers enamored with the cultural legacy of ancient Greece rallied political support for intervention. After years of struggle, Russia, France, and Great Britain forced the Ottoman Empire to recognize Greek independence in 1830.

Revolutionary Fears in France and Britain

The victorious allies placed Louis XVIII, brother of the executed Louis XVI, on the throne of France in 1814. Unlike his ancestors, he ruled as a constitutional monarch until his death in 1824. His brother, the conservative Charles X, inherited the throne. His decision to repudiate the constitution in 1830 provoked a mass uprising in Paris that forced him to abdicate. The crown then went to the king's cousin, Louis Philippe (loo-EE fee-LEEP) (r. 1830–1848), who agreed to accept the constitution and extended voting privileges.

Revolutionary violence in France made the British aristocracy and the conservative Tory Party fearful of democracy and mass movements of any kind. In 1815 the British government passed the Corn Laws, which limited the importation of foreign grains. The laws favored the profits of wealthy landowners who produced grain, rather than the poor who would now be forced to pay more for their bread. When poor consumers organized to overturn these laws, the government outlawed public meetings and used troops to crush protest in Manchester. Reacting against these policies, English reformers increased the power of the House of Commons, redistributed votes from agricultural to industrial districts, and increased the number of voters by nearly 50 percent. Although the most radical demands of reformers, called Chartists, were defeated, new labor and economic reforms addressing the grievances of workers were put in place (see Chapter 23).

The Revolutions of 1848

Revolutions of 1848 Democratic and nationalist revolutions that swept across Europe. The monarchy in France was overthrown. In Germany, Austria, Italy, and Hungary the revolutions failed.

Despite the achievement of Greek independence and limited political reform in France and Great Britain, conservatives continued to hold the upper hand. In 1848 the desire for democratic reform and national self-determination led to upheavals across Europe. The **Revolutions of 1848** began in Paris, where members of the middle class and workers united to overthrow the regime of Louis Philippe and create the Second French Republic. Reformers gave adult men voting rights, abolished slavery in French colonies, ended the death penalty, and legislated the ten-hour workday. But Parisian workers' demands for programs to reduce unemployment and prices provoked conflicts with the middle class, which wanted to protect property rights. When workers rose up against the government, French troops crushed them. Desiring the reestablishment of order, the French elected Louis Napoleon, nephew of the former emperor, president in December 1848. Three years later, he overturned the constitution and, after ruling briefly as dictator, proclaimed himself Emperor Napoleon III.

The Revolution of 1830 in Belgium   After the 1830 uprising that overturned the restored monarchy in France, Belgians rose up to declare their independence from Holland. In Poland and Italy, similar uprisings combining nationalism and a desire for self-governance failed. This painting by Baron Gustaf Wappers romantically illustrates the popular nature of the Belgian uprising by bringing to the barricades men, women, and children drawn from both the middle and the working classes.

In 1848 reformers in Hungary, Italy, Bohemia, and elsewhere pressed for greater national self-determination from the Austro-Hungarian Empire. When the monarchy did not meet their demands, students and workers in Vienna took to the streets to force political reforms similar to those sought in Paris. With revolution spreading throughout the Empire, Metternich, the symbol of reaction, fled Vienna in disguise. Little lasting change occurred, however, because the new Austrian emperor, Franz Joseph (r. 1848–1916), used Russian military assistance and loyal Austrian troops to reestablish his authority.

Similarly, middle-class reformers and workers in Berlin joined forces to force the Prussian king to accept a liberal constitution and seek German unification. But the Constituent Assembly called to write a constitution and negotiate national integration was diverted to deal with diplomatic conflicts with Austria and Denmark. As a result, Frederick William IV (r. 1840–1861) reasserted his authority and thwarted constitutional reform and unification.

Despite their heroism on the barricades of Paris, Vienna, Rome, and Berlin, the revolutionaries of 1848 failed to gain their nationalist and republican objectives. Monarchs retained the support not only of aristocrats but also of professional militaries, largely recruited from among peasants who had little sympathy for urban workers. Revolutionary coalitions, in contrast, proved fragile, as when workers' demands for higher wages and labor reform drove their middle-class allies into the arms of the reactionaries.

SECTION REVIEW

- The slaves of Saint Domingue, led by Toussaint L'Ouverture, overthrew slavery and gained independence.

- The Congress of Vienna and the Holy Alliance attempted to prevent new revolutionary outbreaks in Europe.

- Nationalism and the desire for democracy led to revolutions in 1830 and 1848, but most failed.

CONCLUSION

The last decades of the eighteenth century began a long period of revolutionary upheaval in the Atlantic world. Costly wars in Europe and along Europe's colonial frontiers in the Americas and Asia helped to provoke change, forcing European monarchs to impose new and unpopular taxes. The American Revolution initiated these transformations. Having defeated Britain, the citizens of this new American republic created the most democratic government of the time. While full rights were limited and slavery persisted, many Europeans saw this experiment as demonstrating the efficacy of the Enlightenment's most revolutionary political ideas. In the end, however, the compromises over slavery that had made the Constitution possible in 1787 failed, and, as discussed in Chapter 24, the new nation nearly disintegrated after 1860.

The French Revolution led temporarily to a more radical formulation of representative democracy, but it also led to the Terror, which cost thousands of lives, the militarization of western Europe, and a destructive cycle of wars. Yet, despite these terrible costs, the French Revolution propelled the idea of democracy and the ideal of equality far beyond the boundaries established by the American Revolution. The Haitian Revolution, set in motion by events in France, not only created the second independent nation of the Western Hemisphere but also delivered a powerful blow to the institution of slavery. In Europe the excesses of the French Revolution and the wars that followed in its wake promoted the political ascent of Napoleon Bonaparte and democracy's modern nemesis, popular authoritarianism.

Each revolution had its own character. The revolutions in France and Haiti proved to be more violent and destructive than the American Revolution. American revolutionaries defeated Great Britain and established independence without overturning a colonial social order that depended on slavery in most of the southern colonies. Revolutionaries in France and Haiti faced more strongly entrenched and more powerful oppositions as well as greater social inequalities than American revolutionaries. The resistance of entrenched and privileged elites led inexorably to greater violence. Both French and Haitian revolutionaries also faced powerful foreign interventions that intensified the bloodshed and destructiveness of these revolutions.

The conservative retrenchment that followed the defeat of Napoleon succeeded in the short term. Monarchy, multinational empires, and the established church retained the loyalty of millions of Europeans and could count on the support of many of Europe's wealthiest and most powerful individuals. But liberalism and nationalism continued to stir revolutionary sentiment. The contest between adherents of the old order and partisans of change was to continue well into the nineteenth century. In the end, the nation-state, the Enlightenment legacy of rational inquiry, broadened political participation, and secular intellectual culture prevailed. This outcome was determined in large measure by the old order's inability to satisfy the demands of new social classes tied to an emerging industrial economy. The narrow confines of a hereditary social system could not contain the material transformations generated by industrial capitalism, and the doctrines of traditional religion could not contain the rapid expansion of scientific learning.

These revolutions began the transformation of Western society, but they did not complete it. Only a minority gained full political rights. Women did not achieve full political rights until the twentieth century. Democratic institutions, as in revolutionary France, often failed. Moreover, as Chapter 24 discusses, slavery endured in the Americas past the mid-1800s, despite the revolutionary era's enthusiasm for individual liberty.

KEY TERMS

Enlightenment p. 582
Benjamin
    Franklin p. 584
George
    Washington p. 588
Joseph Brant p. 588

Constitutional
    Convention p. 590
Estates General p. 592
Declaration of the
    Rights of Man and the
    Citizen p. 592

Jacobins p. 594
Maximilien
    Robespierre p. 594
Napoleon
    Bonaparte p. 595
gens de couleur p. 599

François Dominique
    Toussaint
    L'Ouverture p. 599
Congress of Vienna p. 601
Revolutions of 1848 p. 602

EBOOK AND WEBSITE RESOURCES

e Primary Sources

Rousseau Espouses Popular Sovereignty and the General Will

The United States Declaration of Independence

The Declaration of the Rights of Man and the Citizen

e Interactive Maps

Map 22.1 The American Revolutionary War

Map 22.2 Napoleon's Europe, 1810

Map 22.3 The Haitian Revolution

Plus flashcards, practice quizzes, and more. Go to:
www.cengage.com/history/bullietearthpeople5e

SUGGESTED READING

Andress, David. *The Terror: The Merciless War for Freedom in Revolutionary France.* 2006. A recent summary of this era.

Bell, David A. *The First Total War: Napoleon's Europe and the Birth of Warfare as We Know It.* 2008.

Craveri, Benedetta. *The Age of Conversation.* 2005. Illuminates the culture of the French aristocracy prior to the French Revolution.

Damrosch, Leo. *Jean-Jacques Rousseau.* 2005. The best biography of Rousseau.

Dubois, Laurent. *A Colony of Citizens.* 2004. Connects the revolutions in France and Haiti to create a single struggle for liberty and citizenship.

Fenton, William N. *The Great Law and the Long-house: A Political History of the Iroquois Confederacy.* 1998. An essential study of this powerful indigenous alliance.

Fick, Carolyn E. *The Making of Haiti: The Saint Domingue Revolution from Below.* 1990. The best recent synthesis of the Haitian Revolution.

Fitzsimmons, Michael. *The Night the Old Regime Ended: August 14, 1789, and the French Revolution.* 1998.

Godineau, Dominique. *The Women of Paris and Their French Revolution.* 1998. Essential introduction to topic.

Goldstone, Lawrence. *Dark Bargain: Slavery, Profits and the Struggle for the Constitution.* 2005.

Goodman, Dena. *The Republic of Letters: A Cultural History of the Enlightenment.* 1994. Studies male and female intellectuals in the era of revolutions.

Hobsbawm, Eric. *The Age of Revolution.* 1962. Provides a clear analysis of the class issues that appeared during this era.

Holtman, Robert B. *The Napoleonic Revolution.* 1967. Provides a reliable summary of the period.

Hunt, Lynn. *The Family Romance of the French Revolution.* 1992. Examines the gender content of revolutionary politics.

James, C. L. R. *The Black Jacobins*, 2nd ed. 1963. Classic study of the Haitian Revolution.

Lefebvre, Georges. *The Coming of the French Revolution.* Trans. R. R. Palmer. 1947. A classic class-based analysis.

Lindemann, Albert. *History of European Socialism.* 1983. Surveys the development of European social reform movements.

McMahon, Darrin M. *Enemies of the Enlightenment, The French Counter-Enlightenment and the Making of Modernity.* 2001. A helpful discussion of the Counter Enlightenment.

Norton, Mary Beth. *Liberty's Daughters: The Revolutionary Experience of American Women, 1750–1800.* 1980. Studies the role of women in the revolutionary era.

Rudé, George. *The Crowd in History: Popular Disturbances in France and England.* 1981. The best introduction to the role of mass protest in the revolutionary period.

Stearns, Peter, and Herrick Chapman. *European Society in Upheaval.* 1991. Valuable summary of events.

Taylor, Alan. *The Divided Ground. Indians, Settlers, and the Northern Borderland of the American Revolution.* 2006. The best analysis of the topic.

Taylor, Barbara. *Eve and the New Jerusalem: Socialism and Feminism in the Nineteenth Century.* 1983. Analyzes connections between workers' and women's rights issues in England.

Te Brake, Wayne. *Shaping History: Ordinary People in European Politics, 1500–1700.* 1998. Discusses the "underside" of this era and the importance of "folk culture."

Will, Gary. *Inventing America, Jefferson's Declaration of Independence.* 1978. An essential inquiry into this pivotal moment.

Wood, Gordon S. *Revolutionary Characters. What Made the Founders Different.* 2006. A convincing exploration of this crucial generation.

NOTES

1. Quoted in Ray Raphael, *A People's History of the American Revolution* (New York: Perennial, 2001), 141.

2. Quoted in C. L. R. James, *The Black Jacobins*, 2nd ed. (New York: Vintage Books, 1963), 196.

CHAPTER OUTLINE

The Royal Collection ©2006 Her Majesty Queen Elizabeth II

Manchester, the First Industrial City   The first cotton mills, built on the banks of the River Irwell in northern England, transformed Manchester from a country town into a booming industrial city. The use of chemicals to bleach and dye the cloth and the introduction of steam engines in the early nineteenth century to power the spinning and weaving machines made Manchester, for a time, the most polluted city on earth.

 Visit the website and ebook for additional study materials and interactive tools: www.cengage.com/history/bullietearthpeople5e

The Early Industrial Revolution, 1760–1851

M anchester was just a small town in northern England in the early eighteenth century. A hundred years later, it had turned into the fastest-growing city in history. To contemporaries, it was both a marvel and a horror. Cotton mills were interspersed with workers' housing, built as cheaply as possible. The economist Nassau Senior described these workers' quarters:

> But when I went through their habitations . . . my only wonder was that tolerable health could be maintained by the inmates of such houses. These towns . . . have been erected by small speculators with an utter disregard to everything except immediate profit. . . . In one place we saw a whole street following the course of a ditch, in order to have deeper cellars (cellars for people, not for lumber) without the expense of excavation. Not a house in this street escaped cholera. . . . the streets are unpaved, with a dunghill or a pond in the middle; the houses built back to back, without ventilation or drainage, and whole families occupy each a corner of a cellar or of a garret.[1]

Not everyone deplored the living conditions in the new industrial city. Friedrich Engels recounts a meeting with a well-to-do citizen:

> One day I walked with one of these middle-class gentlemen into Manchester. I spoke to him about the disgraceful unhealthy slums and drew his attention to the disgusting condition of that part of the town in which the factory workers lived. I declared that I had never seen so badly built a town in my life. He listened patiently and at the corner of the street at which we parted company, he remarked: "And yet there is a great deal of money made here. Good morning, Sir!"[2]

Manchester's rise as a large, industrial city was a result of what historians call the **Industrial Revolution**, the most profound transformation in human life since the beginnings of agriculture. This revolution involved dramatic innovations in manufacturing, mining, transportation, and communications and equally rapid changes in society and commerce. New relationships between social groups created an environment that was conducive to technical innovation and economic growth. New technologies and new social and economic arrangements allowed the industrializing countries—first Britain, then western Europe and the United States—to unleash massive increases in production and productivity, exploit the world's natural resources as never before, and transform the environment and human life in unprecedented ways.

- What caused the Industrial Revolution?
- What were the key innovations that increased productivity and drove industrialization?
- What was the impact of these changes on the society and environment of the industrializing countries?
- How did the Industrial Revolution influence the rise of new economic and political ideas?
- How did the Industrial Revolution affect the relations between the industrialized and the nonindustrialized parts of the world?

Industrial Revolution
The transformation of the economy, the environment, and living conditions, occurring first in England in the eighteenth century, that resulted from the use of steam engines, the mechanization of manufacturing in factories, and innovations in transportation and communication.

Industrialization widened the gap between rich and poor. The people who owned and controlled the innovations amassed wealth and power over nature and over other people. While some lived in spectacular luxury, workers, including children, worked long hours in dangerous factories and lived crowded together in unsanitary tenements.

The effect of the Industrial Revolution around the world was also very uneven. The first countries to industrialize grew rich and powerful. In Egypt and India, the economic and military power of the European countries stifled the tentative beginnings of industrialization. Regions that had little or no industry were easily taken advantage of. The disparity between the industrial and the developing countries that exists today has its origins in the early nineteenth century.

CAUSES OF THE INDUSTRIAL REVOLUTION

What caused the Industrial Revolution, and why did it begin in England in the late eighteenth century? These are two of the great questions of history. The basic preconditions of this momentous event seem to have been economic development propelled by population growth, an agricultural revolution, the expansion of trade, and an openness to innovation.

Population Growth

The population of Europe rose in the eighteenth century—slowly at first, faster after 1780, even faster in the early nineteenth century. The population of England and Wales rose from 5.5 million in 1688 to 9 million in 1801 and 18 million by 1851—increases never before experienced in European history.

The growth of population resulted from more widespread resistance to disease and more reliable food supplies, thanks to the new crops that originated in the Americas (see Chapter 18). More job opportunities led people to marry at earlier ages and have more children. In the early nineteenth century some 40 percent of the population of Britain was under fifteen years of age. This high proportion of youths explains both the vitality of the British people in that period and the widespread use of child labor. People also migrated at an unprecedented rate—from the countryside to the cities, from Ireland to England, and, more generally, from Europe to the Americas. Thanks to immigration, the population of the United States rose from 4 million in 1791 to 9.6 million in 1820 and 31.5 million in 1860—faster than in any other part of the world at the time.

agricultural revolution
The transformation of farming that resulted in the eighteenth century from the spread of new crops, improvements in cultivation techniques and livestock breeding, and the consolidation of small holdings into large farms from which tenants and sharecroppers were forcibly expelled.

Potatoes and Corn

Enclosure Movement

The Agricultural Revolution

A revolution in farming provided food for city dwellers and forced poorer peasants off the land. This **agricultural revolution** had begun long before the eighteenth century. One important aspect was the acceptance of the potato, introduced from South America in the sixteenth century. In the cool and humid regions of Europe, potatoes yielded two or three times more food per acre than did the wheat, rye, and oats they replaced. Maize (American corn) was grown across Europe from northern Iberia to the Balkans. Turnips, legumes, and clover did not deplete the soil and could be fed to cattle, sources of milk and meat. Manure from cattle in turn fertilized the soil for other crops.

Prosperous landowners with secure titles to their land could afford to bear the risk of trying new methods and new crops. Rich landowners therefore "enclosed" the land—that is, consolidated their holdings—and got Parliament to give them title to the commons that in the past had been open to all. Once in control of the land, they could drain and improve the soil, breed better livestock, and introduce crop rotation. This "enclosure movement" turned tenants and sharecroppers into landless farm laborers. Many moved to the cities to seek work; others became vagrants; still others emigrated to Canada, Australia, and the United States.

CHRONOLOGY

	Technology	Economy, Society, and Politics
	1702–1712 Thomas Newcomen builds first steam engine	
1750	1759 Josiah Wedgwood opens pottery factory	
	1764 Spinning jenny	
	1769 Richard Arkwright's water frame; James Watt patents steam engine	1776 Adam Smith's *Wealth of Nations*
		1776–1783 American Revolution
	1779 First iron bridge	
	1785 Samuel Crompton's mule	1789–1799 French Revolution
		1792 Mary Wollstonecraft's *A Vindication of the Rights of Woman*
	1793 Eli Whitney's cotton gin	
1800	1800 Alessandro Volta's battery	1804–1815 Napoleonic Wars
	1807 Robert Fulton's *North River*	
	1820s Construction of Erie Canal	1820s U.S. cotton industry begins
	1829 *Rocket*, first prize-winning locomotive	1833 Factory Act in Britain
	1837 Wheatstone and Cooke's telegraph; Morse's code	1834 German Zollverein; Robert Owen's Grand National Consolidated Trade Union
	1838 First ships steam across the Atlantic	
	1840 *Nemesis* sails to China	
	1843 Samuel Morse's Baltimore-to-Washington telegraph	1846 Repeal of British Corn Laws
		1847–1848 Irish famine
		1848 Collapse of Chartist movement; revolutions in Europe
1850	1851 Crystal Palace opens in London	
		1854 First cotton mill in India

Trade and Inventiveness

In most of Europe the increasing demand that accompanied the growth of population was met by increasing production in traditional ways. Roads were improved so stagecoaches could travel faster. Royal manufacturers trained craftsmen to produce fine china, silks, and carpets by hand. In rural areas much production was carried out through cottage industries. Merchants delivered raw materials to craftspeople (often farmers in the off-season) and picked up the finished products. The growth of the population and food supply was accompanied by the growth of trade. Most of it was local trade in traditional goods and services, but a growing share came from far away.

During the eighteenth century, sugar from Caribbean slave plantations was the most profitable item in international trade. Even people of modest means began drinking tea, coffee, and cocoa at home and eating pastries and candies. These habits in turn stimulated the demand for porcelain cups and other dinnerware. More and more people wore clothes of silk or cotton imported from Asia.

Technology

Technology and innovation fascinated educated people throughout Europe and eastern North America. The French *Encyclopédie* contained articles and illustrations of crafts and manufacturing (see Diversity and Dominance: Adam Smith and the Division of Labor). The French and British governments sent expeditions around the world to collect plants that could profitably be grown in their colonies. They also offered prizes to anyone who could find a method of determining the longitude of a ship at sea to avoid the shipwrecks that had cost the lives of thousands of sailors. Benjamin Franklin, like many others, experimented with electricity. In France, the Montgolfier brothers invented a hot-air balloon. Claude Chappe (SHAPP) created the first semaphore telegraph. The American Eli Whitney and his associate John Hall invented machine tools, that is, machines capable of making other machines. These machines greatly increased the productivity of manufacturing.

Britain and Continental Europe

Rise of Industrialization in Britain

Industrialization did not take place everywhere at once. To understand why, we must look at the peculiar role of Great Britain. Britain enjoyed a rising standard of living during the eighteenth century, thanks to good harvests and a booming overseas trade. Britain was the world's leading exporter of tools, guns, hardware, clocks, and other craft goods (see Map 23.1). Its mining and metal industries employed engineers willing to experiment with new ideas. It had the largest

© Cengage Learning

MAP 23.1   **The Industrial Revolution in Britain, ca. 1850**   The first industries arose in northern and western England. These regions had abundant coal and iron-ore deposits for the iron industry, as well as moist climate and fast-flowing rivers, factors important for the cotton textile industry.

e   Interactive Map

merchant marine and produced more ships, naval supplies, and navigation instruments than other countries.

Until the mid-eighteenth century the British were known for their cheap imitations, but they put inventions into practice more quickly than other people, as the engineer John Farey told a parliamentary committee in 1829: "The prevailing talent of English and Scotch people is to apply new ideas to use and to bring such applications to perfection, but they do not imagine as much as foreigners."[3]

British Advantages over Europe

Before 1790 Britain also had a more fluid society than the rest of Europe. The court was less ostentatious, its aristocracy was less powerful, and the lines separating the social classes were not as sharply drawn as elsewhere. Political power was not as centralized as on the European continent, and the government employed fewer bureaucrats and officials. Members of the gentry married into merchant families. Intermarriage among the families of petty merchants, yeoman farmers, and town craftsmen was common. Ancestry remained important, but wealth also commanded respect. A businessman with enough money could buy a landed estate, a seat in Parliament, and the social status that accompanied them.

At a time when transportation by land was very costly, Great Britain had good water transportation thanks to its indented coastline, navigable rivers, and growing network of canals. It had a unified internal market with none of the duties and tolls that goods had to pay every few miles in France. This encouraged regional specialization, such as tin mining in Cornwall and cotton manufacturing in Lancashire, and a growing trade between regions.

Britain was also highly commercial; more people were involved in production for export and in trade and finance than in any other major country. It was especially active in overseas trade. It had financial and insurance institutions able to support growing business enterprises and a patent system that offered inventors the hope of rich rewards. The example of men who became wealthy and respected for their inventions stimulated others.

In the eighteenth century, the economies of continental Europe were hampered by high transportation costs, misguided government regulations, and rigid social structures. The Low Countries were laced with canals, but the terrain elsewhere in Europe made canal building costly and difficult. Attempts to import British techniques and organize factory production foundered for lack of markets or management skills. In addition, from 1789 to 1815 Europe was scarred by revolutions and wars. Although war created opportunities for suppliers of weapons, uniforms, and horses, the interruption of trade between Britain and continental Europe slowed the diffusion of new techniques, and the insecurity of countries at war discouraged businessmen from investing in factories and machinery.

Rise of Industrialization in Europe

The political revolutions swept away the restrictions of the old regimes. After 1815 the economies of western Europe were ready to begin industrializing. Industrialization took hold in Belgium and northern France, as businessmen visited Britain to observe the changes and spy out industrial secrets. By the 1820s several thousand Britons were at work on the continent of Europe setting up machines, training workers in the new methods, and even starting their own businesses.

Acutely aware of Britain's head start and the need to stimulate their own industries, European governments took action. They created technical schools. They eliminated internal tariff barriers, tolls, and other hindrances to trade. They encouraged the formation of joint-stock companies and banks to channel private savings into industrial investments. By 1830 the political climate in western Europe was as favorable to business as Britain's had been a half-century earlier.

Abundant coal and iron-ore deposits determined the concentration of industries in a swath of territories running from northern France through Belgium and the Ruhr district of western Germany to Silesia in Prussia (now part of Poland). By the 1850s France, Belgium, and the German states were in the midst of an industrial boom like that of Britain, based on iron, cotton, steam engines, and railroads.

SECTION REVIEW

- The Industrial Revolution arose from population growth, an agricultural revolution, increased trade, and an interest in innovation.
- Britain industrialized first, thanks to its fluid political structures, transportation infrastructure, inventiveness, and society open to talented and enterprising people.
- Among educated Europeans, practical subjects like business, science, and technology became fashionable.
- On the European continent, the revolutions of 1789–1815 swept away the restrictions of the old aristocratic regimes and allowed for more industrial growth.

Adam Smith and the Division of Labor

Adam Smith (1723–1790), a Scottish philosopher, is famous for his book An Inquiry into the Nature and Causes of the Wealth of Nations, *first published in 1776. It was the first work to explain the economy of a nation as a system. Smith criticized the notion, common in the eighteenth century, that a nation's wealth was synonymous with the amount of gold and silver in the government's coffers. Instead, he defined wealth as the amount of goods and services produced by a nation's people. By this definition, labor and its products are an essential element in a nation's prosperity.*

In the passage that follows, Smith contrasts two methods of making pins. In one a team of workers divided up the job of making pins and produced a great many every day; in the other pin workers "wrought separately and independently" and produced very few pins per day. It is clear that the division of labor produces more pins per worker per day. But who benefits? Left unsaid is that a pin factory had to be owned and operated by a manufacturer who hired workers and assigned a task to each one.

The illustration shows a pin-maker's workshop in late-eighteenth-century France. Each worker is performing a specific task on a few pins at once, and all the energy comes from human muscles. These are the characteristics of a proto-industrial workshop.

To take an example, therefore, from a very trifling manufacture—but one in which the division of labour has been very often taken notice of—the trade of the pin-maker: a workman not educated to this business (which the division of labour has rendered a distinct trade), nor acquainted with the use of machinery employed in it (to the invention of which the same division of labour has probably given occasion), could scarce, perhaps, with his utmost industry, make one pin in a day, and certainly could not make twenty. But in the way in which this business is now carried on, not only the whole work is a peculiar trade, but it is divided into a number of branches, of which the greater part are likewise peculiar trades. One man draws out the wire, another straights it, a third cuts it, a fourth points it, a fifth grinds it at the top for receiving the head; to make the head requires two or three distinct operations, to put it on, is a peculiar business, to whiten the pins is another; it is even a trade by itself to put them into the paper; and the important business of making a pin is, in this manner, divided into about eighteen distinct operations, which, in some manufactories, are all performed by distinct hands, though in others the same man will sometimes perform two or three of them. I have seen a small manufactory of this kind where ten men only were employed, and where some of them, consequently, performed two or three distinct operations. But though they were very poor, and therefore but indifferently accommodated with the necessary machinery, they could, when they exerted themselves, make among them about twelve pounds of pins in a day.

There are in a pound upwards of four thousand pins of a middling size. Those ten persons, therefore, could make among them upwards of forty-eight thousand pins in a day. Each person, therefore, making a tenth part of forty-eight thousand pins, might be considered as making four thousand eight hundred pins a day. But if they had all wrought separately and independently, and without any of them having been educated to this peculiar business, they certainly could not each of them have made twenty, perhaps not one pin in a day; that

THE TECHNOLOGICAL REVOLUTION

Five innovations spurred industrialization: (1) mass production through the division of labor, (2) new machines and mechanization, (3) a great increase in the manufacture of iron, (4) the steam engine, and (5) the electric telegraph. China had achieved the first three of these during the Song dynasty (960–1279), but it had not developed the steam engine or electricity. The continued success of Western industrialization depended heavily on these new forms of energy.

mass production The manufacture of many identical products by the division of labor into many small repetitive tasks. This method was introduced into the manufacture of pottery by Josiah Wedgwood and into the spinning of cotton thread by Richard Arkwright.

Mass Production: Pottery

The pottery industry offers a good example of **mass production**, the making of many identical items by breaking the process into simple repetitive tasks. Before the mid-eighteenth century only the wealthy could afford Chinese porcelain. Middle-class people used pewter tableware, and the poor ate from wooden or earthenware bowls. Royal manufactures produced exquisite handmade products for the courts and aristocracy, but their products were much too expensive for mass consumption. As more and more Europeans acquired a taste for tea, cocoa, and coffee, they wanted porcelain that would not spoil the flavor of hot beverages. This demand created opportunities for inventive entrepreneurs.

A Pin-Maker's Workshop   The man in the middle (Fig. 2) is pulling wire off a spindle (G) and through a series of posts. This ensures that the wire will be perfectly straight. The worker seated on the lower right (Fig. 3) takes the long pieces of straightened wire and cuts them into shorter lengths. The man in the lower left-hand corner (Fig. 5) sharpens twelve to fifteen wires at a time by holding them against a grindstone turned by the worker in Fig. 6. The men in Figs. 4 and 7 put the finishing touches on the points. Other operations—such as forming the wire to the proper thickness, cleaning and coating it with tin, and attaching the heads—are depicted in other engravings in the same encyclopedia.

is, certainly, not the two hundred and fortieth, perhaps not the four thousand eight hundredth part of what they are at present capable of performing, in consequence of a proper division and combination of their different operations.

QUESTIONS FOR ANALYSIS

1. **Why does dividing the job of pin-making into ten or more operations result in the production of more pins per worker? How much more productive are these workers than if each one made complete pins from start to finish?**

2. **How closely does the picture of a pin-maker's workshop illustrate Smith's verbal description?**

3. **What disadvantage would there be to working in a pin factory where the job was divided as in Smith's example, compared to making entire pins from start to finish?**

4. **What other examples can you think of, from Adam Smith's day or from more recent times, of the advantages of the division of labor?**

Source: Adam Smith, *An Inquiry into the Nature and Causes of the Wealth of Nations*, ed. Edward Gibbon Wakefield (London: Charles Knight and Co., 1843), 7–9.

Josiah Wedgwood English industrialist whose pottery works were the first to produce fine-quality pottery by industrial methods.

Wedgwood Pottery

division of labor A manufacturing technique that breaks down a craft into many simple and repetitive tasks that can be performed by unskilled workers. Pioneered in the pottery works of Josiah Wedgwood and in other eighteenth-century factories, it greatly increased the productivity of labor and lowered the cost of manufactured goods.

Britain had many small pottery workshops where craftsmen made a few plates and cups at a time. Much of this activity took place in a part of the Midlands that possessed good clay, coal for firing, and lead for glazing. In 1759, **Josiah Wedgwood**, the son of a potter, started his own pottery business. He had a scientific bent and invented a device to measure the extremely high temperatures that are found in kilns during the firing of pottery. Today the name Wedgwood is associated with expensive, highly decorated china. But Wedgwood's most important contribution lay in producing ordinary porcelain cheaply by means of the **division of labor** (see Diversity and Dominance: Adam Smith and the Division of Labor).

Wedgwood subdivided the work into simple repetitive tasks, such as unloading the clay, mixing it, pressing flat pieces, dipping the pieces in glaze, putting handles on cups, packing kilns, and carrying things from one part of his plant to another. To prevent interruptions, he instituted strict discipline among his workers. He substituted molds for the potter's wheel wherever possible, a change that not only saved labor but also created plates and bowls that could be stacked.

Wedgwood's interest in applying technology to manufacturing was sparked by his membership in the Lunar Society, a group of businessmen, scientists, and craftsmen that met each month when the moon was full to discuss the practical application of knowledge. In 1782 the naturalist Erasmus Darwin encouraged him to purchase a steam engine from Boulton and Watt, the firm founded by two other members of the society. The engine that Wedgwood bought to mix clay

Mary Evans Picture Library

Wedgwood's Potteries In Staffordshire, England, Josiah Wedgwood established a factory to mass-produce beautiful and inexpensive china. The bottle-shaped buildings are kilns in which thousands of pieces of china could be fired at one time. Kilns, factories, and housing were all mixed together in pottery towns, and smoke from burning coal filled the air.

and grind flint was one of the first to be installed in a factory. The division of labor and new machinery allowed Wedgwood to lower the cost of his products while improving their quality, and to offer his wares for sale at lower prices. His factory grew far larger than his competitors' factories and employed several hundred workers. His salesmen traveled throughout England touting his goods, and his products were sold on the European continent as well.

Mechanization: The Cotton Industry

The cotton industry, the largest in this period, illustrates the role of **mechanization**, the use of machines to do work previously done by hand. Cotton had long been grown in China, India, and the Middle East, where it was spun and woven by hand. The cloth was so much cooler, softer, and cleaner than wool that wealthy Europeans developed a liking for the costly import. When the powerful English woolen industry persuaded Parliament to forbid the import of cotton cloth, that prohibition stimulated attempts to import cotton fiber and make the cloth locally. Here was an opportunity for enterprising inventors to reduce costs with laborsaving machinery.

Beginning in the 1760s a series of inventions revolutionized the spinning of cotton thread. The first was the jenny, invented in 1764, which mechanically drew out the cotton fibers and twisted them into thread. The jenny was simple, cheap to build, and easy for one person to operate. Early models spun six or seven threads at once, later ones up to eighty. The thread, however, was soft and irregular and could be used only in combination with linen, a strong yarn derived from the flax plant.

In 1769 **Richard Arkwright** invented another spinning machine, the water frame, which produced thread strong enough to be used without linen. Arkwright was both a gifted inventor and a successful businessman. His machine was larger and more complex than the jenny and required a source of power such as a water wheel, hence the name "water frame." To obtain the necessary energy he installed dozens of machines in a building next to a fast-flowing river. The resemblance to a flour mill gave such enterprises the name *cotton mill*.

In 1785 Samuel Crompton patented a machine that combined the best features of the jenny and the water frame. This device, called a mule, produced a strong thread that was thin enough to be used to make a better type of cotton cloth called muslin. The mule could make a finer, more even thread than could any human being, and at a lower cost. At last British industry could undersell high-quality handmade cotton cloth from India. British cotton output increased tenfold between 1770 and 1790.

The boom in thread production and the soaring demand for cloth encouraged inventors to mechanize the rest of textile manufacturing. Power looms were perfected after 1815. Other inventions of the period included carding machines, chlorine bleach, and cylindrical presses to print designs on fabric. By the 1830s large textile mills powered by steam engines were performing all the steps necessary to turn raw cotton into printed cloth.

Mechanization offered two advantages: increased productivity for the manufacturer and lower prices for the consumer. Whereas in India it took five hundred hours to spin a pound of cotton, the mule of 1790 could do so in three person-hours, and the self-acting mule—an improved version introduced in 1830—required only eighty minutes. Cotton mills needed very few skilled

---

mechanization The application of machinery to manufacturing and other activities. Among the first processes to be mechanized were the spinning of cotton thread and the weaving of cloth in late-eighteenth- and early-nineteenth-century England.

Innovations in Cotton Manufacturing

Richard Arkwright English inventor and entrepreneur who became the wealthiest and most successful textile manufacturer of the early Industrial Revolution. He invented the water frame, a machine that, with minimal human supervision, could spin many strong cotton threads at once.

workers, and managers often hired children to tend the spinning machines. The same was true of power looms, which gradually replaced handloom weaving: the number of power looms rose from 2,400 in 1813 to 500,000 by 1850. Meanwhile, the price of cloth fell by 90 percent between 1782 and 1812 and kept on dropping.

The industrialization of Britain made cotton America's most valuable crop. In the 1790s most of Britain's cotton came from India. In 1793 the American Eli Whitney patented his cotton gin, a simple device that separated the bolls or seedpods from the fiber and made cotton growing economical. This invention permitted the spread of cotton farming into Georgia, then into Alabama, Mississippi, and Louisiana, and finally as far west as Texas. By the late 1850s the southern states were producing a million tons of cotton a year, five-sixths of the world's total.

With the help of British craftsmen who introduced jennies, mules, and power looms, Americans developed their own cotton industry in the 1820s. By 1840 the United States had twelve hundred cotton mills, two-thirds of them in New England, that served the booming domestic market.

The Iron Industry

Iron making also was transformed during the Industrial Revolution. Throughout Eurasia and Africa, iron had long been used for tools, weapons, and household items. During the Song period, Chinese forges had produced cast iron in large quantities. Production declined after the Song, but iron continued to be common and inexpensive in China. Wherever iron was produced, however, deforestation eventually drove up the cost of charcoal (used for smelting) and restricted output. Furthermore, iron had to be repeatedly heated and hammered to drive out impurities, a difficult and costly process. Because of limited wood supplies and the high cost of skilled labor, iron was a rare and valuable metal outside China before the eighteenth century.

Innovations in Iron Making

A first breakthrough occurred in 1709 when Abraham Darby discovered that coke (coal from which the impurities have been cooked out) could be used in place of charcoal. The resulting metal was of lower quality than charcoal-smelted iron but much cheaper to produce, for coal was plentiful. In 1784 Henry Cort found a way to remove some of the impurities in coke-iron by puddling—stirring the molten iron with long rods. Cort's process made it possible to turn coal into coke to produce wrought iron (a soft and malleable form of iron) very cheaply. By 1790 four-fifths of Britain's iron was made with coke, while other countries still used charcoal. Coke-iron allowed a great expansion in the size of individual blast furnaces. Britain's iron production rose fast, from 17,000 tons in 1740 to 3 million tons in 1844, as much as in the rest of the world put together.

In turn, there seemed no limit to the novel applications for this cheap and useful material. In 1779 Abraham Darby III (grandson of the first Abraham Darby) built a bridge of iron across

Pit Head of a Coal Mine
This is a small coal mine. In the center of this picture stands a Newcomen engine used to pump water. The work of hauling coal out of the mine was still done by horses and mules. The smoke coming out of the smokestack is a trademark of the early industrial era.

Walker Art Gallery, National Museums Liverpool/The Bridgeman Art Library

Crystal Palace Building erected in Hyde Park, London, for the Great Exhibition of 1851. Made of iron and glass, like a gigantic greenhouse, it was a symbol of the industrial age.

the Severn River. In 1851 Londoners marveled at the **Crystal Palace**, a huge greenhouse made entirely of iron and glass and large enough to enclose the tallest trees.

The availability of cheap iron made the mass production of objects such as guns, hardware, and tools appealing. However, fitting together the parts of these products required a great deal of labor. To reduce labor costs, manufacturers turned to the idea of interchangeable parts. By the mid-nineteenth century, interchangeable-parts manufacturing had been adopted in the manufacture of firearms, farm equipment, and sewing machines. At the Crystal Palace exhibition of 1851, Europeans called it the "American system of manufactures." In the next hundred years the use of machinery to mass-produce consumer items was to become the hallmark of American industry.

The Steam Engine

steam engine A machine that turns the energy released by burning fuel into motion. Thomas Newcomen built the first crude but workable steam engine in 1712. James Watt vastly improved his device in the 1760s and 1770s. Steam power was later applied to moving machinery in factories and to powering ships and locomotives.

In the history of the world, there had been a number of periods of great technological inventiveness and economic growth. But in all previous cases, the dynamism eventually faltered. The Industrial Revolution, in contrast, has only accelerated. One reason has been increased interactions between scientists, technicians, and businesspeople. Another has been access to a source of cheap energy, namely fossil fuels. The first machine to transform fossil fuel into mechanical energy was the **steam engine**, a device that set the Industrial Revolution apart from all previous periods of growth and innovation.

Before the eighteenth century, deep mines filled with water faster than horses could pump it out. Then, between 1702 and 1712 Thomas Newcomen developed the first practical steam engine, a crude but effective device that could pump water out of mines as fast as four horses and could run day and night without getting tired. The Newcomen engine's voracious appetite for fuel mattered little in coal mines, where fuel was cheap, but it made the engine too costly for other uses. In 1764 **James Watt**, a maker of scientific instruments at Glasgow University in Scotland, was asked to repair the university's model Newcomen engine. Watt realized that the engine wasted fuel because the cylinder had to be alternately heated and cooled. He developed a separate condenser—a vessel into which the steam was allowed to escape after it had done its work, leaving the cylinder always hot and the condenser always cold. Watt patented his idea in 1769. He enlisted the help of the iron manufacturer Matthew Boulton to turn his invention into a commercial product. Their first engines were sold to pump water out of copper and tin mines, where fuel was too costly for Newcomen engines. In 1781 Watt invented the sun-and-planet gear, which turned the back-and-forth action of the piston into rotary motion. This allowed steam engines to power machinery in flour and cotton mills, pottery manufactures, and other industries. Because there seemed almost no limit to the amount of coal in the ground, steam-

The Newcomen and Watt Engines

James Watt Scot who invented the condenser and other improvements that made the steam engine a practical source of power for industry and transportation. The watt, an electrical measurement, is named after him.

Transatlantic Steamship Race   In 1838, two ships equipped with steam engines, the *Sirius* and the *Great Western*, steamed from England to New York. Although the *Sirius* left a few days earlier, the *Great Western*—shown here arriving in New York harbor—almost caught up with it, arriving just four hours after the *Sirius*. This race inaugurated regular transatlantic steamship service.

Courtesy of the Mariners' Museum, Newport News, VA

generated energy appeared to be an inexhaustible source of power, and steam engines could be used where animal, wind, and water power were lacking.

Steamboats and Ships

Inspired by the success of Watt's engine, several inventors put steam engines on boats. The first commercially successful steamboat was Robert Fulton's *North River*, which steamed up and down the Hudson River between New York City and Albany, New York, in 1807. Soon steamboats were launched on the Ohio and the Mississippi, gateways to the Midwest. In the 1820s the Erie Canal linked the Atlantic seaboard with the Great Lakes and opened Ohio, Indiana, and Illinois to European settlement. By 1830 some three hundred steamboats plied the Mississippi and its tributaries. The United States was fast becoming a nation that moved by water.

Oceangoing steam-powered ships were much more difficult to build than river boats, for the first steam engines used so much coal that no ship could carry more than a few days' supply. The *Savannah*, which crossed the Atlantic in 1819, was a sailing ship with an auxiliary steam engine that was used for only ninety hours of its twenty-nine-day trip. Engineers soon developed more efficient engines, and in 1838 two steamers, the *Great Western* and the *Sirius*, crossed the Atlantic on steam power alone.

Railroads

After Watt's patent expired in 1800, inventors experimented with lighter, more powerful high-pressure engines—an idea Watt had rejected as too dangerous. In 1804 Richard Trevithick built an engine that consumed twelve times less coal than Newcomen's and three times less than Watt's; with it, he built several steam-powered vehicles able to travel on roads or rails.

By the 1820s England had many railways on which horses pulled heavy wagons. In 1829, the owners of the Liverpool and Manchester Railway organized a contest between steam-powered locomotives and horse-drawn wagons. George Stephenson and his son Robert won the contest with their locomotive *Rocket*, which pulled a 20-ton train at up to 30 miles (48 kilometers) per hour. After that triumph, a railroad-building mania swept Britain. In the late 1830s, as passenger traffic soared, entrepreneurs built lines between the major cities and even to small towns. Railroads were far cheaper, faster, and more comfortable than stagecoaches, and millions of people got in the habit of traveling.

Railroads in America

In the United States entrepreneurs built railroads as quickly and cheaply as possible. By the 1840s, 6,000 miles (10,000 kilometers) of track radiated from Boston, New York, Philadelphia, and Baltimore. In the 1850s, 21,000 miles (34,000 kilometers) of new track were laid, much of it westward across the Appalachians to Memphis, St. Louis, and Chicago. After 1856 the trip from

The *De Witt Clinton* Locomotive, 1835–1840 The *De Witt Clinton* was the first steam locomotive built in the United States. The high smokestack let the hot cinders cool so they would not set fire to nearby trees, an important consideration at a time when eastern North America was still covered with forest. The three passenger cars are clearly horse carriages fitted with railroad wheels.

Bettmann/Corbis

New York to Chicago, which had once taken three weeks by boat and on horseback, could be made in forty-eight hours. It was the railroads that opened up the Midwest, turning the vast prairie into farms to feed the industrial cities of the eastern United States.

Railways also triggered the industrialization of Europe (see Map 23.2). Belgium, independent since 1830, quickly copied the British railways. In France and Prussia, construction was delayed until the mid-1840s. When it began, however, it not only satisfied the long-standing need for transportation but also stimulated the iron, machinery, and construction industries.

Railroads in Europe

electric telegraph A device for rapid, long-distance transmission of information over an electric wire. It was introduced in England and North America in the 1830s and 1840s and replaced telegraph systems that utilized visual signals such as semaphores.

Communication over Wires

After the Italian scientist Alessandro Volta invented the battery in 1800, making it possible to produce an electric current, many inventors tried to apply electricity to communication. The first practical **electric telegraph** systems were developed almost simultaneously in England and America. In 1837 in England Charles Wheatstone and William Cooke introduced a five-wire telegraph, while the American Samuel Morse introduced a code of dots and dashes that could be transmitted with a single wire.

The railroad companies allowed telegraph companies to string wires along the tracks in exchange for the right to send telegrams from station to station announcing the departure and arrival of trains. Such messages made railroads much safer as well as more efficient. By the late 1840s telegraph wires crisscrossed the eastern United States and western Europe. In 1851 the first submarine telegraph cable was laid across the English Channel from England to France; it was the beginning of a network that eventually connected the entire globe. No longer were communications limited to the speed of a sailing ship, a galloping horse, or a fast-moving train.

SECTION REVIEW

- A series of technological and organizational innovations transformed manufacturing, transportation, and communication.

- Mechanization, pioneered by Wedgwood, meant that work formerly done by skilled craftsmen was divided into many simple tasks assigned to workers in factories.

- New machines allowed the mass-production of cotton yarn and cloth.

- The use of coke and new machines made iron cheap and abundant.

- Steam engines provided power for mines, factories, ships, and railroads.

- Electricity found its first practical application in telegraphy.

THE IMPACT OF THE EARLY INDUSTRIAL REVOLUTION

The Industrial Revolution led to profound changes in society, politics, and the economy. At first, the changes were local. Some people became wealthy and built mansions, while others lived in slums with polluted water and air. By the mid-nineteenth century, the worst local effects were being alleviated and cities became cleaner and healthier. Replacing them were more complex problems: business cycles, labor conflicts, and the transformation of entire regions into industrial landscapes. At the global level, industrialization empowered the nations of western Europe and North America at the expense of the rest of the world.

The New Industrial Cities

The most dramatic environmental changes brought about by industrialization occurred in the towns. Never before had towns grown so fast. London, one of the largest cities in Europe in 1700 with 500,000 inhabitants, grew to 959,000 by 1800 and to 2,363,000 by 1850; it was then the largest city the world had ever known. Manchester, a small town of 20,000 in 1758, reached 400,000 a century later, a twentyfold increase. New York City, already 100,000 strong in 1815, reached 600,000 (including Brooklyn) in 1850. In some areas, towns merged and formed megalopolises, such as Greater London, the English Midlands, central Belgium, and the Ruhr district of Germany.

A great deal of money went into the building of fine homes, churches, museums, and theaters in wealthy neighborhoods. Much of the beauty of London dates from the time of the Industrial

Revolution. Yet, by all accounts, the industrial cities grew much too fast, and much of the growth occurred in the poorest neighborhoods. As poor migrants streamed in from the countryside, developers built the cheap, shoddy row houses for them to rent that Nassau Senior described.

Urban Environments

Sudden population growth caused serious urban environmental problems. Town dwellers recently arrived from the country brought country ways with them. People threw their sewage and trash out the windows to be washed down the gutters in the streets. The poor kept pigs and chickens; the rich kept horses; and pedestrians stepped into the street at their own risk. Air pollution from burning coal, a problem since the sixteenth century, got steadily worse. People drank water drawn from wells and rivers contaminated by sewage and industrial runoff. The River Irwell, which ran through Manchester, was, in the words of one visitor, "considerably less a river than a flood of liquid manure."[4]

"Every day that I live," wrote an American visitor to Manchester, "I thank Heaven that I am not a poor man with a family in England."[5] In his poem "Milton," William Blake (1757–1827) expressed the revulsion of sensitive people at the spoliation of England's "mountains green" and "pleasant pastures":

> And did the Countenance Divine
> Shine forth upon our clouded hills?
> And was Jerusalem builded here
> Among these dark Satanic Mills?

Railroads invaded the towns, bringing noise and smoke into densely populated neighborhoods. Railroad companies built their stations as close to the heart of cities as they could. On

e Interactive Map

MAP 23.2 **Industrialization in Europe, ca. 1850** In 1850 industrialization was in its early stages on the European continent. The first industrial regions were comparatively close to England and possessed rich coal deposits: Belgium and the Ruhr district of Germany. Politics determined the location of railroads. Notice the star-shaped French network of rail lines emanating from Paris and the lines linking the different parts of the German Confederation.

© Cengage Learning

Paris Apartment at Night   This cutaway drawing in a French magazine shows the vertical segregation by social class that prevailed in the 1840s. The lower level is occupied by the concierge and her family. The first floor belongs to a wealthy family throwing a party for high-society friends. Middle-class people living on the next floor seem annoyed by the noise coming from below. Above them, a thief has entered an artist's studio. A poor seamstress and her child live in the garret under the roof. When elevators were introduced in the late nineteenth century, people of different income levels became segregated by neighborhoods instead of by floors.

Bibliothèque nationale de France

the outskirts of cities, railroad yards, sidings, and repair shops covered acres of land, surrounded by miles of warehouses and workers' housing.

Under these conditions, diseases proliferated. To the long list of preindustrial diseases, industrialization added new ailments. Rickets, a bone disease caused by lack of sunshine, became endemic in dark and smoky industrial cities. Steamships brought cholera from India, causing great epidemics that struck poor neighborhoods especially hard. Observers documented the horrors of slum life in vivid detail. Their shocking reports led to municipal reforms, such as garbage removal, water and sewage systems, and parks and schools. These measures began to alleviate the ills of urban life after the mid-nineteenth century.

Rural Environments

Long before the Industrial Revolution began, practically no wilderness areas were left in Britain and very few in western Europe. Almost every piece of land was covered with fields, forests, or pastures shaped by human activity, or by towns; yet humans continued to alter the environment. As they had been doing for centuries, people cut timber to build ships and houses, to heat homes, and to manufacture bricks, iron, glass, beer, bread, and many other items.

North American Environments

North Americans transformed their environment faster than Europeans because they saw nature as an obstacle to be overcome and dominated. The Canadian and American governments seized land from the Indians and made it available at low cost to white farmers and logging companies. Settlers viewed forests not as a valuable resource but as a hindrance to development. In their haste to "open up the wilderness," pioneers felled trees and burned them, built houses and abandoned them, and moved on. The cultivation of cotton in the South was especially harmful. Planters cut down forests, grew cotton for a few years until it depleted the soil, then moved west, abandoning the land to scrub pines.

Environments in Europe

In Europe, raw materials once grown on the land—such as wood, hay, and wool—were replaced by materials found underground, like iron ore and coal, or obtained overseas, like cotton. While forested countries continued to smelt iron with charcoal, western Europeans substituted coke made from coal. As the population increased and land grew scarcer, the cost of growing feed for horses rose, creating incentives to find new, less land-hungry means of transportation. Likewise, as iron became cheaper and wood more expensive, ships and many other objects formerly made of wood began to be made of iron.

An Industrial Canal In the late eighteenth and early nineteenth centuries, before railroads were introduced, many canals were constructed in England so that barges could transport heavy materials cheaply, such as coal for industrial works and steam engines, stone and bricks for buildings, clay for pottery works, and ores for metal foundries. Canals such as this one, which ran alongside a copper foundry, contributed greatly to Britain's industrial development.

To contemporaries, the most obvious changes in rural life were brought about by the new transportation systems. In the eighteenth century France had a network of quality roads, which Napoleon extended into Italy and Germany. In Britain local governments' neglect of the roads that served long-distance traffic led to the formation of private "turnpike trusts" that built numerous toll roads. The growing volume of heavy freight triggered canal-building booms in Britain, France, and the Low Countries in the late eighteenth century. Some canals, like the duke of Bridgewater's canal in England, connected coal mines to towns or navigable rivers. Others linked navigable rivers and created national transportation networks.

Canals were where engineers learned skills they were able to apply to the next great transportation system: the railroads. They laid track across rolling country by cutting deeply into hillsides and erecting daringly long bridges across valleys. Soon, trains pulled by puffing, smoke-belching locomotives were invading long-isolated districts.

Working Conditions

Industrialization offered new opportunities to the enterprising. Carpenters, metalworkers, and machinists were in great demand. Some workers became engineers or went into business for themselves. The boldest Britons moved to the European continent, the Americas, or India, using their skills to establish new industries.

The successful, however, were a minority. Most industrial jobs were unskilled, repetitive, and boring. Factory work did not vary with the seasons or the time of day but began and ended by the clock. Gas lighting expanded the working day past sunset (see Environment and Technology: Gas Lighting). Workdays were long, there were few breaks, and foremen watched constantly. Workers who performed one simple task over and over had little sense of achievement or connection to the final product. Industrial accidents were common and could ruin a family. Factory workers had no control over their tools, jobs, or working hours.

Gas Lighting

Before the nineteenth century, the night was a dangerous time to be out. Oil lanterns and candles made of tallow or beeswax were expensive. Almost everyone went to bed at sundown and got up at dawn.

There was a big demand for better lighting. For the managers of industrial establishments, daylight hours were too short, especially in the winter months; they knew that they could keep running after sunset if they had light, but lanterns and candles were costly and dangerous. Wealthy people wanted to light up their homes. Businesses and government offices also needed light. The demand inspired inventors to look for new ways to produce light.

The French engineer Philippe Lebon knew that heating wood to make charcoal produced a flammable gas. In the 1790s he channeled this gas through pipes to illuminate a home and garden. In Britain, the engineer William Murdock used the gas released in the process of making coke to light up a house. Moving from these experiments to commercial applications was a long and complicated process, however. Coal gas was smelly and explosive and full of impurities that gave off toxic fumes when it burned. Engineers had to learn ways to extract the gas efficiently, make strong pipes that did not leak, and market the product. In 1806 Frederick Albert Winsor founded the National Light and Heat Company to produce and distribute gas in London. By 1816, London had 26 miles of gas mains bringing gas to several neighborhoods. That same year, Baltimore became the first American city to install gas mains and streetlamps. In the following decades, engineers developed ways of making gas safer and cleaner. They also invented meters to measure the amount of gas consumed and burners that produced a brighter light. As a result of these improvements, the cost of gas dropped to less than a third that of oil lamps of equivalent lighting power. From the 1840s until the early twentieth century, gaslights were installed in homes, businesses, and factories and along streets in the major cities of Europe and America.

The results were astonishing and delighted city dwellers. Mills and factories could operate on two eight- to ten-hour shifts instead of one long dawn-to-dusk shift. Businesses stayed open late. Theaters gave evening performances. And

Mary Evans Picture Library/The Image Works

Gas Lighting   For city dwellers, one of the most dramatic improvements brought by industrialization was the introduction of gas lighting. The gas used was a byproduct of heating coal to make coke for the iron industry, and the gas was distributed in iron pipes throughout the wealthier neighborhoods of big cities. Every evening at dusk, lamplighters went around lighting the street lamps.

people could now walk the streets safely. Evening illumination also contributed to the tremendous increase in adult education, as working people attended classes after work. Sales of books soared as increasing numbers of people stayed up late reading. Brightly lit cities attracted migrants from the still-dark countryside. Gas lighting had banished the terrors of the night.

Women and Industry

Industrial work had a major impact on women and family life. Women who could not afford servants had always worked, but mostly within the family: spinning and weaving, sewing hats and clothes, preparing food, washing, and doing a myriad other household chores. In rural areas, women also did farmwork, especially caring for gardens and small animals.

In the early years of industrialization, even where factory work was available, it was never the main occupation of working women. Most young women who sought paid employment became domestic servants in spite of the low pay, drudgery, and risk of sexual abuse by male employers. Women with small children tried hard to find work they could do at home, such as laundry, sewing, embroidery, millinery, or taking in lodgers. Those who worked in factories were concentrated in textile mills, because textile work required less strength than metalworking, construction, or hauling. On average, women earned one-third to one-half as much as men. The

"Love Conquers Fear" This is a sentimental Victorian drawing of children in a textile mill. Child labor was common in the first half of the nineteenth century, and workers were exposed to dangerous machines and moving belts, as well as to dust and dirt.

From William Playfair, The Commercial and Political Atlas, 1801. Visual Connection Archive

economist Andrew Ure wrote in 1835: "It is in fact the constant aim and tendency of every improvement in machinery to supersede human labour altogether or to diminish its cost, by substituting the industry of women and children for that of men."[6] Young unmarried women worked to support themselves or to save for marriage. Married women took factory jobs when their husbands were unable to support the family. Mothers of infants faced a hard choice: whether to leave their babies with wet nurses at great expense or bring them to the factory and keep them drugged. Husbands and wives increasingly worked in different places.

As in preindustrial societies, parents thought children should contribute to their upkeep as soon as they were able to. The first generation of workers brought children as young as five or six with them to the factories and mines; there were no public schools or day-care centers. Employers preferred child workers because they were cheaper and more docile than adults and were better able to tie broken threads or crawl under machines to sweep the dust. In Arkwright's cotton mills two-thirds of the workers were children. Children worked fourteen to sixteen hours a day and were beaten if they made mistakes or fell asleep. Mine operators used children to pull coal carts along the low passageways from the coal face to the mine shaft.

In the early nineteenth century Americans still remembered their revolutionary ideals. When Francis Cabot Lowell built a cotton mill in Massachusetts, he hired the unmarried daughters of New England farmers, promising them decent wages and housing in dormitories under careful moral supervision. Other manufacturers eager to combine profits with morality followed his example. But soon the profit motive won out, and manufacturers imposed longer hours, harsher working conditions, and lower wages. When the young women went on strike, the mill owners replaced them with Irish immigrants willing to accept lower pay and worse conditions.

Industry and Slavery

While the cotton boom enriched planters, merchants, and manufacturers, African Americans paid for it with their freedom. In the 1790s, 700,000 slaves of African descent lived in the United States. As the "Cotton Kingdom" expanded, the number of slaves rose, and by 1850 there were 3.2 million slaves in the United States, 60 percent of whom grew cotton. Similarly, demand for sugar prolonged slavery in the plantations of the West Indies and caused it to spread to the coffee-growing regions of southern Brazil. Slavery was not, as white American southerners maintained, a "peculiar institution," a consequence of biological differences or biblical injunctions, but part of the Industrial Revolution.

Changes in Society

In his novel *Sybil*; or, *The Two Nations*, the British politician Benjamin Disraeli (diz-RAY-lee) (1804–1881) spoke of "two nations between whom there is no intercourse and no sympathy, who are as ignorant of each other's habits, thoughts, and feelings as if they were dwellers in different zones, or inhabitants of different planets . . . the rich and the poor."[7]

Handloom Weavers and Factory Workers

In Britain the worst-off were those who clung to an obsolete skill or craft. The high wages and low productivity of handloom weavers in the 1790s induced inventors to develop power looms. As a result, by 1811 handloom weavers' wages had fallen by a third; by 1832, by two-thirds. Even

**Improvements
and Setbacks**

by working longer hours, they could not escape destitution. The standard of living of factory workers did not decline steadily like those of handloom weavers but fluctuated wildly.

During the war years of 1792 to 1815, the price of food, on which the poor spent most of their income, rose faster than wages, causing widespread hardship. Then, in the 1820s real wages and public health began to improve. Prices fell and wages rose. Even the poor could afford comfortable, washable cotton clothes and underwear. Hard times returned in the "hungry forties." In 1847–1848 the potato crop failed in Ireland. One-quarter of the Irish population died in the resulting famine, and another quarter emigrated to England and North America.

The New Middle Class

The real beneficiaries of the early Industrial Revolution were the middle class. In Britain landowning gentry and merchants had long shared wealth and influence. In the late eighteenth century a new group arose: entrepreneurs whose money came from manufacturing. Most, like Arkwright and Wedgwood, were the sons of middling shopkeepers, craftsmen, or farmers. Their enterprises were usually self-financed, for little capital was needed to start a cotton-spinning or machine-building business. A generation later, in the nineteenth century, some newly rich industrialists bought their way into high society. The same happened in western Europe after 1815.

**Middle-Class Women and
Middle-Class Attitudes**

Before the Industrial Revolution, wives of merchants had often participated in the family business; widows occasionally managed sizable businesses on their own. With industrialization came a "cult of domesticity" to justify removing middle-class women from contact with the business world. Instead, they became responsible for the home, the servants, the education of children, and the family's social life (see Chapter 27). Not all women accepted the change; Mary Wollstonecraft (1759–1797) wrote the first feminist manifesto, *Vindication of the Rights of Woman*, in 1792.

Middle-class people who attributed their success to their own efforts and virtues believed that if some people could succeed through hard work, thrift, and temperance, then those who did not succeed had no one but themselves to blame. Many workers, however, were newly arrived from rural districts and earned too little to save for the long stretches of unemployment they experienced. The squalor and misery of life in factory towns led to a noticeable increase in drunkenness on paydays. The moral position of the middle class mingled condemnation with concern, coupled with feelings of helplessness in the face of terrible social problems, such as drunkenness, prostitution, and child abandonment.

SECTION REVIEW

- The Industrial Revolution changed people's lives and the environments in which they lived.

- Cities grew huge and, for most of their inhabitants, unsightly and unhealthy.

- Roads, canals, and railroads crisscrossed open land, changing rural environments.

- Middle-class women were consigned to caring for the home and children, while many working-class women had to earn their living in mines and factories.

- Serious social problems arose, such as unemployment, alcoholism, and the abandonment of children.

NEW ECONOMIC AND POLITICAL IDEAS

Changes as profound as the Industrial Revolution triggered political ferment and ideological conflict. So many wars and revolutions took place during those years that we cannot neatly separate out the consequences of industrialization from the rest. But it is clear that by undermining social traditions and causing a growing gap between rich and poor, the Industrial Revolution strengthened the ideas of laissez faire (LAY-say fair) and socialism and sparked workers' protests.

Laissez Faire and Its Critics

laissez faire The idea that government should refrain from interfering in economic affairs. The classic exposition of laissez-faire principles is Adam Smith's *Wealth of Nations* (1776).

The most celebrated exponent of **laissez faire** ("let them do") was Adam Smith (1723–1790), a Scottish economist. In *The Wealth of Nations* (1776) Smith argued that if individuals were allowed to seek personal gain, the effect, as though guided by an "invisible hand," would be to increase the general welfare. The government should refrain from interfering in business, except to protect private property; it should even allow duty-free trade with foreign countries. By advocating free-market capitalism, Smith was challenging the prevailing economic doctrine,

**Adam Smith
and Laizzez Faire**

mercantilism European government policies of the sixteenth, seventeenth, and eighteenth centuries designed to promote overseas trade between a country and its colonies and accumulate precious metals by requiring colonies to trade only with their motherland country. The British system was defined by the Navigation Acts, the French system by laws known as the *Exclusif*.

mercantilism, which argued that governments should regulate trade in order to maximize their hoard of precious metals (Chapter 19).

Persuaded by Adam Smith's arguments, governments after 1815 dismantled many of their regulations. Britain even lowered its import duties. Nonetheless, it was obvious that industrialization was causing widespread misery. Two other thinkers, Thomas Malthus (1766–1834) and David Ricardo (1772–1832), attempted to explain the poverty they saw without challenging the basic premises of laissez faire. The cause of the workers' plight, they said, was the population boom, which outstripped the food supply and led to falling wages. The workers' poverty, they claimed, was as much a result of "natural law" as the wealth of successful businessmen, and the only way the working class could avoid mass famine was to delay marriage and practice self-restraint and sexual abstinence.

Businesspeople in Britain eagerly adopted laissez-faire ideas that justified their activities and kept the government at bay. But not everyone accepted the grim conclusions of the "dismal science," as economics was then known. The British philosopher Jeremy Bentham (1748–1832) believed that it was possible to maximize "the greatest happiness of the greatest number," if only Parliament would study the social problems of the day and pass appropriate legislation. The German economist Friedrich List (1789–1846) rejected laissez faire and free trade as a British trick "to make the rest of the world, like the Hindus, its serfs in all industrial and commercial relations." To protect their "infant industries" from British competition, he argued, the German states had to erect high tariff barriers against imports from Britain. On the European continent, List's ideas were as influential as those of Smith and Ricardo and led in 1834 to the formation of the Zollverein (TSOLL-feh-rine), a customs union of most of the German states.

Positivism

positivism A philosophy developed by the French count of Saint-Simon. Positivists believed that social and economic problems could be solved by the application of the scientific method, leading to continuous progress. Their ideas became popular in France and Latin America in the nineteenth century.

French social thinkers, moved by sincere concern for the poor, offered a radically new vision of a just civilization. Espousing a philosophy called **positivism**, the count of Saint-Simon (1760–1825) and his disciple Auguste Comte (COMB-tuh) (1798–1857) argued that the scientific method could solve social as well as technical problems. They recommended that the poor, guided by scientists and artists, form workers' communities under the protection of benevolent business leaders. These ideas attracted the enthusiastic support of bankers and entrepreneurs, for whom positivism provided a rationale for investing in railroads, canals, and other symbols of modernity.

Protests and Reforms

Workers benefited little from the ideas of these middle-class philosophers. Instead, they resisted the harsh working conditions in their own ways. Periodically, they rioted or went on strike, especially when food prices were high or when downturns in the business cycle left many unemployed. In some places, craftsmen broke into factories and destroyed the machines that threatened their livelihoods. Such acts of resistance did nothing to change the nature of industrial work.

Workers' Organizations

Gradually, workers organized to demand universal male suffrage and shorter workdays. In 1834 Robert Owen founded the Grand National Consolidated Trade Union to lobby for an eight-hour workday; it quickly gained half a million members but collapsed a few months later in the face of government prosecution. A new movement called Chartism arose soon thereafter, led by William Lovett and Fergus O'Connor, that appealed to miners and industrial workers. It demanded universal male suffrage, the secret ballot, salaries for members of Parliament, and annual elections. It gathered 1.3 million signatures on a petition, but Parliament rejected it. Chartism collapsed in 1848, but it left a legacy of labor organizing.

Eventually, mass movements persuaded the British Parliament to investigate conditions in factories and mines. The Factory Act of 1833 prohibited the employment of children younger than nine in textile mills. It also limited the working hours of children between the ages of nine and thirteen to eight hours a day and of fourteen- to

SECTION REVIEW

- Many people sought explanations and proposed solutions for the changes in society and the economy.

- Some economists defended the growing disparities between rich and poor in the name of laissez faire, the free-market idea proposed by Adam Smith that appealed to businesspeople.

- Positivists deplored the hardships caused by industrialization but asserted that they could be ameliorated by technological advances and wise policies.

- Agitation by workers led politicians to investigate the working conditions in mines and factories, especially the work of women and children.

Reforms   eighteen-year-olds to twelve hours. The Mines Act of 1842 prohibited the employment of women and boys under age ten underground.

Most important was the struggle over the Corn Laws—tariffs on imported grain. Their repeal in 1846, in the name of "free trade," was designed to lower the cost of food for workers and allow employers to pay lower wages. The repeal represented a victory for the rising class of manufacturers over the conservative landowners who had long dominated politics and whose harvests faced competition from cheaper imported food.

The British learned to seek reform through accommodation. On the European continent, in contrast, the revolutions of 1848 revealed widespread discontent with repressive governments but failed to soften the hardships of industrialization (see Chapter 27).

THE LIMITS OF INDUSTRIALIZATION OUTSIDE THE WEST

Egypt

The spread of the Industrial Revolution in the early nineteenth century transformed the relations of western Europe and North America with the rest of the world. Egypt, strongly influenced by European ideas since the French invasion of 1798, began to industrialize in the early nineteenth century. The driving force was its ruler, Muhammad Ali (1769–1849), a man who was to play a major role in the history of the Middle East and East Africa (see Chapters 25 and 26). Muhammad Ali wanted to build up the Egyptian economy and military in order to become less dependent on the Ottoman sultan, his nominal overlord. To do so, he imported advisers and technicians from Europe and built cotton mills, foundries, shipyards, weapons factories, and other industrial enterprises. To pay for all this, he made the peasants grow wheat and cotton, which the government bought at a low price and exported at a profit. He also imposed high tariffs on imported goods to force the pace of industrialization.

Muhammad Ali's efforts fell afoul of the British, who did not want a powerful country threatening to interrupt the flow of travelers and mail across Egypt, the shortest route between Europe and India. When Egypt went to war against the Ottoman Empire in 1839, Britain intervened and forced Muhammad Ali to eliminate all import duties in the name of free trade. Unprotected, Egypt's fledgling industries could not compete with the flood of cheap British products. Thereafter, Egypt exported raw cotton, imported manufactured goods, and became an economic dependency of Britain.

India

Until the late eighteenth century, India had been the world's largest producer and exporter of cotton textiles, handmade by skilled spinners and weavers. The British East India Company took over large parts of India just as the Industrial Revolution was beginning in Britain (see Chapter 26 and Map 26.2). It allowed cheap British factory-made yarn and cloth to flood the Indian market duty-free, putting spinners and handloom weavers out of work. Unlike Britain, India had no factories to which displaced handicraft workers could turn for work. Most of them became landless peasants, eking out a precarious living.

Like other tropical regions, India became an exporter of raw materials and an importer of British industrial goods. To hasten the process, British entrepreneurs and colonial officials introduced railroads into the subcontinent. The construction of India's railroad network began in the mid-1850s, along with coal mining to fuel the locomotives and the installation of telegraph lines to connect the major cities.

Some Indian entrepreneurs saw opportunities in the atmosphere of change that the British created. In 1854 the Bombay merchant Cowasjee Nanabhoy Davar imported an engineer, four skilled workers, and several textile machines from Britain and started India's first textile mill. This was the beginning of India's mechanized cotton industry. Despite many gifted entrepreneurs, however, India's industrialization proceeded at a snail's pace, for the government was in British hands and the British did nothing to encourage Indian industry.

A Railroad Bridge Across the Nile   In the second half of the nineteenth century, industrialized nations, especially Great Britain, sent engineers and equipment to build railroads in less-industrialized parts of the world, such as India, South Africa, Latin America, and the Middle East. One such railway connected Cairo and Alexandria in Egypt. Here a railroad bridge crosses the Nile at Benha near the Pyramids.

China

China stagnated at the very time when first Britain and then western Europe and North America were becoming industrialized. It had the resources, both human and natural, to advance technologically and economically, but a conservative elite stood in the way of change (see Chapter 21). When faced with Western industrial technology, China became weaker rather than stronger.

In January 1840 a shipyard in Britain launched a radically new ship. The *Nemesis* had an iron hull, a flat bottom that allowed it to navigate in shallow waters, and a steam engine to power it upriver and against the wind. In November it arrived off the coast of China, heavily armed. Though ships from Europe had been sailing to China for three hundred years, the *Nemesis* was the first steam-powered iron gunboat in Asian waters. A Chinese observer noted: "Iron is employed to make it strong. The hull is painted black, weaver's shuttle fashion. On each side is a wheel, which by the use of coal fire is made to revolve as fast as a running horse. . . . At the vessel's head is a Marine God, and at the head, stern, and sides are cannon, which give it a terrific appearance. Steam vessels are a wonderful invention of foreigners, and are calculated to offer delight to many."[8]

Instead of offering delight, the *Nemesis* and other steam-powered warships that soon joined it steamed up the Chinese rivers, bombarded forts and cities, and transported troops and supplies from place to place along the coast and up rivers far more quickly than Chinese soldiers could move on foot. With this new weapon, Britain, a small island nation half a world away, was able to defeat the largest and most populated country in the world (see Chapter 25).

The cases of Egypt, India, and China show how the demands of Western nations and the military advantage that industrialization gave them led them to interfere in the internal affairs of nonindustrial societies. As we shall see in Chapter 28, this was the start of a new age of Western dominance.

SECTION REVIEW

- Industrialization gave the newly industrialized nations of the West the power to coerce non-Western societies.

- Britain snuffed out the incipient industrialization in Egypt and India and turned these countries intro producers of raw materials.

- China stagnated and was defeated by Britain and its steam-powered gunboats.

CONCLUSION

The Industrial Revolution was the most momentous transformation in history since the beginning of agriculture. The steam engine and other new machines greatly lowered the cost and increased the production of goods like cotton and iron and the speed of transportation and communication.

The process caused social upheavals and environmental problems, however. Many entrepreneurs and businesspeople became very wealthy, while industrial workers—many of them children—worked under appalling conditions and lived in overcrowded tenements in badly polluted cities. Economists and philosophers proposed many theories and offered many solutions to the radical problems of industrial societies.

Industrialization had political consequences on a global scale. A small number of industrializing nations—first Great Britain, then those of western Europe and North America—grew more powerful. Other parts of the world were left behind to become political or economic dependencies of the powerful nations.

Eventually the industrial nations learned to alleviate their social problems, but the disparity between the rich and poor nations persisted for two centuries or more, and the environmental effects of industrialization changed from local to global.

KEY TERMS

Industrial
   Revolution p. 607
agricultural
   revolution p. 608

mass production p. 612
Josiah Wedgwood p. 613
division of labor p. 613
mechanization p. 614

Richard Arkwright p. 614
Crystal Palace p. 616
steam engine p. 616
James Watt p. 616

electric telegraph p. 618
laissez faire p. 624
mercantilism p. 625
positivism p. 625

EBOOK AND WEBSITE RESOURCES

e Interactive Maps

Map 23.1 The Industrial Revolution in Britain, ca. 1850

Map 23.2 Industrialization in Europe, ca. 1850

Plus flashcards, practice quizzes, and more. Go to:
www.cengage.com/history/bullietearthpeople5e

SUGGESTED READING

Ashton, T. S. *The Industrial Revolution, 1760–1830.* 1948. A classic account the British industrial revolution.

Goodman, J., and K. Honeyman. *Gainful Pursuits: The Making of Industrial Europe: 1600–1914.* 1988. Discusses industrialization outside of Britain.

Inkster, Ian. *Technology and Industrialization: Historical Case Studies and International Perspectives.* 1998. A global view of the Industrial Revolution.

Jeremy, David. *Artisans, Entrepreneurs, and Machines: Essays on the Early Anglo-American Textile Industry, 1770–1840.* 1998. Describes how American industry got started.

Landes, David. *The Unbound Prometheus: Technological Change and Industrial Development in Western Europe from 1750 to the Present,* 2nd ed. 2003. A broad synthesis of modern industrial development.

McClellan, James, III, and Harold Dorn. *Science and Technology in World History.* 1999. Emphasizes the intersection of technology and science.

Mokyr, Joel. *The Gifts of Athena: Historical Origins of the Knowledge Economy.* 2002. Examines the role and institutional bases of knowledge in the growth of the modern industrial world.

Mokyr, Joel. *The Lever of Riches: Technological Creativity and Economic Progress.* 1990. An optimistic overview of technological change.

Pomeranz, Kenneth. *The Great Divergence: Europe, China, and the Making of the Modern World Economy.* 2000. An important work comparing China and Europe in the eighteenth century.

Stearns, Peter. *The Industrial Revolution in World History.* 1993. The first book to treat industrialization as a global phenomenon.

Thompson, E. P. *The Making of the English Working Class.* 1963. Classic work on the impact on workers of industrialization.

Tilly, Louise, and Joan Scott. *Women, Work, and Family.* 1978. The impact of industrialization on women.

Tucker, Richard, and John Richards. *Global Deforestation in the Nineteenth-Century World Economy.* 1983. Looks at the negative consequences of industrialization.

Wilkinson, Richard. *Poverty and Progress: An Ecological Perspective on Economic Development.* 1973. Explores the environmental impact of industrialization.

NOTES

1. Nassau W. Senior, *Letters on the Factory Act, as it affects the cotton manufacture, addressed to the Right Honourable, the President of the Board of Trade*, 2nd ed. (London: Fellows, 1844), 20.

2. Friedrich Engels, *Condition of the Working Class in England*, trans. and ed. by W. O. Henderson and W. H. Chaloner (Oxford: Blackwell, 1958), 312.

3. Quoted in Joel Mokyr, *The Lever of Riches: Technological Creativity and Economic Progress* (New York and Oxford: Oxford University Press, 1990), 240.

4. Quoted in Lewis Mumford, *The City in History* (New York: Harcourt Brace, 1961), 460.

5. Quoted in F. Roy Willis, *Western Civilization: An Urban Perspective*, vol. II (Lexington, MA: D.C. Heath, 1973), 675.

6. Quoted in Joan W. Scott, "The Mechanization of Women's Work," *Scientific American* 247, no. 3 (September 1982): 171.

7. J. P. T. Bury, *The New Cambridge Modern History*, vol. X (Cambridge: Cambridge University Press, 1967), 10.

8. *Nautical Magazine* 12 (1843): 346.

CHAPTER
24

CHAPTER OUTLINE

- Independence in Latin America, 1800–1830
- The Problem of Order, 1825–1890
- The Challenge of Social and Economic Change
- Conclusion

DIVERSITY + DOMINANCE   *The Afro-Brazilian Experience, 1828*

ENVIRONMENT + TECHNOLOGY   *Constructing the Port of Buenos Aires, Argentina*

Estación de Orizaba, 1877. From Casimiro Castro, Album del Ferro-Carril Mexicano Coleccion de Vista Pintadas (Victor Debray and Company, 1877) Typ 887.77.4162 PF, Department of Printing and Graphic Arts, Houghton Library, Harvard College Library

The Train Station in Orizaba, Mexico, 1877   In the last decades of the nineteenth century Mexico's political leaders actively promoted economic development. The railroad became the symbol of this ideal.

Visit the website and ebook for additional study materials and interactive tools: www.cengage.com/history/bullietearthpeople5e

Nation Building and Economic Transformation in the Americas, 1800–1890

During the nineteenth century the newly independent nations of the Western Hemisphere sought to emulate the rapid economic progress of Europe under the influence of the Industrial Revolution. No technology seemed to represent that progress better than railroads. Everywhere from Argentina to Canada, governments sponsored railroad development. By 1850 there were 9,000 miles (14,480 kilometers) of track in the United States, as much as in the rest of the world. Latin American nations committed to this technology later than the United States, but railroads there also soon proved important to exports, to new industries, and to political and cultural integration.

■ What were the causes of the revolutions for independence in Latin America?
■ What major political challenges did Western Hemisphere nations face in the nineteenth century?
■ How did economic modernization and the effects of abolition, immigration, and women's rights change the nations of the Western Hemisphere?

Mexico granted the first concession for railroad construction in 1837, but the first significant rail line was completed in 1873. Few new projects were begun until the presidency of Porfirio Díaz (1876–1880 and 1884–1911), who promoted railroad construction. By the time revolutionaries forced him from office in 1910, Mexico had 12,000 miles (19,300 kilometers) of track. Railroads proved crucial to Mexican economic growth, but there was a downside. Foreign investment helped pay for new railroads, but this dependence on foreign capital led to political protests and economic nationalism. Railroad development also had a powerful effect on native peoples, who still controlled large areas of rural Mexico. Railroads made their lands more valuable, and, as a result, powerful landed families used their political influence to strip this land from indigenous subsistence farmers and use it to produce export crops. As Amerindian villagers lost their traditional lands, the number of rural uprisings increased.

In the nineteenth century the Western Hemisphere witnessed radical political and social changes in addition to technological innovations and economic expansion. Brazil and nearly all of Spain's colonies achieved independence by 1825. As was true in the earlier American and French Revolutions (see Chapter 22), rising nationalism and the ideal of political freedom promoted these changes. Despite the achievement of independence, Mexico and other nations in the hemisphere faced foreign interventions and other threats to sovereignty, including regionalism and civil war.

The new nations of the Western Hemisphere faced difficult questions. If colonies could reject submission to imperial powers, could not regions with distinct cultures, social structures, and economies refuse to accept the political authority of newly formed national governments? How could nations born in revolution accept the political strictures of written constitutions—even those they wrote themselves? How could the ideals of liberty and freedom expressed in those constitutions be reconciled with the denial of rights to Amerindians, slaves, recent immigrants, and women?

While trying to resolve these political questions, the new nations also attempted to promote economic growth. They imported new technologies like railroads, opened new areas to settlement, and promoted immigration. But the legacy of colonial economic development, with its emphasis on agricultural and mining exports, inhibited efforts to promote diversification and industrialization, just as the legacy of class and racial division thwarted the realization of political ideals.

INDEPENDENCE IN LATIN AMERICA, 1800–1830

As the eighteenth century drew to a close, Spain and Portugal held vast colonial possessions in the Western Hemisphere, although their power had declined relative to that of their British and French rivals. Both Iberian empires had reformed their colonial administration and strengthened their military forces in the eighteenth century (see Chapter 18). Despite these efforts, the same economic and political forces that had undermined British rule in its colonies were present in Spanish America and Brazil.

Roots of Revolution, to 1810

The great works of the Enlightenment as well as revolutionary documents like the American Declaration of Independence and the French Declaration of the Rights of Man and the Citizen circulated widely in Latin America, but few colonial residents wanted revolutionary change. While colonial elites and middle classes were frustrated by imperial policies, it was events in Europe that propelled the colonies toward independence. Napoleon's decision to invade Portugal (1807) and Spain (1808), not revolutionary ideas, created a crisis of legitimacy that undermined the authority of colonial officials and ignited Latin America's struggle for independence.

Napoleon Invades Portugal and Spain

As a French army neared Lisbon in 1808, the Portuguese royal family fled to Brazil. King John VI maintained his court there for over a decade. Soon Napoleon forced King Ferdinand VII of Spain to abdicate and placed his own brother, Joseph Bonaparte, on the throne. Spanish patriots fighting against the French created a new political body, the Junta (HUN-tah) Central, to administer the areas they controlled. The junta claimed authority over Spain's colonies, inviting the election of colonial deputies to help write a constitution.

Most residents of colonial Spanish America favored obedience to the Junta Central and many colonies elected deputies, but a vocal minority, including some members of the elite, objected. These dissenters argued that they were subjects of the king, not dependents of the Spanish nation. They wanted to create local juntas and govern their own affairs until Ferdinand regained the throne. Spanish loyalists resisted this assertion of local autonomy, provoking armed uprisings. In late 1808 and 1809 popular movements overthrew Spanish colonial officials in Venezuela, Mexico, and Alto Peru (modern Bolivia) and created local juntas. In each case, Spanish officials quickly reasserted control and punished the leaders. This harsh repression, however, further polarized public opinion in the colonies and gave rise to a greater sense of a separate American nationality. By 1810 Spanish colonial authorities were facing a new round of revolutions now focused on independence.

Spanish South America, 1810–1825

Revolutions Begin

In Caracas (the capital city of modern Venezuela) a revolutionary junta led by creoles (colonial-born whites) declared independence in 1811. Although this group espoused representative

CHRONOLOGY

	United States and Canada	Mexico and Central America	South America
1800	1789 U.S. Constitution ratified 1803 Louisiana Purchase		
			1808 Portuguese royal family arrives in Brazil
			1808–1809 Revolutions for independence begin in Spanish South America
	1812–1815 War of 1812	1810–1821 Mexican movement for independence	
1825			1822 Brazil gains independence
	1836 Texas gains independence from Mexico		1831 Brazil signs treaty with Great Britain to end slave trade. Illegal trade continues.
	1845 Texas admitted as a state	1846–1848 War between Mexico and the United States	
		1847–1870 Caste War	
	1848 Women's Rights Convention in Seneca Falls, New York		
1850			1850 Brazilian illegal slave trade suppressed
		1857 Mexico's new constitution limits power of Catholic Church and military	
	1861–1865 Civil War	1862–1867 French invade Mexico	1865–1870 Argentina, Uruguay, and Brazil wage war against Paraguay
	1867 Creation of Dominion of Canada	1867 Emperor Maximilian executed	
1875	1876 Sioux and allies defeat U.S. Army in Battle of Little Bighorn		1870s Governments of Argentina and Chile begin final campaigns against indigenous peoples
			1879–1881 Chile wages war against Peru and Bolivia; telegraph, refrigeration, and barbed wire introduced in Argentina
			1888 Abolition of slavery in Brazil
	1890 "Jim Crow" laws enforce segregation in South		
	1890s United States becomes world's leading steel producer		

Simón Bolívar The most important military leader in the struggle for independence in South America. Born in Venezuela, he led military forces there and in Colombia, Ecuador, Peru, and Bolivia.

Simón Bolívar

democracy, its leaders were landowners who defended slavery and opposed full citizenship for the black and mixed-race majority. Their aim was to expand their own privileges by eliminating Spaniards from the upper levels of government and the church. The junta's narrow agenda spurred Spanish loyalists to rally thousands of free blacks and slaves to defend the Spanish Empire. Faced with this determined resistance, the revolutionary movement placed overwhelming political authority in the hands of its military leader **Simón Bolívar** (see-MOAN bow-LEE-varh) (1783-1830), who would become the preeminent leader of the independence movement.

The son of wealthy Venezuelan planters, Bolívar had traveled in Europe and studied the works of the Enlightenment. He was a charismatic personality who effectively mobilized political support and held the loyalty of his troops. Defeated on many occasions, Bolívar successfully adapted his objectives and policies to attract new allies and build coalitions. Although initially opposed to the abolition of slavery, for example, he agreed to support emancipation in order to draw slaves and freemen to his cause and to gain supplies from Haiti. Bolívar was also capable of using harsh methods to ensure victory, proclaiming in 1813 that, "any Spaniard who does not . . .

work against tyranny in behalf of this just cause will be considered an enemy and punished; as a traitor to the nation, he will inevitably be shot by a firing squad."[1]

Military advantage shifted back and forth between the patriots and loyalists until Bolívar enlisted demobilized English veterans of the Napoleonic Wars and a military revolt in Spain in 1820 weakened Spanish resolve. The English veterans, hardened by combat, improved the battlefield performance of Bolívar's army, while the revolt in Spain in 1820 forced Ferdinand VII—restored to power in 1814—to accept a constitution that limited the powers of both the monarch and the church. Colonial loyalists who for a decade had fought to maintain the authority of monarch and church viewed these reforms as unacceptably liberal.

With the king's supporters divided, momentum swung to the patriots. After liberating present-day Venezuela, Colombia, and Ecuador, Bolívar's army entered Peru and Bolivia (colonial Alto Peru) and defeated the last Spanish armies in 1824. Bolívar and his supporters then attempted to create a confederation of the former Spanish colonies. The first steps were the creation of Gran Colombia (now Venezuela, Colombia, and Ecuador) and the unification of Peru and Bolivia, but these initiatives had failed by 1830 (see Map 24.1).

Buenos Aires (the capital city of modern Argentina) was the second important center of revolutionary activity in Spanish South America. In Buenos Aires news of French victories in Spain led to the creation of a junta organized by militia commanders, merchants, and ranchers, which overthrew the viceroy in 1810. To deflect the opposition of Spanish loyalists, the junta claimed loyalty to the imprisoned king. Two years after Ferdinand regained the Spanish throne in 1814, junta leaders declared independence as the United Provinces of the Río de la Plata.

Patriot leaders in Buenos Aires at first sought to retain control over the territory of the Viceroyalty of Río de la Plata, but Spanish loyalists in Uruguay and Bolivia and a separatist movement in Paraguay defeated these ambitions. Even within the territory of Argentina, the government in Buenos Aires was unable to control regional rivalries and political differences. As a result, the region rapidly descended into political chaos.

A weak succession of juntas, collective presidencies, and dictators lost control over much of the interior of Argentina. But the government in Buenos Aires did manage to support a mixed force of Chileans and Argentines led by José de San Martín (hoe-SAY deh san mar-TEEN) (1778–1850), who crossed the Andes Mountains to attack Spanish forces in Chile and Peru. During this campaign San Martín's most effective troops were former slaves, who had gained their freedom by enlisting in the army. After gaining victory in Chile, San Martín pushed on to Peru in 1820, but he failed to gain a clear victory there. Unable to make progress, San Martín surrendered command of patriot forces in Peru to Simón Bolívar, who overcame final Spanish resistance in 1824.

Mexico, 1810–1823

In 1810 Mexico was Spain's wealthiest and most populous colony. Its silver mines were the richest in the world, and the colony's capital, Mexico City, was larger than any city in Spain. Mexico also had the largest population of Spanish immigrants among the colonies. When news of Napoleon's invasion of Spain reached Mexico, conservative Spaniards in Mexico City overthrew the local viceroy because he was too sympathetic to the creoles. This action by Spanish loyalists underlined the new reality: with the king removed from his throne by the French, colonial authority now rested on brute force.

The first stage of the revolution against Spain occurred in central Mexico, where ranchers and farmers had aggressively forced Amerindian communities from their traditional agricultural lands. Crop failures and epidemics afflicted the region's rural poor, while miners and the urban poor faced higher food prices and rising unemployment as well. With the power of colonial authorities weakened by events in Spain, anger and fear spread through towns and villages in central Mexico.

On September 16, 1810, the parish priest of the small town of Dolores, **Miguel Hidalgo y Costilla** (mee-GEHL ee-DAHL-go ee cos-TEA-ah), rang the church bells and attracted a crowd. In a fiery speech he urged the crowd to rise up against the oppression of Spanish officials. Tens of thousands of the rural and urban poor soon joined his movement. While they lacked military discipline and weapons, they knew who their oppressors were, the Spanish and colonial-born whites who owned the ranches and mines. Recognizing the threat posed by the angry masses

PRIMARY SOURCE: The Jamaica Letter Simón Bolívar shares his thoughts in 1815 on the present and future of the Latin American independence movement.

Independence of Argentina

San Martín and Chile

Miguel Hidalgo y Costilla Mexican priest who led the first stage of the Mexican independence war in 1810. He was captured and executed in 1811.

Hidalgo and Morelos

OREGON
COUNTRY
(Joint U.S.-British
occupation)

BRITISH NORTH AMERICA
(CANADA)
(Gr. Br.)

Mississippi R.

Colorado R.

New York
Philadelphia
Washington, D.C.

UNITED STATES

MEXICO
1821

Rio Grande

San Antonio

New Orleans

Charleston

Gulf of Mexico

A T L A N T I C
O C E A N

N

40°W

40°N

Mexico City   Veracruz

Havana

CUBA
(Spain)

BAHAMA IS.
(Gr. Br.)

HAITI 1804

PUERTO RICO (Spain)

20°N

BRITISH
HONDURAS (Gr. Br.)
GUATEMALA
Guatemala City

JAMAICA
(Gr. Br.)

Caribbean Sea

UNITED PROVINCES OF
CENTRAL AMERICA
1823–1839

Panama

TRINIDAD (Gr. Br.)

Caracas

VENEZUELA
Socorro
Bogotá

Magdalena R.

Orinoco R.

BR. GUIANA (Gr. Br.)

DUTCH GUIANA (Neth.)

FRENCH GUIANA (France)

GRAN COLOMBIA
1819–1830

Quito

ECUADOR

Amazon R.

Equator 0°

Galápagos
Islands

P A C I F I C

O C E A N

PERU
1824

Lima

EMPIRE OF BRAZIL
1822

Salvador

BOLIVIA
1825
La Paz

Sucre

Paraná R.

20°S

PARAGUAY
1811

São Paulo

Rio de Janeiro

CHILE
1817

UNITED
PROVINCES OF
THE RIO DE
LA PLATA
1816

URUGUAY
1828
Montevideo

Valparaíso
Santiago

ARGENTINA
Buenos Aires
Bahía
Blanca

PATAGONIA
(Disputed between
Argentina and Chile)

Islas Malvinas
(Falkland Islands)

80°W   60°W

0   500   1000 Km.

0   500   1000 Mi.

1811 Year independence gained

Colony

© Cengage Learning

MAP 24.1 **Latin America by 1830** By 1830 patriot forces had overturned the Spanish and Portuguese Empires of the Western Hemisphere. Regional conflicts, local wars, and foreign interventions challenged the survival of many of these new nations following independence.

e Interactive Map

Schaalkwijk/Art Resource, NY

Padre Hidalgo Padre Miguel Hidalgo y Costilla led the first stage of Mexico's revolution for independence by rallying the rural masses. His defeat, trial, and execution made him one of Mexico's most important political martyrs.

following Hidalgo, most wealthy Mexicans supported Spanish authorities. The military tide quickly turned, and Spanish forces captured and executed Hidalgo in 1811.

The revolution continued under the leadership of another priest, **José María Morelos** (hoe-SAY mah-REE-ah moh-RAY-los), a former student of Hidalgo's. A more adept military and political leader than his mentor, Morelos created a formidable fighting force and, in 1813, convened a congress that declared independence and drafted a constitution. Despite these achievements, loyalist forces defeated and executed Morelos in 1815. Although small numbers of insurgents continued to fight Spanish forces, colonial rule seemed secure in 1820, but news of the military revolt in Spain unsettled the conservative groups who had opposed Hidalgo and Morelos. In 1821 Colonel Agustín de Iturbide (ah-goos-TEEN deh ee-tur-BEE-deh) and other loyalist commanders forged an alliance with insurgents to declare Mexico's independence. The conservative origins of Mexico's independence were made clear by the decision to create a monarchial government and crown Iturbide emperor. In early 1823, however, the army overthrew Iturbide and Mexico became a republic. When Iturbide returned to Mexico from exile in 1824, he was captured and, like Hidalgo and Morelos, was executed by a firing squad.

José María Morelos
Mexican priest and former student of Miguel Hidalgo y Costilla, he led the forces fighting for Mexican independence until he was captured and executed in 1815.

Brazil, to 1831

The arrival of the Portuguese royal family in Brazil in 1808 helped maintain the loyalty of the colonial elite. With Napoleon's defeat, the Portuguese government called for King John VI to return to Portugal. At first he resisted, but a liberal revolt in Portugal forced the king to return to Portugal in 1821 to protect his throne. He left his son Pedro in Brazil as regent.

By 1820 the Spanish colonies along Brazil's borders had experienced ten years of revolution and civil war, and some, like Argentina and Paraguay, had gained independence. Unable to ignore these struggles, some Brazilians began to reevaluate Brazil's relationship with Portugal. Many Brazilians resented their homeland's economic subordination to Portugal, while the arrogance of Portuguese soldiers and bureaucrats led others to talk openly of independence.

Pedro I and Brazilian Independence

Unwilling to return to Portugal and committed to maintaining his family's hold on Brazil, Pedro aligned himself with the rising tide of sentiment, and in 1822 he declared Brazilian independence. Pedro's decision launched Brazil on a unique political trajectory. Unlike its neighbors, which became constitutional republics, Brazil gained independence as a constitutional monarchy with Pedro I, son of the king of Portugal, as emperor.

Pedro I was committed to both monarchy and to liberal principles. The constitution of 1824 provided for an elected assembly and granted rights to the political opposition, but Pedro made enemies by protecting the Portuguese who remained in Brazil from arrest and seizure of property. Pedro I also opposed slavery, even though the slave-owning class dominated Brazil. In 1823 he anonymously published an article that characterized slavery as a "cancer eating away at Brazil" (see Diversity and Dominance: The Afro-Brazilian Experience, 1828). His decision in 1831 to ratify a treaty with Great Britain ending Brazilian participation in the slave trade provoked opposition, as did his use of military force to control neighboring Uruguay. As military losses and costs rose, the Brazilian public grew impatient. A vocal minority that sought the creation of a democracy used these issues to rally public opinion against the emperor. Confronted by street demonstrations, Pedro I abdicated the throne in 1831 in favor of his five-year-old son Pedro II. After a nine-year regency, Pedro II assumed full powers as emperor of Brazil and reigned until overthrown by republicans in 1889.

SECTION REVIEW

- The French invasion of Portugal and Spain created a political crisis in their American colonies that in turn led to independence movements.

- Under the leadership of Simón Bolívar, several South American countries gained independence.

- Mexico gained independence after a long and destructive war.

- Led by the son of the Portuguese king, Brazil gained independence as a monarchy.

THE PROBLEM OF ORDER, 1825–1890

All the newly independent nations of the Western Hemisphere encountered difficulties establishing stable political institutions. Popular sovereignty found broad support across the hemisphere as all the new nations sought to establish constitutions and elected assemblies. However, this widespread support for constitutional order and for representative government failed to prevent bitter factional conflict, regionalism, and the threats posed by charismatic political leaders and military uprisings.

Constitutional Experiments

In reaction to what they saw as arbitrary and tyrannical rule by colonial authorities, revolutionary leaders in the United States and Latin America espoused constitutionalism. They believed that the careful description of political powers in written constitutions offered the best protection for individual rights and liberties. In practice, however, many new constitutions proved unworkable. In the United States, George Washington and other leaders became dissatisfied with the first constitution, the Articles of Confederation, and helped write a new constitution. In Latin America few constitutions survived the rough-and-tumble of national politics. For example, Venezuela and Chile ratified and then rejected a combined total of nine constitutions between 1811 and 1833.

Important differences in colonial political experience influenced later political developments in the Americas. The ratification of a new constitution in the United States was the culmination of a long historical process that had begun with the development of English constitutional law and continued under colonial charters. The British colonies provided many opportunities for holding elective offices, and, by the time of independence, citizens had grown accustomed to elections, political parties, and factions. In contrast, neither Brazil nor Spanish America had significant experience with elections and representative institutions.

Canadian Government

Democratic passions and the desire for effective self-rule led to significant political reform in the Americas, even in regions that remained colonies. British Canada included a number of separate colonies and territories, each with a separate government. A provincial governor and appointed advisory council drawn from the local elite dominated political life in each colony, while elected assemblies exercised limited power. The desire to make government responsive to

DIVERSITY + DOMINANCE

The Afro-Brazilian Experience, 1828

Brazil was the most important destination for the Atlantic slave trade. From the sixteenth century to the 1850s it imported more than 2 million African slaves. Beginning in the 1820s, Great Britain, Brazil's main trading partner, began to press for an end to the slave trade. British visitors to Brazil became an important source of critical information for those who sought to end the trade.

A British clergyman, Robert Walsh, who traveled widely in Brazil in 1828 and 1829 left an account of the complex and unexpected ways that slaves and black freedmen were integrated into Brazilian society.

[At the Alfandega, or custom house,] . . . for the first time I saw the Negro population under circumstances so striking to a stranger. The whole labour of bearing and moving burdens is performed by these people, and the state in which they appear is revolting to humanity. Here were a number of beings entirely naked, with the exception of a covering of dirty rags tied about their waists. Their skins, from constant exposure to the weather, had become hard, crusty, and seamed, resembling the coarse black covering of some beast, or like that of an elephant, a wrinkled hide scattered with scanty hairs. On contemplating their persons, you saw them with a physical organization resembling beings of a grade below the rank of man. . . . Some of these beings were yoked to drays, on which they dragged heavy burdens. Some were chained by the necks and legs, and moved with loads thus encumbered. Some followed each other in ranks, with heavy weights on their heads, chattering the most inarticulate and dismal cadence as they moved along. Some were munching young sugar-canes, like beasts of burden eating green provender [animal feed], and some were seen near water, lying on the bare ground among filth and offal, coiled up like dogs, and seeming to expect or require no more comfort or accommodation, exhibiting a state and conformation so un-human, that they not only seemed, but actually were, far below the inferior animals around them. Horses and mules were not employed in this way; they were used only for pleasure, and not for labour. They were seen in the same streets, pampered, spirited, and richly caparisoned, enjoying a state far superior to the negroes, and appearing to look down on the fettered and burdened wretches they were

passing, as on beings of an inferior rank in the creation to themselves. . . .

The first impression of all this on my mind, was to shake the conviction I had always felt, of the wrong and hardship inflicted on our black fellow creatures, and that they were only in that state which God and nature had assigned them; that they were the lowest grade of human existence, and the link that connected it with the brute, and that the gradation was so insensible, and their natures so intermingled, that it was impossible to tell where one had terminated and the other commenced; and that it was not surprising that people who contemplated them every day, so formed, so employed, and so degraded, should forget their claims to that rank in the scale of beings in which modern philanthropists are so anxious to place them. I did not at the moment myself recollect, that the white man, made a slave on the coast of Africa, suffers not only a similar mental but physical deterioration from hardships and emaciation, and becomes in time the dull and deformed beast I now saw yoked to a burden.

A few hours only were necessary to correct my first impressions of the negro population, by seeing them under a different aspect. We were attracted by the sound of military music, and found it proceeded from a regiment drawn up in one of the streets. Their colonel had just died, and they attended to form a procession to celebrate his obsequies. They were all of different shades of black, but the majority were negroes. Their equipment was excellent; they wore dark jackets, white pantaloons, and black leather caps and belts, all which, with their arms, were in high order. Their band produced sweet and agreeable music, of the leader's own composition, and the men went through some evolutions with regularity and dexterity. They were only a militia regiment, yet were as well appointed and disciplined as one of our regiments of the line. Here then was the first step in that gradation by which the black population of this country ascend in the scale of humanity; he advances from the state below that of a beast of burden into a military rank, and he shows himself as capable of discipline and improvement as a human being of any other colour.

Our attention was next attracted by negro men and women bearing about a variety of articles for sale; some in baskets, some on boards and cases carried on their heads. They

---

the will of the assemblies led to armed rebellion in 1837. Britain responded by establishing limited self-rule in each of the Canadian provinces. By the 1860s regional political leaders realized that economic development required a government with a "national" character. Negotiations among Canadian leaders and with the British crown led to a union of Canadian provinces, the **Confederation of 1867**, and to the creation of the Dominion of Canada with a central government in Ottawa (see Map 24.2).

The path to effective constitutional government was rockier to the south. Because neither Spain nor Portugal had permitted anything like the elected legislatures and municipal governments of colonial British America, the drafters of Latin American constitutions were less conbelonged to a class of small shopkeepers, many of whom vend their wares at home, but the greater number send them about in this way, as in itinerant shops. A few of these people were still in a state of bondage, and brought a certain sum every evening to their owners, as the produce of their daily labour. But a large proportion, I was informed, were free, and exercised this little calling on their own account. They were all very neat and clean in their persons, and had a decorum and sense of respectability about them, superior to whites of the same class and calling. All their articles were good in their kind, and neatly kept, and they sold them with simplicity and confidence, neither wishing to take advantage of others, nor suspecting that it would be taken of themselves. I bought some confectionary from one of the females, and I was struck with the modesty and propriety of her manner; she was a young mother, and had with her a neatly dressed child, of which she seemed very fond. I gave it a little comfit [candy covered nut], and it turned up its dusky countenance to her and then to me, taking my sweetmeat, and at the same time kissing my hand. As yet unacquainted with the coin of the country, I had none that was current about me, and was leaving the articles; but the poor young woman pressed them on me with a ready confidence, repeating in broken Portuguese, out of tempo, I am sorry to say, the "other time" never came, for I could not recognize her person afterwards to discharge her little debt, though I went to the same place for the purpose.

It soon began to grow dark, and I was attracted by a number of persons bearing large lighted wax tapers, like torches, gathering before a house. As I passed by, one was put into my hand by a man who seemed in some authority, and I was requested to fall into a procession that was forming. It was the preparation for a funeral, and on such occasions, I learned that they always request the attendance of a passing stranger, and feel hurt if they are refused. I joined the party, and proceeded with them to a neighbouring church. When we entered we arranged ourselves on each side of a platform which stood near the choir, on which was laid an open coffin, covered with pink silk and gold borders. The funeral service was chanted by a choir of priests, one of whom was a negro, a large comely man, whose jet black visage formed a strong and striking contrast to his white vestments. He seemed to perform his part with a decorum and sense of solemnity, which I did not observe in his brethren. After scattering flowers on the coffin, and fumigating it with incense, they retired, the procession dispersed, and we returned on board. I had been but a few hours on shore, for

the first time, and I saw an African negro under four aspects of society; and it appeared to me, that in every one his character depended on the state in which he was placed, and the estimation in which he was held. As a despised slave, he was far lower than other animals of burthen that surrounded him; more miserable in his look, more revolting in his nakedness, more distorted in his person, and apparently more deficient in intellect than the horses and mules that passed him by. Advanced to the grade of a soldier, he was clean and neat in his person, amenable to discipline, expert at his exercises, and showed the port [sic.] and being of a white man similarly placed. As a citizen, he was remarkable for the respectability of his appearance, and the decorum of his manners in the rank assigned him; and as a priest, standing in the house of God, appointed to instruct society on their most important interests, and in a grade in which moral and intellectual fitness is required, and a certain degree of superiority is expected, he seemed even more devout in his impressions, and more correct in his manners, than his white associates. I came, therefore, to the irresistible conclusion in my mind, that colour was an accident affecting the surface of a man, and having no more to do with his qualities than his clothes—that God had equally created an African in the image of his person, and equally given him an immortal soul; and that an European had no pretext but his own cupidity, for impiously thrusting his fellow man from that rank in the creation which the Almighty had assigned him, and degrading him below the lot of the brute beasts that perish.

QUESTIONS FOR ANALYSIS

1. **What is the author's first impression of the Brazilian slave population?**

2. **What does the author later observe that changes this opinion?**

3. **How did slavery dehumanize slaves?**

4. **What circumstances or opportunities permitted Brazil's free blacks to improve their lives?**

Source: Robert Edgar Conrad, *Children of God's Fire: A Documentary History of Black Slavery in Brazil* (Princeton, N.J.: Princeton University Press, 1983), 216–220. Reprinted by permission of the author.

Creating Latin American Nations

strained by practical political experience. As a result, many of the new Latin American nations experimented with untested political institutions.

Latin American nations found it particularly difficult to define the role of the Catholic Church after independence. In the colonial period the Catholic Church was a religious monopoly that controlled all levels of education and dominated intellectual life. Many early constitutions aimed to reduce this power by making education secular and by permitting other religions. The church reacted by organizing and financing conservative movements. Conflicts between liberals who sought the separation of church and state and conservatives who supported the church dominated political life in the nineteenth century.

MAP 24.2 **Dominion of Canada, 1873** Although independence was not yet achieved and settlement remained concentrated along the U.S. border, Canada had established effective political and economic control over its western territories by 1873.

Interactive Map

Limiting the power of the military was another obstacle to the creation of constitutional governments in Latin America. The wars for independence elevated the prestige of military leaders, and, when the wars were over, military commanders seldom proved willing to subordinate themselves to civilian authorities. Frustrated by the chaotic workings of democracy, many citizens saw dictatorship as a better protection for their lives and property.

Personalist Leaders

personalist leaders Political leaders who rely on charisma and their ability to mobilize and direct the masses of citizens outside the authority of constitutions and laws. Nineteenth-century examples include José Antonio Páez of Venezuela and Andrew Jackson of the United States. Twentieth-century examples include Getulio Vargas of Brazil and Juan Perón of Argentina.

Two Personalist Leaders: Jackson and Páez

Patriot leaders in both the United States and Latin America gained mass followings during the wars for independence, and some used these followings to gain political power. George Washington's ability to dominate early republican politics in the United States anticipated the later political ascendancy of revolutionary heroes such as Iturbide in Mexico and Bolívar in Gran Colombia. In each case, military reputation provided the foundation for personal political power. Washington was distinguished from these leaders by his willingness to surrender power. More commonly, **personalist leaders** relied on their mass followings rather than on constitutions and laws to govern. In Latin America, a personalist leader who gained and held political power without constitutional sanction was called a *caudillo* (kouh-DEE-yoh).

Powerful personal followings allowed **Andrew Jackson** of the United States and **José Antonio Páez** (hoe-SAY an-TOE-nee-oh PAH-ays) of Venezuela to challenge constitutional limits to their authority. During the independence wars in Venezuela and Colombia, Páez (1790–1873) was one of Bolívar's most successful generals. Like most of his followers, Páez was uneducated and poor, but his physical strength, courage, and guile made him a natural guerrilla leader and helped him build a powerful political base. Páez described his authority in the following manner: "[The soldiers] resolved to confer on me the supreme command and blindly to obey my will, confident . . . that I was the only one who could save them."[2] Able to count on the personal loyalty of his followers, Páez was seldom willing to accept the constitutional authority of a distant president.

Andrew Jackson First president of the United States to be born in humble circumstances. He was popular among frontier residents, urban workers, and small farmers. He had a successful political career as judge, general, congressman, senator, and president. After being denied the presidency in 1824 in a controversial election, he won in 1828 and was reelected in 1832.

José Antonio Páez Venezuelan soldier who led Simón Bolívar's cavalry force. He became a successful general in the war and built a powerful political base. Unwilling to accept the constitutional authority of Bolívar's government in distant Bogotá, he declared Venezuela's independence from Gran Colombia in 1829.

After defeating the Spanish, Bolívar pursued his dream of forging a union of former Spanish colonies modeled on the United States. But he underestimated the strength of nationalist sentiment unleashed by the independence wars. Páez and other Venezuelan leaders resisted the surrender of their hard-won power to Bolívar's Gran Colombian government in distant Bogotá. When political opponents challenged Bolívar in 1829, Páez declared Venezuela's independence. Merciless to his enemies and indulgent with his followers, Páez ruled the country as president or dictator for the next eighteen years. Despite implementing an economic program favorable to the elite, Páez remained popular with the masses. Even as his personal wealth grew, Páez took care to present himself as a common man.

Andrew Jackson (1767–1845) was the first U.S. president born in humble circumstances. A self-made man who eventually acquired substantial property and owned over a hundred slaves, Jackson was extremely popular among frontier residents, urban workers, and small farmers. Although he was notorious for his untidy personal life as well as for dueling, his courage, individualism, and willingness to challenge authority helped him attain political success as judge, general, congressman, senator, and president.

During his military career, Jackson proved to be impatient with civilian authorities. Widely known because of his victories over the Creek and Seminole peoples, he was elevated to the pinnacle of American politics by his celebrated defeat of the British at the Battle of New Orleans in 1815 and by his seizure of Florida from the Spanish in 1818. In 1824 he received a plurality of the popular votes for president but failed to win a majority of electoral votes. His followers were embittered when the House of Representatives chose John Quincy Adams as president.

Jackson's followers viewed his landslide election victory in 1828 and reelection in 1832 as the triumph of democracy over entrenched aristocracy. In office Jackson challenged constitutional limits on his authority, increasing presidential power at the expense of Congress and the Supreme Court. Like Páez, Jackson was able to dominate national politics by blending a populist political style that celebrated the virtues and cultural enthusiasms of common people with support for policies that promoted the economic interests of powerful propertied groups.

Personalist leaders were common in both Latin America and the United States, but Latin America's weaker constitutional tradition, more limited protection of property rights, lower literacy levels, and less-developed communications systems facilitated the ambitions of popular politicians. Latin America's personalist leaders often ignored constitutional restraints on their authority, and election results seldom determined access to presidential power. As a result, by 1900 every Latin American nation had experienced periods of dictatorship.

The Threat of Regionalism

After independence, national governments were generally weaker than the colonial governments they replaced. Debates over tariffs, tax and monetary policies, and, in many nations, slavery and the slave trade led regional elites to attempt secession. Some of the hemisphere's newly independent nations did not survive these struggles, while others lost territories to aggressive neighbors.

In Spanish America all postindependence efforts to forge large multistate federations failed. The Viceroyalty of New Spain included Central America and Mexico, but after independence this union failed when in 1823 local elites broke with Mexico to form the Republic of Central America. A new round of regional disputes and civil wars led to the creation of five separate nations during the 1820s and 1830s. In South America, Bolívar attempted to maintain the colonial unity of Venezuela, Colombia, and Ecuador by creating Gran Colombia with its capital in Bogotá. But even before his death in 1830, Venezuela and Ecuador had become independent states. In the colonial era Argentina, Uruguay, Paraguay, and Bolivia were organized as a single viceroyalty with its capital in Buenos Aires. After the defeat of Spain the leaders in Paraguay, Uruguay, and Bolivia declared their independence from Argentina.

Regionalism threatened the United States as well. The defense of state and regional interests played an important role in the framing of the U.S. Constitution. Many important constitutional provisions represented compromises forged among competing state and regional leaders. Yet, despite these constitutional compromises, regional rivalries still threatened the nation.

Slavery divided the nation into two separate and competitive societies. A rising tide of immigration to the northern states in the 1830s and 1840s began to move the center of political power away from the south. Southern leaders sought to protect slavery by expanding into new territories. They supported the Louisiana Purchase in 1803 (see Map 24.3), which transferred to the United States a vast French territory extending from the Gulf of Mexico to Canada, and the Mexican-American War in 1846. However, this territorial expansion forced a national debate about slavery that led to the election of Abraham Lincoln as president in 1860.

Lincoln was committed to checking the spread of slavery, and his election provoked the southern planter elite to choose the dangerous course of secession from the Union. The seceding states formed a new government, the Confederate States of America, known as the Confederacy. Lincoln preserved the Union but at an enormous cost. The U.S. Civil War (1861–1865) was the most destructive conflict in the history of the Western Hemisphere. More than 600,000 lives were lost before the Confederacy surrendered in 1865. The Union victory led to the abolition of slavery and also transferred national political power to a northern elite committed to industrial expansion and federal support for the construction of railroads and other internal improvements.

e Interactive Map

MAP 24.3   **Territorial Growth of the United States, 1783–1853**   The rapid western expansion of the United States resulted from aggressive diplomacy and warfare against Mexico and Amerindian peoples. Railroad development helped integrate the trans-Mississippi west and promote economic expansion.

© Cengage Learning

The Confederate States of America was better prepared politically and economically for independence than were the successful secessionist movements that broke up Gran Colombia and other Spanish American federations. Nevertheless, the Confederacy failed, in part because of poor timing. The new nations of the Western Hemisphere were most vulnerable to secessionist movements in the early years of their existence; indeed, all the successful secessions occurred shortly after independence. In the case of the United States, an experienced national government legitimated and strengthened by more than seven decades of relative stability and reinforced by dramatic economic and population growth defeated secession only with enormous effort.

Foreign Interventions and Regional Wars

Wars often determined national borders, access to natural resources, and control of markets in the Western Hemisphere. Even after the achievement of independence, Mexico and other Western Hemisphere nations had to defend themselves against Europe's great powers. Contested national borders and regional rivalries also led to wars between Western Hemisphere nations. By the end of the nineteenth century the United States, Brazil, Argentina, and Chile had all successfully waged wars against their neighbors and established themselves as regional powers.

Wars with European Powers

Within thirty years of independence, the United States fought a second war with England—the War of 1812. The burning of the White House and Capitol by British troops in 1814 symbolized the weakness of the new republic. By the end of the nineteenth century, however, the United States was the hemisphere's greatest military power. Its war against Spain in 1898–1899 created an American empire that reached from the Philippines in the Pacific Ocean to Puerto Rico in the Caribbean Sea (see Chapter 28).

European powers also challenged the sovereignty of Latin American nations. Following independence Argentina faced British and French naval blockades, and British naval forces systematically violated Brazil's territorial waters to stop the importation of slaves. Mexico faced the most serious threats to sovereignty, defeating a weak Spanish invasion in 1829, a French assault on the city of Veracruz in 1838, and a French invasion in 1862.

Threats to Mexican Sovereignty

Mexico also faced a grave threat from the United States. In the 1820s Mexico had encouraged Americans to immigrate to its northern province of Texas. By the early 1830s Americans outnumbered Mexican nationals in Texas and were aggressively challenging Mexican laws such as

Execution of Emperor Maximilian of Mexico This painting by Edouard Manet shows the 1867 execution by firing squad of Maximilian and two of his Mexican generals. The defeat of the French intervention was a great triumph for Mexican patriots led by Benito Juárez.

Erich Lessing/Art Resource, NY

the prohibition of slavery. An alliance of Mexican liberals and American settlers rebelled in 1835 and gained its independence in 1836. In 1845 the United States made Texas a state, provoking war with Mexico a year later. The surrender of Mexico City in 1848 to American forces compelled Mexico to accept a harsh treaty that forced it to cede vast territories to the United States, including present-day New Mexico, Arizona, and California. In return Mexico received $15 million. When gold was discovered in California in 1848, the magnitude of Mexico's loss became clear.

With the very survival of the nation at stake, Mexico's liberals took power and imposed sweeping reforms, including a new constitution in 1857 that limited the power of the Catholic Church and military. This provoked a civil war with conservatives (1858–1861). **Benito Juárez** (beh-NEE-toh WAH-rez) assumed the presidency and defeated the conservatives, who then turned to Napoleon III of France for assistance. In 1862, French forces invaded Mexico, forced Juárez to flee Mexico City, and installed the Austrian Habsburg Maximilian as emperor of Mexico. After years of warfare, Juárez drove the French army out of Mexico in 1867, aided by U.S. diplomatic pressure. After capturing Maximilian, Juárez ordered his execution.

This victory over a powerful foreign enemy redeemed a nation earlier humiliated by the United States. But the creation of democracy proved more elusive than the protection of Mexican sovereignty. Despite the Mexican constitution's prohibition of presidential reelection, Juárez would serve as president until his death in 1872.

As was clear in the Mexican-American War, wars between Western Hemisphere nations could lead to dramatic territorial changes. Chile established itself as the leading military and economic power on the west coast of South America when it fought two successful wars against an alliance of Peru and Bolivia (1836–1839 and 1879–1883). The second contest, the War of the Pacific, forced Bolivia to cede its only outlet to the sea and Peru to yield rich mining districts.

Argentina and Brazil fought for control of Uruguay in the 1820s, but a military stalemate eventually forced them to recognize Uruguayan independence. Then, in 1865, Argentina and Uruguay joined Brazil to wage war against Paraguay (War of the Triple Alliance). After five years of warfare, the Paraguayan dictator Francisco Solano López (fran-CEES-co so-LAN-oh LOH-pehz) and more than 20 percent of the nation's population had died. Paraguay then experienced military occupation, loss of territory, and economic penalties.

Native Peoples and the Nation-State

Both diplomacy and war shaped relations between the Western Hemisphere's new nation-states and indigenous peoples. During late colonial times, Spanish, Portuguese, and British colonial governments attempted to restrict the expansion of settlements into territories occupied by Amerindians. With independence, the colonial powers' role as mediator and protector ended.

Still-independent Amerindian peoples posed a significant military challenge to many Western Hemisphere republics. Weakened by civil wars and constitutional crises, new nations were less able to maintain frontier peace than the colonial governments they replaced. After independence Amerindian peoples in Argentina, the United States, Chile, and Mexico succeeded in pushing back frontier settlements. Despite early victories, native military resistance was overcome by 1890.

After the American Revolution, tens of thousands of settlers entered territories previously guaranteed to Amerindians by treaties with Britain. Indigenous leaders responded by forging military alliances with British officials in Canada and with other native peoples. In the Ohio River Valley two Shawnee brothers, **Tecumseh** (teh-CUM-sah) and Prophet (Tenskwatawa), created a broad, well-organized alliance among Amerindian peoples that gained British support. During the War of 1812, American military forces defeated the alliance. Tecumseh died in battle fighting alongside his British allies.

Throughout the 1820s native peoples lost lands to settlers across the Midwest and Southeast. The 1828 presidential election of Andrew Jackson, a veteran of earlier wars against native peoples, brought matters to a head. The Indian Removal Act of 1830 forced the resettlement of Cherokee, Creek, Choctaw, and other eastern peoples to land west of the Mississippi River. Nearly half these forced migrants died on this journey, known as the Trail of Tears.

The native peoples of the Great Plains offered formidable resistance to the expansion of white settlement. By the time substantial numbers of white buffalo hunters, cattlemen, and

Benito Juárez President of Mexico (1858–1872). Born in poverty in Mexico, he was educated as a lawyer and rose to become chief justice of the Mexican supreme court and then president. He led Mexico's resistance to a French invasion in 1862 and the installation of Maximilian as emperor.

Wars Among American Nations

The United States and Native Peoples

Tecumseh Shawnee leader who attempted to organize an Amerindian confederacy to prevent the loss of additional territory to American settlers. He became an ally of the British in War of 1812 and died in battle.

National Anthropological Archives, Smithsonian Institution, SPC BAE 4420 Vol 6 01007800

Navajo Leaders Gathered in Washington to Negotiate   As settlers pushed west in the nineteenth century, Amerindian peoples were forced to negotiate territorial concessions with the U.S. government. This photo shows Navajo leaders and their Anglo translators in Washington, D.C., in 1874.

settlers reached the American west, indigenous peoples were skilled in the use of horses and firearms. These technologies allowed the Sioux, Comanche, Pawnee, Kiowa, and other plains peoples to hunt more efficiently and develop potent military capacities.

After the Civil War a new wave of settlers pushed onto the plains. Buffalo herds were hunted to near extinction and native lands lost to farmers and ranchers. Amerindian resistance led to four decades of armed conflict with the United States Army. The U.S. government forced the Comanche, who had long dominated the southern plains, to cede their traditional lands in Texas in 1865. The Sioux and their allies held out longer, overwhelming General George Armstrong Custer and the Seventh Cavalry in the Battle of Little Bighorn in 1876, but they were also soon forced to accept reservation life. Military campaigns in the 1870s and 1880s then broke the resistance of the Apache.

Defeat of the Amerindians of Argentina and Chile

The indigenous peoples of Argentina and Chile experienced a similar trajectory of adaptation, resistance, and defeat. Herds of wild cattle provided these peoples with a limitless food supply, and their mastery of the horse increased their military capacities. For a while the natives of Argentina and Chile were able to check the southern expansion of agriculture and ranching. Unable to defeat these resourceful enemies, the governments of Argentina and Chile relied on an elaborate system of gift giving and prisoner exchanges to maintain peace on the frontier.

By the 1860s, however, population increase, political stability, and military modernization allowed Argentina and Chile to take the offensive. In the 1870s the government of Argentina used a large military force armed with modern weapons to crush native resistance on the pampas. In the 1850s, civil war and an economic depression weakened the Chilean government, and the Mapuches (mah-POO-chez) (also called "Araucanians") pushed back frontier settlements, but by the 1870s Chilean forces had overwhelmed Amerindian resistance.

In Chile, Argentina, and the United States, national governments justified military campaigns by demonizing native peoples. Newspaper editorials and the speeches of politicians

Caste War A rebellion of the Maya people against the government of Mexico in 1847 that nearly returned the Yucatán to Maya rule. Some Maya rebels retreated to unoccupied territories, where they held out until 1901.

portrayed Amerindians as brutal and cruel, and as obstacles to progress. In April 1859 a Chilean newspaper commented:

> *The necessity, not only to punish the Araucanian [Mapuche] race, but also to make it impotent to harm us, is well recognized . . . as the only way to rid the country of a million evils. It is well understood that they are odious and prejudicial guests in Chile . . . conciliatory measures have accomplished nothing with this stupid race—the infamy and disgrace of the Chilean nation.*[3]

Political divisions and civil wars within the new nations also provided opportunities for some long-pacified native peoples to rebel. In the Yucatán region of Mexico, large landowners forced many Maya (MY-ah) communities from traditional agricultural lands, reducing thousands to peonage. Weakened by internal rebellions and by the American invasion, the Mexican government faced a mass rebellion by the Maya in 1847. This well-organized and popular uprising, known as the **Caste War**, nearly returned the Yucatán to native control. Grievances accumulated over more than three hundred years led to great violence and property destruction. The end of the war with the United States allowed the government of Mexico to regain control of major towns. Even then, some Maya rebels retreated to unoccupied territories and created an independent state, which they called the "Empire of the Cross." Organized around a mix of traditional beliefs and Christian symbols, this indigenous state resisted Mexican forces until 1870. A few Maya strongholds survived until 1901.

SECTION REVIEW

- The new nations of the Western Hemisphere, including the United States, found it difficult to establish constitutional governments.

- Charismatic military leaders with large followings, like Andrew Jackson and José Antonio Páez, often took power and challenged constitutional limits on presidential power.

- Secessionist movements and civil wars threatened the survival of many Latin American nations and the United States.

- Wars with foreign powers and neighboring states endangered the independence and national borders of many Western Hemisphere nations.

- Native peoples throughout the hemisphere tried to defend their territories, but by the end of the nineteenth century, national governments had overcome native resistance.

THE CHALLENGE OF SOCIAL AND ECONOMIC CHANGE

During the nineteenth century the newly independent nations of the Western Hemisphere struggled to realize the Enlightenment ideals of freedom and individual liberty that had helped ignite the revolutions for independence. The persistence of slavery and other oppressive colonial-era institutions slowed this process. Nevertheless, by century's end reform movements had ended the slave trade, abolished slavery, expanded voting rights, and assimilated immigrants from Asia and Europe.

Industrialization and integration in the world economy sometimes challenged political stability and social arrangements. While a small number of Western Hemisphere nations embraced industrialization, most were dependent on the export of agricultural and mining production. By the end of the century it was clear that the industrializing nations had grown richer than the nations that remained exporters of raw materials. All the region's economies, regardless of development path, had become more vulnerable and volatile as a result of greater dependence on foreign markets. Like contemporary movements for social reform, efforts to assert economic sovereignty produced powerful new political forces.

The Abolition of Slavery

Leaders of the independence movements of the United States and Latin America asserted ideals of universal freedom and citizenship that contrasted sharply with the reality of slavery. Those

abolitionists Men and women who agitated for a complete end to slavery. Abolitionist pressure ended the British transatlantic slave trade in 1808 and slavery in British colonies in 1834. In the United States the activities of abolitionists were one factor leading to the Civil War (1861–1865).

Abolition in the United States

who sought to end the institution were called **abolitionists**. Despite their efforts, slavery survived in most of the hemisphere until the 1850s. It proved most difficult to achieve the abolition of slavery in regions where the export of plantation products was most important—such as the United States, Brazil, and Cuba.

Slavery in the United States was weakened first by the abolition of slavery in some northern states and by the end of the African slave trade in 1808. But the profitable expansion of cotton agriculture after the War of 1812 stalled progress. In Spanish America tens of thousands of slaves gained freedom by joining revolutionary armies during the wars for independence. After independence, most Spanish American republics prohibited the slave trade, but growing international demand for sugar and coffee slowed the achievement of abolition. As prices rose for plantation products, Brazil and Cuba increased their imports of slaves.

During the long struggle to end slavery in the United States, American abolitionists argued that slavery offended Christian morality and the universal rights asserted in the Declaration of Independence. Abolitionist Theodore Weld articulated the religious objection to slavery in 1834:

> No condition of birth, no shade of color, no mere misfortune of circumstance, can annul the birth-right charter, which God has bequeathed to every being upon whom he has stamped his own image, by making him a free moral agent [emphasis in original], and that he who robs his fellow man of this tramples upon right, subverts justice, outrages humanity . . . and sacrilegiously assumes the prerogative of God.[4]

Two groups denied full rights under the Constitution, women and free African Americans, played important roles in the abolition of slavery. Women were among the leaders of the American Anti-Slavery Society and produced effective propaganda against slavery. Eventually, thousands of women joined the abolitionist cause. Social conservatives attacked their highly visible public role, leading many women to become public advocates of female suffrage as well. Frederick Douglass, a former slave, was one of the most visible and effective leaders of the abolitionist movement. Some black leaders, believing that peaceful means would fail, pushed the abolitionist movement to accept the inevitability of violence. In 1843 Henry Highland Garnet stirred the National Colored Convention when he demanded, "Brethren, arise, arise, arise! . . . Let every slave in the land do this and the days of slavery are numbered."[5]

In the 1850s the electoral strength of the newly formed Republican Party forced a confrontation between slave and free states. Following the election of Abraham Lincoln in 1860, eleven southern states seceded from the Union. During the Civil War pressure for emancipation rose as tens of thousands of black freemen and escaped slaves joined the Union army. In 1863, in the midst of the Civil War and two years after the abolition of serfdom in Russia (see Chapter 26), Lincoln issued the Emancipation Proclamation, ending slavery in rebel states not occupied by the Union army. In 1865 the Thirteenth Amendment to the Constitution abolished slavery completely, but most African Americans continued to live in harsh conditions. By the end of the century southern states had instituted "Jim Crow" laws that segregated blacks in public transportation, jobs, and schools. The implementation of these laws coincided with increased racial violence that saw an average of fifty African Americans lynched each year.

Abolition in Brazil

In Brazil slavery survived for more than two decades after abolition in the United States. Britain, Brazil's major trading partner, pressed for an end to the slave trade. Despite an 1830 agreement to end the trade, Brazil imported another half-million African slaves before the British navy forced compliance in the 1850s. The Brazilian emperor, Pedro II, and many liberals worked to abolish slavery, but their effort to find a form of gradual emancipation acceptable to slave owners failed.

During Brazil's war with Paraguay (1865–1870), large numbers of slaves joined the Brazilian army in exchange for freedom. Their patriotism and heroism convinced many Brazilians of the injustice of slavery. Educated Brazilians had also come to view slavery as an obstacle to economic development and an impediment to democratic reform. When political support for slavery weakened in the 1880s, growing numbers of slaves fled their masters and army officers resisted demands to capture and return the runaways. Brazil finally abolished slavery in 1888. A year later a rebellion ended the Brazilian monarchy.

Courtesy, Fundacao Biblioteca Nacional, Brazil

A Former Brazilian Slave Returns from Military Service The heroic actions of black freemen and slaves in the Paraguayan War (1865–1870) led many Brazilians to condemn slavery. The original caption for this drawing reads: "On his return from the war in Paraguay: Full of glory, covered with laurels, after having spilled his blood in defense of the fatherland and to free a people from slavery, the volunteer sees his own mother bound and whipped! Awful reality!"

Abolition in the Caribbean

The Caribbean region received almost 40 percent of all African slaves shipped to the New World. Throughout the region, tiny white minorities lived surrounded by slave and free colored majorities. In the eighteenth century the slave rebellion in Saint Domingue (see Chapter 22) spread terror among slave owners across the Caribbean, convincing slave owners that any effort to overthrow colonial rule would unleash new insurrection. As a result, there was little local support for abolition in the Caribbean. In these colonies abolition would result from decisions made in Europe by imperial governments.

In the Caribbean, as in Brazil and other plantation economies, slaves helped to force abolition by rebelling, running away, and resisting in more subtle ways. Although slave rebellions in Jamaica and Cuba and other Caribbean colonies failed to imitate the success of the Haitian Revolution (1791–1804), they made clear that slaves would never accept their condition.

After 1800, when the profitability of sugar plantations in the British West Indian colonies declined, a coalition of British labor unions, Protestant ministers, and free traders pushed for the abolition of slavery. Britain, the major participant in the eighteenth-century expansion of slavery in the Americas, ended its participation in the slave trade in 1807. It then negotiated treaties with Spain, Brazil, and other importers of slaves to eliminate the slave trade and used its naval forces to force compliance.

Abolition in British colonies occurred in 1834, but "freed" slaves were compelled to remain with former masters as "apprentices." Abuses by planters and resistance to apprenticeship by former slaves led to complete abolition in 1838. A decade later, France abolished slavery in its Caribbean colonies. Abolition of slavery in the Dutch Empire in 1863 freed 33,000 slaves in Surinam and 12,000 in the Antilles.

In the Caribbean, slavery lasted longest in Spain's remaining colonies of Cuba and Puerto Rico. Britain used diplomatic pressure and naval force to undermine the slave trade after 1820, but local support for abolition appeared as well. Both Cuba and Puerto Rico had larger white and free colored populations than did the Caribbean colonies of Britain and France, and there was little fear that abolition would lead to the political ascendancy of former slaves. In Puerto Rico, where slaves numbered approximately 30,000, local reformers secured the abolition of slavery in 1873. In Cuba, where slavery was much more important, forces supporting independence propelled the Spanish colonial government toward abolition. Beginning in the 1870s, Spain passed a series of laws promoting gradual abolition but requiring long periods of service to former masters. Spain finally abolished slavery in 1886.

Immigration

During the colonial period free Europeans were a minority among immigrants to the Western Hemisphere. From 1500 to 1760 African slaves entering the Western Hemisphere outnumbered European immigrants by nearly two to one. Another 4 million African slaves were imported before the end of the slave trade in the 1850s. After the African slave trade came to an end, millions of Europeans and Asians arrived in the Western Hemisphere as immigrants. These

Chinese Funeral in Vancouver, Canada In the 1890s Vancouver was an important destination for Chinese immigrants. This photo shows how an important element of traditional Chinese culture thrived among the storefronts and streetcar lines of the late-Victorian Canadian city.

Vancouver Public Library, Special Collections, VPL #17064

nineteenth-century immigrants helped foster the rapid economic growth and territorial occupation of frontier regions in the United States, Canada, Argentina, Chile, and Brazil. By century's end nearly all of the hemisphere's fastest-growing cities (Buenos Aires, Chicago, New York, and São Paulo, for example) had large immigrant populations. In general, European immigrants avoided regions that had depended on slavery with their tradition of repression and low wages. Tens of thousands of immigrants from China and India arrived with indenture contracts that directed them to plantation zones in the Caribbean.

European Immigration

Europe provided the majority of immigrants to the Western Hemisphere in the nineteenth century. Initially, most came from western Europe, but after 1870 most immigrants were southern or eastern Europeans. The United States received approximately 600,000 European immigrants in the 1830s, 1.5 million in the 1840s, and then 2.5 million per decade until 1880. In the 1890s an astonishing total of 5.2 million immigrants arrived. Immigration helped push national population from 39 million in 1871 to 63 million in 1891. Most of the immigrants settled in cities. Chicago, for example, grew from 444,000 in 1870 to 1.7 million in 1900.

European immigration to Latin America also increased dramatically. Combined immigration to Argentina and Brazil rose from under 130,000 in the 1860s to 1.7 million in the 1890s. By 1910, 30 percent of the Argentine population was foreign-born, more than twice the proportion in the U.S. population. Argentina was an extremely attractive destination for European immigrants, receiving more than twice as many immigrants as Canada between 1870 and 1930. Even so, immigration to Canada increased tenfold during this period.

Asian Immigration

Asian immigration to the Western Hemisphere also increased after 1850. Between 1849 and 1875, approximately 100,000 Chinese immigrants arrived in Peru and another 120,000 entered Cuba. Canada attracted about 50,000 Chinese immigrants in the second half of the century, and the United States received 300,000 immigrants between 1854 and 1882. India also contributed to the social transformation of the Western Hemisphere, sending more than a half-million immigrants to the Caribbean region. British Guiana alone received 238,000 immigrants, mostly indentured laborers, from the Asian subcontinent.

Anti-Immigrant Movements

Despite the obvious economic benefits that accompanied this inflow of people, hostility to immigration mounted in many nations. Nativist political movements argued that it was impossible to integrate large numbers of foreigners into national political cultures. By the end of the century, fear and prejudice led many governments in the Western Hemisphere to limit immigration or to distinguish between "desirable" and "undesirable" immigrants, commonly favoring Europeans over Asians.

Asians faced more obstacles than did Europeans and were more often victims of violence and discrimination. In the 1870s and 1880s anti-Chinese riots erupted in many western cities in the United States. Congress responded to this wave of racism by passing the Chinese Exclusion Act in 1882, which eliminated most Chinese immigration. In 1886 popular fears that "inferior races" threatened Canada led that government to impose a head tax, making immigration more difficult for Chinese families. During this same period strong anti-Chinese prejudice surfaced in Peru, Mexico, and Cuba. Japanese immigrants in Brazil and East Indians in the English-speaking Caribbean faced similar prejudice.

European immigrants faced prejudice and discrimination as well. Popular opinion portrayed Italians as criminals or anarchists. In Argentina and the United States, some social scientists argued that Italian immigrants were more violent and less honest than the native-born population. Immigrants from Spain were widely stereotyped in Argentina as miserly and dishonest. Eastern European Jews seeking to escape pogroms and discrimination at home found themselves barred from many educational institutions and professional careers in both the United States and Latin America. Irish, German, Swedish, Polish, and Middle Eastern immigrants received negative stereotypes as well. The justifications for these prejudices were remarkably similar from Canada to Argentina. Immigrants, critics claimed, threatened the well-being of native-born workers by accepting low wages and threatened national culture by resisting assimilation.

Many intellectuals and political leaders wondered if the evolving mix of culturally diverse populations could sustain a common citizenship. This concern led to efforts to compel immigrants to assimilate. Schools became cultural battlegrounds where language, cultural values, and patriotic attitudes were transmitted to the children of immigrants. Ignoring Canada's large French-speaking population, an English-speaking Canadian reformer commented on recent immigration: "If Canada is to become in a real sense a nation, if our people are to become one people, we must have one language."[6] These fears and prejudices promoted the singing of patriotic songs, the veneration of national flags and other symbols, and the writing of national histories that emphasized patriotism and civic virtue.

Arrest of Labor Activist in Buenos Aires The labor movement in Buenos Aires grew in numbers and became more radical with the arrival of tens of thousands of Italian and Spanish immigrants. Fearful of socialist and anarchist unions, the government of Argentina used an expanded police force to break strikes.

Archivo General de la Nación, Buenos Aires

American Cultures

Despite discrimination, immigrants continued to stream into the Western Hemisphere, where they introduced new languages, living arrangements, technologies, and customs. Immigrants also altered politics in many of the hemisphere's nations as they sought to influence government policies and gain access to power. To compensate for their isolation from home, language, and culture, most immigrant groups created ethnically based mutual aid societies, sports and leisure clubs, and neighborhoods. These organizations provided valuable social and economic support for recent arrivals while sometimes worsening the fears of the native-born that immigration posed a threat to national culture. At the same time, shared experiences in their adopted nations as workers, neighbors, or soldiers changed immigrants individually and collectively as well. The modification of language, customs, values, and behaviors as a result of contact with people from another culture is called **acculturation**.

Immigrants and their children, in turn, made their mark on the cultures of their adopted nations. They learned the language spoken in their adopted countries as fast as possible in order to improve their earning capacity, while words and phrases from their languages entered the vocabularies of the host nations. Languages as diverse as Yiddish and Italian strongly influenced American English, Argentine Spanish, and Brazilian Portuguese. Dietary practices introduced from Europe and Asia altered the cuisine of nearly every American nation. In popular music, the Argentine tango, based on African rhythms, was transformed by new instrumentation and orchestral arrangements brought by Italian immigrants. Mexican ballads blended with English folk music in the U.S. Southwest, and Italian operas played to packed houses in Buenos Aires.

Union movements and electoral politics in the hemisphere also felt the influence of new arrivals who aggressively sought to influence politics and improve working conditions. The anarchist and socialist beliefs of European immigrants influenced the labor movements of Mexico, Argentina, and the United States. Immigrants also helped form new political movements. Their mutual benevolent societies and less-formal ethnic associations pooled resources to help immigrants open businesses, aid the immigration of relatives, or bury family members.

Women's Rights and the Struggle for Social Justice

In 1848 a group of women angered by their exclusion from an international antislavery meeting issued a call for a conference to discuss women's rights. The resulting **Women's Rights Convention** at Seneca Falls, New York, issued a statement that said, in part, "We hold these truths to be self-evident: that all men and women are equal." While moderates focused on the issues of economic independence and legal rights, increasing numbers of women demanded the right to vote. Others lobbied to provide better conditions for women working outside the home, especially in textile factories. Sarah Grimké responded to criticism of women's activism:

> This has been the language of man since he laid aside the whip as a means to keep woman in subjection. He spares her body, but the war he has waged against her mind, her heart, and her soul, has been no less destructive to her as a moral being. How monstrous is the doctrine that woman is to be dependent on man![7]

Progress toward equality between men and women was equally slow in Canada and in Latin America. Canada's first women doctors received their training in the United States because women could not receive medical degrees until 1895. Argentina and Uruguay were among the first Latin American nations to provide public education for women, introducing coeducation in the 1870s. Chilean women gained access to some careers in medicine and law in the 1870s, while in Brazil the first women graduated in medicine in 1882. In Argentina the first woman doctor graduated from medical school in 1899.

Throughout the hemisphere more rapid progress occurred in lower-status careers that threatened male economic power less directly, and, by the end of the century, women dominated elementary school teaching. From Canada to Argentina and Chile, the majority of working-class women, although having no direct involvement in reform movements, succeeded in transforming gender relations in their daily lives. By the end of the nineteenth century, large numbers of poor women worked outside the home on farms, in markets, and, increasingly, in factories.

acculturation The adoption of the language, customs, values, and behaviors of host nations by immigrants.

The Immigrant Legacy

Women's Rights Convention An 1848 gathering of women angered by their exclusion from an international antislavery meeting. They met at Seneca Falls, New York, to discuss women's rights.

Access to Education and the Professions

Many bore full responsibility for providing for their children. Whether men thought women should remain in the home or not, by the end of the century women were unambiguously present in the economy (see also Chapter 27).

The Search for Racial Justice

There was little progress toward eliminating racial discrimination in the nineteenth century. Blacks were denied the vote throughout the southern United States and were subjected to the indignity of segregation—consigned to separate schools, hotels, restaurants, seats in public transportation, and even water fountains. Racial discrimination against men and women of African descent was also common in Latin America. Unlike the southern states of the United States, however, Latin American nations did not insist on formal racial segregation or permit lynching. Nor did they enforce a strict color line. Many men and women of mixed background were able to enter the skilled working class or middle class. Latin Americans tended to view racial identity across a continuum of physical characteristics rather than in the narrow terms of black and white that defined race relations in the United States.

The abolition of slavery in Latin America did not end discrimination. Some leaders of the abolition struggles later organized to promote racial integration. They demanded access to education, the right to vote, and greater economic opportunity, pointing out the economic and political costs of denying full rights to all citizens. Their success depended on effective political organization and on forging alliances with sympathetic white politicians. Black intellectuals also struggled to overturn racist stereotypes. In Brazil, Argentina, and Cuba, as in the United States, political and literary magazines celebrating black cultural achievement became powerful weapons in the struggle against racial discrimination. While men and women of African descent continued to experience prejudice and discrimination everywhere in the Americas, successful men and women of mixed descent in Latin America confronted fewer obstacles to advancement than did similar groups in the United States.

Development and Underdevelopment

While the Atlantic economy experienced three periods of severe economic contraction during the nineteenth century, nearly all the nations of the Western Hemisphere were richer in 1900 than in 1800. The Industrial Revolution, worldwide population growth, and an increasingly integrated world market stimulated economic expansion (see Environment and Technology: Constructing the Port of Buenos Aires, Argentina). Wheat, corn, wool, meats, and nonprecious minerals joined the region's earlier exports of silver, sugar, dyes, coffee, and cotton. The United States was the only Western Hemisphere nation to industrialize, but nearly every government promoted new industries and technologies. Governments invested in roads, railroads, canals, and telegraph systems to better serve distant markets, while adopting tariff and monetary policies to foster economic diversification and growth. Despite these efforts, by 1900 only three Western Hemisphere nations—the United States, Canada, and Argentina—achieved individual income levels similar to those of western Europe. All three nations had open land, temperate climates, diverse resources, and large inflows of immigrants.

New demands for copper, zinc, lead, coal, and tin unleashed by the Industrial Revolution led to mining booms in the western United States, Mexico, and Chile. The mining companies of the late nineteenth century were heavily capitalized international corporations that could bully governments and buy political favors. European and North American corporations owned nearly all the largest mining enterprises in Latin America. Petroleum development, which occurred at the end of the century in Mexico and elsewhere, followed this pattern as well (see the discussion of the Mexican economy during the Díaz dictatorship in Chapter 31).

The Role of Technology

New technology accelerated economic integration, but the high cost of this technology often increased dependence on foreign capital. Many governments promoted railroads by granting tax benefits, free land, and monopoly rights to both domestic and foreign investors. As a result, by 1890 vast areas of the Great Plains in the United States, the Canadian prairie, the Argentine pampas, and parts of northern Mexico were producing grain and livestock for foreign markets opened by the development of railroads. Steamships also lowered the cost of transportation to

Constructing the Port of Buenos Aires, Argentina

Located on the banks of the Río de la Plata, Buenos Aires had been a major commercial center and port since the late eighteenth century. But Buenos Aires was not a natural harbor. Because of the shallowness of the river, the largest oceangoing ships were forced to anchor hundreds of yards offshore while goods and passengers were unloaded by small boats or by specially built ox carts with huge wheels. Smaller vessels docked at a river port to the city's south.

By the 1880s the Argentine economy was transformed by the growing demands of European consumers for meat and grain. As exports surged and land values exploded, the wages of Argentines rose, and the nation became a favored destination for European immigrants. Argentina was becoming the wealthiest nation in Latin America.

The nation's political and economic elites decided that future growth required the modernization and expansion of port facilities. They debated two competing plans. The first emphasized the incremental expansion and dredging of the river port and was supported by local engineers and political groups suspicious of foreign economic interests. The second, and ultimately successful, plan involved dredging a port and deepwater channel from the low mud flats near the city center. Argentine economic interests closely tied to the European export trade and national political leaders who believed progress and prosperity required the imitation of European models supported this more expensive plan, which relied on British engineering firms, British banks, and British technology. The British were also Argentina's primary creditors, as well as developers of the nation's railroads, streetcar lines, and gas works.

The photograph shows the construction of Puerto Madero, the new port of Buenos Aires, in the 1890s. Recent immigrants provided most of the labor, and British experts dominated the engineering staff. The local elite found their profits in real estate deals and commissions associated with construction. Puerto Madero opened in stages beginning in 1890. However, cost overruns and corruption stretched out completion to 1898. By 1910 arrivals and departures reached thirty thousand ships and 18 million tons, but design problems forced "improvements" into the 1920s.

Why had the government of Argentina chosen the costliest and most difficult design? Argentine politicians sought to demonstrate their nation's modernity and so chose the most complex and technologically sophisticated solution to the port problem. They also believed that British engineering and British capital were guarantees of modernity. While the new port facilities facilitated a boom in exports and imports and the huge public works budget did provide incomes for thousands of laborers, debts, design flaws, and the increased influence of foreign capital in Argentina left a legacy of problems. (See the discussion of Juan Perón in Chapter 31.)

Courtesy, Hack Hoffenburg

Excavation of Port of Buenos Aires, Argentina   Relying on foreign capital and engineering, the government of Argentina improved the port to facilitate the nation's rapidly expanding export economy.

distant markets, and the telegraph stimulated expansion by speeding information about the demand for and availability of products.

The simultaneous acquisition of several new technologies could have a dramatic effect. In Argentina the railroad, the telegraph, barbed wire, and refrigeration all appeared in the 1870s and 1880s. Although Argentina had had abundant livestock herds since the colonial period,

New Technologies Change the Mining Industry Powerful hydraulic technologies were introduced in western mining sites in the United States. This early photo shows how high-power water jets could transform the natural environment.

Image courtesy Colorado Historical Society

development In the nineteenth and twentieth centuries, the economic process that led to industrialization, urbanization, the rise of a large and prosperous middle class, and heavy investment in education.

Rich and Poor Nations

underdevelopment The condition experienced by economies that depend on colonial forms of production such as the export of raw materials and plantation crops with low wages and low investment in education.

the distance from Europe's markets prevented Argentine cattle raisers from exporting fresh meat or live animals. Technology overcame these obstacles. The combination of railroads and the telegraph lowered freight costs and improved information about markets. Steamships shortened trans-Atlantic crossings, and refrigerated ships made it possible to sell meat in distant markets. As land values rose and livestock breeding improved, ranchers protected new investments with barbed wire, the first inexpensive fencing available on the nearly treeless plains.

Growing interdependence and increased competition produced deep structural differences among Western Hemisphere economies by 1900. Two distinct economic tracks became visible. One led to industrialization and prosperity: **development**. The other continued colonial dependence on exporting raw materials and on low-wage industries: **underdevelopment**. By 1900 prosperity was greater and economic development more diversified in English-speaking North America than in the nations of Latin America. With a temperate climate, vast fertile prairies, and an influx of European immigrants, Argentina was the only Latin American nation to approach the prosperity of the United States and Canada.

Changes in the performance of international markets helped determine the trajectory of Western Hemisphere economies as new nations promoted economic development. When the United States gained independence, the world economy enjoyed rapid growth. With a large merchant fleet, a diversified economy that included some manufacturing, and adequate banking and insurance services, the United States benefited from this expansion. Rapid population growth due in large measure to immigration, high levels of individual wealth, widespread land-ownership, and relatively high literacy rates also fostered rapid economic development. In 1865 the United States had the world's largest railroad network, but by 1915, it had multiplied elevenfold (see Map 24.4). Steel production grew rapidly as well, with the United States overtaking Britain and Germany in the 1890s.

Canada's achievement of greater political autonomy, the Confederation of 1867, coincided with a second period of global economic expansion. Canada also benefited from a special trading relationship with Britain, the world's preeminent industrial nation, and from a rising tide

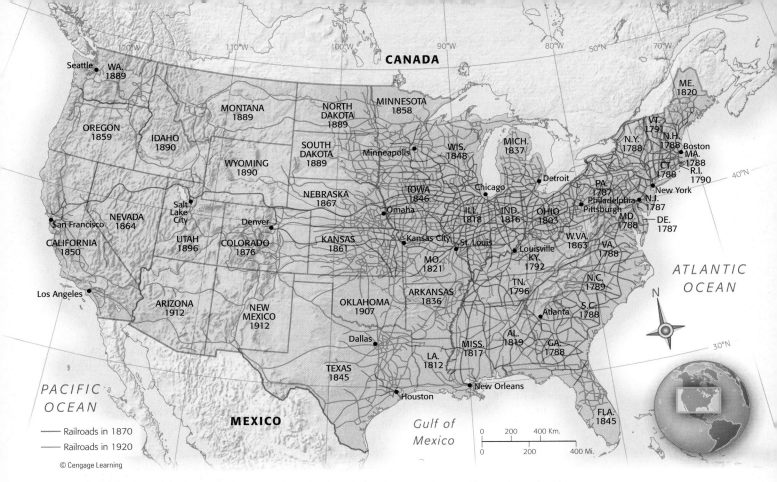

Seattle WA. 1889
OREGON 1859
IDAHO 1890
MONTANA 1889
NORTH DAKOTA 1889
MINNESOTA 1858
ME. 1820
WYOMING 1890
SOUTH DAKOTA 1889
Minneapolis
WIS. 1848
MICH. 1837
VT. 1791
N.H. 1788
N.Y. 1788 Boston
MA. 1788
San Francisco
NEVADA 1864
Salt Lake City
Denver
NEBRASKA 1867
Omaha
IOWA 1846
Chicago
Detroit
IND. 1816
OHIO 1803
Pittsburgh
PA. 1787
CT. 1788
R.I. 1790
New York
Philadelphia
N.J. 1787
CALIFORNIA 1850
UTAH 1896
COLORADO 1876
KANSAS 1861
Kansas City
St. Louis
ILL. 1818
MD. 1788
DE. 1787
W.VA. 1863
VA. 1788
Louisville
KY. 1792
MO. 1821
Los Angeles
ARIZONA 1912
NEW MEXICO 1912
OKLAHOMA 1907
ARKANSAS 1836
TN. 1796
N.C. 1789
Atlanta
S.C. 1788
Dallas
AL. 1819
MISS. 1817
GA. 1788
TEXAS 1845
LA. 1812
Houston
New Orleans
FLA. 1845

CANADA
MEXICO
PACIFIC OCEAN
ATLANTIC OCEAN
Gulf of Mexico
N

Railroads in 1870
Railroads in 1920
© Cengage Learning

0   200   400 Km.
0   200   400 Mi.

MAP 24.4 **The Expansion of the United States, 1850–1920** The settlement of western territories and their admission as states depended on migration, the exploitation of natural resources, and important new technologies like railroads and telegraphs that facilitated economic and political integration.

e Interactive Map

of immigrants after 1850. Nevertheless, some regions within each of these prosperous North American nations—Canada's Maritime Provinces and the southern part of the United States—demonstrated the same patterns of underdevelopment found in Latin America.

Most Latin American nations gained independence in the 1820s when the global economy contracted. In the colonial period, Spain and Portugal had promoted the production of agricultural and mining exports in their colonies. After independence these exports faced increased competition. Although these sectors experienced periods of great prosperity in the nineteenth century, they also faced stiff competition and falling prices as new regions began production or competing products captured markets.

The history of the Latin American economies, subject to periodic problems of oversupply and low prices, was one of boom and bust. Many Latin American governments sought to promote exports in the face of increased competition and falling prices by resisting union activity and demands for higher wages and by opening domestic markets to foreign manufactures. The resulting low wages and an abundance of foreign manufactured goods, in turn, undermined efforts to promote industrialization in Latin America.

Weak governments, political instability, and, in some cases, civil war also slowed Latin American economic development. Because Latin America was also dependent on importing foreign capital and technology, Great Britain and, by the end of the century, the United States often imposed unfavorable trade conditions or even intervened militarily to protect their investments. The combined impact of these domestic and international impediments to development became clear when Mexico, Chile, and Argentina failed to achieve high levels of domestic investment in manufacturing late in the nineteenth century, despite a rapid accumulation of wealth derived from traditional exports.

Altered Environments

Population growth, economic expansion, new technologies, and the introduction of foreign plants and animals had dramatically altered American environments. Cuba's planters cut down the island's forests in the early nineteenth century to expand sugar production. Growing demand for meat led ranchers to expand livestock-raising into fragile environments in Argentina, Uruguay, southern Brazil, and the southwestern United States. Other forms of commercial agriculture also threatened the environment. Farmers in South Carolina and Georgia gained a short-term increase in cotton production by abandoning crop rotation after 1870, but this practice quickly led to soil exhaustion and erosion. Similarly, coffee planters in Brazil exhausted fertility with a destructive cycle of overplanting followed by expansion onto forest reserves cleared by cutting and burning. The transfers of land from public to private ownership in order to promote livestock-raising and agriculture also altered landscapes. Finally, new technologies had environmental effects. For example, the use of steel plows on North American prairies and Argentine pampas eliminated many native grasses and increased the threat of soil erosion.

Rapid urbanization also imposed environmental costs. New York, Chicago, Rio de Janeiro, Buenos Aires, and Mexico City were among the world's fastest-growing cities in the nineteenth century, and governments strained to provide sewers, clean water, and garbage disposal. Timber companies clear-cut large areas of Michigan, Wisconsin, and the Appalachian Mountains in the United States to provide lumber for railroad ties and housing, pulp for paper, and fuel for locomotives and foundries. At the same time, the forest industries of British Honduras (now Belize), Nicaragua, and Guatemala grew rapidly in response to demand in Europe and North America for tropical hardwoods like mahogany. As forests throughout the hemisphere were cleared, animal habitats and native plant species disappeared.

The scale of mining in Nevada, Montana, and California accelerated erosion and pollution. Similar results occurred in other mining areas as well. Nitrate mining and open-pit copper mining in Chile scarred and polluted the environment. The state of Minas Gerais (ME-nas JER-aize) in Brazil experienced a series of mining booms that began with gold in the late seventeenth century and continued with iron ore in the nineteenth. By the end of the nineteenth century, its red soil had been ripped open, its forests depleted, and erosion uncontrolled. Similar devastation afflicted parts of Bolivia and Mexico.

By the end of the nineteenth century, small-scale conservation efforts were under way in many nations, and the first national parks and nature reserves were created. In the United States large areas remained undeveloped. In 1872 Yellowstone in Wyoming became the first national park. President Theodore Roosevelt (1901–1909) and the naturalist John Muir played major roles in preserving large areas of the western states. Canada created its first national park in Banff in 1885 and expanded it from 10 to 260 square miles (26 to 673 square kilometers) two years later. When confronted with a choice between economic growth and environmental protection, however, the hemisphere's nations embraced growth.

CONCLUSION

While the new nations of the Western Hemisphere faced similar challenges in the nineteenth century, they had developed from different colonial traditions. The effort to establish stable constitutional systems proved difficult nearly everywhere. While the constitution of the United States endured, conflict over slavery led to a civil war that threatened the nation's survival. Elsewhere most new constitutions failed within a generation. In Argentina, for example, fifty years passed before a stable national government was in place. Personalist political leaders with large followings, like José Antonio Páez and Andrew Jackson, resisted the constraints of constitutions. Regionalism, ideological confrontations, racial divisions, and conflict with native peoples all threatened stability as well.

New nations also faced foreign interventions and local wars with regional powers. By 1850 Mexico had lost 50 percent of its territory to the United States and then faced a French invasion in 1862. Bolivia and Peru lost territory to an expansive Chile, while Paraguay lost a disastrous war to an alliance of Argentina, Brazil, and Uruguay. The nations of the Americas also fought numerous wars with indigenous peoples, crushing resistance by the 1890s.

The nations of the hemisphere also experienced a series of dramatic social and economic changes in this period. The slave trade and slavery persisted long after independence (see Chapter 19) but after a century of protest and political mobilization, the hemisphere's last slave state, Brazil, freed its slaves in 1888. Slavery left a legacy of racism and discrimination across the Americas. In places where the institution was most important, the plantation regions of Brazil, the Caribbean, and the American South, racial prejudice, discrimination, and persistent low levels of investment in education and internal improvements slowed economic growth and weakened democracy. By 1890 many of the hemisphere's poorest nations or poorest regions within nations were those that had depended on slavery.

Amerindian populations experienced centuries of exploitation, forced integration in market economies, and compulsory removal to marginal lands. In most of Latin America, Amerindians had been subjected to exploitation for centuries when the Spanish and Portuguese empires finally fell. Once in place, forced labor and other abuses persisted in nations like Guatemala and Bolivia. With independence, new national governments undertook the pacification of the hemisphere's remaining independent native peoples. By the 1890s nearly all were reduced to reservations or forced onto marginal lands. As a result, Amerindians were among the poorest peoples in the hemisphere, suffering oppression, poverty, and disenfranchisement.

Immigration transformed many Western Hemisphere nations. As a general rule, the millions of European immigrants that entered the Western Hemisphere in the nineteenth century avoided regions where slavery dominated or where indigenous populations were compelled to labor. Argentina, Brazil, Canada, and the United States were the most popular destinations, and immigrants to Brazil and the United States avoided the former plantation zones. Instead, hundreds of thousands of Chinese and East Indians, migrating as indentured laborers, were directed to plantation regions, where they faced racism and discrimination.

Industrialization had a transforming effect on the hemisphere. Wealth, political power, and population were increasingly concentrated in urban areas, and bankers and manufacturers, rather than farmers and plantation owners, increasingly directed national destinies. Industrialization altered the natural environment in dramatic ways. Modern factories consumed huge amounts of raw materials and energy. Copper mines in Chile and Mexico, Cuban sugar plantations, Brazilian coffee plantations, and Canadian lumber companies all left their mark on the natural environment, and all had ties to markets in the United States.

In 1900 nearly every American nation was wealthier, better educated, more democratic, and more populous than at independence. But these nations were also more vulnerable to distant economic forces, more profoundly split between haves and have-nots, and more clearly divided into a rich north and a poorer south. A small number of nations located in the temperate regions—Canada, the United States, Argentina, and Chile—had become prosperous regional powers relative to their neighbors. While most of the hemisphere's growth continued to depend on the export of agricultural goods and raw materials—sugar, cotton, grains, minerals, and livestock products—the United States had become a major industrial nation by 1890.

KEY TERMS

Simón Bolívar p. 633

**Miguel Hidalgo y
  Costilla** p. 634

José María Morelos p. 636

**Confederation of
  1867** p. 638

personalist leaders p. 640

Andrew Jackson p. 641

José Antonio Páez p. 641

Benito Juárez p. 644

Tecumseh p. 644

Caste War p. 646

abolitionists p. 647

acculturation p. 651

**Women's Rights
  Convention** p. 651

development p. 654

underdevelopment p. 654

EBOOK AND WEBSITE RESOURCES

e Primary Source

The Jamaica Letter

e Interactive Maps

Map 24.1 Latin America by 1830

Map 24.2 Dominion of Canada, 1873

Map 24.3 Territorial Growth of the United States, 1783–1853

Map 24.4 The Expansion of the United States, 1850–1920

Plus flashcards, practice quizzes, and more. Go to:
www.cengage.com/history/bullietearthpeople5e

SUGGESTED READING

Andrews, George Reid. *Afro-Latin America, 1800–2000*. 2004. An excellent synthesis of the Latin American experience.

Barth, Gunther. *Bitter Strength: A History of Chinese in the United States, 1850–1870*. 1964. A reliable introduction to this topic.

Brands, H. W. *Andrew Jackson, His Life and Times*. 2005.

Burns, E. Bradford. *The Poverty of Progress: Latin America in the Nineteenth Century*. 1980. A useful examination of the politics of development.

Bushnell, David, and Neil Macaulay. *The Emergence of Latin America in the Nineteenth Century*. 1988.

Careless, J. M. S. *The Union of the Canadas: The Growth of Canadian Institutions, 1841–1857*. 1967.

Cronon, William. *Nature's Metropolis: Chicago and the Great West*. 1991. An excellent discussion of the environment during nineteenth-century development.

Crosby, Alfred. *Ecological Imperialism: The Biological Expansion of Europe, 900–1900*. 1986. A seminal study of environment.

Dean, Warren. *With Broadax and Firebrand: The Destruction of the Brazilian Atlantic Forest*. 1995.

Dickason, Olive Patricia. *Canada's First Nations*. 1993.

Du Bois, Ellen C. *Feminism and Suffrage: The Emergence of an Independent Woman's Movement in the Nineteenth Century*. 1984.

Ginzberg, Lori D. *Women and the Work of Benevolence: Morality, Politics, and Class in the Nineteenth-Century United States*. 1990.

Graden, Dale T. *From Slavery to Freedom in Brazil: Bahia, 1835–1900*. 2006.

Green, William A. *British Slave Emancipation: The Sugar Colonies and the Great Experiment, 1830–1865*. 1973.

Halperin-Donghi, Tulio. *The Contemporary History of Latin America*. 1993.

Kinsbruner, Jay. *Independence in Spanish America*, 2nd ed. 2000. The best short analysis of the independence period.

Kohl, Lawrence Frederick. *The Politics of Individualism: Parties and the American Character in the Jacksonian Era*. 1989.

Krech III, Shepard. *The Ecological Indian*. 1999.

Larson, John Lauritz. *Internal Improvement: National Public Works and the Promise of Popular Government in the Early United States*. 2001.

Martin, Ged, ed. *The Causes of Canadian Confederation*. 1990.

Miller, Francesca. *Latin American Women and the Search for Social Justice*. 1991.

Nugent, Walter. *Crossing: The Great Transatlantic Migrations, 1870–1914*. 1992.

Petulla, Joseph M. *American Environmental History*. 1973.

Quarles, Benjamin. *Black Abolitionists*. 1969.

Remini, Robert V. *Andrew Jackson and His Indian Wars*. 2001.

Rodriguez O., Jaime. *The Origins of Mexican National Politics*. 1997.

Scott, Rebecca. *Slave Emancipation in Cuba: The Transition to Free Labor, 1860–1899*. 1985.

Thomas, Victor Bulmer. *The Economic History of Latin America Since Independence*. 2003.

Worster, Donald. *Rivers of Empire: Water, Aridity, and the Growth of the American West*. 1985.

NOTES

1. Quoted in Lyman L. Johnson, "Spanish American Independence and Its Consequences," in *Problems in Modern Latin American History: A Reader*, ed. John Charles Chasteen and Joseph S. Tulchin (Wilmington, DE: Scholarly Resources, 1994), 21.

2. José Antonio Páez, *Autobiografía del General José Antonio Páez*, vol. 1 (New York: Hallety Breen, 1869), 83.

3. Quoted in Brian Loveman, *Chile: The Legacy of Hispanic Capitalism* (New York: Oxford University Press, 1979), 170.

4. Quoted in Bernard Bailyn, David Brion Davis, David Herbert Donald, John L. Thomas, Robert H. Wiebe, and Gordon S. Wood, *The Great Republic: A History of the American People* (Lexington, MA: D. C. Heath, 1981), 398.

5. Quoted in Mary Beth Norton et al., *A People and a Nation: A History of the United States*, 6th ed. (Boston: Houghton Mifflin, 2001), 284.

6. J. S. Woodsworth in 1909, quoted in R. Douglas Francis, Richard Jones, and Donald B. Smith, *Destinies: Canadian History Since Confederation*, 2nd ed. (Toronto: Holt, Rinehart and Winston, 1992), 141.

7. Sarah Grimké, "Reply to the Massachusetts Clergy," in *Early American Women: A Documentary History, 1600–1900*, ed. Nancy Woloch (Belmont, CA: Wadsworth, 1992), 343.

Peabody Essex Museum, Salem, Massachusetts/The Bridgeman Art Library

Trade Warehouse in Guangzhou   A European merchant enters in the background while Chinese workers pack tea and porcelain.

Visit the website and ebook for additional study materials and interactive tools: www.cengage.com/history/bullietearthpeople5e

Land Empires in the Age of Imperialism, 1800–1870

When the emperor of the Qing (ching) (the last empire to rule China) died in 1799, the imperial court received a shock. For decades officials had known that the emperor was indulging his handsome young favorite, Heshen (huh-shun), allowing him extraordinary privileges and power. Senior bureaucrats hated Heshen, suspecting him of overseeing a widespread network of corruption. They believed he had been scheming to prolong the inconclusive wars against the native Miao (mee-ow) peoples of southwest China in the late 1700s. Glowing reports of successes against the rebels had poured into the capital, and enormous sums of government money had flowed to the battlefields. But there was no adequate accounting for the funds, and the war persisted.

After the emperor's death, Heshen's enemies ordered his arrest. When they searched his mansion, they discovered a magnificent hoard of silk, furs, porcelain, furniture, and gold and silver. His personal cash alone exceeded what remained in the imperial treasury. The new emperor ordered Heshen to commit suicide with a rope of gold silk. The government seized Heshen's fortune, but the financial damage could not be undone. The declining agricultural base could not replenish the state coffers, and much of the income that did flow in was squandered by an increasingly corrupt bureaucracy. In the 1800s the Qing Empire faced increasing challenges from Europe and the United States with an empty treasury, a stagnant economy, and a troubled society.

The Qing Empire's problems were not unique. They were common to all the land-based empires of Eurasia, where old and inefficient ways of governing put states at risk. The international climate was increasingly dominated by industrializing European economies drawing on the wealth of their overseas colonies. During the early 1800s rapid population growth and slow agricultural growth affected much of Eurasia. In addition, earlier military expansion had stretched the resources of imperial treasuries (see Chapter 21), leaving the land-based empires vulnerable to European military pressure. Responses to this pressure varied, with reform and adaptation gaining headway in some lands and tradition being reasserted in others. In the long run, attempts to meet western Europe's economic and political demands produced financial indebtedness to France, Britain, and other Western powers.

This chapter contrasts the experiences of the Qing Empire with those of the Russian and Ottoman Empires. Whereas the Qing opted for resistance, the others

- What were the benefits and the drawbacks to the Ottoman Empire of the reforms adopted during the Tanzimat period?
- How did the Russian Empire maintain its status as both a European power and a great Asian land empire?
- How did the impact of European imperialism on China differ from its impact on Russia and the Ottoman Empire?

made varying attempts to adapt and reform. Russia eventually became part of Europe and shared in many aspects of European culture, while the Ottomans and the Qing became subject to ever-greater imperialist pressure. These different responses raise the question of the role of culture in shaping western Europe's relations with the rest of the world in the nineteenth century.

THE OTTOMAN EMPIRE

Fragmentation of Power

During the eighteenth century the central government of the Ottoman Empire lost much of its power to provincial governors, military commanders, ethnic leaders, and bandit chiefs. In several parts of the empire local officials and large landholders tried to increase their independence and divert imperial funds into their own coffers.

A kingdom in Arabia led by the Saud family, following the puritanical and fundamentalist religious views of an eighteenth-century leader named Muhammad ibn Abd al-Wahhab (moo-HAH-muhd ib-uhn ab-dahl-wa-HAHB), took control of the holy cities of Mecca and Medina and deprived the sultan of the honor of organizing the annual pilgrimage. In Egypt factions of mamluk slave-soldiers purchased as boys in Georgia and nearby parts of the Caucasus and educated for war reasserted their influence. Such soldiers had ruled Egypt between 1260 and 1517, when they were defeated by the Ottomans. Now Ottoman weakness allowed mamluk factions based on a revival of the slave-soldier tradition to reemerge as local military forces.

For the sultans, the outlook was bleak. At the end of the eighteenth century, the inefficient Janissary corps used the political power it enjoyed in Istanbul to force Sultan Selim III to abandon efforts to train a modern, European-style army. This situation unexpectedly changed when France invaded Egypt.

Egypt and the Napoleonic Example

Napoleon Bonaparte and an invasion force of 36,000 men and four hundred ships invaded Egypt in May 1798. The French quickly defeated the mamluk forces that for several decades had dominated the country under the loose jurisdiction of the Ottoman sultan in Istanbul. Fifteen months later, after being stopped by Ottoman land and British naval forces in an attempted invasion of Syria, Napoleon secretly left Cairo and returned to France. Three months later he seized power and made himself emperor.

Muhammad Ali

Muhammad Ali Leader of Egyptian modernization in the early nineteenth century. He ruled Egypt as an Ottoman governor but had imperial ambitions. His descendants ruled Egypt until overthrown in 1952.

Back in Egypt, his generals tried to administer a country that they only poorly understood. Cut off from France by British ships in the Mediterranean, they had little hope of remaining in power and agreed to withdraw in 1801. For the second time in three years, a collapse of military power produced a power vacuum in Egypt. The winner of the ensuing contest was **Muhammad Ali** (moo-HAM-mad AH-lee), the commander of a contingent of Albanian soldiers sent by the sultan to restore imperial control. By 1805 he had taken the place of the official Ottoman governor, and by 1811 he had dispossessed the mamluks of their lands and privileges.

Muhammad Ali's rise to power coincided with the meteoric career of Emperor Napoleon I. It is not surprising, therefore, that he adopted many French practices in rebuilding the Egyptian state. Militarily, he established special schools for training artillery and cavalry officers, army surgeons, military bandmasters, and others. The curricula of these schools featured European skills and sciences, and Muhammad Ali began to send promising officer trainees to France for education. In 1824 he started a gazette devoted to official affairs, the first newspaper in the Islamic world.

Reforms on European Models

As discussed in Chapter 23, Muhammad Ali built all sorts of factories to outfit his new army. These did not prove efficient enough to survive, but they showed a determination to achieve independence and parity with the European powers.

Egypt in Syria and Greece

In the 1830s Muhammad Ali's son Ibrahim invaded Syria and instituted some of the changes already under way in Egypt. The improved quality of the new Egyptian army had been proven during the Greek war of independence (see below), when Ibrahim had commanded an expeditionary force to help the sultan. In response, the sultan embarked on building his own new

CHRONOLOGY

	Ottoman Empire	Russian Empire	Qing Empire
			1794–1804 White Lotus Rebellion
1800		1801–1825 Reign of Alexander I	
	1805–1849 Muhammad Ali governs Egypt		
	1808–1839 Rule of Mahmud II	1812 Napoleon's retreat from Moscow	
		1825 Decembrist revolt	
	1826 Janissary corps dissolved	1825–1855 Reign of Nicholas I	
	1829 Greek independence		
	1839 Abdul Mejid begins Tanzimat reforms		1839–1842 Opium War
1850	1853–1856 Crimean War	1853–1856 Crimean War	1850–1864 Taiping Rebellion
		1855–1881 Reign of Alexander II	1856–1860 Arrow War
		1861 Emancipation of the serfs	
	1876 First constitution by an Islamic government		

army in 1826. The two armies met when Ibrahim attacked northward into Anatolia in 1839 and defeated the army of his suzerain, the Ottoman sultan. The road to Istanbul seemed open until the European powers intervened and forced a withdrawal to the present-day border between Egypt and Israel.

Muhammad Ali remained Egypt's ruler, under the suzerainty of the sultan, until his death in 1849; and his family continued to rule the country until 1952. But his dream of making Egypt a mighty country capable of standing up to Europe faded. What survived was the example he had set for the sultans in Istanbul.

Ottoman Reform and the European Model, 1807–1853

At the end of the eighteenth century Sultan Selim (seh-LEEM) III (r. 1789–1807), a forward-looking ruler who stayed abreast of events in Europe, introduced reforms to create European-style military units, bring provincial governors under central government control, and standardize taxation. The rise in government expenditures to implement the reforms was supposed to be offset by taxes on selected items, primarily tobacco and coffee.

The reforms failed for political more than economic reasons. The most violent and persistent opposition came from the **Janissary** (JAN-nih-say-ree) military corps (see Chapter 20). Originally Christian boys taken from their homes in the Balkans, converted to Islam, and required to serve for life in the Ottoman army, in the eighteenth century the Janissaries became a significant political force in Istanbul and in provincial capitals like Damascus and Aleppo. Their interest in preserving special economic privileges made them resist the creation of new military units.

At times, Janissary power produced military uprisings. In the Ottoman territory of **Serbia**, local residents intensely resented the control exercised by Janissary governors. The Orthodox Christians claimed that the Janissaries abused them. In response, Selim threatened to reassign the Janissaries to Istanbul. Suspecting that the sultan wanted to curb their political power, in 1805 the Janissaries revolted and massacred Christians in Serbia. Unable to reestablish central Ottoman rule over Serbia, the sultan had to rely on the ruler of Bosnia, another Balkan province, who joined his troops with the peasants of Serbia to suppress the Janissary uprising. The threat

Janissaries Infantry, originally of slave origin, armed with firearms and constituting the elite of the Ottoman army from the fifteenth century until the corps was abolished in 1826.

Janissary Problems

Serbia The Ottoman province in the Balkans that rose up against Janissary control in the early 1800s. After World War II the central province of Yugoslavia. Serb leaders struggled to maintain dominance as the Yugoslav federation dissolved in the 1990s.

MAP 25.1 **The Ottoman and Russian Empires, 1829–1914** At its height the Ottoman Empire controlled most of the perimeter of the Mediterranean Sea. But in the 1800s Ottoman territory shrank as many countries gained their independence. The Black Sea, where the Turkish coast was vulnerable to assault, became a weak spot as Russian naval power grew. Russian challenges to the Ottomans at the eastern end of the Black Sea and to the Persians east and west of the Caspian aroused fears in Europe that Russia was trying to reach the Indian Ocean.

Map legend:

The Ottoman Empire
- Territory lost, 1829–1877
- Territory lost, 1878–1813
- Ottoman Empire in 1914

The Russian Empire
- Russia in 1802
- Territory gained, by 1914

- Persia

© Cengage Learning

e Interactive Map

of Russian intervention prevented the Ottomans from disarming the victorious Serbians, so Serbia became effectively independent.

Other opponents of reform included ulama, or Muslim religious scholars, who distrusted the secularization of law and taxation that Selim proposed. In the face of widespread rejection of his reforms, Selim suspended his program in 1806. Nevertheless, a massive military uprising occurred at Istanbul, and the sultan was deposed and imprisoned. Reform forces recaptured the capital, but not before Selim had been executed. Selim's cousin, Sultan Mahmud (mah-MOOD) II (r. 1808–1839), cautiously revived Selim's program, but he realized that reforms needed to be more systematic and imposed more forcefully. The effectiveness of radical reform in Muhammad Ali's Egypt drove this lesson home, as did the insurrection in Greece, during which the Egyptian military performed much better than the main Ottoman army.

Greek independence in 1829 had dramatic international significance. A combination of Greek nationalist organizations and interlopers from Albania formed the independence movement. Europe's interest in the classical age of Greece and Rome led many Europeans to consider the Greeks' struggle for independence a campaign to recapture their classical glory from Muslim oppression. Some—including the "mad, bad and dangerous to know" English poet Lord Byron, who lost his life in the war—went to Greece to fight as volunteers. When the combined squadrons of the British, French, and Russian fleets, under orders to observe but not intervene in the war, made an unauthorized attack that sank the Ottoman fleet at the Battle of Navarino, Greek victory was assured (see Map 25.1).

Sultan Mahmud II

Destruction of the Janissaries

Mahmud II concurred with the pro-Greek Europeans in viewing Ottoman military reversals in Greece as a sign of profound weakness. With popular outrage over the military setbacks strong, the sultan made his move in 1826. First he announced the creation of a new artillery unit, which he had secretly been training. When the Janissaries rose in revolt, he ordered the new unit to bombard the Janissary barracks. The Janissary corps was officially dissolved.

Like Muhammad Ali, Mahmud felt he could not implement major changes without reducing the political power of the religious elite. He visualized restructuring the bureaucracy and the educational and legal systems, where ulama power was strongest. Before such strong measures could be undertaken, however, Ibrahim attacked from Syria in 1839. Battlefield defeat, the decision of the rebuilt Ottoman navy to switch sides and support Egypt, and the death of Mahmud, all in the same year, left the empire completely dependent on the European powers for survival.

The Tanzimat

Tanzimat Restructuring reforms by the nineteenth-century Ottoman rulers, intended to move civil law away from the control of religious elites and make the military and the bureaucracy more efficient.

Mahmud's reforming ideas received their widest expression in the **Tanzimat** (TAHNZ-ee-MAT) ("reorganization"), a series of reforms announced by his sixteen-year-old son and successor, Abdul Mejid (ab-dul meh-JEED), in 1839 and strongly endorsed by the European ambassadors. One proclamation called for public trials and equal protection under the law for all, whether Muslim, Christian, or Jew. It also guaranteed some rights of privacy, equalized the eligibility of men for conscription into the army (a practice copied from Egypt), and provided for a new, formalized method of tax collection that legally ended tax farming in the Ottoman Empire. It took many years and strenuous efforts by reforming bureaucrats, known as the "men of the Tanzimat," to give substance to these reforms.

Over time, one legal code after another—commercial, criminal, civil procedure—was introduced to take the place of the corresponding areas of religious legal jurisdiction. All the codes were modeled closely on those of Europe. The Shari'a, or Islamic law, gradually became restricted to matters of family law such as marriage and inheritance. As the Shari'a was displaced, job opportunities for the ulama shrank.

e **PRIMARY SOURCE: Tanzimat Decree** This document marks the beginning of the Tanzimat.

European observers praised the reforms for their noble principles and rejection of religious influence. Ottoman citizens were more divided; the Christians and Jews, for whom the Europeans showed the greatest concern, were generally more enthusiastic than the Muslims. Many historians see the Tanzimat as the dawn of modern thought and enlightened government in the Middle East. Others point out that removing the religious elite from influence in government also removed the one remaining check on authoritarian rule.

Military Reforms

Like Muhammad Ali, Sultan Mahmud sent military cadets to France and the German states for training. In the 1830s an Ottoman imperial school of military sciences, later to become Istanbul University, was established. Instructors from western Europe taught chemistry, engineering, mathematics, and physics in addition to military history. Military education became the model for more general educational reforms. In 1838 the first medical school was established to train army doctors and surgeons. Later, a national system of preparatory schools was created to feed graduates into the military schools. The subjects that were taught and many of the teachers were foreign, raising the issue of whether Turkish should be a language of instruction. Because it was easier to import and use foreign textbooks than to write new ones in Turkish, French became the preferred language in all advanced professional and scientific training. In numerical terms, however, the great majority of students still learned to read and write in Quran schools down to the twentieth century.

In the capital city of Istanbul, the reforms stimulated the growth of a small but cosmopolitan milieu embracing European language and culture. The first Turkish newspaper, a government gazette modeled on that of Muhammad Ali, appeared in 1831. Other newspapers followed, many written in French. Travel to Europe—particularly to England and France—became popular among wealthy Turks. Interest in importing European military, industrial, and communications technology remained strong through the 1800s.

Introduction of the Fez

Changes in military practice had unforeseen cultural and social effects. Accepting the European notion that modern weapons and drill required modern military dress, beards were deemed unhygienic and, in artillery units, a fire hazard. Military headgear also became controversial. European military caps, which had leather bills on the front to protect against the glare of the sun, were not acceptable because they interfered with Muslim soldiers' touching their foreheads to the ground in prayer. The compromise was the brimless cap now called the *fez*, which was adopted by the military and then by Ottoman civil officials in the early years of Mahmud II's reign.

Modernized Ottoman Troops
This photograph of a contingent of Imperial Guards in the late nineteenth century shows them equipped and uniformed much like any other European army of the time. The only distinctive feature is the fez, a brimless hat adopted earlier in the century as a symbol of reform. Comparison with the soldiers in the funeral procession of Suleiman the Magnificent (page 530) shows the degree of change from the traditional military uniforms that were still being worn in the eighteenth century.

From one of the original photographic albums of Sultan Abdul Hamid II, 1842–1918/Library of Congress

The empire's new orientation spread beyond the military. Government ministries that normally recruited from traditional bureaucratic families and relied on on-the-job training were gradually transformed into formal civil services hiring men educated in the new schools. Among self-consciously progressive men, particularly those in government service, European dress became the fashion in the Ottoman cities of the later 1800s, while traditional dress became a symbol of the religious, the rural, and the parochial.

Legal Reforms

Secularization of the legal code particularly affected non-Muslim Ottoman subjects. Islamic law had required non-Muslims to pay a special head tax that was sometimes explained as a substitute for military service. Under the Tanzimat, the tax was abolished and non-Muslims became liable for military service—unless they bought their way out by paying a new military exemption tax. The new law codes gave all male subjects equal access to the civil courts, while the operations of the Islamic law courts shrank. What enhanced the status of non-Muslims most, however, was the strong concern for their welfare consistently expressed by the European powers. The Ottoman Empire became a rich field of operation for Christian missionaries and European supporters of Jewish community life in the Muslim world.

Status of Women

The public rights and political participation granted during the Tanzimat applied specifically to men. Private life, including everything connected to marriage and divorce, remained within the sphere of religious law, and at no time was there a question of political participation or reformed education for women. Indeed, the reforms may have decreased the influence of women. The political changes ran parallel to economic changes that also narrowed women's opportunities.

After silver from the Americas began to flood the empire in the 1600s, workers were increasingly paid in cash rather than in goods, and businesses associated with banking and finance developed. But women were barred from the early industrial labor and the professions, and traditional "woman's work" such as weaving was increasingly mechanized and done by men.

Nevertheless, in the early 1800s women retained considerable power in the management and disposal of their own property, gained mostly through fixed shares of inheritance. After marriage a woman was often pressured to convert her landholdings to cash in order to transfer her personal wealth to her husband's family, with whom she and her husband would reside. However, this was not a requirement, since men were legally obligated to support their families single-handedly. Until the 1820s many wealthy women retained their say in the distribution of property through the creation of charitable trusts for their sons. Because these trusts were set up in the religious courts, they could be designed to conform to the wishes of family members. Then, in the 1820s and 1830s the secularizing reforms of Mahmud II, which did not always pro-

Interior of the Ottoman Financial Bureau This engraving from the eighteenth century depicts the governing style of the Ottoman Empire before the era of westernizing reforms. By the end of the Tanzimat period in 1876, government offices and the costumes of officials looked much more like those in contemporary European capitals.

From Ignatius Mouradgea d'Ohsson, *Tableau General de l'Empire Ottoman*, large folio edition, Paris, 1787–1820, pl. 178, following p. 340

duce happy results, transferred jurisdiction over the charitable trusts from religious courts to the state and ended women's control over this form of property.

The Crimean War and Its Aftermath

Since the reign of Peter the Great (r. 1689–1725), the Russian Empire had been attempting to expand southward at the Ottomans' expense (see the section on Russia and Asia). By 1815 Russia had pried the Georgian region of the Caucasus away from the Ottomans, and the threat of Russian intervention had prevented the Ottomans from crushing Serbian independence. When Muhammad Ali's Egyptian army invaded Syria in 1833, Russia signed a treaty in support of the Ottomans. In return, the sultan recognized Russia's claim to being the protector of all of the empire's Orthodox subjects. This set the stage for an obscure dispute that resulted in war.

The Eastern Question

Bowing to British and French pressure, the sultan named France Protector of the Holy Sepulchre in Jerusalem in 1852. Russia protested, but the sultan held firm. So Russia invaded Ottoman territories in what is today Romania, and Britain and France went to war as allies of the sultan. The real causes of the war went beyond church quarrels in Jerusalem and involved diplomatic maneuvering among European powers over whether the Ottoman Empire should continue to exist and, if not, who should take over its territory. The Eastern Question was the simple name given to this complex issue. Though the powers, including Russia, had agreed to save the empire in 1839, Britain subsequently became suspicious of Russian ambitions. Prominent anti-Russian politicians in Britain feared that Russia would threaten the British hold on India.

Siege of Sevastopol

Crimean War Conflict between the Russian and Ottoman Empires fought primarily in the Crimean Peninsula. To prevent Russian expansion, Britain and France sent troops to support the Ottomans.

Between 1853 and 1856 the **Crimean** (cry-ME-uhn) **War** raged in Romania, on the Black Sea, and on the Crimean peninsula. Britain, France, and the Italian kingdom of Sardinia-Piedmont sided with the Ottomans. Austria mediated the outcome. Britain and France trapped the Russian fleet in the Black Sea, where its commanders decided to sink the ships to protect the approaches to Sevastopol, their main base in Crimea. However, an army largely made up of British and French troops landed and laid siege to the city. Official corruption and lack of railways hampered the Russians' attempts to supply their forces. On the Romanian front, the Ottomans resisted effectively. At Sevastopol, the Russians were outmatched militarily and suffered badly from disease. Tsar Nicholas died as defeat loomed, leaving his successor, Alexander II (r. 1855–1881), to sue for peace when Sevastopol finally fell three months later.

The Crimean War brought significant changes to all the combatants. The tsar and his government, already beset by demands for the reform of serfdom, education, and the military (discussed later), were further discredited. In Britain and France, the conflict was accompanied by massive propaganda campaigns. For the first time newspapers effectively mobilized public support for a war. British press accounts so glamorized British participation that the false impression has lingered that Ottoman troops played a negligible role in the conflict. At the time, how-

From Edward William Lane, *The Manners and Customs of the Modern Egyptians* (London: J. M. D & Co. 1860)

Street Scene in Cairo This engraving from Edward William Lane's influential travel book, *Account of the Manners and Customs of the Modern Egyptians Written in Egypt During the Years 1833–1835* conveys the image of narrow lanes and small stores that became stock features of European thinking about Middle Eastern cities.

ever, British and French commanders noted the massive losses among Turkish troops in particular. The French press, dominant in Istanbul, promoted a sense of unity between Turkish and French society that continued to influence many aspects of Turkish urban culture.

The larger significance of the Crimean War was that it marked the transition from traditional to modern warfare (see Environment and Technology: The Web of War). All the combatants had previously prided themselves on the use of highly trained cavalry to smash through the front lines of infantry. Cavalry coexisted with firearms until the early 1800s, primarily because early rifles were awkward to load and not very accurate. Cavalry could attack during the intervals between volleys. Then in the 1830s and 1840s percussion caps that did away with pouring gunpowder into the barrel of a musket came into use. In Crimean War battles many cavalry units were destroyed by the rapid fire of rifles that loaded at the breech rather than down the barrel. That was the fate of the famed British Light Brigade, which was sent to relieve an Ottoman unit surrounded by Russian troops.

After the Crimean War, the Ottoman Empire increased its involvement with European commerce. The Ottoman imperial bank was founded in 1840, and a few years later currency reform pegged the value of Ottoman gold coins to the British pound. Sweeping changes in the 1850s expedited the creation of banks, insurance companies, and legal firms throughout the empire. Bustling trade also encouraged a migration from country to city between about 1850 and 1880. Many of the major cities of the empire—Istanbul, Damascus, Beirut, Alexandria, Cairo—expanded. A small but influential urban professional class emerged, as did a considerable class of wage laborers. Other demographic shifts involved refugees from Poland and Hungary, where rivalry between the European powers and the Russian Empire caused political tension and sporadic warfare, and from Georgia and other parts of the Caucasus, where Russian expansion forced many Muslims to emigrate (discussed later).

Commercial Expansion

extraterritoriality The right of foreign residents in a country to live under the laws of their native country and disregard the laws of the host country. In the nineteenth and early twentieth centuries, European and American nationals living in certain areas of Chinese and Ottoman cities were granted this right.

Foreign Debt

However, commercial vigor and urbanization could not make up for declining revenues and the chronic insolvency and corruption of the imperial government. From the conclusion of the Crimean War in 1856 on, the Ottoman government became heavily dependent on foreign loans. In return it lowered tariffs to favor European imports and allowed European banks to open in Ottoman cities. Europeans living in Istanbul and other commercial centers enjoyed **extraterritoriality**, the right to be subject to their own laws and exempt from Ottoman jurisdiction.

As the result of these measures, imported goods multiplied, but—apart from tobacco and the Turkish opium that American traders took to China to compete against British opium from India—Anatolia produced few exports. As foreign debt grew, so did inflationary trends that left urban populations in a precarious position. By contrast, Egyptian cotton exports soared during the American Civil War, when American cotton exports plummeted; but the profits benefited Muhammad Ali's descendants, who had become the hereditary governors of Egypt, rather than the Ottoman government. The Suez Canal, which was partly financed by cotton profits, opened in 1869, and Cairo was redesigned and beautified. Eventually overexpenditure on such projects plunged Egypt into the same debt crisis that plagued the empire as a whole.

The decline of Ottoman power and prosperity had a strong impact on a group of well-educated young urban men who aspired to wealth and influence. They doubted that the empire's

The Web of War

The lethal military technologies of the mid-nineteenth century that were used on battlefields in the United States, Russia, India, and China were rapidly transmitted from one conflict to the next. This dissemination was due not only to the rapid development of communications but also to the existence of a new international network of soldiers who moved from one trouble spot to another, bringing expertise in the use of new techniques.

General Charles Gordon (1833–1885), for instance, was commissioned in the British army in 1852, then served in the Crimean War after Britain entered on the side of the Ottomans. In 1860 he was dispatched to China. He served with British forces during the Arrow War and took part in the sack of Beijing. Afterward, he stayed in China and was assigned to the Qing imperial government until the suppression of the Taipings in 1864, earning himself the nickname "Chinese" Gordon. Gordon later served the Ottoman rulers of Egypt as governor of territory along the Nile. He was killed in Egypt in 1885 while leading his Egyptian troops in defense of the city of Khartoum against an uprising by the Sudanese religious leader, the Mahdi.

Journalism played an important part in the developing web of telegraph communications that sped orders to and from the battlefields. Readers in London could learn details of the drama occurring in the Crimea or in China within a week—or in some cases days—after they occurred. Print and, later, photographic journalism created new "stars" from these war experiences. Charles Gordon was one. Florence Nightingale was another.

In the great wars of the 1800s, the vast majority of deaths resulted from infection or excessive bleeding, not from the wounds themselves. Florence Nightingale (1820–1910), while still a young woman, became interested in hospital management and nursing. She went to Prussia and France to study advanced techniques. Before the outbreak of the Crimean War she was credited with bringing about marked improvement in British health care. When the public reacted to news reports of the suffering in the Crimea, the British government sent Nightingale to the region. Within a year of her arrival the death rate in the military hospitals there dropped from 45 percent to under 5 percent. Her techniques for preventing septicemia and dysentery, essentially sanitary measures like washing bed linens after a death and emptying toilet buckets outside, were quickly adopted by those working for and with her. On her return to London, Nightingale established institutes for nursing that soon were recognized as leaders around the world. She herself was lionized by the British public and received the Order of Merit in 1907, three years before her death.

The importance of Nightingale's innovations in public hygiene is underscored by the life of her contemporary, Mary Seacole (1805–1881). A Jamaican woman who volunteered to nurse British troops in the Crimean War, Seacole was repeatedly excluded from nursing service by British authorities. She eventually went to Crimea and used her own funds to run a hospital there, bankrupting herself in the process. The drama of the Crimean War moved the British public to support Seacole after her sacrifices were publicized. She was awarded medals by the British, French, and Turkish governments and today is recognized with her contemporary Florence Nightingale as an innovative field nurse and a champion of public hygiene in peacetime.

Florence Nightingale During Crimean War This 1856 lithograph shows Florence Nightingale supervising nursing care in a hospital in Scutari (Uskudar) across the Bosphorus strait from Istanbul. Though the artist may have exaggerated the neatness and cleanliness of the ward, sanitary measures proved the key to Nightingale's raising of the survival rate of sick and wounded soldiers.

rulers and the Tanzimat officials who worked for them would ever stand up to European domination. Though lacking a sophisticated organization, these Young Ottomans (sometimes called Young Turks, though that term properly applies to a later movement) promoted a mixture of liberal ideas derived from Europe, national pride in Ottoman independence, and modernist views of Islam. Prominent Young Ottomans helped draft a constitution that was promulgated in 1876 by a new and as yet untried sultan, Abdul Hamid II. This apparent triumph of liberal reform was short-lived. With war against Russia again threatening in the Balkans in 1877, Abdul Hamid suspended the constitution and the parliament that had been elected that year. Though he ruthlessly opposed further political reforms, the Tanzimat programs of extending modern schooling, utilizing European military practices and advisers, and making the government bureaucracy more orderly continued during his reign.

SECTION REVIEW

- After French withdrawal from Egypt, Muhammad Ali seized control and began a French-influenced modernization program.

- His successors continued the program and attacked the Ottoman Empire, but they were thwarted by the European powers.

- The Greek insurrection, European intervention, and Egyptian attack drove the westernizing reform efforts of Mahmud II and his successors.

- The most comprehensive reform initiative was Abdul Mejid's Tanzimat program.

- The Crimean War marked the transition from traditional to modern warfare and drew the Ottoman Empire into greater involvement with European commerce.

- Declining power and prosperity led to the rise of the Young Ottomans.

THE RUSSIAN EMPIRE

In 1812, when Napoleon's march on Moscow ended in a disastrous retreat brought on more by what a later tsar called "Generals January and February" than by Russian military action, the European image of Russia changed. Just as Napoleon's withdrawal from Egypt led to Muhammad Ali briefly becoming a political power, so his withdrawal from Russia conferred status on Tsar Alexander I (r. 1801–1825). Conservative Europeans still saw Russia as alien, backward, and oppressive, but they acknowledged its immensity and potential and included the tsar in efforts to suppress revolutionary tendencies throughout Europe.

Russia Compared with Ottomans

In several important respects Russia resembled the Ottoman Empire more than the conservative kingdoms of Europe whose autocratic practices it so staunchly supported. Socially dominated by nobles whose country estates were worked by unfree serfs, Russia had almost no middle class. Industry was still at the threshold of development by the standards of the rapidly industrializing European powers, though it was somewhat more dynamic than Ottoman industry. Like Egypt and the Ottoman Empire, Russia engaged in reforms from the top down under Alexander I, but when his conservative brother Nicholas I (r. 1825–1855) succeeded to the throne, iron discipline and suspicion of modern ideas took priority over reform.

Russia and Europe

In 1700 only three Russians out of a hundred lived in cities, two-thirds of them in Moscow alone. By the mid-1800s the town population had grown tenfold, though it still accounted for only 6 percent of the total because the territories of the tsars had grown greatly through wars and colonization (see Chapter 21). These figures demonstrate that, like the Ottoman Empire, Russia was an overwhelmingly agricultural land. However, it had poorer transportation than the Ottoman Empire, since many Ottoman cities were seaports. Both empires encompassed peoples speaking many different languages.

Slow Pace of Reform

Well-engineered roads did not begin to appear until 1817, and steam navigation commenced on the Volga in 1843. Tsar Nicholas I built the first railroad from St. Petersburg, the Russian capital, to his summer palace in 1837. A few years later his commitment to strict discipline led him to insist that the trunk line from St. Petersburg to Moscow run in a perfectly straight line. American engineers, among them the father of the painter James McNeill Whistler, who learned to paint in St. Petersburg, oversaw the laying of track and built locomotive workshops. Industrialization projects depended heavily on foreign expertise. British engineers set up the textile mills that gave woolens and cottons a prominent place among Russia's industries.

Until the late nineteenth century the Russian government's interest in industry was limited. An industrial revolution required educated and independent-minded artisans and entrepreneurs, but Nicholas feared the spread of literacy and modern education—especially anything smacking of liberalism, socialism, or revolution—beyond the minimum needed to train the officer corps and the bureaucracy. He preferred serfs to factory workers, and he paid for imported industrial goods with exports of grain and timber.

Like Egypt and the Ottoman Empire, Russia aspired to Western-style economic development. But when France and Britain entered the Crimean War, they faced a Russian army equipped with obsolete weapons and bogged down by lack of transportation. At a time when European engineers were making major breakthroughs in loading cannon through an opening at the breech end, muzzle-loading artillery remained the Russian standard.

Russia and Europe

Slavophiles Russian intellectuals in the early nineteenth century who favored resisting western European influences and taking pride in the traditional peasant values and institutions of the Slavic people.

Yet in some ways Russia bore a closer resemblance to other European countries than the Ottoman Empire did. From the point of view of the French and the British, the Cyrillic alphabet and the Russian Orthodox form of Christianity seemed foreign, but they were not nearly as foreign as the Arabic alphabet and the Muslim faith. Britain and France feared Russia as a rival for power in the east, but they increasingly accepted Tsar Nicholas's view of the Ottoman Empire as "the sick man of Europe," capable of surviving only so long as the European powers permitted.

From the Russian point of view, kinship with western Europe was of questionable value. Westernizers, like the men of the Tanzimat in the Ottoman Empire, put their trust in technical advances and governmental reform. Opposing them were intellectuals known as **Slavophiles**, who considered the Orthodox faith, the solidity of peasant life, and the tsar's absolute rule to be the proper bases of Russian civilization. After Russia's humiliation in the Crimea, the Slavophile tendency gave rise to **Pan-Slavism**, a militant political doctrine advocating unity of all the Slavic peoples, including those living under Austrian and Ottoman rule.

Pan-Slavism

Pan-Slavism Movement among Russian intellectuals in the second half of the nineteenth century to identify culturally and politically with the Slavic peoples of eastern Europe.

On the diplomatic front, the tsar's inclusion as a major European ruler contrasted sharply with the sultan's exclusion. However, this did not prevent a powerful sense of Russophobia from developing in the West. Britain in particular saw Russia as a threat to India and despised the subjection of the serfs, who gained their freedom from Tsar Alexander II only in 1861, twenty-seven years after the British had abolished slavery. In addition, the passions generated by the Crimean War and its outcome affected the relations of Russia, Europe, and the Ottoman Empire for the remainder of the nineteenth century.

Russia and Asia

The Russian drive to the east in the eighteenth century brought the tsar's empire to the Pacific Ocean and the frontiers of China (see Map 21.1) by century's end. In the nineteenth century Russian expansionism focused on the south. There the backwardness of the Russian military did not matter since the peoples they faced were even less industrialized and technologically advanced. In 1860 Russia established a military outpost on the Pacific coast that would eventually grow into the great naval port of Vladivostok, today Russia's most southerly city. In Central Asia the steppe lands of the Kazakh nomads came under Russian control early in the century, setting the stage for a confrontation with three Uzbek states farther south. They succumbed one by one, beginning in 1865, giving rise to the new province of Turkestan, with its capital at Tashkent in present-day Uzbekistan.

In the region of the Caucasus Mountains, the third area of southward expansion, Russia first took over Christian Georgia (1786), Muslim Azerbaijan (ah-zer-by-JAHN) (1801), and Christian Armenia (1813) before gobbling up the many small principalities in the heart of the mountains. Between 1829 and 1864 Dagestan, Chechnya (CHECH-nee-yah), Abkhazia (ab-KAH-zee-yah), and other regions that would one day gain political prominence after the breakup of the Soviet Union became parts of the Russian Empire.

The drive to the south intensified political friction with Russia's new neighbors: Qing China and Japan in the east, Iran on the Central Asian and Caucasus frontiers, and the Ottoman Empire at the eastern end of the Black Sea. In the latter two instances, Muslim refugees from the territories newly absorbed by Russia spread anti-Russian feelings, though some of them brought with them modern skills and ideas gained from exposure to Russian administration and education.

Russia Confronts British India

The Russian drive to the south added a new element to the Eastern Question. Many British statesmen and strategists reckoned that a warlike Russia would press on until it had conquered all the lands separating it from British India, a prospect that made them shudder, given India's enormous contribution to Britain's prosperity. The competition that ensued over which power would control southern Central Asia resulted in a standoff in Afghanistan, which became a buffer zone under the control of neither. In Iran, the standoff between the powers helped preserve the weak Qajar dynasty of shahs.

Cultural Trends

Tsar Alexander I

Unlike Egypt and the Ottoman Empire, which began to send students to Europe for training only in the nineteenth century, Russia had been in cultural contact with western Europe since the time of Peter the Great (r. 1689–1725). Members of the Russian court knew Western languages, and the tsars employed officials and advisers from Western countries. Peter had also enlisted the well-educated Ukrainian clerics who headed the Russian Orthodox Church to help spread a Western spirit of education. As a result, Alexander I's reforms met a more positive reception than those of Muhammad Ali and Mahmud II. However, his reforms promised more on paper than they brought about in practice. It took many years to develop a sufficient pool of trained bureaucrats to make the reforms effective.

Ironically, much of the opposition to Alexander's reforms came from well-established families that were not at all unfriendly to Western ideas. Their fear was that the new government bureaucrats, who often came from humbler social origins, would act as agents of imperial tyranny. This fear was realized during the conservative reign of Nicholas I in the same way that the Tanzimat-inspired bureaucracy of the Ottoman Empire served the despotic purposes of Sultan Abdul Hamid II after 1877. Individuals favoring more liberal reforms, including military officers who had served in western Europe, intellectuals who read Western political tracts, and members of Masonic lodges who exchanged views with Freemasons in the West, formed secret societies of opposition. Some placed their highest priority on freeing the serfs; others advocated a constitution and a republican form of government. When Alexander I died in December 1825, confusion over who was to succeed him encouraged a group of reform-minded army officers to try to take over the government and provoke an uprising. This so-called **Decembrist revolt** failed, and many of the participants were severely punished. These events ensured that the new tsar, Nicholas I, would pay little heed to calls for reform over the next thirty years.

Decembrist revolt Abortive attempt by army officers to take control of the Russian government upon the death of Tsar Alexander I in 1825.

Tsar Alexander II

The great powers meeting in Paris to settle the Crimean War in 1856 forced Russia to return land to the Ottomans in both Europe and Asia. This humiliation spurred Nicholas's son and successor, Alexander II (r. 1855–1881), to institute major new reforms to reinvigorate the country. The greatest of his reforms was the emancipation of the serfs in 1861. He also authorized new joint-stock companies, projected a railroad network to tie the country together, and modernized the legal and administrative arms of government.

Raising of the Alexander Monument in St. Petersburg The death of Alexander I in 1825 brought to power his conservative brother Nicholas I. Yet Alexander remained a heroic figure for his resistance to Napoleon. This monument in Winter Palace Square was erected in 1829.

Visual Connection Archive

Intellectual Awakening

Earlier intellectual and cultural trends flourished under Alexander II. More and more people became involved in intellectual, artistic, and professional life. Most prominent intellectuals received some amount of instruction at Moscow University or some German university. Universities also appeared in provincial cities like Kharkov in Ukraine and Kazan on the Volga River. Student clubs, along with Masonic lodges, became places for discussing new ideas. As Russian scholars and scientists began to achieve recognition for their contributions to European thought, scholarly careers attracted young men from clerical families, who in turn helped stimulate reforms in religious education.

Just as the Tanzimat reforms of the Ottoman Empire preceded the emergence of the Young Ottomans as a new and assertive political and intellectual force in the second half of the nineteenth century, so the initially ineffective reforms of Alexander I set in motion cultural currents that would make Russia a dynamic center of intellectual, artistic, and political life under his nephew Alexander II. Thus Russia belonged to two different spheres of development. It entered the nineteenth century a recognized force in European politics, but in other ways it resembled the Ottoman Empire. Rulers in both empires instituted reforms, overcame opposition, and increased the power of their governments. These activities stimulated intellectual and political trends that would ultimately work against the absolute rule of tsar and sultan. Yet Russia would eventually develop much closer relations with western Europe and become an arena for every sort of European intellectual, artistic, and political tendency, while the Ottoman Empire would ultimately succumb to European imperialism.

SECTION REVIEW

- Russian society resembled Ottoman society, but Alexander I undertook top-down westernizing reforms.
- Nicholas I's suspicion of Western ideas stalled reform and slowed industrial development.
- Slavophiles opposed westernizers and, after the Crimean War, embraced Pan-Slavism, contributing to Russophobia in the West.
- Russian expansion southward and eastward added vast territories to the empire and caused friction with China, Japan, Iran, and the Ottoman Empire.
- Resistance to Alexander I's bureaucratic reforms sparked the Decembrist revolt, which stiffened Nicholas I's hostility to Western ideas.
- The humiliation of the Crimean War drove Alexander II's reforms, including emancipation of the serfs.

THE QING EMPIRE

In 1800 the Qing Empire faced many problems, but no reform movement of the kind initiated by Sultan Selim III emerged in China. The reasons are not difficult to understand. The Qing emperors had skillfully countered Russian strategic and diplomatic moves in the 1600s. Instead of having a Napoleon threatening them with invasion, they enjoyed the admiration of Jesuit priests, who likened them to enlightened philosopher-kings. In 1793, however, a British attempt to establish diplomatic and trade relations—the Macartney mission—turned European opinion against China (see Chapter 21).

"Canton System"

China's most serious crises were domestic, not foreign: rebellions by displaced indigenous peoples and the poor, and protests against the injustice of the local magistrates. The Qing dealt with these problems in the usual way, by suppressing rebels and dismissing incompetent or untrustworthy officials. They paid little attention to the far-off Europeans and brushed aside the complaints from European merchants who chafed against the restrictions of the "Canton system" by which the Qing limited and controlled foreign trade.

Economic and Social Disorder

Population Pressure

Early Qing successes and territorial expansion sowed the seeds of the domestic and political chaos of the later period. The early emperors encouraged the recovery of farmland, the opening of previously uncultivated areas, and the restoration and expansion of the road and canal systems. These measures expanded the agricultural base and supported a doubling of the population between about 1650 and 1800. Enormous numbers of farmers, merchants, and day laborers migrated in search of less crowded conditions, and a permanent floating population of the unemployed and homeless emerged. By 1800 population strain had caused serious environmental damage in some parts of central and western China.

While farmers tried to cope with agricultural deterioration, other groups vented grievances against the government: minority peoples in central and southwestern China complained about being driven off their lands during the boom of the 1700s; Mongols resented appropriation of their grazing lands and the displacement of their traditional elites. In some regions, village vigilante organizations took over policing and governing functions from Qing officials who had lost control. Growing numbers of people mistrusted the government, suspecting that all officials were corrupt. The increasing presence of foreign merchants and missionaries in Canton and in the Portuguese colony of Macao aggravated discontent in neighboring districts.

White Lotus Rebellion

In some parts of China the Qing were hated as foreign conquerors and were suspected of sympathy with the Europeans. In 1794 the White Lotus Rebellion—partly inspired by a messianic ideology that predicted the restoration of the Chinese Ming dynasty and the coming of the Buddha—raged across central China and was not suppressed until 1804. It initiated a series of internal conflicts that continued through the 1800s. Ignited by deepening social instabilities, these movements were sometimes intensified by local ethnic conflicts and by unapproved religions. The ability of some village militias to defend themselves and attack others intensified the conflicts, though the same techniques proved useful to southern coastal populations attempting to fend off British invasion.

The Opium War and Its Aftermath, 1839–1850

Imports from India

Unlike the Ottomans, the Qing knew little about the enormous fortunes being made in the early 1800s by European and American merchants smuggling opium into China. They did not know that silver gained in this illegal trade was helping finance the industrial transformation of England and the United States. Only slowly did Qing officials become aware of British colonies in India that grew and exported opium, and of the major naval base at Singapore through which British opium reached East Asia.

In 1729 the first Qing law banning opium imports was promulgated. By 1800, however, opium smuggling had swelled the annual import level to as many as four thousand chests. Though British merchants had pioneered this profitable trade, Chinese merchants likewise profited from distributing the drugs. A price war in the early 1820s stemming from competition between British and American importers raised demand so sharply that as many as thirty thousand chests were being imported by the 1830s. Addiction spread to people at all levels of Qing society, including high-ranking officials. The Qing emperor and his officials debated whether to legalize and tax opium or to enforce the existing ban more strictly. Having decided to root out the use and importation of opium, in 1839 they sent a high official to Canton to deal with the matter.

Military Weakness

Britain considered the ban on opium importation an intolerable limitation on trade, a direct threat to Britain's economic health, and a cause for war. British naval and marine forces arrived on the south China coast in late 1839. The **Opium War** (1839–1842) broke out when negotiations between the Qing official and British representatives reached a stalemate. The war exposed the fact that the traditional, hereditary soldiers of the Qing Empire—the **Bannermen**—were, like the Janissaries of the Ottoman Empire, hopelessly obsolete. As in the Crimean War, the British excelled at sea, where they deployed superior technology. British ships landed marines who pillaged coastal cities and then sailed to new destinations (see Map 25.2). The Qing had no imperial navy. Thus until they were able to engage the British in prolonged fighting on land, they were unable to defend themselves against British attacks. Even in the land engagements, Qing resources proved woefully inadequate. The British could quickly transport their forces by sea along the coast, whereas Qing troops moved primarily on foot. Moving Qing reinforcements from central to eastern China took more than three months; and when the defense forces arrived, they were exhausted and basically without weapons.

Opium War War between Britain and the Qing Empire that was, in the British view, occasioned by the Qing government's refusal to permit the importation of opium into its territories. The victorious British imposed the one-sided Treaty of Nanking on China.

The Bannermen used the few muskets the Qing had imported during the 1700s. The weapons were matchlocks, which required the soldiers to ignite the load of gunpowder in them by hand. Firing the weapons was dangerous, and the canisters of gunpowder that each musketeer carried on his belt were likely to explode if a fire broke out nearby—a frequent occurrence in encounters with British artillery. Most of the Bannermen, however, had no guns at all and fought with swords, knives, spears, and clubs. Soldiers under British command—many of them Indians—carried percussion-cap rifles, which were far quicker, safer, and more accurate than

Bannermen Hereditary military servants of the Qing Empire, in large part descendants of peoples of various origins who had fought for the founders of the empire.

the matchlocks. In addition, the long-range British artillery could be moved from place to place and proved deadly in the cities and villages of eastern China.

Qing commanders thought that British gunboats rode so low in the water that they could not sail up the Chinese rivers. So they evacuated the coastal areas to counter the British threat. But the British deployed new gunboats for shallow waters and moved without difficulty up the Yangzi River (see Chapter 23).

When the invaders approached Nanjing, the former Ming capital, the Qing decided to negotiate. In 1842 the terms of the **Treaty of Nanking** (the British name for Nanjing) dismantled the old Canton system. The number of **treaty ports**—cities opened to foreign residents—increased from one (Canton) to five (Canton, Xiamen, Fuzhou, Ningbo, and Shanghai [shahng-hie]). The island of Hong Kong became a British colony, and British residents in China gained extraterritorial rights. The Qing government agreed to set a low tariff of 5 percent on imports and to pay Britain an indemnity of 21 million ounces of silver as a penalty for having started the war. A supplementary treaty the following year guaranteed **most-favored-nation status** to Britain: any privileges that China granted to another country would be automatically extended to Britain as well. This provision effectively prevented the colonization of China, because giving land to one country would have necessitated giving it to all.

With each round of treaties came a new round of privileges for foreigners. In 1860 a new treaty legalized their right to import opium. Later, French treaties established the rights of foreign missionaries to travel in the Chinese countryside and preach their religion. The number of treaty ports grew, too; by 1900 they numbered more than ninety.

The treaty system and the principle of extraterritoriality resulted in the colonization of small pockets of Qing territory, where foreign merchants lived at ease. Greater territorial losses resulted when outlying regions gained independence or were ceded to neighboring countries. Districts north and south of the Amur River in the northeast fell to Russia by treaty in 1858 and 1860; parts of modern Kazakhstan and Kyrgyzstan in the northwest met the same fate in 1864. From 1865 onward the British gradually gained control of territories on China's Indian frontier. In the late 1800s France forced the court of Vietnam to end its tribute relationship to the Qing, while Britain encouraged Tibetan independence.

In Canton, Shanghai, and other coastal cities, Europeans and Americans maintained offices and factories that employed local Chinese as menial laborers. The foreigners built comfortable housing in zones where Chinese were not permitted to live, and they entertained themselves in exclusive restaurants and bars. Around the foreign establishments, gambling and prostitution offered employment to part of the local urban population.

Whether in town or in the countryside, Christian missionaries whose congregations sponsored hospitals, shelters, and soup kitchens or gave stipends to Chinese who attended church enjoyed a good reputation. But just as often the missionaries themselves were regarded as another evil. They seemed to subvert Confucian beliefs by condemning ancestor worship, pressuring poor families to put their children into orphanages, or fulminating against footbinding. The growing numbers of foreigners, and their growing privileges, became targets of resentment for a deeply dissatisfied, daily more impoverished, and increasingly militarized society.

The Taiping Rebellion, 1850–1864

The inflammatory mixture of social unhappiness and foreign intrusion exploded in the great civil war usually called the **Taiping (tie-PING) Rebellion**. In Guangxi, where the Taiping movement originated, entrenched social problems had been generating disorders for half a century. Agriculture in the region was unstable, and many people made their living from arduous and despised trades such as disposing of human waste, making charcoal, and mining. Ethnic divisions complicated economic distress. The lowliest trades frequently involved a minority group, the Hakkas, and tensions between them and the majority were rising. Problems may have been intensified by sharp fluctuations in the opium trade and reactions to the cultural and economic impact of the Europeans and Americans in Canton.

Hong Xiuquan (hoong shee-OH-chew-an), the founder of the Taiping movement, experienced all of these influences. Hong came from a humble Hakka background. After years of study, he competed in the provincial Confucian examinations, hoping for a post in government. He failed the examinations repeatedly, and it appears that he suffered a nervous breakdown in his late thirties. Afterward he spent some time in Canton, where he met both Chinese and American

British Gunboats

Most Favored Nation

Treaty of Nanking The treaty that concluded the Opium War. It awarded Britain a large indemnity from the Qing Empire, denied the Qing government tariff control over some of its own borders, opened additional ports of residence to Britons, and ceded the island of Hong Kong to Britain.

treaty ports Cities opened to foreign residents as a result of the forced treaties between the Qing Empire and foreign signatories. In the treaty ports, foreigners enjoyed extraterritoriality.

most-favored-nation status A clause in a commercial treaty that awards to any later signatories all the privileges previously granted to the original signatories.

European Zones

Taiping Rebellion A Christian-inspired rural rebellion that threatened to topple the Qing Empire.

"Younger Brother of Jesus"

Protestant missionaries, who inspired him with their teachings. Hong had his own interpretation of the Christian message. He saw himself as the younger brother of Jesus, commissioned by God to found a new kingdom on earth and drive the Manchu conquerors, the Qing, out of China. The result would be universal peace. Hong called his new religious movement the "Heavenly Kingdom of Great Peace."

Hong quickly attracted a community of believers, primarily Hakkas like himself. They believed in the prophecy of dreams and claimed they could walk on air. Hong and his rivals for leadership in the movement went in and out of ecstatic trances. They denounced the Manchus as creatures of Satan. News of the sect reached the government, and Qing troops arrived to arrest the Taiping leaders. But the Taipings soundly repelled the imperial troops. Local loyalty to the Taipings spread quickly; their numbers multiplied; and they began to enlarge their domain.

e Interactive Map

MAP 25.2 **Conflicts in the Qing Empire, 1839–1870** In both the Opium War of 1839–1842 and the Arrow War of 1856–1860, the seacoasts saw most of the action. Since the Qing had no imperial navy, the well-armed British ships encountered little resistance as they shelled the southern coasts. In inland conflicts, such as the Taiping Rebellion, the opposing armies were massive and slow moving. Battles on land were often prolonged attempts by one side to starve out the other side before making a major assault.

© Cengage Learning

南京行劵圖

門音觀

門儀鳳

燕子磯

馬飛

Roger-Viollet/Getty Images

Nanjing Encircled   For a decade the Taipings held the city of Nanjing as their capital. For years Qing and international troops attempted to break the Taiping hold. By the summer of 1864, Qing forces had built tunnels leading to the foundations of Nanjing's city walls and had planted explosives. The detonation of the explosives signaled the final Qing assault on the rebel capital. As shown here, the common people of the city, along with their starving livestock, were caught in the crossfire. Many of the Taiping leaders escaped the debacle at Nanjing, but nearly all were hunted down and executed.

Hakkas versus Manchus

The Taipings relied at first on Hakka sympathy and the charismatic appeal of their religious doctrine to attract followers. But as their numbers and power grew, they altered their methods of preaching and governing. They replaced the anti-Chinese appeals used to enlist Hakkas with anti-Manchu rhetoric designed to enlist Chinese. They forced captured villages to join their movement. Once people were absorbed, the Taipings strictly monitored their activities. They segregated men and women and organized them into work and military teams. Women were forbidden to bind their feet (the Hakkas had never practiced footbinding) and participated fully in farming and labor. Brigades of women soldiers took to the field against Qing forces.

Capture of Nanjing

As the movement grew, it began to move toward eastern and northern China (see Map 25.2). Panic preceded the Taipings. Villagers feared being forced into Taiping units, and Confucian elites recoiled in horror from the bizarre ideology of foreign gods, totalitarian rule, and walking, working, warring women. But the huge numbers the Taipings were able to muster overwhelmed attempts at local defense. The tremendous growth in the number of Taiping followers required the movement to establish a permanent base. When the rebel army conquered Nanjing in 1853, the Taiping leaders decided to settle there and make it the capital of the new "Heavenly Kingdom of Great Peace."

Military Reforms

Qing forces attempting to defend north China became more successful as problems of organization and growing numbers slowed Taiping momentum. Increasing Qing military success resulted mainly from the flexibility of the imperial military commanders in the face of an unprecedented challenge. In addition, the military commanders received strong backing from a group of civilian provincial governors who had studied the techniques developed by local militia forces for self-defense. Certain provincial governors combined their knowledge of civilian

Photo by John Thomson/George Eastman House/Getty Images

Street Scene in Guangzhou This photograph taken in the 1860s by an Englishman shows a comparatively wide market street with signs advertising drugs, cushions, seals, ink, etc. The engraving of a Cairo street scene (page 668) shows a much more exotic stereotype of the orient, complete with young girl displaying her body while covering her face.

self-defense and local terrain with more efficient organization and the use of modern weaponry. The result was the formation of new military units, in which many of the Bannermen voluntarily served under civilian governors. The Qing court agreed to special taxes to fund the new armies and acknowledged the new combined leadership.

When the Taipings settled into Nanjing, the new Qing armies surrounded the city, hoping to starve out the rebels. The Taipings, however, had provisioned and fortified themselves well. They also had the services of several brilliant young military commanders, who mobilized enormous campaigns in nearby parts of eastern China, scavenging supplies and attempting to break the encirclement of Nanjing. For more than a decade the Taiping leadership remained ensconced at Nanjing, and the "Heavenly Kingdom" endured.

European Intervention

In 1856 Britain and France, freed from their preoccupation with the Crimean War, turned their attention to China. European and American missionaries had visited Nanjing, curious to see what their fellow Christians were up to. Their reports were discouraging. Hong Xiuquan and the other leaders appeared to lead lives of indulgence and abandon, and more than one missionary accused them of homosexual practices. Relieved of the possible accusation of quashing a pious Christian movement, the British and French surveyed the situation. Though the Taipings were not going to topple the Qing, rebellious Nian ("Bands") in northern China added a new threat in the 1850s. A series of simultaneous large insurrections might indeed destroy the empire. Moreover, since the Qing had not observed all the provisions of the treaties signed after the Opium War, Britain and France were now considering renewing war on the Qing themselves.

In 1856 the British and French launched a series of swift, brutal coastal attacks—a second opium war, called the Arrow War (1856–1860)—which culminated in a British and French invasion of Beijing and the sacking of the Summer Palace in 1860. A new round of treaties punished the Qing for not enacting all the provisions of the Treaty of Nanking. Having secured their principal objective, the British and French forces then joined the Qing campaign against the Taipings. Attempts to coordinate the international forces were sometimes riotous and sometimes tragic, but the injection of European weaponry and money helped quell both the Taiping and the Nian rebellions during the 1860s.

The Taiping Rebellion ranks as the world's bloodiest civil war and the greatest armed conflict before the twentieth century. Estimates of deaths range from 20 million to 30 million. The loss of life came primarily from starvation and disease, for most engagements consisted of surrounding fortified cities and waiting until the enemy forces died, surrendered, or were so weakened that they could be easily defeated. Many sieges continued for months. Reports of people eating grass, leather, hemp, and human flesh were widespread. The dead were rarely buried properly, and epidemic disease was common.

Death and Disease

The area of early Taiping fighting was close to the regions of southwest China in which bubonic plague had been lingering for centuries. When the rebellion was suppressed, many Taiping followers sought safety in the highlands of Laos and Vietnam, which soon showed infestation by plague. Within a few years the disease reached Hong Kong. From there it spread to Singapore, San Francisco, Calcutta, and London. In the late 1800s there was intense apprehension over the possibility of a worldwide outbreak, and Chinese immigrants were regarded as likely carriers. This fear became a contributing factor in the passage of discriminatory immigration bans on Chinese in the United States in 1882.

Lasting Devastation

The Taiping Rebellion devastated the agricultural centers of China. Many of the most intensely cultivated regions of central and eastern China were depopulated. Some were still uninhabited decades later, and major portions of the country did not recover until the twentieth century.

Cities, too, were hard hit. Shanghai, a treaty port of modest size before the rebellion, saw its population multiplied many times by the arrival of refugees from war-blasted neighboring provinces. The city then endured months of siege by the Taipings. Major cultural centers in eastern China lost masterpieces of art and architecture; imperial libraries were burned or their collections exposed to the weather; and the printing blocks used to make books were destroyed. While the empire faced the mountainous challenge of dealing with the material and cultural destruction of the war, it also was burdened by a major ecological disaster in the north. The Yellow River changed course in 1855, destroying the southern part of impoverished Shandong province with flood and initiating decades of drought along the former riverbed in northern Shandong.

Decentralization at the End of the Qing Empire, 1864–1875

The Qing government emerged from the 1850s with no hope of achieving solvency. The corruption of the 1700s, attempts in the very early 1800s to restore waterworks and roads, and declining yields from land taxes had bankrupted the treasury. By 1850, before the Taiping Rebellion, Qing government expenditures were ten times revenues. The indemnities demanded by Europeans

Cixi's Allies In the 1860s and 1870s, Cixi was a supporter of reform (see page 682). In later years she was widely regarded as corrupt and self-centered and as an obstacle to reform. Her greatest allies were the court eunuchs. Introduced to palace life in early China as managers of the imperial harems, eunuchs became powerful political parties at court. The first Qing emperors refused to allow the eunuchs any political influence, but by Cixi's time the eunuchs once again were a political factor.

Freer Gallery of Art and Arthur M. Sackler Gallery Archives, Smithsonian Institution, Washington, D.C., Purchase, 1963–1964. Neg #SC-GR 261

DIVERSITY + DOMINANCE

Chinese Responses to Imperialism

The Opium War, followed by the Taiping Rebellion, revealed China's weakness for all to see, but there was no agreement on what should be done to restore its strength. A few provincial officials were able to take effective action, but the competing ideas that were heard at the imperial court tended to cancel each other out.

Feng Guifen, an official and a scholar, came into contact with Westerners defending Shanghai when he took refuge there from the Taipings. The following is from a book of essays he published in 1861.

According to a general geography compiled by an Englishman, the territory of China is eight times that of Russia, ten times that of the United States, one hundred times that of France, and two hundred times that of Great Britain. . . . Yet we are shamefully humiliated by the four nations, not because our climate, soil, or resources are inferior to theirs, but because our people are inferior. . . . Now, our inferiority is not due to our allotment from Heaven [i.e., our inherent nature], but is rather due to ourselves. . . .

Why are the Western nations small and yet strong? Why are we large and yet weak? We must search for the means to become their equal, and that depends solely upon human effort. . . .

We have only one thing to learn from the barbarians, and that is strong ships and effective guns. . . . Funds should be allotted to establish a shipyard and arsenal in each trading port. A few barbarians should be employed, and Chinese who are good in using their minds should be selected to receive instruction so that in turn they may teach many craftsmen. When a piece of work is finished and is as good as that made by the barbarians, the makers should be rewarded with an official *juren* degree and be permitted to participate in the metropolitan examinations on the same basis as other schol-

ars. Those whose products are of superior quality should be rewarded with the *jinshi* degree [ordinarily conferred in the metropolitan examinations] and be permitted to participate in the palace examinations like others. The workers should be paid double so that they will not quit their jobs.

Our nation's emphasis on civil service examinations has sunk deep into people's minds for a long time. Intelligent and brilliant scholars have exhausted their time and energy in such useless things as the stereotyped examination essays, examination papers, and formal calligraphy. . . . We should now order one-half of them to apply themselves to the manufacturing of instruments and weapons and to the promotion of physical studies. . . . The intelligence and ingenuity of the Chinese are certainly superior to those of the various barbarians; it is only that hitherto we have not made use of them. When the government above takes delight in something, the people below will pursue it further: their response will be like an echo carried by the wind. There ought to be some people of extraordinary intelligence who can have new ideas and improve on Western methods. At first they may take the foreigners as their teachers and models; then they may come to the same level and be their equals; finally they may move ahead and surpass them. Herein lies the way to self-strengthening.

In 1867 the debate over how to resist foreign military pressure surged through the imperial court. Woren, a Mongol who held the rank of grand secretary, spoke for the conservatives.

Mathematics, one of the six arts, should indeed be learned by scholars as indicated in the imperial decree, and it should not be considered an unworthy subject. But according to the viewpoint of your servant, astronomy and mathematics are of very little use. If these subjects are going to be taught by Westerners as regular studies, the damage will be great. . . . Your servant

after the Opium and Arrow Wars compounded the problem. Vast stretches of formerly productive rice land were devastated, and the population was dispersed. Refugees pleaded for relief, and the imperial, volunteer, foreign, and mercenary troops that had suppressed the Taipings demanded unpaid wages.

Foreign Debt

Britain and France became active participants in the period of recovery that followed the rebellion (see Diversity and Dominance: Chinese Responses to Imperialism). To ensure repayment of the debt to Britain, Robert Hart was installed as inspector-general of a newly created Imperial Maritime Customs Service. Britain and the Qing split the revenues he collected. Britons and Americans worked for the Qing government as advisers and ambassadors, attempting to smooth communications between the Qing, Europe, and the United States.

Strength in the Provinces

The real work of the recovery, however, was managed by provincial governors who had come to the forefront in the struggle against the Taipings. To prosecute the war, they had won the right to levy their own taxes, raise their own troops, and run their own bureaucracies. These special powers were not entirely canceled when the war ended. Chief among these governors was Zeng Guofan (zung gwoh-FAN), who oversaw programs to restore agriculture, communications, has learned that the way to establish a nation is to lay emphasis on rites and rightness, not on power and plotting. The fundamental effort lies in the minds of people, not in techniques. Now, if we seek trifling arts and respect barbarians as teachers . . . all that can be accomplished is the training of mathematicians. From ancient down to modern times, your servant has never heard of anyone who could use mathematics to raise the nation from a state of decline or to strengthen it in time of weakness. . . .

Since the conclusion of the peace, Christianity has been prevalent, and half of our ignorant people have been fooled by it. The only thing we can rely on is that our scholars should clearly explain to the people the Confucian tenets, which may be able to sustain the minds of the ignorant populace. Now if these brilliant and talented scholars, who have been trained by the nation and reserved for great future usefulness, have to change from their regular course of study to follow the barbarians, then the correct spirit will not be developed, and accordingly the evil spirit will become stronger. After several years it will end in nothing less than driving the multitudes of the Chinese people into allegiance to the barbarians.

The opposing group of ministers who backed the idea of "self-strengthening" responded.

Your ministers have examined the memorial of Woren: the principles he presents are very lofty and the opinion he maintains is very orthodox. Your ministers' point of view was also like that before they began to manage foreign affairs; and yet today they do not presume to insist on such ideas, because of actual difficulties that they cannot help. . . .

From the beginning of foreign relations to the present there have been twenty or thirty years. At first the officials inside and outside the capital did not grasp the crux of the matter, and whether they negotiated peace or discussed war, generally these were empty words without effect. . . . Therefore your ministers have pondered a long-term policy and discussed the situation thoroughly with all the provincial officials. Propos-

als to learn the written and spoken languages of foreign countries, the various methods of making machines, the training of troops with foreign guns, the dispatching of officials to travel in all countries, the investigation of their local customs and social conditions . . . all these painstaking and special decisions represent nothing other than a struggle for self-strengthening. . . .

We too are afraid that the people who are learning these things will have no power of discrimination and are likely to be led astray by foreigners, as Woren fears. Therefore we have deliberated and decided that those who participate in these examinations must be persons from regular scholastic channels. It is indeed those students who have read widely and who understand right principles and have their minds set upon upright and grand purposes—and the present situation is just what causes the scholars and officials to feel pain in heart and head—who would certainly be able to lie on faggots and taste gall [i.e., nurse vengeance] in order to encourage each other vigorously to seek the actual achievement of self-strengthening. They are different from those who have vague, easygoing, or indifferent ideas.

QUESTIONS FOR ANALYSIS

1. How do the views of the writers reflect their own backgrounds as officials who achieved their offices through the traditional examination system?

2. In what ways do these passages indicate a deep or a shallow understanding of the West?

3. How do the ideas expressed here compare with the attitudes toward reform in the Ottoman and Russian Empires as discussed elsewhere in this chapter?

Source: Wm. Theodore de Bary and Richard Lafrano, *Sources of Chinese Tradition*, vol. 2, 2nd ed. (New York: Columbia University Press, 2000), 235–236, 238–239.

education, and publishing, as well as efforts to reform the military and industrialize armaments manufacture.

Like many provincial governors, Zeng preferred to look to the United States rather than to Britain for models and aid. He therefore hired American advisers to run his weapons factories, shipyards, and military academies. He also sponsored a daring program in which promising Chinese boys were sent to Hartford, Connecticut, a center of missionary activity, to learn English, science, mathematics, engineering, and history. They returned to China to assume some of the positions previously held by foreign advisers. Though Zeng was never an advocate of participation in public life by women, his Confucian convictions taught him that educated mothers were more than ever a necessity. He not only encouraged but also partly oversaw the advanced classical education of his own daughters. Zeng's death in 1872 deprived the empire of a major force for reform.

Dowager Empress Cixi The period of recovery marked a fundamental structural change in the Qing Empire. Although the emperors after 1850 were ineffective rulers, a coalition of aristocrats supported the reform and recovery programs. Without their legitimization of the new powers of provincial governors like Zeng Guofan, the empire might have evaporated within a generation. A crucial member of this alliance was Cixi **(TSUH-shee)**, who was known as the "Empress Dowager" after the 1880s. Later observers, both Chinese and foreign, reviled her as a monster of corruption and arrogance. But in the 1860s and 1870s Cixi supported the provincial governors, some of whom became so powerful that they were managing Qing foreign policy as well as domestic affairs.

No longer a conquest regime dominated by a Manchu military caste and its Chinese civilian appointees, the empire came under the control of a group of reformist aristocrats and military men, independently powerful civilian governors, and a small number of foreign advisers. The Qing lacked strong, central, unified leadership and could not recover their powers of taxation, legislation, and military command once these had been granted to the provincial governors. From the 1860s forward, the Qing Empire disintegrated into a number of large power zones in which provincial governors handed over leadership to their protégés in a pattern that the Qing court eventually could only ritually legitimate.

SECTION REVIEW

- Social unrest grew in Qing China through a combination of discontent among the poor and displaced indigenous peoples and resentment of growing European influence.

- Qing attempts to ban opium imports provoked the Opium War with Britain, which exposed Qing military inferiority.

- The Treaty of Nanking gave extraterritoriality and other privileges to Britain and led to further losses to other Western powers.

- Social resentment and foreign intrusion ignited the Taiping Rebellion, which, after the Arrow War, the Qing quelled with British and French aid.

- The rebellion encouraged epidemics, devastated agriculture, produced overcrowded cities filled with refugees, and coincided with environmental disasters.

- The rebellion and China's recovery afterward resulted in a process of decentralization led by reformist aristocrats.

CONCLUSION

Most of the subjects of the Ottoman, Russian, and Qing rulers did not think of European pressure or competition as determining factors in their lives during the first half of the nineteenth century. They continued to live according to the social and economic institutions they inherited from previous generations. By the 1870s, however, the challenge of Europe had become widely realized. The Crimean War, where European allies achieved a hollow victory for the Ottomans and then pressured the sultan for more reforms, confirmed both Ottoman and Russian military weakness. The Opium War did the same for China. But China, unlike the other empires, was also stricken by rampaging civil war and regional uprisings.

Though all three empires faced similar problems of reform, military rebuilding, and financial disarray, China was geographically remote from Europe and thus removed from the geostrategic tug-of-war between Britain and Russia. Despite British fears about Russian threats to India, the tsars enjoyed the advantage of being included in high-level deliberations among European powers. The Ottoman Empire, which had once dominated eastern Europe, was largely excluded from these deliberations. To many European diplomats and overseas investors, its final demise seemed only a matter of time, leaving up in the air the question of who would reap the benefits.

In analyzing the crises of the three empires, historians today stress European economic pressures and observe that all three empires ultimately became insolvent and saw the overthrow of their ruling dynasties. However, at the time what most impressed the Ottomans, Russians, and Chinese was European military superiority, as demonstrated in the Greek war of independence, the Crimean War, and the Opium War. Thus for all three empires, dealing with military emergency took priority over deeper reforms throughout most of the time period of this chapter.

KEY TERMS

Muhammad Ali p. 662
Janissaries p. 663
Serbia p. 663
Tanzimat p. 665

Crimean War p. 667
extraterritoriality p. 668
Slavophiles p. 671
Pan-Slavism p. 671

Decembrist revolt p. 672
Opium War p. 674
Bannermen p. 674
Treaty of Nanking p. 675

treaty ports p. 675
most-favored-nation status p. 675
Taiping Rebellion p. 675

EBOOK AND WEBSITE RESOURCES

e **Primary Source**

Tanzimat Decree

e **Interactive Maps**

Map 25.1 The Ottoman and Russian Empires, 1829–1914

Map 25.2 Conflicts in the Qing Empire, 1839–1870

Plus flashcards, practice quizzes, and more. Go to:
www.cengage.com/history/bullietearthpeople5e

SUGGESTED READING

Bassin, Mark. *Imperial Visions: Nationalist Imagination and Geographical Expansion in the Russian Far East, 1840–1865*. 1999. Addresses Russia's little-studied eastward expansion.

Blackwell, W. L. *The Beginnings of Russian Industrialization, 1800–1860*. 1968. A standard introduction.

Crossley, Pamela Kyle. *Orphan Warriors: Three Manchu Generations and the End of the Qing World*. 1990. Presents a Manchu perspective on the late Qing.

Deringil, Selim. *The Well-Protected Domains: Ideology and the Legitimation of Power in the Ottoman Empire, 1876–1909*. 1998. A revisionist view of the reign of Abdul Hamid II.

Field, Daniel. *The End of Serfdom: Nobility and Bureaucracy in Russia, 1855–1861*. 1976. Studies the primary problem besetting Russian society during this period.

Kappeler, Andreas. *The Russian Multi-Ethnic Empire*. 2001. Puts an emphasis on ethnic diversity.

Lewis, Bernard. *The Emergence of Modern Turkey*, 3rd ed. 2001. A treatment of late Ottoman history based on Europeanization as a sign of progress.

Mardin, Serif. *The Genesis of Young Ottoman Thought: A Study in the Modernization of Turkish Political Ideas*. Reprint, 2000. Classic study of intellectual developments.

Pamuk, Sevket. *The Ottoman Empire and European Capitalism, 1820–1913: Trade, Investment, and Production*. 1987. An economic analysis of the Ottoman Empire.

Polachek, James M. *The Inner Opium War*. 1992. Details a major event in Chinese-Western confrontation.

Quataert, Donald. *The Ottoman Empire, 1700–1922*, 2nd ed. 2005. A survey of late Ottoman history.

Raeff, Marc. *Understanding Imperial Russia*. 1984. Sets nineteenth-century Russian developments in a broad context and challenges many standard ideas.

Spence, Jonathan D. *God's Chinese Son: The Taiping Heavenly Kingdom of Hong Xiuquan*. 1996. A highly readable account of the Taiping movement that focuses on religious leadership.

Walicki, Andrzej. *The Slavophile Controversy*. 1975. A study in intellectual history.

Zelin, Madeleine. *The Merchants of Zigong: Industrial Entrepreneurship in Early Modern China*. 2005. A revealing study of indigenous economic development.

CHAPTER
26

CHAPTER OUTLINE

- Changes and Exchanges in Africa
- India Under British Rule
- Britain's Eastern Empire
- Conclusion

DIVERSITY + DOMINANCE   *Ceremonials of Imperial Domination*

ENVIRONMENT + TECHNOLOGY   *Whaling*

Private Collection

Indian Railroad Station, 1866   British India built the largest network of railroads in Asia. People of every social class traveled by train.

Visit the website and ebook for additional study materials and interactive tools: www.cengage.com/history/bullietearthpeople5e

684

Africa, India, and the New British Empire, 1750–1870

I n 1782 Tipu Sultan inherited the throne of the state of Mysore (my-SORE), which his father had made the most powerful state in south India. The ambitious and talented new ruler distrusted the territorial ambitions of Great Britain's East India Company. In 1785, before the company could invade Mysore, Tipu Sultan launched his own attack. He then sent an embassy to France in 1788, seeking an alliance against Britain. Tipu's struggle with the East India Company went badly. A military defeat in 1792 forced him to surrender most of his coastal lands. Despite the loose alliance with France, he was unable to stop further British advances. Tipu lost his life in 1799 while defending his capital against a British assault. Mysore was divided between the British and their Indian allies.

As these events illustrate, local leaders and European powers all tried to expand their influence in South Asia and Africa between 1750 and 1870. Midway through that period, it was by no means clear who would gain the upper hand. Britain and France were as likely to fight each other as they were to fight an Asian or African state. In 1800 the two nations were engaged in their third major war for overseas supremacy since 1750.

By 1870, Britain had gained a decisive advantage. The new British Empire included the subcontinent of India, settler colonies in Australia and New Zealand, and a growing network of trading outposts. By 1870 Britain had completed the campaign to replace the overseas slave trade from Africa with "legitimate" trade and had spearheaded new Asian and South Pacific labor migrations into a new string of tropical colonies.

- How did different African leaders and peoples interact with each other, and how did European nations' relationship to African peoples change during this period?
- How did Britain secure its hold on India, and what colonial policies led to the beginnings of Indian nationalism?
- What role did the abolition of slavery and the continued growth of British overseas trade play in the immigration to the Caribbean and elsewhere of peoples from Africa, India, and Asia?

CHANGES AND EXCHANGES IN AFRICA

In the century before 1870 Africa underwent dynamic political changes and a great expansion of foreign trade. Indigenous African leaders and Middle Eastern and European imperialists built powerful new states and expanded old ones. As the slave trade died under British pressure, trade in other goods grew sharply. In return Africans imported large quantities of machine-made textiles and firearms. These complex changes are best understood by looking at African regions separately.

New African States

Internal forces produced clusters of new states in two parts of sub-Saharan Africa between 1750 and 1870. In southern Africa a powerful Zulu kingdom arose. In inland West Africa Islamic reformers created the Sokoto (SOH-kuh-toh) Caliphate and companion states (see Map 26.1).

Shaka Zulu

Zulu A people of modern South Africa whom King Shaka united in 1818.

For many centuries the Nguni (ng-GOO-nee) peoples had farmed and raised cattle in the fertile coast-lands of southeastern Africa. When a serious drought hit the region at the beginning of the nineteenth century, an upstart military genius named Shaka (r. 1818–1828) created the **Zulu** kingdom in 1818. Strict military drill and close-combat tactics featuring ox-hide shields and lethal stabbing spears made the Zulu the most powerful and most feared fighters in southern Africa.

Shaka expanded his kingdom by raiding his African neighbors, seizing their cattle, and capturing their women and children. Breakaway military bands spread this system of warfare and state building inland to the high plateau country as far north as Lake Victoria. As the power and population of these new kingdoms increased, so too did the number of displaced and demoralized refugees around them.

To protect themselves from the Zulu, some neighboring Africans created their own states. The Swazi kingdom consolidated north of the Zulu, and the kingdom of Lesotho (luh-SOO-too) grew by attracting refugees to strongholds in southern Africa's highest mountains. Both Lesotho and Swaziland survive as independent states to this day.

Although Shaka ruled for little more than a decade, he succeeded in creating a new national identity as well as a new kingdom. He grouped all the young people in his domains by age into regiments. Regiment members lived together and immersed themselves in Zulu lore and customs, including fighting methods. A British trader named Henry Francis Fynn expressed his "astonishment at the order and discipline" he found everywhere in the Zulu kingdom. He witnessed public festivals of loyalty to Shaka at which regiments of young men and women numbering in the tens of thousands danced around the king for hours. Parades showed off the king's enormous herds of cattle, a Zulu measure of wealth.

Killie Campbell Africana Library. Photo: Jane Taylor/Sonia Halliday Photographs

Zulu in Battle Dress, 1838 Elaborate costumes helped impress opponents with the Zulus' strength. Shown here are long-handled spears and thick leather shields.

Meanwhile, Islamic reform movements were creating another cluster of powerful states in the savannas of West Africa. Islam had been a force in the politics and cities of this region for centuries, but it had made slow progress among rural people, and most Muslim rulers had found it prudent to tolerate the older religious practices of their subjects. In the 1770s, however, Muslim scholars began preaching the need to reform Islamic practices. They condemned the accommodations Muslim rulers had made with older traditions and called for a forcible conquest of rural "pagans." Their *jihad* (holy war) added new lands where governments enforced Islamic laws and promoted the religion's spread.

The largest of the new Muslim reform movements occurred in the Hausa (HOW-suh) states (in northern Nigeria) under the leadership of Usuman dan Fodio (OO-soo-mahn dahn FOH-dee-oh) (1745–1817). He charged that the Hausa kings, despite their official profession of Islam, were "undoubtedly unbelievers . . . because they practice polytheistic rituals and turn people away from the path of God." Distressed by the lapses of the king of Gobir, Usuman issued a call in 1804 for a jihad to overthrow him.

CHRONOLOGY

	Empire	Africa	India
1750			1756 Black Hole of Calcutta
	1763 End of Seven Years War		1765 East India Company (EIC) rule of Bengal begins
	1769–1778 Captain James Cook explores New Zealand and eastern Australia		
	1795 End of Dutch East India Company	1795 Britain takes Cape Colony	1796 Britain annexes Ceylon
		1798 Napoleon invades Egypt	1799 EIC defeats Mysore
1800		1805 Muhammad Ali seizes Egypt	
	1807 Britain outlaws slave trade	1808 Britain takes over Sierra Leone	
		1809 Sokoto Caliphate founded	
		1818 Shaka founds Zulu kingdom	1818 EIC creates Bombay Presidency
		1821 Foundation of Liberia	
			1826 EIC annexes Assam and northern Burma
		1831–1847 Algerians resist French takeover	1828 Brahmo Samaj founded
	1834 Britain frees slaves in its colonies	1836–1839 Afrikaners' Great Trek	1834 Indentured labor migrations begin
		1840 Omani sultan moves capital to Zanzibar	
1850			1857–1858 Sepoy Rebellion leads to end of EIC rule and Mughal rule
	1867 End of Atlantic slave trade	1869 Jaja founds Opobo	
	1877 Queen Victoria becomes Empress of India		

Sokoto Caliphate

Sokoto Caliphate A large Muslim state founded in 1809 in what is now northern Nigeria.

modernization The process of reforming political, military, economic, social, and cultural traditions in imitation of the early success of Western societies, often with regard for accommodating local traditions in non-Western societies.

Muhammad Ali

Muslims unhappy with their social or religious position spread the movement to other Hausa states. The successful armies united the conquered Hausa states and neighboring areas under a caliph (sultan) who ruled from the city of Sokoto. The **Sokoto Caliphate** (1809–1906) was the largest state in West Africa since the sixteenth century.

These new Muslim states became centers of Islamic learning and reform. Schools for training boys in Quranic subjects spread rapidly, and the great library at Sokoto attracted many scholars. Officials permitted non-Muslims within the empire to follow their religions in exchange for paying a special tax, but they suppressed dances and ceremonies associated with traditional religions. During the jihads, many who resisted the expansion of Muslim rule were killed, enslaved, or forced to convert.

Sokoto's leaders sold many captives into the trans-Saharan slave trade, which carried ten thousand slaves a year, mostly women and children, across the desert to North Africa and the Middle East. Slavery also increased greatly within the Sokoto Caliphate and other new Muslim states. It is estimated that by 1865 there were more slaves in the Sokoto Caliphate than in any remaining slave-holding state in the Americas.[1] Most of the slaves raised food, making possible the seclusion of free women in their homes in accordance with reformed Muslim practice.

Modernization in Egypt and Ethiopia

While new states were arising elsewhere, in northeastern Africa the ancient states of Egypt and Ethiopia were undergoing growth and **modernization**. Napoleon's invading army had withdrawn from Egypt by 1801, but the shock of this display of European strength and Egyptian weakness

Muhammad Ali Leader of Egyptian modernization in the early nineteenth century. He ruled Egypt as an Ottoman governor but had imperial ambitions. His descendants ruled Egypt until overthrown in 1952.

was long-lasting. The successor to Napoleon's rule was **Muhammad Ali** (see Chapter 25), who ruled Egypt from 1805 to 1849 and who began the reforms that created modern Egypt. In the 1830s Muhammad Ali headed the strongest state in the Islamic world and the first to employ Western methods and technology. The technical expertise of the West was combined with Islamic religious and cultural traditions. For example, the Egyptian printing industry, begun to provide Arabic translations of technical manuals, turned out critical editions of Islamic classics and promoted a revival of Arabic writing and literature.

By the end of Muhammad Ali's reign in 1849, the population had nearly doubled; trade with Europe had expanded by almost 600 percent; and a new class of educated Egyptians had begun to replace the old ruling aristocracy. Egyptians were replacing many of the foreign experts, and the fledgling program of industrialization was providing the country with its own textiles, paper, weapons, and military uniforms. The demands on peasant families for labor and military service, however, were acutely disruptive.

Ismail

Ali's grandson Ismail (is-MAH-eel) (r. 1863–1879) placed even more emphasis on westernizing Egypt. "My country is no longer in Africa," Ismail declared, "it is in Europe."[2] His efforts increased the number of European advisers in Egypt, as well as Egypt's debts to French and British banks. In the first decade of his reign, revenues increased thirtyfold and exports doubled (largely because of a huge increase in cotton exports during the American Civil War). By 1870 Egypt had a network of new irrigation canals, 800 miles (1,300 kilometers) of railroads, a modern postal service, and the dazzling new capital city of Cairo. When the market for Egyptian cotton collapsed after the American Civil War, however, Egypt's debts to British and French investors led to the country's partial occupation.

Ethiopia

State building and reform were also under way in Ethiopia, whose rulers had been Christian for fifteen hundred years. Beginning in the 1840s, Ethiopian rulers purchased modern weapons from European sources and created strong armies loyal to the ruler. Emperor Téwodros (tay-WOH-druhs) II (r. 1833–1868) also encouraged the manufacture of weapons locally. With the aid of Protestant missionaries his craftsmen even constructed a giant cannon capable of firing a half-ton shell. However, his efforts to coerce more technical aid by holding some British officials captive backfired when the British invaded instead. As the British forces advanced, Téwodros

Téwodros's Mighty Cannon Like other modernizers in the nineteenth century, Emperor Téwodros of Ethiopia sought to reform his military forces. In 1861 he forced resident European missionaries and craftsmen to build guns and cannon, including this 7-ton behemoth. It took five hundred men to haul it across Ethiopia's hilly terrain.

From Hormuzd Rassam, *Narrative of the British Mission to Theodore, King of Abyssinia, II*, London 1869, John Murray

MAP 26.1 **Africa in the Nineteenth Century** Expanding trade drew much of Africa into global networks, but foreign colonies in 1870 were largely confined to Algeria and southern Africa. Growing trade, Islamic reform movements, and other internal forces created important new states throughout the continent.

Legend:
- Zanzibari trading post
- Nguni/Ngoni states
- Reformist Muslim states
- Nyamwezi states
- Ethiopia, 1880
- Ethiopia, 1900
- Other states
- European colonies
- → Migrations of the Nguni/Ngoni
- → The Great Trek
- → Trade routes
- 1857 External slave trade and date of suppression

© Cengage Learning

Interactive Map

committed suicide to avoid being taken prisoner. Satisfied that their honor was avenged, the British withdrew. Under Téwodros and his successor Yohannes (yoh-HAHN-nehs) IV (r. 1872–1889), most highland regions were brought back under imperial rule. The only large part of ancient Ethiopia that remained outside Emperor Yohannes's rule was the Shoa kingdom, ruled by King Menelik (MEN-uh-lik) from 1865.

European Penetration

Algeria

France's conquest of Algeria anticipated the general European "scramble" for Africa after 1870. Long an exporter of grain and olive oil to France, Algeria had even supplied Napoleon with grain for his 1798 invasion of Egypt. The failure of French governments to repay this debt led to many disputes between Algeria and France and eventually to a severing of diplomatic relations in 1827. Three years later an unpopular French government, hoping to stir French nationalism with an easy overseas victory, attacked Algeria.

The French government was soon overthrown, but the war in Algeria dragged on for eighteen years. The attack by an alien Christian power united the Algerians behind 'Abd al-Qadir (AHB-dahl-KAH-deer), a gifted and resourceful Muslim holy man. To achieve victory, the French built up an army of over 100,000 that broke Algerian resistance by destroying farm animals and crops and massacring villagers by the tens of thousands. After 'Abd al-Qadir was captured and exiled in 1847, the resistance movement fragmented, but the French occupiers faced resistance in the mountains for another thirty years. European settlers, who rushed in to take possession of Algeria's rich coastlands, numbered 130,000 by 1871.

Explorers

Meanwhile, small expeditions of adventurous explorers, using their own funds or financed by private geographical societies, were seeking to uncover the mysteries of inner Africa. Besides discovering the course of Africa's rivers, they wished to assess the continent's mineral wealth or convert Africans to Christianity.

Many of them were concerned with tracing the course of Africa's great rivers. Explorers learned that the Niger River flowed from west to east and that the small streams entering the Gulf of Guinea were in fact the Niger Delta.

The north-flowing Nile similarly attracted explorers bent on finding its headwaters. In 1770 Lake Tana in Ethiopia was established as a major source, and in 1861–1862 Lake Victoria was found to be the other main source.

The Scottish missionary doctor David Livingstone (1813–1873) explored southern and central Africa. His primary goal was to scout out locations for Christian missions, but he also traced the course of the Zambezi River between 1853 and 1856, naming its greatest waterfall for the British Queen Victoria. In 1871, while tracing the course of the upper Congo River, he encountered the journalist Henry Morton Stanley (1841–1904) on a publicity-motivated search for the "lost" missionary doctor. Stanley's large expeditions fought their way across the continent, but Livingstone's modest expeditions, which posed no threat to anyone, regularly received warm hospitality.

Abolition and Legitimate Trade

No sooner was the mouth of the Niger River discovered than eager entrepreneurs began to send expeditions up the river to assess its potential for trade. The value of trade between West Africa and the West more than doubled between the 1730s and the 1780s, then doubled again by 1870.[3] Before about 1825 the slave trade accounted for most of that increase, but thereafter African exports of vegetable oils, gold, ivory, and other goods drove overseas trade to new heights.

Slave Trade

The successful slave revolt in Saint Domingue in the 1790s (see Chapter 22) ended slavery in the largest plantation colony in the West Indies. Elsewhere in the Americas slave revolts were brutally repressed. As news of the slave revolts and their repression spread, humanitarians and religious reformers called for an end to the trade. Support for abolition of the trade was found even among Americans wanting to preserve slavery. In 1807 both Great Britain and the United States made importing slaves from Africa illegal for their citizens. Most other Western countries followed suit by 1850, but few enforced abolition with the vigor of the British.

Once the world's greatest slave traders, the British became the most aggressive abolitionists. Britain sent a naval patrol to enforce the ban along the African coast and negotiated treaties allowing the patrol to search other nations' vessels suspected of carrying slaves. Although British patrols captured 1,635 slave ships and liberated over 160,000 enslaved Africans, the trade proved difficult to stop. Cuba and Brazil continued to import huge numbers of slaves, which drove prices up and persuaded some African rulers and merchants to continue to sell slaves and to help foreign slavers evade the British patrols. Because the slave trade moved to other parts of Africa, the transatlantic slave trade did not end until 1867.

"legitimate" trade Exports from Africa in the nineteenth century that did not include the newly outlawed slave trade.

In exchange for slaves, Africans purchased cloth, metals, and other goods. To continue those imports, Africans expanded their **"legitimate" trade** (exports other than slaves). They revived old exports or developed new ones as the Atlantic slave trade was shut down. The most successful of the new exports from West Africa was palm oil, used by British manufacturers for soap,

Palm Oil

Reproduced from *West Africa: An Introduction to Its History*, by Michael Crowder, by courtesy of the publishers, Addison Wesley Longman

King Jaja of Opobo This talented man rose from slavery in the Niger Delta port of Bonny to head one of the town's major palm-oil trading firms, the Anna Pepple House, in 1863. Six years later, Jaja founded and ruled his own trading port of Opobo.

candles, and lubricants. Though still a major source of slaves until the mid-1830s, the trading states of the Niger Delta emerged as the premier exporters of palm oil. Coastal African traders bought the palm oil at inland markets and delivered it to European ships at the coast.

The dramatic increase in palm-oil exports—from a few hundred tons at the beginning of the century to tens of thousands of tons by midcentury—altered the social structure of the coastal trading communities. Coastal traders used their wealth to buy slaves to paddle the giant dugout canoes that transported palm oil from inland markets along the narrow delta creeks to the trading ports. Niger Delta slavery could be as harsh and brutal as slavery on New World plantations, but it offered some slaves a chance to gain wealth and power. Male slaves who supervised canoe fleets were well compensated, and a few even became wealthy enough to take over the leadership of coastal "canoe houses" (companies). The most famous, known as "Jaja" (ca. 1821–1891), rose from canoe slave to become the head of a major canoe house. In 1869, to escape discrimination by free-born Africans, he founded the new port of Opobo, which he ruled as king. In the 1870s Jaja of Opobo was the greatest palm-oil trader in the Niger Delta.

Another effect of the suppression of the slave trade was the spread of Western cultural influences in West Africa. To serve as a base for their anti-slave-trade naval squadron, the British had taken over the small colony of Sierra Leone (see-AIR-uh lee-OWN) in 1808. Over the next several years, 130,000 men, women, and children taken from "captured" vessels were liberated in Sierra Leone. Christian missionaries helped settle these **recaptives** in and around Freetown, the capital. Mission churches and schools made many converts among such men and women.

Recaptives

recaptives Africans rescued by Britain's Royal Navy from the illegal slave trade of the nineteenth century and restored to free status.

Sierra Leone's schools also produced a number of distinguished graduates. Samuel Adjai Crowther (1808–1891), freed from a slave ship in 1821, became the first Anglican bishop in West Africa in 1864, administering a pioneering diocese along the lower Niger River. James Africanus Horton (1835–1882), the son of slaves liberated in Sierra Leone, became a doctor and the author of many studies of West Africa.

Other Western cultural influences came from people of African birth or descent returning to their ancestral homeland. In 1821, free black Americans founded a settlement that grew into the Republic of Liberia, a place of liberty at a time when slavery was legal and flourishing in the United States. After their emancipation in 1865 other African Americans moved to Liberia. Emma White, a literate black woman from Kentucky, moved from Liberia to Opobo in 1875, where King Jaja employed her to write his commercial correspondence and run a school for his children. Edward Wilmot Blyden (1832–1912), born in the West Indies and proud of his West African parentage, emigrated to Liberia in 1851 and became a professor of Greek, Latin, and Arabic at the fledgling Liberia College. Free blacks from Brazil and Cuba chartered ships to return to their West African homelands, bringing Roman Catholicism, architectural motifs, and clothing fashions from the New World. Although the number of Africans exposed to Western culture in 1870 was still small, their influence grew rapidly.

Secondary Empires in Eastern Africa

When British patrols hampered the slave trade in West Africa, slavers moved to eastern Africa. There the Atlantic slave trade joined an existing trade in slaves to the Islamic world that also was expanding. Two-thirds of the 1.2 million slaves exported from eastern Africa in the nineteenth century went to markets in North Africa and the Middle East; the other third went to plantations in the Americas and to European-controlled Indian Ocean islands.

Zanzibar

Slavery also became more prominent within eastern Africa itself. Between 1800 and 1873 Arab and Swahili (swah-HEE-lee) owners of clove plantations along the coast purchased some 700,000 slaves to do the hard work of harvesting this spice. The plantations were on Zanzibar Island and in neighboring territories belonging to the Sultanate of Oman, an Arabian kingdom on the Persian Gulf that had been expanding its control over the East African coast since 1698. The sultan had even moved his court to Zanzibar in 1840 to take advantage of the burgeoning trade in cloves. Zanzibar also was an important center of slaves and ivory. Most of the ivory was shipped to India, where much of it was carved into decorative objects for European markets.

Tippu Tip

Ivory caravans came to the coast from hundreds of miles inland under the direction of African and Arab merchants. Some of these merchants brought large personal empires under their control by using capital they borrowed from Indian bankers and modern firearms they bought from Europeans and Americans. The largest of these personal empires, along the upper Congo River, was created by Tippu Tip (ca. 1830–1905), a trader from Zanzibar. Livingstone, Stanley, and other explorers who received Tippu Tip's gracious hospitality in the remote center of the continent praised their host's intelligence and refinement. On an 1876 visit, Stanley recorded in his journal that Tippu Tip was "a remarkable man," a "picture of energy and strength" with "a fine intelligent face: almost courtier-like in his manner."

Tippu Tip also composed a detailed memoir of his adventures in the heart of Africa, written in the Swahili language of the coast. In it he mocked innocent African villagers for believing that his gunshots were thunder. Modern rifles not only felled countless elephants for their ivory tusks but also inflicted widespread devastation and misery on the people of this isolated area.

Europeans supplied the weapons and were major consumers of ivory and cloves. For this reason histories refer to the states carved out of eastern Africa by the sultans of Oman, Tippu Tip, and others as "secondary empires," in contrast to the empire that Britain was establishing directly. At the same time, British officials pressured the sultan of Oman into halting the Indian Ocean slave trade from Zanzibar in 1857 and ending the import of slaves into Zanzibar in 1873.

SECTION REVIEW

- Shaka established a powerful Zulu kingdom in the south.

- Usuman dan Fodio conquered the former Hausa states in the west and formed the Sokoto Caliphate.

- In Egypt Muhammad Ali combined Western expertise with Islamic traditions; his grandson Ismail developed the country's infrastructure.

- Under Emperor Téwodros and his successor, Ethiopia grew stronger by purchasing and manufacturing modern weapons.

- When France invaded Algeria in 1830, Algerians united behind the Muslim cleric 'Abd al-Qadir, but were defeated.

- Commercial ties between Europe and Africa grew enormously.

- No country enforced the abolition of slavery more effectively than Britain. British antislavery naval operations settled freed captives in Sierra Leone.

- The slave trade exploited the market for slaves in North Africa and the Middle East.

INDIA UNDER BRITISH RULE

The people of South Asia felt the impact of European commercial, cultural, and colonial expansion more immediately and profoundly than did the people of Africa. While Europeans were laying claim to only small parts of Africa between 1750 and 1870, nearly all of India (with three times the population of all of Africa) came under British rule. During the 250 years after the founding of the East India Company in 1600, British interests commandeered the colonies and trade of the Dutch, fought off French and Indian challenges, and picked up the pieces of the decaying Mughal (MOO-guhl) Empire. By 1763 the French were stymied; in 1795 the Dutch East India Company was dissolved; and in 1858 the last Mughal emperor was dethroned, leaving the vast subcontinent in British hands.

Company Men

As Mughal power weakened, Iranian armies defeated the Mughal forces in 1739, sacked Delhi, and returned home with vast amounts of booty. Indian states also took advantage of Mughal weakness to assert their independence. By midcentury, the Maratha (muh-RAH-tuh) Confederation, a coalition of states in central India, controlled more land than the Mughals did (see Map 26.2). Also ruling their own powerful states were the **nawabs** (NAH-wab), a term used for Muslim princes who were deputies of the Mughal emperor, though in name only.

British, Dutch, and French companies were also eager to expand their profitable trade into India in the eighteenth century. Such far-flung European trading companies were speculative and risky ventures in 1750. Their success depended on ambitious young "company men," who used hard bargaining, and hard fighting when necessary, to persuade Indian rulers to allow them to establish trading posts at strategic points along the coast. To protect their fortified warehouses from attack, they trained Indian troops known as **sepoys** (SEE-poy). In divided India these private armies came to hold the balance of power.

In 1691 Great Britain's East India Company (EIC) had convinced the nawab of the large state of Bengal in northeast India to let the company establish a fortified outpost at the fishing port of Calcutta. A new nawab, pressing claims for additional tribute from the prospering port, overran the fort in 1756 and imprisoned a group of EIC men in a cell so small that many died of suffocation. To avenge their deaths in this "Black Hole of Calcutta," a large EIC force from Madras, led by Robert Clive, overthrew the nawab. The weak Mughal emperor was persuaded to acknowledge

nawab A Muslim prince allied to British India; technically, a semi-autonomous deputy of the Mughal emperor.

sepoy A soldier in South Asia, especially in the service of the British.

East India Company

MAP 26.2 **India, 1707–1805** As Mughal power weakened during the eighteenth century, other Indian states and the East India Company expanded their territories.

 Interactive Map

the East India Company's right to rule Bengal in 1765. The EIC profited from the tax revenues of Bengal as well as from trade. Calcutta grew into a city of 250,000 by 1788.

In southern India, Clive had used EIC forces from Madras to secure victory for the British Indian candidate for nawab of Arcot during the Seven Years War (1756–1763), thereby gaining an advantage over French traders who had supported the loser. The defeat of Tipu Sultan of Mysore at the end of the century secured south India for the company and prevented a French resurgence.

Along with Calcutta and Madras, the third major center of British power in India was Bombay. There, in 1818, the East India Company annexed large territories to form the core of what was called the "Bombay Presidency." Some states were taken over completely, as Bengal had been, but very many others remained in the hands of local princes who accepted the political control of the company.

Raj and Rebellion, 1818–1857

British raj The rule over much of South Asia between 1765 and 1947 by the East India Company and then by a British government.

British Rule

In 1818 the East India Company controlled an empire with more people than in all of western Europe and with fifty times the population of the colonies the British had lost in North America. One goal of the **British raj** (reign) was to remake India on a British model through administrative and social reform, economic development, and the introduction of new technology. Yet the company men—like the Mughals before them—had to temper their interference with Indian social and religious customs lest they provoke rebellion or lose the support of their Indian princely allies.

The EIC's main goal was to create a powerful and efficient system of government, backed by military power. It also gave free rein to Christian missionaries eager to convert and uplift India's masses. Few converts were made, but the missionaries kept up steady pressure for social reforms.

Another key British policy was to substitute private property for India's complex and overlapping patterns of landholding. In Bengal this reform worked to the advantage of large landowners, but in Mysore the peasantry gained. Private ownership made it easier for the state to collect the taxes that were needed to pay for administration, the army, and economic reform.

Such policies of "westernization, Anglicization, and modernization," as they have been called, were only one side of British rule. The other side was the bolstering of "traditions"—both real and newly invented. In the name of tradition the Indian princes who ruled nearly half of British India were frequently endowed by their British overlords with greater power and splendor and longer tenure than their predecessors had ever had. Likewise, Hindu and Muslim holy men were able to expand their "traditional" power over property and people far beyond what had been the case in earlier times. At the same time, princes, holy men, and other Indians frequently used claims of tradition to resist British rule as well as to turn it to their advantage. The British rulers themselves invented many "traditions"—including elaborate parades and displays—half borrowed from European royal pomp, half from Mughal ceremonies.

The British and Indian elites worked sometimes in close partnership, sometimes in opposition, but always at the expense of the ordinary people of India. Women of every status, members of subordinate Hindu castes, the "untouchables" and "tribals" outside the caste system, and the poor experienced few benefits from the British reforms and much new oppression from the taxes and "traditions" that exalted their superiors' status.

The transformation of British India's economy was also doubled-edged. On the one hand, British raj created many new jobs as a result of the growth of trade and expanded crop production, such as opium in Bengal, largely for export to China (see Chapter 25); coffee in Ceylon; and tea in Assam in northeastern India. On the other hand, competition from cheap cotton goods produced in Britain's industrial mills drove many Indians out of the handicraft textile industry. In the eighteenth century India had been the world's greatest exporter of cotton textiles; in the nineteenth century India increasingly shipped raw cotton fiber to Britain.

Sepoy Rebellion

Even the beneficial economic changes introduced under British rule were disruptive, and local rebellions were common. During the first half of the nineteenth century, British rulers readily handled these isolated uprisings, but they were more concerned about the continuing loyalty of Indian sepoys in the East India Company's army. The EIC employed 200,000 sepoys in 1857, along with 38,000 British troops. Armed with modern rifles and disciplined in fighting methods, the sepoys had a potential for successful rebellion that other groups lacked.

In fact, discontent was growing among Indian soldiers. In the early decades of EIC rule, most sepoys came from Bengal, one of the first states the company had annexed. The Bengali sepoys resented the active recruitment of other ethnic groups into the army after 1848, such as Sikhs (seek) from Punjab and Gurkhas from Nepal. In addition, many high-caste Hindus objected to a new law in 1856 requiring new recruits to be available for service overseas in the growing Indian Ocean empire, for their religion prohibited ocean travel. Finally, the replacement of the standard military musket by the far more accurate Enfield rifle in 1857 also caused problems. Soldiers were ordered to use their teeth to tear open the ammunition cartridges, which were greased with animal fat. Hindus were offended by this order if the fat came from cattle, which they considered sacred. Muslims were offended if the fat came from pigs, which they considered unclean.

Although the cartridge-opening procedure was quickly changed, the initial discontent grew into rebellion by Hindu sepoys in May 1857. British troubles mushroomed when Muslim sepoys, peasants, and discontented elites joined in. The rebels asserted old traditions to challenge British authority: sepoy officers in Delhi proclaimed their loyalty to the Mughal emperor; others rallied behind the Maratha leader Nana Sahib. The rebellion was put down by March 1858, but it shook this empire to its core.

Historians have attached different names and meanings to the events of 1857 and 1858. Concentrating on the fact that the uprising was an unlawful action by soldiers, nineteenth-century British historians labeled it the **"Sepoy Rebellion"** or "Mutiny." Seeing in these events the beginnings of the later movement for independence, some modern Indian historians have termed it the "Revolution of 1857." In reality, it was much more than a simple mutiny, because it involved more than soldiers, but it was not yet a nationalist revolution, for the rebels had little sense of a common Indian national identity.

Sepoy Rebellion The revolt of Indian soldiers in 1857 against certain practices that violated religious customs; also known as the Sepoy Mutiny.

Political Reform and Industrial Impact

The events of 1857–1858 marked a turning point in the history of modern India. In their wake Indians gained a new centralized government, entered a period of rapid economic growth, and began to develop a new national consciousness.

In 1858 Britain eliminated the last traces of Mughal and Company rule. In their place, a new secretary of state for India in London oversaw Indian policy, and a new governor-general in Delhi acted as the British monarch's viceroy. In November 1858 Queen Victoria guaranteed all Indians equal protection of the law and the freedom to practice their religions and social customs, but she also assured Indian princes that so long as they were loyal to the queen British India would respect their control of territories and "their rights, dignity and honour."[4]

Durbars

durbar An elaborate display of political power and wealth in British India in the nineteenth century, ostensibly in imitation of the pageantry of the Mughal Empire.

British rule continued to emphasize both tradition and reform after 1857. At the top, the British viceroys lived in enormous palaces amid hundreds of servants and gaudy displays of luxury meant to convince Indians that the British viceroys were legitimate successors to the Mughal emperors. They treated the quasi-independent Indian princes with elaborate ceremonial courtesy and maintained them in splendor. When Queen Victoria was proclaimed "Empress of India" in 1877 and periodically thereafter, the viceroys put on great pageants known as **durbars**. At the durbar in Delhi in 1902–1903 to celebrate the coronation of King Edward VII, Viceroy Lord Curzon honored himself with a 101-gun salute and a parade of 34,000 troops in front of 50 princes and 173,000 visitors (see Diversity and Dominance: Ceremonials of Imperial Domination).

Indian Civil Service

Indian Civil Service The elite professional class of officials who administered the government of British India. Originally composed exclusively of well-educated British men, it gradually added qualified Indians.

Meanwhile, a powerful and efficient bureaucracy controlled India. Members of the elite **Indian Civil Service** (ICS) held the senior administrative and judicial posts. Numbering only a thousand at the end of the nineteenth century, these men visited the villages in their districts, heard lawsuits and complaints, and passed judgments.

Recruitment into the ICS was by open examinations. In theory any British subject could take these exams; since they were given in England, however, in practice the system worked to exclude Indians. In 1870 only one Indian was a member of the ICS. Subsequent reforms led to fifty-seven Indian appointments by 1887, but there the process stalled. Working under the ICS were thousands of lesser Indian officials.

Ceremonials of Imperial Domination

This letter to Queen Victoria from Edward Robert Bulwer-Lytton, Earl of Lytton and viceroy of India, describes the elaborate durbar that the government of India staged in 1876 in anticipation of her being named "Empress of India." It highlights the effects these ceremonies had on the Indian princes who governed many parts of India as agents ("feudatories") of the British or as independent rulers.

British India's power rested on the threat of military force, but the letter points up how much it also depended on cultivating the allegiance of powerful Indian rulers. For their part, as the letter suggests, such rulers were impressed with such displays of majesty and organization and found much to be gained from granting the British their support.

The day before yesterday (December 23), I arrived, with Lady Lytton and all my staff at Delhi. . . . I was received at the [railroad] station by all the native chiefs and princes, and, . . . after shaking hands . . . , I immediately mounted my elephant, accompanied by Lady Lytton, our two little girls following us on another elephant. The procession through Delhi to the camp . . . lasted upwards of three hours. . . . The streets were lined for many miles with troops; those of the native princes being brigaded with those of your Majesty. The crowd along the way, behind the troops, was dense, and apparently enthusiastic; the windows, walls, and housetops being thronged with natives, who salaamed, and Europeans, who cheered as we passed along. . . .

My reception by the native princes at the station was most cordial. The Maharaja of Jeypore informed Sir John Strachey that India had never seen such a gathering as this, in which not only all the great native princes (many of whom have never met before), but also chiefs and envoys from Khelat, Burmah, Siam, and the remotest parts of the East, are assembled to do homage to your Majesty. . . .

On Tuesday (December 26) from 10 A.M. till past 7 P.M., I was, without a moment's intermission, occupied in receiving visits from native chiefs, and bestowing on those entitled to them the banners, medals, and other honours given by your Majesty. The durbar, which lasted all day and long after dark, was most successful. . . . Your Majesty's portrait, which was placed over the Viceregal throne in the great durbar tent, was thought by all to be an excellent likeness of your Majesty. The native chiefs examined it with special interest.

On Wednesday, the 27th, I received visits from native chiefs, as before, from 10 A.M. til 1 P.M., and from 1:30 P.M. to 7:30 P.M., was passed in returning visits. I forgot to mention that on Tuesday and Wednesday evenings I gave great State dinners to the Governors of Bombay and Madras. Every subsequent evening of my stay at Delhi was similarly occupied by state banquets and receptions [for officials, foreign dignitaries, and] many distinguished natives. After dinner on Thursday, I held a levee [reception], which lasted till one o'clock at night, and is said to have been attended by 2,500 persons—the largest, I believe, ever held by any Viceroy or Governor-General in India. . . .

The satisfactory and cordial assurances received from [the ruler of] Kashmir are, perhaps, less important, because his loyalty was previously assumed. But your Majesty will, perhaps, allow me to mention, in connection with the name of this prince, one little circumstance which appears to me very illustrative of the effect which the assemblage has had on him and others. In the first interviews which took place months ago between myself and Kashmir, which resulted in my securing his assent to the appointment of a British officer at Gilgit, I noticed that, though perfectly courteous, he was extremely mistrustful of the British Government and myself. He seemed to think that every word I had said to him must have a hidden meaning against which he was bound to be on his guard. During our negotiations he carefully kept all his councillors round him, and he referred to them before answering any question I put to him, and, although he finally agreed to my proposals, he did so with obvious reluctance and suspicion, after taking a night to think them over. On the day following the Imperial assemblage, I had another private interview with Kashmir for the settlement of some further details. His whole manner and language on this last occasion were strikingly different. [He said:] "I am now convinced that you mean nothing that is not

The reason qualified Indians were denied entry into the upper administration of their country was the racist contempt most British officials felt for the people they ruled. When he became commander-in-chief of the Indian army in 1892, Lord Kitchener declared:

> *It is this consciousness of the inherent superiority of the European which had won for us India. However well educated and clever a native may be, and however brave he may have proved himself, I believe that no rank we can bestow on him would cause him to be considered an equal of the British officer.*[5]

After 1857 the government invested millions of pounds sterling in harbors, cities, irrigation canals, and other public works. Forests were felled to make way for tea plantations. Indian farmers were persuaded to grow cotton and jute for export. Engineers built great irrigation systems to alleviate the famines that periodically decimated whole provinces. As a result, India's trade expanded rapidly.

for the good of me and mine. Our interests are identical with those of the empire. Give me your orders and they shall be obeyed."

I have already mentioned to your Majesty that one of the sons of Kashmir acted as my page at the assemblage. I can truly affirm that all the native princes, great and small, with whom I was previously acquainted vied with each other in doing honor to the occasion, and I sincerely believe that this great gathering has also enabled me to establish the most cordial and confidential personal relations with a great many others whom I then met for the first time.

. . . If the vast number of persons collected together at Delhi, and all almost entirely under canvas, be fairly taken into consideration—a number alluding the highest executive officers of your Majesty's administration from every part of India, each with his own personal staff; all the members of my own Council, with their wives and families, who were entertained as the Viceroy's personal guests; all the representatives of the Press, native and European; upwards of 15,000 British troops, besides about 450 native princes and nobles, each with a following of from 2 to 500 attendants; the foreign ambassadors with their suites; the foreign consuls; a large number of the rudest and most unmanageable transfrontier chieftains with their horses and camels, Etc.; and then an incalculably large concourse of private persons attracted by curiosity from every corner of the country—I say if all this be fairly remembered, no candid person will, I think, deny that to bring together, lodge, and feed so vast a crowd without a single case of sickness, or a single accident due to defective arrangements, without a moment's confusion or an hour's failure in the provision of supplies, and then to have sent them all away satisfied and loud in their expressions of gratitude for the munificent hospitality with which they had been entertained (at an expenditure of public money scrupulously moderate), was an achievement highly creditable to all concerned in carrying it out. Sir Dinkur Rao (Sindiah's great Minister) said to one of my colleagues: "If any man would understand why it is that the English are, and must necessarily remain, the masters of India, he need only go up to the Flagstaff Tower, and look down upon this marvellous camp. Let him notice the method, the order, the cleanliness, the discipline, the perfection of its whole organisation, and he will recognise in it at once the epitome of every title to command and

govern which one race can possess over others." This anecdote reminds me of another which may perhaps please your Majesty. [The ruler of] Holkar said to me when I took leave of him: "India has been till now a vast heap of stones, some of them big, some of them small. Now the house is built, and from roof to basement each stone of it is in the right place."

The Khan of Khelat and his wild Sirdars were, I think, the chief objects of curiosity and interest to our Europeans. . . . On the Khan himself and all his Sirdars, the assemblage seems to have made an impression more profound even than I had anticipated. Less than a year ago they were all at war with each other, but they have left Delhi with mutual embraces, and a very salutary conviction that the Power they witnessed there is resolved that they shall henceforth keep the peace and not disturb its frontiers with their squabbles. The Khan asked to have a banner given to him. It was explained to His Highness that banners were only given to your Majesty's feudatories, and that he, being an independent prince, could not receive one without compromising his independence. He replied: "But I am a feudatory of the Empress, a feudatory quite as loyal and obedient as any other. I don't want to be an independent prince, and I do want to have my banner like all the rest. Pray let me have it."

QUESTIONS FOR ANALYSIS

1. What is significant about the fact that Lord Lytton and his family arrived in Delhi by train and then chose to move through the city on elephants?

2. What impression did the viceroy intend to create in the minds of the Indian dignitaries by assembling so many of them together and bestowing banners, medals, and honors on them?

3. What might account for some Indians' remarkable changes of attitude toward the viceroy and the empire? How differently might a member of the Indian middle class or an unemployed weaver have reacted?

Source: Lady Betty Balfour, *The History of Lord Lytton's Indian Administration, 1876 to 1880* (London: Longmans, Green, and Co., 1899), 116–125.

Most of the exports were agricultural commodities: cotton fiber, opium, tea, silk, and sugar. In return India imported manufactured goods from Britain, including machine-made cotton textiles that undercut Indian hand-loom weavers. Some women found jobs at very low pay on plantations or in the growing cities, where prostitution flourished. Others struggled to hold families together or ran away from abusive husbands. Everywhere in India poverty remained the norm.

Railroads
The Indian government also promoted the introduction of new technologies into India. Earlier in the century there were steamboats on the rivers and a massive program of canal building for irrigation. Beginning in the 1840s a railroad boom gave India its first national transportation network, followed by telegraph lines, and by 1870 India had the fifth largest rail network in the world. Originally designed to serve British commerce, the railroads were owned by British companies, constructed with British rails and equipment, and paid dividends to British investors. Ninety-nine percent of the railroad employees were Indians, but Europeans occupied all the top

Delhi Durbar, January 1, 1903 The parade of Indian princes on ornately decorated elephants and accompanied by retainers fostered their sense of belonging to the vast empire of India that British rule had created.

positions—"like a thin film of oil on top of a glass of water, resting upon but hardly mixing with [those] below," as one official report put it.

Although some Indians opposed the railroads at first because the trains mixed people of different castes, faiths, and sexes, the Indian people took to rail travel with great enthusiasm. Indians rode trains on business, on pilgrimage, and in search of work. In 1870 over 18 million passengers traveled along the network's 4,775 miles (7,685 kilometers) of track, and more than half a million messages were sent up and down the 14,000 miles (22,500 kilometers) of telegraph wires.

But the freer movement of Indian pilgrims and the flood of poor Indians into the cities also promoted the spread of cholera (KAHL-uhr-uh), a disease transmitted through water contaminated by human feces. Cholera deaths rose rapidly during the nineteenth century, and eventually the disease spread to Europe. In many Indian minds *kala mari* ("the black death") was a divine punishment for failing to prevent the British takeover. This chastisement also fell heavily on British residents, who died in large numbers. In 1867 officials demonstrated the close connection between cholera and pilgrims who bathed in and drank from sacred pools and rivers. The installation of a new sewerage system (1865) and a filtered water supply (1869) in Calcutta dramatically reduced cholera deaths there. Similar measures in Bombay and Madras also led to great reductions, but most Indians lived in small villages where famine and lack of sanitation kept cholera deaths high.

Indian Nationalism

Indian National Congress A movement and political party founded in 1885 to demand greater Indian participation in government. Its membership was middle class, and its demands were modest until World War I. Led after 1920 by Mohandas K. Gandhi, it appealed increasingly to the poor, and it organized mass protests demanding self-government and independence.

Rammohun Roy

Both the successes and the failures of British India stimulated the development of Indian nationalism. After the failure of the rebellion of 1857 to overthrow British rule, some Indians argued that the only way for Indians to regain control of their destiny was to reduce their country's social and ethnic divisions and promote Pan-Indian nationalism.

Individuals such as Rammohun Roy (1772–1833) had promoted development along these lines a generation earlier. A Western-educated Bengali from a Brahmin family, Roy was a suc-

Rammohun Roy This portrait of the Indian reformer emphasizes his scholarly accomplishments and India's traditional architecture and natural beauty.

Bristol City Museum and Art Gallery, UK/The Bridgeman Art Library

cessful administrator for the East India Company and a student of comparative religion. His Brahmo Samaj (BRAH-moh suh-MAHJ) (Divine Society), founded in 1828, attracted Indians who sought to reconcile the values of the West with the religious traditions of India. They advocated reforming some Hindu customs, such as the caste system and child marriage, and urged a return to the founding principles of the *Upanishads*, ancient sacred writings of Hinduism. They also backed British efforts to ban practices they found repugnant. Widow burning (*sati* [suh-TEE]) was outlawed in 1829 and slavery in 1843. Reformers sought to correct other abuses of women: prohibitions against widows remarrying were revoked in 1856, and female infanticide was made a crime in 1870.

Although Brahmo Samaj remained influential after the rebellion of 1857, many Indian intellectuals turned to Western secular values and nationalism as the way to reclaim India. In this process the spread of Western education played an important role, a process aided by European and American missionaries. Roy had studied both Indian and Western subjects and helped found the Hindu College in Calcutta in 1816. Other Western-curriculum schools quickly followed, including Bethune College in Calcutta, the first secular school for Indian women, in 1849. India's three universities were established in 1857. In 1870 there were over 24,000 elementary and secondary schools, whose graduates articulated a new Pan-Indian nationalism that transcended regional and religious differences.

Indian National Congress

Many of the new nationalists came from the Indian middle class, which had prospered from the increase of trade and manufacturing. Educated people were angered by the obstacles that British rules and prejudices put in the way of their advancement. Hoping to increase their influence and improve their employment opportunities in the Indian government, they convened the first **Indian National Congress** in 1885. The members sought a larger role for Indians in the Civil Service. They also called for reductions in military expenditures, which consumed 40 percent of the government's budget, so that more could be spent on alleviating the poverty of the Indian masses. But although the Indian National Congress promoted unity among the country's many religions and social groups, most early members were upper-caste Western-educated Hindus and Parsis. Until it attracted the support of the masses, it could not hope to challenge British rule.

SECTION REVIEW

- Between 1757 and 1857, Britain gained nearly complete control of India.

- With its armies of sepoys, the British East India Company was able to secure control of Calcutta, Madras, and Bombay.

- The British instituted a powerful colonial government and skillfully exploited native traditions and local rulers. The power given to Indians who governed on their behalf increased, while the life of the masses deteriorated.

- The Sepoy Rebellion of 1857–1858 prompted a wave of reforms. Great sums of money were invested in harbors, canals, trains, and telegraph lines, but profits remained in colonial hands.

- In response to modernization, Indian nationalism arose in the increasingly educated middle class.

BRITAIN'S EASTERN EMPIRE

In 1750 Britain's empire was centered on slave-based plantation and settler colonies in the Americas. A century later its main focus was on commerce and colonies in the East. Several distinct changes facilitated the expansion and transformation of Britain's overseas empire. A string of military victories pushed aside rivals for overseas trade and colonies; new policies favored free trade over mercantilism; and changes in shipbuilding techniques increased the speed and volume of maritime commerce. Linked to these changes were new European settlements in southern Africa, Australia, and New Zealand and the growth of a new long-distance trade in indentured labor.

Colonies and Commerce

At the end of the eighteenth century, France was still a serious rival for dominion in the Indian Ocean. However, defeats in the wars of the French Revolution (see Chapter 22) ended Napoleon's dream of restoring French dominance overseas. The wars also dismantled much of the Netherlands' Indian Ocean empire. When French armies occupied the Netherlands, the Dutch ruler, who had fled to Britain in January 1795, authorized the British to take over Dutch possessions overseas in order to keep them out of French hands. During 1795 and 1796 British forces quickly occupied the Cape Colony at the southern tip of Africa, the strategic Dutch port of Malacca on the strait between the Indian Ocean and the South China Sea, and the island of Ceylon (see Map 26.3).

Then the British occupied Dutch Guiana (ghee-AH-nuh) and Trinidad in the southern Caribbean. In 1811 they even seized the island of Java, the center of the Netherlands' East Indian empire. British forces also seized the French islands of Mauritius (moh-RIHS-uhs) and Réunion in the Indian Ocean. At the end of the Napoleonic Wars in 1814, Britain returned Java to the Dutch and Réunion to the French but kept the Cape Colony, British Guiana (once part of Dutch Guiana), Trinidad, Ceylon, Malacca, and Mauritius.

Afrikaners

The Cape Colony was valuable because of Cape Town's strategic importance as a supply station for ships making the long voyages between Britain and India. With the port city came some twenty thousand descendants of Dutch and French settlers who occupied farms and ranches in its hinterland. Despite their European origins, these people thought of themselves as permanent residents of Africa and were beginning to refer to themselves as "Afrikaners" (af-rih-KAHN-uhr). British governors prohibited any expansion of the white settler frontier because such expansion invariably led to wars with indigenous Africans. This decision, along with the imposition of laws protecting African rights within Cape Colony (including the emancipation of slaves in 1834), alienated many Afrikaners.

Between 1836 and 1839 parties of Afrikaners embarked on a "Great Trek," leaving British-ruled Cape Colony for the fertile high *veld* (plateau) to the north that two decades of Zulu wars had depopulated. The Great Trek laid the foundation of three new settler colonies in southern Africa: the Afrikaners' Orange Free State and Transvaal on the high veld and the British colony of Natal on the Indian Ocean coast. Although firearms enabled the settlers to win some important battles against the Zulu and other Africans, they were still a tiny minority surrounded by the populous and powerful independent African kingdoms that had grown up at the beginning of the century.

Singapore

Meanwhile, another strategic British outpost was being established in Southeast Asia. One prong of the advance was led by Thomas Stamford Raffles, who had governed Java from 1811 to 1814. After Java's return to the Dutch, Raffles helped establish a new free port at Singapore in 1824, on the site of a small Malay fishing village with a superb harbor. By attracting British merchants and Chinese businessmen and laborers, Singapore soon became the center of trade and shipping between the Indian Ocean and China. Along with Malacca and other possessions on the strait, Singapore formed the "Straits Settlements," which British India administered until 1867.

Burma

Further British expansion came more quickly in neighboring Burma. Burma had emerged as a powerful kingdom by 1750. In 1785 Burma tried to annex neighboring territories of Siam (now Thailand) to the east, but a coalition of Thai leaders thwarted Burmese advances by 1802. Burma next attacked Assam to the west, but this provoked a war with British India. After a two-year war, India annexed Assam in 1826 and occupied two coastal provinces of northern Burma. As the rice and timber trade from these provinces grew important, the occupation became permanent, and in 1852 British India annexed the rest of coastal Burma.

Great Trek Aided by African servants, the ox-drawn wagons of the Afrikaners struggled over the Drakensberg Mountains to the high plains in an effort to escape British control.

Hulton Archive/Getty Images

Imperial Policies and Shipping

Free Trade

Through such piecemeal acquisitions, by 1870 Britain had added several dozen colonies to the twenty-six colonies it had in 1792. The underlying goal of most British imperial expansion during these decades was trade rather than territory. Most of the new colonies were meant to serve as ports in the growing network of shipping that encircled the globe or as centers of production and distribution for those networks.

This new commercial expansion was closely tied to the needs of Britain's growing industrial economy and reflected a new philosophy of overseas trade. Rather than rebuilding the closed mercantilist network of trade with its colonies, Britain sought to trade freely with all parts of the world. Free trade was also a wise policy in light of the independence of so many former colonies in the Americas (see Chapter 24).

Whether colonized or not, more and more lands were being drawn into the commercial networks created by British expansion and industrialization. Uncolonized parts of West Africa became major exporters to Britain of vegetable oils and forest products, while areas of eastern Africa free of European control exported ivory that ended up as piano keys and decorations in the homes of the middle and upper classes. From the far corners of the world came coffee, cocoa, tea, and sugar for the tables of Western consumers, and indigo dyes and cotton fibers for the expanding textile factories.

In return, the factories of the industrialized nations supplied manufactured goods at very attractive prices. By the mid-nineteenth century a major part of their textile production was destined for overseas markets. Sales of cotton cloth to Africa increased 950 percent from the 1820s to the 1860s. British trade to India grew 350 percent between 1841 and 1870, while India's exports increased 400 percent. Trade with other regions also expanded rapidly. In most cases

MAP 26.3 European Possessions in the Indian Ocean and South Pacific, 1870 By 1870 the British controlled much of India, were settling Australia and New Zealand, and possessed important trading enclaves throughout the region.

Colonial possessions
- British
- Dutch
- French
- Portuguese
- Spanish
- Afrikaners
- ◆ Penal colony

e Interactive Map

© Cengage Learning

RUSSIA

ASIA

JAPAN

PACIFIC OCEAN

Yellow R. (Yellow R.)

Huang He R.

OTTOMAN EMPIRE

PERSIA

AFGHANISTAN

HIMALAYA MTS.

CHINA

East China Sea

Yellow Sea

Tropic of Cancer   20°N

Tigris R.

Euphrates R.

Persian Gulf

BAHRAIN (Gr. Br. 1861)

Indus R.

Ganges R.

ASSAM

BURMA (1826)

LAOS

ANNAM

Taiwan

Macao (Portugal 1555)

Hong Kong (Gr. Br. 1842)

South China Sea

Arabian Sea

INDIA

Diu (Portugal 1535)

Daman (Portugal 1558)

Goa (Portugal 1510)

Bay of Bengal

Rangoon (1852)

SIAM

Mekong R.

CAMBODIA (1863)

COCHIN CHINA

Andaman Is. (Gr. Br. 1852)

MALAYA

Penang (Gr. Br. 1786)

Malacca (Gr. Br. 1796)

SARAWAK (1824)

Singapore (Gr. Br. 1824)

PHILIPPINES (1570)

Pondicherry (France 1764)

Karikal (France 1738)

Nicobar Is. (Gr. Br. 1869)

Ceylon (1798)

SUMATRA

BORNEO

Moluccas

NEW GUINEA

DUTCH EAST INDIES

Java

Timor

Laccadive Is. (Gr. Br. 1791)

Maldives Is. (Gr. Br. 1796)

Kuria Muria Is. (Gr. Br. 1854)

ARABIAN DESERT

Aden (Gr. Br. 1839)

Red Sea

Nile R.

Cairo

Mediterranean Sea

AFRICA

Assab (Italy 1870)

Obok (France 1862)

Seychelles (Gr. Br. 1810)

Comoro Is. (France 1841)

Pemba
Zanzibar

PORTUGUESE EAST AFRICA

MADAGASCAR

Mauritius (Gr. Br. 1810)

Réunion (France 1642)

INDIAN OCEAN

N

ANGOLA

Congo R.

TRANSVAAL

ORANGE FREE STATE

NATAL

CAPE COLONY

Cape Town

GREAT SANDY DESERT

GREAT VICTORIA DESERT

AUSTRALIA

GREAT DIVIDING RANGE

Adelaide

Melbourne

Macquarie Harbour

Tasmania

Maria I.

Hobart

Port Arthur

Moreton Bay

Brisbane

Port Macquarie

Newcastle

Sydney

NEW CALEDONIA (France 1853)

Tropic of Capricorn   20°S

NEW ZEALAND

Wellington

0° Equator

20°E   40°E   60°E   80°E   100°E   120°E   140°E   160°E   180°

0   500   1000 Km.
0   500   1000 Mi.

such trade benefited both sides, but there is no question that the industrial nations were the dominant partners.

A second impetus to global commercial expansion was the technological revolution in the construction of oceangoing ships under way in the nineteenth century. The middle decades of the century were the golden age of the sailing ship. Using iron to fasten timbers together permitted shipbuilders to construct much larger vessels. Merchant ships in the eighteenth century rarely exceeded 300 tons, but after 1850 **clipper ships** of 2,000 tons were commonplace in the British merchant fleet. Huge canvas sails made the streamlined clippers faster than earlier vessels. Ships from the East Indies or India had taken six months to reach Europe in the seventeenth century; after 1850 the new ships could complete the voyage in half that time.

This increase in size and speed lowered shipping costs and further stimulated maritime trade. The tonnage of British merchant shipping quadrupled between 1778 and 1860. Clippers intended for eastern service generally were built of teak and other tropical hardwoods from new British colonies in South and Southeast Asia.

Clipper Ships

clipper ship Large, fast, streamlined sailing vessel, often American built, of the mid-to-late nineteenth century rigged with vast canvas sails hung from tall masts.

Colonization of Australia and New Zealand

Australia

In the once-remote South Pacific, British settlers displaced the indigenous populations of Australia and New Zealand, just as they had done in North America. Portuguese mariners had sighted Australia in the early seventeenth century, but it was too remote to be of much interest to Europeans. However, after the English captain James Cook explored New Zealand and the eastern coast of Australia between 1769 and 1778, expanding shipping networks brought in growing numbers of visitors and settlers.

At the time of Cook's visits, Australia was the home of about 650,000 hunting-and-gathering people, whose Melanesian (mel-uh-NEE-zhuhn) ancestors had settled there some forty thousand years earlier. New Zealand was inhabited by about 250,000 Maori (MOW-ree [ow as in cow]), who practiced hunting, fishing, and simple forms of agriculture, which their Polynesian ancestors had introduced around 1200. Because of their long isolation from the rest of humanity, the populations of Australia and New Zealand were as vulnerable as the Amerindians had been to unfamiliar diseases introduced by new overseas contacts. By the 1890s, only 93,000 aboriginal Australians and 42,000 Maori survived, and British settler populations outnumbered and dominated the indigenous peoples.

The first permanent British settlers in Australia were 736 convicts, of whom 188 were women, sent into exile in 1788. Over the next few decades, Australian penal colonies grew slowly and had only slight contact with the indigenous population, whom the British called "Aborigines." However, the discovery of gold in 1851 brought a flood of free European settlers (and some Chinese) and hastened the end of the penal colonies. When the gold rush subsided, government subsidies enabled tens of thousands of British settlers to settle "down under." Though it still took more than three months to reach Australia from Britain, by 1860 Australia had a million immigrants, and the settler population doubled during the next fifteen years.

New Zealand

British settlers were drawn more slowly to New Zealand. Some of the first were temporary residents along the coast who slaughtered seals and exported pelts to Western countries to be made into men's felt hats. A single ship in 1806 took away sixty thousand sealskins. By the early 1820s overhunting had nearly exterminated the seal population. Special ships also hunted sperm whales extensively near New Zealand for their oil, used for lubrication, soap, and lamps; ambergris (AM-ber-grees), an ingredient in perfume; and bone, used in women's corsets (see Environment and Technology: Whaling). A brief gold rush and faster ships and subsidized passages attracted more British immigrants after 1860. The colony especially courted women immigrants to offset the preponderance of single men. By the early 1880s this most distant frontier of the British Empire had a settler population of 500,000. Britain encouraged the settlers in Australia and New Zealand to become self-governing, following the 1867 model that had formed the Dominion of Canada out of the diverse and thinly settled colonies of British North America. Britain's policies toward its settler colonies in Canada and the South Pacific reflected a desire to avoid the conflicts that had led to the American Revolution. By gradually turning over governing power to the colonies' inhabitants, Britain accomplished three things. It satisfied the settlers' desire for greater control over their own territories; it muted demands for independence; and it made the colonial governments responsible for most of their own expenses. Indigenous peoples were outvoted by the settlers or excluded from voting.

New Zealand Sheep Farming
In New Zealand, populist government policies made land available at low cost to European settlers. Here, two sheep farmers are immersing their animals in sheep dip, an insecticide solution that kills parasites.

North American patterns also shaped the indigenous peoples' fate. Aborigines lacked the rights of Australian citizens. The requirement that voters had to be able to read and write English kept Maori from voting in early New Zealand elections, but four seats in the lower house of the legislature were reserved for Maori from 1867 on.

New Labor Migrations

Between 1834 and 1870 many thousands of Indians, Chinese, and Africans went overseas to work, especially on sugar plantations. In the half-century after 1870, tens of thousands of Asians and Pacific islanders made similar voyages.

In part these migrations were linked to the end of slavery. After their emancipation in British colonies in 1834, many slaves left the plantations. To compete with sugar plantations in Cuba, Brazil, and the French Caribbean that were still using slave labor, British colonies had to recruit new laborers.

India's impoverished people seemed one obvious alternative. After planters on Mauritius successfully introduced Indian laborers, the Indian labor trade moved to the British Caribbean in 1838. In 1841 the British government also allowed Caribbean planters to recruit Africans whom British patrols had rescued from slave ships and liberated in Sierra Leone and elsewhere. By 1870 nearly 40,000 Africans had settled in British colonies, along with over a half-million Indians and over 18,000 Chinese. After the French and Dutch abolished slavery in 1848, their colonies also recruited new laborers from Asia and Africa.

Slavery was not abolished in Cuba until 1886, but the rising cost of slaves led the burgeoning sugar plantations to recruit 138,000 new laborers from China between 1847 and 1873. Inden-

Whaling

The rapid expansion of whaling aptly illustrates the growing power of technology over nature in this period. Many contemporaries, like many people today, were sickened by the killing of the planet's largest living mammals. American novelist Herman Melville captured the conflicting sentiments in his epic whaling story, *Moby Dick* (1851). One of his characters enthusiastically explains why the grisly and dangerous business existed:

> But, though the world scorns us as whale hunters, yet does it unwittingly pay us the profoundest homage; yea, an all abounding adoration! for almost all the tapers, lamps, and candles that burn around the globe, burn, as before so many shrines, to our glory!

Melville's character overstates the degree to which whale oil dominated illumination and does not mention its many other industrial uses. Neither does he describe the commercial importance of whalebone (baleen). For a time its use in corsets allowed fashionable women to achieve the hourglass shape that fashion dictated. Whalebone's use for umbrella stays, carriage springs, fishing rods, suitcase frames, combs, brushes, and many other items made it the plastic of its day.

New manufacturing technologies went hand in hand with new hunting technologies. The revolution in ship design enabled whalers from Europe and North America to extend the hunt into the southern oceans off New Zealand. By the nineteenth century whaling ships were armed with guns that shot a steel harpoon armed with vicious barbs deep into the whale. In the 1840s explosive charges on harpoon heads ensured the whale's immediate death. Yet, as this engraving of an expedition off New Zealand shows, flinging small harpoons from rowboats in the open sea continued to be part of the dangerous work.

Another century of extensive hunting devastated many whale species before international agreements finally limited the killing of these giant sea creatures.

The Granger Collection, New York

South Pacific Whaling   One boat was swamped, but the hunters killed the huge whale.

---

contract of indenture A voluntary agreement binding a person to work for a specified period of years in return for free passage to an overseas destination. Before 1800 most indentured servants were Europeans; after 1800 most indentured laborers were Asians.

Indenture

tured labor recruits also became the mainstay of new sugar plantations in places that had never known slave labor. After 1850 American planters in Hawaii recruited labor from China and Japan; British planters in Natal recruited from India; and those in Queensland (in northeastern Australia) relied on laborers from neighboring South Pacific islands.

Larger, faster ships made transporting laborers halfway around the world affordable, though voyages from Asia to the Caribbean still took an average of three months. Despite close regulation and supervision of shipboard conditions, the crowded accommodations encouraged the spread of cholera and other contagious diseases that took many migrants' lives.

All of these laborers served under **contracts of indenture**, which bound them to work for a specified period (usually from five to seven years) in return for free passage to their overseas destination. They were paid a small salary and were provided with housing, clothing, and medical care. Indian indentured laborers also received the right to a free passage home if they

SECTION REVIEW

- By 1850 the British Empire was no longer focused on slave-based colonies in the Americas but on commercial networks and colonies in the East.

- Fast and large clipper ships facilitated the expansion of the British merchant fleet.

- The British took control of the Cape Colony in southern Africa, Ceylon, and the port of Malacca. Singapore soon became the center of trade between the Indian Ocean and China.

- After 1778, growing numbers of settlers to Australia and New Zealand displaced the native Australian and Maori peoples. New and devastating diseases killed over 80 percent of native New Zealanders and Australians.

- After Britain, France, and the Netherlands abolished slavery, thousands of Indians, Chinese, Africans, and Pacific islanders immigrated to British colonies under contracts of indenture.

worked a second five-year contract. British Caribbean colonies required forty women to be recruited for every hundred men as a way to promote family life. So many Indians chose to stay in Mauritius, Trinidad, British Guiana, and Fiji that they constituted a third or more of the total population of these colonies by the early twentieth century.

The indentured labor trade reflected the unequal commercial and industrial power of the West, but it was not an entirely one-sided creation. The men and women who signed indentured contracts were trying to improve their lives by emigrating, and many succeeded. Whether for good or ill, more and more of the world's peoples saw their lives being influenced by the existence of Western colonies, Western ships, and Western markets.

CONCLUSION

What is the global significance of these complex political and economic changes in southern Asia, Africa, and the South Pacific? One perspective stresses the continuing exploitation of African, Asian, and Pacific peoples by more powerful Europeans. In this view, the emergence of Britain as a dominant power continues the European expansion that the Portuguese, the Spanish, and the Dutch pioneered. Likewise, Britain's control over South and Southeast Asia and over Australia and New Zealand can be seen as a continuation of the conquest and colonization of the Americas.

From another perspective what was most important about this period was not the political and military strength of the Europeans but their growing domination of the world's commerce, especially long-distance ocean shipping. Like other Europeans, the British were drawn to Africa and southern Asia by a desire to obtain new materials. However, Britain's commercial expansion in the nineteenth century was also the product of Easterners' demand for industrial manufactures. The growing exchanges could be mutually beneficial. African and Asian consumers found industrially produced goods far cheaper and sometimes better than the handicrafts they replaced. Industrialization also created new markets for African and Asian goods, as in the case of the vegetable-oil trade in West Africa or cotton in Egypt and India. There were also negative impacts, as in the case of the weavers of India and the damage to species of seals and whales.

Europeans' military and commercial strength did not reduce Africa, Asia, and the Pacific to mere appendages of Europe. While the balance of power shifted in the Europeans' favor between 1750 and 1870, other cultures were still vibrant and local initiatives often dominant. Islamic reform movements and the rise of the Zulu nation had greater significance for their respective regions of Africa than did Western forces. Despite European power, Southeast Asians were still largely in control of their own destinies. Even in India, most people's lives and beliefs showed continuity with the past.

Asians and Africans were not powerless in dealing with European expansion. The Indian princes who extracted concessions from the British in return for their cooperation and the Indians who rebelled against the raj both forced the system to accommodate their needs. Some Asians and Africans were also beginning to use European education, technology, and methods to transform their own societies. Leaders in Egypt, India, and other lands were learning to challenge the power of the West on its own terms. In 1870 no one could say how long and how difficult that learning process would be, but Africans and Asians would continue to shape their own futures.

KEY TERMS

Zulu p. 686
Sokoto Caliphate p. 687
modernization p. 687
Muhammad Ali p. 688
"legitimate" trade p. 690

recaptives p. 691
nawab p. 693
sepoy p. 693
British raj p. 694
Sepoy Rebellion p. 695

durbar p. 695
Indian Civil Service p. 695
Indian National
  Congress p. 698
clipper ship p. 703

contract of
  indenture p. 705

EBOOK AND WEBSITE RESOURCES

e Interactive Maps

Map 26.1 Africa in the Nineteenth Century

Map 26.2 India, 1707–1805

Map 26.3 European Possessions in the Indian Ocean and South Pacific, 1870

Plus flashcards, practice quizzes, and more. Go to:
www.cengage.com/history/bullietearthpeople5e

SUGGESTED READING

Bayly, C. A. *Indian Society and the Making of the British Empire*. 1987. How Indians adapted to, and resisted, British rule.

Bennett, Norman R. *Arab Versus European: Diplomacy and War in Nineteenth Century East Central Africa*. 1986. Describes the wars and rivalries over northeastern Africa.

Bose, Sugata. *A Hundred Horizons: The Indian Ocean in the Age of Global Empire*. 2006. Discusses British dominance in South Asia and the Indian Ocean.

Bose, Sugata, and Ayeshia Jalal. *Modern South Asia: History, Culture, Political Economy*, 2nd ed. 2003. A readable introduction to India in the age of the British raj.

Eltis, David. *Economic Growth and the Ending of the Transatlantic Slave Trade*. 1987. Discusses the British naval patrols against slavers and their effects.

Gadgil, Madhav, and Ramachandra Guha. *This Fissured Land: An Ecological History of India*. 1993. Describes the environmental changes in India that resulted from modernization.

Headrick, Daniel. *The Tentacles of Progress: Technology Transfer in the Age of Imperialism, 1850–1940*. 1988. Describes the impact of Western technology on India.

Jackson, Gordon. *The British Whaling Trade*. 2005. An outstanding analysis of British whaling.

Keith Sinclair, ed. *The Oxford Illustrated History of New Zealand*. 1996. A wide-ranging introduction to that nation.

Morris, Donald R. *The Washing of the Spears*. 1965. A very readable account of the rise and fall of Shaka's Zulu kingdom.

Northrup, David. *Indentured Labor in the Age of Imperialism, 1834–1922*. 1995. Summarizes recent scholarship on the indentured labor trade.

Rotberg, Robert I., ed., *Africa and Its Explorers: Motives, Methods, and Impact*. 1970. A classic account of the "opening" of Africa to Europeans.

SarDesai, D. R. *Southeast Asia: Past and Present*, 5th ed. 2004. A good introduction to the complexities of Southeast Asian history.

Whitlock, Gillian, and David Carter, eds. *Images of Australia: An Introductory Reader in Australian Studies*. 1992. Presents a multicultural and gendered perspective.

Woodruff, William. *Impact of Western Man: A Study of Europe's Role in the World Economy, 1750–1960*. 1982. A general overview of the period covered in this chapter.

NOTES

1. Paul E. Lovejoy and Jan S. Hogendorn, *Slow Death for Slavery: The Course of Abolition in Northern Nigeria, 1897–1936* (New York: Cambridge University Press, 1993).

2. Quoted in P. J. Vatikiotis, *The History of Modern Egypt: From Muhammad Ali to Mubarak*, 4th ed. (Baltimore: Johns Hopkins University Press, 1991), 74.

3. David Eltis, "Precolonial Western Africa and the Atlantic Economy," in *Slavery and the Rise of the Atlantic Economy*, ed. Barbara Solow (New York: Cambridge University Press, 1991), table 1.

4. Quoted by Bernard S. Cohn, "Representing Authority in Victorian India," in *The Invention of Tradition*, ed. Eric Hobsbawm and Terence Ranger (Cambridge, England: Cambridge University Press, 1983), 165.

5. James Truslow, *Empire of the Seven Seas: The British Empire 1784–1939* (New York: Charles Scribners Sons, 2007), 268.

STATE POWER, THE CENSUS, AND THE QUESTION OF IDENTITY

Between the American Revolution and the last decades of the nineteenth century, Europe and the Americas were transformed. The ancient power of kings and the authority of religion were eclipsed by muscular new ways of organizing political, economic, and intellectual life. The Western world was vastly different in 1870 than it had been a century earlier. One of the less heralded but enduringly significant changes was the huge expansion of government statistical services.

The rise of the nation-state was associated with the development of modern bureaucratic departments that depended on reliable statistics to measure the nation's achievements and discover its failures. The nation-state, whether democratic or not, mobilized resources on a previously unimaginable scale. Modern states were more powerful and wealthier, and they were also more ambitious and more intrusive. The growth of their power can be seen in the modernization of militaries, the commitment to internal improvements such as railroads, and the growth in state revenues. In recent years historians have begun to examine a less visible but equally important manifestation of growing state power: census taking.

Governments and religious authorities have counted people since early times. Our best estimates of the Amerindian population of the Western Hemisphere in 1500 rest almost entirely on what were little more than missionaries' guesses about the numbers of people they baptized. Spanish and Portuguese kings were eager to count native populations, since "indios" (adult male Amerindians) were subject to special labor obligations and tribute payments. So, from the mid-sixteenth century onward, imperial officials conducted regular censuses of Amerindians, adapting practices already in place in Europe.

The effort to measure and categorize populations was transformed in the last decades of the eighteenth century when the nature of European governments began to change. The Enlightenment belief that the scientific method could be applied to human society proved to be attractive both to political radicals, like the French Revolutionaries, and to reforming monarchs like Maria Theresa of Austria. Enlightenment philosophers had argued that a science of government could remove the inefficiencies and irrationalities that had long subverted the human potential for prosperity and happiness. The French intellectual Condorcet wrote in 1782:

> Those sciences, created almost in our own days, the object of which is man himself, the direct goal of

> which is the happiness of man, will enjoy a progress no less sure than that of the physical sciences. . . . In meditating on the nature of the moral sciences [what we now call the social sciences], one cannot help seeing that, as they are based like the physical sciences on the observation of fact, they must follow the method, acquire a language equally exact and precise, attaining the same degree of certainty.[1]

As confidence in this new "science" grew, the term previously used to describe the collection of numbers about society, *political arithmetic*, was abandoned by governments and practitioners in favor of *statistics*, a term that clearly suggests its close ties to the "state." In the nineteenth century the new objectives set out by Condorcet and others led to both the formal university training of statisticians and the creation of government statistical services.

The ambitions of governments in this new era were great. Nation-states self-consciously sought to transform society, sponsoring economic development, education, and improvements in health and welfare. They depended on statistics to measure the effectiveness of their policies and, as a result, were interested in nearly everything. They counted taverns, urban buildings, births and deaths, and arrests and convictions. They also counted their populations with a thoroughness never before seen. As statistical reporting became more uniform across Europe and the Americas, governments could measure not only their own progress but also that of their neighbors and rivals.

The revolutionary governments of France modernized the census practices of the overthrown monarchy. They spent much more money, hired many more census takers, and devoted much more energy to training the staff that designed censuses and analyzed results. Great Britain set up an official census in 1801, but it established a special administrative structure only in the 1830s. In the Western Hemisphere nearly every independent nation provided for "scientific" censuses. In the United States the federal constitution required that a census be taken every ten years. Latin American nations, often torn by civil war in the nineteenth century, took censuses less regularly, but even the poorest nations took censuses when they could. It was as if the census itself confirmed the existence of the government, demonstrating its modernity and seriousness.

Until recently, historians who relied on these documents in their research on economic performance, issues of race and ethnicity, family life, and fertility and mortality asked few questions about the politics of census design. What could be more objective than rows of numbers? But the advocates of statistics who managed census taking were uninhibited in advertising the usefulness of reliable numbers to the governments that employed them. At the 1860 International Statistical Congress held in London one speaker said, "I think the true meaning to be attached to 'statistics' is not every collection of figures, but figures collected with the sole purpose of applying the principles deduced from them to questions of importance to the state."[2] The desire to be useful meant that statistics could not be fully objective.

Subjectivity was an unavoidable problem with censuses. Censuses identified citizens and foreign residents by place of residence, sex, age, and family relationships within households as well as profession and literacy. These determinations were sometimes subjective. Modern scholars have demonstrated that census takers also often undercounted the poor and those living in rural areas.

Because census takers, as agents of nation-states, were determined to be useful, they were necessarily concerned with issues of nationality and, in the Americas, with race because these characteristics commonly determined political rights and citizenship. The assessment and recording of nationality and race would prove to be among the most politically problematic objectives of the new social sciences.

Nationality had not been a central question for traditional monarchies. For the emerging nation-state, however, nationality was central. A nation's strength was assumed to depend in large measure on the growth of its population, a standard that, once articulated, suggested that the growth of minority populations was dangerous. Who was French? Who was Austrian or Hungarian? European statisticians relied on both *language of use* and *mother tongue* as proxies for *nationality*, the first term being flexible enough to recognize the assimilation of minorities, the second suggesting a more permanent identity based on a person's original language. Both terms forced bilingual populations to simplify their more complex identities. Ethnic minorities, once identified, were sometimes subject to discrimination such as exclusion from military careers or from universities. In parts of Spanish America language was used as a proxy for *race*. Those who spoke Spanish were citizens in the full sense, even if they were indistinguishable from Amerindians in appearance. Those who spoke indigenous languages were "indios" and therefore subject to special taxes and labor obligations and effectively denied the right to vote.

Beyond providing a justification for continuing discrimination, census categories compressed and distorted the complexity and variety of human society to fit the preconceptions of bureaucrats and politicians. Large percentages of the residents of Mexico, Peru, and Bolivia, among other parts of the Americas, were descended from both Europeans and Amerindians and, in the Caribbean region, from Europeans and Africans. Census categories never adequately captured the complexities of these biological and cultural mixtures. We now know that the poor were often identified as "indios" or "blacks" and the better-off were often called something else, "Americanos," "criollos" (creoles), or even whites. Since this process flattened and streamlined the complexities of identity, censuses on their own are not reliable guides to the distribution of ethnicity and race in a population.

In Europe the issue of nationality proved similarly perplexing for census takers and similarly dangerous to those identified as minorities. Linguistic and ethnic minorities had always lived among the politically dominant majorities: Jewish and Polish minorities in areas controlled by German speakers, German speakers among the French, and Serbo-Croatian speakers among Hungarians, for example. The frontiers between these minority populations and their neighbors were always porous. Sexual unions and marriages were common, and two or more generations of a family often lived together in the same household, with the elder members speaking one language and the younger members another. Who was what? In a very real sense, nationality, like race in the Americas, was ultimately fixed by the census process, where the nation-state forced a limited array of politically utilitarian categories onto the rich diversity of ethnicity and culture.

NOTES

1. Quoted in James C. Scott, *Seeing like a State. How Certain Schemes to Improve the Human Condition Have Failed* (New Haven: Yale University Press, 1998), 91.
2. This discussion relies heavily on Eliza Johnson (now Ablovatski), "Counting and Categorizing: The Hungarian Gypsy Census of 1893" (M.A. Thesis, Columbia University, 1996), especially Chapter III. She quotes from the *Proceedings of the Sixth International Statistical Congress Held in London, 1860*, 379.

PART VII

Victoria & Albert Museum, London/Art Resource, NY

Highways of the Empire   In the late nineteenth century, Europeans believed the world revolved around their subcontinent. World maps printed in Great Britain showed the British Empire in red, with informal dependencies and protectorates in pink. This map, a polar projection with Britain in the exact center, shows the major shipping routes and submarine telegraph cable lines that made London the center of global commerce and finance and ensured the supremacy of the Royal Navy around the world.

Global Diversity and Dominance, 1850–1945

In 1850, the world embraced a huge diversity of societies and cultures. During the century that followed, Europe, the United States, and Japan dominated much of the world and tried to convert other peoples to their own cultures and ways of life.

In Europe, mounting tensions led to the Great War of 1914–1918. Russia and China erupted in revolution. Soon after, the heartland of the Ottoman Empire became modern Turkey, while its Arab provinces were taken over by France and Britain.

The political and economic system the European powers crafted after the war fell apart in the 1930s. While the capitalist nations fell into a depression, the Soviet Union industrialized at breakneck speed. In Germany and Japan, extremists sought to solve their countries' grievances by military conquest.

World War II caused the death of millions of people and the destruction of countless cities. The war also weakened Europe's overseas empires. Nationalists in Asia, Latin America, and Africa yearned for independence and the benefits of industrialization. India gained its independence in 1947. Two years later, Mao Zedong led the Chinese communists to victory. Latin American leaders embraced nationalist economic and social policies. Of all the once great powers, only the United States and the Soviet Union remained to compete for global dominance.

CHAPTER OUTLINE

Courtesy of the Trustees of the British Museum/The Art Archive

Arrivals from the East   In 1853, Commodore Matthew Perry's fleet sailed into Edo (now Tokyo) Bay. The first steam-powered warships to appear in Japanese waters caused a sensation among the Japanese. In this print done after the Meiji Restoration, the traditionally dressed local samurai go out to confront the mysterious "black ships."

 Visit the website and ebook for additional study materials and interactive tools: www.cengage.com/history/bullietearthpeople5e

The New Power Balance, 1850–1900

On July 8, 1853, four American warships, two of them steam-powered, appeared in Edo Bay, close to the capital of Japan. The commander of the fleet, **Commodore Matthew Perry**, delivered a letter from the president of the United States, demanding that Japan open its ports to foreign trade. Perry's "black ships" were the first to break through the barriers that had kept Japan isolated from the rest of the world for two and a half centuries. It was not the foreign interlopers who created such a sensation among the Japanese, but the machines they came in.

A year later, Perry returned to receive the answer from the Japanese government. The Americans also brought a miniature railroad, a short telegraph line, and other marvels of Western technology. For the next twenty years, Japanese society was torn between those who wanted to retreat into isolation and those who wished to embrace the foreign ways and acquire their machines. For it was clear that only by industrializing could Japan escape the fate of weaker nations then being taken over by Europe and the United States.

In the late nineteenth century a very small number of states, known as "great powers," dominated the world. Great Britain, France, and Russia had been recognized as great powers long before the industrial age. Russia began industrializing in the late nineteenth century, as did Germany, the United States, and Japan. The rise of the United States was covered in Chapter 24; here we will turn to the other great powers of the age. In the next chapter, which deals with the "New Imperialism" (1870–1914), we will see how these nations used their power to establish colonial empires in Asia and Africa and to control Latin America. Together, Chapters 27 and 28 describe an era in which a handful of wealthy industrialized nations imposed on the other peoples of the world a domination more powerful than any experienced before or since.

- What new technologies and industries appeared between 1850 and 1900, and how did they affect the world economy?
- How did the societies of the industrial countries change during this period?
- How did industrialization contribute to the socialist and labor movements?
- How was nationalism transformed from a revolutionary to a conservative ideology?
- How did the forces of nationalism affect the major powers of Europe?

Commodore Matthew Perry A navy commander who, on July 8, 1853, became the first foreigner to break through the barriers that had kept Japan isolated from the rest of the world for 250 years.

NEW TECHNOLOGIES AND THE WORLD ECONOMY

The Industrial Revolution marked the beginning of a massive transformation of the world. In the nineteenth century the technologies discussed in Chapter 23—textile mills, railroads, steamships, the telegraph, and others—spread from Britain to other parts of the world. By 1890 Germany and the United States had surpassed Great Britain as the world's leading industrial powers. Industrialization also introduced entirely new technologies that revolutionized everyday life and transformed the world economy. The motive force behind this second phase of industrialization consisted of potent combinations of business, engineering, and science. By the mid-nineteenth century this combination was institutionalized in engineering schools and research laboratories, first in Germany and then in the United States. Electricity and the steel and chemical industries were the first results of this new force.

Railroads

railroads Networks of iron (later steel) rails on which steam (later electric or diesel) locomotives pulled long trains at high speeds. The first railroads were built in England in the 1830s. Their success caused a railroad-building boom throughout the world that lasted well into the twentieth century.

By the mid-nineteenth century, steam engines had become the prime mover of industry and commerce. Nowhere was this more evident than in the spread of **railroads**. By 1850 the first railroads had proved so successful that every industrializing country, and many that aspired to become industrial, began to build lines. The next fifty years saw a tremendous expansion of the world's rail networks. After a rapid spurt of building new lines, British railroad mileage leveled off in the 1870s at around 20,000 miles (over 32,000 kilometers). France and Germany built networks longer than Britain's, as did Canada and Russia. When Japan began building its railway network in the 1870s, it imported several hundred engineers from the United States and Britain, then replaced them with newly trained Japanese engineers in the 1880s.

Railroads were not confined to the industrialized nations; they could be constructed almost anywhere they would be of value to business or government. That included regions with abundant raw materials or agricultural products, like South Africa, Mexico, and Argentina, and densely populated countries like Egypt. The British built the fourth largest rail network in the world in India in order to reinforce their presence and develop trade with their largest colony.

With one exception, European or American engineers built these railroads with equipment imported from the West. In 1855, barely a year after Commodore Perry's visit, the Japanese instrument maker Tanaka Hisashige built a model steam train that he demonstrated to an admiring audience. In the 1870s the Japanese government hired British engineers to build the first line from Tokyo to Yokohama, then sent them home again as soon as they had trained Japanese engineers. Within a few years, Japan began manufacturing its own equipment.

Railroads consumed huge amounts of land. Many old cities doubled in size to accommodate railroad stations, sidings, tracks, warehouses, and repair shops. In the countryside, railroads required bridges, tunnels, and embankments. Railroads also consumed vast quantities of timber for ties to hold the rails and for bridges, often consuming trees for miles on either side of the tracks. Throughout the world, they opened new land to agriculture, mining, and other human exploitation of natural resources.

Steamships and Telegraph Cables

In the mid-nineteenth century, a series of developments radically transformed ocean shipping. First iron, then steel, replaced the wood that had been used for hulls since shipbuilding began. Propellers replaced paddle wheels, and engineers built more powerful and fuel-efficient engines. The average size of freighters increased from 200 tons in 1850 to 7,500 tons in 1900. Coaling stations and ports able to handle large ships were built around the world. The Suez Canal, constructed in 1869, shortened the distance between Europe and Asia and triggered a massive switch from sail power to steam (see Chapter 28).

submarine telegraph cables Insulated copper cables laid along the bottom of a sea or ocean for telegraphic communication. The first short cable was laid across the English Channel in 1851; the first successful transatlantic cable was laid in 1866.

The world's fleet of merchant ships grew from 9 million tons in 1850 to 35 million tons in 1910. Shipping lines offered fast, punctual, and reliable service on a fixed schedule for passengers, mail, and perishable freight. Meanwhile, tramp freighters sailed from one port to another under orders from their company headquarters in Europe or North America.

To control their ships, shipping companies used a new medium of communications: **submarine telegraph cables**. By the turn of the century cables connected every country and almost every inhabited island. As cables became the indispensable tools of modern shipping and business, the public and the press extolled the "annihilation of time and space."

CHRONOLOGY

Political Events	Social, Cultural, and Technological Events
1850	1851 Majority of British population living in cities
1853–1854 Commodore Matthew Perry visits Japan	1856 Bessemer converter; first synthetic dye
	1859 Charles Darwin, *On the Origin of Species*
1860 1860–1870 Unification of Italy	
1861–1865 American Civil War	1861 Emancipation of serfs (Russia)
1862–1908 Rule of Empress Dowager Cixi (China)	1866 Alfred Nobel develops dynamite
	1867 Karl Marx, *Das Kapital*
1868 Meiji Restoration begins modernization drive in Japan	1868–1894 Japan undergoes Western-style industrialization and societal changes
1870 1870–1871 Franco-Prussian War	
1871 Unification of Germany	
1880	1879 Thomas Edison develops incandescent lamp
1890	
1894 Sino-Japanese War	
1900 1900 Boxer Uprising (China)	
1904–1905 Russo-Japanese War	
1905 Revolution in Russia	
1910 Japan annexes Korea	

The Steel and Chemical Industries

steel A form of iron that is both durable and flexible. It was first mass-produced in the 1860s and quickly became the most widely used metal in construction, machinery, and railroad equipment.

Until the nineteenth century **steel** could be made only by skilled blacksmiths in very small quantities and was reserved for swords, knives, axes, and watch springs. Then came a series of inventions that made it the cheapest and most versatile metal ever known. In the 1850s the American William Kelly and the Englishman Henry Bessemer discovered that air forced through molten pig iron by powerful pumps turned it into steel without additional fuel. Other new processes permitted steel to be made from scrap iron, an increasingly important raw material, and from the phosphoric iron ores common in western Europe. Steel became cheap and abundant enough to make rails, bridges, ships, and even "tin" cans meant to be used once and thrown away.

The chemical industry followed a similar pattern. In 1856 the Englishman William Perkin created the first synthetic dye, aniline purple, from coal tar; the next few years were known in Europe as the "mauve decade" from the color of fashionable women's clothes. Industry began mass-producing other organic chemicals—compounds containing carbon atoms. Toward the end of the century German chemists synthesized red, violet, blue, brown, and black dyes as well. These bright, long-lasting colors were cheaper to manufacture and could be produced in much greater quantities than natural dyes. They delighted consumers but ruined the indigo plantations of India. Chemistry also made important advances in the manufacture of explosives. The first of these, nitroglycerin, was so dangerous that it exploded when shaken. In 1866 the Swedish scientist Alfred Nobel found a way to turn nitroglycerin into a stable solid—dynamite. This and other new explosives were useful in mining and were critical in the construction of railroads and canals. They also enabled the armies and navies of the great powers to arm themselves with increasingly accurate and powerful rifles and cannon.

The growing complexity of industrial chemistry made it one of the first fields where science and technology interacted on a daily basis. This development gave a great advantage to Germany, which had the most advanced engineering schools and scientific institutes of the time and whose government funded research and encouraged cooperation between universities and industries. By the end of the nineteenth century, Germany was the world's leading producer of dyes, drugs, synthetic fertilizers, ammonia, and nitrates used in making explosives.

Environmental Problems   Industrialization affected entire regions such as the English Midlands, the German Ruhr, parts of Pennsylvania in the United States, and the regions around Tokyo and Osaka in Japan.

The new steel mills took up as much space as whole towns, belched smoke and particulates, and left behind huge hills of slag and other waste products. Railroad locomotives and other steam engines polluted the air with coal smoke. The dyestuff and other chemicals produced toxic effluents that were dumped into nearby rivers. Industrialization unrestrained by environmental regulations caused considerable damage to nature and to the health of nearby inhabitants.

Electricity

Thomas Edison

electricity A form of energy used in telegraphy from the 1840s on and for lighting, industrial motors, and railroads beginning in the 1880s.

Thomas Edison American inventor best known for inventing the electric light bulb, acoustic recording on wax cylinders, and motion pictures.

No innovation of the late nineteenth century changed people's lives as radically as **electricity**. As an energy source, electricity was more flexible and much easier to use than water power or stationary steam engines. At first, producing electric current was so costly that it was used only for electroplating and telegraphy. Then in 1831 the Englishman Michael Faraday showed that the motion of a copper wire through a magnetic field induced an electric current in the wire. Based on his discovery, inventors in the 1870s devised generators that turned mechanical energy into electric current.

Electricity now had a host of new applications. Arc lamps lit up public squares, theaters, and stores. For a while, homes continued to rely on gas lamps, which produced a softer light. Then in 1879 in the United States **Thomas Edison** developed an incandescent lamp well suited to lighting small rooms. In 1882 Edison created the world's first electrical distribution network in New York City. By the turn of the century electric lighting was rapidly replacing gas lamps in the cities of Europe and North America.

Other uses of electricity quickly appeared. Electric streetcars and subways transported people throughout the cities of Europe and North America. Electric motors replaced steam engines and power belts, increasing productivity and improving workers' safety. As demand for electricity grew, engineers built hydroelectric plants. The plant at Niagara Falls, on the border between Ontario, Canada, and New York State, produced an incredible 11,000 horsepower when it opened in 1895. At the newly created Imperial College of Engineering in Japan, an Englishman, William Ayrton, became the first professor of electrical engineering anywhere in the world; his students later went on to found major corporations and government research institutes.

Paris Lit Up by Electricity, 1900 The electric light bulb was invented in the United States and Britain, but Paris made such extensive use of the new technology that it was nicknamed "City of Lights." To mark the Paris Exposition of 1900, the Eiffel Tower and all the surrounding buildings were illuminated with strings of light bulbs while powerful spotlights swept the sky.

World Trade and Finance

World trade expanded tenfold between 1850 and 1913. Europe imported wheat from the United States and India, wool from Australia, and beef from Argentina, while it exported coal, railroad equipment, textiles, and machinery to Asia and the Americas. Because steamships were much more efficient than sailing ships, the cost of freight dropped between 50 and 95 percent, making it worthwhile to ship even cheap and heavy products over very long distances.

The growth of world trade transformed different parts of the world in different ways. The economies of western Europe and North America, the first to industrialize, grew more diversified and prosperous. Industries mass-produced consumer goods for a growing number of middle-class and even working-class customers: soap, canned and packaged foods, ready-made clothes, household items, and small luxuries like cosmetics and engravings.

Business Cycles and Globalization

Capitalist economies, however, were prey to sudden swings in the business cycle—booms followed by deep depressions in which workers lost their jobs and investors their fortunes. Because of the close connections among the industrial economies, the collapse of a bank in Austria in 1873 triggered a depression that spread to the United States, causing mass unemployment. Worldwide recessions occurred in the mid-1880s and mid-1890s as well.

Tariffs could not insulate countries from the business cycle, for money continued to flow almost unhindered around the world. One of the main causes of the growing interdependence of the global economy was the financial power of Great Britain, which dominated the flow of trade, finance, and information. In 1900 two-thirds of the world's submarine cables were British or passed through Britain, and over half of the world's shipping was British owned. Britain invested one-fourth of its national wealth overseas, much of it in the United States and Argentina. British money financed many of the railroads, harbors, mines, and other big projects outside Europe. While other currencies fluctuated, the pound sterling was as good as gold, and nine-tenths of international transactions used sterling.

Nonindustrial areas also were tied to the world economy as never before. They were more vulnerable to changes in price and demand than were the industrialized nations, for many of them produced raw materials that could be replaced by synthetic substitutes (like dyestuffs) or alternative sources of supply. Nevertheless, until 1913 the value of exports from the tropical countries generally kept up with the growth of their populations.

SECTION REVIEW

- Industrialization spread throughout the world through trade and new technologies.

- Railroads, almost always financed by Western nations, spread to all continents, changing and enlarging cities.

- Steamships and telegraph cables connected continents and encouraged trade.

- In three new industries—steel, chemicals, and electricity—the United States and Germany surpassed Great Britain.

- World trade boomed in an age of globalization.

SOCIAL CHANGES

As fast-growing population swelled cities to unprecedented size, millions of Europeans emigrated to the Americas. Strained relations between industrial employers and workers spawned labor movements and new forms of radical politics. Women found their lives dramatically altered, both in the home and in the public sphere.

Population and Migrations

European Migrations

The population of Europe grew faster from 1850 to 1914 than ever before or since, almost doubling from 265 million to 468 million. In non-European countries with predominantly white populations—the United States, Canada, Australia, New Zealand, and Argentina—the increase was even greater because of the inflow of Europeans. There were many reasons for the mass migrations of this period: the Irish famine of 1847–1848; the persecution of Jews in Russia; poverty and population growth in Italy, Spain, Poland, and Scandinavia; and the cultural ties between Great Britain and English-speaking countries overseas. Equally important was the availability of cheap and rapid steamships and railroads serving travelers at both ends (see Environment and Technology: Railroads and Immigration). Between 1850 and 1900, on average,

400,000 Europeans migrated overseas every year; between 1900 and 1914 the flood rose to over 1 million a year. From 1850 to 1910 the population of the United States and Canada rose from 25 million to 98 million, and the proportion of people of European ancestry in the world's population rose from one-fifth to one-third.

Why did the number of Europeans and their descendants overseas jump so dramatically? Much of the increase came from a drop in the death rate, as epidemics and starvation became less common. The Irish famine was the last peacetime famine in European history. As farmers plowed up the plains of North America and planted wheat, much of which was shipped to Europe, food supplies increased faster than the population. Canning and refrigeration made food abundant year-round. The diet of Europeans and North Americans improved as meat, fruit, vegetables, and oils became part of the daily fare of city dwellers in winter as well as in summer.

Asian Migrations

During this period Asians also migrated in large numbers as indentured laborers recruited to work on plantations, in mines, and on railroads. Indians went to Africa, Southeast Asia, and other tropical colonies of Great Britain. Chinese and Indians emigrated to Southeast Asia, the East Indies, and the Caribbean to work on sugar plantations. Japanese migrated to Brazil and other parts of Latin America. Many Japanese, as well as Chinese and Filipinos, went to work in agriculture and menial trade in Hawaii and California, where they encountered growing hostility from European-Americans.

Urbanization and Urban Environments

In 1851 Britain became the first nation with a majority of its population living in towns and cities. By 1914, 80 percent of its population was urban, as were 60 percent of Germans and 45 percent of the French. Cities grew to unprecedented size. London grew from 2.7 million in 1850 to 6.6 million in 1900. New York, a small town of 64,000 people in 1800, reached 3.4 million by 1900, a fiftyfold increase. In 1800 New York had covered only the southernmost quarter of Manhattan Island, some 3 square miles (nearly 8 square kilometers); by 1900 it covered 150 square miles (390 square kilometers). In the English Midlands, in the German Ruhr, and around Tokyo Bay, towns fused into one another, filling in the fields and woods that once had separated them.

As cities grew, they changed in character. Newly built railroads not only brought goods into the cities on a predictable schedule but also allowed people to live farther apart. At first, only the well-to-do could afford to commute by train; by the end of the century, electric streetcars and subways allowed working-class people to live miles from their workplaces.

Sanitation

In preindustrial and early industrial cities, the poor crowded together in tenements; sanitation was bad; water often was contaminated with sewage; and darkness made life dangerous. New urban technologies and the growing powers and responsibilities of governments transformed city life for all but the poorest residents. The most important change was the installation of pipes to bring in clean water and to carry away sewage. First gas lighting and then electric lighting made cities safer at night. By the turn of the twentieth century municipal governments provided police and fire protection, sanitation and garbage removal, building and health inspection, schools, parks, and other amenities unheard of a century earlier.

As sanitation improved, epidemics became rare. For the first time, urban death rates fell below birthrates. The decline in infant mortality was especially significant. Confident that their children would survive infancy, couples began to limit the number of children they had, and ancient scourges like infanticide and child abandonment became less frequent.

Housing

To accommodate the growing population, builders created new neighborhoods, from crowded tenements for the poor to opulent mansions for the newly rich. In the United States planners laid out new cities, such as Chicago, on rectangular grids, and middle-class families moved to new developments on the edges of cities. In Paris older neighborhoods with narrow crooked streets and rickety tenements were torn down to make room for broad boulevards and modern apartment buildings. Brilliantly lit by gas and electricity, Paris became the "city of lights," a model for city planners from New Delhi to Buenos Aires. The rich continued to live in inner cities that contained the monuments, churches, and palaces of preindustrial times, while workers moved to the outskirts.

Lower population densities and better transportation divided cities into industrial, commercial, and residential zones occupied by different social classes. Improvements such as water and sewerage, electricity, and streetcars always benefited the wealthy first, then the middle

Railroads and Immigration

Why did so many Europeans emigrate to North America in the late nineteenth and early twentieth centuries? The quick answer is that millions of people longed to escape the poverty or tyranny of their home countries and start new lives in a land of freedom and opportunity. Personal desire alone, however, does not account for the migrations. After all, poverty and tyranny existed long before the late nineteenth century. Two other factors helped determine when and where people migrated: whether they were allowed to migrate, and whether they were able to.

In the nineteenth century Asians were recruited to build railroads and work on farms. But from the 1890s on, the United States and Canada closed their doors to non-Europeans, so regardless of what they wanted, they could not move to North America. In contrast, emigrants from Europe were admitted until after the First World War.

The ability to travel was a result of improvements in transportation. Until the 1890s most immigrants came from Ireland, England, or Germany—countries with good rail transportation to their own harbors and low steamship fares to North America. As rail lines were extended into eastern and southern Europe, more and more immigrants came from Italy, Austria-Hungary, and Russia.

Similarly, until the 1870s most European immigrants to North America settled on the east coast. Then, as the railroads pushed west, more of them settled on farms in the central and western parts of the continent. The power of railroads moved people as much as their desires did.

Library of Congress

Emigrant Waiting Room   The opening of the western region of the United States attracted settlers from the east coast and from Europe. These migrants are waiting for a train to take them to the Black Hills of Dakota during one of the gold rushes of the late nineteenth century.

class, and finally the working class. In the complex of urban life, businesses of all kinds arose, and the professions—engineering, accounting, research, journalism, and the law, among others—took on increased importance. The new middle class exhibited its wealth in fine houses with servants and in elegant entertainment.

Air Pollution   While urban environments improved in many ways, air quality worsened. Coal, burned to power steam engines and heat buildings, polluted the air, creating unpleasant and sometimes dangerous "pea-soup" fog and coating everything with a film of grimy dust. The thousands of horses that pulled the carts and carriages covered the streets with their wastes, causing a terrible stench. The introduction of electricity helped alleviate some of these environmental problems. Electric motors and lamps did not pollute the air. Power plants were built at a distance from cities. As electric trains and streetcars began replacing horse-drawn trolleys and coal-burning locomotives, cities became cleaner and healthier. However, most of the environmental benefits of electricity were to come in the twentieth century.

Middle-Class Women's "Separate Sphere"

Victorian Age The reign of Queen Victoria of Great Britain (r. 1837–1901). The term is also used to describe late-nineteenth-century society, with its rigid moral standards and sharply differentiated roles for men and women and for middle-class and working-class people.

Middle-Class Homes

"separate spheres" Nineteenth-century idea in Western societies that men and women, especially of the middle class, should have clearly differentiated roles in society: women as wives, mothers, and homemakers; men as breadwinners and participants in business and politics.

In English-speaking countries the period from about 1850 to 1901 is known as the "**Victorian Age**." The expression refers not only to the reign of Queen Victoria of England (r. 1837–1901) but also to rules of behavior and to an ideology surrounding the family and the relations between men and women. The Victorians contrasted the masculine ideals of strength and courage with the feminine virtues of beauty and kindness, and they idealized the home as a peaceful and loving refuge from the dog-eat-dog world of competitive capitalism.

Victorian morality claimed to be universal, yet it best fit upper- and middle-class European families. Men and women were thought to belong in "**separate spheres**." Successful businessmen spent their time at work or relaxing in men's clubs. They put their wives in charge of rearing the children, running the household, and spending the family money to enhance the family's social status.

Before electric appliances, maintaining a middle-class home involved enormous amounts of work. Not only were families larger, but middle-class couples entertained often and lavishly. Carrying out these tasks required servants. A family's status and the activities and lifestyle of the "mistress of the house" depended on the availability of servants to help with household tasks. Only families that employed at least one full-time servant were considered middle class.

Toward the turn of the century modern technology began to transform middle-class homes. Plumbing eliminated the pump and the outhouse. Central heating replaced fireplaces, stoves, trips to the basement for coal, and endless dusting. Gas and electricity lit houses and cooked food without soot, smoke, and ashes. In the early twentieth century wealthy families acquired the first vacuum cleaners and washing machines. These technological advances did not mean less housework for women. As families acquired new household technologies, they raised their standards of cleanliness, thus demanding just as much labor as before.

The most important duty of middle-class women was raising children. Victorian mothers nursed their own babies and showered their children with love and attention. Even those who could afford governesses remained personally involved in their children's education. Girls' edu-

Separate Spheres in Great Britain In the Victorian Age, men and women of the middle and upper classes led largely separate lives. In *Aunt Emily's Visit* (1845), we see women and children at home, tended by a servant. *The Royal Exchange*, meanwhile, was a place for men to transact business.

cation was very different from that of boys. While boys were being prepared for the business world or the professions, girls were taught embroidery, drawing, and music, skills that enhanced their social graces and marriage prospects.

Jobs and Careers

Young middle-class women could work until they got married, but only in genteel places like stores and offices, never in factories. When the typewriter and telephone were introduced into the business world in the 1880s, businessmen found that they could get better work at lower wages from educated young women than from men, and operating these machines was typecast as women's work.

Most professional careers were closed to women, and few universities granted women degrees. In the United States higher education was available to women only at elite colleges in the East and teachers' colleges in the Midwest. European women had fewer opportunities. Before 1914 very few women became doctors, lawyers, or professional musicians. Instead, women were considered well suited to teaching young children and girls—an extension of the duties of Victorian mothers—but only until marriage. A married woman was expected to become pregnant right away and to stay home taking care of her own children rather than other people's.

Suffragists

A home life, no matter how busy, did not satisfy all middle-class women. Some became volunteer nurses or social workers, receiving little or no pay. Others organized to fight prostitution, alcohol, and child labor. By the turn of the century a few challenged male domination of politics and the law. Suffragists, led in Britain by Emmeline Pankhurst and in the United States by Elizabeth Cady Stanton and Susan B. Anthony, demanded the right to vote. By 1914 U.S. women had won the right to vote in twelve states. British women did not vote until 1918.

Working-Class Women

Domestic Servants

In the new industrial cities, men and women no longer worked together at home or in the fields. The separation of work and home affected women even more than men. While working-class women formed a majority of the workers in the textile industries and in domestic service, they also needed to keep homes and raise children. As a result, they led lives of toil and pain. Parents expected girls as young as ten to contribute to the household. In Japan, as in Ireland and New England, tenant farmers, squeezed by rising taxes and rents, were forced to send their daughters to work in textile mills. Others became domestic servants, commonly working sixteen or more hours a day, six and a half days a week, for little more than room and board, usually in attics or basements. Without appliances, much of their work was physically hard: hauling coal and water up stairs, washing laundry by hand.

Young women often preferred factory work to domestic service. Men worked in construction, iron and steel, heavy machinery, or on railroads; women worked in textiles and the clothing trades, extensions of traditional women's household work (see Material Culture: Cotton Clothing). Appalled by the abuses of women and children in the early years of industrialization, most industrial countries passed protective legislation limiting the

Mary Evans Picture Library

Emmeline Pankhurst Under Arrest The leader of the British women's suffrage movement frequently called attention to her cause by breaking the law to protest discrimination against women. Here she is being arrested and carried off to jail by the police.

Cotton Clothing

Of all the things that bring us comfort, nothing compares to cotton. For clothes, sheets, and towels, it is the world's favorite textile. And no wonder: cotton is cool next to the skin, can be dyed in bright colors, absorbs moisture, and, unlike other fabrics such as wool, can be washed easily.

The use of cotton for clothing has a long history dating back to 3000 B.C.E., when it was grown in the Indus River Valley. Originally, the cotton plant was grown and the cloth woven only in India, Mexico, Peru, and a few other places in the tropics. The Maya wove fine textiles from cotton and traded them with other parts of Mesoamerica. Indian cottons were particularly fine and exported as luxury items to China and Rome. Cotton replaced hemp clothing in China and was used extensively by the Mongols for turbans, pants, and other items of clothing. The Arabs spread cotton growing and weaving to the Middle East and Spain. By the tenth century, it was a major crop in Iran and elsewhere in the region. Many of our names for particular kinds of cotton fabric come from cities in India, like *calico* (from Calicut) or *madras,* or in the Middle East, like *damask* (from Damascus) or *muslin* (from Mosul in Iraq).

Around 800 C.E., Arab merchants brought cotton cloth to Europe, where it became as precious as silk. With the invention of machines like the spinning jenny and the water frame in the eighteenth century (see Chapter 23), cotton became less precious and more available. Cotton yarn and cloth were the first items to be mass-produced in the Industrial Revolution, with important consequences for India, the American South, and other countries.

Mass production means mass consumption. In the nineteenth century, for the first time, the poor could afford to wear bright, colorful clothes and—even more important—to wash them. These clothes were made almost exclusively by women. Wealthy European families hired seamstresses who came to the house, took measurements, and returned a few days later with finished clothes. Other women sewed clothes for themselves and their families.

Sewing by hand was very time-consuming and increasingly costly compared to the declining price of cloth. By the mid-nineteenth century, prosperity and a faster pace of life in Europe and America provided an incentive for inventors to devise a machine that could sew. In 1850, Isaac Singer manufactured the first practical machine for commercial use. A few years later, he designed the "Singer Family Sewing Machine" with an iron stand and a foot-treadle for home use. By 1891 Singer alone had manufactured 10 million machines in the United States and Europe. Some were industrial machines sold to makers of ready-to-wear clothes in the new garment districts. Others were home models, some inexpensive enough for the working class. There were even portable

Private Collection

The Sewing Machine The Japanese imported many innovations from the West after the Meiji Restoration of 1868. Among the most popular were Western-style clothing and sewing machines. Sewing was a gendered activity in Japan as in the West, with the woman sewing and the man looking on.

models that seamstresses could take with them to their clients' homes.

The combination of cotton cloth and sewing machines revolutionized clothing. A shirt that took fourteen and a half hours to sew by hand could be made in an hour and a quarter on a machine; an apron could be made in nine minutes instead of an hour and a half. Now the poor could afford to own several shirts, skirts, or pants, even underwear. Better-off homemakers subscribed to fashion magazines, bought patterns, and made blouses and dresses, even complicated items like crinolines and hoopskirts, which would once have been too tedious to sew by hand.

Today, the world uses more cotton than any other fiber. China is the largest producer (and consumer) of cotton, followed by the United States, India, and Pakistan. Almost all of the cotton clothing sold is produced on powerful computerized machines in the developing countries of Asia and Latin America.

Factory Workers

hours or forbidding the employment of women in the hardest and most dangerous occupations, such as mining and foundry work. Such legislation reinforced gender divisions in industry, keeping women in low-paid, subordinate positions. Female factory workers earned between one-third and two-thirds of men's wages.

Workers' Homes

Married women with children were expected to stay home, even if their husbands did not make enough to support the family. Yet they had to contribute to the family's income. Families who had room to spare, even a bed or a corner in the kitchen, took in boarders. Many women did piecework such as sewing dresses, making hats or gloves, or weaving baskets. The hardest and worst-paid work was washing other people's clothes. Many women worked at home ten to twelve hours a day and enlisted the help of their small children, perpetuating practices long outlawed in factories. Without electric lighting and indoor plumbing, even ordinary household duties like cooking and washing remained heavy burdens.

SECTION REVIEW

- As European population grew, millions migrated to other continents.

- Cities grew to enormous size, changing in character and posing difficult housing, sanitation, and environmental problems.

- Middle-class women inhabited a "separate sphere" from men and devoted their lives to their homes and families, but a few fought for equal rights.

- Working-class women, who had to keep a home while earning a living, led hard lives.

SOCIALISM AND LABOR MOVEMENTS

socialism A political ideology that originated in Europe in the 1830s. Socialists advocated government protection of workers from exploitation by property owners and government ownership of industries. This ideology led to the founding of socialist or labor parties throughout Europe in the second half of the nineteenth century.

labor union An organization of workers in a particular industry or trade, created to defend the interests of members through strikes or negotiations with employers.

Industrialization combined with the revolutionary ideas of the late eighteenth century to produce two kinds of movements calling for further changes: socialism and labor unions. **Socialism** was an ideology developed by radical thinkers who questioned the sanctity of private property and argued in support of industrial workers against their employers. **Labor unions** were organizations formed by industrial workers to defend their interests in negotiations with employers. The socialist and labor movements were never identical. Most of the time they were allies; occasionally they were rivals.

Marx and Socialism

The Communist Manifesto

Karl Marx German journalist and philosopher, founder of the Marxist branch of socialism. He is known for two books: *Manifesto of the Communist Party* (1848) and *Das Kapital* (Vols. I–III, 1867–1894).

By far the best-known socialist was **Karl Marx** (1818–1883), a German journalist and writer who spent most of his life in England and collaborated with another socialist, Friedrich Engels (1820–1895), author of *The Condition of the Working Class in England in 1844* (1845). Together, they combined German philosophy, French revolutionary ideas, and knowledge of British industrial conditions.

Marx expressed his ideas succinctly in the *Manifesto of the Communist Party* (1848) (see Diversity and Dominance: Marx and Engels on Global Trade and the Bourgeoisie) and in great detail in *Das Kapital* (DUSS cop-ee-TAHL) (1867). He saw history as a long series of conflicts between social classes, the latest being between property owners (the bourgeoisie) and workers (the proletariat). He argued that the capitalist system allowed the bourgeoisie to extract the "surplus value" of workers' labor—that is, the difference between their wages and the value of the goods they manufactured. He saw business enterprises becoming larger and more monopolistic and workers growing more numerous and impoverished with every downturn in the business cycle. He concluded that this conflict would inevitably lead to a revolution and the overthrow of the bourgeoisie, after which the workers would establish a communist society without classes.

What Marx called "scientific socialism" provided an intellectual framework for the growing dissatisfaction with raw industrial capitalism. In the late nineteenth century business tycoons spent money lavishly on displays of wealth that contrasted sharply with the poverty of the workers. Even though industrial workers were not becoming poorer as Marx believed, the class struggle between workers and employers was brutally real. Marx offered a persuasive explanation of the causes of this contrast and the antagonisms it bred.

Marx and Engels on Global Trade and the Bourgeoisie

In 1848 Karl Marx (1818–1883) and Friedrich Engels (1820–1895) published the Manifesto of the Communist Party. *In it, they tried to explain why business owners—the "bourgeoisie"—had become the wealthiest and most powerful class of people in industrializing countries like Britain, and why industrial workers—the "proletariat"—lived in poverty. In their view, the dominance of the bourgeoisie was destroying the diversity of human cultures, reducing all classes in Europe and all cultures to the status of proletarians selling their labor.*

In the Manifesto, *Marx and Engels called for a revolution in which the workers would overthrow the bourgeoisie and establish a new society without private property or government. Their* Manifesto *was soon translated into many languages and became the best-known expression of radical communist ideology.*

Marx and Engels's ideas are especially interesting from the perspective of global history because of the way in which they connect the rise of the bourgeoisie with world trade and industrial technology. The following paragraphs explain these connections.

The history of all hitherto existing society is the history of class struggles. . . .

In the earlier epochs of history, we find almost everywhere a complicated arrangement of society into various orders, a manifold gradation of social rank. In ancient Rome we have patricians, knights, plebeians, slaves; in the middle ages, feudal lords, vassals, guild-masters, journeymen, apprentices, serfs; in almost all of these classes, again, subordinate gradations.

The modern bourgeois society that has sprouted from the ruins of feudal society, has not done away with class antagonisms. It has but established new classes, new conditions of oppression, new forms of struggle in place of the old ones.

Our epoch, the epoch of the bourgeoisie, possesses, however, this distinctive feature; it has simplified the class antagonisms. Society as a whole is more and more splitting up into two great hostile camps, into two great classes directly facing each other: Bourgeoisie and Proletariat. . . .

The discovery of America, the rounding of the Cape, opened up fresh ground for the rising bourgeoisie. The East-Indian and Chinese markets, the colonization of America, trade with the colonies, the increase in the means of exchange and in commodities generally, gave to commerce, to navigation, to industry, an impulse never before known, and thereby, to the revolutionary element in the tottering feudal society, a rapid development. . . .

Modern industry has established the world-market, for which the discovery of America paved the way. This market has given an immense importance to commerce, to navigation, to communication by land. This development has, in its turn, reacted on the extension of industry; and in proportion as industry, commerce, navigation, railways extended, in the same proportion the bourgeoisie developed, increased its capital, and pushed into the background every class handed down from the Middle Ages. . . .

The bourgeoisie, historically, has played a most revolutionary part. . . .

It has been the first to show what man's activity can bring about. It has accomplished wonders far surpassing Egyptian pyramids, Roman aqueducts, and Gothic cathedrals; it has conducted expeditions that put in the shade all former Exoduses of nations and crusades. . . .

The need of a constantly expanding market for its products chases the bourgeoisie over the whole surface of the globe. It must nestle everywhere, settle everywhere, establish connexions everywhere.

---

e PRIMARY SOURCE: Working Men of All Countries, Unite! Read these excerpts from the *Manifesto of the Communist Party* and find out why "the proletarians have nothing to lose but their chains."

Universal Male Suffrage

Labor Unions and Movements

Since the beginning of the nineteenth century, workers had united to create "friendly societies" for mutual assistance in times of illness, unemployment, or disability. Laws that forbade workers to strike were abolished in Britain in the 1850s and in the rest of Europe soon thereafter. Labor unions sought not only better wages but also improved working conditions and insurance against illness, accidents, disability, and old age. They grew slowly because they required a permanent staff and a great deal of money to sustain their members during strikes. Still, by the end of the century British labor unions counted 2 million members, and German and American unions had 1 million members each.

Just as labor unions strove to share in the benefits of a capitalist economy, so did electoral politics persuade workers to become part of the existing political system. The nineteenth century saw a gradual extension of the right to vote throughout Europe and North America. Universal male suffrage became law in the United States in 1870, in France and Germany in 1871, in Britain in 1885, and in the rest of Europe soon thereafter. With so many newly enfranchised workers, socialist politicians hoped to capture many seats in their nations' parliaments. Rather than seize power through revolution, the socialists expected to obtain concessions from government and eventually even to form a government.

The bourgeoisie has through its exploitation of the world-market given a cosmopolitan character to production and consumption in every country. To the great chagrin of Reactionists, it has drawn from under the feet of industry the national ground on which it stood. All old-fashioned national industries have been destroyed or are daily being destroyed. They are dislodged by new industries, whose introduction becomes a life or death question for all civilised nations, by industries that no longer work up indigenous raw material, but raw material drawn from the remotest zones; industries whose products are consumed, not only at home, but in every quarter of the globe. In place of the old wants, satisfied by the productions of the country, we find new wants, requiring for their satisfaction the products of distant lands and climes. In place of the old local and national seclusion and self-sufficiency, we have intercourse in every direction, universal inter-dependence of nations. And as in material, so also in intellectual production. The intellectual creations of individual nations become common property. National one-sidedness and narrow-mindedness become more and more impossible, and from the numerous national and local literatures there arises a world-literature.

The bourgeoisie, by the rapid improvement of all instruments of production, by the immensely facilitated means of communication, draws all, even the most barbarian, nations into civilisation. The cheap prices of its commodities are the heavy artillery with which it batters down all Chinese walls, with which it forces the barbarians' intensely obstinate hatred of foreigners to capitulate. It compels all nations, on pain of extinction, to adopt the bourgeois mode of production; it compels them to introduce what it calls civilisation into their midst, i.e., to become bourgeois themselves. In a word, it creates a world after its own image.

The bourgeoisie has subjected the country to the rule of the towns. It has created enormous cities, has greatly increased the urban population as compared with the rural, and has thus rescued a considerable part of the population from the idiocy of rural life. Just as it has made the country dependent on the towns, so it has made barbarian and semi-barbarian countries dependent on the civilised ones, nations of peasants on nations of bourgeois, the East on the West. . . .

The bourgeoisie, during its rule of scarce one hundred years, has created more massive and more colossal productive forces than have all preceding generations together. Subjection of Nature's forces to man, machinery, application of chemistry to industry and agriculture, steam-navigation, railways, electric telegraphs, clearing of whole continents for cultivation, canalization of rivers, whole populations conjured out of the ground—what earlier century had even a presentiment that such productive forces slumbered in the lap of social labour?

QUESTIONS FOR ANALYSIS

1. How did the growth of world trade since the European discovery of America affect relations between social classes in Europe?

2. Compare Marx and Engels's views on industrial production with those of Adam Smith that you read in Chapter 23. Do they contradict each other? Or does Smith's description of pin-making explain the rise of what Marx and Engels call "the giant, Modern Industry"?

3. What effect did the growth of trade and industry have on products, intellectual creations, and consumer tastes around the world?

Source: Karl Marx and Frederick Engels, *Manifesto of the Communist Party,* Authorized English Translation: Edited and Annotated by Frederick Engels (Chicago: Charles H. Kerr & Company, 1906), pp. 12–20.

Women Revolutionaries

anarchists Revolutionaries who wanted to abolish all private property and governments, usually by violence, and replace them with free associations of groups.

Working-class women, burdened with both job and family responsibilities, found little time for politics and were not welcome in the male-dominated trade unions or radical political parties. A few radicals such as the German socialist Rosa Luxemburg and the American **anarchist** Emma Goldman in the United States became famous but did not have a large following. It was never easy to reconcile the demands of workers and those of women. In 1889 the German socialist Clara Zetkin wrote: "Just as the male worker is subjected by the capitalist, so is the woman by the man, and she will always remain in subjugation until she is economically independent. Work is the indispensable condition for economic independence." Six years later, she recognized that the liberation of women would have to await a change in the position of the working class as a whole: "The proletarian woman cannot attain her highest ideal through a movement for the equality of the female sex, she attains salvation only through the fight for the emancipation of labor."[1]

SECTION REVIEW

- Karl Marx expected a workers' revolution, but later socialists hoped to gain influence through elections.

- Labor movements and unions worked to improve workers' pay and working conditions.

NATIONALISM AND THE RISE OF ITALY, GERMANY, AND JAPAN

nationalism A political ideology that stresses people's membership in a nation—a community defined by a common culture and history as well as by territory. In the late eighteenth and early nineteenth centuries, nationalism was a force for unity in western Europe. In the late nineteenth century it hastened the disintegration of the Austro-Hungarian and Ottoman Empires. In the twentieth century it provided the ideological foundation for scores of independent countries emerging from colonialism.

The most influential idea of the nineteenth century was **nationalism**. Whereas people had previously been considered the subjects of a sovereign, the French revolutionaries defined people as the citizens of a *nation*—a concept identified with a territory, the state that ruled it, and the culture of its people.

Language and National Identity in Europe Before 1871

Language was usually the crucial element in creating a feeling of national unity. It was important both as a way to unite the people of a nation and as the means of persuasion by which political leaders could inspire their followers. Language was the tool of the new generation of political activists, most of them lawyers, teachers, students, and journalists. Yet language and citizenship seldom coincided.

The fit between France and the French language was closer than in most large countries, though some French-speakers lived outside of France and some French people spoke other languages. Italian- and German-speaking people, however, were divided among many small states. Living in the Austrian Empire were peoples who spoke German, Czech, Slovak, Hungarian, Polish, and other languages. Even where people spoke a common language, they could be divided by religion or institutions. The Irish, though English-speaking, were mostly Catholic, whereas the English were primarily Protestant.

The idea of redrawing the boundaries of states to accommodate linguistic, religious, or cultural differences was revolutionary. In Italy and Germany it led to the forging of large new states out of many small ones in 1871. In central and eastern Europe, nationalism threatened to break up large states into smaller ones.

Liberalism

liberalism A political ideology that emphasizes the civil rights of citizens, representative government, and the protection of private property. This ideology, derived from the Enlightenment, was especially popular among the property-owning middle classes of Europe and North America.

Until the 1860s nationalism was associated with **liberalism**, the revolutionary middle-class ideology that emerged from the French Revolution, asserted the sovereignty of the people, and demanded constitutional government, a national parliament, and freedom of expression. The most famous nationalist of the early nineteenth century was the Italian liberal Giuseppe Mazzini (jew-SEP-pay mots-EE-nee) (1805–1872), the leader of the failed revolution of 1848 in Italy. Mazzini sought to unify the Italian peninsula into one nation and associated with revolutionaries elsewhere to bring nationhood and liberty to all peoples oppressed by tyrants and foreigners. The governments of Russia, Prussia, and Austria censored the new ideas but could not quash them.

The revolutions of 1848 convinced conservatives that governments could not forever keep their citizens out of politics and that mass politics, if properly managed, could strengthen rather than weaken the state. A new generation of conservative political leaders learned how to preserve the status quo through public education, universal military service, and colonial conquests, all of which built a sense of national unity.

The Unification of Italy, 1860–1870

By midcentury, popular sentiment was building throughout Italy for unification. Opposing it were Pope Pius IX, who abhorred everything modern, and Austria, which controlled two Italian provinces, Lombardy and Venetia (see Map 27.1). The prime minister of Piedmont-Sardinia, Count Camillo Benso di Cavour, saw the rivalry between France and Austria as an opportunity to unify Italy. He secretly formed an alliance with France, then instigated a war with Austria in 1858. The war was followed by uprisings throughout northern and central Italy in favor of joining Piedmont-Sardinia, a moderate constitutional monarchy under King Victor Emmanuel.

Giuseppe Garibaldi Italian nationalist and revolutionary who conquered Sicily and Naples and added them to a unified Italy in 1860.

If the conservative, top-down approach to unification prevailed in the north, a more radical approach was still possible in the south. In 1860 the fiery revolutionary **Giuseppe Garibaldi** (jew-SEP-pay gary-BAHL-dee) and a small band of followers landed in Sicily and then in southern Italy, overthrew the Kingdom of the Two Sicilies, and prepared to found a democratic republic. The royalist Cavour, however, took advantage of the unsettled situation to sideline Garibaldi

Cavour and Garibaldi

MAP 27.1 **Unification of Italy, 1859–1870** The unification of Italy was achieved by the expansion of the kingdom of Piedmont-Sardinia, with the help of France.

e Interactive Map

Kingdom of Sardinia before 1859
To Kingdom of Sardinia, 1859
To Kingdom of Sardinia, 1860
To Kingdom of Italy, 1866, 1870
★ Major battle
Boundary of Kingdom of Italy after unification

© Cengage Learning

and expand Piedmont-Sardinia into a new Kingdom of Italy. Unification was completed with the addition of Venetia in 1866 and the Papal States in 1870.

The process of unification illustrates the shift of nationalism from a radical democratic idea to a conservative method of building popular support for a strong centralized government, even an aristocratic and monarchical one.

The Unification of Germany, 1866–1871

The unification of most German-speaking people into a single state in 1871 had momentous consequences for the world. Until the 1860s the region of central Europe where people spoke German consisted of Prussia, the western half of the Austrian Empire, and numerous smaller states (see Map 27.2). Some German nationalists wanted to unite all Germans under the Austrian throne. Others wanted to exclude Austria with its many non-Germanic peoples and unite all other German-speaking areas under Prussia. The divisions were also religious: Austria and southwestern Germany were Catholic; Prussia and the northeast were Lutheran. The Prussian state had two advantages: (1) the newly developed industries of the Rhineland, and (2) the first European army to make use of railroads, telegraphs, breechloading rifles, steel artillery, and other products of modern industry.

**Bismarck Attacks
Austria and France**

Otto von Bismarck Chancellor (prime minister) of Prussia from 1862 until 1871, when he became chancellor of Germany. A conservative nationalist, he led Prussia to victory against Austria (1866) and France (1870) and was responsible for the creation of the German Empire in 1871.

During the reign of King Wilhelm I (r. 1861–1888), Prussia was ruled by a brilliant and authoritarian aristocrat, Chancellor **Otto von Bismarck** (UTT-oh von BIS-mark) (1815–1898). Bismarck was determined to use Prussian industry and German nationalism to make his state the dominant power in Germany. In 1866 Prussia attacked and defeated Austria. To everyone's surprise, Prussia took no Austrian territory. Instead, Prussia and some smaller states formed the North German Confederation, the nucleus of a future Germany. Then in 1870 Bismarck attacked France. Prussian armies, joined by troops from other German states, used their superior firepower and tactics to achieve a quick victory. "Blood and iron" were the foundation of the new German Empire.

The spoils of victory included a large indemnity and two provinces of France bordering on Germany: Alsace and Lorraine. The French paid the indemnity easily enough but resented the loss of their provinces. To the Germans, this region was German because a majority of its inhabitants spoke German. To the French, it was French because most of its inhabitants considered themselves French. These two conflicting definitions of nationalism kept enmity between France and Germany smoldering for decades. In this case, nationalism turned out to be a divisive rather than a unifying force.

The West Challenges Japan

The Shogunate

In Japan the emperor was revered but had no power. Instead, Japan was governed by the Tokugawa Shogunate—a secular government under a military leader, or *shogun*, that had come to power in 1600 (see Chapter 21). Local lords, called *daimyos,* were permitted to control their lands and populations with very little interference from the shogunate.

When threatened from outside, this system showed many weaknesses. For one thing, it did not permit the coordination of resources necessary to resist a major invasion. Attempting to minimize exposure to foreign powers, in the early 1600s the shoguns prohibited foreigners from entering Japan and Japanese from going abroad. The penalty for breaking these laws was death, but many Japanese ignored them. The most flagrant violators were powerful lords in southern Japan who ran large and very successful pirate or black-market operations. In their entrepreneurial activities they benefited from the decentralization of the shogunal political system. But when a genuine foreign threat was suggested—as when, in 1792, Russian and British ships were spotted off the Japanese coast—the local lords realized that Japan was too weak and decentralized to resist a foreign invasion. As a result, a few of the regional lords began to develop their own reformed armies, arsenals, and shipyards.

By the 1800s Satsuma (SAT-soo-mah) and Choshu (CHOE-shoo), two large domains in southern Japan, had become wealthy and ambitious, enjoying high rates of revenue and population growth. Their remoteness from the capital Edo (now Tokyo) and their economic vigor also fostered a strong sense of local self-reliance.

Commodore Perry's Fleet

In 1853 the American commodore Matthew C. Perry arrived off the coast of Japan and demanded that Japan open its ports to trade and allow American ships to refuel and take on supplies during their voyages between China and California. He promised to return a year later to receive the Japanese answer. Perry's demands sparked a crisis in the shogunate. After consultation with the provincial daimyos, the shogun's advisers advocated capitulation to Perry, pointing to China's humiliating defeats in the Opium and Arrow Wars. In 1854, when Perry returned, representatives of the shogun indicated their willingness to sign the Treaty of Kanagawa (KAH-nah-GAH-wah), modeled on the unequal treaties between China and the Western powers. Angry and disappointed, some provincial governors began to encourage an underground movement calling for the destruction of the Tokugawa regime and the banning of foreigners from Japan.

Tensions between the shogunate and some provincial leaders, particularly in Choshu and Satsuma, increased in the early 1860s. Young, ambitious, educated men who faced mediocre prospects under the rigid Tokugawa class system emerged as provincial leaders. When British and French ships shelled the southwestern coasts in 1864 to protest the treatment of foreigners, the action enraged the provincial samurai who rejected the Treaty of Kanagawa and resented the shogunate's inability to protect the country. In 1867 the Choshu leaders Yamagata Aritomo and Ito Hirobumi finally realized that they should stop warring with their rival province, Satsuma, and join forces to lead a rebellion against the shogunate.

MAP 27.2 **Unification of Germany, 1866–1871** Germany was united after a series of short, successful wars by the kingdom of Prussia against Austria in 1866 and against France in 1871.

© Cengage Learning

 Interactive Map

The Meiji Restoration and the Modernization of Japan, 1868–1894

Meiji Restoration The political program that followed the destruction of the Tokugawa Shogunate in 1868, in which a collection of young leaders set Japan on the path of centralization, industrialization, and imperialism.

The civil war was intense but brief. In 1868 provincial rebels overthrew the Tokugawa Shogunate and declared young emperor Mutsuhito (moo-tsoo-HE-toe) (r. 1868–1912) "restored." The new leaders called their regime the **"Meiji (MAY-gee) Restoration"** after Mutsuhito's reign name (*Meiji* means "enlightened rule"). The "Meiji oligarchs," as the new rulers were known, were extraordinarily talented and far-sighted. Determined to protect their country from Western imperialism, they encouraged its transformation into "a rich country with a strong army" with world-class industries. Though imposed from above, the Meiji Restoration marked as profound a change as the French Revolution (see Map 27.3).

MAP 27.3 **Expansion and Modernization of Japan, 1868–1918** As Japan acquired modern industry, it followed the example of the European powers in seeking overseas colonies. Its colonial empire grew at the expense of its neighbors: Taiwan was taken from China in 1895; Karafutu (Sakhalin) from Russia in 1905; and all of Korea became a colony in 1910.

e Interactive Map

The oligarchs were under no illusion that they could fend off the Westerners without changing their institutions and their society. In the Charter Oath issued in 1868, the young emperor included a prophetic phrase: "Knowledge shall be sought throughout the world and thus shall be strengthened the foundation of the imperial polity." It was to be the motto of a new Japan, which embraced all foreign ideas, institutions, and techniques that could strengthen the nation. The literacy rate in Japan was the highest in Asia at the time, and the oligarchs shrewdly exploited it in their introduction of new educational systems, a conscript army, and new communications. The government was able to establish heavy industry, thanks to decades of industrial development and financing in the provinces in the earlier 1800s. With a conscript army and a revamped educational system, the oligarchs attempted to create a new citizenry that was literate and competent but also loyal and obedient.

The Meiji leaders copied the government structure of imperial Germany and modeled the new Japanese navy on the British and the army on the Prussian. They also introduced Western-style postal and telegraph services, railroads and harbors, banking, clocks, and calendars. To

Japan's New Army　After the Meiji Restoration in 1868, the leaders of the new government set out to make Japan "a rich country with a strong army." They modeled the new army on the European armies of the time, with Western-style uniforms, rifles, cannon, and musical instruments.

Laurie Platt Winfrey/The Granger Collection, New York

learn the secrets of Western strength, they sent hundreds of students to Britain, Germany, and the United States. Western-style clothing and hairstyles and garden parties and formal dances became popular.

The government was especially interested in Western technology. It opened vocational, technical, and agricultural schools, founded four imperial universities, and brought in foreign experts to advise on medicine, science, and engineering. To encourage industrialization, the government set up state-owned enterprises to manufacture cloth and inexpensive consumer goods for sale abroad. The first Japanese industries exploited their workers ruthlessly, just as the first industries in Europe and America had done. In 1881 the government sold these enterprises to private investors, mainly large *zaibatsu* (zye-BOT-soo), or conglomerates, and also encouraged individual technological innovation. Thus the carpenter Toyoda Sakichi founded the Toyoda Loom Works (now Toyota Motor Company) in 1906; ten years later he patented the world's most advanced automatic loom.

**e PRIMARY SOURCE:
Letter to Mitsubishi
Employees** Iwasaki Yaturo announces government aid in the effort to defeat foreign competition for control of Japanese coastal trade.

Charles Darwin

Nationalism and Social Darwinism

The Franco-Prussian War of 1870–1871 changed the political climate of Europe, making France more liberal. The kingdom of Italy completed the unification of the peninsula. Germany, Austria-Hungary (as the Austrian Empire had renamed itself in 1867), and Russia remained conservative and used nationalism to maintain the status quo.

Nationalism and parliamentary elections made politicians of all parties appeal to public opinion. They were greatly aided by the press, especially cheap daily newspapers that sought to increase circulation by publishing sensational articles about overseas conquests and foreign threats. As governments increasingly came to recognize the advantages of an educated population in the competition between states, they opened public schools in every town and admitted women into public-service jobs for the first time. Politicians and journalists appealed to the emotions of the poor, diverting their anger from their employers to foreigners and their votes from socialist to nationalist parties.

In many countries the dominant group used nationalism to impose its language, religion, or customs on minority populations. The Russian Empire attempted to "Russify" its diverse ethnic populations. The Spanish government made Spanish compulsory in the schools, newspapers, and courts of its Basque- and Catalan-speaking provinces. Immigrants to the United States were expected to learn English.

Western culture in the late nineteenth century exalted the powerful over the weak, men over women, rich over poor, Europeans over other races, and humans over nature. Some people looked to science for support of political dominance. One of the most influential scientists of the century, and the one whose ideas were most widely cited and misinterpreted, was the English biologist Charles Darwin (1809–1882).

In his 1859 book *On the Origin of the Species,* Darwin argued that the earth was much older than previously believed. He proposed that over the course of hundreds of thousands of years living beings had either evolved in the struggle for survival or become extinct.

The philosopher Herbert Spencer (1820–1903) and others took up Darwin's ideas of "natural selection" and "survival of the fittest" and applied them to human society. Social Darwinists developed elaborate pseudo-scientific theories of racial differences, claiming that they were the result not of history but of biology. They saw social and racial differences as resulting from natural processes and opposed state intervention to alleviate inequities. Although not based on any research, these ideas gave a scientific-sounding justification for the power of the privileged.

SECTION REVIEW

- Nationalism, the most powerful new ideology of the nineteenth century, defined nations primarily on the basis of language.

- Garibaldi helped unify Italy between 1860 and 1870, and Bismarck unified Germany from 1866 to 1871.

- In response to Western intrusion, provincial Japanese lords launched the Meiji Restoration and quickly transformed Japan into a modern industrial nation.

- During this era, Charles Darwin's theory of evolution was often misinterpreted to justify the power of the privileged few.

THE GREAT POWERS OF EUROPE, 1871–1900

After the middle of the century, politicians and journalists discovered that minor events involving foreigners could be used to stir up popular indignation against neighboring countries. Military officers, impressed by the awesome power of the weapons that industry provided, began to think that the weapons were invincible. Rivalries over colonial territories, ideological differences, even minor border incidents or trade disagreements contributed to a growing international tension.

e PRIMARY SOURCE: **Extracts from History of Germany in the Nineteenth Century and Historical and Political Writings** A nineteenth-century German historian proclaims a racist and militarist ideology.

Germany at the Center of Europe

International relations revolved around Germany because it was located in the center of Europe and had the most powerful army on the European continent. After creating a unified Germany in 1871, Bismarck declared that his country had no further territorial ambitions, and he put his effort into maintaining the peace in Europe. To isolate France, he forged a loose coalition with Austria-Hungary and Russia, the other two conservative powers. Despite their competing ambitions in the Balkans, he was able to keep his coalition together for twenty years.

German Social Policies

Bismarck proved equally adept at strengthening German unity at home. To weaken the influence of middle-class liberals, he extended the vote to all adult men, thereby allowing Socialists to win seats in the *Reichstag* or parliament. By imposing high tariffs on manufactured goods and wheat, he gained the support of both the wealthy industrialists of the Rhineland and the great landowners of eastern Germany, traditional rivals for power. He also introduced social legislation—medical, unemployment, and disability insurance and old-age pensions—long before other industrial countries. His government supported public and technical education. Under his leadership, the German people developed a strong sense of national unity and pride in their industrial and military power.

Wilhelm II

In 1888 Wilhelm I was succeeded by his grandson Wilhelm II (r. 1888–1918), an insecure and arrogant man who tried to gain respect by making belligerent speeches. Within two years he had dismissed Chancellor Bismarck and surrounded himself with yes men. He talked about his "global policy" and demanded a colonial empire. Ruler of the nation with the mightiest army and the largest industrial economy in Europe, he felt that Germany deserved "a place in the sun."

The Liberal Powers: France and Great Britain

France

France, once the dominant nation in Europe, had difficulty reconciling itself to being in second place. Though a prosperous country with flourishing agriculture and a large colonial empire, the French republic had some serious weaknesses. For example, its population was scarcely growing; in 1911 France had only 39 million people compared to Germany's 64 million. In an age when the power of nations was roughly proportional to the size of their armies, France could field an army only two-thirds the size of Germany's.

The French people were also deeply divided over the very nature of the state: some were monarchists and Catholic, but a growing number held republican and anticlerical views. Yet if French political life seemed fragile and frequently in crisis, a long tradition of popular participation in politics and a strong sense of nationhood, reinforced by a fine system of public education, gave the French people a deeper cohesion than appeared on the surface.

Britain and the Irish

Great Britain had a long experience with parliamentary elections and competing parties. The British government alternated smoothly between the Liberal and Conservative Parties, and the income gap between rich and poor gradually narrowed. Nevertheless, Britain had problems that grew more apparent as time went on. One was Irish resentment of English rule. Nationalism had strengthened the allegiance of the English, Scots, and Welsh to the British state. But the Irish, excluded because they were Catholic and predominantly poor, saw the British as a foreign occupying force.

Another problem was the British economy. Great Britain had fallen behind the United States and Germany in such important industries as steel, chemicals, electricity, and textiles. Even in shipbuilding and shipping, Britain's traditional specialty, Germany was catching up.

Britain's Empire

Britain was preoccupied with its enormous and fast-growing empire. A source of wealth for investors and the envy of other imperialist nations, the empire was a constant drain on Britain's finances, for it required Britain to maintain costly fleets of warships throughout the world.

For most of the nineteenth century Britain pursued a policy of "splendid isolation." Britain's preoccupation with India led British statesmen to exaggerate the Russian threat to the Ottoman Empire and to the Central Asian approaches to India. Periodic "Russian scares" and Britain's age-old rivalry with France for overseas colonies diverted the attention of British politicians from the rise of Germany.

The Conservative Powers: Russia and Austria-Hungary

The forces of nationalism weakened rather than strengthened Russia and Austria-Hungary. Their populations were far more divided, socially and ethnically, than were the German, French, or British peoples.

Balkan Rivalries

Nationalism was most divisive in south-central Europe, where many different language groups lived in close proximity. In 1867 the Austrian Empire renamed itself the Austro-Hungarian Empire to appease its Hungarian critics. Its attempts to promote the cultures of its Slavic-speaking minorities failed to gain their political allegiance. However, it still thought of itself as a great power and attempted to dominate the Balkans. This strategy irritated Russia, which thought of itself as the protector of Slavic peoples everywhere.

Minorities in Russia

Ethnic diversity also contributed to the instability of imperial Russia. The Polish people rebelled in 1830 and 1863–1864. The tsarist empire also included Finland, Estonia, Latvia, Lithuania, and Ukraine; the Caucasus; and the Muslim population of Central Asia conquered between 1865 and 1881. Furthermore, Russia had the largest Jewish population in Europe, and the harshness of its anti-Semitic laws and periodic *pogroms* (massacres) prompted many Jews to flee to America. The state's attempts to impose the Russian language on its subjects were divisive instead of unifying forces.

Emancipation of the Serfs

In 1861 the moderate conservative Tsar Alexander II (r. 1855–1881) emancipated the peasants from serfdom. He did so partly out of a genuine desire to strengthen the bonds between the monarchy and the Russian people, and partly to promote industrialization by enlarging the labor pool. That half-hearted measure, however, only turned serfs into farm workers with few skills and little capital. Though "emancipated," the great majority of Russians had little education, few legal rights, and no say in the government. After Alexander's assassination in 1881, his successors Alexander III (r. 1881–1894) and Nicholas II (r. 1894–1917) reluctantly permitted half-hearted attempts at social change. The Russian commercial middle class was small and had little influence. Industrialization consisted largely of state-sponsored projects, such as railroads, iron foundries, and armament factories, and led to social unrest among urban workers. Wealthy landowning aristocrats dominated the Russian court and administration and blocked most reforms.

© 2009 The State Russian Museum, St. Petersburg

The Doss House Late-nineteenth-century cities showed more physical than social improvements. This painting by Makovsky of a street in St. Petersburg contrasts the broad avenue and impressive new buildings with the poverty of the crowd.

The Russo-Japanese War and Revolution

The weaknesses in Russia's society and government became glaringly obvious during a war with Japan in 1904 and 1905. The fighting took place in Manchuria, a province in northern China far from European Russia. The Russian army, which received all its supplies by means of the inefficient Trans-Siberian Railway, was defeated by the better-trained and better-equipped Japanese. After a long journey around Eurasia and Africa, the Russian navy was sunk by the Japanese fleet at Tsushima Strait in 1905.

The shock of defeat caused a revolution in 1905 that forced Tsar Nicholas II to grant a constitution and an elected Duma (parliament). But as soon as he was able to rebuild the army and the police, he reverted to the traditional despotism of his forefathers. Small groups of radical intellectuals, angered by the contrast between the wealth of the elite and the poverty of the common people, began plotting the violent overthrow of the tsarist autocracy.

SECTION REVIEW

- A united Germany, the most powerful state in Europe, became a threat to peace under Wilhelm II.

- France and Great Britain, though liberal democracies, faced difficulties at home and overseas.

- Russia and Austria-Hungary, two conservative empires, failed to adapt their politics to the modernization of their societies.

CHINA, JAPAN, AND THE WESTERN POWERS

After 1850 China and Japan—the two largest countries in East Asia—felt the influence of the Western powers as never before, but their responses were completely opposite. China resisted Western influence and became weaker, while Japan transformed itself into a major industrial and military power. One reason for this difference was the Western powers' heavy involvement in China and the distance to Japan, the nation most remote from Europe by ship. More important was the difference between the Chinese and Japanese elites' attitudes toward foreign cultures.

China in Turmoil

China had been devastated by the Taiping (tie-PING) Rebellion that raged from 1850 to 1864 (see Chapter 25). The French and British took advantage of China's weakness to demand treaty

Le Petit Parisien

SUPPLÉMENT LITTÉRAIRE ILLUSTRÉ

DIRECTION: 18, rue d'Enghien, PARIS

Les Événements de Chine

MORT AUX ÉTRANGERS !

Mary Evans Picture Library/The Image Works

Empress Dowager Cixi
Empress of China and mother of Emperor Guangxi. She put her son under house arrest, supported antiforeign movements, and resisted reforms of the Chinese government and armed forces.

Japanese Imperialism

Yamagata Aritomo One of the leaders of the Meiji Restoration.

The Boxer Rebellion

The Boxer Uprising In 1900 a Chinese secret society, the Righteous Fists, rose up with the encouragement of the Empress Dowager Cixi and attacked foreigners and their establishments. In the Western press they were known as "Boxers." These men are putting up a poster that reads "Death to Foreigners!"

ports where they could trade at will. The British took over China's customs and allowed the free import of opium until 1917. A Chinese "self-strengthening movement" tried in vain to bring about significant reforms by reducing government expenditures and eliminating corruption. The **Empress Dowager Cixi** (TSUH-shee) (r. 1862–1908) opposed railways and other foreign technologies that could carry foreign influences to the interior. Government officials, who did not dare resist the Westerners outright, secretly encouraged crowds to attack and destroy the intrusive devices. They were able to slow the foreign intrusion, but in doing so, they denied themselves the best means of defense against foreign pressure.

Japan Confronts China

The late nineteenth century marked the high point of European power and arrogance, as the nations of Europe, in a frenzy known as the "New Imperialism," rushed to gobble up the last remaining unclaimed pieces of the world. Yet at that very moment two nations outside Europe were becoming great powers. One of them, the United States, was inhabited mainly by people of European origin. Its rise to great-power status had been predicted early in the nineteenth century by astute observers like the French statesman Alexis de Tocqueville. The other one, Japan, seemed so distant and exotic in 1850 that no European guessed that it would join the ranks of the great powers.

The motive for the transformation of Japan was to protect the nation from the Western powers, but the methods that strengthened Japan against the imperial ambitions of others could also be used to carry out its own conquests. Japan's path to imperialism was laid out by **Yamagata Aritomo**, a leader of the Meiji oligarchs. He believed that to be independent Japan had to define a "sphere of influence" that included Korea, Manchuria, and part of China (see Map 27.3). If other countries controlled this sphere, Japan would be at risk. To protect this sphere of influence, Yamagata insisted, Japan must sustain a vigorous program of military industrialization, culminating in the building of battleships.

As Japan grew stronger, China was growing weaker. In 1894 the two nations went to war over Korea. The Sino-Japanese War lasted less than six months, and it forced China to evacuate Korea, cede Taiwan and the Liaodong (li-AH-oh-dong) Peninsula, and pay a heavy indemnity. France, Germany, Britain, Russia, and the United States, upset at seeing a newcomer join the ranks of the imperialists, made Japan give up Liaodong in the name of the "territorial integrity" of China. In exchange for their "protection," the Western powers then made China grant them territorial and trade concessions, including ninety treaty ports.

In 1900 Chinese officials around the Empress Dowager Cixi encouraged a series of antiforeign riots known as the Boxer Uprising. Military forces from the European powers, Japan, and the United States put down the riots and occupied Beijing. Emboldened by China's obvious weakness, Japan and Russia competed for possession of the mineral-rich Chinese province of Manchuria.

SECTION REVIEW

- China was weakened by the Taiping Rebellion, a reactionary government under Empress Dowager Cixi, and the demands of the West.

- Japan, in contrast, built up its military and industrial strength and became another imperial power, taking advantage of China's weakness to seize Korea, Taiwan, and southern Manchuria.

Japan's participation in the suppression of the Boxer Uprising demonstrated its military power in East Asia. Then in 1905 Japan surprised the world by defeating Russia in the Russo-Japanese War. By the Treaty of Portsmouth that ended the war, Japan established a protectorate over Korea. In spite of Western attempts to restrict it to the role of junior partner, Japan continued to increase its influence. It gained control of southern Manchuria, with its industries and railroads, and in 1910 it finally annexed Korea, joining the ranks of the world's colonial powers.

CONCLUSION

After World War I broke out in 1914, many people, especially in Europe, looked back on the period from 1850 to 1914 as a golden age. For some, and in certain ways, it was. Industrialization was a powerful torrent changing Europe, North America, and East Asia. While shipping and railroads increased their global reach, new technologies—electricity, the steel and chemical industries, and the global telegraph network—contributed to the enrichment and empowerment of the industrial nations.

With these new technologies, memories of the great scourges—famines, wars, and epidemics—faded. Clean water, electric lights, and railways began to improve the lives of city dwellers, even the poor. Municipal services made city life less dangerous and chaotic. Goods from distant lands, even travel to other continents, came within the reach of millions. Middle-class women continued to focus on domestic pursuits and lived in a "separate sphere" from men. Many working-class women took jobs in the textile industry, yet their work outside the home did not lessen their domestic and child-rearing responsibilities.

Though Karl Marx predicted a class struggle between workers and employers, socialism became more of an intellectual movement. Through labor unions, workers achieved some measure of recognition and security. By the turn of the century, liberal political reforms had taken hold in western Europe. Universal male suffrage became law in the United States in 1870 and in various parts of Europe by the 1880s.

The framework for all these changes was the nation-state. Until the 1860s nationalism was associated with liberalism, but later generations of conservatives used public education, military service, and colonial conquests to build a sense of national unity. By 1871 both Italy and Germany had become unified states. In Japan, the Meiji Restoration restored power to the emperor and ushered in a period of Western influences.

The world economy, international politics, and even cultural and social issues revolved around a handful of countries—the great powers—that believed they controlled the destiny of the world. These included the most powerful European nations of the previous century, as well as three newcomers—Germany, the United States, and Japan.

KEY TERMS

Commodore Matthew Perry p. 713
railroads p. 714
submarine telegraph cables p. 714
steel p. 715

electricity p. 716
Thomas Edison p. 716
Victorian Age p. 720
"separate spheres" p. 720
socialism p. 723
labor union p. 723

Karl Marx p. 723
anarchists p. 725
nationalism p. 726
liberalism p. 726
Giuseppe Garibaldi p. 726
Otto von Bismarck p. 728

Meiji Restoration p. 729
Empress Dowager Cixi p. 735
Yamagata Aritomo p. 735

EBOOK AND WEBSITE RESOURCES

Primary Sources

Working Men of All Countries, Unite!

Letter to Mitsubishi Employees

Extracts from History of Germany in the Nineteenth Century and Historical Political Writings

Interactive Maps

Map 27.1 Unification of Italy, 1859–1870

Map 27.2 Unification of Germany, 1866–1871

Map 27.3 Expansion and Modernization of Japan, 1868–1918

Plus flashcards, practice quizzes, and more. Go to:
www.cengage.com/history/bullietearthpeople5e

SUGGESTED READING

Anderson, Benedict. *Imagined Communities: Reflections on the Origin and Spread of Nationalism.* 1991. Describes how nationalism spread beyond Europe.

Branca, Patricia. *Silent Sisterhood: Middle-Class Women in the Victorian Home.* 1975. Discusses how "Victorian morality" affected women.

Craig, Gordon A. *Germany, 1866–1945.* 1980. The classic overview.

Duus, Peter. *The Rise of Modern Japan,* 2nd ed. 1998. A clear explanation of the Meiji Restoration.

Fairbank, John King. *The Great Chinese Revolution, 1800–1985.* 1987. The classic synthesis of China's decline and recovery.

Hobsbawm, E. J. *Nation and Nationalism Since 1780.* 1990. Deals mainly with Europe.

Landes, David. *The Unbound Prometheus: Technological Change and Industrial Development in Western Europe from 1750 to the Present.* 1969. A classic narrative history.

Lindemann, Albert. *A History of European Socialism.* 1983. Covers the labor movements as well.

Moore, Barrington. *The Social Origins of Dictatorship and Democracy.* 1966. A classic essay on European society.

Pflanze, Otto. *Bismarck and the Development of Germany.* 1990. The best biography of Bismarck.

Read, Donald. *The Age of Urban Democracy: England, 1868–1914.* 1994. An excellent social history.

Rogger, Hans. *Russia in the Age of Modernization and Revolution, 1881–1917.* 1983. Discusses how Western influences corroded the tsarist empire.

Sked, Alan. *The Decline and Fall of the Habsburg Empire, 1815–1918.* 1989. Discusses how nationalism destroyed the Austrian state.

Spence, Jonathan D. *The Search for Modern China.* 1990. A monumental account of a complex society.

Stearns, Peter. *The Industrial Revolution in World History.* 1993. The first truly global history of industrialization.

Tilly, Louise, and Joan Scott. *Women, Work, and Family.* 1987. A wide-ranging history of Western women.

Weber, Eugen. *Peasants into Frenchmen.* 1976. Describes the creation of French nationhood.

NOTES

1. Quoted in Bonnie S. Anderson and Judith P. Zinsser, *A History of Their Own: Women in Europe from Prehistory to the Present,* vol. 2 (New York: Harper & Row, 1988), 372, 387.

CHAPTER OUTLINE

Bildarchiv Preussischer Kulturbesitz/Art Ressource, NY

Opening the Suez Canal   When the canal opened in 1869, thousands of dignitaries and ordinary people gathered to watch the ships go by.

   Visit the website and ebook for additional study materials and interactive tools: www.cengage.com/history/bullietearthpeople5e

The New Imperialism, 1869–1914

In 1869 Ismail (is-mah-EEL), the khedive (kuh-DEEV) (ruler) of Egypt, invited all the Christian princes of Europe and all the Muslim princes of Asia and Africa—except the Ottoman sultan, his nominal overlord—to celebrate the inauguration of the greatest construction project of the century: the **Suez Canal**. Sixteen hundred dignitaries from the Middle East and Europe assembled at Port Said (port sah-EED). A French journalist wrote:

> This multitude, coming from all parts of the world, presented the most varied and singular spectacle. All races were represented. . . . We saw, coming to attend this festival of civilization, men of the Orient wearing clothes of dazzling colors, chiefs of African tribes wrapped in their great coats, Circassians in war costumes, officers of the British army of India with their shakos [hats] wrapped in muslin, Hungarian magnates wearing their national costumes.[1]

Ismail used the occasion to emphasize the harmony and cooperation between the peoples of Africa, Asia, and Europe and to show that Egypt was not only independent but was also an equal of the great powers. To bless the inauguration, Ismail had invited clergy of the Muslim, Orthodox, and Catholic faiths. A reporter noted: "The Khedive . . . wished to symbolize thereby the unity of men and their brotherhood before God, without distinction of religion; it was the first time that the Orient had seen such a meeting of faiths to celebrate and bless together a great event and a great work."[2]

The canal was a great success, but not in the way Ismail intended. Ships using it could travel between Europe and India in less than two weeks—much less time than the month or longer consumed by sailing around Africa and across the Indian Ocean. By lowering freight costs, the canal stimulated shipping and the construction of steamships, giving an advantage to nations that had heavy industry and a large maritime trade over land-based empires and countries with few merchant ships. Great Britain benefited more than any other nation. France, which provided half the capital and most of the engineers, came in a distant second, for it had less trade with Asia than Britain did. Egypt, which contributed the other half of the money and most of the labor, was the loser. Instead of making Egypt powerful and independent, the Suez Canal provided the excuse for a British invasion and occupation of that country.

- What motivated the industrial nations to conquer new territories, and what means did they use?
- Why were imperialists drawn to the natural resources of Africa, and how did their presence on that continent change the environment?
- What were the social and cultural effects of imperialism in Asia?
- What were the economic motives behind imperialism in Latin America?
- How did imperialism contribute to the growth and globalization of the world economy?

Suez Canal Ship canal dug across the isthmus of Suez in Egypt, designed by Ferdinand de Lesseps. It opened to shipping in 1869 and shortened the sea voyage between Europe and Asia. Its strategic importance led to the British conquest of Egypt in 1882.

PRIMARY SOURCE: Convention on Free Navigation of the Suez Canal Between the European Powers and the Ottoman Empire, October 29, 1888 Read about the laws governing the Suez Canal and the code of conduct for parties sharing this passage.

Far from inaugurating an era of harmony among the peoples of three continents and three faiths, the canal triggered a wave of European domination over Africa and Asia. Between 1869 and 1914 Germany, France, Britain, Russia, Japan, and the United States used industrial technology to impose their will on the nonindustrial parts of the world. Historians call this exercise of power the **New Imperialism**.

THE NEW IMPERIALISM: MOTIVES AND METHODS

New Imperialism Historians' term for the late-nineteenth- and early-twentieth-century wave of conquests by European powers, the United States, and Japan, which were followed by the development and exploitation of the newly conquered territories for the benefit of the colonial powers.

Europe had a long tradition of imperialism reaching back to the twelfth century. During the first two-thirds of the nineteenth century the European powers continued to increase their influence overseas (see Chapter 26). The New Imperialism was characterized by an explosion of territorial conquests even more rapid than the Spanish conquests of the sixteenth century. Between 1869 and 1914, in a land grab of unprecedented speed, Europeans seized territories in Africa and Central Asia, and both Europeans and Americans took territories in Southeast Asia and the Pacific. Approximately 10 million square miles (26 million square kilometers) and 150 million people fell under the rule of Europe and the United States in this period.

The New Imperialism was more than a land grab. The imperial powers used economic and technological means to reorganize dependent regions and bring them into the world economy as suppliers of foodstuffs and raw materials and as consumers of industrial products. In Africa and other parts of the world, this was done by conquest and colonial administration. The Latin American republics, though remaining politically independent, became economic dependencies of the United States and Europe.

What inspired Europeans and Americans to venture overseas and impose their will on other societies? Economic, cultural, and political motives were involved in all cases.

Political Motives

The great powers of the late nineteenth century, as well as less powerful countries like Italy, Portugal, and Belgium, were competitive and hypersensitive about their status. French leaders, humiliated by their defeat by Prussia in 1871 (see Chapter 27), sought to reestablish their nation's prestige through territorial acquisitions overseas. Great Britain, already in possession of the world's largest empire, felt the need to protect India by acquiring colonies in East Africa and Southeast Asia. German Chancellor Otto von Bismarck had little interest in acquiring colonies, but many Germans believed that a country as important as theirs required an impressive empire overseas.

Political motives were not limited to statesmen in the capital cities. Colonial governors, even officers posted to the farthest colonial outposts, practiced their own diplomacy. They often decided on their own to claim a piece of land before some rival got it. Armies fighting frontier wars found it easier to defeat their neighbors than to make peace with them. In response to border skirmishes with neighboring states, colonial agents were likely to send in troops, take over their neighbors' territories, and then inform their home governments. Governments felt obligated to back up their men-on-the-spot. The great powers of Europe acquired much of West Africa, Southeast Asia, and the Pacific islands in this manner.

Cultural Motives

The late nineteenth century saw a Christian revival in Europe and North America, as both Catholics and Protestants founded new missionary societies. Their purpose was not only religious—to convert nonbelievers, whom they regarded as "heathen"—but also cultural. They were determined to abolish slavery in Africa and bring Western education, medicine, hygiene, and monogamous marriage to all the world's peoples.

Among those attracted by religious work overseas were many women who joined missionary societies to become teachers and nurses. Although they did not challenge colonialism directly, their influence often helped soften the harshness of colonial rule—for example, by calling attention to issues of maternity and women's health. Mary Slessor, a British missionary who lived for

CHRONOLOGY

	Africa	Asia and the Pacific	Latin America
1870	1869 Opening of the Suez Canal	1862–1895 French conquer Indochina	
	1874 Warfare between Britain and Asante (Gold Coast)	1865–1876 Russian forces advance into Central Asia	1870–1910 Railroad building boom in Argentina, Brazil, and Mexico
	1877–1879 Warfare between Britain and the Xhosa and the Zulu (South Africa)	1878 United States obtains Pago Pago Harbor (Samoa)	
	1882 British forces occupy Egypt		
	1884–1885 Berlin Conference; Leopold II obtains Congo Free State	1885 Britain completes conquest of Burma	
		1887 United States obtains Pearl Harbor (Hawaii)	
1890			
	1896 Ethiopians defeat Italian army at Adowa	1894–1895 China defeated in Sino-Japanese War	1895–1898 Cubans revolt against Spanish rule
	1898 Battle of Omdurman	1898 United States annexes Hawaii and Guam and purchases Philippines from Spain	1898 Spanish-American War; United States annexes Puerto Rico and Hawaii
1900	1899–1902 South African War between Afrikaners and British	1899–1902 U.S. forces conquer and occupy Philippines	1901 United States imposes Platt Amendment on Cuba
	1902 First Aswan Dam completed (Egypt)	1903 Russia completes Trans-Siberian Railway	1903 United States backs secession of Panama from Colombia
		1904–1905 Russia defeated in Russo-Japanese War	1904–1907, 1916 U.S. troops occupy Dominican Republic
			1904–1914 United States builds Panama Canal
1910	1908 Belgium annexes Congo		1912 U.S. troops occupy Nicaragua and Honduras

forty years among the people of southeastern Nigeria, campaigned against slavery, human sacrifice, and the killing of twins and, generally, for women's rights. In India missionaries denounced the customs of child marriages and *sati* (the burning of widows on their husbands' funeral pyres). Such views often clashed with the customs of the people among whom they settled.

Racism

The sense of moral duty and cultural superiority was not limited to missionaries. Many Europeans and Americans equated technological innovations with progress. They believed that Western technology proved the superiority of Western ideas, customs, and culture. More harmful were racist ideas that relegated non-Europeans to a status of permanent inferiority. Racists assigned different stages of biological development to peoples of different races and cultures (see Chapter 27). They divided humankind into several races based on physical appearance and ranked these races in a hierarchy that ranged from "civilized" down through "semibarbarous," "barbarian," and finally, at the bottom, "savage." Whites were always at the top of this ranking. Such ideas were often presented as an excuse for permanent rule over Africans and Asians.

Young men, finding few opportunities for adventure and glory at home in an era of peace, sought them overseas. At first, European people and parliaments were indifferent or hostile to overseas adventures, but a few easy victories in the 1880s helped to overcome their reluctance. The United States was fully preoccupied with its westward expansion until the 1880s, but in the 1890s popular attention shifted to lands outside U.S. borders. Newspapers, which achieved wide readership in the second half of the nineteenth century, discovered that they could boost circulation with reports of wars and conquests. By the 1890s imperialism was a popular cause, the overseas extension of the nationalism of the time.

Economic Motives

The industrialization of Europe and North America stimulated the demand for minerals— copper for electrical wiring, tin for canning, chrome and manganese for the steel industry, coal for steam engines, and, most of all, gold and diamonds. The demand for such industrial crops as cotton and rubber and for stimulants such as sugar, coffee, tea, and tobacco also grew. These products were found in the tropics, but never in sufficient quantities.

An economic depression lasting from the mid-1870s to the mid-1890s caused European businessmen to seek protection against foreign competition (see below). They argued that their respective countries needed secure sources of tropical raw materials and protected markets for their industries. Declining business opportunities at home prompted entrepreneurs and investors to look for profits in Asia, Africa, and Latin America. Since investment in countries so different from their own was extremely risky, businessmen sought the backing of their governments, preferably with soldiers.

These reasons explain why Europeans and Americans wished to expand their influence over other societies. Yet motives do not adequately explain the events of that time. What made it possible to conquer a piece of Africa, convert the "heathen," and start plantations was the sudden increase in the power that industrial peoples could wield over nonindustrial peoples and over the forces of nature. Technological advances explain both the motives and the outcome of the New Imperialism.

The Tools of the Imperialists

To succeed, empire builders needed the means to achieve their objectives at a reasonable cost. These means were provided by the Industrial Revolution (see Chapter 23). In the early nineteenth century technological innovations began to tip the balance of power in favor of Europe.

Shipping

Europeans had dominated the oceans since about 1500, and their naval power increased still more with the introduction of steamships. The first steamer reached India in 1825 and was soon followed by regular mail service in the 1830s. The building of the Suez Canal and the development of increasingly efficient engines led to a boom in shipping to the Indian Ocean and East Asia. Submarine telegraph cables connected Europe with North America in the 1860s, with Latin America and Asia in the 1870s, with Africa in the 1880s, and finally across the Pacific in 1904.

Gunboats

Europeans used gunboats with considerable success in China, Burma, Indochina, and the Congo Basin. Although gunboats opened the major river basins to European penetration, the invaders often found themselves hampered by other natural obstacles. *Falciparum* malaria, found only in Africa, was so deadly to Europeans that few explorers survived before the 1850s. In 1854 a British doctor discovered that the drug quinine, taken regularly during one's stay in Africa, could prevent the disease. This and a few sanitary precautions reduced the annual death rate among whites in West Africa from between 250 and 750 per thousand in the early nineteenth century to between 50 and 100 per thousand after 1850. This reduction was sufficient to open the continent to merchants, officials, and missionaries.

Firearms

The development of new and much deadlier firearms in the 1860s and 1870s shifted the balance of power on land between Westerners and other peoples. One of these was the breechloader, which could be fired accurately ten times as fast as, and five or six times farther than, a musket. By the 1870s all armies in Europe and the United States had switched to these new rifles. Repeating rifles could shoot fifteen rounds in fifteen seconds. In the 1890s European and American armies began using machine guns, which could fire eleven bullets per second. As European firearms improved, the firepower gap widened, making colonial conquests easier than ever before. By the 1880s and 1890s European-led forces of a few hundred could defeat non-European armies of thousands. Against the latest weapons, African and Asian soldiers armed with muskets or spears did not stand a chance, no matter how numerous and courageous they were.

Battle of Omdurman British victory over the Mahdi in the Sudan in 1898. General Kitchener led a mixed force of British and Egyptian troops armed with rapid-firing rifles and machine guns.

A classic example is the **Battle of Omdurman** in Sudan. On September 2, 1898, forty thousand Sudanese attacked an Anglo-Egyptian expedition that had come up the Nile on six steamers and four other boats to avenge the defeat of General Charles Gordon in 1885 (see Chapter 25). General Horatio Kitchener's troops had twenty machine guns and four artillery pieces; the

The Battle of Omdurman   In the late nineteenth century, most battles between European-led troops and African forces were one-sided encounters because of the disparity in the opponents' firearms and tactics. The Battle of Omdurman in Sudan in 1898 is a dramatic example. The forces of the Mahdi, some on horseback, were armed with spears and single-shot muskets. The British troops and their Egyptian allies, lined up in the foreground, used repeating rifles and machine guns able to shoot much farther than the Sudanese weapons. As a result, there were many Sudanese casualties but very few British and Egyptian casualties.

Sudanese were equipped with muskets and spears. Within a few hours eleven thousand Sudanese and forty-eight British lay dead.

Colonial Agents and Administration

Once colonial agents took over a territory, their home government expected them to cover their own costs and, if possible, return some profit to the home country. The system of administering and exploiting colonies for the benefit of the home country is known as **colonialism**. In some cases, such as along the West African coast or in Indochina, there was already a considerable trade that could be taxed. In other places profits could come only from investments and a thorough reorganization of the indigenous societies. In applying modern scientific and industrial methods to their colonies, colonialists started the transformation of Asian and African societies and landscapes that has continued to our day.

colonialism Policy by which a nation administers a foreign territory and develops its resources for the benefit of the colonial power.

One important factor was the presence or absence of European settlers. In Canada, Australia, and New Zealand, whites were already in the majority by 1869, and Britain encouraged them to elect parliaments and rule themselves. Where European settlers were numerous but still a minority of the population, as in Algeria and South Africa, settlers and the home country struggled for control over the indigenous population. In colonies with few white settlers, the European governors ruled autocratically.

White Settlers

In the early years of the New Imperialism, colonial administrations consisted of a governor and his staff, a few troops to keep order, and a small number of tax collectors and magistrates. Nowhere could colonialism operate without the cooperation of indigenous elites, because no colony was wealthy enough to pay the salaries of more than a handful of European officials. In most cases the colonial governors exercised power through traditional rulers willing to cooperate.

A Colonial Lady In many tropical colonies in the nineteenth century, there were few good roads, but labor was abundant. European colonial officials and their wives often traveled in a tonjon, or sedan chair carried by porters. This image of a lady in India dates from 1828.

A Tonjon, or Ladies' Carriage.

Colonial governments also educated a few local youths for "modern" jobs as clerks, nurses, policemen, customs inspectors, and the like. Thus colonialism relied on two rival indigenous elites.

White Women

European and American women seldom took part in the early stages of colonial expansion. As conquest gave way to peaceful colonialism and as steamships and railroads made travel less difficult, colonial officials and settlers began bringing their wives to the colonies. The arrival of white women in Asia and Africa led to increasing racial segregation. Sylvia Leith-Ross, wife of a colonial officer in Nigeria, explained: "When you are alone, among thousands of unknown, unpredictable people, dazed by unaccustomed sights and sounds, bemused by strange ways of life and thought, you need to remember who you are, where you come from, what your standards are."[3] Many colonial wives found themselves in command of numerous servants and expected to follow the complex etiquette of colonial entertainment in support of their husbands' official positions. Some found opportunities to exercise personal initiative, usually charitable work involving indigenous women and children. However well meaning, their efforts were always subordinate to the work of men.

SECTION REVIEW

- From 1864 to 1914 Europeans and Americans conquered 10 million square miles and 150 million people.

- The European powers were motivated by political rivalries.

- Missionaries and the press supported the conquests. So did businessmen eager to invest capital, sell their products, and obtain raw materials.

- New industrial technologies—gunboats, rifles, and quinine—made it possible for Europeans to conquer other lands.

- Colonial agents transformed the societies and peoples they ruled; white women participated in the enterprise.

THE SCRAMBLE FOR AFRICA

"scramble" for Africa Sudden wave of conquests in Africa by European powers in the 1880s and 1890s. Britain obtained most of eastern Africa, France most of northwestern Africa. Other countries (Germany, Belgium, Portugal, Italy, and Spain) acquired lesser amounts.

Until the 1870s African history was largely shaped by internal forces and the spread of Islam (see Chapter 26). Outside Algeria and southern Africa, only a handful of Europeans had ever visited the interior of Africa, and European countries possessed only small enclaves on the coasts. As late as 1879 Africans ruled more than 90 percent of the continent. Then, within a decade, Africa was invaded and divided among the European powers in a movement often referred to as the **"scramble" for Africa** (see Map 28.1). Let us look at the most significant cases, beginning with Egypt, the wealthiest and most populated part of the continent.

Egypt

Ironically, European involvement in Egypt resulted from Egypt's attempt to free itself from Ottoman rule. Throughout the mid-nineteenth century the khedives of Egypt had tried to modernize their armed forces; build canals, harbors, railroads, and other public works; and reorient

MAP 28.1 **Africa in 1878 and 1914** In 1878 the European colonial presence was limited to a few coastal enclaves, plus portions of Algeria and South Africa. By 1914, Europeans had taken over all of Africa except Ethiopia and Liberia.

e Interactive Map

agriculture toward export crops, especially cotton (see Chapters 23 and 26). Their interest in the Suez Canal was also part of this policy. Khedive Ismail even tried to make Egypt the center of an empire reaching south into Sudan and Ethiopia.

These ambitions cost vast sums of money, which the khedives borrowed from European creditors at high interest rates. By 1876 Egypt's foreign debt had risen to £100 million sterling, and the interest payments alone consumed one-third of its foreign export earnings. To avoid bankruptcy the Egyptian government sold its shares in the Suez Canal to Great Britain and accepted four foreign "commissioners of the debt" to oversee its finances. French and British bankers, still not satisfied, lobbied their governments to secure the loans by stronger measures. In 1878 the two governments obliged Ismail to appoint a Frenchman as minister of public works and a Briton as minister of finance. When high taxes caused hardship and popular discontent,

Britain Occupies Egypt

Henry Morton Stanley
British-American explorer of Africa, famous for his expeditions in search of Dr. David Livingstone. Stanley helped King Leopold II establish the Congo Free State.

King Leopold II King of Belgium (r. 1865–1909). He was active in encouraging the exploration of Central Africa and became the ruler of the Congo Free State (to 1908).

Savorgnan de Brazza
Franco-Italian explorer sent by the French government to claim part of equatorial Africa for France. Founded Brazzaville, capital of the French Congo, in 1880.

The Berlin Conference

Berlin Conference Conference that German chancellor Otto von Bismarck called to set rules for the partition of Africa. It led to the creation of the Congo Free State under King Leopold II of Belgium.

the French and British persuaded the Ottoman sultan to depose Ismail. This foreign intervention provoked a military uprising under Egyptian army colonel Arabi Pasha, which threatened the Suez Canal.

Fearing for their investments, the British sent an army into Egypt in 1882. So important was the Suez Canal to Britain's maritime supremacy that they stayed for seventy years. During those years the British ruled Egypt "indirectly"—that is, they maintained the Egyptian government and the fiction of Egyptian sovereignty but retained real power in their own hands.

Eager to develop Egyptian cotton production, the British brought in engineers and contractors to build the first dam across the Nile, at Aswan in upper Egypt. When completed in 1902, it captured the annual Nile flood and released its waters throughout the year, allowing farmers to grow two, sometimes three, crops a year. The economic development of Egypt by the British enriched a small elite of landowners and merchants, many of them foreigners. Egyptian peasants got little relief from the heavy taxes collected to pay for their country's crushing foreign debt and the expenses of the British army of occupation. Western ways that conflicted with the teachings of Islam—such as the drinking of alcohol and the relative freedom of women—offended Muslim religious leaders. Most Egyptians found British rule more onerous than that of the Ottomans. By the 1890s Egyptian politicians and intellectuals were demanding that the British leave.

Western and Equatorial Africa

While the British were taking over Egypt, the French were planning to extend their empire into the interior of West Africa. Starting from the coast of Senegal, which had been in French hands for centuries, they hoped to build a railroad from the upper Senegal River to the upper Niger in order to open the interior to French merchants. This in turn led the French military to undertake the conquest of western Sudan.

Meanwhile, the actions of three individuals, rather than a government, brought about the occupation of the Congo Basin, an enormous forested region in the heart of equatorial Africa (see Map 28.1). In 1879 the American journalist **Henry Morton Stanley**, who had explored the area (see Chapter 26), persuaded **King Leopold II** of Belgium to invest his personal fortune in "opening up" equatorial Africa. With Leopold's money, Stanley returned to Africa from 1879 to 1884 to establish trading posts along the southern bank of the Congo River. At the same time, **Savorgnan de Brazza**, an Italian officer serving in the French army, obtained from an African ruler living on the opposite bank a treaty that placed the area under the "protection" of France.

These events sparked a flurry of diplomatic activity. German chancellor Bismarck called the **Berlin Conference** on Africa of 1884 and 1885. There the major powers agreed that henceforth "effective occupation" would replace the former trading relations between Africans and Europeans. Every country with colonial ambitions had to send troops into Africa and participate in the division of the spoils. As a reward for triggering the "scramble" for Africa, Leopold II acquired a personal domain under the name "Congo Free State," while France and Portugal took most of the rest of equatorial Africa. In this manner, the European powers and King Leopold managed to divide Africa among themselves, at least on paper.

"Effective occupation" required many years of effort. In the interior of West Africa, Muslim rulers resisted the French invasion for up to thirty years. The French advance encouraged the Germans to stake claims to parts of the region and the British to move north from their coastal enclaves, until the entire region was occupied by Britain, France, and Germany.

Because West Africa had long had a flourishing trade, the new rulers took advantage of existing trade networks, taxing merchants and farmers, investing the profits in railroads and harbors, and paying dividends to European stockholders. In the Gold Coast (now Ghana) British trading companies bought the cocoa grown by African farmers at low prices and resold it for large profits. The interior of French West Africa lagged behind. Although the region could produce cotton, peanuts, and other crops, the difficulties of transportation limited its development before 1914.

Compared to West Africa, equatorial Africa had few inhabitants and little trade. Rather than try to govern these vast territories directly, authorities in the Congo Free State, the French Congo, and the Portuguese colonies of Angola and Mozambique farmed out huge pieces of land to private concession companies, offering them monopolies on the natural resources and trade of their territories and the right to employ soldiers and tax the inhabitants. Freed from outside supervision, the companies forced the African inhabitants at gunpoint to produce cash crops

From H. M. Stanley, *The Congo*, vol. 2, London, 1885

A Steamboat for the Congo River   Soon after the Congo Basin was occupied by Europeans, the new colonial rulers realized they needed to improve transportation. Since access from the sea was blocked by rapids on the lower Congo River, steamboats had to be brought in sections, hauled from the coast by thousands of Congolese over very difficult terrain. This picture shows the pieces arriving at Stanley Pool, ready to be reassembled.

and carry them, on their heads or backs, to the nearest railroad or navigable river. The worst abuses took place in the Congo Free State, where a rubber boom made it profitable for private companies to coerce Africans to collect latex from vines that grew in the forests. One Congolese refugee told the British consul Roger Casement who investigated the atrocities:

> We begged the white men to leave us alone, saying we could get no more rubber, but the white men and their soldiers said: "Go. You are only beasts yourselves, you are only nyama (meat)." We tried, always going further into the forest, and when we failed and our rubber was short, the soldiers came to our towns and killed us. Many were shot, some had their ears cut off; others were tied up with ropes around their necks and bodies and taken away.[4]

After 1906 the British press began publicizing the horrors. The public outcry that followed, coinciding with the end of the rubber boom, convinced the Belgian government to take over Leopold's private empire in 1908.

Southern Africa

The history of southern Africa between 1869 and 1914 differs from that of the rest of the continent in several important respects. One was that the land had long attracted settlers. African pastoralists and farmers had inhabited the region for centuries. **Afrikaners**, descendants of Dutch settlers on the Cape of Good Hope, moved inland throughout the nineteenth century; British prospectors and settlers arrived later in the century; and, finally, Indians were brought over by the British and stayed.

Southern Africa attracted European settlers because of its good pastures and farmland and its phenomenal deposits of diamonds, gold, and copper, as well as coal and iron ore. This was the new El Dorado that imperialists had dreamed of since the heyday of the Spanish Empire.

The discovery of diamonds at Kimberley in 1868 lured thousands of European prospectors as well as Africans looking for work. Great Britain, colonial ruler of the Cape Colony, annexed the diamond area in 1871, angering the Afrikaners. Once in the interior, the British defeated the

Afrikaners South Africans descended from Dutch and French settlers of the seventeenth century. Their Great Trek founded new settler colonies in the nineteenth century. Though a minority among South Africans, they held political power after 1910, imposing a system of racial segregation called apartheid after 1949.

Diamonds

Xhosa (KOH-sah) people in 1877 and 1878. Then in 1879 they confronted the Zulu, militarily the most powerful of the African peoples in the region.

The Zulu, led by their king Cetshwayo (set-SHWAH-yo), resented their encirclement by Afrikaners and British. Their proud military tradition led them into a war with the British in 1879. They defeated the British at Isandhlwana (ee-sawn-dull-WAH-nuh), but a few months later they were in turn defeated. Cetshwayo was captured and sent into exile, and the Zulu lands were given to white ranchers. Yet throughout those bitter times, the Zulu's sense of nationhood remained strong.

Relations between the British and the Afrikaners, already tense as a result of British encroachment, took a turn for the worse when gold was discovered in the Afrikaner republic of Transvaal (trans-VAHL) in 1886. In the gold rush that ensued, the British soon outnumbered the Afrikaners.

Britain's invasion of southern Africa was driven in part by the ambition of **Cecil Rhodes** (1853–1902), who once declared that he would "annex the stars" if he could. Rhodes made his fortune in the Kimberley diamond fields, founding De Beers Consolidated, a company that has dominated the world's diamond trade ever since. He then turned to politics. He encouraged a concession company, the British South Africa Company, to push north into Central Africa, where he named two new colonies after himself: Southern Rhodesia (now Zimbabwe) and Northern Rhodesia (now Zambia). The Ndebele (en-duh-BELL-ay) and Shona peoples, who inhabited the region, resisted this invasion, but the machine guns of the British finally defeated them.

British attempts to annex the two Afrikaner republics, Transvaal and Orange Free State, and the inflow of English-speaking whites into the gold- and diamond-mining areas led to the South African War, which lasted from 1899 to 1902. At first the Afrikaners had the upper hand, for they were highly motivated, possessed modern rifles, and knew the land. In 1901, however, Great Britain brought in 450,000 troops and crushed the Afrikaner armies. Ironically, the Afrikaners' defeat in 1902 led to their ultimate victory. Wary of costly commitments overseas, the British government expected European settlers in Africa to manage their own affairs, as they were doing in Canada, Australia, and New Zealand. Thus, in 1910 the European settlers created the Union of South Africa, in which the Afrikaners eventually emerged as the ruling element.

Unlike Canada, Australia, and New Zealand, South Africa had a majority of indigenous inhabitants and substantial numbers of Indians and "Cape Coloureds" (people of mixed ancestry). Yet the Europeans were both numerous enough to demand self-rule and powerful enough to deny the vote and other civil rights to the majority. In 1913 the South African parliament passed the Natives Land Act, assigning Africans to reservations and forbidding them to own land elsewhere. This and other racial policies turned South Africa into a land of segregation and oppression.

Political and Social Consequences

At the time of the European invasion, Africa contained a wide variety of societies. Some parts of the continent had long-established kingdoms with aristocracies or commercial towns dominated by a merchant class. In other places agricultural peoples lived in villages without any outside government. Elsewhere pastoral nomads were organized along military lines. In some remote areas people lived from hunting and gathering. Not surprisingly, these societies responded in very different ways to the European invasion.

Some peoples welcomed the invaders as allies against local enemies. Once colonial rule was established, they sought work in government service or in European firms and sent their children to mission schools. In exchange, they were often the first to receive benefits such as clinics and roads. Peoples with a pastoral or a warrior tradition, however, fought tenaciously. Examples abound, from the Zulu and Ndebele of southern Africa to the pastoral Herero (hair-AIR-oh) people of Southwest Africa (now Namibia), who rose up against German invaders in 1904; in repressing their uprising, the Germans exterminated two-thirds of them. In the Sahel, a belt of grasslands south of the Sahara, charismatic leaders rose up in the name of a purified Islam, gathered a following of warriors, and led them on part religious, part empire-building campaigns called *jihads*. All of them eventually came into conflict with European-led military expeditions and were defeated.

Some commercial states with long histories of contact with Europeans also fought back. The kingdom of **Asante** (uh-SHAWN-tee) in Gold Coast rose up in 1874, 1896, and 1900 before it was

---

Cecil Rhodes British entrepreneur and politician involved in the expansion of the British Empire from South Africa into Central Africa. The colonies of Southern Rhodesia (now Zimbabwe) and Northern Rhodesia (now Zambia) were named after him.

Britain Versus Afrikaners

Collaborators and Resisters

Asante African kingdom on the Gold Coast that expanded rapidly after 1680. Asante participated in the Atlantic economy, trading gold, slaves, and ivory. It resisted British imperial ambitions for a quarter century before being absorbed into Britain's Gold Coast colony in 1902.

Victorious Ethiopians   Among the states of Africa, Ethiopia alone was able to defend itself against European imperialism. In the 1880s, Ethiopia purchased modern weapons and trained its army to use them. Thus prepared, the Ethiopians defeated an Italian invasion at Adowa in 1896. These Ethiopian army officers wore their most elaborate finery to pose for a photograph after their victory.

National Archives

Ethiopian Success

Menelik   Emperor of Ethiopia (r. 1889–1911). He enlarged Ethiopia to its present dimensions and defeated an Italian invasion at Adowa (1896).

African Land and Labor

finally overwhelmed. In the Niger Delta, the ancient city of Benin, rich with artistic treasures, resisted colonial control until 1897, when a British "punitive expedition" set it on fire and carted its works of art off to Europe.

One resistance movement succeeded, to the astonishment of Europeans and Africans alike. When **Menelik** became emperor of Ethiopia in 1889 (see Chapter 26), his country was threatened by Sudanese Muslims to the west and by France and Italy, which controlled the coast of the Red Sea to the east. For many years, Ethiopia had been purchasing European and American weapons. When Italians attempted to establish a protectorate over Ethiopia, they found the Ethiopians armed with thousands of rifles and even machine guns and artillery pieces. Although Italy sent twenty thousand troops to attack Ethiopia, in 1896 they were defeated at Adowa (AH-do-ah) by a larger and better-trained Ethiopian army.

Most Africans neither joined nor fought the European invaders but tried to continue living as before. They found this increasingly difficult because colonial rule disrupted every traditional society. The presence of colonial officials meant that rights to land, commercial transactions, and legal disputes were handled very differently and that traditional rulers lost all authority, except where Europeans used them as local administrators.

Changes in landholding were especially disruptive, for most Africans were farmers or herders for whom access to land was a necessity. In areas with a high population density, such as Egypt and West Africa, colonial rulers left peasants in place, encouraged them to grow cash crops, and collected taxes on the harvest. Elsewhere, the new rulers declared any land that was not farmed to be "vacant" and gave it to private concession companies or to European planters and ranchers. In Kenya, Northern Rhodesia, and South Africa, Europeans found the land and climate to their liking. White settlers forced Africans to become squatters, sharecroppers, or ranch hands on land they had farmed for generations. In South Africa they forced many Africans off their lands and onto "reserves."

Although the colonial rulers harbored designs on the land, they were even more interested in African labor. They did not want to pay wages high enough to attract workers voluntarily. Instead, they imposed various taxes, such as the hut tax and the head tax, which Africans had to pay regardless of their income. To find the money, Africans had little choice but to accept whatever work the Europeans offered. In this way Africans were recruited to work on plantations, railroads, and other modern enterprises. In the South African mines Africans were paid, on average, one-tenth as much as Europeans.

Two Africans Recall the Arrival of the Europeans

We know a great deal about the arrival of the Europeans into the interior of Africa from the perspective of the conquerors, but very little about how the events were experienced by Africans. Here are two accounts by African women, one from northern Nigeria whose land was occupied by the British, the other from the Congo Free State, a colony of King Leopold II of Belgium. They show not only how Africans experienced European colonial dominance but also how diverse these African experiences were.

Baba of Karo, a Nigerian Woman, Remembers Her Childhood

When I was a maiden the Europeans first arrived. Ever since we were quite small the *malams* had been saying that the Europeans would come with a thing called a train, they would come with a thing called a motor-car, in them you would go and come back in a trice. They would stop wars, they would repair the world, they would stop oppression and lawlessness, we should live at peace with them. We used to go and sit quietly and listen to the prophecies.

I remember when a European came to Karo on a horse, and some of his foot soldiers went into the town. Everyone came out to look at them, but in Zerewa they didn't see the European. Everyone at Karo ran away—"There's a European, there's a European!"

At that time Yusufu was the king of Karo. He did not like the Europeans, he did not wish them, he would not sign their treaty. Then he say that perforce he would have to agree, so he did. We Habe wanted them to come, it was the Fulani who did not like it. When the Europeans came the Habe saw that if you worked for them they paid you for it, they didn't say, like the Fulani, "Commoner, give me this! Commoner, bring me that!" Yes, the Habe wanted them; they saw no harm in them.

The Europeans said that there were to be no more slaves; if someone said "Slave!" you could complain to the *alkali* who would punish the master who said it, the judge said, "That is what the Europeans have decreed." The first order said that any slave, if he was younger than you, was your younger brother, if he was older than you was your elder brother—they were all brothers of their master's family. No one used the word "slave" any more. When slavery was stopped, nothing much happened at our *rinji* except that some slaves whom we had bought in the market ran away. Our own father went to his farm and worked, he and his son took up their large hoes; they loaned out their spare farms. Tsoho our father and Kadiri my brother with whom I live now and Babambo worked, they farmed guinea-corn and millet and groundnuts and everything; before this they had supervised the slaves' work—now they did their own.

In the old days if the chief liked the look of your daughter he would take her and put her in his house; you could do nothing about it. Now they don't do that.

Ilanga, a Congolese Woman, Recounts Her Capture by Agents of the Congo Free State

. . . we were all busy in the fields hoeing our plantations, for it was the rainy season, and the weeds sprang quickly up, when a runner came to the village saying that a large band of men was coming, that they all wore red caps and blue cloth, and carried guns and long knives, and that many white men were with them, the chief of whom was *Kibalanga* (Michaux). Niendo at once called all the chief men to his house, while the drums were beaten to summon the people to the village. A long consultation was held, and finally we were all told to go quietly to the fields and bring in ground-nuts, plantains, and cassava for the warriors who were coming, and goats and fowl for the white men. The women all went with baskets and filled them, and put them in the road, which was blocked up, so many were there. Niendo then commanded everyone to go and sit quietly

Some Africans came to the cities and mining camps seeking a better life than they had on the land. Many migrated great distances and stayed away for years at a time. Most migrant workers were men who left their wives and children behind in villages and on reserves. In some cases the authorities did not allow them to bring their families and settle permanently in the towns. This caused great hardship for African women, who had to grow food for their families during the men's absences and care for sick and aged workers. Long separations between spouses also led to an increase in prostitution and to the spread of sexually transmitted diseases.

African Women
Some African women welcomed colonial rule, for it brought an end to fighting and slave raiding, but others were led into captivity (see Diversity and Dominance: Two Africans Recall the Arrival of the Europeans). A few succeeded in becoming wealthy traders or owners of livestock. On the whole, however, African women benefited less than men from the economic changes that colonialism introduced. In areas where the colonial rulers replaced communal property with private property, property rights were assigned to the head of the household—that is, to the man. Almost all the jobs open to Africans, even those considered "women's work" in Europe, such as nursing and domestic service, were reserved for men.

in the houses until he gave other orders. This we did, everyone remaining quietly seated while Niendo went up the road with the head men to meet the white chief. We did not know what to think, for most of us feared that so many armed men coming boded evil; but Niendo thought that, by giving presents of much food, he would induce the strangers to pass on without harming us. And so it proved, for the soldiers took the baskets, and were then ordered by the white men to move off through the village. Many of the soldiers looked into the houses and shouted at us words we did not understand. We were glad when they were all gone, for we were much in fear of the white men and the strange warriors, who are known to all the people as being great fighters, bringing war wherever they go. . . .

When the white men and their warriors had gone, we went again to our work, and were hoping that they would not return; but this they did in a very short time. As before, we brought in great heaps of food; but this time *Kibalanga* did not move away directly, but camped near our village, and his soldiers came and stole all our fowl and goats and tore up our cassava; but we did not mind as long as they did not harm us. The next morning it was reported that the white men were going away; but soon after the sun rose over the hill, a large band of soldiers came into the village, and we all went into the houses and sat down. We were not long seated when the soldiers came rushing in shouting, and threatening Niendo with their guns. They rushed into the houses and dragged the people out. Three or four came to our house and caught hold of me, also my husband Oleka and my sister Katinga. We were dragged into the road, and were tied together with cords about our necks, so that we could not escape. We were all crying, for now we knew that we were to be taken away to be slaves. The soldiers beat us with the iron sticks from their guns, and compelled us to march to the camp of *Kibalanga*, who ordered the women to be tied up separately, ten to each cord, and the men in the same way. When we were all collected—and there were many from other villages whom we now saw, and many from Waniendo— the soldiers brought baskets of food for us to carry, in some of which was smoked human flesh (*niama na nitu*).

We then set off marching very quickly. My sister Katinga had her baby in her arms, and was not compelled to carry a basket;

but my husband Oleka was made to carry a goat. We marched until the afternoon, when we camped near a stream, where we were glad to drink, for we were much athirst. We had nothing to eat, for the soldiers would give us nothing, so we lay upon the ground, and at night went to sleep. The next day we continued the march, and when we camped at noon were given some maize and plantains, which were gathered near a village from which the people had run away. So it continued each day until the fifth day, when the soldiers took my sister's baby and threw it in the grass, leaving it to die, and made her carry some cooking pots which they found in the deserted village. On the sixth day we became very weak from lack of food and from constant marching and sleeping in the damp grass, and my husband, who marched behind us with the goat, could not stand up longer, and so he sat down beside the path and refused to walk more. The soldiers beat him, but still he refused to move. Then one of them struck him on the head with the end of his gun, and he fell upon the ground. One of the soldiers caught the goat, while two or three others stuck the long knives they put on the ends of their guns into my husband. I saw the blood spurt out, and then saw him no more, for we passed over the brow of a hill and he was out of sight. Many of the young men were killed the same way, and many babies thrown into the grass to die. A few escaped; but we were so well guarded that it was almost impossible.

QUESTIONS FOR ANALYSIS

1. How do Baba and Ilanga recall their existence before the Europeans came?

2. What did they expect when they first heard of the arrival of Europeans? Instead, what happened to them, their relatives, and their towns?

3. How do you explain the difference between these two accounts?

Source: From M. F. Smith, ed., *Baba of Karo: A Woman of the Muslim Hausa* (New York: Philosophical Library, 1955), 66–68. Edgar Canisius, *A Campaign Amongst Cannibals* (London: R. A. Everett & Co., 1903), 250–256. Used by permission of the Philosophical Library.

Cultural Responses

Africans had more contact with missionaries than with any other Europeans. Missionaries, both men and women, opened schools to teach reading, writing, and arithmetic to village children. Boys were taught crafts such as carpentry and blacksmithing, while girls learned domestic skills such as cooking, laundry, and childcare.

Mission Schools

Along with basic skills, the first generation of Africans educated in mission schools acquired Western ideas of justice and progress. Samuel Ajayi Crowther, a Yoruba rescued from slavery as a boy and educated in mission schools in Sierra Leone, went on to become an Anglican minister and, in 1864, the first African bishop. Crowther thought that Africa needed European assistance in achieving both spiritual and economic development:

> *Africa has neither knowledge nor skill . . . to bring out her vast resources for her own improvement. . . . Therefore to claim Africa for the Africans alone, is to claim for her the right of a continued ignorance. . . . For it is certain, unless help [comes] from without, a nation can never rise above its present state.*[5]

After the first generation, many of the teachers in mission schools were African, themselves the products of a mission education. They discovered that Christian ideals clashed with the reality of colonial exploitation. One convert wrote in 1911:

> There is too much failure among all Europeans in Nyasaland. The three combined bodies— Missionaries, Government and Companies or gainers of money—do form the same rule to look upon the native with mockery eyes. . . . If we had enough power to communicate our- selves to Europe, we would advise them not to call themselves Christendom, but European- dom. Therefore the life of the three combined bodies is altogether too cheaty, too thefty, too mockery. Instead of "Give," they say "Take away from." There is too much breakage of God's pure law.[6]

Christian missionaries from Europe and America were not the only ones to bring religious change to Africa. In southern and Central Africa indigenous preachers adapted Christianity to African values and customs and founded new denominations known as "Ethiopian" churches.

Christianity proved successful in converting followers of traditional religions but made no inroads among Muslims. Instead, Islam, long pre- dominant in northern and eastern Africa, spread southward as Muslim teachers established Quranic schools in the villages and founded Muslim brotherhoods. European colonialism unwittingly helped the diffusion of Islam. By building cities and increas- ing trade, colonial rule permitted Mus- lims to settle in new areas. As Islam— a universal religion without the taint of colonialism—became increasingly relevant to Africans, the number of Muslims in sub-Saharan Africa prob- ably doubled between 1869 and 1914.

SECTION REVIEW

- In the late nineteenth century, the European powers divided Africa among themselves.

- Britain took over Egypt when it could not repay its debts.

- King Leopold II of Belgium initiated the partition of Africa by claiming the Congo.

- The discovery of gold and diamonds in southern Africa triggered clashes between British and Afrikaners, with the British emerging victorious.

- African reactions to the invasion varied widely; some collaborated, others resisted, but few benefited.

- Only Ethiopia, because it had adequate firearms, was able to defend its independence.

- Many African men lost their lands and migrated to cities and mines, leaving families behind.

- Many Africans turned to Christianity or Islam.

IMPERIALISM IN ASIA AND THE PACIFIC

Europeans had traded along the coasts of Asia and the East Indies since the early sixteenth cen- tury. By 1869 Britain already controlled most of India and Burma; Spain occupied the Philip- pines; and the Netherlands held large parts of the East Indies (now Indonesia). Between 1862 and 1895 France conquered Indochina (now Vietnam, Kampuchea, and Laos). Let us look at the impact of the New Imperialism on Central and Southeast Asia, Indonesia, the Philippines, and Hawaii (see Map 28.2).

Central Asia

For over seven centuries Russians had been at the mercy of the nomads of the Eurasian steppe extending from the Black Sea to Manchuria. When the nomadic tribesmen were united, as they were under the Mongol ruler Genghis Khan (r. 1206–1227), they could defeat the Russians; when they were not, the Russians moved into the steppe. This age-old ebb and flow ended when Rus- sia acquired modern rifles and artillery.

Russian Imperialism   Between 1865 and 1876 Russian forces advanced into Central Asia. The Kazakhs, who lived east of the Caspian Sea, fought bravely but in vain. The fertile agricultural land of Kazakhstan attracted 200,000 Russian settlers. Although the governments of Tsars Alexander II (r. 1855–1881) and Alexander III (r. 1881–1894) claimed not to interfere in indigenous customs, they declared communally owned grazing lands "vacant" and turned them over to farmers from Russia. By the end of the nineteenth century the nomads were reduced to starvation. Echoing the beliefs of other European imperialists, an eminent Russian jurist declared: "International rights cannot be taken into account when dealing with semibarbarous peoples."

South of the Kazakh steppe land were deserts dotted with oases where the fabled cities of Tashkent, Bukhara, and Samarkand served the caravan trade between China and the Middle East. By the 1860s and 1870s it was fairly easy for Russian expeditions to conquer the indigenous peoples in these areas. Russia thereby acquired land suitable for cotton, along with a large and growing Muslim population. The Russians abolished slavery, built railroads to link the region with Europe, and planted hundreds of thousands of acres of cotton. Unlike the British in India, however, they did not attempt to change the customs, languages, or religious beliefs of their subjects.

Southeast Asia and Indonesia

The peoples of the Southeast Asian peninsula and the Indonesian archipelago had been in contact with outsiders—Chinese, Indians, Arabs, Europeans—for centuries. Java and the Spice Islands had long been subject to Portuguese and later Dutch domination. Until the mid-nineteenth century, however, most of the region was made up of independent kingdoms.

As in Africa, there is considerable variation in the history of different parts of the region, yet all came under intense imperialist pressure during the nineteenth century. Burma (now Myanmar), nearest India, was gradually taken over by the British in the course of the century, until the last piece was annexed in 1885. Indochina fell under French control piece by piece until it was finally subdued in 1895. Similarly, Malaya (now Malaysia) came under British rule in stages during the 1870s and 1880s. By the early 1900s the Dutch had subdued northern Sumatra. Only Siam (now Thailand) remained independent, although it lost several border provinces.

Tropical Agriculture

Despite their varied political histories, all these regions had features in common. They all had fertile soil, constant warmth, and heavy rains. Furthermore, the peoples of the region had a long tradition of intensive gardening, irrigation, and terracing. In parts of the region where the population was not very dense, Europeans found it easy to import landless laborers from China and India. Another reason for the region's wealth was the transfer of commercially valuable plants from other parts of the world. Tobacco, cinchona (sin-CHO-nah) (an antimalarial drug), manioc (an edible root crop), maize (corn), and natural rubber were brought from the Americas; sugar from India; tea from China; and coffee and oil palms from Africa. By 1914 much of the world's supply of these valuable products—in the case of rubber, almost all—came from Southeast Asia and Indonesia (see Environment and Technology: Imperialism and Tropical Ecology).

Most of the wealth of Southeast Asia and Indonesia was exported to Europe and North America. In exchange, the inhabitants of the region received two benefits from colonial rule: peace and a reliable food supply. As a result, their numbers increased at an unprecedented rate. For

Mary Evans Picture Library/The Image Works

A Rubber Plantation   As bicycles and automobiles proliferated in the early twentieth century, the demand for rubber outstripped the supply available from wild rubber trees in the Amazon forest. Rubber grown on plantations in Southeast Asia came on the market from 1910 on. The rubber trees had to be tapped very carefully and on a regular schedule to obtain the latex or sap from which rubber was extracted. In this picture a woman and a boy perform this operation on a plantation in British Malaya.

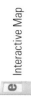
Interactive Map

MAP 28.2   Asia in 1914 By 1914, much of Asia was claimed by colonial powers. The southern rim, from the Persian Gulf to the Pacific, was occupied by Great Britain, France, the Netherlands, and the United States. Central Asia had been incorporated into the Russian Empire. Japan, now industrialized, had joined the Western imperialist powers in expanding its territory and influence at the expense of China.

© Cengage Learning

Territories held by Western powers

- Great Britain
- France
- Netherlands
- United States
- Russian Empire

- Japan and its territories
- Independent Asian states
- Ottoman Empire
- Major railroads

Imperialism and Tropical Ecology

Like all conquerors before them, the European imperialists of the nineteenth century exacted taxes and rents from the peoples they conquered. But they also sent botanists and agricultural experts to their tropical colonies to increase the production of commercial crops, radically changing the landscapes.

The most dramatic effects were brought about by the deliberate introduction of new crops. In the early nineteenth century tea was transferred from China to India and Ceylon. In the 1850s British and Dutch botanists smuggled seeds of the cinchona tree from the Andes to India and Java. With the seeds, the Europeans established cinchona plantations to produce quinine, used as an antimalarial drug and a flavoring for tonic water. In the 1870s British agents stole seeds of rubber trees from the Amazon rain forest and transferred them to Malaya and Sumatra.

Before these transfers, vast forests covered the highlands of India, Southeast Asia, and Indonesia, the lands where the new plants grew best. So European planters had the forests cut down and replaced with thousands of acres of commercially profitable trees and bushes, all lined up in perfect rows and tended by indigenous laborers to satisfy the demands of customers in faraway lands. The crops that poured forth from the transformed environments brought great wealth to the European planters and the imperial powers. In 1909 the British botanist John Willis justified the transformation in these terms:

> *Whether planting in the tropics will always continue to be under European management is another question, but the northern powers will not permit that the rich and as yet comparatively undeveloped countries of the tropics should be entirely wasted by being devoted merely to the supply of the food and clothing wants of their own people, when they can also supply the wants of the colder zones in so many indispensable products.*

This quotation raises important questions about trade versus self-sufficiency. If a region's economy supplies the food and clothing wants of its own people, is its output "entirely wasted"? What is the advantage of trading the products of one region (such as the tropics) for those of another (such as the colder zones)? Is this trade an obligation? Should one part of the world (such as the "northern powers") let another refuse to develop and sell its "indispensable products"? Can you think of a case where a powerful country forced a weaker one to trade?

CINCHONA OFFICINALIS, *Linn*

Branch of a Cinchona Tree The bark of the cinchona tree was the source of quinine, the only antimalarial drug known before the 1940s. Quinine made it much safer for Europeans to live in the tropics.

Source: The quotation is from John Christopher Willis, *Agriculture in the Tropics: An Elementary Treatise* (Cambridge: Cambridge University Press, 1909), 38–39.

instance, the population of Java (an island the size of Pennsylvania) doubled from 16 million in 1870 to over 30 million in 1914.

Social Changes

Colonialism and the growth of population brought many social changes. Agricultural and commercial peoples gradually moved into mountainous and forested areas, displacing the earlier inhabitants who practiced hunting and gathering or shifting agriculture. The migrations of the Javanese to Borneo and Sumatra are but one example. Immigrants from China and India (see Chapter 26) changed the ethnic composition and culture of every country in the region. Thus the population of the Malay Peninsula became part Malay, part Chinese, and part Indian.

As in Africa, European missionaries attempted to spread Christianity under the colonial umbrella. Islam, however, was much more successful in gaining new converts, for it had been established in the region for centuries and people did not consider it a religion imposed on them by foreigners.

Nationalism

Education and European ideas had an impact on the political perceptions of the peoples of Southeast Asia and Indonesia. Just as important was their awareness of events in neighboring Asian countries: India, where a nationalist movement arose in the 1880s; China, where modernizers were undermining the authority of the Qing; and especially Japan, whose rapid industrialization culminated in its brilliant victory over Russia in the Russo-Japanese War (1904–1905; see Chapter 27). The spirit of a rising generation was expressed by a young Vietnamese writing soon after the Russo-Japanese War:

> I, . . . an obscure student, having had occasion to study new books and new doctrines, have discovered in a recent history of Japan how they have been able to conquer the impotent Europeans. This is the reason why we have formed an organization. . . . We have selected from young Annamites [Vietnamese] the most energetic, with great capacities for courage, and are sending them to Japan for study. . . . Several years have passed without the French being aware of the movement. . . . Our only aim is to prepare the population for the future.[7]

Hawaii and the Philippines, 1878–1902

By the 1890s the United States had a fast-growing population and industries that produced more manufactured goods than they could sell at home. Merchants and bankers began to look for export markets. The political mood was also expansionist, and many echoed the feelings of the naval strategist Alfred T. Mahan (mah-HAHN): "Whether they will or no, Americans must now begin to look outward. The growing production of the country requires it."

Annexation of Hawaii

Some Americans had been looking outward for quite some time, especially across the Pacific to China and Japan. In 1878 the United States obtained the harbor of Pago Pago in Samoa as a coaling and naval station, and in 1887 it secured the use of Pearl Harbor in Hawaii for the same purpose. By 1898 the United States under President William McKinley (1897–1901) had become openly imperialistic and annexed Hawaii as a steppingstone to Asia. As the United States became ever more involved in Asian affairs, Hawaii's strategic location brought an inflow of U.S. military personnel, and its fertile land caused planters to import laborers from Japan, China, and the Philippines. These immigrants soon outnumbered the native Hawaiians.

The United States Conquers the Philippines

While large parts of Asia were falling under colonial domination, the people of the Philippines were chafing under their Spanish rulers. **Emilio Aguinaldo**, leader of a secret society, rose in revolt and proclaimed a republic in 1899. The revolutionaries had a good chance of winning independence, for Spain had its hands full with a revolution in Cuba. Unfortunately for Aguinaldo and his followers, the United States declared war against Spain in April 1898 and quickly overcame Spanish forces in the Philippines and Cuba. After the Spanish defeat, President McKinley realized that a weakened Spain might lose the islands to another imperialist power. Japan, having recently defeated China in the Sino-Japanese War (1894–1895) and annexed Taiwan (see Chapter 27), was eager to expand its empire. So was Germany, which had taken over parts of New Guinea and Samoa and several Pacific archipelagoes during the 1880s. To forestall them, McKinley purchased the Philippines from Spain for $20 million.

Emilio Aguinaldo Leader of the Filipino independence movement against Spain (1895–1898). He proclaimed the independence of the Philippines in 1899, but his movement was crushed and he was captured by the United States Army in 1901.

The Filipinos were not eager to trade one master for another. For a while, Aguinaldo cooperated with the Americans in the hope of achieving full independence. When his plan was rejected, he rose up again in 1899 and proclaimed the independence of his country. In spite of protests by anti-imperialists in the United States, the U.S. government decided that its global interests outweighed the interests of the Filipino people. In rebel areas, a U.S. army of occupation tortured prisoners, burned villages and crops, and forced the inhabitants into "reconcentration camps." By the end of the insurrection in 1902, the war had cost the lives of 5,000 Americans and 200,000 Filipinos.

SECTION REVIEW

- Once it had modern firearms, Russia easily conquered and settled the countries of Central Asia.

- Britain, France, and the Netherlands turned their colonies in Southeast Asia and Indonesia into producers of tropical crops.

- The United States took over Hawaii in 1898; after four years of war, it secured the Philippines from Spain and crushed a Filipino rebellion.

Emilio Aguinaldo   In 1896, a revolt led by Emilio Aguinaldo attempted to expel Spaniards from the Philippines. When the United States purchased the Philippines from Spain two years later, the Filipino people were not consulted. Aguinaldo continued his campaign, this time against the American occupation forces, until his capture in 1901. In this picture, he appears on horseback, surrounded by some of his troops.

After the insurrection ended, the United States attempted to soften its rule with public works and economic development projects. New buildings went up in the city of Manila; roads, harbors, and railroads were built; and the Philippine economy was tied ever more closely to that of the United States. In 1907 Filipinos were allowed to elect representatives to a legislative assembly, but ultimate authority remained in the hands of a governor appointed by the president of the United States. In 1916 the Philippines were the first U.S. colony to be promised independence, a promise fulfilled thirty years later.

IMPERIALISM IN LATIN AMERICA

free-trade imperialism
Economic dominance of a weaker country by a more powerful one, while maintaining the legal independence of the weaker state. In the late nineteenth century, free-trade imperialism characterized the relations between the Latin American republics, on the one hand, and Great Britain and the United States, on the other.

Nations in the Americas followed two divergent paths (see Chapter 24). In Canada and the United States manufacturing industries, powerful corporations, and wealthy financial institutions arose. Latin America and the Caribbean exported raw materials and foodstuffs and imported manufactured goods. The poverty of their people, the preferences of their elites, and the pressures of the world economy made them increasingly dependent on the industrialized countries. Their political systems saved them from outright annexation, but their natural resources made them attractive targets for manipulation by the industrial powers, including the United States, in a form of economic dependence called **free-trade imperialism**. In the larger republics of South America, the pressure was mostly financial and economic. In Central America and the Caribbean, it also included military intervention by the United States.

Railroads and the Imperialism of Free Trade

Latin America's economic potential was huge, for the region could produce many agricultural and mineral products in demand in the industrial countries. What was needed was a means of opening the interior to development. Railroads seemed the perfect answer.

Foreign merchants and bankers and Latin American landowners and politicians embraced the new technology. Starting in the 1870s, almost every country in Latin America acquired railroads, usually connecting mines or agricultural regions with the nearest port rather than linking up the different parts of the interior. All the equipment and building material came from Britain or the United States. So did the money to build the networks, the engineers who designed and maintained them, and the managers who ran them.

Argentina, a land of rich soil that produced wheat, beef, and hides, gained the longest and best-developed rail network south of the United States. By 1914, 86 percent of the railroads in Argentina were owned by British firms; 40 percent of the employees were British; and the official language of the railroads was not Spanish but English. The same was true of mining and industrial enterprises and public utilities throughout Latin America.

In many ways, the situation resembled those of India and Ireland, which also obtained rail networks in exchange for raw materials and agricultural products. The Argentine nationalist Juan Justo saw the parallel:

> *English capital has done what English armies could not do. Today our country is tributary to England . . . the gold that the English capitalists take out of Argentina or carry off in the form of products does us no more good than the Irish get from the revenues that the English lords take out of Ireland.*[8]

The difference was that the Indians and Irish had little say in the matter because they were under British rule. But in Latin America the political elites encouraged foreign companies with generous concessions as the most rapid way to modernize their countries and enrich the property owners. The majority were neither consulted nor allowed to benefit from the railroad boom.

American Expansionism and the Spanish-American War, 1898

The United States had long had interests in Cuba, the closest and richest of the Caribbean islands and a Spanish colony. American businesses had invested great sums of money in Cuba's sugar and tobacco industries, and thousands of Cubans had migrated to the United States. In 1895 the Cuban nationalist José Martí started a revolution against Spanish rule. American newspapers thrilled readers with lurid stories of Spanish atrocities; businessmen worried about their investments; and politicians demanded that the U.S. government help liberate Cuba.

On February 15, 1898, the U.S. battleship *Maine* accidentally blew up in Havana harbor, killing 266 American sailors. The U.S. government immediately blamed Spain and issued an ultimatum that the Spanish evacuate Cuba. Spain agreed to the ultimatum, but the American press and Congress were eager for war, and President McKinley did not restrain them.

The Spanish-American War was over quickly. On May 1, 1898, U.S. warships destroyed the Spanish fleet at Manila in the Philippines. Two months later the United States Navy sank the Spanish Atlantic fleet off Santiago, Cuba. By mid-August Spain was suing for peace. U.S. Secretary of State John Hay called it "a splendid little war." The United States purchased the Philippines from Spain but took over Puerto Rico and Guam as war booty. The two islands remain American possessions to this day. Cuba became an independent republic, subject to interference by the United States.

American Intervention in the Caribbean and Central America, 1901–1914

The nations of the Caribbean and Central America were small and poor, and their governments were corrupt, unstable, and often bankrupt. They seemed to offer an open invitation to foreign interference. A government would borrow money to pay for railroads, harbors, electric power, and other symbols of modernity. When it could not repay the loan, the lending banks in Europe or the United States would ask for assistance from their home governments, which sometimes threatened to intervene. To ward off European intervention, the United States sent in the marines on more than one occasion.

Presidents Theodore Roosevelt (1901–1909), William Taft (1909–1913), and Woodrow Wilson (1913–1921) felt impelled to intervene in the region, though they differed sharply on the proper policy the United States should follow toward the small nations to the south. Roosevelt

Panama Canal Ship canal cut across the isthmus of Panama by United States Army engineers; it opened in 1915. The canal greatly shortened the sea voyage between the east and west coasts of North America. The United States turned the canal over to Panama on January 1, 2000.

encouraged regimes friendly to the United States; Taft sought to influence them through loans from American banks; and the moralist Wilson tried to impose clean governments by military means.

Having "liberated" Cuba from Spain, in 1901 the United States forced the Cuban government to accept the Platt Amendment, which gave the United States the "right to intervene" to maintain order on the island. The United States used this excuse to occupy Cuba militarily from 1906 to 1909, in 1912, and again from 1917 to 1922. In all but name Cuba became an American protectorate. U.S. troops also occupied the Dominican Republic from 1904 to 1907 and again in 1916, Nicaragua and Honduras in 1912, and Haiti in 1915. They brought sanitation and material progress but no political improvements.

The United States was especially forceful in Panama, which was a province of Colombia. Here the issue was not corruption or debts but a more vital interest. When the United States acquired Hawaii and the Philippines, it recognized the need for a canal that would allow warships to move quickly between the Atlantic and Pacific Oceans. The main obstacle was Colombia, which refused to give the United States a piece of its territory. In 1903 the U.S. government supported a Panamanian rebellion against Colombia and quickly recognized the independence of Panama. In exchange, it obtained the right to build a canal and to occupy a zone 5 miles (8 kilometers) wide on either side of it. Work began in 1904, and the **Panama Canal** opened on August 15, 1914.

SECTION REVIEW

- Britain and the United States collaborated with Latin American elites to exploit the Latin American republics economically; a key factor was the expansion of railroads.

- After defeating Spain in 1898, the United States sent troops to Cuba and other Caribbean and Central American republics; through the Platt Amendment, it also claimed the right to interfere in Cuban affairs.

- The United States helped Panama secede from Colombia so that it could build the Panama Canal.

THE WORLD ECONOMY AND THE GLOBAL ENVIRONMENT

The New Imperialists were not traditional conquerors or empire builders like the Spanish conquistadors. Although their conquests were much larger (see Map 28.3), their aim was not only to extend their power over new territories and peoples but also to control both the natural world and indigenous societies and put them to work more efficiently than had ever been done before. They expressed their belief in progress and their good intentions in the clichés of the time: "the conquest of nature," "the annihilation of time and space," "the taming of the wilderness," and "our civilizing mission."

Expansion of the World Economy

For centuries Europe had been a ready market for spices, sugar, silk, and other exotic or tropical products. The Industrial Revolution vastly expanded this demand. Imports of foods and stimulants such as tea, coffee, and cocoa increased substantially during the nineteenth century. The trade in industrial raw materials grew even faster. Some were the products of agriculture, such as cotton, jute for bags, and palm oil for soap and lubricants. Others were minerals such as diamonds, gold, and copper. There also were wild forest products that only later came to be cultivated: timber for buildings and railroad ties, cinchona bark, rubber for rainwear and tires, and gutta-percha (gut-tah-PER-cha) (the sap of a Southeast Asian tree) to insulate electric cables.

The growing needs of the industrial world could not be met by the traditional methods of production and transportation of the nonindustrial world. When the U.S. Civil War interrupted the export of cotton to England in the 1860s, the British turned to India and Egypt, but they found that Indian cotton was ruined by exposure to rain and dust during the long trip from the interior of the country to the harbors. To prevent the expansion of their industry from being stifled by the technological backwardness of their newly conquered territories, the imperialists made every effort to bring those territories into the mainstream of the world market.

The Transportation Revolution

One great change was in transportation. The Suez and Panama Canals cut travel time and lowered freight costs dramatically. Steamships became more numerous, and as their size increased, new, deeper harbors were needed. The Europeans also built railroads throughout the

MAP 28.3 **The Great Powers and Their Colonial Possessions in 1913** By 1913, a small handful of countries claimed sovereignty over more than half the land area of the earth. Global power was closely connected with industries and a merchant marine, rather than with a large territory. This explains why Great Britain, the smallest of the great powers, possessed the largest empire.

The colonial powers and their possessions

- Germany
- France
- Great Britain
- Belgium
- Netherlands
- Portugal
- Italy
- Spain
- Russia
- United States
- Japan
- Major shipping route

© Cengage Learning

e Interactive Map

0   1,000   2,000 Km.
0   1,000   2,000 Mi.

world; India alone had 37,000 miles (nearly 60,000 kilometers) of track by 1915, almost as much as Germany or Russia. Railroads reached into the interior of Latin America, Canada, China, and Australia. In 1903 the Russians completed the Trans-Siberian Railway from Moscow to Vladivostok on the Pacific. Visionaries even made plans for railroads from Europe to India and from Egypt to South Africa.

Transformation of the Global Environment

The economic changes brought by Europeans and Americans also altered environments around the world. The British, whose craving for tea could not be satisfied with the limited exports available from China, introduced tea into Ceylon and northeastern India. In those areas and in Java, thousands of square miles of tropical rain forests were felled to make way for tea plantations.

Economic Botany

Economic botany and agricultural science were applied to every promising plant species. European botanists had long collected and classified exotic plants from around the world. In the nineteenth century they founded botanical gardens in Java, India, Mauritius (maw-REE-shuss), Ceylon, Jamaica, and other tropical colonies. These gardens not only collected local plants but also transferred commercially valuable plant species from one tropical region to another. Cinchona, tobacco, sugar, and other crops were introduced, improved, and vastly expanded in the colonies of Southeast Asia and Indonesia (see Environment and Technology: Imperialism and Tropical Ecology). Cocoa and coffee growing spread over large areas of Brazil and Africa; oil-palm plantations were established in Nigeria and the Congo Basin. After 1910, rubber, used to make waterproof garments and bicycle tires, came from plantations in Southeast Asia.

Throughout the tropics, land once covered with forests or devoted to shifting slash-and-burn agriculture was transformed into permanent farms and plantations. Even in areas not developed to export crops, growing populations put pressure on the land. In Java and India farmers felled trees to obtain arable land and firewood. They terraced hillsides, drained swamps, and dug wells.

Irrigation

Irrigation and water control transformed the dry parts of the tropics as well. British engineers in India built new irrigation canals, turning thousands of previously barren acres into well-watered, densely populated farmland. The migration of European experts spread the newest techniques of irrigation engineering around the world. By the turn of the century irrigation projects were under way wherever rivers flowed through dry lands. In Egypt and Central Asia irrigation brought more acres under cultivation in one forty-year span than in all previous history.

Railroads had voracious appetites for land and resources. They cut into mountains, spanned rivers and canyons, and covered as much land with their freight yards as whole cities had needed in previous centuries. They also consumed vast quantities of iron, timber for ties, and coal or wood for fuel. Most important of all, railroads brought people and their cities, farms, and industries to areas previously occupied by small, scattered populations.

Gardiner F. Williams/NGS Image Collection

South African Diamond Mine   When diamonds were found in Kimberley, South Africa, in 1868, the discovery precipitated a rush of prospectors from Europe and America. As soon as surface deposits were exhausted, their claims were bought by large companies that could afford the heavy equipment needed to mine deep underground. By the early twentieth century, diamonds came from major industrial mines like the Premier Mine shown here.

SECTION REVIEW

- The world economy, fueled by European ideas of "progress," expanded quickly between 1860 and 1914, thanks to cheaper and faster transportation made possible with canals and railroads.

- Europeans made Latin America, Africa, and Asia into producers of raw materials and crops and into markets for industrial goods.

- Europeans studied botany and brought huge areas of land into cultivation through irrigation.

- Railroads transformed the land, and mining often polluted it.

Prospectors looking for valuable minerals opened the earth to reveal its riches. Where mines were dug deep inside the earth, the dirt and rocks brought up with the ores formed huge mounds near mine entrances. Open mines dug to obtain ores lying close to the surface created a landscape of lunar craters, and runoff from the minerals poisoned the water for miles around. Refineries that processed the ores fouled the environment with slag heaps and more toxic runoff.

The transformation of the land by human beings, a constant throughout history, accelerated sharply. Only the changes occurring since 1914 can compare with the transformation of the global environment that took place between 1869 and 1914.

CONCLUSION

The imperial powers were driven by many motives. Governments used colonies to enhance their prestige and power. Missionaries sought not only to convert native peoples but also to "civilize" their behavior. Colonizers were led by the growing demand for natural resources. The imperialists used steamships, gunboats, and improved firearms to build their empires.

The "scramble" for Africa began in the 1870s. Britain secured the Suez Canal and constructed a dam across the Nile. Elsewhere, European companies exploited rubber plantations, diamond mines, and other resources. Local reaction to colonial rule varied greatly, as traditional land use patterns were disrupted. All Africans were affected by changes in social and cultural customs.

The effects of colonialism varied throughout Asia, although in all regions the economic changes benefited the Europeans rather than the indigenous peoples. Southeast Asia's fertile soil and heavy rains made various crops, especially rubber, very profitable. In Hawaii, Americans and foreign laborers eventually outnumbered the native Hawaiians. Europeans differed in their approach to indigenous cultures and religions. Russians did not attempt to impose their customs, language, or religious beliefs on Central Asians, whereas Christian missionaries in Southeast Asia worked to spread their beliefs. Their efforts gained only limited success in lands in which Islam or Hinduism had been dominant for centuries.

Latin America had great economic potential. The construction of railroads, using equipment and funding from Britain and the United States, helped to connect the interior regions with the ports. Americans invested heavily in the sugar and tobacco industries of Cuba. The United States also supported a Panamanian rebellion against Colombia in order to build the Panama Canal.

Imperialism, both formal and informal, opened up the world to increased trade and communication. Shipping, canals, and railroads were the most visible means of globalization. Farming, mining, labor migrations, and urbanization were profoundly affected as well. In the process, natural environments were transformed as never before. Forests were replaced by plantations. Irrigation schemes opened dry lands to agriculture. And railroads and mines cut into the landscape, leaving scars and pollution.

KEY TERMS

EBOOK AND WEBSITE RESOURCES

Primary Source

Convention on Free Navigation of the Suez Canal Between the European Powers and the Ottoman Empire, October 29, 1888

Interactive Maps

Map 28.1 Africa in 1878 and 1914

Map 28.2 Asia in 1914

Map 28.3 The Great Powers and Their Colonial Possessions in 1913

Plus flashcards, practice quizzes, and more. Go to:
www.cengage.com/history/bullietearthpeople5e

SUGGESTED READING

Achebe, Chinua. *Things Fall Apart.* 1958. A classic novel describing the impact of colonialism in Nigerian society.

Cook, Scott B. *Colonial Encounters in the Age of High Imperialism.* 1996. A brief, well-written account of the New Imperialism.

Headrick, Daniel R. *The Tools of Empire: Technology and European Imperialism in the Nineteenth Century,* 1981; and *The Tentacles of Progress: Technology Transfer in the Age of Imperialism, 1850–1940.* 1988. Two books emphasizing the importance of technology in the conquests and the colonial era.

Healy, David. *Drive to Hegemony: The United States in the Caribbean, 1898–1917.* 1989. The best summary of "dollar diplomacy."

Hochschild, Adam. *King Leopold's Ghost: A Story of Greed, Terror, and Heroism in Colonial Africa.* 1998. A dramatic account of the conquest and exploitation of the Belgian Congo.

Hopkirk, Peter. *The Great Game: The Struggle for Empire in Central Asia.* 1994. Describes the rivalry between Russia and Great Britain.

Huttenback, Robert. *Racism and Empire: White Settlers and Colored Immigrants in the British Self-Governing Colonies, 1830–1910.* 1976. Analyzes racism and race relations in Australia, Canada, New Zealand, and South Africa.

Iriye, Akira. *Across the Pacific: An Inner History of American-East Asian Relations.* 1992. Describes American policy toward Japan and China.

Karnow, Stanley. *In Our Image: America's Empire in the Philippines.* 1989. How the United States conquered and rule the Philippines.

MacKenzie, John. *Imperialism and the Natural World.* 1990. The impact of economic development and agriculture on colonial environments.

McCracken, Donal. *Gardens of Empire: Botanical Institutions of the Victorian British Empire.* 1997. How British botanists contributed to plant transfers and commercial agriculture in the tropics.

Northrup, David. *Indentured Labor in the Age of Imperialism, 1834–1922.* 1995. How colonial enterprises imported workers from China and India to work in mines and plantations in Southeast Asia, Oceania, the Caribbean, and Africa.

Oliver, Caroline. *Western Women in Colonial Africa.* 1982. On the role of wives of colonial officials and women missionaries in the colonies.

Oliver, Roland, and Anthony Atmore. *Africa Since 1800,* new ed. 1994. A classic account of modern African history.

Vandervort, Bruce. *Wars of Imperial Conquest in Africa, 1830–1914.* 1998. A brief account of the conflicts between Europeans and Africans during the New Imperialism.

NOTES

1. *Journal Officiel* (November 29, 1869), quoted in Georges Douin, *Histoire du Règne du Khédive Ismaïl* (Rome: Reale Società di Geografia d'Egitto, 1933), 453.

2. E. Desplaces in *Journal de l'Union des Deux Mers* (December 15, 1869), quoted ibid., 453.

3. Michael Adas, *Islamic and European Expansion* (Philadelphia: Temple University Press, 1993), 365.

4. "Correspondence and Report from His Majesty's Consul at Boma respecting the Administration of the Independent State of the Congo," *British Parliamentary Papers, Accounts and Papers, 1904* (Cd. 1933), lxii, 357.

5. Robert W. July, *A History of the African People,* 3d ed. (New York: Charles Scribner's Sons, 1980), 323.

6. George Shepperson and Thomas Price, *Independent African* (Edinburgh: University Press, 1958), 163–164, quoted in Roland Oliver and Anthony Atmore, *Africa Since 1800,* 4th ed. (Cambridge: Cambridge University Press, 1994), 150.

7. Thomas Edson Ennis, *French Policy and Development in Indochina* (Chicago: University of Chicago Press, 1936), 178, quoted in K. M. Panikkar, *Asia and Western Dominance* (New York: Collier, 1969), 167.

8. Quoted in Stanley J. Stein and Barbara H. Stein, *The Colonial Heritage of Latin America* (New York: Oxford University Press, 1970), 151.

CHAPTER
29

CHAPTER OUTLINE

- Origins of the Crisis in Europe and the Middle East
- The "Great War" and the Russian Revolutions, 1914–1918
- Peace and Dislocation in Europe, 1919–1929
- China and Japan: Contrasting Destinies
- The New Middle East
- Society, Culture, and Technology in the Industrialized World
- Conclusion

DIVERSITY + DOMINANCE   *The Middle East After World War I*
ENVIRONMENT + TECHNOLOGY   *The Birth of Civil Aviation*

Imperial War Museum/The Art Archive

The Western Front in World War I   In a landscape ravaged by artillery fire, two soldiers dash for cover amid shell holes and the charred remains of a forest.

Visit the website and ebook for additional study materials and interactive tools: www.cengage.com/history/bullietearthpeople5e

The Crisis of the Imperial Order, 1900–1929

On June 28, 1914, Archduke Franz Ferdinand, heir to the throne of Austria-Hungary, was riding in an open carriage through Sarajevo, a city Austria had annexed six years earlier. When the carriage stopped momentarily, Gavrilo Princip, member of a pro-Serbian conspiracy, fired his pistol twice, killing the archduke and his wife.

Those shots ignited a global conflict. All previous wars had caused death and destruction, but they were also marked by heroism and glory. In this new war, four years of bitter fighting produced no victories, no gains, and no glory, only death for millions of soldiers. The war became global as the Ottoman Empire fought against Britain and Japan attacked German positions in China. France and Britain involved their empires in the war and brought Africans, Indians, Australians, and Canadians to Europe to fight and labor on the front lines. Finally, in 1917, the United States entered the fray.

The next three chapters tell a story of violence and hope. In this chapter, we will look at the causes of war between the great powers, the consequences of that conflict in Europe, the Middle East, and Russia, and the upheavals in China and Japan. At the same time, we will review the technological changes that made war more dangerous, yet also allowed far more people to live healthier, more comfortable, and more interesting lives than ever before.

- What led to the outbreak of the First World War?
- How did the war lead to revolution in Russia?
- What role did the war play in eroding European dominance in the world?
- Why did China and Japan follow such divergent paths in this period?
- How did the Middle East change as a result of the war?
- How did European and North American society and technology change in the aftermath of the war?

ORIGINS OF THE CRISIS IN EUROPE AND THE MIDDLE EAST

When the twentieth century opened, the world seemed firmly under the control of the great powers (see Chapter 27). The first decade of the twentieth century was a period of relative peace and economic growth in most of the world. Several new technologies—airplanes, automobiles, radio, and cinema—aroused much excitement. The great powers consolidated their colonial conquests of the previous decades, and their alliances were evenly matched. The only international war of the period, the Russo-Japanese War (1904–1905), ended quickly with a decisive Japanese victory.

However, two major changes undermined the apparent stability of the world. In Europe, tensions mounted as Germany, with its growing industrial and military might, challenged

Britain at sea and France in Morocco. The Ottoman Empire grew weaker, leaving a dangerous power vacuum. The resulting chaos in the Balkans gradually drew the European powers into a web of hostilities.

The Ottoman Empire and Balkans

From the fifteenth to the nineteenth centuries the Ottoman Empire was one of the most powerful states. By the late nineteenth century, however, it had fallen behind economically, technologically, and militarily. Europeans referred to it as the "sick man of Europe."

As the Ottoman Empire weakened, it began losing provinces closest to Europe: Macedonia in 1902–1903, Bosnia in 1908, Crete in 1909, Albania in 1910. In 1912 Italy conquered Libya, the Ottomans' last foothold in Africa. In 1912–1913 Serbia, Bulgaria, Romania, and Greece chased the Turks out of Europe, except for a small enclave around Constantinople.

The Young Turks

In reaction, the Turks began to assert themselves against rebellious minorities and meddling foreigners. Many officers in the army, the most Europeanized segment of Turkish society, blamed Sultan Abdul Hamid II (r. 1876–1909) for the decline of the empire. A group known as "Young Turks" plotted to force a constitution on the sultan. They alienated other anti-Ottoman groups by advocating centralized rule and the Turkification of ethnic minorities.

In 1909 the parliament, dominated by Young Turks, overthrew Abdul Hamid. The new regime began to reform the police, the bureaucracy, and the educational system. At the same time, it cracked down on Greek and Armenian minorities. Galvanized by their defeat in the Balkan Wars, the Turks hired a German general to modernize their armed forces. The dangerous mixture of modern armies and nationalism was not limited to the Ottoman Empire, however.

Nationalism, Alliances, and Military Strategy

The assassination of Franz Ferdinand triggered a chain of events over which military and political leaders lost control. The escalation from assassination to global war had causes that went back many years. One was nationalism, which bound citizens to their ethnic group and led them, when called upon, to kill people they viewed as enemies. Another was the system of alliances and military plans that the great powers had devised to protect themselves from their rivals. A third was Germany's yearning to dominate Europe.

Nationalism

Nationalism united the citizens of France, Britain, and Germany behind their respective governments and gave them tremendous cohesion and strength of purpose. Only the most powerful feelings could inspire millions of men to march into battle and could sustain civilian populations through years of hardship.

Nationalism could also be a dividing force. The large but fragile multinational Russian, Austro-Hungarian, and Ottoman Empires contained numerous ethnic and religious minorities. Having repressed the other minorities for centuries, the governments could never count on their full support. The very existence of an independent Serbia threatened Austria-Hungary by stirring up the hopes and resentments of its Slavic populations.

Imbued with nationalism, most people viewed war as a crusade for liberty or as long-overdue revenge for past injustices. During the nineteenth century, as memories of the misery and carnage caused by the Napoleonic Wars faded, revulsion against war gradually weakened. The Crimean War of 1853–1856 and the Franco-Prussian War of 1871 had caused few casualties or long-term consequences. And in the wars of the New Imperialism (see Chapter 28), Europeans almost always had been victorious at a small cost in money and manpower.

What turned an incident in the Balkans into a conflict involving all the great powers was the system of alliances. At the center of Europe stood Germany, the most heavily industrialized country in Europe. Its army was the best trained and equipped, and it challenged Great Britain's naval supremacy by building "dreadnoughts"—heavily armed battleships. In 1882 it joined Austria-Hungary and Italy in the Triple Alliance, while France allied itself with Russia. In 1904 Britain and France reached an Entente (on-TONT) ("understanding"), joined by Russia in 1907. Europe was thus divided into two blocs of roughly equal power (see Map 29.1).

The alliance system was cursed by inflexible military planning. In 1914 western and central Europe had highly developed railroad networks but very few motor vehicles, and European

CHRONOLOGY

	Europe and North America	Middle East	East Asia
1900			1900 Boxer uprising in China
	1904 British-French Entente		1904–1905 Russo-Japanese War
	1907 British-Russian Entente		
		1909 Young Turks overthrow Sultan Abdul Hamid	
1910			
	1912–1913 Balkan Wars	1912 Italy conquers Libya, last Ottoman territory in Africa	1911 Chinese revolutionaries led by Sun Yat-sen overthrow Qing dynasty
	1914 Assassination of Archduke Franz Ferdinand sparks World War I	1915 British defeat at Gallipoli	1915 Japan presents Twenty-One Demands to China
	1916 Battles of Verdun and the Somme	1916 Arab Revolt in Arabia	
	1917 Russian Revolutions; United States enters the war	1917 Balfour Declaration	
	1918 Armistice ends World War I		
	1918–1921 Civil war in Russia		
	1919 Treaty of Versailles	1919–1922 War between Turkey and Greece	1919 May Fourth Movement in China
1920	1920 First commercial radio broadcast (United States)	1922 Egypt nominally independent	
	1923–1928 New Economic Policy in Russia	1923 Mustafa Kemal proclaims Turkey a republic	
	1927 Charles Lindbergh flies alone across the Atlantic		1927 Guomindang forces occupy Shanghai and expel Communists

armies had grown to include millions of soldiers and reservists. To mobilize these forces and transport them to battle would require thousands of trains running on precise schedules. Once under way, a country's mobilization could not be canceled or postponed without causing chaos.

In the years before World War I, military planners in France and Germany had worked out elaborate railroad timetables to mobilize their respective armies in a few days. Russia, a large country with an underdeveloped rail system, needed several weeks to mobilize its forces. Britain, with a tiny volunteer army, had no mobilization plans, and German planners believed that the British would stay out of a war on the European continent. So that Germany could avoid having to fight France and Russia at the same time, German war planners expected to defeat France in a matter of days, then transport the entire army across Germany to the Russian border by train before Russia could fully mobilize.

The War Begins On July 28, Austria-Hungary declared war on Serbia. The declaration of war triggered the general mobilization plans of Russia, France, and Germany. On July 29 the Russian government ordered general mobilization to force Austria to back down. On August 1 France ordered general mobilization. Minutes later Germany did likewise. Because of the rigid railroad timetables, war was now automatic.

The German plan was to wheel around through neutral Belgium and into northwestern France. The German General Staff expected France to capitulate before the British could get involved. But on August 3, when German troops entered Belgium, Britain demanded their withdrawal. When Germany refused, Britain declared war on Germany.

SECTION REVIEW

- As the Ottoman Empire declined, nationalists calling themselves Young Turks tried to create a new Turkish nation.

- Nationalism, competing alliances, and inflexible military plans based on railroads turned an assassination into a cause for war.

MAP 29.1 **Europe in 1913**   On the eve of World War I, Europe was divided between two great alliance systems—the Triple Alliance (Germany, Austria-Hungary, and Italy) and the Entente (France, Great Britain, and Russia)—and their respective colonial empires. These alliances were not stable. When war broke out, the Triple Alliance lost Italy but gained the Ottoman Empire.

© Cengage Learning

e Interactive Map

THE "GREAT WAR" AND THE RUSSIAN REVOLUTIONS, 1914–1918

Throughout Europe, people greeted the outbreak of war with parades and flags, expecting a quick victory. German troops marched off to the front shouting "To Paris!" Spectators in France encouraged marching French troops with shouts of "Send me the Kaiser's moustache!" The German sociologist Max Weber wrote: "This war, with all its ghastliness, is nevertheless grand and wonderful. It is worth experiencing."[1] When the war began, very few imagined that their side might not win. No one foresaw that everyone would lose.

Stalemate, 1914–1917

The war that erupted in 1914 was known as the "Great War" until the 1940s, when a far greater one overshadowed it. Its form came as a surprise to all belligerents, from the generals on down. In the classic battles that every officer studied, the advantage always went to the fastest-moving army led by the boldest general. In 1914 the generals' carefully drawn plans went awry from the start. Believing that a spirited attack would always prevail, French generals hurled their troops, dressed in bright blue-and-red uniforms, against the well-defended German border and suffered a crushing defeat. In battle after battle the much larger German armies defeated the French and the British. By early September the Germans held Belgium and northern France and were fast approaching Paris.

German victory seemed assured. But German troops, who had marched and fought for a month, were exhausted, and their generals wavered. A gap opened between two German armies along the Marne River, into which General Joseph Joffre moved France's last reserves. At the Battle of the Marne (September 5–12, 1914), the Germans were thrown back several miles.

Trench Warfare

Western Front A line of trenches and fortifications in World War I that stretched without a break from Switzerland to the North Sea. Scene of most of the fighting between Germany, on the one hand, and France and Britain, on the other.

During the next month, both sides spread out until they formed an unbroken line extending over 300 miles (some 500 kilometers) from the North Sea to the border of Switzerland. All along this **Western Front**, the opposing troops prepared their defenses. Their most potent weapons were machine guns, which provided an almost impenetrable defense against advancing infantry but were useless for the offensive because they were too heavy for one man to carry and took too much time to set up.

To escape the deadly streams of bullets, soldiers dug holes in the ground, connected the holes to form shallow trenches, then dug communications trenches to the rear. Within weeks, the battlefields were scarred by lines of trenches several feet deep, their tops protected by sandbags and their floors covered with planks. Trenches were nothing new. What was extraordinary was that the trenches along the entire Western Front were connected, leaving no gaps through which armies could advance (see Map 29.2). How, then, could either side ever hope to win?

For four years, generals on each side again and again ordered their troops to attack. In battle after battle, thousands of young men on one side climbed out of their trenches, raced across the open fields, and were mowed down by enemy machine-gun fire. Hoping to destroy the machine guns, the attacking force would saturate the entrenched enemy lines with artillery barrages. But this tactic alerted the defenders to an impending attack and allowed them to rush in reinforcements and set up new machine guns.

The year 1916 saw the bloodiest and most futile battles of the war. The Germans attacked French forts at Verdun, losing 281,000 men and causing 315,000 French casualties. In retaliation, the British attacked the Germans at the Somme River and suffered 420,000 casualties—60,000 on the first day alone—while the Germans lost 450,000 and the French 200,000.

Warfare had never been waged this way before. It was mass slaughter in a moonscape of mud, steel, and flesh. Both sides attacked and defended, but neither side could win, for the armies were stalemated by trenches and machine guns. During four years of the bloodiest fighting the world had ever seen, the Western Front moved no more than a few miles one way or another.

The War at Sea

At sea, the war was just as inconclusive. As soon as war broke out, the British cut the German overseas telegraph cables, blockaded the coasts of Germany and Austria-Hungary, and set out to capture or sink all enemy ships still at sea. The German High Seas Fleet, built at enormous cost, seldom left port. Only once, in May 1916, did it confront the British Grand Fleet. At the Battle of Jutland, off the coast of Denmark, the two fleets lost roughly equal numbers of ships, and the Germans escaped back to their harbors.

In early 1915, in retaliation for the British naval blockade, Germany announced a blockade of Britain by submarines. German submarines attacked every vessel they could. One of their victims was the British ocean liner *Lusitania*. The death toll from that attack was 1,198 people, 139 of them Americans. When the United States protested, Germany ceased its submarine campaign, hoping to keep America neutral.

Airplanes were used for reconnaissance and engaged in spectacular but inconsequential dogfights above the trenches. Poison gas, introduced on the Western Front in 1915, killed and wounded attacking soldiers as well as their intended victims, adding to the horror of battle. Primitive tanks aided, but did not cause, the collapse of the German army in the last weeks of the war. Although these weapons were of limited effectiveness in World War I, they offered an insight into the future of warfare.

MAP 29.2 **The First World War in Europe** After an initial surge through Belgium into northern France, the German offensive bogged down for four years along the Western Front. To the East, the German armies conquered a large part of Russia during 1917 and early 1918. Despite spectacular victories in the east, Germany lost the war because its armies collapsed along the strategically important Western Front.

e Interactive Map

© Cengage Learning

Triple Entente and its Allies
Central Powers
Neutral nations
Greatest extent of territory gained
by Germany-Austria
Battle line

Germany, 1914
German offensive, 1915
Greatest extent of territory
gained by Germany, Sept. 1914
Front at beginning of 1915
German offensive, Summer 1918
Armistice line, November 1918
Major battle

Treaty of Brest-Litovsk, March 1918

Armistice line, December 1917

Farthest Russian advance, 1914

Western front

Balkan front

Italian front

British blockade line

*Inset map labels:*
NETHERLANDS
GERMANY
BELGIUM
LUXEMBOURG
FRANCE
Antwerp
Brussels
Liège
Coblenz
Cologne
Ostend
Ghent
FLANDERS
Arras
St. Quentin
Sedan
ARDENNES
ARGONNE FOREST
Verdun
St-Mihiel
Nancy
LORRAINE
Strasbourg
ALSACE
Épinal
Mulhouse
Basel
Calais
Dover
Amiens
Compiègne
Somme
Belleau Wood
Marne I
Paris
Marne II
Château-Thierry
Reims
Châlons-sur-Marne
English Channel
Ruhr R.
Rhine R.
Moselle R.
Saar R.
Meuse R.
Aisne R.
Marne R.
Seine R.
Somme R.
Scheldt R.

*Main map labels:*
ATLANTIC OCEAN
GREAT BRITAIN
London
IRELAND
North Sea
NORWAY
SWEDEN
DENMARK
Jutland 1916
Kiel
NETHERLANDS
GERMANY
Berlin
Elbe R.
Baltic Sea
FINLAND
Helsinki
Petrograd (St. Petersburg)
Moscow
RUSSIA
Don R.
ESTONIA
LATVIA
Riga
COURLAND
LITHUANIA
Wilno (Vilnius)
BELARUS
Masurian Lakes 1914
E. PRUSSIA
Tannenberg 1914
Warsaw
KINGDOM OF POLAND (Russia)
Vistula R.
Brest-Litovsk
Kiev
UKRAINE
Dnieper R.
Dniester R.
GALICIA
MAY 1915
Black Sea
ROMANIA
Bucharest
Danube R.
TRANSYLVANIA
AUSTRIA-HUNGARY
Budapest
Vienna
SWITZERLAND
ALSACE-LORRAINE
LUXEMBOURG
BELGIUM
Louvain
Paris
FRANCE
Bordeaux
Loire R.
Garonne R.
Seine R.
Rhine R.
Rhône R.
Po R.
ITALY
Rome
Caporetto 1917
AUG. 1917
MAR. 1918
SPAIN
Ebro R.
Corsica
Sardinia
Balearic Is.
Elba
Sicily
TUNISIA (France)
Tunis
Malta
Mediterranean Sea
Adriatic Sea
SERBIA
MONTENEGRO
Sarajevo
ALBANIA
BULGARIA
GREECE
1915
1916
1917
1918
Constantinople
Dardanelles
Gallipoli 1915
OTTOMAN EMPIRE
Crete
Cyprus

N

0   200   400 Km.
0   200   400 Mi.

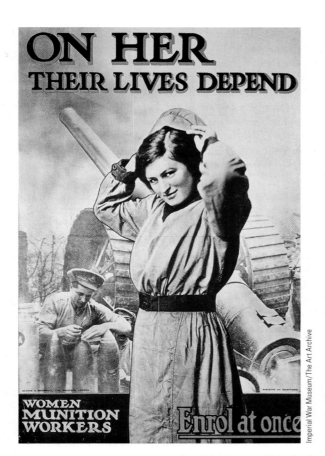

ON HER
THEIR LIVES DEPEND

WOMEN MUNITION WORKERS

Enrol at once

Imperial War Museum/The Art Archive

Women in World War I   Women played a more important role in World War I than in previous wars. As the armies drafted millions of men, employers hired women for essential war work. This poster extolls the importance of women workers in supplying munitions.

The Home Front and the War Economy

Trench-bound armies demanded ever more weapons, ammunition, and food, so civilians had to work harder, eat less, and pay higher taxes. Textiles, coal, meat, fats, and imported products such as tea and sugar were strictly rationed. Governments gradually imposed stringent controls over all aspects of their economies.

The war economy transformed civilian life. In France and Britain food rations were allocated according to need, improving nutrition among the poor. Unemployment vanished. Thousands of Africans, Indians, and Chinese were recruited for heavy labor in Europe. Employers hired women to fill jobs vacated by men off to war. Some women became streetcar drivers, mail carriers, and police officers. Others found work in the burgeoning government bureaucracies. Many joined auxiliary military services as doctors, nurses, mechanics, and ambulance drivers; after 1917, as the war took its toll of young men, the British government established women's auxiliary units for the army, navy, and air force. These positions gave thousands of women a sense of participation in the war effort and a taste of personal and financial independence.

German civilians paid an especially high price for the war, for the British naval blockade severed their overseas trade. Wheat flour disappeared, replaced first by rye, then by potatoes and turnips, then by acorns and chestnuts, and finally by sawdust. After the failure of the potato crop in 1916 came the "turnip winter," when people had to survive on 1,000 calories per day, half the normal amount that an active adult needed. Women, children, and the elderly were especially hard hit. Soldiers at the front raided enemy lines to scavenge food.

Africa in the War

The war also brought hardships to Europe's African colonies. When the war began, the British and French overran German Togo on the West African coast. The much larger German colonies of Southwest Africa and German Cameroon were conquered in 1915. In German East Africa, the Germans remained undefeated until the end of the war. The Europeans requisitioned foodstuffs, imposed heavy taxes, and forced Africans to grow export crops and sell them at low prices. As Europeans stationed in Africa joined the war, the combination of increased demands on Africans and fewer European officials led to uprisings that lasted for several years. Over a million Africans served in the various armies, and perhaps three times that number were drafted as porters to carry army equipment. Faced with a shortage of young Frenchmen, France drafted Africans into its army, where many fought side by side with Europeans.

The United States

One country grew rich during the war: the United States. For two and a half years the United States stayed technically neutral but did a roaring business supplying France and Britain. When the United States entered the war in 1917, businesses engaging in war production made spectacular profits. Civilians were exhorted to help the war effort by investing their savings in war bonds and growing food in backyard "victory gardens." Employment opportunities created by the war played a major role in the migration of African Americans from the rural south to the cities of the north.

PRIMARY SOURCE: Letter from Turkey, Summer 1915   Read an eyewitness account of the Armenian genocide, by an American missionary from Massachusetts.

The Ottoman Empire at War

On August 2, 1914, the Turks signed a secret alliance with Germany. In November they joined the fighting, hoping to gain land at Russia's expense. During the campaign in the Caucasus the Turks expelled the Armenians, whom they suspected of being pro-Russian, from their

Gallipoli and the Arab Revolt

Faisal Arab prince, leader of the Arab Revolt in World War I. The British made him king of Iraq in 1921, and he reigned under British protection until 1933.

Britain and the Jewish National Homeland

Theodore Herzl Austrian journalist and founder of the Zionist movement urging the creation of a Jewish national homeland in Palestine.

 PRIMARY SOURCE: The Balfour Declaration Learn which questions were considered—and which were ignored—as Britain prepared to support the Zionist movement.

Balfour Declaration Statement issued by Britain's Foreign Secretary Arthur Balfour in 1917 favoring the establishment of a Jewish national homeland in Palestine.

Bolsheviks Radical Marxist political party founded by Vladimir Lenin in 1903. Under Lenin's leadership, the Bolsheviks seized power in November 1917 during the Russian Revolution.

Lenin and the Bolsheviks

Vladimir Lenin Leader of the Bolshevik (later Communist) Party. He lived in exile in Switzerland until 1917, then returned to Russia to lead the Bolsheviks to victory during the Russian Revolution and the civil war that followed.

homelands in eastern Anatolia. During the forced march across the mountains in the winter, hundreds of thousands died of hunger and exposure.

The Turks also closed the Dardanelles, the strait between the Mediterranean and Black Seas (see Map 29.2). Seeing little hope of victory on the Western Front, Britain tried to open the Dardanelles by landing troops on the nearby Gallipoli Peninsula in 1915. Turkish troops pushed the invaders back into the sea. The British then promised the emir (prince) of Mecca, Hussein ibn Ali, a kingdom of his own if he would lead an Arab revolt against the Turks. In 1916 Hussein rose up and was proclaimed king of Hejaz (hee-JAHZ) (western Arabia). His son **Faisal** (FIE-sahl) then led an Arab army in support of the British advance from Egypt into Palestine and Syria. The Arab Revolt of 1916 did not affect the struggle in Europe, but it did contribute to the defeat of the Ottoman Empire.

The British made promises to Jews as well as Arabs. For centuries, Jewish minorities in eastern and central Europe had developed a thriving culture despite frequent persecutions. By the early twentieth century a nationalist movement called Zionism, led by **Theodore Herzl**, arose among those who wanted to return to their ancestral homeland in Palestine. The concept of a Jewish homeland appealed to many Europeans as a humanitarian solution to the problem of anti-Semitism.

By 1917 Chaim Weizmann (hi-um VITES-mun), leader of the British Zionists, had persuaded several British politicians that a Jewish homeland in Palestine should be carved out of the Ottoman Empire and placed under British protection, thereby strengthening the Allied cause. In November, as British armies were advancing on Jerusalem, Foreign Secretary Sir Arthur Balfour wrote:

> *His Majesty's Government view with favor the establishment in Palestine of a national home for the Jewish people and will use their best endeavours to facilitate the achievement of that object, it being clearly understood that nothing shall be done which may prejudice the civil and religious rights of existing non-Jewish communities in Palestine.*[2]

The British did not foresee that this statement, known as the **Balfour Declaration**, would lead to conflicts between Palestinians and Jewish settlers.

Double Revolution in Russia

At the beginning of the war Russia had the largest army in the world, but its generals were incompetent, supplies were lacking, and soldiers were poorly trained and equipped. In August 1914 two Russian armies invaded eastern Germany but were thrown back.

In 1916, after a string of defeats, the Russian army ran out of ammunition and other essential supplies. Soldiers were ordered into battle unarmed and told to pick up the rifles of fallen comrades. Railroads broke down for lack of fuel and parts, and crops rotted in the fields. Civilians faced shortages and widespread hunger. In the cities food and fuel became scarce. During the bitterly cold winter of 1916–1917 factory workers and housewives had to line up in front of grocery stores before dawn to get food. The court of Tsar Nicholas II, however, remained as extravagant and corrupt as ever.

In early March 1917 (February by the old Russian calendar), food ran out in Petrograd (St. Petersburg), the capital. Women staged mass demonstrations, and soldiers mutinied and joined striking workers to form soviets (councils) to take over factories and barracks. A few days later the tsar abdicated, and leaders of the parliamentary parties, led by Alexander Kerensky, formed a Provisional Government. Thus began what Russians called the "February Revolution."

Revolutionaries formerly hunted by the tsar's police came out of hiding. Most numerous were the Social Revolutionaries, who advocated the redistribution of land to the peasants. The Mensheviks advocated electoral politics and reform in the tradition of European socialists and had a large following among intellectuals and factory workers. The **Bolsheviks**, their rivals, were a small but tightly disciplined group of radicals obedient to the will of their leader, **Vladimir Lenin** (1870–1924).

Lenin, the son of a government official, became a revolutionary in his teens when his older brother was executed for plotting to kill the tsar. He spent years in exile, first in Siberia and later in Switzerland, where he devoted his full attention to organizing his followers. His goal was to create a party that would lead the revolution rather than wait for it. He explained: "The will of a class is sometimes fulfilled by a dictator. . . . Soviet socialist democracy is not in the least incompatible with individual rule and dictatorship."[3]

In early April 1917 the German government, hoping to destabilize Russia, allowed Lenin to travel from Switzerland to Russia in a sealed railway car. As soon as he arrived in Petrograd, he announced his program: immediate peace, all power to the soviets, and transfers of land to the peasants and factories to the workers. This plan proved immensely popular among soldiers and workers exhausted by the war.

The next few months witnessed a tug-of-war between the Provisional Government and the various revolutionary factions in Petrograd. When Kerensky ordered another offensive against the Germans, Russian soldiers began to desert by the hundreds of thousands, throwing away their rifles and walking back to their villages. As the Germans advanced, the government lost the little support it had.

Meanwhile, the Bolsheviks were gaining support among the workers of Petrograd and the soldiers and sailors stationed there. On November 6, 1917 (October 24 in the Russian calendar), they rose up and took over the city, calling their action the "October Revolution." Their sudden move surprised rival revolutionary groups that believed that a "socialist" revolution could happen only after many years of "bourgeois" rule. Lenin, more interested in power than in the fine points of Marxist doctrine, overthrew the Provisional Government and arrested Mensheviks, Social Revolutionaries, and other rivals.

Seizing Petrograd was only the first step, for the rest of Russia was in chaos. The Bolsheviks nationalized all private land and ordered the peasants to hand over their crops without compensation. The peasants, having seized their landlords' estates, resisted. In the cities the Bolsheviks took over the factories and drafted the workers into compulsory labor brigades. To enforce his rule Lenin created the Cheka, a secret police force with powers to arrest and execute opponents.

The Bolsheviks also sued for peace with Germany and Austria-Hungary. By the Treaty of Brest-Litovsk, signed on March 3, 1918, Russia lost territories containing a third of its population and wealth. Poland, Finland, and the Baltic states (Estonia, Latvia, and Lithuania) became independent republics. Russian colonies in Central Asia and the Caucasus broke away temporarily.

The End of the War in Western Europe, 1917–1918

Like many Americans, President **Woodrow Wilson** wanted to stay out of the European conflict. For nearly three years he kept the United States neutral and tried to persuade the belligerents to compromise. But in late 1916 German leaders decided to starve the British into submission by using submarines to sink ships carrying food supplies to Great Britain. The Germans knew that unrestricted submarine warfare was likely to bring the United States into the war, but they were willing to gamble that Britain and France would collapse before the United States could send enough troops to help them.

The submarine campaign resumed on February 1, 1917, and the German gamble failed. The British organized their merchant ships into convoys protected by destroyers, and on April 6 President Wilson asked the United States Congress to declare war on Germany.

In January 1918, President Wilson presented his **Fourteen Points**, a peace plan that called for the German evacuation of occupied lands, the settling of territorial disputes by the decisions of the local populations, and the formation of an association of nations to guarantee the independence and territorial integrity of all states. In response, General Erich von Ludendorff launched a series of surprise attacks that pushed to within 40 miles (64 kilometers)

Woodrow Wilson President of the United States (1913–1921) and the leading figure at the Paris Peace Conference of 1919. He was unable to persuade the U.S. Congress to ratify the Treaty of Versailles or join the League of Nations.

The October Revolution

Fourteen Points A peace program presented to the U.S. Congress by President Woodrow Wilson in January 1918. It called for the evacuation of German-occupied lands, the drawing of borders and the settling of territorial disputes by the self-determination of the affected populations, and the founding of an association of nations to preserve the peace and guarantee their territorial integrity. It was rejected by Germany, but it made Wilson the moral leader of the Allies in the last year of World War I.

SECTION REVIEW

- Europeans greeted the outbreak of war with joy.
- After a month-long German advance into Belgium and France, armies got bogged down in a line of trenches along the Western Front.
- Huge battles cost tens of thousands of casualties but did not bring victory.
- On the home fronts, civilians suffered shortages and women entered the work force, while the United States grew richer.
- The entry of the Ottoman Empire into the war did not tip the balance.
- Great Britain promised Jews a "national homeland" in Palestine.
- As Russia weakened, Lenin's Bolsheviks seized power in November 1917.
- In 1917 the United States entered the war on the Allied side, and Germany began to retreat.
- The war ended on November 11, 1918, with the defeat of Germany.

of Paris, but victory eluded him. Meanwhile, every month brought another 250,000 American troops to the front. In August the Allies counterattacked, and the Germans began a retreat that could not be halted.

In late October Ludendorff resigned, and sailors in the German fleet mutinied. Two weeks later, a new German government signed an armistice. At 11 A.M. on November 11, the guns on the Western Front went silent.

PEACE AND DISLOCATION IN EUROPE, 1919–1929

The Great War lasted four years. Millions of people had died or been disabled; political tensions and resentments lingered; and national economies remained depressed until the mid-1920s. In the late 1920s peace and prosperity finally seemed assured, but this hope proved to be illusory.

The Impact of the War

Between 8 million and 10 million people died in the war, almost all of them young men. Among the dead were about 2 million Germans, 1.7 million Russians, and 1.7 million Frenchmen. Austria-Hungary lost 1.5 million, the British Empire a million, Italy 460,000, and the United States 115,000. Perhaps twice that many returned home wounded, gassed, or shell-shocked, many of them injured for life.

Refugees and Immigrants

War and revolution forced almost 2 million Russians, 750,000 Germans, and 400,000 Hungarians to flee their homes. War also led to the expulsion of hundreds of thousands of Greeks from Anatolia and Turks from Greece. Many refugees found shelter in France, which welcomed 1.5 million people to bolster its declining population. About 800,000 immigrants reached the United States before immigration laws passed in 1921 and 1924 closed the door to eastern and southern Europeans. Canada, Australia, and New Zealand adopted similar restrictions on immigration. The Latin American republics welcomed European refugees, but their poverty discouraged potential immigrants.

The Flu Epidemic

One unexpected byproduct of the war was the great influenza epidemic of 1918–1919, which started among soldiers heading for the Western Front. This virulent strain infected almost everyone on earth and killed one person in every forty. Half a million Americans perished in the epidemic—five times as many as died in the war. Worldwide, some 20 million people died.

Environmental Damage

The war also caused serious damage to the environment. No place was ever so completely devastated as the scar across France and Belgium known as the Western Front. The fighting ravaged forests and demolished towns. The earth was gouged by trenches, pitted with craters, and littered with ammunition, broken weapons, chunks of concrete, and the bones of countless soldiers. After the war, it took a decade to clear away the debris, rebuild the towns, and create dozens of military cemeteries with neat rows of crosses stretching for miles.

The Peace Treaties

In early 1919 delegates of the victorious powers met in Paris. The defeated powers were kept out until the treaties were ready for signing. Russia was not invited.

From the start, three men dominated the Paris Peace Conference: U.S. president Wilson, British prime minister David Lloyd George, and French premier Georges Clemenceau (zhorzh cluh-mon-SO). They ignored the Italians, who had joined the Allies in 1915. They paid even less attention to the delegates of smaller European nations. They rejected the Japanese proposal that all races be treated equally. They ignored the Pan-African Congress organized by the African American W. E. B. Du Bois to call attention to the concerns of African peoples around the world. They also ignored the ten thousand other delegates of various nationalities that did not represent sovereign states—the Arab leader Faisal, the Zionist Chaim Weizmann, and several Armenian delegations—who came to Paris to lobby for their causes. They were, in the words of Britain's Foreign Secretary Balfour, "three all-powerful, all-ignorant men, sitting there and carving up continents"[4] (see Map 29.3).

The League of Nations

Wilson, a high-minded idealist, wanted to apply the principle of self-determination to European affairs, by which he meant creating nations that reflected ethnic or linguistic divisions. He

League of Nations International organization founded in 1919 to promote world peace and cooperation but greatly weakened by the refusal of the United States to join. It proved ineffectual in stopping aggression by Italy, Japan, and Germany in the 1930s, and it was superseded by the United Nations in 1945.

The Treaty of Versailles

e **PRIMARY SOURCE: Comments of the German Delegation to the Paris Peace Conference on the Conditions of Peace, October 1919** Read Germany's response to the Treaty of Versailles, which deprived it of its colonies, 13 percent of its land, and 10 percent of its population.

Treaty of Versailles The treaty imposed on Germany by France, Great Britain, the United States, and other Allied Powers after World War I. It demanded that Germany dismantle its military and give up some lands to Poland. It was resented by many Germans.

e **PRIMARY SOURCE: An Economist Analyzes the Versailles Treaty and Finds It Lacking** Read how an American economist condemned the Allies for ignoring, in the provisions of the Versailles Treaty, "the economic rehabilitation of Europe."

New Economic Policy Policy proclaimed by Vladimir Lenin in 1923 to encourage the revival of the Soviet economy by allowing small private enterprises. Joseph Stalin ended the NEP in 1928 and replaced it with a series of Five-Year Plans.

Stalin and Trotsky

proposed a **League of Nations**, a world organization to safeguard the peace and foster international cooperation. His idealism clashed with the more hardheaded and self-serving nationalism of the Europeans. Lloyd George insisted that Germany pay a heavy indemnity. Clemenceau wanted Germany to return Alsace and Lorraine, provinces of France before 1871.

The result was a series of compromises that satisfied no one. The European powers formed a League of Nations, but the United States Congress refused to let the United States join. France recovered Alsace and Lorraine but had to content itself with vague promises of British and American protection if Germany ever rebuilt its army. Britain acquired new territories in Africa and the Middle East but was greatly weakened by human losses and the disruption of its trade.

On June 28, 1919, the German delegates reluctantly signed the **Treaty of Versailles** (vuhr-SIGH). Germany was forbidden to have an air force and was permitted only a token army and navy. It also gave up large parts of its eastern territory to a newly reconstituted Poland. The Allies made Germany promise to pay reparations to compensate the victors for their losses, but they did not set a figure or a period of time for payment. A "guilt clause," which was to rankle for years to come, obliged the Germans to accept "responsibility for causing all the loss and damage" of the war. The treaty left Germany humiliated but largely intact. Establishing a peace neither of punishment nor of reconciliation, it was one of the great failures in history.

Meanwhile, the Austro-Hungarian Empire fell apart. New countries appeared in the lands lost by Russia, Germany, and Austria-Hungary: Poland, resurrected after over a century; Czechoslovakia, created from the northern third of Austria-Hungary; and Yugoslavia, combining Serbia and the former south Slav provinces of Austria-Hungary. The new boundaries coincided with the major linguistic groups of eastern Europe, but they all contained disaffected minorities. These small nations were safe only as long as Germany and Russia lay defeated and prostrate.

Russian Civil War and the New Economic Policy

In December 1918, civil war broke out in Russia. The Communists—as the Bolsheviks called themselves after March 1918—held central Russia, but all the surrounding provinces rose up against them. Counter-revolutionary armies led by former tsarist officers obtained weapons and supplies from the Allies. For three years the two sides burned farms and confiscated crops, causing a famine that claimed 3 million victims, more than had died in Russia in seven years of fighting. By 1921 the Communists had defeated most of their enemies.

Finland, the Baltic states, and Poland remained independent, but the Red Army reconquered other parts of the tsar's empire one by one. In 1922, Ukraine merged with Russia to create the Union of Soviet Socialist Republics (USSR), or Soviet Union. In 1920–1921 the Red Army reconquered the Caucasus and replaced the indigenous leaders with Russians. In 1922 the new Soviet republics of Georgia, Armenia, and Azerbaijan joined the USSR. In this way the Bolsheviks retained control over lands and peoples that had been part of the tsar's empire.

Years of warfare, revolution, and mismanagement had ruined the Russian economy. Factories and railroads had shut down for lack of fuel, raw materials, and parts. Farmland had been devastated and livestock killed, causing hunger in the cities. Finding himself master of a country in ruin, Lenin announced the **New Economic Policy** (NEP) in 1923. It allowed peasants to own land and sell their crops, private merchants to trade, and private workshops to produce goods and sell them on the free market. Only the biggest businesses, such as banks, railroads, and factories, remained under government ownership.

The relaxation of controls had an immediate effect. Production began to climb, and food and other goods became available. But the NEP reflected no change in the ultimate goals of the Communist Party. It merely provided breathing space, what Lenin called "two steps back to advance one step forward." The Communists had every intention of creating a modern industrial economy without private property. This meant investing in heavy industry and electrification and moving farmers to the cities to work in the new industries. It also meant providing food for the urban workers without spending scarce resources to purchase it from the peasants. In other words, it meant making the peasants, the great majority of the Soviet people, pay for the industrialization of Russia. This policy turned them into bitter enemies of the Communists.

When Lenin died in January 1924, his associates jockeyed for power. The leading contenders were Leon Trotsky, commander of the Red Army, and Joseph Stalin, general secretary of the Communist Party. Trotsky had the support of many "Old Bolsheviks" who had joined the party before the revolution. Having spent years in exile, he saw the revolution as a spark that would

MAP 29.3 **Territorial Changes in Europe After World War I** Although the heaviest fighting took place in western Europe, the territorial changes there were relatively minor. In eastern Europe, in contrast, the changes were enormous. The disintegration of the Austro-Hungary Empire and the defeat of Russia allowed a belt of new countries to arise, stretching from Finland in the north to Yugoslavia in the south.

e Interactive Map

ignite a world revolution of the working class. Stalin, the only leading Communist who had never lived abroad, insisted that socialism could survive "in one country."

Stalin filled the party bureaucracy with individuals loyal to himself. In 1926–1927 he had Trotsky expelled for "deviation from the party line," and in January 1929 he forced Trotsky to flee the country. Then, as absolute master of the party, he prepared to industrialize the Soviet Union at breakneck speed.

An Ephemeral Peace

After the enormous sacrifices made during the war, the survivors developed hugely unrealistic expectations and were soon disillusioned. Conservatives in Britain and France longed for a return to the stability of the prewar era—the hierarchy of social classes, prosperous world trade, and European dominance over the rest of the world. All over the rest of the world, people's hopes had been raised by the rhetoric of the war, then dashed by its outcome. In Europe, Germans felt

Lenin the Orator   The leader of the Bolshevik revolutionaries was a spellbinding orator. Here Lenin is addressing Red Army soldiers in Sverdlov Square, Moscow, in 1920.

cheated out of a victory that had seemed within their grasp, and Italians were disappointed that their sacrifices had not been rewarded with large territorial gains. Arabs and Indians longed for independence; the Chinese looked for social justice and a lessening of foreign intrusion; and the Japanese hoped to expand their influence in China. In Russia, the Communists were eager to consolidate their power and export their revolution to the rest of the world.

German Hyperinflation

In 1923 Germany suspended reparations payments. In retaliation for the French occupation of the Ruhr, the German government began printing money recklessly, causing the most severe inflation the world had ever seen. Soon German money was worth so little that it took a wheel-barrow full of it to buy a loaf of bread. As Germany teetered on the brink of civil war, radical nationalists tried to overthrow the government. Finally, the German government issued a new currency and promised to resume reparations payments, and the French agreed to withdraw their troops from the Ruhr.

Beginning in 1924 the world enjoyed a few years of calm and prosperity. After the end of the German crisis of 1923, the western European nations became less confrontational, and Germany joined the League of Nations. The vexed issue of reparations also seemed to vanish, as Germany borrowed money from New York banks to make its payments to France and Britain,

SECTION REVIEW

- The war caused millions of deaths and injuries and millions of refugees.

- France, Britain, and the United States dominated the Paris Peace Conference, refusing to listen to other voices.

- The United States refused to join the League of Nations, thereby weakening it.

- The Treaty of Versailles humiliated Germany but did not weaken it, thus becoming one of the big mistakes in history.

- When Austria-Hungary and Russia fell apart, several smaller nations arose in Europe, creating another source of potential conflict.

- After the Bolshevik victory in the Civil War, the Russian economy was in ruins, and Stalin took power.

- After the German hyperinflation of 1923 was resolved, the world economy began to prosper in 1924.

Mid-Twenties Prosperity

which used the money to repay their wartime loans from the United States. This triangular flow of money, based on credit, stimulated the rapid recovery of the European economies. France began rebuilding its war-torn northern zone; Germany recovered from its hyperinflation; and a boom began in the United States that was to last for five years.

While their economies flourished, governments grew more cautious and businesslike. Even the Communists, after Lenin's death, seemed to give up their attempts to spread revolution abroad. Yet neither Germany nor the Soviet Union accepted its borders with the small nations that had arisen between them. In 1922 they signed a secret pact allowing the German army to conduct maneuvers in Russia (in violation of the Versailles treaty) in exchange for German help in building up Russian industry and military potential.

The League of Nations proved adept at resolving numerous technical issues pertaining to health, labor relations, and postal and telegraph communications. Without U.S. participation, however, sanctions against states that violated League rules carried little weight.

CHINA AND JAPAN: CONTRASTING DESTINIES

China and Japan were both subject to Western pressures, but their modern histories have been completely opposite. China clung much longer than Japan to a traditional social structure and economy, then collapsed into chaos and revolution. Japan experienced reform from above (see Chapter 27), acquiring industry and a powerful military, which it used to take advantage of China's weakness. Their different reactions to the pressures of the West put these two great nations on a collision course.

The Bund in Shanghai   On the Bund, the most important street in Shanghai, banks, corporate headquarters, and luxury hotels faced the waterfront where ships from around the world docked. Although Shanghai was China's industrial and commercial center, many of its workers loaded and unloaded ships by hand or pulled wealthy customers in rickshaws.

Bettmann/Corbis

Social and Economic Change

China's population—about 400 million in 1900—was the largest of any country in the world and growing fast. In 1900 peasant plots averaged between 1 and 4 acres (less than 2 hectares) apiece, half as large as they had been two generations earlier. Farming methods had not changed in centuries, and landlords and tax collectors took more than half of the harvest. Most Chinese worked incessantly, survived on a diet of grain and vegetables, and spent their lives in fear of floods, bandits, and tax collectors.

Above the peasantry, Chinese society was divided into many groups and strata. Landowners lived off the rents of their tenants. Officials, chosen through an elaborate examination system, enriched themselves from taxes and the government's monopolies on salt, iron, and other products. Shanghai, China's financial and commercial center, was famous for its wealthy foreigners and its opium addicts, prostitutes, and gangsters.

Although foreign trade represented only a small part of China's economy, contact with the outside world had a tremendous impact on Chinese politics. Young men living in the treaty ports saw no chance for advancement in the old system of examinations and official positions. Some learned foreign ideas in Christian mission schools or abroad. The contrast between the squalor in which most urban residents lived and the luxury of the foreigners' enclaves in the treaty ports sharpened the resentment of educated Chinese.

Japan had few natural resources and very little arable land on which to grow food for its rising population. Typhoons regularly hit its southern regions, and earthquakes periodically shook the country, which lies on the great ring of tectonic fault lines that surround the Pacific Ocean. The Kanto earthquake of 1923 destroyed all of Yokohama and half of Tokyo and killed some 200,000 people.

Japan's population reached 60 million in 1925 and was increasing by a million a year. The crash program of industrialization begun in 1868 by the Meiji oligarchs (see Chapter 27) accelerated during the First World War, when Japan's economy grew four times as fast as western Europe's and eight times faster than China's.

The "New Rich"

Economic growth aggravated social tensions. The *narikin* ("new rich") affected Western ways and lifestyles that clashed with the austerity of earlier times. In the big cities *mobos* (modern boys) and *mogas* (modern girls) shocked traditionalists with their foreign ways: dancing together, wearing short skirts and tight pants, and behaving like Americans. Students who flirted with dangerous thoughts were called "Marx boys."

The main beneficiaries of prosperity were the *zaibatsu* (zie-BOT-soo), or conglomerates, four of which—Mitsubishi, Sumitomo, Yasuda, and Mitsui—controlled most of Japan's industry and commerce. Farmers, who constituted half of the population, remained poor; in desperation some sold their daughters to textile mills or into domestic service. Labor unions were weak and repressed by the police.

Japanese prosperity depended on foreign trade. The country exported silk and light manufactures and imported almost all its fuel, raw materials, and machine tools, and even some of its food. Though less at the mercy of the weather than China, Japan was much more vulnerable to swings in the world economy.

e PRIMARY SOURCE: Two Proclamations of the Boxer Rebellion The secret society known as "The Righteous and Harmonious Fists" announces its intention to kill the "foreign devils" plaguing China.

Sun Yat-sen Chinese nationalist revolutionary, founder and leader of the Guomindang until his death. He attempted to create a liberal democratic political movement in China but was thwarted by military leaders.

Sun Yat-sen and Yuan Shikai

Revolution and War, 1900–1918

In 1900 China's Empress Dowager Cixi (TSUH-shee), who had seized power in a palace coup two years earlier, encouraged a secret society, the Righteous Fists, or Boxers, to rise up and expel all the foreigners from China. When the Boxers threatened the foreign legation in Beijing, an international force from the Western powers and Japan captured the city and forced China to pay a huge indemnity. Shocked by these events, many Chinese students became convinced that China needed a revolution to get rid of the Qing dynasty and modernize their country.

When Cixi died in 1908, the Revolutionary Alliance led by **Sun Yat-sen** (soon yot-SEN) (1867–1925) prepared to take over. Sun had spent much of his life in Japan, England, and the United States, plotting the overthrow of the Qing dynasty. His ideas were a mixture of nationalism, socialism, and Confucian philosophy. His patriotism, his powerful ambition, and his tenacious spirit attracted a large following.

Yuan Shikai Chinese general and first president of the Chinese Republic (1912–1916). He stood in the way of the democratic movement led by Sun Yat-sen.

Guomindang Nationalist political party founded on democratic principles by Sun Yat-sen in 1912. After 1925, the party was headed by Chiang Kai-shek, who turned it into an increasingly authoritarian movement.

e PRIMARY SOURCE: The Three People's Principles and the Future of the Chinese People Decrying the gulf between rich and poor in Europe and America, Sun Yat-sen calls for a revolution in China that will ensure prosperity and social justice.

Chiang Kai-shek Chinese military and political leader. Succeeded Sun Yat-sen as head of the Guomindang in 1925; headed the Chinese government from 1928 to 1949; fought against the Chinese Communists and Japanese invaders. After 1949 he headed the Chinese Nationalist government in Taiwan.

Chiang Kai-shek

The military thwarted Sun's plans. After China's defeat in the war with Japan in 1895, the government had agreed to equip the army with modern rifles and machine guns. This, combined with the fact that local armies were beholden to warlords rather than to the central government, created a threatening situation for the Qing. When a regional army mutinied in October 1911, **Yuan Shikai** (you-AHN she-KIE), the most powerful of the regional generals, refused to defend the Qing. A revolutionary assembly at Nanjing elected Sun Yat-sen president of China in December 1911, but he had no military forces at his command. To avoid a clash with the army, he resigned after a few weeks, and a new national assembly elected Yuan president of the new Chinese republic.

Yuan was an able military leader, but he had no political program. When Sun reorganized his followers into a political party called **Guomindang** (gwo-min-dong) (National People's Party), Yuan quashed every attempt at creating a Western-style government and harassed Sun's followers. Victory in the first round of the struggle to create a new China went to the military.

Meanwhile, the Japanese were quick to join the Allied side in World War I, since they saw the war as an opportunity to advance their interests while the Europeans were occupied elsewhere. They quickly conquered the German colonies in the northern Pacific and on the coast of China, then turned their attention to the rest of China. In 1915 Japan presented China with Twenty-One Demands, which would have turned it into a virtual protectorate. Britain and the United States persuaded Japan to soften the demands but could not prevent it from keeping the German coastal enclaves and extracting railroad and mining concessions at China's expense. In protest, anti-Japanese riots and boycotts broke out throughout China. Thus began a bitter struggle between the two countries that was to last for thirty years.

Chinese Warlords and the Guomindang, 1919–1929

At the Paris Peace Conference, the great powers accepted Japan's seizure of the German enclaves in China. To many Chinese, this decision was a cruel insult. On May 4, 1919, students demonstrated in front of the Forbidden City of Beijing. Despite a government ban, the May Fourth Movement spread to other parts of China. A new generation was growing up to challenge the old officials, the regional generals, and the foreigners.

Sun Yat-sen tried to make a comeback in Guangzhou (Canton) in the early 1920s. Though not a Communist, he was impressed with the efficiency of Lenin's revolutionary tactics and let a Soviet adviser reorganize the Guomindang along Leninist lines. He also welcomed members of the newly created Chinese Communist Party into the Guomindang.

When Sun died in 1925, the leadership of his party passed to Jiang Jieshi, known in the West as **Chiang Kai-shek** (chang kie-shek) (1887–1975). An officer and director of the military academy, Chiang trained several hundred young officers who remained loyal to him thereafter. In 1927 he determined to defeat the regional warlords. As his army moved north from its base in Canton, he briefly formed an alliance with the Communists. Once his troops occupied Shanghai, however, he crushed the labor unions and decimated the Communists, whom he considered a threat. He then defeated or co-opted most of the other warlords and established a dictatorship.

Chiang's government issued ambitious plans to build railroads, develop agriculture and industry, and modernize China from the top down. However, his followers were neither competent administrators nor ruthless modernizers. Instead, his government attracted thousands of opportunists whose goals were to "become officials and get rich" by taxing and plundering businesses. In the countryside tax collectors and landowners squeezed the peasants ever harder, even in times of natural disasters. What little money reached the government's coffers went to the military. Thus for twenty years after the fall of the Qing, China remained mired in poverty, subject to corrupt officials and the whims of nature.

SECTION REVIEW

- Japan prospered during the war and quickly modernized; it also began preying on China.
- When the Qing dynasty ended in 1911, the regional general Yuan Shikai took over China and repressed Sun Yat-sen's party, the Guomindang.
- After Sun Yat-sen's death, Chiang Kai-shek established a corrupt military dictatorship.

THE NEW MIDDLE EAST

After the war, the Arab peoples expected to have a say in the outcome of the Great War. But the victorious French and British planned to treat the Middle East like a territory open to colonial rule. The result was a legacy of instability that has persisted to this day.

The Mandate System

mandate system Allocation of former German colonies and Ottoman possessions to the victorious powers after World War I, to be administered under League of Nations supervision.

At the Paris Peace Conference, France, Britain, Italy, and Japan proposed to divide the former German colonies and the territories of the Ottoman Empire among themselves, but their ambitions clashed with President Wilson's ideal of national self-determination. Eventually, the victors arrived at a compromise solution called the **mandate system**: colonial rulers would administer the territories but would be accountable to the League of Nations for "the material and moral well-being and the social progress of the inhabitants."

Class C Mandates—those with the smallest populations—were treated as colonies by their conquerors. South Africa replaced Germany in Southwest Africa (now Namibia); Britain, Australia, New Zealand, and Japan took over the German islands in the Pacific. Class B Mandates, larger than Class C but still underdeveloped, were to be ruled for the benefit of their inhabitants under League of Nations supervision. Most of Germany's African colonies fell into this category.

The Arab-speaking territories of the old Ottoman Empire were Class A Mandates. The League of Nations declared that they had "reached a state of development where their existence as independent nations can be provisionally recognized subject to the rendering of administrative advice and assistance by a Mandatory, until such time as they are able to stand alone." While Arabs interpreted this ambiguous wording as a promise of independence, Britain and France sent troops into the region "for the benefit of its inhabitants." Palestine (now Israel), Transjordan (now Jordan), and Iraq (formerly Mesopotamia) became British mandates; France claimed Syria and Lebanon (see Map 29.4). (See Diversity and Dominance: The Middle East After World War I.)

The Rise of Modern Turkey

At the end of the war, as the Ottoman Empire teetered on the brink of collapse, France, Britain, and Italy saw an opportunity to expand their empires, and Greece eyed those parts of Anatolia inhabited by Greeks. In 1919 French, British, Italian, and Greek forces occupied Constantinople and parts of Anatolia. By the Treaty of Sèvres (1920) the Allies made the sultan give up most of his lands.

In 1919 Mustafa Kemal had formed a nationalist government in central Anatolia with the backing of fellow army officers. In 1922, after a short but fierce war against invading Greeks, his armies reconquered Anatolia and the area around Constantinople. The victorious Turks forced hundreds of thousands of Greeks from their ancestral homes in Anatolia. In response the Greek government expelled all Muslims from Greece.

Mustafa Kemal Atatürk After World War I, Mustafa Kemal was determined to modernize Turkey on the Western model. Here he is shown wearing a European-style suit and teaching the Latin alphabet.

Stock Montage

DIVERSITY + DOMINANCE

The Middle East After World War I

During the First World War, Entente forces invaded and occupied Palestine, Mesopotamia, and Syria. This raised the question of what to do with these territories after the war. Would they be returned to the Ottoman Empire? Would they simply be added to the colonial empires of Britain and France? Or would they become independent Arab states?

The following documents illustrate the diversity of opinions among various groups planning the postwar settlement: Great Britain, concerned with defeating Germany and maintaining its empire; the United States, basing its policies on lofty principles; and Arab delegates from the Middle East, seeking self-determination.

In the early twentieth century, in response to the rise of anti-Semitism in Europe, a movement called Zionism had arisen among European Jews. Zionists, led by Theodore Herzl, hoped for a return to Israel, the ancestral homeland of the Jewish people. For two thousand years this land had been a province of various empires—the Roman, Byzantine, Arab, and Ottoman—and was inhabited by Arabic-speaking people, most of whom practiced the Islamic religion.

During the war the British government was receptive to the idea of establishing a Jewish homeland in Palestine. It was motivated by the need to win the war, but it also considered the more distant future. The result was a policy statement, sent by Foreign Secretary Arthur James Balfour to Baron Rothschild, a prominent supporter of the Zionist movement in England. This statement, called the "Balfour Declaration," has haunted the Middle East ever since.

The Balfour Declaration of 1917

Foreign Office
November 2nd, 1917

Dear Lord Rothschild:

I have much pleasure in conveying to you, on behalf of His Majesty's Government, the following declaration of sympathy with Jewish Zionist aspirations which have been submitted to, and approved by, the Cabinet:

His Majesty's Government view with favor the establishment in Palestine of a national home for the Jewish people, and will use their best endeavors to facilitate the achievement of this object, it being clearly understood that nothing shall be done which may prejudice the civil and religious rights of existing non-Jewish communities in Palestine, or the rights and political status enjoyed by Jews in any other country.

I should be grateful if you would bring this declaration to the knowledge of the Zionist Federation.

Yours,
Arthur James Balfour

On January 8, 1918, the American president Woodrow Wilson issued his famous Fourteen Points proposal to end the war. Much of his speech was devoted to European affairs or to international relations in general, but two of his fourteen points referred to the Arab world.

Woodrow Wilson's Fourteen Points

What we demand in this war . . . is that the world be made fit and safe to live in; and particularly that it be made safe for every peace-loving nation which, like our own, wishes to live its own life, determine its own institutions, be assured of justice and fair dealing by the other peoples of the world as against force and selfish aggression. All the peoples of the world are in effect partners in this interest, and for our own part we see very clearly that unless justice be done to others it will not be done to us. The programme of the world's peace, therefore, is our programme; and that programme, the only possible programme, as we see it, is this:

XII. The Turkish portions of the present Ottoman Empire should be assured a secure sovereignty, but the other nationalities which are now under Turkish rule should be assured an undoubted security of life and an

Atatürk The founder of modern Turkey. He distinguished himself in the defense of Gallipoli in World War I and expelled a Greek expeditionary army from Anatolia in 1921–1922. He replaced the Ottoman Empire with the Turkish Republic in 1923. As president, he pushed through a radical Westernization and reform of Turkish society.

As a war hero and proclaimed savior of his country, Kemal was able to impose wrenching changes on his people. An outspoken modernizer, he was eager to bring Turkey closer to Europe as quickly as possible. He abolished the sultanate, declared Turkey a secular republic, and introduced European laws. In a radical break with Islamic tradition, he suppressed Muslim courts, schools, and religious orders and replaced the Arabic alphabet with the Latin alphabet.

Kemal attempted to westernize the traditional Turkish family. Women received civil equality, including the right to vote and to be elected to the national assembly. Kemal forbade polygamy and instituted civil marriage and divorce. He even changed people's clothing, strongly discouraging women from veiling their faces, and replaced the fez, until then the traditional Turkish men's hat, with the European brimmed hat. He ordered everyone to take a family name, choosing the name **Atatürk** ("father of the Turks") for himself. His reforms spread quickly in the cities; but in rural areas, where Islamic traditions remained strong, people resisted them for a long time.

absolutely unmolested opportunity of autonomous development. . . .

When the war ended, the victorious Allies assembled in Paris to determine, among other things, the fate of the former Arab provinces of the Ottoman Empire. Arab leaders had reason to doubt the intentions of the great powers, especially Britain and France. When the Allies decided to create mandates in the Arab territories on the grounds that the Arab peoples were not ready for independence, Arab leaders expressed their misgivings, as in the following statement:

Memorandum of the General Syrian Congress, July 2, 1919

We the undersigned members of the General Syrian Congress, meeting in Damascus on Wednesday, July 2nd, 1919, made up of representatives from the three Zones, viz., The Southern, Eastern, and Western, provided with credentials and authorizations by the inhabitants of our various districts, Moslems, Christians, and Jews, have agreed upon the following statement of the desires of the people of the country who have elected us. . . .

1. We ask absolutely complete political independence for Syria. . . .

3. Considering the fact that the Arabs inhabiting the Syrian area are not naturally less gifted than other more advanced races and that they are by no means less developed than the Bulgarians, Serbians, Greeks, and Roumanians at the beginning of their independence, we protest against Article 22 of the Covenant of the League of Nations, placing us among the nations in their middle stage of development which stand in need of a mandatory power.

4. . . . . relying on the declarations of President Wilson that his object in waging war was to put an end to the ambition of conquest and colonization, . . . and believing that the American Nation is furthest from any thought of colonization and has no political ambition in our country, we will seek the technical and economic assistance from the United States of America, provided that such assistance does not exceed 20 years.

5. In the event of America not finding herself in a position to accept our desire for assistance, we will seek this assistance from Great Britain, also provided that such does not prejudice our complete independence and unity of our country and that the duration of such assistance does not exceed that mentioned in the previous article.

6. We do not acknowledge any right claimed by the French Government in any part whatever of our Syrian country and refuse that she should assist us or have a hand in our country under any circumstances and in any place.

7. We opposed the pretensions of the Zionists to create a Jewish commonwealth in the southern part of Syria, known as Palestine, and oppose Zionist migration to any part of our country; for we do not acknowledge their title but consider them a grave peril to our people from the national, economical, and political points of view. Our Jewish compatriots shall enjoy our common rights and assume our common responsibilities.

QUESTIONS FOR ANALYSIS

1. Was there a contradiction between Balfour's proposal to establish "a national home for the Jewish people" and the promise "that nothing shall be done which may prejudice the civil and religious rights of existing non-Jewish communities in Palestine"? If so, why did he make two contradictory promises?

2. How would Woodrow Wilson's statements about "an absolutely unmolested opportunity of autonomous development" apply to Palestine?

3. Why did the delegates to the Syrian General Congress object to the plan to create mandates in the former Ottoman provinces? What alternatives did they offer?

4. Why did the delegates object to the creation of a Jewish commonwealth?

Source: The Balfour Declaration, *The Times* (London), November 9, 1917. Memorandum of the General Syrian Congress, *Foreign Relations of the United States: Paris Peace Conference,* vol. 12 (Washington, DC: Government Printing Office, 1919), 780–781.

Arab Lands and the Question of Palestine

Among the Arab people, the thinly disguised colonialism of the mandate system set off protests and rebellions. Arabs viewed the European presence not as liberation from Ottoman oppression, but as foreign occupation.

After World War I Middle Eastern society underwent dramatic changes. Trucks replaced camel caravans. Landless peasants migrated to the swelling cities. The population of the region is estimated to have increased by 50 percent between 1914 and 1939, while that of large cities such as Constantinople, Baghdad, and Cairo doubled.

The urban and mercantile middle class, encouraged by the transformation of Turkey, adopted Western ideas, customs, and styles of housing and clothing. Some families sent their sons to European secular or mission schools, then to Western colleges in Cairo and Beirut or universities abroad, to prepare for jobs in government and business. A few women became

MAP 29.4 **Territorial Changes in the Middle East After World War I** The defeat and dismemberment of the Ottoman Empire at the end of World War I resulted in an entirely new political map of the region. The Turkish Republic inherited Anatolia and a small piece of the Balkans, while the Ottoman Empire's Arab provinces were divided between France and Great Britain. Only Iran and Egypt did not change.

Map legend:
- Ottoman Empire in 1914
- British protectorate in 1914
- Area controlled under mandates from the League of Nations, 1920
- British Mandate
- French Mandate
- International boundaries, 1923

© Cengage Learning

e Interactive Map

schoolteachers or nurses. There were great variations, ranging from Lebanon, with its strong French influence, to Arabia and Iran, which retained their cultural traditions.

The region in closest contact with Europe was the Maghrib—Algeria, Tunisia, and Morocco—which the French army considered its private domain. Alongside the old native quarters, the French built modern neighborhoods inhabited mainly by Europeans. France had occu-

Hulton Archive/Getty Images

The Jewish Settlement of Palestine   Thousands of Jews fleeing persecution and discrimination in Europe settled on the land and founded *kibbutzim*, or collective farms. In this picture taken in 1912, an eighty-four-year-old immigrant from Russia learns to plow the land.

pied Algeria since 1830 and had encouraged European immigration. The settlers owned the best lands and monopolized government jobs and businesses, while Arabs and Berbers remained poor and suffered intense discrimination.

Britain in the Middle East

The British attempted to control the Middle East with a mixture of bribery and intimidation. They made Faisal, leader of the Arab Revolt, king of Iraq and used bombers to quell rural insurrections. In 1931 they reached an agreement with King Faisal's government: official independence for Iraq in exchange for the right to keep two air bases, a military alliance, and an assured flow of petroleum. France, meanwhile, sent thousands of troops to Syria and Lebanon to crush nationalist uprisings.

In Egypt, as in Iraq, the British substituted a phony independence for official colonialism. They declared Egypt independent in 1922 but reserved the right to station troops along the Suez Canal to secure their link with India in the event of war. Most galling to the Wafd (Nationalist) Party was the British attempt to remove Egyptian troops from Sudan, a land many Egyptians considered a colony of Egypt. Britain was successful in keeping Egypt in limbo—neither independent nor a colony—thanks to an alliance with King Fouad and conservative Egyptian politicians who feared both secular and religious radicalism.

Before the war, a Jewish minority lived in Palestine, as in other Arab countries. Small numbers of Jews had been immigrating to Palestine since the nineteenth century, but as soon as Palestine became a British mandate in 1920, many more came from Europe, encouraged by the Balfour Declaration of 1917. Most settled in the cities, but

Jewish Migration to Palestine

some established *kibbutzim,* or communal farms. Their goals were to become self-sufficient and to reestablish their ties to the land of their ancestors. The purchases of land by Jewish agencies angered the indigenous Palestinians, especially tenant farmers who had been evicted to make room for settlers. In 1920–1921 riots erupted between Jews and Arabs. When far more Jewish immigrants arrived than they had anticipated, the British tried to limit immigration, thereby alienating the Jews without mollifying the Arabs. Increasingly, Jews arrived without papers, smuggled in by militant Zionist organizations. In the 1930s the country was torn by strikes and guerrilla warfare that the British could not control. In the process, Britain earned the hatred of both sides and of many other people in the Arab world.

SOCIETY, CULTURE, AND TECHNOLOGY IN THE INDUSTRIALIZED WORLD

With the signing of the peace treaties, the countries that had fought for four years turned their efforts toward building a new future. Advances in science offered astonishing new insights into the mysteries of nature and the universe. New technologies, many of them pioneered in the United States, promised to change the daily lives of millions of people.

Class and Gender

The war had left a deep imprint on European society and culture. After the war, class distinctions began to fade. Many European aristocrats had died on the battlefields, and with them went their class's long domination of the army, the diplomatic corps, and other elite sectors of society. The United States and Canada had never had as rigidly defined a class structure as European societies or as elaborate a set of traditions and manners. On both sides of the Atlantic, engineers, businessmen, lawyers, and other professionals rose to prominence, increasing the relative importance of the middle class.

The activities of governments had expanded during the war and continued to grow, creating a need for thousands more bureaucrats. Governments provided housing, highways, schools, public health facilities, broadcasting, and other services. Department stores, banks, insurance companies, and other businesses also increased the white-collar work force. The working class did not expand, however. The introduction of new machines and new ways of organizing work, such as the automobile assembly line that Henry Ford devised, increased workers' productivity so that greater outputs could be achieved without a larger labor force.

Women's Lives

Women's lives changed more rapidly in the 1920s than ever before. Although the end of the war marked a retreat from wartime job opportunities, some women remained in the work force. The young and wealthy enjoyed more personal freedoms than their mothers had before the war; they drove cars, played sports, traveled alone, and smoked in public. For others, the upheavals of war brought more suffering than liberation. Millions of women had lost their fathers, brothers, sons, husbands, and fiancés in the war or in the great influenza epidemic. After the war many single women led lives of loneliness and destitution.

In Europe and North America advocates of women's rights had been demanding the vote for women since the 1890s. New Zealand was the only nation to grant women the vote before the twentieth century. Women in Norway were the first to obtain it in Europe, in 1915. Russian women followed in 1917, and Canadians and Germans in 1918. Britain gave women over age thirty the vote in 1918 and later extended it to younger women. The Nineteenth Amendment to the U.S. Constitution granted suffrage to American women in 1920. Women in Turkey began voting in 1934. Most other countries did not allow women to vote until after 1945. Everywhere, their influence on politics was less radical than feminists had hoped and conservatives had feared. Even when it did not alter politics and government, however, the right to vote was a potent symbol.

Women were active in many other areas besides the suffrage movement. On both sides of the Atlantic women participated in social reform movements to prevent mistreatment of women and children and of industrial workers. In the United States such reforms were championed by Progressives such as Jane Addams (1860–1935), who founded a settlement house in a poor neighborhood and received the Nobel Peace Prize in 1931. In Europe reformers were generally aligned with Socialist or Labour Parties.

Among the most controversial, and eventually most effective, of the reformers were those who advocated contraception, such as the American **Margaret Sanger** (1883–1966). Her campaign brought her into conflict with the authorities, who equated birth control with pornography. Finally, in 1923 she was able to found a birth control clinic in New York. In France, the government prohibited contraception and abortion in 1920 in an effort to increase the birthrate and make up for the loss of so many young men in the war. Russian communists allowed abortion for ideological reasons.

Revolution in the Sciences

At the end of the nineteenth century, a revolution in physics undermined all the old certainties about nature. Physicists discovered that atoms, the building blocks of matter, are not indivisible, but consist of far smaller subatomic particles. In 1900 the German physicist **Max Planck** (1858–1947) found that atoms emit or absorb energy in discrete amounts called *quanta*. These findings seemed strange enough, but what really undermined Newtonian physics was the general theory of relativity developed by **Albert Einstein** (1879–1955). In 1916 Einstein announced that not only is matter made of insubstantial particles, but that time, space, energy, and mass are not fixed but are relative to one another. Other physicists said that light is made up of either waves or particles, depending on the observer, and that an experiment could determine either the speed or the position of a particle of light, but never both.

To nonscientists it seemed as though theories expressed in arcane mathematical formulas were replacing truth and common sense. Far from being mere speculation, however, the new physics promised to unlock the secrets of matter and provide humans with plentiful—and potentially dangerous—sources of energy.

The new social sciences were even more unsettling than the new physics, for they challenged Victorian morality, middle-class values, and notions of Western superiority. **Sigmund Freud** (1856–1939), a Viennese physician, developed the technique of psychoanalysis to probe the minds of his patients. He found not only rationality but also hidden layers of emotion and desire repressed by social restraints. "The primitive, savage and evil impulses have not vanished from any individual, but continue their existence, although in a repressed state,"[5] he warned. Meanwhile, sociologists and anthropologists had begun the empirical study of societies, both Western and non-Western. Before the war the French sociologist Emile Durkheim (1858–1917) had come to the then-shocking conclusion that "there are no religions that are false. All are true after their own fashion."[6]

If the words *primitive* and *savage* applied to Europeans as well as to other peoples, and if religions were all equally "true," then what remained of the superiority of Western civilization? Cultural relativism, as the new approach to human societies was called, was as unnerving as relativity in physics.

Although these ideas had been expressed before 1914, wartime experiences called into question the West's faith in reason and progress. Some people accepted the new ideas with enthusiasm. Others condemned and rejected them, clinging to the sense of order and faith in progress that had energized European and American culture before the war. Yet others were overcome with feelings of uncertainty and despair in a world in which human existence seemed to have lost its meaning and purpose.

New Technologies of Modernity

Some people viewed the sciences with mixed feelings, but the new technologies aroused almost universal excitement. In North America even working-class people could afford some of the new products of scientific research, inventors' ingenuity, and industrial production. Mass consumption lagged in Europe, but science and technology were just as advanced, and public fascination with the latest inventions—the cult of the modern—was just as strong.

Margaret Sanger American nurse and author; pioneer in the movement for family planning; organized conferences and established birth control clinics.

The New Physics

Max Planck German physicist who developed quantum theory and was awarded the Nobel Prize for physics in 1918.

Albert Einstein German physicist who developed the theory of relativity, which states that time, space, and mass are relative to each other and not fixed.

The New Social Sciences

Sigmund Freud Austrian psychiatrist, founder of psychoanalysis. He argued that psychological problems were caused by traumas, especially sexual experiences in early childhood, that were repressed in later life. His ideas caused considerable controversy among psychologists and in the general public. Although his views on repressed sexuality are no longer widely accepted, his psychoanalytic methods are still very influential.

Aviation

Wilbur and Orville Wright American bicycle mechanics; the first to build and fly an airplane, at Kitty Hawk, North Carolina, December 7, 1903.

Electricity and Radio

Cinema

Health

Of all the innovations of the time, none attracted public interest as much as airplanes. In 1903 two young American mechanics, **Wilbur and Orville Wright**, built the first aircraft that was heavier than air and could be maneuvered in flight. From that moment on, airplanes fascinated people. During the war the exploits of air aces relieved the tedium of news from the front. In the 1920s aviation became a sport and a form of entertainment, and flying daredevils achieved extraordinary fame. Among the most celebrated pilots were three Americans. Amelia Earhart was the first woman to fly across the Atlantic Ocean, and her example encouraged other women to fly. Richard Byrd flew over the North Pole in 1926. The most admired of all was Charles Lindbergh, the first person to fly alone across the Atlantic in 1927 (see Environment and Technology: The Birth of Civil Aviation).

Electricity, produced in industrial quantities since the 1890s (see Chapter 27), began to transform home life. The first home use of electricity was for lighting, thanks to the economical and long-lasting tungsten bulb. Then, having persuaded people to wire their homes, electrical utilities joined manufacturers in advertising electric irons, fans, washing machines, hot plates, and other appliances.

Radio had served ships and the military during the war as a means of point-to-point telecommunication. After the war, amateurs used surplus radio equipment to talk to one another. The first commercial station began broadcasting in Pittsburgh in 1920. By the end of 1923 six hundred stations were broadcasting news, sports, soap operas, and advertising to homes throughout North America. By 1930, 12 million families owned radio receivers. In Europe radio spread more slowly because governments reserved the airwaves for cultural and official programs and taxed radio owners to pay for the service.

Another medium that spread explosively in the 1920s was film. Motion pictures had begun in France in 1895 and flourished there and elsewhere in Europe, where the dominant concern was to reproduce stage plays. American filmmakers, however, aimed to entertain audiences rather than preserve outstanding theatrical performances. In competing for audiences they looked to cinematic innovation, broad humor, and exciting spectacles.

Diversity was a hallmark of the early film industry. After World War I filmmaking took root and flourished in Japan, India, Turkey, Egypt, and Hollywood, California. American and European movie studios were successful in exporting films, since silent movies presented no language problems. Then in 1927 the United States introduced the first "talking" motion picture, *The Jazz Singer,* which changed all the rules.

The number of Americans who went to see their favorite stars in thrilling adventures and heart-breaking romances rose from 40 million in 1922 to 100 million in 1930, at a time when the population of the country was about 120 million. Europeans had the technology and the art but neither the wealth nor the huge market of the United States. Hollywood studios began the diffusion of American culture that has continued to this day.

Health and hygiene were also part of the cult of modernity. Advances in medicine—some learned in the war—saved many lives. Wounds were regularly disinfected, and x-ray machines helped diagnose fractures. Cities built costly water supply and sewage treatment systems. By the 1920s indoor plumbing and flush toilets were becoming common even in working-class neighborhoods.

Interest in cleanliness altered private life. Doctors and home economists bombarded women with warnings and advice on how to banish germs. Soap and appliance manufacturers filled women's magazines with advertisements for products to help housewives keep their family's homes and clothing spotless and their meals fresh and wholesome. The decline in infant mortality and improvements in general health and life expectancy in this period owe as much to the cult of cleanliness as to advances in medicine.

Technology and the Environment

The New Architecture

Two new technologies—the skyscraper and the automobile—transformed the urban environment even more radically than the railroad had done in the nineteenth century. At the end of the nineteenth century architects had begun to design ever-higher buildings using load-bearing

ENVIRONMENT + TECHNOLOGY

The Birth of Civil Aviation

Antoine de Saint-Exupéry, best known for his children's book *The Little Prince*, was a pilot for Aéropostale, a French airline that served South America. In his book *Vol de Nuit* (Night Flight), he tells a harrowing tale of a pilot blown out to sea in a storm over Argentina:

> One of the radio operators at the Comodoro Rivadavia station in Patagonia made a sudden gesture and all those who were keeping a helpless vigil there crowded around him....
>
> "Storm?"
>
> He nodded yes; static prevented him from hearing the message. Then he scrawled some illegible signs, then words. Then the text came out:
>
> "Cut off at 12,000 feet above the storm. Proceeding due west toward interior; we were carried out to sea. No visibility below. Do not know if still flying over sea. Report if storm extends interior." . . .
>
> Buenos Aires transmitted a reply.
>
> "Storm covers all interior. How much gasoline left?"
>
> "Half an hour."
>
> These words sped from post to post back to Buenos Aires. The plane was doomed to plunge in less than half an hour into a hurricane that would smash it to earth. . . .

Today, airplanes are safer than cars, but in the 1920s, when regular airline service began, air travel was dangerous. Airplanes, many of them converted World War I bombers, were made of wood and cloth, with open cockpits for the pilot and navigator and wicker chairs for passengers. Pilots located their position by looking for towns and railroad tracks. At night and in cloudy weather, they often got lost. And yet, with these machines they conquered the skies.

Source: Antoine de Saint-Exupéry, *Vol de nuit* (Paris: Gallimard, 1939), 147–149.

An Early Passenger Plane After World War I, aviators and aircraft manufacturers turned their attention to civil aviation, using planes to distribute mail, dust crops, and carry passengers. This British-made De Havilland-34 biplane, photographed before 1924, was designed to carry up to ten passengers.

Mary Evans Picture Library/The Image Works

steel frames and passenger elevators. Major corporations in Chicago and New York competed to build the most daring buildings in the world, such as New York's fifty-five-story Woolworth Building (1912). A building boom in the late 1920s produced dozens of skyscrapers, culminating with the eighty-six-story Empire State Building in New York in 1932.

Herald Examiner Collection/Los Angeles Public Library

The Archetypal Automobile City As Los Angeles grew from a modest town into a sprawling metropolis, broad avenues, parking lots, and garages were built to accommodate automobiles. By 1929, most families owned a car and streetcar lines had closed for lack of passengers.

European cities restricted the height of buildings to protect their architectural heritage; Paris forbade buildings over 56 feet (17 meters) high. In the 1920s the Swiss architect Charles Edouard Jeanneret (1887–1965), known as Le Corbusier (luh cor-booz-YEH), outlined a new approach to architecture that featured simplicity of form, absence of surface ornamentation, easy manufacture, and inexpensive materials. Other architects—including the Finn Eero Saarinen, the Germans Ludwig Mies van der Rohe (LOOD-vig MEES fon der ROW-uh) and Walter Gropius, and the American Frank Lloyd Wright—also contributed to what became known as the International Style.

Automobiles and Suburbs

Meanwhile, outlying areas were spreading far into the countryside, thanks to the automobile. The assembly line pioneered by Henry Ford mass-produced vehicles in ever-greater volume and at falling prices. By 1929 the United States had one car for every five people, five-sixths of the world's automobiles. Automobiles were praised as the solution to urban pollution; as they replaced carts and carriages, horses disappeared from city streets, as did tons of manure.

The most important environmental effect of automobiles was suburban sprawl. Middle-class families could now live in single-family homes too far apart to be served by public transportation. As middle- and working-class families bought cars, cities acquired rings of automobile suburbs. Los Angeles, the first true automobile city, consisted of suburbs spread over hundreds of square miles and linked together by broad avenues. Many Americans saw Los Angeles as the portent of a glorious future in which everyone would have a car.

Technological advances also transformed rural environments. Automobile owners drove out to the country on weekends or holidays. Farmers bought cars and light trucks to transport produce as well as passengers. Governments obliged by building new roads and paving old ones to make automobile travel smoother and safer.

In 1915 Ford introduced a gasoline-powered tractor, and by the mid-1920s these versatile machines began replacing horses. Larger farms profited most from this innovation, while small farmers sold their land and moved to the cities. Tractors and other expensive equipment hastened the transformation of agriculture from family enterprises to large agribusinesses.

In India, Australia, and the western United States, where there was little virgin rain-watered land left to cultivate, engineers built dams and canals to irrigate dry lands. Dams offered the added advantage of producing electricity, for which there was a booming demand. The immediate benefits of irrigation—land, food, and electricity—far outweighed such distant consequences as salt deposits on irrigated lands and harm to wildlife.

CONCLUSION

In the late 1920s it seemed as though the victors in the Great War might reestablish the prewar prosperity and European dominance of the globe. But the spirit of the 1920s was not real peace; instead it was the eye of a hurricane.

The Great War caused a major realignment among the nations of the world. France and Britain, the two leading colonial powers, emerged economically weakened despite their victory. The war brought defeat and humiliation to Germany but did not reduce its military or industrial potential. It destroyed the old regime of Russia, leading to civil war and revolution from which the victorious powers sought to isolate themselves. Two other old empires—the Austro-Hungarian and the Ottoman—were divided into many smaller and weaker nations.

Japan took advantage of the European conflict to develop its industries and press its demands on a China weakened by domestic turmoil and social unrest. The United States emerged as the most prosperous and potentially most powerful nation, restrained only by the isolationist sentiments of many Americans.

In the Middle East, the fall of the Ottoman Empire awakened aspirations of nationhood among the Turkish and Arab inhabitants and Jewish immigrants. These aspirations were thwarted when France and Great Britain tried to impose their rule upon the former Ottoman lands, causing conflicts and bitter enmities.

The war challenged social traditions in many ways. Many women who had participated in the war effort remained in the work force and demanded voting and other rights. Governments took on new responsibilities for education, public health, and social welfare. Automobiles, movies, and radio broadcasts were eagerly adopted by western Europeans and North Americans, and aviation aroused tremendous enthusiasm. Advances in the sciences, especially in physics and psychology, undermined the old cultural certainties, while birth control and family planning provoked considerable opposition from traditionalists.

KEY TERMS

EBOOK AND WEBSITE RESOURCES

 Primary Sources

Letter from Turkey, Summer 1915

The Balfour Declaration

Comments of the German Delegation to the Paris Peace Conference on the Conditions of Peace, October 1919

An Economist Analyzes the Versailles Treaty and Finds It Lacking

Two Proclamations of the Boxer Rebellion

The Three People's Principles and the Future of the Chinese People

Interactive Maps

Map 29.1 Europe in 1913

Map 29.2 The First World War in Europe

Map 29.3 Territorial Changes in Europe After World War I

Map 29.4 Territorial Changes in the Middle East After World War I

Plus flashcards, practice quizzes, and more. Go to:
www.cengage.com/history/bullietearthpeople5e

SUGGESTED READING

Bianco, Lucien. *Origins of the Chinese Revolution, 1915–1949.* 1971. A succinct account of the rise of communism in China.

DuBois, Ellen. *Woman Suffrage and Women's Rights.* 1998. The best description of the women's movement at the beginning of the twentieth century.

Figes, Orlando. *A People's Tragedy: The Russian Revolution, 1891–1924.* 1996. A well-written overview of the Russian Revolution.

Fritzsche, Peter. *A Nation of Fliers: German Aviation and the Popular Imagination.* 1992. On the rise of aviation in Germany.

Fromkin, David. *A Peace to End All Peace.* 1989. An excellent introduction of twentieth-century Middle Eastern history.

Higonnet, Margaret, et al., eds. *Behind the Lines: Gender and the Two World Wars.* 1987. Describes the contributions of women during wartime.

Hughes, H. Stuart. *Consciousness and Society: The Reorientation of European Social Thought, 1890–1930.* 1958. An intellectual and cultural history of early twentieth-century Europe.

Keegan, John. *The First World War.* 1999. A short account of the war by an eminent military historian.

Nye, David E. *Electrifying America: Social Meanings of a New Technology.* 1990. The cultural history of American electrification and modernization.

Remarque, Erich Maria. *All Quiet on the Western Front.* 1928. The classic novel about war from the soldiers' viewpoint.

Roberts, A. D., ed. *Cambridge History of Africa,* vol. 7, *1905–1940.* 1986. A complete but readable analysis of early twentieth-century African history.

Sontag, Raymond. *A Broken World, 1919–1939.* 1971. Describes how the problems left by the First World War led to the Second World War.

Tuchman, Barbara. *The Guns of August.* 1962. A classic and very readable account of the first month of the Great War.

NOTES

1. Frank B. Tipton, *A History of Modern Germany since 1815* (Berkeley: University of California Press, 2003), 295.

2. Walter Z. Laqueur and Barry Rubin, eds., *The Arab-Israeli Reader: A Documentary History of the Middle East Conflict*, 4th ed. (New York: Penguin Books, 1984), 18.

3. David Shub, *Lenin: A Biography* (Garden City, N.Y.: Doubleday, 1948), 257.

4. David Vital, *A People Apart: The Jews of Europe*, 1789–1939 (Oxford: Oxford University Press, 1999), 756.

5. Ragnhild Fiebig von Hase and Ursula Lehmkuhl, *Enemy Images in American History* (Oxford: Berghahn Books, 1997), 5.

6. Emile Durkheim, *The Elementary Forms of Religious Life*, trans. by Karen Elise Fields (New York: Free Press, 1995), 2.

CHAPTER OUTLINE

German Dive-Bomber over Eastern Europe   A German Messerschmidt Bf-110 fighter plane attacks a Soviet troop convoy on the Eastern Front.

Visit the website and ebook for additional study materials and interactive tools: www.cengage.com/history/bullietearthpeople5e

The Collapse of the Old Order, 1929–1949

Before the First World War the Italian poet Filippo Marinetti exalted violence as noble and manly: "We want to glorify war, the world's only hygiene—militarism, deed, destroyer of anarchisms, the beautiful ideas that are death-bringing, and the subordination of women."[1] His friend Gabriele d'Annunzio added: "If it is a crime to incite citizens to violence, I shall boast of this crime."[2] Poets are sometimes more prescient than they imagine.

In the nineteenth century the governments of the great powers were manipulated by politicians through appeals to popular nationalism. Internationally, the world order relied on the maintenance of empires by military or economic means. And the global economy was based on free-market capitalism in which the industrial countries exchanged manufactured goods for the agricultural and mineral products of the nonindustrial world.

- How did the Soviet Union change under Stalin, and at what cost?
- What caused the Depression, and what effects did it have on the world?
- How did fascism in Italy and Germany lead to the Second World War?
- What were the economic reasons behind Japan's invasion of Manchuria?
- How was the war fought, and why did Japan and Germany lose?
- How did science and technology change the nature of warfare?

After the trauma of World War I the world seemed to return to what U.S. president Warren Harding called "normalcy": prosperity in Europe and America, European colonialism in Asia and Africa, American domination of Latin America, and peace almost everywhere. But in 1929 normalcy vanished. As the Great Depression spread around the world, governments turned against one another in desperate attempts to protect their people's livelihood.

Most survivors of the war had learned to abhor violence. For a few, however, war and domination became a creed, a goal, and a solution to their problems. The Japanese military tried to save their country from the Depression by conquering China, which erupted in revolution. In Germany many blamed their troubles on Communists and Jews and turned to the Nazis, who promised to save German society by crushing others. In the Soviet Union, Stalin used energetic and murderous means to force his country into a Communist version of the Industrial Revolution.

As the old order collapsed, the world was engulfed by a second Great War, one far more global and destructive than the first. Unlike World War I, this was a war of movement in which entire countries were conquered in a matter of weeks. It was also a war of machines: fighter planes and bombers that targeted civilians, tanks, aircraft carriers, and, finally, atomic bombs that obliterated entire cities.

At the end of World War II much of Europe and East Asia lay in ruins, and millions of destitute refugees sought safety in other lands. The colonial powers were either defeated or so weakened that they could no longer prevent their Asian and African subjects from demanding independence.

THE STALIN REVOLUTION

Joseph Stalin Bolshevik revolutionary, head of the Soviet Communist Party after 1924, and dictator of the Soviet Union from 1928 to 1953. He led the Soviet Union with an iron fist, using Five-Year Plans to increase industrial production and terror to crush all opposition.

Five-Year Plans Plans that Joseph Stalin introduced to industrialize the Soviet Union rapidly, beginning in 1928. They set goals for the output of steel, electricity, machinery, and most other products and were enforced by the police powers of the state. They succeeded in making the Soviet Union a major industrial power before World War II.

During the 1920s the Soviet Union recovered from the Revolutions of 1917 and the civil war that followed (see Chapter 29). After Stalin achieved total mastery over this huge nation in 1929, he led it through an economic and social transformation that turned it into a great industrial and military power and intensified both admiration for and fear of communism throughout the world.

Five-Year Plans

Joseph Stalin (1879–1953) was the son of a poor shoemaker. Before becoming a revolutionary, he studied for the priesthood. Under the name *Stalin* (Russian for "man of steel"), he played a small part in the Revolutions of 1917. He was a hard-working and skillful administrator who rose within the party bureaucracy and filled its upper ranks with men loyal to himself. He then proceeded to make himself absolute dictator and transform Soviet society.

Stalin's ambition was to turn the USSR into an industrial nation. However, industrialization was to serve a different purpose than in other countries. It was not expected to produce consumer goods for a mass market or to enrich individuals. Instead, its aim was to increase the power of the Communist Party domestically and that of the Soviet Union in relation to other countries.

Stalin was determined to prevent a repetition of the humiliating defeat Russia had suffered at the hands of Germany in 1917. His goal was to quintuple the output of electricity and double that of heavy industry—iron, steel, coal, and machinery—in five years. To do so, he devised the first of a series of **Five-Year Plans**. Beginning in October 1928, the Communist Party and government created whole industries and cities from scratch, then trained millions of peasants to work in the new factories, mines, and offices. In every way except actual fighting, Stalin's Russia resembled a nation at war.

Rapid industrialization hastened environmental changes. Hydroelectric dams turned rivers into strings of reservoirs. Roads, canals, and railroad tracks cut the landscape. Forests and grassland were turned into farmland. From an environmental perspective, the Five-Year Plans resembled the transformation that had occurred in the United States and Canada a few decades earlier.

Collectivization of Agriculture

Since the Soviet Union was still a predominantly agrarian country, the only way to pay for these massive investments, provide the labor, and feed the millions of new industrial workers was to squeeze the peasantry. Stalin therefore proceeded with the most radical social experiment conceived up to that time: the collectivization of agriculture.

David King Collection

The Collectivization of Soviet Agriculture   One of the goals of collectivization was to introduce modern farm machinery. This poster shows delighted farmers operating new tractors and threshers.

CHRONOLOGY

United States, Europe, and North Africa	Asia and the Pacific
1920	
1928 Stalin introduces Five-Year Plans and the collectivization of agriculture	
1929 Great Depression begins in U.S.	
1930 1931 Great Depression reaches Europe	1931 Japanese forces occupy Manchuria
1933 Hitler comes to power in Germany	1934–1935 Mao leads Communists on Long March
1935 1936 Hitler invades the Rhineland	1937 Japanese troops invade China, conquer coastal provinces; Chiang Kai-shek flees to Sichuan
1939 (Sept. 1) German forces invade Poland	1937–1938 Japanese troops take Nanjing
1940 1940 (March–April) German forces conquer Denmark, Norway, the Netherlands, and Belgium	
1940 (May–June) German forces conquer France	
1940 (June–Sept.) Battle of Britain	
1941 (June 21) German forces invade USSR	1941 (Dec. 7) Japanese aircraft bomb Pearl Harbor
1942–1943 Allies and Germany battle for control of North Africa	1942 (Jan.–March) Japanese conquer Thailand, Philippines, Malaya
	1942 (June) United States Navy defeats Japan at Battle of Midway
1943 Soviet victory in Battle of Stalingrad	
1943–1944 Red Army slowly pushes Wehrmacht back to Germany	
1944 (June 6) D-day: U.S., British, and Canadian troops land in Normandy	
1945 1945 (May 7) Germany surrenders	1945 (Aug. 6) United States drops atomic bomb on Hiroshima
	1945 (Aug. 14) Japan surrenders
	1945–1949 Civil war in China
	1949 (Oct. 1) Communists defeat Guomindang; Mao proclaims People's Republic of China

Collectivization meant consolidating small private farms into vast collectives and making the farmers work together in commonly owned fields. Each collective was expected to supply the government with a fixed amount of food and distribute what was left among its members. Collectives were to become outdoor factories where food was manufactured through the techniques of mass production and the application of machinery. The purpose of this collectivization was to bring the peasants under government control so they never again could withhold food supplies, as they had done during the Russian civil war of 1918-1921.

Kulaks

When collectivization was announced, the government mounted a massive propaganda campaign and sent party members into the countryside to enlist the farmers' support. At first all seemed to go well, but soon *kulaks* (COO-lox) ("fists"), the better-off peasants, began to resist giving up all their property. When soldiers came to force them into collectives at gunpoint, they burned their crops, smashed their equipment, and slaughtered their livestock. Within a few months they slaughtered half of the Soviet Union's horses and cattle and two-thirds of the sheep and goats. In retaliation, Stalin ruthlessly ordered the "liquidation of kulaks as a class" and incited the poor peasants to attack their wealthier neighbors. Over 8 million kulaks were arrested. Many were executed, and the rest were sent to slave labor camps, where most starved to death.

Famine

The peasants who were left had been the least successful before collectivization and proved to be the least competent after. Many were sent to work in factories. The rest were forbidden to leave their farms. With half of their draft animals gone, they could not plant or harvest enough to meet the swelling demands of the cities. Yet government agents took whatever they could find, leaving little or nothing for the farmers themselves. After bad harvests in 1933 and 1934, a famine swept through the countryside, killing some 5 million people, about one in every twenty farmers.

Stalin's second Five-Year Plan, designed to run from 1933 to 1937, was originally intended to produce consumer goods. But when the Nazis took over Germany in 1933 (see below), Stalin changed the plan to emphasize heavy industries that could produce armaments. Between 1927 and 1937 the Soviet output of metals and machines increased fourteen-fold while consumer goods became scarce and food was rationed. After a decade of Stalinism, the Soviet people were more poorly clothed, fed, and housed than they had been before the war.

Terror and Opportunities

The 1930s brought both terror and opportunities to the Soviet people. The forced pace of industrialization, the collectivization of agriculture, and the uprooting of millions of people could be accomplished only under duress. To prevent any possible resistance or rebellion, the NKVD, Stalin's secret police force, created a climate of suspicion and fear.

As early as 1930 Stalin had hundreds of engineers and technicians arrested on trumped-up charges of counterrevolutionary ideas and sabotage. Three years later, he expelled a million members of the Communist Party—one-third of the membership—on similar charges. He then turned on his most trusted associates.

The Purge Trials

In December 1934 Sergei Kirov, the party boss of Leningrad (now St. Petersburg), was assassinated, perhaps on Stalin's orders. Stalin made a public display of mourning Kirov while blaming others for the crime. He then ordered a series of spectacular purge trials in which he accused most of Lenin's associates of treason. In 1937 he had his eight top generals and many lower officers executed, leaving the Red Army dangerously weakened. Under torture or psychological pressure, almost all the accused confessed to the "crimes" they were charged with.

Gulags

While "Old Bolsheviks" and high officials were being put on trial, terror spread steadily downward. The government regularly made demands that people could not meet, so everyone was guilty of breaking some regulation or other. People from all walks of life were arrested, some on mere suspicion or because of a false accusation by a jealous coworker or neighbor, some for expressing a doubt or working too hard or not hard enough, some for being related to someone previously arrested, some for no reason at all. Millions of people were sentenced without trials. At the height of the terror, some 8 million were sent to *gulags* (GOO-log) (labor camps), where perhaps a million died each year of exposure or malnutrition. To its victims the terror seemed capricious and random. Yet it turned a sullen and resentful people into docile hard-working subjects of the party.

In spite of the fear and hardships, many Soviet citizens supported Stalin's regime. Suddenly, with so many people gone and new industries and cities being built everywhere, there were opportunities for those who remained, especially the poor and the young. Women entered careers and jobs previously closed to them, becoming steelworkers, physicians, and office managers; but they retained their household and child-rearing duties, receiving little help from men (see Diversity and Dominance: Women, Family Values, and the Russian Revolution). People who moved to the cities, worked enthusiastically, and asked no questions could hope to rise into the upper ranks of the Communist Party, the military, the government, or the professions—where the privileges and rewards were many.

Stalin's brutal methods helped the Soviet Union industrialize faster than any country had ever done. By the late 1930s the USSR was the world's third largest industrial power, after the United States and Germany. To foreign observers it seemed to be booming with construction projects and labor shortages. Even anti-Communist observers admitted that government planning worked. To millions of Soviet citizens who took pride in the new strength of their country and to many foreigners who contrasted conditions in the Soviet Union with the unemployment and despair in the West, Stalin's achievement seemed worth any price.

THE DEPRESSION

On October 24, 1929—"Black Thursday"—the New York stock market went into a dive. Within days stocks had lost half their value. The fall continued for three years, ruining millions of investors. People with bank accounts rushed to make withdrawals, causing thousands of banks to collapse.

Economic Crisis

What began as a stock market crash soon turned into the deepest depression in history. As consumers reduced their purchases, businesses cut production, laying off thousands of workers. Female employees were the first laid off on the grounds that men had to support families while women worked only for "pin money." Jobless men deserted their families. Small farmers went bankrupt and lost their land. By mid-1932 the American economy had shrunk by half, and unemployment had risen to an unprecedented 25 percent of the work force. Many observers thought that free-enterprise capitalism was doomed.

In 1930 the U.S. government, hoping to protect American industries from foreign competition, imposed the Smoot-Hawley tariff, the highest in American history. In retaliation, other countries raised their tariffs in a wave of "beggar thy neighbor" protectionism. The result was crippled export industries and shrinking world trade. While global industrial production declined by 36 percent between 1929 and 1932, world trade dropped by a breathtaking 62 percent.

Two Views of the American Way In this classic photograph, *Life* magazine photographer Margaret Bourke-White captured the contrast between advertisers' view of the ideal American family and the reality of bread lines for the poor.

Time Life Pictures/Getty Images

Women, Family Values, and the Russian Revolution

The Bolsheviks were of two minds on the subject of women. They were opposed to bourgeois morality and to the oppression of women, especially working-class women, under capitalism. But what to put in its place?

Alexandra Kollontai was the most outspoken of the Bolsheviks on the subject of women's rights. She advocated the liberation of women, the replacement of housework by communal kitchens and laundries, and divorce on demand. Under socialism, love, sex, and marriage would be entirely equal, reciprocal, and free of economic obligations. Childbearing would be encouraged, but children would be raised communally: "The worker mother . . . must remember that there are henceforth only our children, those of the communist state, the common possession of all workers."

In a lecture she gave at Sverdlov University in 1921, Kollontai declared:

. . . it is important to preserve not only the interests of the woman but also the life of the child, and this is to be done by giving the woman the opportunity to combine labour and maternity. Soviet power tries to create a situation where a woman does not have to cling to a man she has learned to loathe only because she has nowhere else to go with her children, and where a woman alone does not have to fear for her life and the life of her child. In the labour republic it is not the philanthropists with their humiliating charity but the workers and peasants, fellow-creators of the new society, who hasten to help the working woman and strive to lighten the burden of motherhood. . . . I would like to say a few words about a question which is closely connected with the problem of maternity—the question of abortion, and Soviet Russia's attitude toward it. On 20 November 1920 the labour republic issued a law abolishing the penalties that had been attached to abortion. What is the reason behind this new attitude? Russia after all suffers not from an overproduction of living labour but rather from a lack of it. Russia is thinly, not densely populated. Every unit of labour power is precious. Why then have we declared abortion to be no longer a criminal offence? . . .

Abortion exists and flourishes everywhere, and no laws or punitive measures have succeeded in rooting it out. A way round the law is always found. But "secret help" only cripples women; they become a burden on the labour government, and the size of the labour force is reduced. Abortion, when carried out under proper medical conditions, is less harmful and dangerous, and the woman can get back to work quicker. Soviet power realizes that the need for abortion will only disappear on the one hand when Russia has a broad and developed network of institutions protecting motherhood and providing social education, and on the other hand when women understand that *childbirth is a social obligation*; Soviet power has therefore allowed abortion to be performed openly and in clinical conditions.

Besides the large-scale development of motherhood protection, the task of labour Russia is to strengthen in women the healthy instinct of motherhood, to make motherhood and labour for the collective compatible and thus do away with the need for abortion. This is the approach of the labour republic to the question of abortion, which still faces women in the bourgeois countries in all its magnitude. In these countries women are exhausted by the dual burden of hired labour for capital and motherhood. In Soviet Russia the working woman and peasant woman are helping the Communist Party to build a new society and to undermine the old way of life that has enslaved women. As soon as woman is viewed as being essentially a labour unit, the key to the solution of the complex question of maternity can be found. . . . The emancipation of women can only be completed when a fundamental transformation of living is effected; and life-styles will change only

Depression in Industrial Nations

By 1931 the Depression had spread to Europe. Governments canceled reparations payments and war loans, but it was too late to save the world economy. Though their economies stagnated, France and Britain weathered the Depression by making their colonial empires purchase their products rather than the products of other countries. Nations that relied on exports to pay for imported food and fuel suffered much more. In Germany unemployment reached 6 million by 1932, twice as high as in Britain. Half the German population lived in poverty, while those who kept their jobs saw their salaries cut and their living standards fall. In Japan the burden of the Depression fell hardest on the farmers and fishermen.

This massive economic upheaval had profound political repercussions. Nationalists everywhere called for autarchy, or independence from the world economy. In the United States Franklin D. Roosevelt was elected president in 1932 on a "New Deal" platform of government programs to stimulate and revitalize the economy. Although the American, British, and French governments intervened in their economies, they remained democratic. In Germany and Japan, with the fundamental transformation of all production and the establishment of a communist economy. The revolution in everyday life is unfolding before our very eyes, and in this process the liberation of women is being introduced in practice.

Fifteen years later Joseph Stalin reversed the Soviet policy on abortion.

The published draft of the law prohibiting abortion and providing material assistance to mothers has provoked a lively reaction throughout the country. It is being heatedly discussed by tens of millions of people and there is no doubt that it will serve as a further strengthening of the Soviet family. . . .

When we speak of strengthening the Soviet family, we are speaking precisely of the struggle against the survivals of a bourgeois attitude towards marriage, women, and children. So-called "free love" and all disorderly sex life are bourgeois through and through, and have nothing to do with either socialist principles or the ethics and standards of conduct of the Soviet citizens. Socialist doctrine shows this, and it is proved by life itself.

The elite of our country, the best of the Soviet youth, are as a rule also excellent family men who dearly love their children. And vice versa: the man who does not take marriage seriously, and abandons his children to the whims of fate, is usually also a bad worker and a poor member of society. . . .

It is impossible even to compare the present state of the family with that which obtained before the Soviet regime—so great has been the improvement towards greater stability and, above all, greater humanity and goodness. The single fact that millions of women have become economically independent and are no longer at the mercy of men's whims, speaks volumes. Compare, for instance, the modern woman collective farmer who sometimes earns more than her husband, with the pre-revolutionary peasant woman who completely depended on her husband and was a slave in the household. Has not this fundamentally changed family relations, has it not rationalized and strengthened the family? The very motives for setting up a family, for getting married, have changed for the better, have been cleansed of atavistic and barbaric elements. Marriage has ceased to be a matter of sell-and-buy. Nowadays a girl from a collective farm is not given away (or should we say "sold away"?) by her father, for now she is her own mistress, and no one can give her away. She will marry the man she loves. . . .

We alone have all the conditions under which a working woman can fulfill her duties as a citizen and as a mother responsible for the birth and early upbringing of her children.

A woman without children merits our pity, for she does not know the full joy of life. Our Soviet women, full-blooded citizens of the freest country in the world, have been given the bliss of motherhood. We must safeguard the family and raise and rear healthy Soviet heroes!

QUESTIONS FOR ANALYSIS

1. How does Kollontai expect women to be both workers and mothers without depending on a man? How would Soviet society make this possible?

2. Why does Alexandra Kollontai advocate the legalization of abortion in Soviet Russia? Does she view abortion as a permanent right or as a temporary necessity?

3. Why does Stalin characterize a "lighthearted, negligent attitude toward marriage" and "all disorderly sex life" as "bourgeois through and through"?

4. How does Stalin's image of the Soviet family differ from Kollontai's? Are his views a variation of her views, or the opposite?

Source: First selection from Alexandra Kollontai, "The Labour of Women in the Revolution of the Economy," in *Selected Writings of Alexandra Kollontai*, translated by Alix Holt (Lawrence Hill & Company, 1978), pp. 148–149. Used with permission of Lawrence Hill Books. Second selection from Joseph Stalin, *Law on the Abolition of Legal Abortion* (1936).

as economic grievances worsened long-festering political resentments, radical leaders came to power and turned their nations into military machines, hoping to acquire, by war if necessary, empires large enough to support self-sufficient economies.

Depression in Nonindustrial Regions

The Depression also spread to Asia, Africa, and Latin America, but very unevenly. In 1930 India erected a wall of import duties to protect its infant industries from foreign competition; its living standards stagnated but did not drop. China was little affected by trade with other countries; its problems were more political than economic.

Asia

Countries that depended on exports were hard hit by the Depression. Malaya, Indochina, and the Dutch East Indies produced most of the world's natural rubber; when automobile production in the United States and Europe dropped by half, so did imports of rubber, devastating their economies. Egypt, dependent on cotton exports, was also affected, and in the resulting political strife, the government became autocratic and unpopular.

Latin America

Throughout Latin America unemployment and homelessness increased markedly. The industrialization of Argentina and Brazil was set back a decade or more. Disenchanted with liberal politics, military officers seized power in several Latin American countries. Consciously imitating dictatorships emerging in Europe, they imposed authoritarian control over their economies, hoping to stimulate local industries and curb imports.

Africa

Other than the USSR, only southern Africa boomed during the 1930s. As other prices dropped, gold became relatively more valuable. Copper deposits, found in Northern Rhodesia (now Zambia) and the Belgian Congo, proved to be cheaper to mine than Chilean copper. But this mining boom benefited only a small number of European and white South African mine owners. For Africans it was a mixed blessing; mining provided jobs and cash wages to men while women stayed behind in the villages, farming, herding, and raising children without their husbands' help.

SECTION REVIEW

- The New York stock market crash of 1929 caused business and bank failures and massive unemployment.

- The Depression soon spread to all industrial nations, especially Germany and Japan.

- Nonindustrial countries, especially those that depended on exports to industrial countries, were also hard hit; only southern Africa was spared.

- In the face of this threat, some countries turned to dictatorship to save their economies.

THE RISE OF FASCISM

The Russian Revolution and its Stalinist aftermath frightened property owners in Europe and North America. In western Europe and North America, middle- and upper-income voters took refuge in conservative politics. In southern and central Europe, the war had turned people's hopes of victory to bitter disappointment. Many blamed ethnic minorities, especially Jews, for their troubles. In their yearning for a mythical past of family farms and small shops, increasing numbers rejected representative government and sought more dramatic solutions.

Radical politicians quickly learned to apply wartime propaganda techniques to appeal to a confused citizenry. They promised to use any means necessary to bring back full employment, stop the spread of communism, and achieve the territorial conquests that World War I had denied them. While defending private property from communism, they borrowed the communist model of politics: a single party and a secret police that ruled by terror and intimidation.

Benito Mussolini Fascist dictator of Italy (1922–1943). He led Italy to conquer Ethiopia (1935), joined Germany in the Axis pact (1936), and allied Italy with Germany in World War II. He was overthrown in 1943 when the Allies invaded Italy.

Fascist Party Italian political party created by Benito Mussolini during World War I. It emphasized aggressive nationalism and was Mussolini's instrument for the creation of a dictatorship in Italy from 1922 to 1943.

Fascism

Mussolini's Italy

The first country to seek radical answers was Italy. World War I, which had never been popular, left thousands of veterans who found neither pride in their victory nor jobs in the postwar economy. Unemployed veterans and violent youths banded together into *fasci di combattimento* (fighting units) to demand action and intimidate politicians. When workers threatened to strike, factory and property owners hired gangs of these *fascisti* to defend them.

Benito Mussolini (1883–1945) had supported Italy's entry into the war. A spellbinding orator, he quickly became the leader of the **Fascist Party**, which glorified warfare and the Italian nation. By 1921 the party had 300,000 members, many of whom used violent methods to repress strikes, intimidate voters, and seize municipal governments. A year later Mussolini threatened to march on Rome if he was not appointed prime minister. The government, composed of timid parliamentarians, gave in.

Mussolini proceeded to install Fascist Party members in all government jobs, crush all opposition parties, and jail anyone who criticized him. The party took over the press, public education, and youth activities and gave employers control over their workers. The Fascists lowered living standards but reduced unemployment and provided social security and public services. They proved to be neither ruthless radicals nor competent administrators.

What Mussolini and the Fascist movement really excelled at was bombastic speeches, spectacular parades, and signs everywhere proclaiming "Il Duce (eel DOO-chay) [the Leader] is always right!" Mussolini's genius was to apply the techniques of modern mass communications and advertisement to political life. Movie footage and radio news bulletins galvanized the masses in ways never before done in peacetime. His techniques of whipping up public enthusiasm were not lost on other radicals. By the 1930s fascist movements had appeared in most European countries, as well as in Latin America, China, and Japan. Fascism appealed to many people who were frightened by rapid changes and placed their hopes in charismatic leaders. Of all of Mussolini's imitators, none was as sinister as Adolf Hitler.

Hitler's Germany

Adolf Hitler Born in Austria, Hitler became a radical German nationalist during World War I. He led the National Socialist German Workers' Party—the Nazis—in the 1920s and became dictator of Germany in 1933. He led Europe into World War II.

Nazis German political party led by Adolf Hitler, emphasizing nationalism, racism, and war. When Hitler became chancellor of Germany in 1933, the Nazis became the only legal party and an instrument of Hitler's absolute rule. The party's formal name was National Socialist German Workers' Party.

Nazi Racism

The Third Reich

Germany had lost the First World War after coming very close to winning. The hyperinflation of 1923 wiped out the savings of middle-class families. Less than ten years later the Depression caused more unemployment and misery than in any other country. Millions of Germans blamed Socialists, Jews, and foreigners for their troubles.

Adolf Hitler (1889–1945) joined the German army in 1914 and was wounded at the front. He later looked back fondly on the clear lines of authority and the camaraderie he had experienced in battle. After the war he used his gifts as an orator to lead a political splinter group called the National Socialist German Workers' Party—**Nazis** for short. While serving a brief jail sentence he wrote *Mein Kampf* (mine compf) (*My Struggle*), in which he outlined his goals and beliefs.

When it was published in 1925, *Mein Kampf* attracted little notice. Its ideas seemed so insane that almost no one took it, or its author, seriously. Hitler's ideas went far beyond ordinary nationalism. He believed that Germany should incorporate all German-speaking areas, even those in neighboring countries. He distinguished among a "master race" of Aryans (he meant Germans, Scandinavians, and Britons), a degenerate "Alpine" race of French and Italians, and an inferior race of Russian and eastern European Slavs, fit only to be slaves of the master race. He reserved his most intense hatred for Jews, on whom he blamed every disaster that had befallen Germany, especially the defeat of 1918. He glorified violence and looked forward to a future war in which the "master race" would defeat and subjugate all others.

Hitler's first goal was to repeal the humiliation and military restrictions of the Treaty of Versailles. Then he planned to annex all German-speaking territories to a greater Germany, then gain *Lebensraum* (LAY-bens-rowm) (room to live) at the expense of Poland and the USSR. Finally, he planned to eliminate all Jews from Europe.

From 1924 to 1930 Hitler's followers remained a tiny minority, for most Germans found his ideas too extreme. But when the Depression hit, the Nazis gained supporters among the unemployed, who believed their promises of jobs for all, and among property owners frightened by the growing popularity of Communists.

In March 1933 Hitler became chancellor of Germany. Once in office, he quickly assumed dictatorial powers. He put Nazis in charge of all government agencies, educational institutions, and professional organizations; banned all other political parties; and threw their leaders into concentration camps. The Nazis deprived Jews of their citizenship and civil rights, prohibited them from marrying "Aryans," ousted them from the professions, and confiscated their property. In August 1934 Hitler proclaimed himself *Führer* (FEW-rer) ("leader") and called Germany the "Third Reich," the third German empire after the Holy Roman Empire of medieval times and the German Empire of 1871 to 1918.

The Nazis' economic and social policies were spectacularly effective. The government undertook massive public works projects. Businesses got contracts to manufacture weapons. Women who had entered the work force were urged to release their jobs to men. By 1936 business was booming; unemployment was at its lowest level since the 1920s; and living standards were rising. Most Germans believed that their economic well-being outweighed the loss of liberty.

The Road to War, 1933–1939

However, Hitler's goal was not prosperity or popularity, but conquest. As soon as he came to office, he began to build up the armed forces. Meanwhile, he tested the reactions of the other powers through a series of surprise moves followed by protestations of peace.

In 1933 Hitler withdrew Germany from the League of Nations. Two years later he announced that Germany was going to introduce conscription, build up its army, and create an air force—in violation of the Versailles treaty. Neither Britain nor France was willing to risk war by standing up to Germany.

A Nazi Rally Hitler organized mass rallies at Nuremberg to whip up popular support for his regime and to indoctrinate young Germans with a martial spirit. Thousands of men in uniform marched in torch-lit parades before Hitler and his top officials.

AP Images

Fascist Aggression

In 1935, emboldened by the weakness of the democracies, Italy invaded Ethiopia, the last independent state in Africa and a member of the League of Nations. The League and the democracies protested but refused to close the Suez Canal to Italian ships or impose an oil embargo. The following year, when Hitler sent troops into the Rhineland on the borders of France and Belgium, the other powers merely protested.

By 1938 Hitler decided that his rearmament plans were far enough advanced that he could afford to escalate his demands. In March Germany invaded Austria. Most Austrians were German-speakers and accepted the annexation of their country without protest. Then came Czechoslovakia, where a German-speaking minority lived along the German border. Hitler first demanded their autonomy from Czech rule, then their annexation to Germany. Throughout the summer he threatened to go to war. At the Munich Conference of September 1938, the leaders of France, Britain, and Italy gave him everything he wanted without consulting Czechoslovakia. Once again, Hitler learned that aggression paid off.

Appeasement

The weakness of the democracies—now called "appeasement"—had three causes. The first was the deep-seated fear of war among people who had lived through World War I. Unlike the dictators, politicians in the democracies could not ignore their constituents' yearnings for peace. Most people believed that the threat of war might go away if they wished for peace fervently enough. The second cause of appeasement was fear of communism among conservatives, who feared Stalin more than Hitler because Hitler claimed to respect Christianity and private property. The third cause was the very novelty of fascist tactics. Britain's prime minister Neville Chamberlain assumed that political leaders (other than the Bolsheviks) were honorable men and that an agreement was as valid as a business contract. Thus, when Hitler promised to incorporate only German-speaking people into Germany and said he had "no further territorial demands," Chamberlain believed him.

After Munich it was too late to stop Hitler, short of war. Germany and Italy signed an alliance called the Axis, and in March 1939 Germany invaded what was left of Czechoslovakia. Belatedly realizing that Hitler could not be trusted, France and Britain sought Soviet help. Stalin, however, distrusted the

SECTION REVIEW

- The Depression gave opportunities to ultranationalist politicians who promised prosperity and order.

- Mussolini, head of the Fascist Party, became dictator of Italy in 1922 and proceeded to quell all opposition.

- After gaining power in 1933, Hitler began to transform the German economy and society and to build up the German armed forces.

- Germany and Italy made aggressive moves that the democracies, fearing another war, did not oppose, but when Germany invaded Poland, Hitler's aggressive objectives were clear.

Alliances

"capitalists" as much as they distrusted him. When Hitler offered to divide Poland between Germany and the Soviet Union, Stalin accepted. The Nazi-Soviet Pact of August 23, 1939, freed Hitler from the fear of a two-front war and gave Stalin time to build up his armies. One week later, on September 1, German forces swept into Poland, and the war was on.

EAST ASIA, 1931–1945

When the Depression hit, the collapse of demand for silk and rice ruined thousands of Japanese farmers; to survive, many sold their daughters into prostitution while their sons flocked to the military. Ultranationalists resented their country's dependence on foreign trade. If only Japan had a colonial empire, they thought, it would not be beholden to the rest of the world. But Europeans and Americans had already taken most potential colonies in Asia. Japanese nationalists saw the conquest of China, with its vast population and resources, as the solution to their country's problems.

The Manchurian Incident of 1931

Meanwhile, in China the Guomindang (gwo-min-dong) was becoming stronger and preparing to challenge the Japanese presence in Manchuria, a province rich in coal and iron ore. Junior officers in the Japanese army, frustrated by the caution of their superiors, took action. In September 1931 an explosion on a railroad track, probably staged, gave them an excuse to conquer the entire province. In Tokyo weak civilian ministers acquiesced to the attack to avoid losing face. Japan thereupon recognized the "independence" of Manchuria under the name *Manchukuo* (man-CHEW-coo-oh).

Chiang Kai-shek Chinese military and political leader. Succeeded Sun Yat-sen as head of the Guomindang in 1925; headed the Chinese government from 1928 to 1948; fought against the Chinese Communists and Japanese invaders. After 1949 he headed the Chinese Nationalist government in Taiwan.

The U.S. government condemned the Japanese conquest, and the League of Nations refused to recognize Manchukuo and urged the Japanese to remove their troops from China. Persuaded that the Western powers would not fight, Japan resigned from the League.

During the next few years the Japanese built railways and heavy industries in Manchuria and northeastern China and sped up their rearmament. At home, production was diverted to the military, especially to building warships. The government grew more authoritarian, jailing thousands of dissidents. On several occasions, superpatriotic junior officers mutinied or assassinated leading political figures. The mutineers received mild punishments, and generals and admirals sympathetic to their views replaced more moderate civilian politicians.

The Long March

Until the Japanese seized Manchuria, the Chinese government seemed to be creating conditions for a national recovery. The main challenge to the government of **Chiang Kai-shek** (chang kie-shek) came from the Communists. The Chinese Communist Party had been founded in 1921 by a handful of intellectuals, and for several years it lived in the shadow of the Guomindang. Its efforts to recruit members among industrial workers came to naught in 1927, when Chiang Kai-shek arrested and executed Communists and labor leaders alike. The few Communists who escaped the mass arrests fled to the remote mountains of Jiangxi (jang-she), in southeastern China.

Mao Zedong Leader of the Chinese Communist Party (1927–1976). He led the Communists on the Long March (1934–1935) and rebuilt the Communist Party and Red Army during the Japanese occupation of China (1937–1945). After World War II, he led the Communists to victory over the Guomindang. He ordered the Cultural Revolution in 1966.

Mao Zedong and Maoism

Among them was **Mao Zedong** (ma-oh zay-dong) (1893–1976), a farmer's son who had left home to study philosophy. Mao was a man of action whose first impulse was to call for violent effort: "To be able to leap on horseback and to shoot at the same time; to go from battle to battle; to shake the mountains by one's cries, and the colors of the sky by one's roars of anger." In the early 1920s Mao discovered the works of Karl Marx, joined the Communist Party, and soon became one of its leaders.

In Jiangxi Mao began studying conditions among the peasants, in whom Communists had previously shown no interest. He planned to redistribute land from the wealthier to the poorer peasants, thereby gaining adherents for the coming struggle with the Guomindang army. His goal was a complete social revolution from the bottom up. Mao's reliance on the peasantry was a radical departure from Marxist-Leninist ideology, which stressed the backwardness of the peasants and pinned its hopes on industrial workers. Mao therefore had to be careful to cloak his pragmatic tactics in Communist rhetoric to allay the suspicions of Stalin and his agents.

Mao was an advocate of women's equality. Before 1927 the Communists had organized the women who worked in Shanghai's textile mills, the most exploited of all Chinese workers. Later, in their mountain stronghold in Jiangxi, they organized women farmers, allowed divorce, and banned arranged marriages and footbinding. But the party was still run by men whose primary task was warfare.

The Guomindang army pursued the Communists into the mountains, building small forts throughout the countryside. Rather than risk direct confrontations, Mao responded with guerrilla warfare. He harassed the army at its weak points with hit-and-run tactics, relying on the terrain and the support of the peasantry. Whereas government troops often mistreated civilians, Mao insisted that his soldiers help the peasants, pay a fair price for food and supplies, and treat women with respect.

Long March The 6,000-mile flight of Chinese Communists from southeastern to northwestern China. The Communists, led by Mao Zedong, were pursued by the Chinese army under orders from Chiang Kai-shek. The four thousand survivors of the march formed the nucleus of a revived Communist movement that defeated the Guomindang after World War II.

In spite of their good relations with the peasants of Jiangxi, the Communists gradually found themselves encircled by government forces. In 1934 Mao and his followers decided to break out of the southern mountains and trek to Shaanxi (SHAWN-she), an even more remote province in northwestern China. The so-called **Long March** took them 6,000 miles (nearly 9,700 kilometers) in one year over desolate mountains and through swamps and deserts, pursued by the army and bombed by Chiang's aircraft. Of the 100,000 Communists who left Jiangxi in October 1934, only 4,000 reached Shaanxi a year later (see Map 30.1). Chiang's government thought it was finally rid of the Communists.

The Sino-Japanese War, 1937–1945

In Japan politicians, senior officers, and business leaders disagreed on how to solve their country's economic problems. Some proposed a quick conquest of China; others advocated war with the Soviet Union. While their superiors hesitated, junior officers decided to take matters into their own hands.

On July 7, 1937, Japanese troops attacked Chinese forces near Beijing. The junior officers who ordered the attack quickly obtained the support of their commanders and then, reluctantly, of the government. Within weeks Japanese troops seized Beijing, Tianjin, Shanghai, and other coastal cities, and the Japanese navy blockaded the entire coast of China.

Once again, the United States and the League of Nations denounced the Japanese aggression. Yet the Western powers were too preoccupied with events in Europe and with their own economic problems to risk a military confrontation in Asia. When the Japanese sank a U.S. gunboat and shelled a British ship on the Yangzi River, the U.S. and British governments responded only with righteous indignation and pious resolutions.

The Chinese armies were large and fought bravely, but they were poorly led and armed and lost every battle. Japanese planes bombed cities while soldiers broke dikes and burned villages, killing thousands of civilians. Within a year Japan controlled the coastal provinces of China and the lower Yangzi and Yellow River Valleys, China's richest and most populated regions (see Map 30.1).

In spite of Japanese organizational and fighting skills, the attack on China did not bring the victory Japan had hoped for. The Chinese people continued to resist, either in the army or with the Communist guerrilla forces. As Japan sank deeper into the Chinese quagmire, life became harsher and more repressive for the Japanese people, as taxes rose, food and fuel became scarce, and more and more young men were drafted.

Warfare between the Chinese and Japanese was incredibly violent. In the winter of 1937–1938 Japanese troops took Nanjing, raped 20,000 women, killed 200,000 prisoners and civilians, and looted and burned the city. To slow them down, Chiang ordered the Yellow River dikes blasted open, causing a flood that destroyed four thousand villages, killed 890,000 people, and made 12.5 mil-

- Seeing conquest as a solution to its economic problems, in 1931 Japan conquered Manchuria.
- The Chinese government under Chiang Kai-shek fought both the Japanese and the Communists led by Mao Zedong, who fled into the mountains of northern China.
- In 1937, Japanese forces conquered the coastal provinces of China; in the ensuing violent war, however, Japan gained few real advantages.
- Chiang Kai-shek fled to the interior and prepared to fight the Communists.

MAP 30.1 **Chinese Communist Movement and the Sino-Japanese War, to 1938** During the 1930s, China was the scene of a three-way war. The Nationalist government attacked and pursued the Communists, who escaped into the mountains of Shaanxi. Meanwhile, Japanese forces, having seized Manchuria in 1931, attacked China in 1937 and quickly conquered its eastern provinces.

 Interactive Map

lion homeless. Two years later, when the Communists ordered a massive offensive, the Japanese retaliated with a "kill all, burn all, loot all" campaign, destroying hundreds of villages down to the last person, building, and farm animal.

The Guomindang

The Chinese government, led by Chiang Kai-shek, escaped to the mountains of Sichuan in the center of the country. There Chiang built up a huge army, not to fight Japan but to prepare for a future confrontation with the Communists. The army drafted over 3 million men, even though it had only a million rifles and could not provide food or clothing for all its soldiers. The Guomindang raised farmers' taxes, even when famine forced farmers to eat the bark of trees. Such taxes were not enough to support both a large army and the thousands of government officials and hangers-on who had fled to Sichuan. To avoid taxing its wealthy supporters the government printed money, causing inflation, hoarding, and corruption.

The Communists

From his capital of Yan'an in Shaanxi province, Mao also built up his army and formed a government. Unlike the Guomindang, the Communists listened to the grievances of the peasants, especially the poor, to whom they distributed land confiscated from wealthy landowners. They imposed rigid discipline on their officials and soldiers and tolerated no dissent or criticism from intellectuals. Though they had few weapons, the Communists obtained support and intelligence from farmers in Japanese-occupied territory. They turned military reversals into propaganda victories, presenting themselves as the only group in China that was serious about fighting the Japanese.

THE SECOND WORLD WAR

Many people feared that the Second World War would be a repetition of the First. Instead, it was much bigger in every way. It was fought around the world, from Norway to New Guinea and from Hawaii to Egypt, and on every ocean. It killed far more people than World War I, involved all civilians and productive forces, and showed how effectively industry, science, and nationalism could be channeled into mass destruction.

The War of Movement

In World War II motorized weapons gave back the advantage to the offensive. Opposing forces moved fast, their victories hinging as much on the aggressive spirit of their commanders and the military intelligence they obtained as on numbers of troops and firepower.

Blitzkrieg

The Wehrmacht (VAIR-mokt), or German army, was the first to learn this lesson. It not only had tanks, trucks, and fighter planes but had also perfected their combined use in a tactic called *Blitzkrieg* (BLITS-creeg) (lightning war): fighter planes scattered enemy troops and disrupted communications, tanks punctured the enemy's defenses, and then, with the help of the infantry, they encircled and captured enemy troops. At sea, both Japan and the United States had developed aircraft carriers that could launch planes against targets hundreds of miles away.

Armies ranged over vast theaters of operation, and countries were conquered in days or weeks. The belligerents mobilized the economies of entire continents, squeezing them for every possible resource. They tried not only to defeat their enemies' armed forces but—by blockades, submarine attacks, and bombing raids—to damage the economies that supported those armed forces. They thought of civilians as legitimate targets and, later, as vermin to be exterminated.

War in Europe and North Africa

It took less than a month for the Wehrmacht to conquer Poland (see Map 30.2). Britain and France declared war on Germany but took no military action. Meanwhile, the Soviet Union invaded eastern Poland and the Baltic republics. Although the Poles fought bravely, their infantry and cavalry were no match for German and Russian tanks. During the winter of 1939–1940 Germany and the Western democracies faced each other in what soldiers called a "phony war."

In March 1940 Hitler went on the offensive again, conquering Denmark, Norway, the Netherlands, and Belgium in less than two months. In May he attacked France. Although the French army had as many soldiers, tanks, and aircraft as the Wehrmacht, its morale was low and it quickly collapsed. By the end of June Hitler was master of all of Europe between Russia and Spain.

The Battle of Britain

Germany still had to face Britain. The British had no army to speak of, but they had other assets: the English Channel, the Royal Navy and Air Force, and a tough new prime minister, Winston Churchill. The Germans knew they could invade Britain only by gaining control of the airspace over the Channel, so they launched a massive air attack—the Battle of Britain—lasting from June through September. The attack failed because the Royal Air Force used radar and code-breaking to detect approaching German planes.

The Nazi-Soviet War

Frustrated in the west, Hitler turned his attention eastward, even though it meant fighting a two-front war. So far he had gotten the utmost cooperation from Stalin, who supplied Germany with grain, oil, and strategic raw materials. Yet he had always wanted to conquer Lebensraum in the east and enslave the Slavic peoples who lived there, and he feared that if he waited, Stalin would build a dangerously strong army. In June 1941 Hitler launched the largest attack in history, with 3 million soldiers and thousands of planes and tanks. Within five months the Wehrmacht conquered the Baltic states, Ukraine, and half of European Russia, captured a million prisoners of war, and reached the very gates of Moscow and Leningrad. The USSR seemed on the

e Interactive Map

MAP 30.2 **World War II in Europe and North Africa** In a series of quick and decisive campaigns from September 1939 to December 1941, German forces overran much of Europe and North Africa. There followed three years of bitter fighting as the Allies slowly pushed the Germans back.

© Cengage Learning

Soviet Tanks at Stalingrad In the winter of 1942–1943, the Red Army encircled a German army at Stalingrad, a strategic city in southern Russia that marked the furthest eastward advance of the Wehrmacht. The Soviets deployed their new T-34s, the best tanks in the world at the time. Unlike the Germans, Soviet soldiers were equipped with warm winter uniforms with a white outer layer for camouflage in the snow.

TASS-Sovfoto

Stalingrad City in Russia, site of a Red Army victory over the German army in 1942–1943. The Battle of Stalingrad was the turning point in the war between Germany and the Soviet Union. Today Volgograd.

Stalingrad

North Africa

El Alamein Town in Egypt, site of the victory by Britain's Field Marshal Bernard Montgomery over German forces led by General Erwin Rommel (the "Desert Fox") in 1942–1943.

Japanese War Plans

verge of collapse. Then the weather turned cold, machines froze, and the fighting came to a halt. Like Napoleon, Hitler had ignored the environment of Russia to his peril.

The next spring the Wehrmacht renewed its offensive. It surrounded Leningrad in a siege that was to cost a million lives. Leaving Moscow aside, it turned toward the Caucasus and its oil wells. In August the Germans attacked **Stalingrad** (now Volgograd), the key to the Volga River and the supply of oil. For months German and Soviet soldiers fought over every street and every house. When winter came, the Red Army counterattacked and encircled the city. In February 1943 the remnants of the German army in Stalingrad surrendered. Hitler had lost an army of 200,000 men and his last chance of defeating the Soviet Union and of winning the war (see Map 30.2).

From Europe the war spread to Africa. When France fell in 1940, Mussolini decided that the time had come to realize his imperial ambitions. Italian forces quickly overran British Somaliland, then invaded Egypt. Their victories were ephemeral, however, for when the British counterattacked, Italian resistance crumbled. During 1941 British forces conquered Italian East Africa and invaded Libya as well. The Italian rout in North Africa brought the Germans to their rescue, and during 1942 the German army and the forces of the British Commonwealth seesawed back and forth across the deserts of Libya and Egypt. At **El Alamein** in northern Egypt the British prevailed because they had more weapons and supplies and were better informed about their enemies' plans. The Germans were finally expelled from Africa in May 1943.

War in Asia and the Pacific

The fall of France and the involvement of Britain and the USSR against Germany presented Japan with the opportunity it had been looking for. Suddenly the European colonies in Southeast Asia, with their abundant oil, rubber, and other strategic materials, seemed ripe for the taking. In July 1941, when the French government allowed Japanese forces to occupy Indochina, the United States stopped shipments of steel, scrap iron, oil, and other products that Japan desperately needed. This left Japan with three alternatives: giving up its conquests, as the Americans insisted; facing economic ruin; or widening the war. Japan chose war.

Admiral Isoroku Yamamoto, commander of the Japanese fleet, told Prime Minister Fumimaro Konoye: "If I am told to fight regardless of the consequences, I shall run wild for the first six months or a year, but I have utterly no confidence for the second or third year. . . . I hope that you will endeavor to avoid a Japanese-American war." Ignoring his advice, the war cabinet made plans for a surprise attack on the United States Navy, followed by an invasion of Southeast Asia. They knew they could not hope to defeat the United States, but they calculated that the shock of the attack would be so great that isolationist Americans would accept the Japanese conquest of Southeast Asia as readily as they had acquiesced to Hitler's conquests in Europe.

MAP 30.3 **World War II in Asia and the Pacific** Having conquered much of China between 1937 and 1941, Japanese forces launched a sudden attack on Southeast Asia and the Pacific in late 1941 and early 1942. American forces slowly reconquered the Pacific islands and the Philippines. In August 1945, the atomic bombing of Hiroshima and Nagasaki forced Japan's surrender.

Pearl Harbor

Pearl Harbor Naval base in Hawaii attacked by Japanese aircraft on December 7, 1941. The sinking of much of the U.S. Pacific Fleet brought the United States into World War II.

Battle of Midway U.S. naval victory over the Japanese fleet in June 1942, in which the Japanese lost four of their best aircraft carriers. It marked a turning point in World War II.

On December 7, 1941, Japanese planes bombed the U.S. naval base at **Pearl Harbor**, sinking or damaging scores of warships but missing the aircraft carriers, which were at sea. Then, in early 1942, the Japanese conquered all of Southeast Asia and the Dutch East Indies. They soon began to confiscate food and raw materials and demand heavy labor from the inhabitants.

Japan's dream of an East Asian empire seemed within reach, for its victories surpassed even Hitler's in Europe. The United States, however, quickly began preparing for war. In April 1942 American planes bombed Tokyo. In May the United States Navy defeated a Japanese fleet in the Coral Sea, ending Japanese plans to conquer Australia. A month later, at the **Battle of Midway**, Japan lost four of its six largest aircraft carriers. Without them, Japan faced a long and hopeless war (see Map 30.3).

The End of War

After the Battle of Stalingrad the advantage on the Eastern Front shifted to the Soviet Union. By 1943 the Red Army was receiving a growing stream of supplies from factories in Russia and the United States. Slowly at first and then with increasing vigor, it pushed the Wehrmacht back toward Germany.

D-day

e **PRIMARY SOURCE: The Decision to Use the Atomic Bomb** Learn why President Truman was advised to drop atomic bombs on Japan—from the chairman of the committee that gave him that advice.

The Pacific War

Hiroshima and Nagasaki

Hiroshima City in Japan, the first to be destroyed by an atomic bomb, on August 6, 1945. The bombing hastened the end of World War II.

The Western powers, meanwhile, staged two invasions of Europe. Beginning in July 1943 they captured Sicily and invaded Italy. Italy signed an armistice, but German troops held off the Allied advance for two years. On June 6, 1944—forever after known as D-day—156,000 British, American, and Canadian troops landed on the coast of Normandy in western France—the largest shipborne assault ever staged. Within a week the Allies had more troops in France than Germany did, and by September Germany faced an Allied army of over 2 million men and half a million vehicles.

Although the Red Army was on the eastern border of Germany, ready for the final push, Hitler transferred part of the Wehrmacht westward. Despite overwhelming odds, Germany held out for almost a year, a result of the fighting qualities of its soldiers and the terror inspired by the Nazi regime, which commanded obedience to the end. On May 7, 1945, a week after Hitler committed suicide, German military leaders surrendered.

Japan fought on a while longer because the United States had aimed most of its war effort at Germany. Pacific islands had to be captured by amphibious landings, with high casualty rates on both sides. In June 1944 U.S. bombers began attacking Japan and American submarines sank Japanese merchant ships, cutting Japan off from its sources of oil and other raw materials. After May 1945, with Japanese fighters grounded for lack of fuel, U.S. planes began destroying Japanese shipping, industries, and cities at will.

Even as their homeland was being pounded, the Japanese still held strong positions in Asia. Despite its name, "Greater East Asian Co-Prosperity Sphere," the Japanese occupation was harsh and brutal. By 1945 Asians were eager to see the Japanese leave, but not to welcome back the Europeans. Instead, they looked forward to independence (see Chapters 31 and 32).

On August 6, 1945, the United States dropped an atomic bomb on **Hiroshima**, killing some 80,000 people in a flash and leaving about 120,000 more to die in agony from burns and radiation. Three days later another atomic bomb destroyed Nagasaki. On August 14 Emperor Hirohito gave the order to lay down arms. Two weeks later Japanese leaders signed the terms of surrender. The war was officially over.

Were these atomic weapons necessary? At the time, Americans believed that the conquest of the Japanese homeland would take more than a year and cost the lives of hundreds of thousands

Hiroshima After the Atomic Bomb   On August 6, 1945, an atomic bomb destroyed the city, killing some eighty thousand people. This photo shows the devastation of the city center, where only a few concrete buildings remained standing.

Corbis

Sale of Gold in the Last Days of the Guomindang   This picture was taken by famed French photojournalist Henri Cartier-Bresson in Shanghai just before the arrival of the Communist-led People's Liberation Army in 1949. It shows people desperate to buy gold before their Guomindang currency becomes worthless.

of American soldiers. Although some believed the Japanese were determined to fight to the bitter end, others thought they would surrender if they could retain their emperor. Winston Churchill wrote: "It would be a mistake to suppose that the fate of Japan was settled by the atomic bomb. Her defeat was certain before the first bomb fell."[3]

Collapse of the Guomindang and Communist Victory

The formal Japanese surrender in September 1945 surprised the Guomindang. The United States gave millions of dollars of aid and weapons to the Guomindang, all the while urging "national unity" and a "coalition government" with the Communists. But Chiang used all means available to prepare for a civil war. By late 1945 he had U.S. support, control of China's cities, and an army of 2.7 million, more than twice the size of the Communist forces. But the Guomindang's behavior eroded whatever popular support they had. As they moved into formerly Japanese-held territory, they acted like an occupation force. They taxed the people they "liberated" more heavily than the Japanese had, confiscated supplies, and enriched themselves at the expense of the population. Chiang's government printed money so fast that it soon lost all its value. In the countryside the Guomindang's brutality alienated the peasants.

Meanwhile, the Communists obtained Japanese equipment seized by the Soviets in the last weeks of the war and American weapons brought over by deserting Guomindang soldiers. In Manchuria, where they were strongest, they pushed through a radical land reform program, distributing the properties of wealthy landowners among the poorest peasants. In battles against government forces, the higher morale and popular support they enjoyed outweighed the heavy equipment of the Guomindang, whose soldiers began deserting by the thousands.

By 1949 the Guomindang armies were collapsing everywhere, defeated more by their own greed

SECTION REVIEW

- World War II was a war of machines and movement covering entire continents and oceans.
- Hitler's armies quickly overran western Europe, but Hitler failed to defeat Britain by air.
- In 1941 Germany attacked the USSR, but its defeat at Stalingrad in the winter of 1942–1943 sealed its fate.
- After the United States stopped shipments of vital supplies to Japan, in December 1941 Japanese planes bombed Pearl Harbor; a few months later Japan conquered Southeast Asia and Indonesia.
- After mid-1942, however, American forces pushed the Japanese back across the Pacific and began bombing Japan.
- In 1944, on D-day, the Allies landed troops on Norway and then fought their way into Germany; meanwhile, two atomic bombs forced Japan to surrender.
- After Japan's defeat, Chiang Kai-shek's army failed from its own ineptness and Mao's Communists took over China.

and ineptness than by the Communists. As the Communists advanced, high-ranking members of the Guomindang fled to Taiwan, protected from the mainland by the U.S. Navy. On October 1, 1949, Mao Zedong announced the founding of the People's Republic of China.

THE CHARACTER OF WARFARE

The war left an enormous death toll. Recent estimates place the figure at close to 60 million deaths, six to eight times more than in World War I. Over half of the dead were civilian victims of massacres, famines, and bombs. The Soviet Union lost between 20 million and 25 million people, more than any other country. China suffered 15 million deaths; Poland lost some 6 million, of whom half were Jewish; the Jewish people lost another 3 million outside Poland. Over 4 million Germans and over 2 million Japanese died. Great Britain lost 400,000 people, and the United States 300,000. In much of the world, families mourned one or more of their members.

Many parts of the world were flooded with refugees. Some 90 million Chinese fled the Japanese advance. In Europe millions fled from the Nazis or the Red Army or were herded back and forth on government orders. Many refugees never returned to their homes.

Belligerents identified not just soldiers but entire peoples as enemies. Some even labeled their own ethnic minorities as "enemies." Another reason for the devastation was the appearance of new technologies that carried destruction deep into enemy territory, far beyond the traditional battlefields. New technologies of warfare and changes in morality formed a lethal combination.

The Science and Technology of War

As fighting spread around the world, the mobilization of manpower and economies and the mobility of the armed forces grew increasingly important, while new aspects of war took on a growing importance. Chemists found ways to make synthetic rubber from coal or oil. Physicists perfected radar, which warned of approaching enemy aircraft and submarines. Cryptanalysts broke enemy codes and were able to penetrate secret military communications (see Environment and Technology: The Enigma Machine). Pharmacologists developed antibiotics that saved the lives of wounded soldiers, who in any earlier war would have died of infections.

Warplanes   Aircraft development was especially striking. As war approached, German, British, and Japanese aircraft manufacturers developed fast, maneuverable fighter planes. U.S. industry was especially noted for heavy bombers designed to fly in huge formations and drop tons of bombs on enemy cities. Germany responded with radically new designs, including the first jet fighters, low-flying buzz bombs, and, finally, V-2 missiles against which there was no warning or defense.

Atom Bombs   Military planners expected scientists to furnish secret weapons that could doom the enemy. In October 1939 President Roosevelt received a letter from physicist Albert Einstein, a Jewish refugee from Nazism, warning of the dangers of nuclear power: "There is no doubt that subatomic energy is available all around us, and that one day man will release and control its almost infinite power. We cannot prevent him from doing so and can only hope that he will not use it exclusively in blowing up his next door neighbor." Roosevelt placed the vast resources of the U.S. government at the disposal of physicists and engineers. By 1945 they had built two atomic bombs, each one powerful enough to annihilate an entire city.

Bombing Raids

Since it was very hard to pinpoint individual buildings, especially at night, British air chief marshal Arthur "Bomber" Harris decided that "operations should now be focused on the morale of the enemy civilian population and in particular the industrial workers."

In May 1942, 1,000 British planes dropped incendiary bombs on Cologne, setting fire to the old city. Between July 24 and August 2, 1943, 3,330 British and American planes fire-bombed Hamburg, killing 50,000 people, mostly women and children. Later raids destroyed Berlin, Dresden, and other German cities. The bombing raids against Germany killed 600,000 people—more than half of them women and children—and injured 800,000, but they failed to break the morale of the German people. German armament production continued to increase until late 1944, and

ENVIRONMENT + TECHNOLOGY

The Enigma Machine

Since ancient times, governments and armies have used various methods of encrypting messages, that is, making them unreadable to people who do not possess the proper code (words replaced by other words using a codebook) or cipher (letters replaced by numbers). The introduction of radio, which could be easily monitored by agents of foreign powers, turned cryptography (secret writing) into a necessity of diplomacy and war. Yet encrypting and decrypting messages required expert code clerks and took time. Furthermore, since each nation used several codes and ciphers and changed them periodically, a breakthrough in one code or cipher did not necessarily make other messages easier to decrypt.

After World War I, inventors in several countries set out to create machines that could encrypt and decrypt messages automatically while also making them harder to crack than manual codes and ciphers. The invention that was most successful was the Enigma, first produced by a German company in 1923. It consisted of a typewriter keyboard, a set of rotors containing electrical wires and contacts, and a series of lights marked with letters. When the operator entered a letter on the keyboard, an electrical current went through the rotors and lit up a letter different from the one entered. With each keystroke, the rotors also turned, so that the next time the same key was pushed, a different light went on. At the receiving end, if the operator had set his rotors in the same pattern as the sender, entering the encrypted letters on the keyboard lit up the letters of the original plaintext. Anyone who had an Enigma but was not privy to the rotor settings and attempted to read an encrypted message would have to try an almost infinite number of settings. This might take months or years, by which time the information would no longer have any value.

As war approached, the German armed forces purchased thousands of Enigma machines, each the size of a portable typewriter. They accompanied ships at sea, frontline troops, and squadrons of airplanes. The Germans considered their cipher unbreakable and their secrets safe from enemy eyes. They were wrong. Before the war began, Polish cryptanalysts had figured out how the Enigma worked and built some replicas. They also devised an electromechanical device they called "bomba" that went through rotor settings at blazing speed until it encountered an expression, such as "Heil Hitler," that often appeared in German messages. When the war broke out, these cryptanalysts fled to France. From there, the secret of the bomba passed to British cryptanalysts at a secret installation at Bletchley Park, north of London.

With this breakthrough, the British were able to read many Luftwaffe signals during the Battle of Britain in 1940. Cracking the German navy and army Enigmas proved to be much more difficult, for the other services used more rotors, changed the settings more frequently, and, most importantly, learned to avoid stock phrases. Nonetheless, by the spring of 1942, Bletchley Park had a staff of 1,500 handling some 40,000 German military messages a month. Their ability to read German messages was instrumental in the Allied victories against General Rommel in North Africa in 1942 and against the German U-boats in the Battle of the Atlantic in 1943.

Courtesy, Brian Johnson

The Enigma Machine   During World War II, German armed forces used Enigma machines like the one seen here in the vehicle of a German tank commander. With Enigmas, they could encrypt and decrypt radio messages, keeping them secret (they believed) from enemy code-breakers.

the population remained obedient and hard working. However, bombing raids against oil depots and synthetic fuel plants almost brought the German war effort to a standstill by early 1945.

Japanese cities were also the targets of American bombing raids. As early as April 1942 sixteen planes launched from an aircraft carrier bombed Tokyo. Later, as American forces captured islands close to Japan, the raids intensified. Their effect was even more devastating than the fire-bombing of German cities, for Japanese cities were made of wood. In March 1945 bombs set Tokyo ablaze, killing 80,000 people and leaving a million homeless.

Hulton Deutsch Collection/Corbis

U.S. Army Medics and Holocaust Victims When Allied troops entered the Nazi concentration camps, they found the bodies of thousands of victims of the Holocaust. In Dachau in southern Germany, two U.S. Army medics are overseeing a truckload of corpses to be taken to a burial site.

The Holocaust

In World War II, for the first time, more civilians than soldiers were deliberately put to death. The champions in the art of killing defenseless civilians were the Nazis. Their murders were not the accidental byproducts of some military goal but a calculated policy of exterminating whole races of people.

Their first targets were Jews. Soon after Hitler came to power, he deprived German Jews of their citizenship and legal rights. When eastern Europe fell under Nazi rule, the Nazis herded its large Jewish population into ghettos in the major cities, where many died of starvation and disease. Then, in early 1942, the Nazis decided to carry out Hitler's "final solution to the Jewish problem" by applying modern industrial methods to the slaughter of human beings. Thousands of ordinary German citizens supported and aided the genocide. Every day trainloads of cattle cars arrived at the extermination camps in eastern Europe and disgorged thousands of captives and the corpses of those who had died along the way. The strongest survivors were put to work and fed almost nothing until they died. Women, children, the elderly, and the sick were shoved into gas chambers and asphyxiated with poison gas. **Auschwitz**, the biggest camp,

Auschwitz Nazi extermination camp in Poland, the largest center of mass murder during the Holocaust. Close to a million Jews, Gypsies, Communists, and others were killed there.

Holocaust Nazis' program during World War II to kill people they considered undesirable. Some 6 million Jews perished during the Holocaust, along with millions of Poles, Gypsies, Communists, Socialists, and others.

was a giant industrial complex designed to kill up to twelve thousand people a day. This mass extermination, now called the **Holocaust** ("burning"), claimed some 6 million Jewish lives.

Besides the Jews, the Nazis also killed 3 million Polish Catholics—especially professionals, army officers, and the educated—in an effort to reduce the Polish people to slavery. They also exterminated homosexuals, Jehovah's Witnesses, Gypsies, the disabled, and the mentally ill—all in the interests of "racial purity." Whenever a German was killed in an occupied country, the Nazis retaliated by burning a village and all its inhabitants. After the invasion of Russia the Wehrmacht was given orders to execute all captured communists, government employees, and officers. They also worked millions of prisoners of war to death or let them die of starvation.

The Home Front in Europe and Asia

In the First World War there had been a clear distinction between the "front" and the "home front." Not so in World War II, where rapid military movements and air power carried the war into people's homes. For the civilian populations of China, Japan, Southeast Asia, and Europe, the war was far more terrifying than their worst nightmares. Armies swept through the land, confiscating food, fuel, and anything else of value. Bombers and heavy artillery pounded cities into rubble, leaving only the skeletons of buildings, while survivors cowered in cellars. Even when a city was not targeted, air-raid sirens awakened people throughout the night. In countries occupied by the Germans, the police arrested civilians, deporting many to die in concentration camps or to work as slave laborers in armaments factories. Millions fled their homes in terror, losing their families and friends. Even in Britain, children and the elderly were sent to live in the countryside.

The war demanded an enormous and sustained effort from all civilians, but more so in some countries than in others. In 1941, the Soviets dismantled over fifteen hundred factories and rebuilt them in the Ural Mountains and Siberia, where they soon turned out more tanks and artillery than the Axis.

e **PRIMARY SOURCE:**
Memoirs Read what the man responsible for administering and overseeing the Holocaust thought and felt about his "work."

Civilian Contributions

Half of the ships afloat in 1939 were sunk during the war, but the Allied losses were more than made up for by American shipyards, while Axis shipping was reduced to nothing by 1945. The production of aircraft, trucks, tanks, and other materiel showed a similar imbalance. Although the Axis powers made strenuous efforts to increase their production, they could not compete with the vast outpouring of Soviet tanks and American materiel.

Women at War

The Red Army eventually mobilized 22 million men; Soviet women took over half of all industrial and three-quarters of all agricultural jobs. In the other Allied countries, women also played major roles in the war effort, replacing men in fields, factories, and offices. The Nazis, in contrast, believed that German women should stay home and bear children, and they imported 7 million "guest workers"—a euphemism for captured foreigners.

The Home Front in the United States

The United States flourished during the war. Safe behind their oceans, Americans felt no bombs, saw no enemy soldiers, had almost no civilian casualties, and suffered fewer military casualties than other countries. The economy went into a prolonged boom after 1940. By 1944 the United States was producing twice as much as all the Axis powers combined. Thanks to huge military orders, jobs were plentiful, bread lines disappeared, and nutrition and health improved. Most Americans saved part of their paychecks, laying the basis for a phenomenal postwar consumer boom. Many Americans later looked back on the conflict as the "good war."

American Women

World War II also did much to weaken the hold of traditional ideas, as employers recruited women and members of racial minorities to work in jobs once reserved for white men. Six million women entered the labor force during the war, 2.5 million of them in manufacturing jobs previously considered "men's work." In a book entitled *Shipyard Diary of a Woman Welder* (1944), Augusta Clawson recalled her experiences in a shipyard in Oregon:

> *The job confirmed my strong conviction—I have stated it before—what exhausts the woman welder is not the work, not the heat, nor the demands upon physical strength. It is the apprehension that arises from inadequate skill and consequent lack of confidence; and this can be overcome by the right kind of training. . . . And so, in spite of the discomforts of climbing, heavy equipment, and heat, I enjoyed the work today because I could do it.[4]*

Many men opposed women doing work that would take them away from their families. As the labor shortage got worse, however, employers and politicians grudgingly admitted that the government ought to help provide day care for the children of working mothers. The entry of women into the labor force proved to be one of the most significant consequences of the war.

Racial Minorities

The war loosened racial bonds as well. Seeking work in war industries, 1.2 million African Americans migrated to the north and west. In the southwest Mexican immigrants took jobs in agriculture and war industries. But no new housing was built to accommodate the influx of migrants to the industrial cities, and many suffered from overcrowding and discrimination. In addition, 112,000 Japanese-Americans living on the west coast of the United States were arrested and herded into internment camps in the desert until the war was over, ostensibly for fear of spying and sabotage, but actually because of their race.

War and the Environment

During the Depression, construction and industry had slowed to a crawl, reducing environmental stress. The war reversed this trend, sharply accelerating pressures on the environment.

One reason for the change was the fighting itself. Battles scarred the

---

SECTION REVIEW

- World War II caused 60 million deaths, most of them civilians, as well as many refugees.

- Scientific technology, especially aircraft design, contributed to the mobility and violence of warfare.

- Allied bombing raids set fire to entire cities in both Europe and Japan.

- In the Holocaust, the Nazis murdered millions of Jews, Poles, Gypsies, and other minorities.

- Industrial economies, especially in the United States and Russia, mobilized civilians to manufacture war materiel.

- A booming American economy provided jobs for women and African Americans.

- Environments in war zones were badly damaged, and construction for the war transformed the environments of many countries.

landscape, leaving behind spent ammunition and damaged equipment. Retreating armies flooded large areas of China and the Netherlands. The bombing of cities left ruins that remained visible for a generation or more.

Construction

The main cause of environmental stress, however, was not the fighting but the economic development that sustained it. The war's half-million aircraft required thousands of air bases, many of them in the Pacific, China, Africa, and other parts of the world that had seldom seen an airplane before. Barracks, shipyards, docks, warehouses, and other military construction sprouted on every continent.

As war industries boomed, so did the demand for raw materials. Mining companies opened new mines and towns in Africa to supply strategic minerals. Latin American countries deprived of manufactured imports began building their own steel mills, factories, and shipyards. In India, China, and Europe, timber felling accelerated far beyond the reproduction rate of trees, replacing forests with denuded land. In a few instances, however, the war was good for the environment. For example, submarine warfare made fishing and whaling so dangerous that fish and whale populations had a few years in which to increase.

CONCLUSION

After the Great War ended, the world seemed to return to its prewar state, but it was an illusion. In the Soviet Union, Joseph Stalin was determined to turn his country into a modern industrial state at breakneck speed, regardless of the human cost. Several million people—most of them peasants—died, and millions more were enslaved during the Five-Year Plans and the collectivization of agriculture. By 1941 the USSR was much better prepared for a war with Germany than Russia had been in 1914–1917.

In 1929, after a few years of prosperity, the New York stock market collapsed. Within a few months, the world economy fell into the Great Depression, throwing millions out of work throughout the world. France and Britain survived the Depression by making their colonial empires purchase their products. Countries that were dependent on exports, such as Germany and Japan, suffered more. Only the USSR and southern Africa boomed during the 1930s.

In Italy, Mussolini installed Fascist Party members in all government jobs and jailed anyone who criticized him. In Germany, economic collapse led people to entrust their government to Adolf Hitler and his Nazi followers, who quickly set to work establishing a totalitarian government. Nazi Germany's rebuilding of its military and its invasion of Austria and Czechoslovakia were greeted with a policy of appeasement by Western democracies, until finally they could no longer overlook Germany's intentions.

Hard hit by the Depression, Japan saw China as a potential colony with resources to help solve its economic problems. In 1931, Japan conquered Manchuria. The United States and the League of Nations protested but did little else. Starting in 1937, a long and brutal war with China became a drain on the Japanese economy and resources. Meanwhile, the Communists, led by Mao Zedong, were slowly gaining support in the Chinese countryside.

The war spread to Europe in 1939 when Germany conquered Poland, then Denmark, Norway, the Low Countries, and France in 1940. The war turned global in 1941 when Germany invaded the Soviet Union and Japan attacked the United States. In 1943, the Red Army began to push the Germans back. Beginning in June 1944, Anglo-American forces, backed by the overwhelming industrial resources of the United States, drove German forces back from the west. U.S. naval victories in the Pacific and atomic weapons defeated Japan and ended the war in 1945.

The Second World War was by far the deadliest in history. Modern mechanized forces swept across entire nations and oceans. Their targets were not only each other's armed forces, but their civilian populations as well. Though Germany had considerable scientific and technical talent, the war favored the nations with the most heavy industries, namely, the United States and the Soviet Union. The Allies destroyed German and Japanese cities with fire-bombs, and the United States dropped atomic bombs on Hiroshima and Nagasaki. Of the roughly 60 million people who died in the war, most were civilians.

KEY TERMS

Joseph Stalin p. 796
Five-Year Plans p. 796
Benito Mussolini p. 802
Fascist Party p. 802

Adolf Hitler p. 803
Nazis p. 803
Chiang Kai-shek p. 805
Mao Zedong p. 805

Long March p. 806
Stalingrad p. 810
El Alamein p. 810
Pearl Harbor p. 811

Battle of Midway p. 811
Hiroshima p. 812
Auschwitz p. 816
Holocaust p. 816

EBOOK AND WEBSITE RESOURCES

e **Primary Sources**

The Decision to Use the Atomic Bomb

Memoirs

e **Interactive Maps**

Map 30.1 Chinese Communist Movement and the Sino-Japanese War, to 1938

Map 30.2 World War II in Europe and North Africa

Map 30.3 World War II in Asia and the Pacific

Plus flashcards, practice quizzes, and more. Go to:
www.cengage.com/history/bullietearthpeople5e

SUGGESTED READING

Burleigh, Michael. *Third Reich: A New History*. 2000. A thorough and up-to-date analysis of the history of Nazi Germany.

Chang, Iris. *The Rape of Nanking: The Forgotten Holocaust of World War II*. 1997. A best-selling account of one of the most sordid events of the Sino-Japanese War.

Chang, Jung. *Wild Swans: Three Daughters of China*. 1991. A biography of three generations of Chinese women who lived through the wars and revolutions of twentieth-century China.

Conquest, Robert. *The Great Terror: A Reassessment*. 1990. The definitive account of Stalin's purges and terror during the 1930s.

Dower, John. *War Without Mercy: Race and Power in the Pacific War*. 1987. An analysis of the role of racism—on both sides—that made the Pacific War especially brutal.

Frank, Anne. *The Diary of a Young Girl*. 1952. A classic account of the life of a Jewish family in hiding during the Nazi occupation of the Netherlands.

Hsiung, James, and Steven Levine, eds. *China's Bitter Victory: The War with Japan, 1937–1945*. 1992. Documents and accounts of the war in China.

Keegan, John. *The Second World War*. 1990. The best short history of the war by an eminent military historian.

McElvaine, Robert. *The Great Depression: America, 1929–1941*. 1993. A brief but well written account of the hardships of the 1930s.

Rhodes, Richard. *The Making of the Atomic Bomb*. 1986. A fascinating account of the Manhattan Project and its consequences.

Solzhenitsyn, Alexander. *One Day in the Life of Ivan Denisovich*. 1978. The novel that first revealed the existence of Stalin's concentration camps.

Spector, Ronald. *Eagle Against the Sun*. 1988. A popular history of the Pacific War.

Terkel, Studs. *"The Good War": An Oral History of World War Two*. 1984. Interviews with Americans about their experiences during World War II.

Volkogonov, Dmitrii. *Stalin: Triumph and Tragedy*. 1991. A classic biography of the great tyrant.

Wiesel, Eli. *Night*. 1960. The classic work recounting the horrors of the Holocaust.

NOTES

1. Apollonio Umbro, ed., *Documents of Twentieth Century Art: Futurist Manifestos* (New York: Viking Press, 1973), 23.

2. Richard F. Hamilton and Holger H. Herwig, *Decisions for War, 1914–1917* (Cambridge: Cambridge University Press, 2004), 199.

3. Gar Alperowitz, *Atomic Diplomacy: Hiroshima and Potsdam* (New York: Simon & Schuster, 1965), 176–181 and 236–242.

4. Rosalyn Fraad Baxandall, Linda Gordon, and Susan Reverby, eds., *America's Working Women* (New York: Random House, 1976), 253.

CHAPTER

31

CHAPTER OUTLINE

- The Indian Independence Movement, 1905–1947
- Sub-Saharan Africa, 1900–1945
- Mexico, Argentina, and Brazil, 1900–1949
- Conclusion

ENVIRONMENT + TECHNOLOGY   *Gandhi and Technology*

DIVERSITY + DOMINANCE   *A Vietnamese Nationalist Denounces French Colonialism*

Rush Hour in Brazil   In Latin American countries, modern conveniences, when first introduced, were often insufficient to meet the demand from eager customers. This streetcar in Rio de Janeiro carries twice as many passengers as it was designed for.

 Visit the website and ebook for additional study materials and interactive tools: www.cengage.com/history/bullietearthpeople5e

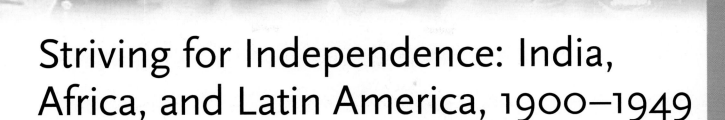

Striving for Independence: India, Africa, and Latin America, 1900–1949

Modern technologies first appeared in the wealthier countries of Europe and North America. When they were transferred to Asia, Africa, and Latin America, they reinforced those countries' dependence on the industrialized countries and widened the gap between their social classes. The tensions of modernization contributed to popular movements for independence and social justice.

The previous two chapters focused on a world convulsed by war and revolution. The world wars involved Europe, East Asia, the Middle East, and the United States and sparked violent revolutions in Russia and China. Parts of the world that were little touched by war also underwent profound changes in this period, partly for internal reasons and partly because of the warfare and revolution in other parts of the world.

In this chapter we examine the changes that took place in India, in sub-Saharan Africa, and in Mexico, Brazil, and Argentina. These three regions represent three very distinct cultures, yet they had much in common. India and Africa were colonies of Europe, both politically and economically. Though politically independent, the Latin American republics were dependent on Europe and the United States for the sale of commodities and for imports of manufactured goods, technology, and capital. In all three regions independence movements tried to wrest control from distant foreigners and improve the livelihood of their peoples. Their success was partial at best.

- Why did the educated elites of India want independence? What were ordinary Indians hoping for?
- What changes did foreign rule bring to Africa, and how did Africans respond?
- What could Latin Americans do to achieve social justice and economic development? Were these two goals compatible?

THE INDIAN INDEPENDENCE MOVEMENT, 1905–1947

Under British rule India acquired railroads, harbors, modern cities, and cotton and steel mills, as well as an active and worldly middle class. The economic transformation of the region awakened in this educated middle class a sense of national dignity that demanded political fulfillment. In response, the British gradually granted India a limited amount of political autonomy while maintaining overall control. Religious and communal tensions among the Indian peoples were carefully papered over, and when the British withdrew in 1947, violent conflicts tore India apart (see Map 31.1).

Interactive Map

MAP 31.1 **The Partition of India, 1947** Before the British, India was divided among many states, ethnic groups, and religions. When the British left in 1947, the subcontinent split along religious lines. The predominantly Muslim regions in the northwest and East Bengal in the east formed the new nation of Pakistan. The predominantly Hindu center became the Republic of India. Jammu and Kashmir remained disputed territories and poisoned relations between the two new countries.

The Land and the People

Much of India is fertile land, but it is vulnerable to droughts caused by the periodic failure of the monsoons. When the rains failed from 1896 to 1900, 2 million people died of starvation.

Despite periodic famines, the Indian population grew from 250 million in 1900 to 319 million in 1921 and 389 million in 1941. This growth created pressures in many areas. Landless young men converged on the cities, exceeding the number of jobs available in the slowly expanding industries. To produce timber for construction and railroad ties and to clear land for tea and rubber plantations, foresters cut down most of the tropical hardwood forests that had covered the subcontinent in the nineteenth century. But in spite of deforestation and extensive irrigation, the amount of land available to peasant families shrank with each successive generation. Economic development hardly benefited the average Indian.

Classes and Languages   Indians were divided into many classes. Peasants, always the great majority, paid rents to landowners, interest to village moneylenders, and taxes to the government and had little left to improve their land or raise their standard of living. The government protected property owners, from village moneylenders all the way up to the maharajahs (mah-huh-RAH-juh) or ruling princes, who owned huge tracts of land. The cities were crowded with craftsmen, traders, and

CHRONOLOGY

	India	Africa	Latin America
			1876–1910 Porfirio Díaz, dictator of Mexico
1900	1905 Viceroy Curzon splits Bengal; mass demonstrations	1900s Railroads connect ports to the interior	
	1906 Muslims found All-India Muslim League		
	1911 British transfer capital from Calcutta to Delhi	1912 African National Congress founded	1911–1919 Mexican Revolution
			1917 New constitution proclaimed in Mexico
1920	1919 Amritsar Massacre	1920s J. E. Casely Hayford organizes political movement in British West Africa	
	1929 Gandhi leads Walk to the Sea		1928 Plutarco Elías Calles founds Mexico's National Revolutionary Party
1930	1930s Gandhi calls for independence; he is repeatedly arrested		1930–1945 Getulio Vargas, dictator of Brazil
			1934–1940 Lázaro Cárdenas, president of Mexico
	1939 British bring India into World War II	1939–1945 A million Africans serve in World War II	1938 Cárdenas nationalizes Mexican oil industry; Vargas proclaims Estado Novo in Brazil
1940	1940 Muhammad Ali Jinnah demands a separate nation for Muslims		
			1943 Juan Perón leads military coup in Argentina
			1946 Perón elected president of Argentina
	1947 Partition and independence of India and Pakistan		

workers of all sorts, most very poor. Although the British had banned the burning of widows on their husbands' funeral pyres, in other respects women's lives changed little under British rule.

Indians also spoke many different languages. As a result of British rule and increasing trade and travel, English became the common medium of communication of the Western-educated middle class. This new class of English-speaking bureaucrats, professionals, and merchants was to play a leading role in the independence movement.

Religions

The majority of Indians who practiced Hinduism were subdivided into hundreds of castes, each affiliated with a particular occupation. Hinduism discouraged intermarriage and other social interactions among the castes and with non-Hindus. Until they were displaced by the British in the eighteenth century, Muslim rulers had dominated northern and central India, and Muslims now constituted one-quarter of the people of India but formed a majority in the northwest and in eastern Bengal. They felt discriminated against by both British and Hindus.

British Rule and Indian Nationalism

Colonial India was ruled by a viceroy appointed by the British government and administered by a few thousand members of the Indian Civil Service. These men, drawn mostly from the English gentry, believed it was their duty to protect the Indian people from the dangers of industrialization and to defend their own positions from Indian nationalists.

As Europeans they admired modern technology. They encouraged railroads, harbors, telegraphs, and other communications technologies, as well as irrigation and plantations, because these increased India's foreign trade and strengthened British control. Yet, they discouraged the cotton and steel industries and limited the training of Indian engineers, to spare India the social upheavals that had accompanied the Industrial Revolution in Europe while protecting British industry from Indian competition.

Construction Site in Colonial India British civil engineers were active throughout India building roads, railroads, and canals. Here, a British official supervises Indian workers building a bridge.

Indian National Congress A movement and political party founded in 1885 to demand greater Indian participation in government. Its membership was middle class, and its demands were modest until World War I. Led after 1920 by Mohandas K. Gandhi, it appealed increasingly to the poor, and it organized mass protests demanding self-government and independence.

Racism and the Indian National Congress

Bengal Region of northeastern India. It was the first part of India to be conquered by the British in the eighteenth century and remained the political and economic center of British India throughout the nineteenth century. The 1905 split of the province into predominantly Hindu West Bengal and predominantly Muslim East Bengal (now Bangladesh) sparked anti-British riots.

The Muslim League

All-India Muslim League Political organization founded in India in 1906 to defend the interests of India's Muslim minority. Led by Muhammad Ali Jinnah, it attempted to negotiate with the Indian National Congress. In 1940, the League began demanding a separate state for Muslims, to be called Pakistan.

The Indian Steel Industry

The Billie Love Collection

At the turn of the century most Indians—especially peasants, landowners, and princes—accepted British rule. But the Europeans' racist attitude toward dark-skinned people increasingly offended Indians who had learned English and absorbed English ideas of freedom and representative government, only to discover that racial quotas excluded them from the Indian Civil Service, the officer corps, and prestigious country clubs.

In 1885 a small group of English-speaking Hindu professionals founded a political organization called the **Indian National Congress**. For twenty years its members respectfully petitioned the government for access to higher administrative positions and for a voice in official decisions, but they had little influence. Then, in 1905, Viceroy Lord Curzon divided the province of **Bengal** in two to improve the efficiency of its administration. This decision, made without consulting anyone, angered not only educated Indians, who saw it as a way to lessen their influence, but also millions of uneducated Hindu Bengalis, who found themselves outnumbered by Muslims in East Bengal. Soon Bengal was the scene of demonstrations, boycotts of British goods, and even incidents of violence against the British.

In 1906, while the Hindus of Bengal were protesting the partition of their province, Muslims, fearful of Hindu dominance elsewhere in India, founded the **All-India Muslim League**. The government responded by granting Indians a limited franchise based on wealth. Muslims, however, were on average poorer than Hindus, for many poor and low-caste Hindus had converted to Islam to escape caste discrimination. Taking advantage of these religious divisions, the British instituted separate representation and different voting qualifications for Hindus and Muslims. Then, in 1911, the British transferred the capital of India from Calcutta to Delhi (DEL-ee), the former capital of the Mughal (MOO-guhl) emperors. These changes disturbed Indians of all classes and religions and raised their political consciousness. Politics, once primarily the concern of westernized intellectuals, turned into two mass movements: one by Hindus and one by Muslims.

British geologists looked for minerals, such as coal or manganese, that British industry required. However, when the only Indian member of the Indian Geological Service, Pramatha Nath Bose, wanted to prospect for iron ore, he had to resign because the government wanted no part of an Indian steel industry that could compete with that of Britain. Bose joined forces with Jamsetji Tata, a Bombay textile magnate who decided to produce steel in spite of British opposition. With the help of German and American engineers and equipment, Tata's son Dorabji opened the first steel mill in India in 1911, in a town called Jamshedpur in honor of his father. Although it produced only a fraction of the steel that India required, Jamshedpur became a pow-

The Amritsar Massacre

Mohandas K. Gandhi Leader of the Indian independence movement and advocate of nonviolent resistance. After being educated as a lawyer in England, he returned to India and became leader of the Indian National Congress in 1920. He appealed to the poor, led nonviolent demonstrations against British colonial rule, and was jailed many times. Soon after independence he was assassinated for attempting to stop Hindu-Muslim rioting.

erful symbol of Indian national pride. It also prompted Indian nationalists to ask why a country that could produce its own steel needed foreigners to run its government.

During World War I Indians supported Britain enthusiastically; 1.2 million men volunteered for the army, and millions more voluntarily contributed money to the government. Many expected the British to reward their loyalty with political concessions. Others organized to demand a voice in the government. In 1917, in response to the agitation, the British government announced "the gradual development of self-governing institutions with a view to the progressive realization of responsible government in India as an integral part of the British Empire." This sounded like a promise of self-government, but the timetable was so vague that nationalists denounced it as a devious maneuver to postpone India's independence.

On April 13, 1919, in the city of Amritsar, General Reginald Dyer ordered his troops to fire into a peaceful crowd of some 10,000 demonstrators, killing at least 379 and wounding 1,200. While waves of angry demonstrations swept over India, the British House of Lords voted to approve Dyer's actions, and a fund was raised in appreciation of his services. Indians interpreted these gestures as showing British contempt for their colonial subjects. In the charged atmosphere of the time, the period of gradual accommodation between the British and the Indians came to a close.

Mahatma Gandhi and Militant Nonviolence

For the next twenty years India teetered on the edge of violent uprisings and harsh repression, possibly even war. That it did not succumb was due to **Mohandas K. Gandhi** (GAHN-dee) (1869–1948), a man known to his followers as "Mahatma," the "great soul."

Gandhi began life with every advantage. His family was wealthy enough to send him to England for his education. After his studies he lived in South Africa and practiced law for the small Indian community there. During World War I he returned to India and was one of many Western-educated Hindu intellectuals who joined the Indian National Congress.

Unlike many radical political thinkers of his time, Gandhi denounced the popular ideals of power, struggle, and combat. Instead, inspired by both Hindu and Christian ideals, he preached the saintly virtues of *ahimsa* (uh-HIM-sah) (nonviolence) and *satyagraha* (suh-TYAH-gruh-huh) (the search for truth). He refused to countenance violence among his followers and called off several demonstrations when they turned violent.

In 1921 Gandhi gave up the Western-style suits worn by lawyers and the fine raiment of wealthy Indians and henceforth wore simple peasant garb: a length of homespun cloth below his waist and a shawl to cover his torso (see Environment and Technology: Gandhi and Technology). He spoke for the farmers and the outcasts, whom he called *harijan* (HAH-ree-jahn), "children of God." He attracted ever-larger numbers of followers among the poor and the illiterate, who soon began to revere him; and he transformed the cause of Indian independence from an elite movement of the educated into a mass movement with a quasi-religious aura.

Gandhi was a brilliant political tactician and a master of public relations gestures. In 1929, for instance, he led a few followers on an 80-mile (129-kilometer) walk, camped on a beach, and gathered salt from the sea in a blatant and well-publicized act of civil disregard for the government's monopoly on salt. But he discovered that unleashing the power of popular participation was one thing and controlling its direction was quite another. Within days of his "Walk to the Sea," demonstrations of support broke out all over India, in which the police killed a hundred demonstrators and arrested over sixty thousand.

Many times during the 1930s Gandhi threatened to fast "unto death," and several times he came close to death, to protest the violence of both the police and his followers and to demand independence. He was repeatedly arrested and spent a total of six years in jail. But every arrest made him more popular. He became a cult figure not only in his own country but also in the Western media. In the words of historian Percival Spear, he made the British "uncomfortable in their cherished field of moral rectitude," and he gave Indians the feeling that theirs was the ethically superior cause.

India Moves Toward Independence

In the 1920s, slowly and reluctantly, the British handed over control of "national" areas such as education, the economy, and public works to Indians. They also gradually admitted more Indians into the Civil Service and the officer corps.

Gandhi and Technology

In the twentieth century all political leaders but one embraced modern industrial technology. That one exception is Gandhi.

After deciding to wear only handmade cloth, Gandhi made a bonfire of imported factory-made cloth and began spending half an hour every day spinning yarn on a simple spinning wheel, a task he called a "sacrament." The spinning wheel became the symbol of his movement and was later incorporated into the Indian flag. Any Indian who wished to come before him had to dress in handwoven cloth.

Gandhi had several reasons for reviving this ancient craft. One was his revulsion against "the incessant search for material comforts," an evil to which Europeans were "becoming slaves." He blamed the impoverishment of the Indian people on the cotton industries of England and Japan, which had ruined the traditional cotton manufacturing by which India had once supplied all her own needs. Gandhi looked back to a time before India became a colony of Britain, when "our women spun fine yarns in their own cottages, and supplemented the earnings of their husbands." The spinning wheel, he believed, was "presented to the nation for giving occupation to the millions who had, at least four months of the year, nothing to do." A return to the spinning wheel would provide employment to millions of Indians and would also become a symbol of "national consciousness and a contribution by every individual to a definite constructive national work."

Nevertheless, Gandhi was a shrewd politician who understood the usefulness of modern devices for mobilizing the masses and organizing his followers. He wore a watch and used the telephone and the printing press to keep in touch with his followers. When he traveled by train, he rode third class—but in a third-class railroad car of his own. His goal was

Time Life Pictures/Getty Images

Gandhi at the Spinning Wheel Mahatma Gandhi chose the spinning wheel as his symbol because it represented the traditional activity of millions of rural Indians whose livelihoods were threatened by industrialization.

the independence of his country, and he pursued it with every nonviolent means he could find.

Gandhi's ideas challenge us to rethink the purpose of technology. Was he opposed on principle to all modern devices? Was he an opportunist who used those devices that served his political ends and rejected those that did not? Or did he have a higher principle that accounts for his willingness to use the telephone and the railroad but not factory-made cloth?

Jawaharlal Nehru Indian statesman who succeeded Mohandas K. Gandhi as leader of the Indian National Congress. He negotiated the end of British colonial rule in India and became India's first prime minister (1947–1964).

India in World War II

In the years before the Second World War, Indian politicians obtained the right to erect high tariff barriers against imports to protect India's infant industries from foreign competition. Behind these barriers, Indian entrepreneurs built plants to manufacture iron and steel, cement, paper, textiles, sugar, and other products. This early industrialization did not provide enough jobs to improve the lives of the Indian peasants or urban poor, but it created a class of wealthy Indian businessmen who supported the Indian National Congress and its demands for independence. Though paying homage to Gandhi, they preferred his designated successor as leader of the Indian National Congress, **Jawaharlal Nehru** (NAY-roo) (1889–1964). Unlike Gandhi, Nehru looked forward to creating a modern industrial India.

Congress politicians won regional elections but continued to be excluded from the viceroy's cabinet, the true center of power. When World War II began, Viceroy Lord Linlithgow declared war without consulting a single Indian. The Congress-dominated provincial governments resigned in protest and found that boycotting government office increased their popular support. When the British offered to give India its independence once the war ended, Gandhi demanded full independence immediately. His "Quit India" campaign aroused popular demonstrations against the British and provoked a wave of arrests, including his own. The Second World War divided the Indian people. Most Indian soldiers felt they were fighting to defend their country rather than to support the British Empire. As in World War I, Indians contributed heav-

Margaret Bourke-White, Time Life Pictures/Getty Images

The Partition of India   When India became independent, Muslims fled from Hindu regions, and Hindus fled from Muslims. Margaret Bourke-White photographed a long line of refugees, with their cows, carts, and belongings, trudging down a country road toward safety.

ily to the Allied war effort, supplying 2 million soldiers and enormous amounts of resources, especially the timber needed for emergency construction. A small number of Indians, however, were so anti-British that they joined the Japanese side.

Partition and Independence

Muhammad Ali Jinnah
Indian Muslim politician who founded the state of Pakistan. A lawyer by training, he joined the All-India Muslim League in 1913. As leader of the League from the 1920s on, he negotiated with the British and the Indian National Congress for Muslim participation in Indian politics. From 1940 on, he led the movement for the independence of India's Muslims in a separate state of Pakistan, founded in 1947.

Violence

When the war ended, Britain's new Labour Party government prepared for Indian independence, but deep suspicions between Hindus and Muslims complicated the process. The break between the two communities had started in 1937, when the Indian National Congress won provincial elections and refused to share power with the Muslim League. In 1940 the leader of the League, **Muhammad Ali Jinnah** (JEE-nah) (1876–1948), demanded what many Muslims had been dreaming of for years: a country of their own, to be called Pakistan.

As independence approached, talks between Jinnah and Nehru broke down and battle lines were drawn. Violent rioting between Hindus and Muslims broke out. Gandhi's appeals for tolerance and cooperation fell on deaf ears. The British made frantic proposals to keep India united, but their authority was waning fast.

In early 1947 the Indian National Congress accepted the partition of India into two states, one secular but dominated by Hindus, the other Muslim. On August 15 British India gave way to a new India and Pakistan. The Indian National Congress, led by Nehru, formed the first government of India; Jinnah and the Muslim League established a government for the provinces that made up Pakistan.

The rejoicing over independence was marred by violent outbreaks between Muslims and Hindus. In protest against the mounting chaos, Gandhi refused to attend the independence day celebration. Throughout the land, Muslim and Hindu neighbors turned on one another, and armed members of one faith hunted down people of the other faith. Leaving most of their possessions behind, Hindus fled from predominantly Muslim areas, and Muslims fled from Hindu areas. Trainloads of desperate refugees of one faith were attacked and massacred by members of the other or were left stranded in the middle of deserts. Within a few months some 12 million people had abandoned their ancestral homes and a half-million lay dead. In January 1948 Gandhi died too, gunned down by an angry Hindu refugee.

After the sectarian massacres and flights of refugees, Muslims were a minority in all but one state of India. That state was Kashmir, a strategically important region in the foothills of the Himalayas. India annexed Kashmir because the local maharajah was Hindu and because the state held the headwaters of the rivers that irrigated millions of acres of farmland. Most inhabitants would have joined Pakistan if they had been allowed to vote on the matter. The annexation of Kashmir turned India and Pakistan into bitter enemies that have fought several wars in the past half-century.

SECTION REVIEW

- Under British rule, India's population grew but remained divided by religion and caste.

- The British introduced certain modern technologies but discouraged Indian industry that might compete with British industry.

- British racial policies, brutality, and arrogance awakened a sense of nationhood among educated Indians.

- The Indian National Congress and the All-India Muslim League demanded independence.

- Mahatma Gandhi led the independence movement using nonviolent tactics and turned an upper-class rebellion into one involving all of India.

- Nehru, Gandhi's successor, wanted to modernize India, and the Indian National Congress resisted British rule during World War II.

- When the British left India in 1947, it split into two nations amidst widespread riots and massacres between Hindus and Muslims.

SUB-SAHARAN AFRICA, 1900–1945

Of all the continents, Africa was the last to come under European rule (see Chapter 28). The first half of the twentieth century, the time when nationalist movements threatened European rule in Asia (see Diversity and Dominance: A Vietnamese Nationalist Denounces French Colonialism), was Africa's period of classic colonialism. After World War I Britain, France, Belgium, and South Africa divided Germany's African colonies among themselves. Then in the 1930s Italy invaded Ethiopia. The colonial empires reached their peak shortly before World War II.

Colonial Africa: Economic and Social Changes

Outside of Algeria, Kenya, and South Africa, few Europeans lived in Africa. In 1930 Nigeria, with a population of 20 million, was ruled by 386 British officials and by 8,000 policemen and military, of whom 150 were European. Yet even such a small presence stimulated deep social and economic changes.

The colonial powers had built railroads from coastal cities to mines and plantations in the interior to transport raw materials to the industrial world, but few Africans benefited from these changes. Colonial governments took lands from Africans and sold or leased them to European companies or to white settlers. Large European companies dominated wholesale commerce, while Indians, Greeks, and Syrians handled much of the retail trade.

African Farmers Where land was divided into small farms, some Africans benefited from the boom. Farmers in the Gold Coast (now Ghana [GAH-nuh]) profited from the high price of cocoa, as did palm-oil producers in Nigeria and coffee growers in East Africa. In most of Africa women played a major role in the retail trades, selling cloth, food, pots and pans, and other items in the markets. Many maintained their economic independence and kept their household finances separate from those of their husbands, following a custom that predated the colonial period.

For many Africans, however, economic development meant working in European-owned mines and plantations, often under compulsion. Colonial governments were eager to develop the resources of the territories under their control but would not pay wages high enough to attract

Making Palm Oil Palm oil is one of the most important crops of West Africa. Here two farm women are extracting the oil from palm kernels with a simple press.

workers. Instead, they used their police powers to force Africans to work under harsh conditions for little or no pay. In the 1920s, when the government of French Equatorial Africa decided to build a railroad from Brazzaville to the Atlantic coast, a distance of 312 miles (502 kilometers), it drafted 127,000 men to carve a roadbed across mountains and through rain forests. For lack of food, clothing, and medical care, 20,000 of them died, an average of 64 deaths per mile of track.

African Health

Europeans prided themselves on bringing modern health care to Africa; yet before the 1930s other aspects of colonialism actually worsened public health. Migrants and soldiers spread syphilis, gonorrhea, tuberculosis, and malaria. Sleeping sickness and smallpox epidemics raged throughout Central Africa. In recruiting men to work, colonial governments also depleted rural areas of farmers needed to plant and harvest crops. Forced requisitions of food to feed the workers left the remaining populations undernourished and vulnerable to diseases. Not until the 1930s did colonial governments realize the negative consequences of their labor policies and begin to invest in agricultural development and health care for Africans.

In 1900 Ibadan (ee-BAH-dahn) in Nigeria was the only city in sub-Saharan Africa with more than 100,000 inhabitants; fifty years later, dozens of cities had reached that size. Africans migrated to cities because they offered hope of jobs and excitement and, for a few, the chance to become wealthy.

However, migrations damaged the family life of those involved, for almost all the migrants were men leaving women in the countryside to farm and raise children. Reflecting the colonialists' attitudes, cities built during the colonial period had racially segregated housing, clubs, restaurants, hospitals, and other institutions. Patterns of racial discrimination were most rigid in the white-settler colonies of eastern and southern Africa.

Religious and Political Changes

Traditional religious belief could not explain the dislocations that foreign rule, migrations, and sudden economic changes brought to the lives of Africans. Many therefore turned to Christianity or Islam.

A Vietnamese Nationalist Denounces French Colonialism

Movements for independence were a worldwide phenomenon. The tactics that different peoples used to achieve their goals differed widely. Among countries that were formal colonies, the case of India is unique in that its nationalist movement was led by Mahatma Gandhi, a man committed to nonviolent passive resistance. Elsewhere, revolutionary movements were often associated with violent uprisings. French Indochina is a case in point.

Indochina was conquered by the French from 1862 to 1895, after overcoming fierce resistance. Thereafter, France modernized the cities and irrigation systems and transformed the country into a leading producer of tea, rice, and natural rubber. This meant transferring large numbers of landless peasants to new plantations and destroying the traditional social structure. To govern Indochina, the French brought in more soldiers and civil administrators than the British had in all of India, a far larger colony. While they succeeded in crushing the resistance of the peasants and the old elites, the French were educating a new elite in the French language. These youths, inspired by French ideas of liberty and nationhood and by the example of neighboring China, formed the core of two new revolutionary movements.

One movement was the Vietnamese Revolutionary Youth League founded by Ho Chi Minh (1890-1969) in 1925, which later became the Indochinese Communist Party. The other was the Vietnamese Nationalist Party, founded in 1927 by a schoolteacher named Nguyen Thai Hoc (1904-1930). This party attracted government employees, soldiers, and small businessmen. At first Nguyen Thai Hoc lobbied the colonial government for reforms, but in vain. Two years later he turned to revolutionary action. In February 1930 he led an uprising at Yen Bay that the French quickly crushed. He and many of his followers were executed four months later, leaving Ho Chi Minh's Communists as the standard-bearers of nationalist revolution in Vietnam.

While awaiting his execution, Nguyen Thai Hoc wrote the following letter to the French Chamber of Deputies to justify his actions.

Gentlemen:

I, the undersigned, Nguyen Thai Hoc, a Vietnamese citizen, twenty-six years old, chairman and founder of the Vietnamese Nationalist Party, at present arrested and imprisoned at the jail of Yen Bay, Tongking, Indochina, have the great honor to inform you of the following facts:

According to the tenets of justice, everyone has the right to defend his own country when it is invaded by foreigners, and according to the principles of humanity, everyone has the duty to save his compatriots when they are in difficulty or in danger. As for myself, I have assessed the fact that my country has been annexed by you French for more than sixty years. I realize that under your dictatorial yoke, my compatriots have experienced a very hard life, and my people will without doubt be completely annihilated, by the naked principle of natural selection. Therefore, my right and my duty have compelled me to seek every way to defend my country which has been invaded and occupied, and to save my people who are in great danger.

At the beginning, I had thought to cooperate with the French in Indochina in order to serve my compatriots, my country and my people, particularly in the areas of cultural and economic development. As regards economic development, in 1925 I sent a memorandum to Governor General Varenne, describing to him all our aspirations concerning the protection of local industry and commerce in Indochina. I urged strongly in the same letter the creation of a Superior School of Industrial Development in Tongking. In 1926 I again addressed another letter to the then Governor General of Indochina in which I included some explicit suggestions to relieve the hardships of our poor people. In 1927, for a third time, I sent a letter to the Résident Supérieur [provincial administrator] in Tongking, requesting permission to publish a weekly magazine with the aim of safeguarding and encouraging local industry and com-

Christianity and Islam   Christianity was introduced into Africa by Western missionaries, except in Ethiopia, where it was indigenous. It was most successful in West and South Africa, where the European influence was strongest. A major attraction of the Christian denominations was their mission schools, which taught both craft skills and basic literacy, providing access to employment as minor functionaries, teachers, and shopkeepers. These schools educated a new elite, many of whom learned not only skills and literacy but Western political ideas as well. Many Africans accepted Christianity enthusiastically, reading the suffering of their own peoples into the biblical stories of Moses and the parables of Jesus. The churches trained some of the brighter pupils to become catechists, teachers, and clergymen. Independent Christian churches associated Christian beliefs with radical ideas of racial equality and participation in politics.

Islam spread inland from the East African coast and southward from the Sahel (SAH-hel) through the influence and example of Arab and African merchants. Islam also emphasized merce. With regard to the cultural domain, I sent a letter to the Governor General in 1927, requesting (1) the privilege of opening tuition-free schools for the children of the lower classes, particularly children of workers and peasants; (2) freedom to open popular publishing houses and libraries in industrial centers.

It is absolutely ridiculous that every suggestion has been rejected. My letters were without answer; my plans have not been considered; my requests have been ignored; even the articles that I sent to newspapers have been censored and rejected. From the experience of these rejections, I have come to the conclusion that the French have no sincere intention of helping my country or my people. I also concluded that we have to expel France. For this reason, in 1927, I began to organize a revolutionary party, which I named the Vietnamese Nationalist Party, with the aim of overthrowing the dictatorial and oppressive administration of our country. We aspire to create a Republic of Vietnam, composed of persons sincerely concerned with the happiness of the people. My party is a clandestine organization, and in February 1929, it was uncovered by the security police. Among the members of my party, a great number have been arrested. Fifty-two persons have been condemned to forced labor ranging from two to twenty years. Although many have been detained and many others unjustly condemned, my party has not ceased its activity. Under my guidance, the Party continues to operate and progress towards its aim.

During the Yen Bay uprising someone succeeded in killing some French officers. The authorities accused my party of having organized and perpetrated this revolt. They have accused me of having given the orders for the massacre. In truth, I have never given such orders, and I have presented before the Penal Court of Yen Bay all the evidence showing the inanity of this accusation. Even so, some of the members of my party completely ignorant of that event have been accused of participating in it. The French Indochinese government burned and destroyed their houses. They sent French troops to occupy their villages and stole their rice to divide it among the soldiers. Not just members of my party

have been suffering from this injustice—we should rather call this cruelty rather than injustice—but also many simple peasants, interested only in their daily work in the rice fields, living miserable lives like buffaloes and horses, have been compromised in this reprisal. At the present time, in various areas there are tens of thousands of men, women, and children, persons of all ages, who have been massacred. They died either of hunger or exposure because the French Indochinese government burned their homes. I therefore beseech you in tears to redress this injustice which otherwise will annihilate my people, which will stain French honor, and which will belittle all human values. . . .

If France wants to stay in peace in Indochina, if France does not want to have increasing troubles with revolutionary movements, she should immediately modify the cruel and inhuman policy now practiced in Indochina. The French should behave like friends to the Vietnamese, instead of being cruel and oppressive masters. They should be attentive to the intellectual and material sufferings of the Vietnamese people, instead of being harsh and tough. Please, Gentlemen, receive my gratitude.

QUESTIONS FOR ANALYSIS

1. When he first became involved in politics, what were Nguyen Thai Hoc's views of French colonialism?

2. What were his first initiatives, and what response did he get from the French colonial administration?

3. What motivated Nguyen Thai Hoc to organize an uprising, and what was the response of the French?

4. Compare Nguyen Thai Hoc's views and methods and the French response with the situation in India.

Source: Harry Benda and John Larkin, *The World of Southeast Asia* (New York: Harper & Row, 1967), 182–185. Reprinted by permission of the author.

A Quranic School In Muslim countries, religious education is centered on learning to read, write, and recite the Quran, the sacred book of the Islamic religion, in the original Arabic. This picture shows boys in a Libyan madrasa (Quranic school) studying writing and religion.

Olivier Martel/Corbis

literacy—in Arabic rather than in a European language—and was less disruptive of traditional African customs such as polygamy.

Early Political Movements

Blaise Diagne Senegalese political leader. He was the first African elected to the French National Assembly. During World War I, in exchange for promises to give French citizenship to Senegalese, he helped recruit Africans to serve in the French army. After the war, he led a movement to abolish forced labor in Africa.

Africa in World War II

In Dakar in Senegal and Cape Town in South Africa, small numbers of Africans could obtain secondary education. Even smaller numbers went on to college in Europe or America. Though few in number, they became the leaders of political movements. The contrast between the liberal ideas imparted by Western education and the realities of racial discrimination under colonial rule contributed to the rise of nationalism among educated Africans. In Senegal **Blaise Diagne** (dee-AHN-yuh) agitated for African participation in politics and fair treatment in the French army during World War I, and in the 1920s J. E. Casely Hayford began organizing a movement for greater autonomy in British West Africa. These nationalist movements were inspired by the ideas of Pan-Africanists from America such as W. E. B. Du Bois and Marcus Garvey, who advocated the unity of African peoples around the world, as well as by European ideas of liberty and nationhood. To defend the interests of Africans, Western-educated lawyers and journalists in South Africa founded the **African National Congress** in 1912. Before World War II, however, these nationalist movements were small and had little influence.

The Second World War had a profound effect on the peoples of Africa, even those far removed from the theaters of war. The war brought hardships, such as increased forced labor, inflation, and requisitions of raw materials. Yet it also brought hope. During the campaign to oust the Italians from Ethiopia, Emperor **Haile Selassie** (HI-lee seh-LASS-ee) (r. 1930–1974) led his own troops into Addis Ababa, his capital, and reclaimed his title. A million Africans served as soldiers and carriers in Burma, North Africa, and Europe, where many became aware of Africa's role in helping the Allied war effort. They listened to Allied propaganda in favor of European liberation movements and against Nazi racism and returned to their countries with new and radical ideas.

SECTION REVIEW

- Colonial rule developed Africa's economies at the expense of its peoples' livelihoods and health.

- Many Africans turned to Christianity or Islam; some, especially those who participated in World War II, began to demand independence.

MEXICO, ARGENTINA, AND BRAZIL, 1900–1949

African National Congress An organization dedicated to obtaining equal voting and civil rights for black inhabitants of South Africa. Founded in 1912 as the South African Native National Congress, it changed its name in 1923. Though it was banned and its leaders were jailed for many years, it eventually helped bring majority rule to South Africa.

Haile Selassie Emperor of Ethiopia (r. 1930–1974) and symbol of African independence. He fought the Italian invasion of his country in 1935 and regained his throne during World War II, when British forces expelled the Italians. He ruled Ethiopia as a traditional autocracy until he was overthrown in 1974.

Latin America achieved independence from Spain and Portugal in the nineteenth century but did not industrialize. Most Latin American republics, suffering from ideological divisions, unstable governments, and violent upheavals, traded their commodities for foreign manufactured goods and investments and became economically dependent on the United States and Great Britain. Their societies remained deeply split between wealthy landowners and desperately poor peasants.

Mexico, Brazil, and Argentina contained well over half of Latin America's land, population, and wealth, and their relations with other countries and their economies were quite similar. Mexico, however, underwent a traumatic social revolution, while Argentina and Brazil evolved more peaceably.

Background to Revolution: Mexico in 1910

At the beginning of the twentieth century Mexican society was divided into rich and poor and into persons of Spanish, Indian, and mixed ancestry. A few very wealthy families of Spanish origin, less than 1 percent of the population, owned 85 percent of Mexico's land, mostly in huge *haciendas* (estates). A handful of American and British companies controlled most of Mexico's railroads, silver mines, plantations, and other productive enterprises. At the other end of the social scale were Indians, many of whom did not speak Spanish. *Mestizos* (mess-TEE-so), people of mixed Indian and European ancestry, were only slightly better off; most of them were peasants who worked on the haciendas or farmed small communal plots near their ancestral villages.

After independence in 1821 wealthy Mexican families and American companies used bribery and force to acquire millions of acres of good agricultural land from villages in southern

Mexico. Peasants lost not only their fields but also their access to firewood and pasture for their animals and had little choice but to work on haciendas. To survive, they had to buy food and other necessities on credit from the landowner's store; eventually, they fell permanently into debt.

The Díaz Regime

For thirty-four years General Porfirio Díaz (DEE-as) (1830–1915) had ruled Mexico under the motto "Liberty, Order, Progress." To Díaz "liberty" meant freedom for rich hacienda owners and foreign investors to acquire more land. The government imposed "order" through rigged elections, bribes to Díaz's supporters, and summary justice for those who opposed him. "Progress" meant mainly the importing of foreign capital, machinery, and technicians to take advantage of Mexico's labor, soil, and natural resources.

During the Díaz years (1876–1910) Mexico City became a showplace with paved streets, streetcar lines, electric street lighting, and public parks. New telegraph and railroad lines connected cities and towns throughout Mexico. But this material progress benefited only a handful of well-connected businessmen and lowered the average Mexican's standard of living.

Emiliano Zapata Revolutionary and leader of peasants in the Mexican Revolution. He mobilized landless peasants in south-central Mexico in an attempt to seize and divide the lands of the wealthy landowners. Though successful for a time, he was ultimately defeated and assassinated.

Though a mestizo himself, Díaz discriminated against the nonwhite majority of Mexicans. He and his supporters tried to eradicate what they saw as Mexico's rustic traditions. On many middle- and upper-class tables French cuisine replaced traditional Mexican dishes, and the wealthy replaced sombreros and ponchos with European garments. To the educated middle class—the only group with a strong sense of Mexican nationhood—this devaluation of Mexican culture became a symbol of the Díaz regime's failure to defend national interests against foreign influences.

Revolution and Civil War in Mexico

Brown Brothers

Emiliano Zapata Zapata, the leader of a peasant rebellion in southern Mexico during the Mexican Revolution, stands in full revolutionary regalia: sword, rifles, bandoleers, boots, and sombrero.

The Mexican Revolution was a social revolution that developed haphazardly under ambitious but limited leaders, each representing a different segment of Mexican society. The first was Francisco I. Madero (1873–1913), the son of a wealthy landowning and mining family, educated in the United States. When minor uprisings broke out in 1911, the government collapsed and Díaz fled into exile. The Madero presidency was welcomed by some, but it aroused opposition from peasant leaders like **Emiliano Zapata** (sah-PAH-tah) (1879–1919). In 1913, after two years as president, Madero was overthrown and murdered by one of his former supporters, General Victoriano Huerta. Woodrow Wilson (1856–1924), president of the United States, showed his displeasure by sending the United States Marines to occupy Veracruz.

The inequities of Mexican society and foreign intervention angered Mexico's middle class and industrial workers. They found leaders in Venustiano Carranza, a landowner, and in Alvaro Obregón (oh-bray-GAWN), a schoolteacher. Calling themselves Constitutionalists, Carranza and Obregón organized private armies and overthrew Huerta in 1914. By then, the revolution had spread to the countryside.

Francisco "Pancho" Villa   Francisco "Pancho" Villa led an army of cowboys and ranch hands in northern Mexico during the revolution. He became very popular by confiscating large haciendas and dividing them among the poor. In March 1916 he entered the United States with 500 soldiers and attacked the town of Columbus, New Mexico, provoking an American invasion of Mexico. He was assassinated in 1923.

Zapata and Villa

Zapata, an Indian farmer, had led a revolt against the haciendas in the mountains of Morelos, south of Mexico City (see Map 31.2). His soldiers were peasants mounted on horseback and armed with pistols and rifles. For several years they periodically came down from the mountains, burned hacienda buildings, and returned land to the Indian villages to which it had once belonged.

Another leader appeared in Chihuahua, a northern state where seventeen individuals owned two-fifths of the land and 95 percent of the people had no land at all. Starting in 1913, **Francisco "Pancho" Villa** (1877–1923), a former ranch hand, mule driver, and bandit, organized an army of three thousand men, most of them cowboys, and divided large haciendas into family ranches.

Francisco "Pancho" Villa
A popular leader during the Mexican Revolution. An outlaw in his youth, when the revolution started, he formed a cavalry army in the north of Mexico and fought for the rights of the land-less in collaboration with Emiliano Zapata. He was assassinated in 1923.

Zapata and Villa enjoyed tremendous popular support but could never rise above their regional and peasant origins and lead a national revolution. The Constitutionalists had fewer soldiers than Zapata and Villa, but they held the major cities and used the proceeds of oil sales to buy modern weapons. Gradually the Constitutionalists took over most of Mexico. In 1919 they defeated and killed Zapata; Villa was assassinated four years later. An estimated 2 million people lost their lives in the civil war, and much of Mexico lay in ruins.

During their struggle to win support against Zapata and Villa, the Constitutionalists adopted many of their rivals' agrarian reforms, such as restoring communal lands to the Indians of Morelos. The Constitutionalists also proposed social programs designed to appeal to workers and the middle class. The Constitution of 1917 promised universal suffrage and a one-term presidency; state-run education to free the poor from the hold of the Catholic Church; the end of debt peonage; restrictions on foreign ownership of property; and laws specifying minimum wages and maximum hours to protect laborers. Although these reforms were too costly to implement right away, they had important symbolic significance, for they enshrined the dignity of Mexicans and the equality of Indians, mestizos, and whites, as well as of peasants and city people.

The Constitution of 1917

Lázaro Cárdenas President of Mexico (1934–1940). He brought major changes to Mexican life by distributing millions of acres of land to the peasants, bringing representatives of workers and farmers into the inner circles of politics, and nationalizing the oil industry.

In the early 1920s, after a decade of violence that exhausted all classes, the Mexican Revolution lost momentum, and President Obregón and his closest associates made all the important decisions. His successor, Plutarco Elías Calles (KAH-yace), founded the National Revolutionary Party, or PNR (the abbreviation of its name in Spanish). The PNR was a forum where all the pressure groups and vested interests—labor, peasants, businessmen, landowners, the military, and others—worked out compromises. The establishment of the PNR gave the Mexican Revolution a second wind.

Lázaro Cárdenas (LAH-sah-roe KAHR-dih-nahs), chosen by Calles to be president in 1934, brought peasants' and workers' organizations into the party and removed the generals from government positions. Then he set to work implementing the reforms promised in the Constitution of 1917. Cárdenas redistributed 44 million acres (17.6 million hectares) to peasant com-

The Cárdenas Reforms

munes, replaced church-run schools with government schools, and nationalized the railroads and numerous other businesses.

In 1938 Cárdenas seized the foreign-owned oil industry. The American and British oil companies expected their governments to come to their rescue, perhaps with military force. But Mexico and the United States chose to resolve the issue through negotiation, and Mexico retained control of its oil industry.

When Cárdenas's term ended in 1940, Mexico was still a land of poor farmers with a small industrial base. The Revolution had brought great changes, however. The political system was free of both chaos and dictatorships. A few wealthy people no longer monopolized land and other resources. The military was tamed; the Catholic Church no longer controlled education; and the nationalization of oil had demonstrated Mexico's independence from foreign corporations and military intervention.

The Mexican Revolution did not fulfill the democratic promise of Madero's campaign, for it brought to power a party that monopolized the government for eighty years. However, it allowed far more sectors of the population to participate in politics and made sure no president stayed in office more than six years. The Revolution also promised far-reaching social reforms, such as free education, higher wages for workers, and the redistribution of land to the peasants. These long-delayed reforms began to be implemented during the Cárdenas administration. They fell short of the ideals expressed by the revolutionaries, but they laid the foundation for the later industrialization of Mexico.

e | Interactive Map

MAP 31.2   **The Mexican Revolution** The Mexican Revolution began in two distinct regions of the country. One was the mountainous and densely populated area south of Mexico City, particularly Morelos, homeland of Emiliano Zapata. The other was the dry and thinly populated ranch country of the north, home of Pancho Villa. The fighting that ensued crisscrossed the country along the main railroad lines, shown on the map.

© Cengage Learning

Revolutionary Art

In the arts the Mexican Revolution sparked a surge of creativity. The political murals of José Clemente Orozco and Diego Rivera and the paintings of Frida Kahlo focused on social themes, showing scenes from the Revolution. These works of art gave Mexicans a sense of national unity and pride in the achievements of the Revolution that lasted long after the revolutionary fervor had dissipated.

The Transformation of Argentina

Most of Argentina consists of *pampas* (POM-pus), flat, fertile land that is easy to till, much like the prairies of the midwestern United States and Canada. At the end of the nineteenth century railroads and refrigerator ships, which allowed the safe transportation of meat, changed not only the composition of Argentina's exports but even the land itself. European consumers preferred the soft flesh of Lincoln sheep and Hereford cattle, but these valuable animals were carefully bred and fed alfalfa and oats. To safeguard them, the pampas had to be divided, plowed, cultivated, and fenced with barbed wire. Once fenced, the land could be used to produce wheat as well as beef and mutton. Within a few years grasslands that had stretched to the horizon were transformed into farmland. Like the North American Midwest, the pampas became one of the world's great producers of wheat and meat.

The *Oligarquía*

Argentina's government represented the interests of the *oligarquía* (oh-lee-gar-KEE-ah), a small group of wealthy landowners who raised cattle and sheep and grew wheat for export. They owned fine homes in Buenos Aires (BWAY-nos EYE-res), a city that was built to resemble Paris, traveled frequently to Europe, and spent lavishly. However, they showed little interest in any business other than farming and were content to let British companies build Argentina's railroads, processing plants, and public utilities. In exchange for its agricultural exports, Argentina imported almost all its manufactured goods from Europe and the United States. So important were British interests in the Argentinean economy that English, not Spanish, was used on the railroads, and the biggest department store in Buenos Aires was a branch of Harrods of London.

Brazil and Argentina, to 1929

Before the First World War, Brazil produced most of the world's coffee and cacao, grown on vast estates, and natural rubber, gathered by Indians from rubber trees growing wild in the Amazon rain forest. Thus Brazil's elite was made up of coffee and cacao planters and rubber exporters. Like their Argentinean counterparts, they spent their money lavishly, building palaces in Rio de Janeiro (REE-oh day zhuh-NAIR-oh) and an opera house deep in the Amazon. Also as in Argentina, they let British companies build railroads, harbors, and other infrastructure and imported most manufactured goods. At the time this seemed to allow each country to do what it did best. If Britain did not grow coffee, why should Brazil build locomotives?

Both Argentina and Brazil had small but outspoken middle classes that demanded a share in government and looked to Europe as a model. Beneath each middle class were the poor. In Argentina these were mainly Spanish and Italian immigrants who had ended up as landless farm laborers or workers in urban packing plants. In Brazil there was a large class of sharecroppers and plantation workers, many of them descendants of slaves.

Hipólito Irigoyen Argentine politician, president of Argentina from 1916 to 1922 and 1928 to 1930. The first president elected by universal male suffrage, he began his presidency as a reformer but later became conservative.

Rubber exports collapsed after 1912, replaced by cheaper plantation rubber from Southeast Asia. Then the outbreak of war in 1914 put an end to imports from Europe as Britain and France focused all their industries on war production and Germany was cut off entirely. The disruption of the old trade patterns weakened the landowning class. In Argentina the urban middle class obtained the secret ballot and universal male suffrage in 1916 and elected a liberal politician, **Hipólito Irigoyen** (ee-POH-lee-toe ee-ree-GO-yen), as president. To a certain extent, the United States replaced the European countries as suppliers of machinery and consumers of coffee. European immigrants built factories to manufacture textiles and household goods.

Postwar Prosperity

The postwar years were a period of prosperity in South America. Trade with Europe resumed; prices for agricultural exports remained high; and both Argentina and Brazil used profits accumulated during the war to industrialize and improve their transportation systems and public utilities. Yet it was also a time of social turmoil, as workers and middle-class professionals demanded social reforms and a larger voice in politics. In Argentina students' and workers' demonstrations were brutally crushed. In Brazil junior officers rose up several times against the government. Though they accomplished little, they laid the groundwork for later reformist movements. In neither country did the urban middle class take power away from the wealthy landowners. Instead, the two classes shared power at the expense of both the landless peasants and the urban workers.

Yet as Argentina and Brazil were moving forward, new technologies again left them dependent on the advanced industrial countries. Aviation reached Latin America after World War I, when European and American companies such as Aéropostale and Pan American Airways introduced airmail service between cities and linked Latin America with the United States and Europe.

Before and during World War I, radio was used only for point-to-point communications. Transmitters powerful enough to send messages across oceans or continents were extraordinarily complex and expensive: their antennas covered many acres, and they used as much electricity as a small town. Right after the war, the major powers scrambled to build powerful transmitters on every continent to take advantage of the boom in international business and news reporting. At the time, no Latin American country possessed the knowledge or funds to build its own transmitters. Four powerful radio companies—one British, one French, one German, and one American—formed a cartel to control all radio communications in Latin America. Thus, even as Brazil and Argentina were taking over their railroads and older industries, the major industrial countries controlled the diffusion of the newer aviation and radio technologies.

The Depression and the Vargas Regime in Brazil

The Depression hit Latin America as hard as it hit Europe and the United States; in many ways, it marks a more important turning point for the region than either of the world wars. As long-term customers cut back their orders, the value of agricultural and mineral exports fell by two-thirds between 1929 and 1932. Argentina and Brazil could no longer afford to import manufactured goods. An imploding economy also undermined their shaky political systems. Like European countries, Argentina and Brazil veered toward authoritarian regimes that promised to solve their economic problems.

In 1930 **Getulio Vargas** (jay-TOO-lee-oh VAR-gus) (1883–1954), a state governor, staged a coup and proclaimed himself president of Brazil. He proved to be a masterful politician. He wrote a new constitution that broadened the franchise and limited the president to one term. He also raised import duties and promoted national firms and state-owned enterprises. By 1936 industrial production had doubled, especially in textiles and small manufactures. Under his guidance, Brazil was on its way to becoming an industrial country. Vargas's policy became a model for other Latin American countries as they attempted to break away from neocolonial dependency.

The Environment

The industrialization of Brazil brought all the familiar environmental consequences. Powerful new machines allowed the reopening of old mines and the digging of new ones. Cities grew as poor peasants looking for work arrived from the countryside. In Rio de Janeiro and São Paulo (sow PAL-oh), the poor turned steep hillsides and vacant lands into immense *favelas* (feh-VEL-luhs) (slums) of makeshift shacks.

The countryside also was transformed. Scrubland was turned into pasture or planted in wheat, corn, and sugar cane. Even the Amazon rain forest—half of the land area of Brazil—was affected. In 1930 American industrialist Henry Ford invested $8 million to clear land along the Tapajós River and prepare it to become the site of the world's largest rubber plantation. Ford encountered opposition from Brazilian workers and politicians; the rubber trees proved vulnerable to diseases; and he had to abandon the project—but not before leaving 3 million acres (1.2 million hectares) denuded of trees.

Vargas's Legacy

Although Vargas instituted many reforms favorable to urban workers, he refused to take any measures that might help the millions of landless peasants or harm the interests of the great landowners. In 1938, prohibited by his own constitution from being reelected, Vargas staged another coup, abolished the constitution, and instituted the Estado Novo (esh-TAH-doe NO-vo), or "New State," with himself as supreme leader. He abolished political parties, jailed

Getulio Vargas Dictator of Brazil from 1930 to 1945 and from 1951 to 1954. Defeated in the presidential election of 1930, he overthrew the government and created Estado Novo ("New State"), a dictatorship that emphasized industrialization and helped the urban poor but did little to alleviate the problems of the peasants.

Juan and Eva Perón Juan Perón's presidency of Argentina (1946–1955) relied on his, and especially on his wife Eva's, popularity with the working class. To sustain their popularity, they often organized parades and demonstrations in imitation of the fascist dictators of Europe. This picture shows them riding in a procession in Buenos Aires in 1952.

Bettmann/Corbis

Juan Perón President of Argentina (1946–1955, 1973–1974). As a military officer, he championed the rights of labor. Aided by his wife Eva Duarte Perón, he was elected president in 1946. He built up Argentinean industry, became very popular among the urban poor, but harmed the economy.

Juan Perón

opposition leaders, and turned Brazil into a fascist state. When the Second World War broke out, Vargas contributed troops and ships to the Allied war effort.

Despite his economic achievements, Vargas harmed Brazil. By running roughshod over laws, constitutions, and rights, he infected not only Brazil but also all of South America with the temptations of political violence.

Argentina After 1930

Economically, the Depression hurt Argentina almost as badly as it hurt Brazil. Politically, however, the consequences were delayed for many years. In 1930 General José Uriburu (hoe-SAY oo-ree-BOO-roo) overthrew the popularly elected President Irigoyen. For thirteen years the generals and the oligarchy ruled, doing nothing to lessen the poverty of the workers or the frustrations of the middle class. When World War II broke out, Argentina remained officially neutral.

In 1943 another military revolt flared, this one among junior officers led by Colonel **Juan Perón** (hoo-AHN pair-OWN) (1895–1974). The intentions of the rebels were clear:

> *Civilians will never understand the greatness of our ideal; we shall therefore have to eliminate them from the government and give them the only mission which corresponds to them: work and obedience.*[1]

Once in power the officers took over the highest positions in government and business and began to lavish money on military equipment and their own salaries. Their goal, inspired by Nazi victories, was nothing less than the conquest of South America.

As the war turned against the Nazis, the officers saw their popularity collapse. Perón, however, had other plans. Inspired by his charismatic wife **Eva Duarte Perón** (AY-vuy doo-AR-tay pair-OWN) (1919–1952), he appealed to the urban workers. Eva Perón became the champion of the *descamisados* (des-cah-mee-SAH-dohs), or "shirtless ones," and campaigned tirelessly for social benefits and for the cause of women and children. With his wife's help, Perón won the presidency in 1946 and created a populist dictatorship in imitation of the Vargas regime in Brazil.

Like Brazil, Argentina industrialized rapidly under state sponsorship. Perón spent lavishly on social welfare projects as well as on the military, depleting the capital that Argentina had earned during the war. Though a skillful demagogue who played off the army against the navy and both against the labor unions, Perón could not create a stable government. When Eva died in 1952, he lost his political skills (or perhaps they were hers), and soon thereafter was overthrown in yet another military coup.

Eva Duarte Perón Wife of Juan Perón and champion of the poor in Argentina. She was a gifted speaker and popular political leader who campaigned to improve the life of the urban poor by founding schools and hospitals and providing other social benefits.

SECTION REVIEW

- Mexican society was deeply split between rich landowners and the poor.
- The Díaz regime introduced modern technologies while also lowering the living standards of the poor still further.
- Revolution broke out in Mexico in 1910, as different leaders vied for power.
- In the 1920s a single party, the Constitutionalists, emerged to rule Mexico.
- Lázaro Cárdenas fulfilled some of the promises of the revolution and nationalized the oil industry.
- Under its landowning oligarchy, Argentina became a major exporter of beef and wheat and depended on Europeans for its industrial products.
- After World War I, Argentina and Brazil prospered but were still dependent on the United States and Europe for advanced technology.
- Brazil and Argentina suffered greatly from the Depression; in the 1930s Vargas's dictatorship modernized Brazil but left the majority in poverty.
- Argentina, under Juan Perón, also industrialized, but his unstable government came to an end in the 1950s.

CONCLUSION

The wars and revolutions that engulfed the Northern Hemisphere between 1900 and 1949 affected India, sub-Saharan Africa, and Latin America by placing heavy demands on their peoples and raising their hopes for a better life. Sub-Saharan Africa and India were still under colonial rule, and their political life revolved around the desire of their elites for political independence while ordinary people yearned for social justice. Mexico, Argentina, and Brazil were politically independent, but their economies, like those of Africa and India, were closely tied to the economies of the industrial nations with which they traded. When the Depression hit, all three turned to state intervention. Like all industrializing countries, they did so at the expense of the natural environment. Their deeply polarized societies and the stresses caused by their dependence on the industrial countries clashed with the expectations of their peoples.

In Mexico these stresses brought about a long and violent social revolution, out of which Mexicans forged a lasting sense of national identity. Argentina and Brazil moved toward greater economic independence, but the price was social unrest, militarism, and dictatorship. They languished under conservative regimes devoted to the interests of wealthy landowners, sporadically interrupted by military coups and populist demagogues. In India the conflict between growing expectations and the reality of colonial rule produced both a movement for independence and an ethnic split that tore the nation apart. In sub-Saharan Africa demands for national self-determination and economic development were only beginning to be voiced by 1949.

Nationalism and the yearning for social justice were the two most powerful forces for change in the early twentieth century. These ideas originated in the industrialized countries but resonated in the independent countries of Latin America as well as in colonial regions such as India and sub-Saharan Africa. However, they did not always unite people against their colonial rulers or foreign oppressors; instead, they often divided them along social, ethnic, or religious lines. Western-educated elites looked to industrialization as a means of modernizing their country and ensuring their position in it, while peasants and urban workers supported nationalist and revolutionary movements in the hope of improving their lives. Often these goals were not compatible.

KEY TERMS

Indian National Congress p. 824
Bengal p. 824
All-India Muslim League p. 824
Mohandas K. Gandhi p. 825
Jawaharlal Nehru p. 826
Muhammad Ali Jinnah p. 827
Blaise Diagne p. 832
African National Congress p. 832
Haile Selassie p. 832
Emiliano Zapata p. 833
Francisco "Pancho" Villa p. 834
Lázaro Cárdenas p. 834
Hipólito Irigoyen p. 836
Getulio Vargas p. 837
Juan Perón p. 838
Eva Duarte Perón p. 839

EBOOK AND WEBSITE RESOURCES

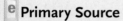

Primary Source

An Indian Nationalist Condemns the British Empire

Interactive Maps

Map 31.1 The Partition of India, 1947

Map 31.2 The Mexican Revolution

Plus flashcards, practice quizzes, and more. Go to:
www.cengage.com/history/bullietearthpeople5e

SUGGESTED READING

Achebe, Chinua. *Arrow of God*. 1964. A classic novel about the conflict between traditional beliefs and Christianity in a Nigerian village.

Adelman, Jeremy. *Frontier Development: Land, Labour and Capital on the Wheatlands of Argentina and Canada, 1890–1914*. 1994. An analysis of the contrasting development of two major American nations.

Boahen, Adu. *African Perspectives on Colonialism*. 1987. A work recounting the African reactions to colonial rule.

Brown, Judith M. *Gandhi: Prisoner of Hope*. 1989. The classic biography of the Indian leader.

Burns, E. Bradford. *A History of Brazil*, 3rd ed. 1993. The definitive history of a great nation.

Collins, Larry, and Dominique Lapierre. *Freedom at Midnight*. 1975. A popular account of the coming of independence and the partition of India.

Dean, Warren. *Brazil and the Struggle for Rubber: A Study in Environmental History*. 1987. Describes the destruction of the rainforest and of its inhabitants who were coerced to produce rubber for the automobile boom.

Gadgil, M., and R. Guha, *This Fissured Land: An Ecological History of India*. 1993. The classic work on the history of the Indian environment.

Jefferson, Mark. *Peopling the Argentine Pampas*. 1971. How immigrants from Spain and Italy made the Argentine nation.

Knight, Alan. *The Mexican Revolution*, 2 vols. 1986. The definitive history of the revolution.

Krauze, Enrique. *Mexico: Biography of Power: A History of Modern Mexico, 1810–1996*. 1997. The political history of a nation in turmoil.

Machado, Manuel. *Centaur of the North: Francisco Villa, the Mexican Revolution, and Northern Mexico*. 1988. A biography of the famous bandit-revolutionary.

Meyer, Michael, and William Beezley, *Oxford History of Mexico*. 2000. The definitive account.

Oliver, Roland, and Anthony Atmore, *Africa Since 1800*, 4th ed. 1994. The best-known history of modern Africa.

Sarkar, Sumit. *Modern India, 1885–1947*. 1983. The classic history of the independence movement.

NOTES

1. George Blankstein, *Perón's Argentina* (Chicago: University of Chicago Press, 1953), 37.

FAMINES AND POLITICS

Human history is filled with tales of famines—times when crops failed, food supplies ran out, and people starved.

Natural Famines

India, dependent on the monsoon rains, has been particularly prone to such calamities, with famines striking two to four times a century, whenever the rains fail for several years in succession. Three times in the eighteenth century famines killed several million people. The nineteenth century was worse, with famines in 1803–1804, 1837–1838, 1868–1870, and 1876–1878. The famine of 1876–1878 also afflicted northern China, causing between 9 and 13 million deaths from hunger and from the diseases of malnutrition. There were even incidents of cannibalism, as starving adults ate starving children.

When drought hit a region, it decimated not only the human population but also the animals they relied on to transport crops or plow the land. When water levels dropped in rivers and canals, food could not be transported by boat to areas where people were starving.

Commercial Famines

That all changed in the nineteenth century. Railroads and steamships could transport foodstuffs quickly across great distances, regardless of the weather. Great Britain became dependent on imports of wheat and beef. Yet the global death toll from starvation has been far higher since the mid-nineteenth century than ever before. Why?

Consider Ireland. By the early nineteenth century the potato had become the main source of nutrition for the Irish people. Potatoes grew abundantly and produced more calories per acre than any other crop, allowing the population to increase dramatically.

In 1845 a blight turned the potatoes in the fields black, mushy, and inedible. The harvest was ruined the following year as well. It recovered slightly in 1847 but was bad again in 1848. Tens of thousands died of starvation, while hundreds of thousands died from dysentery, typhus, or cholera. Travelers saw corpses rotting in their hovels or on the sides of roads. Altogether, a million or more people died, while another million emigrated, reducing the population of Ireland by half.

Throughout those years, Ireland exported wheat to England, where people had money to pay for it. Food cost money, and the Irish, poor even before the famines, were destitute and could not afford to buy wheat or bread. The British government was convinced that interfering with the free market would only make things worse. Relief efforts were half-hearted at best; the official responsible for Irish affairs preferred to leave the situation to "the operation of natural causes."

The same held true in India, like Ireland a colony of Great Britain. The drought of 1876–1878 killed over 5 million Indians in the Deccan region, while British officials stood by helpless or indifferent. Part of the problem was transportation. In the 1870s most goods were still transported in bullock carts, but the bullocks starved during the drought. Another obstacle was political. The idea that a government should be responsible for feeding the population was unthinkable at the time. And so, while millions were starving in the Deccan, the Punjab was exporting wheat to Britain.

Over the next twenty years, so-called famine railways were built in the regions historically most affected by the failures of the monsoon. When drought struck again at the end of the century, the railways were ready to transport food to areas that had previously been accessible only by bullock carts. However, the inhabitants of the affected regions had no money with which to buy what little food there was, and the government was still reluctant to interfere with free enterprise. Grain merchants bought all the stocks, hoarded them until the price rose, then used the railways to transport them out of the famine regions to regions where the harvests were better and people had more money.

In the twentieth century, commercial famines became rare as governments realized that they had a responsibility to provide food not only for their own people but also for people in other countries. Yet commercial famines have not entirely disappeared. In 1974, when a catastrophic flood covered half of Bangladesh, the government was too disorganized to distribute its stocks of rice, while merchants bought what they could and exported it to India. Thousands died, and thousands more survived only because of belated shipments of food from donor countries.

Political Famines

To say that governments are responsible for food supplies does not mean that they exercise that responsibility for the good of the people. Some do, but in many instances food is used as a weapon. In the twentieth century global food supplies were always adequate for the population of the world, and transportation was seldom a problem. Yet the century witnessed the most murderous famines ever recorded.

As commercial famines declined, war famines became common. The destruction or requisitioning of crops caused famines in the Russian civil war of 1921–1922, the Japanese occupation of Indochina in 1942–1945, and the Biafran war in Nigeria in 1967–1969.

In 1942 the Japanese army had conquered Burma, a rich rice-producing colony. Food supplies in Bengal, which imported rice from Burma, dropped by 5 percent. As prices began to rise, merchants bought stocks of rice and held them in the hope that prices would continue to increase. Sharecroppers sold their stocks to pay off their debts to landlords and village moneylenders. Meanwhile, the railroads that in peacetime would have carried food from other parts of India were fully occupied with military traffic. By the time Viceroy Lord Wavell ordered the army to transport food to Bengal in October 1943, between 1.5 and 2 million Bengalis had died.

Worst of all were the famines caused by deliberate government policies. The most famous was the famine of 1932–1933 caused by Stalin's collectivization of agriculture. The Communists tried to force the peasants to give up their land and livestock and join collectives, where they could be made to work harder and provide food for the growing cities and industries. When the peasants resisted, their crops were seized. Millions were sent to prison camps, and millions of others died of starvation.

An even worse famine took place in China from 1958 to 1961 during the "Great Leap Forward" (see Chapter 32). Communist Party Chairman Mao Zedong decided to hasten the transformation of China into a communist state by relying not on the expertise of economists and technocrats but on the enthusiasm of the masses. Farms were consolidated into huge communes. Peasants were told to make steel out of household utensils in backyard furnaces. The harvest of 1959 was poor, and later ones were even worse. The amount of grain per person declined from 452 pounds (205 kilograms) in 1957 to 340 pounds (154 kilograms) in 1961. Since the Central Statistical Bureau had been shut down, the central government was unaware of the shortages and demanded ever higher requisitions of food to feed the army and urban and industrial workers and to export to the Soviet Union to pay off China's debts. The amount of food left to the farmers was between one-fifth and one-half of their usual subsistence diet. From 1958 to 1961 between 20 and 30 million Chinese are estimated to have starved or died of the diseases of malnutrition. It was the worst famine in the history of the world. Mao denied its existence.

Nothing quite as horrible has happened since the Great Leap Forward. During the droughts in Africa in the 1970s and 1980s, most people in the affected regions received international food aid. However, to crush rebellions, the governments of Ethiopia and Sudan denied that their people were hungry and prevented food shipments from reaching drought victims.

In the world today, natural disasters are as frequent as ever, and many countries are vulnerable to food shortages. No one now claims that governments have no business providing food to the starving. Though food is not equitably distributed, there is enough for all human beings now, and there will be enough for the foreseeable future. However, humanitarian feelings compete with other political agendas, and the specter of politically motivated famines still stalks the world.

PART VIII

NASA/Getty Images

Satellite Photograph of the Globe   Photography from space revolutionized mapping, making physical features more important than political boundaries and clearly displaying transient features, such as cloud coverage and storm patterns. In this photograph the distinctive whorl of a tropical storm is visible off the east coast of Japan. More specialized photographic techniques are used to appraise natural resources and environmental problems.

Perils and Promises of a Global Community, 1945 to the Present

An increasingly interconnected world faced new hopes and fears after World War II. The United Nations promoted peace, international cooperation, and human rights. Colonized peoples gained independence, and global trade expanded.

However, Cold War rhetoric and nuclear stalemate dispelled dreams of world peace. Wars in Korea and Vietnam, as well as proxy conflicts from Nicaragua to Afghanistan, pitted the United States against communist regimes. Following the Cold War nuclear proliferation and terrorism became top concerns. The 9/11 attacks by Muslim extremists on the World Trade Center and the Pentagon triggered an American "global war on terrorism." The ensuing invasions of Afghanistan and Iraq made the Middle East a top danger spot.

The industrialized nations, including Germany and Japan, recovered well from World War II. Elsewhere economic development came slowly, except in a handful of countries: South Korea, Taiwan, Brazil, Argentina, and, after 2000, China and India. In Africa and other poor regions, population growth usually offset economic gains.

Although the Green Revolution of the 1960s and genetic engineering thirty years later alleviated much world hunger, industrial growth and automobile use increased pollution and competition for petroleum supplies. Global warming became an international concern, along with overfishing, deforestation, and endangerment of wild species.

Globalization affected culture as well. Transnational corporations selling uniform products threatened localized economic enterprises, and Western popular culture aroused fears of cultural imperialism. The Internet and the emergence of English as the global language improved international communication but also stimulated fears that cultural diversity would be lost.

Bettmann/Corbis

Fidel Castro Arrives in Havana   Castro and his supporters overthrew a brutal dictatorship and began the revolutionary transformation of Cuba that led to a confrontation with the United States.

Visit the website and ebook for additional study materials and interactive tools: www.cengage.com/history/bullietearthpeople5e

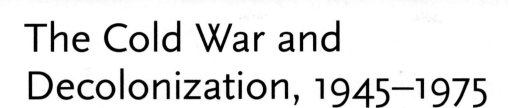

The Cold War and Decolonization, 1945–1975

On January 1, 1959, Fidel Castro entered Havana, Cuba, after having successfully defeated the dictatorship of Fulgencio Batista (ful-HEHN-see-oh bah-TEES-tah). Castro had initiated his revolution in 1953 with an attack on a military barracks, but the attack failed. At his trial, Castro put on a spirited defense that he later published as *History Will Absolve Me*. He proclaimed his objectives as the restoration of Cuban democracy and an ambitious program of social and economic reforms designed to ameliorate the effects of underdevelopment.

On September 26, 1960, Castro addressed the United Nations General Assembly. Relations between the Castro government and the United States were already heading toward confrontation as a result of Castro's policies. In his speech, Castro offered a broad internationalist and anti-imperialist criticism of the world's developed nations and of the United Nations. He criticized the role of the United Nations in the Congo, suggesting that it had supported Colonel Mobutu Sese Seko, a client of imperialism, rather than Patrice Lumumba, identified by the United States as a dangerous radical. He also strongly supported the independence struggle of the Algerians against the French.

In this speech, Castro outlined an ambitious program of new revolutionary reforms in Cuba, claiming that the United States had supported the Batista dictatorship to protect American investors. Once back in Cuba, Castro pressed ahead with economic reforms that included nationalizing most American investments. Cuba became a flash point in the Cold War when the United States tried and failed to overthrow Castro in 1961. Castro declared himself to be a socialist and forged an economic and military alliance with the Soviet Union that led in 1962 to the Cuban missile crisis.

The intensity of the Cold War, with its accompanying threat of nuclear destruction, obscured a postwar phenomenon of more enduring importance. The colonial empires of the New Imperialism disappeared, and Western power and influence declined in Asia, Africa, and Latin America. The leaders who headed these new nations were sometimes able to use Cold War antagonism to their own advantage when they sought economic or military assistance. Some, like Castro, became front-line participants in this struggle, but most focused on nation building.

Each former colony had its own history and followed its own route to independence. Thus these new nations had difficulty finding a collective voice in a world

■ What were the major threats to world peace during the Cold War?

■ How were the experiences of Asia, Africa, and Latin America similar in this period?

■ How did the rivalry between the Cold War superpowers affect the rest of the world?

increasingly oriented toward two superpowers, the United States and the Soviet Union. Some former colonies sided openly with one or the other, while others banded together in a posture of neutrality. All spoke with one voice about their need for economic and technical assistance and the obligation of the wealthy nations to satisfy those needs.

The Cold War military rivalry led to extraordinary advances in weaponry and associated technologies, but many new nations faced basic problems of educating their citizens, nurturing industry, and escaping the economic constraints imposed by their former imperialist masters. The environment suffered severe pressures from oil exploration and transport to support the growing economies of the wealthy nations and from deforestation and urbanization in poor regions. Neither rich nor poor nations fully understood the costs associated with these environmental changes.

THE COLD WAR

iron curtain Winston Churchill's term for the Cold War division between the Soviet-dominated East and the U.S.-dominated West.

Cold War The ideological struggle between communism (Soviet Union) and capitalism (United States) for world influence. The Cold War came to an end when the Soviet Union dissolved in 1991.

North Atlantic Treaty Organization (NATO) Organization formed in 1949 as a military alliance of western European and North American states against the Soviet Union and its east European allies.

Warsaw Pact The 1955 treaty binding the Soviet Union and countries of eastern Europe in an alliance against the North Atlantic Treaty Organization.

United Nations International organization founded in 1945 to promote world peace and cooperation. It replaced the League of Nations.

Political Divisions and the United Nations

For more than a century, political and economic leaders in the industrialized West had viewed socialism as a threat to free markets and untrammeled capital investment. The wartime alliance between the United States, Great Britain, and the Soviet Union had succeeded despite these deep structural differences. With the defeat of Germany, however, growing Soviet assertiveness in Europe and communist insurgencies in China and elsewhere confirmed to Western leaders the threat of worldwide revolution.

Western leaders saw the Soviet Union as the sponsor of world revolution and as a military power capable of launching a war as destructive and terrible as the one recently ended. As early as 1946 Great Britain's wartime leader, Winston Churchill, said in a speech in Missouri, "From Stettin in the Baltic to Trieste in the Adriatic, an iron curtain has descended across the Continent. . . . I am convinced there is nothing they [the communists] so much admire as strength, and there is nothing for which they have less respect than weakness, especially military weakness." The phrase "**iron curtain**" became a watchword of the **Cold War**, the state of political tension and military rivalry then beginning between the United States and its allies and the Soviet Union and its allies.

Once the United States and the nations of western Europe established the **North Atlantic Treaty Organization (NATO)** military alliance in 1949, Soviet leaders felt surrounded by hostile forces as they struggled to recover from the terrible losses sustained in the war against the Axis. In response, the Soviet Union created its own military alliance, the **Warsaw Pact**, in 1955. The distrust and suspicion between the two sides played out on a worldwide stage, and the United Nations was often the location of confrontational debate.

The United Nations

In 1944 representatives from the United States, Great Britain, the Soviet Union, and China drafted proposals that led to a treaty called the United Nations Charter, ratified on October 24, 1945. Like the earlier League of Nations, the **United Nations** had two main bodies: the General Assembly, with representatives from all member states; and the Security Council, with five permanent members—China, France, Great Britain, the United States, and the Soviet Union—and seven rotating members. A full-time bureaucracy headed by a Secretary General carried out the organization's day-to-day business and directed agencies focused on specialized international problems—for example, UNICEF (United Nations Children's Emergency Fund), FAO (Food and Agriculture Organization), and UNESCO (United Nations Educational, Scientific and Cultural Organization) (see Environment and Technology: The Green Revolution). Unlike the League of Nations, which required unanimous agreement in both deliberative bodies, the United Nations operated by majority vote, except that the five permanent members of the Security Council had veto power in that chamber.

All signatories to the United Nations Charter renounced war and territorial conquest. Nevertheless, peacekeeping, the sole preserve of the Security Council, became a vexing problem as

CHRONOLOGY

	Cold War	Decolonization
1945	1947–1948 Soviet blockade of Berlin	1947 Partition of India
	1949 NATO formed	1949 Dutch withdraw from Indonesia
1950	1950–1953 Korean War	
	1952 United States detonates first hydrogen bomb	
	1954 Jacobo Arbenz overthrown in Guatemala, supported by CIA	1954 CIA intervention in Guatemala; defeat at Dienbienphu ends French hold on Vietnam
1955	1955 Warsaw Pact created	1955 Bandung Conference
	1956 Soviet Union suppresses Hungarian revolt	
	1957 Soviet Union launches first artificial satellite into earth orbit	1957 Ghana becomes first British colony in Africa to gain independence
		1959 Triumph of Fidel Castro's revolution in Cuba
1960		1960 Shootings in Sharpeville intensify South African struggle against apartheid; Nigeria becomes independent
	1961 East Germany builds Berlin Wall	
	1961 Bay of Pigs (Cuba)	
	1962 Cuban missile crisis	1962 Algeria wins independence
	1968 Nuclear Non-Proliferation Treaty	
1970		1971 Bangladesh secedes from Pakistan
	1975 Helsinki Accords; end of Vietnam War	

permanent members exercised their vetoes to protect their allies and interests. Throughout the Cold War the United Nations was seldom able to forestall or quell international conflicts, though from time to time it sent observers or peacekeeping forces to monitor truces or other international agreements.

The decolonization of Africa and Asia greatly swelled the size of the General Assembly but not the Security Council. Many newly independent nations looked to the United Nations for material assistance and access to a wider political world. While the rivalry of the Security Council's permanent members stymied actions that even indirectly touched on Cold War concerns, the General Assembly became an arena for debates over issues like decolonization and development.

In the early years of the United Nations, General Assembly resolutions carried great weight. An example is a 1947 resolution that sought to divide Palestine into sovereign Jewish and Arab states. Gradually, though, the flood of new members produced a voting majority concerned more with poverty, racial discrimination, and the struggle against imperialism than with the Cold War. As a result, Western powers increasingly disregarded the General Assembly, in effect allowing new nations to have their say but effectively preventing any collective action contrary to their interests.

World Bank A specialized agency of the United Nations that makes loans to countries for economic development, trade promotion, and debt consolidation. Its formal name is the International Bank for Reconstruction and Development.

Capitalism and Communism

In July 1944, with Allied victory inevitable, economic specialists representing over forty countries met at Bretton Woods, a New Hampshire resort, to devise a new international monetary system. The signatories eventually agreed to fix exchange rates and to create the International Monetary Fund (IMF) and World Bank. The IMF used currency reserves from member nations to finance temporary trade deficits, while the **World Bank** provided funds for reconstructing Europe and helping needy countries after the war.

The Soviet Union attended the Bretton Woods Conference and signed the agreements that went into effect in 1946. But growing hostility between the Soviet Union and the United States and Britain undermined cooperation. While the United States held reserves of gold and the rest of the world held reserves of dollars to maintain the stability of the monetary system, the Soviet

Two Distinct Economic Systems

The Green Revolution

Concern about world food supplies grew from the serious shortages caused by the devastation and trade disruptions of World War II. The Food and Agriculture Organization of the United Nations, the Rockefeller Foundation, and the Ford Foundation took leading roles in fostering crop research and agricultural education. In 1966 the International Rice Research Institute (established in 1960–1962) began distributing seeds for an improved rice variety known as IR-8. Crop yields from this and other new varieties, along with improved farming techniques, were initially so impressive that a hoped-for new era in agriculture was called the *Green Revolution*.

After the successful introduction of new rice strains, scientists developed new varieties of corn and wheat. Building on twenty years of Rockefeller-funded research in Mexico, the Centro Internacional de Mejoramiento de Maiz y Trigo (International Center for the Improvement of Maize and Wheat) was established in 1966 under Norman Borlaug, who was awarded the Nobel Peace Prize four years later. This organization distributed new varieties of wheat that were resistant to disease and responsive to fertilizer.

By 1970 other centers for research on tropical agriculture were established, but experts believed that the success of the Green Revolution required a more comprehensive effort. The Consultative Group on International Agricultural Research brought together World Bank expertise, private foundations, international organizations, and national foreign aid agencies to undertake worldwide support of efforts to increase food productivity and improve natural resource management.

Early optimism about these innovations is now muted. Although crop yields often improved as a result of new seeds, improved fertilizers, and irrigation, these improvements were too expensive for poor farmers to employ. This meant in practice that, as agricultural production rose, land was increasingly concentrated in the hands of the rich and the rural poor were forced to become laborers or migrate to cities.

Miracle Rice New strains of so-called miracle rice made many nations in South and Southeast Asia self-sufficient in food production after decades of worry that population growth would outstrip agricultural productivity.

Victor Englebert

Union established a closed monetary system for itself and allied communist regimes in eastern Europe. In Western countries, supply and demand determined production priorities and prices; in the Soviet command economy, government agencies allocated goods and set prices according to governmental priorities, irrespective of market forces.

Many leaders of newly independent states, having won their nation's independence from European colonial powers, preferred the Soviet Union's socialist example to the capitalism of their former masters. Thus, the relative success of economies patterned on Eastern or Western

Cold War Confrontation in 1959
U.S. vice president Richard M. Nixon and Soviet premier Nikita Khrushchev had a heated exchange of views during Nixon's visit to a Moscow trade fair. Two years earlier, the Soviet Union launched the world's first space satellite.

Seymour Raskin/Magnum Photos, Inc.

models became part of the Cold War argument. Each side trumpeted economic successes measured by industrial output, changes in per capita income, and productivity gains.

During World War II the U.S. economy escaped the lingering effects of the Great Depression (see Chapter 30) as increased military spending and the military draft raised employment and wages. During the war, U.S. factories were converted from the production of consumer goods to weapons. With peace, the pent-up demand for consumer goods led to a period of rapid economic growth and prosperity. Europe, still rebuilding from the destruction of the war, at first lagged behind.

Recovery in the United States and Western Europe

World War II had heavily damaged the economy of western Europe. Bombs had flattened cities and destroyed railroads, port facilities, and communication networks. Populations had lost their savings and struggled to find employment. Seeking to forestall the radicalization of European politics, the United States decided to support the reconstruction of Europe. The **Marshall Plan** and other aid programs provided more than $20 billion to Europe by 1961. European determination backed by American aid spurred recovery, and by 1963 the resurgent European economies had doubled their total 1940 output.

Marshall Plan U.S. program to support the reconstruction of western Europe after World War II. By 1961 more than $20 billion in economic aid had been dispersed.

Recovering western European governments sought a greater role in economic management than did the United States during this period. In Great Britain, for example, the Labour Party government of the early 1950s nationalized coal, steel, railroads, and health care. Similarly, the French government nationalized public utilities; the auto, banking, and insurance industries; and parts of the mining industry. These steps provided large infusions of capital for rebuilding and acquiring new technologies.

European Economic Integration

In 1948 European nations initiated a process of economic cooperation and integration with the creation of the Organization of European Economic Cooperation (OEEC). They began by cooperating on coal and steel. Located in disputed border areas, these industries had previously been flash points that led to war. With success in these areas, some OEEC countries lowered tariffs to encourage trade. Then in 1957 France, West Germany, Italy, the Netherlands, Belgium, and Luxembourg signed a treaty creating the **European Economic Community**, also known as the **Common Market**. By the 1970s this economic alliance had nearly overtaken the United States in industrial production. Then between 1973 and 1995, Great Britain, Denmark, Greece, Ireland, Spain, Portugal, Finland, Sweden, and Austria joined the alliance, renamed the European Union (EU) in 1993 to reflect growing political integration.

European Economic Community (Common Market) An organization promoting economic unity in Europe, formed in 1957 by consolidation of earlier, more limited, agreements. With the addition of many new nations it became the European Union (EU) in 1993.

The resulting prosperity brought dramatic changes to the societies of western Europe. Wages increased and social welfare benefits grew. Governments increased spending on health care, unemployment benefits, old-age pensions, public housing, and grants to poor families. The combination of economic growth and income redistribution raised living standards and fueled demand for consumer goods, leading to the development of a mass consumer society.

The Soviet Model

The Soviet experience was dramatically different. The rapid growth of the Soviet state after 1917 had challenged traditional Western assumptions about economic development and social policy. From the 1920s the Soviet state relied on bureaucratic agencies and political processes to determine the production, distribution, and price of goods. The government regulated and administered nearly every area of the society, including housing, medical services, retail shops, factories, and the land. Despite many problems, the Soviet state achieved a dramatic expansion in basic industrial production.

As in western Europe, the economies of the Soviet Union and its eastern European allies were devastated at the end of the Second World War, but they took a different path to reconstruction. The Soviet command economy had enormous natural resources, a large population, and abundant energy at its disposal. It also benefited from the state's large investments in technical and scientific education and heavy industries during the 1930s and war years.

As a result, recovery was rapid at first, creating the structural basis for modernization and growth. However, as industrial production throughout the world refocused on consumer goods such as television sets and automobiles rather than coal and steel, the inefficiencies of bureaucratic control became obvious. By the 1970s the gap with the West had widened. Soviet industry failed to meet domestic demand for clothing, housing, food, automobiles, and consumer electronics, while Soviet agricultural production failed to meet domestic needs.

West Versus East in Europe and Korea

In Germany, Austria, and Japan, the end of the war meant foreign military occupation and governments controlled by the victors. The Soviet Union initially seemed willing to accept governments in neighboring states that included a mix of parties as long as they were not hostile to local communist groups or to the Soviets. In the nations of central and eastern Europe, many remembered the Soviets as enemies of the fascists and were eager to support local communist parties. As relations between the Soviets and the West worsened in the late 1940s, communists gained a series of political victories across eastern Europe. Western leaders saw the emergence of communist regimes in Poland, Czechoslovakia, Hungary, Bulgaria, Romania, Yugoslavia, and Albania as a sign of growing Soviet aggressiveness.

The Cold War

By 1948 the United States viewed the Soviet Union as an adversary and threat. While the United States had seemed amenable to the Soviet desire for access to the Mediterranean through the Bosporus and Dardanelles straits at war's end, by 1947 it acted to strengthen Turkey and Greece to resist Soviet military pressure and local communist subversion. This decision to hold the line against further Soviet expansion led to the admission of Turkey and Greece to NATO and to the decision to allow West Germany to rearm (see Map 32.1). The Soviets created the Warsaw Pact in 1955 as a strategic counterweight.

Increased hostility did not lead to a direct military confrontation between the two great alliances. But the Soviet Union did test Western resolve, first by blockading the British, French, and American zones of Berlin (located in Soviet-controlled East Germany) in 1947–1948 and then in 1961 by building the Berlin Wall to prevent East Germans from fleeing to West Berlin.

In turn, the West tested the East by encouraging divisions within the Warsaw Pact. This policy contributed to an armed anti-Soviet revolt in Hungary that Soviet troops crushed in 1956. In 1968 Soviet troops repressed a peaceful reform effort in Czechoslovakia, making clear that, like the West, it would defend its sphere of influence. By failing to support either of these challenges to Soviet control, the West effectively accepted the political and ideological boundaries established by the Cold War.

Korean War Conflict that began with North Korea's invasion of South Korea and that came to involve the United Nations (primarily the United States) allying with South Korea and the People's Republic of China allying with North Korea.

The Korean War

By the end of the Second World War, Soviet troops controlled the Korean peninsula north of the thirty-eighth parallel, while American troops controlled the south. When these two powers could not reach an agreement to hold countrywide elections, a communist North Korea and a noncommunist South Korea emerged as independent states in 1948. Two years later North Korea invaded South Korea. The United Nations Security Council, in the absence of the Soviet delegation, condemned the invasion and called on its members to come to the defense of South Korea. In the ensuing **Korean War**, which lasted until 1953, the United States was the primary ally of South Korea, while the People's Republic of China supported North Korea.

Because the United States feared that launching attacks into China might prompt China's ally, the Soviet Union, to retaliate, the conflict remained limited to the Korean peninsula. Victories by American and South Korean forces forced North Korean forces north until China entered the war. The contending armies eventually reached a stalemate along the thirty-eighth parallel. The two sides formally agreed to a truce but never signed a peace treaty. As a result, fear of renewed warfare between the two Koreas continued well past the end of the Cold War.

United States Defeat in Vietnam

The most important postwar communist movement arose in French Indochina in Southeast Asia. The Vietnamese leader Ho Chi Minh (hoe chee min) (1890–1969) had spent several years in France during World War I and helped form the French Communist Party. In 1930, after training in Moscow, he returned to Vietnam to found the Indochina Communist Party. Forced to take refuge in China during World War II, Ho cooperated with the United States while Japan controlled Vietnam.

At war's end the French government was determined to keep its colonial possessions. Ho Chi Minh's nationalist coalition, called the Viet Minh, fought the French with help from the People's Republic of China. After a brutal struggle, the French stronghold of Dienbienphu (dee-yen-bee-yen-FOO) fell in 1954, marking the end of France's colonial enterprise. Ho's Viet Minh government took over in the north, and a noncommunist nationalist government ruled in the south.

Under President Dwight D. Eisenhower (1953–1961), the United States provided limited support to the French but ultimately decided not to prop up French colonial rule in Vietnam, perceiving that the European colonial empires were doomed. After winning independence, communist North Vietnam supported a communist guerrilla movement—the Viet Cong—against the noncommunist government of South Vietnam. At issue was the ideological and economic orientation of an independent Vietnam.

Vietnam War Conflict pitting North Vietnam and South Vietnamese communist guerrillas against the South Vietnamese government, aided after 1961 by the United States.

America in Vietnam

President John F. Kennedy (served 1961–1963) changed American policy to support the South Vietnamese government of President Ngo Dinh Diem (dee-YEM). Although he knew that the Diem government was corrupt and unpopular, he feared that a communist victory would encourage communist movements throughout Southeast Asia and alter the Cold War balance of power. Kennedy increased the number of American military advisers while encouraging the overthrow of the Diem government, an event that led to Diem's execution.

Following the assassination of Kennedy, President Lyndon Johnson (served 1963–1969) gained congressional support for an unlimited U.S. military deployment that eventually reached 500,000 troops. Because South Vietnam's new rulers were as corrupt and unpopular as the earlier Diem government, many South Vietnamese supported the Viet Cong. Despite battlefield success in the **Vietnam War**, the United States failed to achieve a comprehensive victory. In the massive 1968 Tet Offensive, the Viet Cong guerrillas and their North Vietnamese allies gained significant military credibility while suffering significant losses. With a clear victory unlikely, the antiwar movement in the United States grew in strength (see below).

Dana Stone/Black Star

The Vietnamese People at War   American and South Vietnamese troops burned many villages to deprive the enemy of civilian refuges. This policy undermined support for the South Vietnamese government in the countryside.

MAP 32.1 **Cold War Confrontation** A polar projection is shown on this map because Soviet and U.S. strategists planned to attack one another by missile in the polar region; hence the Canadian-American radar lines.

© Cengage Learning

e Interactive Map

Legend:

NATO nations
Warsaw Pact nations
Soviet military base
U.S. military base
U.S. Strategic Air Command base
U.S. Intercontinental Ballistic Missile base
U.S. naval fleet
Cold War point of conflict

HAWAI'I (U.S.)

CZECHOSLOVAKIA 1948, 1968
EAST GERMANY 1948–1949, 1953, 1958–1962
POLAND 1956
YUGOSLAVIA 1948–1953
HUNGARY 1956

PACIFIC OCEAN

UNITED STATES

1st fleet

2nd fleet

CANADA

Pinetree Radar Line

Mid-Canada Radar Line

ALASKA (U.S.)

Distant Early Warning (DEW) Radar Line

GREENLAND (DEN.)

ARCTIC OCEAN

ICELAND

NORWAY

Azores (Port.)

ATLANTIC OCEAN

GREAT BRITAIN

DEN.
NETH.
BELG.
FRANCE
PORT.
SPAIN

E. GER.
W. GER.
POLAND
CZECH.
ITALY
ALB.
HUNG.
YUGO.
ROMANIA
BULG.
GREECE 1946–1949

6th fleet

MOROCCO

LIBYA

EGYPT 1956 1967 1973

SAUDI ARABIA

IRAQ 1958

TURKEY 1945–1947

LEBANON 1958

IRAN 1945–1946 1951–1953

AFGHANISTAN 1979

PAKISTAN

SOVIET UNION

MONGOLIA

CHINA

JAPAN

SOUTH KOREA 1950–1953

7th fleet

Okinawa (U.S.)

FORMOSA (TAIWAN) 1958

SOUTH VIETNAM 1957–1975

LAOS 1960–1975

THAILAND

CAMBODIA 1969–1975

PHILIPPINES 1945–1954

INDONESIA 1965

INDIAN OCEAN

ETHIOPIA 1975–1991

SOMALIA 1970s–1980s

DEMOCRATIC REPUBLIC OF THE CONGO 1961–1965

ANGOLA 1976–1992

Equator

GUATEMALA 1954

EL SALVADOR 1979–1992

NICARAGUA 1981–1990

PANAMA

CUBA 1961–1962

DOMINICAN REPUBLIC 1965–1966

Puerto Rico (U.S.)

GRENADA 1983

PACIFIC OCEAN

0 500 1000 Km.
0 500 1000 Mi.

30°N
60°N
120°E
150°E
90°E
60°E
30°E
0°
30°W
60°W
90°W
120°W
150°W

In 1973 a treaty between North Vietnam and the United States ended U.S. involvement in the war and promised future elections. Two years later, in violation of the treaty, Viet Cong and North Vietnamese troops overran the South Vietnamese army and captured the southern capital of Saigon, renaming it Ho Chi Minh City. They then united the two Vietnams in a single state ruled from the north. Over a million Vietnamese and 58,000 Americans had died during the war.

Protests in the United States

President Johnson began his administration committed to a broad program of social reforms and civil rights initiatives, called the Great Society, and was instrumental in passing major civil rights legislation that responded to the heroic campaign for voting rights and integration led by Martin Luther King, Jr. As the commitment of U.S. troops in Vietnam grew, a massive antiwar movement applied the tactics of the civil rights movement to end the war. Growing economic problems and a rising tide of antiwar rallies, now international in character, undermined support for Johnson, who declined to seek reelection.

The Race for Nuclear Supremacy

The terrible devastation of Hiroshima and Nagasaki by atomic weapons (see Chapter 30) framed the strategic decisions in the Korean and Vietnamese wars. In both cases the United States took care not to expand the wars and challenge the Soviet Union or China (nuclear power from 1964). The Soviet Union had exploded its first nuclear device in 1949. The United States claimed a new advantage when it exploded a more powerful hydrogen bomb in 1952, but the Soviet Union followed suit less than a year later. In a world deeply scared by two world wars, the threat of nuclear war spread despair around the world.

In 1954 President Eisenhower warned Soviet leaders against attacking western Europe. In response to such an attack, he said, the United States would reduce the Soviet Union to "a smoking, radiating ruin at the end of two hours." A few years later the Soviet leader Nikita Khrushchev (KROOSH-chef) made an equally stark promise: "We will bury you." He was referring to economic competition, but Americans interpreted the statement to mean literal burial. Rhetoric aside, both men—and their successors—had the capacity to deliver on their threats, and everyone in the world knew that all-out war with nuclear weapons would produce the greatest global devastation in human history.

Cuban missile crisis Brink-of-war confrontation between the United States and the Soviet Union over the latter's placement of nuclear-armed missiles in Cuba.

The Soviet Union's deployment of nuclear missiles to Cuba in 1962 pushed the two sides to the brink of war. Reacting to U.S. efforts to overthrow the Cuban government, Khrushchev and Fidel Castro decided that the deployment of nuclear weapons in Cuba would force the United States to accept the status quo. When the missiles were discovered, the United States declared a naval blockade and prepared to invade Cuba, forcing Khrushchev to remove the missiles. As frightening as the **Cuban missile crisis** was, the fact that the superpowers chose diplomacy over war gave reason to hope that nuclear weapons might be contained.

Nuclear Nonproliferation

Fear of a nuclear holocaust produced an international effort to limit proliferation. In 1963 Great Britain, the United States, and the Soviet Union agreed to ban the testing of nuclear weapons in the atmosphere, in space, and under water, reducing the danger of radioactive fallout. In 1968 the United States and the Soviet Union together proposed a world treaty against further proliferation, leading ultimately to the Nuclear Non-Proliferation Treaty (NPT) signed by 137 countries. Not until 1972, however, did the two superpowers begin the arduous and extremely slow process of negotiating weapons limits.

Helsinki Accords Political and human rights agreement signed in Helsinki, Finland, by the Soviet Union and western European countries.

The atomic powers France and Britain were economically unable to keep up with the Soviet-American arms race. Instead, they led the European states in an effort to relax tensions. Between 1972 and 1975 the Conference on Security and Cooperation in Europe (CSCE) brought delegates from thirty-seven European states, the United States, and Canada to Helsinki. The Soviet Union sought European acceptance of the political boundaries of the Warsaw Pact nations as a condition for broad cooperation. In the end, the **Helsinki Accords** affirmed these boundaries and also called for economic, social, and governmental contacts and for cooperation in humanitarian fields between the two alliances.

Space exploration was another offshoot of the nuclear arms race. The contest to build larger and more accurate missiles prompted the superpowers to prove their skills in rocketry by launching space satellites. The Soviet Union placed a small *Sputnik* satellite into orbit around the earth in October 1957, and the United States responded with its own satellite three months later. The space race was on, a contest in which accomplishments in space were understood to signify equivalent achievements in the military sphere. In 1969, when Neil A. Armstrong and Edwin E. ("Buzz") Aldrin became the first humans to walk on the moon, America had demonstrated its technological superiority.

SECTION REVIEW

- The United Nations was created to manage international disputes and facilitate decolonization and development.

- The United States developed the Marshall Plan to aid European recovery from the devastation of World War II.

- The Cold War was a confrontation between two military alliances, NATO and the Warsaw Pact, and two distinct economic systems, capitalism and communism.

- The United States and the Soviet Union avoid a direct conflict, but the Cold War led to wars in Korea and Vietnam.

- The development of nuclear weapons made the Cold War a threat to the survival of the human race and led to nonproliferation treaties.

DECOLONIZATION AND NATION BUILDING

After World War I Germany, Austria-Hungary, and the Ottoman Empire lost their empires, and many colonies and dependencies were transferred to the victors, especially to Great Britain and France. In the two decades following World War II, nearly all remaining colonies gained independence (see Map 32.2). Circumstances differed profoundly from place to place. In some Asian countries, where colonial rule was of long standing, new states possessed viable industries, communications networks, and education systems. In other countries, notably in Africa, decolonized nations faced dire economic problems and disunity resulting from language and ethnic differences.

Most Latin American nations had achieved political independence in the nineteenth century (see Chapter 22). Following World War II, mass political movements in this region focused on the related issue of economic sovereignty—freedom from growing American economic domination. Great Britain and other European nations still retained colonies in the Caribbean after World War II. In the 1960s Barbados, Guyana, Jamaica, and Trinidad Tobago gained independence from Britain, and the smaller British colonies followed in the 1970s and 1980s, as did Surinam, which gained independence from the Netherlands.

Despite their differences, a sense of kinship arose among the nations of Latin America, Africa, and Asia. All shared feelings of excitement and rebirth. As North Americans, Europeans, and the Chinese settled into the exhausting deadlock of the Cold War, visions of independence and national development captivated the rest of the world.

New Nations in South and Southeast Asia

After partition in 1947 the independent states of India and Pakistan were strikingly dissimilar. Muslim Pakistan defined itself according to religion and quickly fell under the control of military leaders. India, a secular republic led by Prime Minister Jawaharlal Nehru, was much larger and inherited the considerable industrial and educational resources developed by the British, along with a large share of trained civil servants and military officers. Ninety percent of its population was Hindu and most of the rest Muslim.

India and Pakistan   Adding to the tensions of independence (see Chapter 31) was the decision by the Hindu ruler of the northwestern state Jammu and Kashmir, now commonly called Kashmir, without consulting his overwhelmingly Muslim subjects, to join India. War between India and Pakistan over Kashmir broke out in 1947 and ended with an uneasy truce. In 1965 war broke out again, this time involving large military forces and the use of air power by both sides. Kashmir has remained a flash point, with new clashes in 1999 and 2000.

Despite recurrent predictions that multilingual India might break up into a number of linguistically homogeneous states, most Indians recognized that unity benefited everyone; and the country pursued a generally democratic and socialist line of development. Pakistan, in contrast, did break up. In 1971 the Bengali-speaking eastern section seceded to become the independent country of Bangladesh. During the fighting Indian military forces again struck against Pakistan. Despite their shared political heritage, India, Pakistan, and Bangladesh have found cooperation difficult and have pursued markedly different economic, political, religious, and social paths.

Independence in Southeast Asia

During the war the Japanese supported anti-British Indian nationalists as a way to weaken their enemy; they also encouraged the aspirations of nationalists in the countries they occupied in Southeast Asia. Many Asian nationalists saw Japanese victories over British, French, and Dutch colonial armies as a demonstration of the political and military capacities of Asian peoples. In the Dutch East Indies, Achmad Sukarno (1901–1970) cooperated with the Japanese in the hope that the Dutch, who had dominated the region economically since the seventeenth century, could be expelled. The Dutch finally negotiated withdrawal in 1949, and Sukarno became the dictator of the resource-rich but underdeveloped nation of Indonesia. He ruled until 1965, when a military coup ousted him and brutally eliminated the nation's once powerful communist party.

Britain granted independence to Burma (now Myanmar [my-ahn-MAR]) in 1948 and established the Malay Federation the same year. Singapore, once a member of the federation, became an independent city-state in 1965. In 1946 the United States kept its promise of postwar independence for the Philippine Islands but retained close economic ties and leases on military bases.

The Struggle for Independence in Africa

Algerian Independence

Between 1952 and 1956 France granted independence to Tunisia and Morocco, but it sought to retain Algeria. France had controlled this colony for nearly 150 years and had encouraged settlement; in 1950, 10 percent of the Algerian population was of French or other European origin. France also granted political rights to the settler population and asserted the fiction of Algeria's political and economic integration in the French nation. In reality few Algerians benefited from this arrangement, and most resented their continued colonial status.

The Vietnamese military victory over France in 1954 helped provoke a nationalist uprising in Algeria, during which both sides acted brutally. The Algerian revolutionary organization, the Front de Libération National (FLN), was supported by Egypt and other Arab countries who sought the emancipation of all Arab peoples. French colonists considered the country theirs and fought to the bitter end. When Algeria finally won independence in 1962, a flood of angry colonists returned to France. Since few Arabs had received technical training, this departure undermined the economy. Despite harsh feelings left by the war, Algeria retained close and seemingly indissoluble economic ties to France, and Algerians in large numbers emigrated to France to take low-level jobs.

Independence in Africa

Independence was achieved in most of sub-Saharan Africa through negotiation, not revolution. In colonies with significant white settler minorities, however, the path to independence followed the violent experience of Algeria. African nationalists were forced to overcome many obstacles, but they were also able to take advantage of many consequential changes put in place during colonial rule. In the 1950s and 1960s world economic expansion and growing support for liberation overcame African worries about potential economic and political problems that might follow independence. Moreover, improvements in medical care and public health had led to rapid population growth in Africa, and the continent's young population embraced the idea of independence.

Western nationalist and egalitarian ideals also helped fuel resistance to colonialism. Most of the leaders of African independence movements were among the most westernized members of these societies. African veterans of Allied armies during World War II had exposure to Allied propaganda that emphasized ideas of popular sovereignty and self-determination. In addition, many leaders were recent graduates of educational institutions created by colonial governments, and a minority had obtained advanced education in Europe and the United States.

African nationalists were able to take advantage of other legacies of colonial rule as well. Schools, labor associations, and the colonial bureaucracy itself proved to be fertile nationalist recruiting centers. Languages introduced by colonial governments were useful in building multiethnic coalitions, while networks of roads and railroads built to promote colonial exports forged new national identities and a new political consciousness.

MAP 32.2 **Decolonization, 1947–1990** Independence was achieved a decade or so earlier in South and Southeast Asia than in Africa.

© Cengage Learning

Interactive Map

Former ruler

Great Britain	Belgium
France	Portugal
Netherlands	United States
Italy	Other

1960 Year independence achieved

Jomo Kenyatta   Kenya's newly elected premier, Jomo Kenyatta, cheered by crowds in Nairobi in 1963. Kenyatta (waving ceremonial "wisk") had led the struggle to end British colonial rule in Kenya.

Corbis

The young politicians who led the nationalist movements devoted their lives to ridding their homelands of foreign occupation. An example is Kwame Nkrumah (KWAH-mee nn-KROO-muh) (1909–1972), who in 1957 became prime minister of Ghana (formerly the Gold Coast), the first British colony in West Africa to achieve independence. After graduating from a Catholic mission school and a government teacher-training college, Nkrumah spent a decade studying philosophy and theology in the United States, where he absorbed ideas about black pride and independence propounded by W. E. B. Du Bois and Marcus Garvey.

During a brief stay in Britain, Nkrumah joined Kenyan nationalist Jomo Kenyatta, a Ph.D. in anthropology, to found an organization devoted to African freedom. In 1947 Nkrumah returned to the Gold Coast to work for independence. The time was right. There was no longer strong public support in Britain for colonialism, and Britain's political leadership was not enthusiastic about investing resources to hold restive colonies. When Nkrumah's party won a decisive election victory in 1951, the British Gold Coast governor appointed him prime minister. Full independence came in 1957. Although Nkrumah remained an effective international spokesman for colonized peoples, he was overthrown in 1966 by a group of army officers.

Britain soon granted independence to its other West African colonies, including large and populous Nigeria in 1960. In some British colonies in eastern and southern Africa, however, white settler opposition resisted independence. In Kenya a small but influential group of wealthy coffee planters claimed that a protest movement among the Kikuyu (kih-KOO-you) people was proof that Africans were not ready for self-government. The settlers called the movement "Mau Mau," a made-up name meant to evoke primitive savagery. When violence between settlers and anticolonial fighters escalated after 1952, British troops hunted down movement leaders and resettled the Kikuyu in fortified villages. They also declared a state of emergency, banned all African political protest, and imprisoned Kenyatta and other nationalists. Released in 1961, Kenyatta negotiated with the British to write a constitution for an independent Kenya, and in 1964 he was elected the first president. Kenyatta proved to be an effective, though autocratic, ruler, and Kenya benefited from greater stability and prosperity than Ghana and many other former colonies.

Independence in French Africa

African leaders in the sub-Saharan French colonies were more reluctant than their counterparts in British colonies to call for full independence. Promises made in 1944 by the Free French movement of General Charles de Gaulle at a conference in Brazzaville, in French Equatorial Africa, seemed to offer dramatic changes without independence. Dependent on the troops and supplies of French African colonies, de Gaulle had promised Africans a more democratic government, broader suffrage, and greater access to employment in the colonial government. He had also promised better education and health services and an end to many abuses in the colonial system. He had not promised independence, but the politics of postwar colonial self-government led in that direction.

Most Africans elected to office following the reforms were trained civil servants. Because of the French policy of job rotation, they had typically served in a number of different colonies and

e PRIMARY SOURCE:
Comments on Algeria,
April 11, 1961 Read excerpts
of a press conference held by
Charles de Gaulle, in which he
declares France's willingness to
accept Algerian independence.

thus had a broad regional outlook. They realized that some colonies—such as Ivory Coast, with coffee and cacao exports, fishing, and hardwood forests—had good economic prospects, while others, such as landlocked, desert Niger, did not. Furthermore, they recognized the importance of French public investment in the region—a billion dollars between 1947 and 1956—and their own dependence on civil service salaries. As a result, they generally looked to achieve greater self-government incrementally.

When Charles de Gaulle returned to power in France in 1958, at the height of the Algerian war, he warned that a rush to independence would have costs, saying: "One cannot conceive of both an independent territory and a France which continues to aid it." Ultimately, however, African patriotism prevailed in all of France's West African and Equatorial African colonies. Guinea, under the dynamic leadership of Sékou Touré (SAY-koo too-RAY), gained full independence in 1958 and the others in 1960.

The Belgian Congo

Independence in the Belgian Congo was chaotic and violent. Contending political and ethnic groups found external allies; some were supported by Cuba and the Soviet Union, while others were supported by the West or by business groups tied to the rich mines. Civil war, the introduction of foreign mercenaries, and the rhetoric of Cold War confrontation roiled the waters and led to a heavy loss of life and great property destruction. In 1965 Mobuto Sese Seko seized power in a military coup that included the assassination of Patrice Lumumba, the first prime minister. Mobuto controlled one of the region's most corrupt governments until driven from power in 1997.

South Africa

The opposition of European settlers delayed decolonization in southern Africa. While the settler minority tried to defend white supremacy, African-led liberation movements were committed to the creation of nonracial societies and majority rule. In the 1960s African guerrilla movements successfully fought to end Portuguese rule in Angola and Mozambique. Their efforts led to the overthrow of the antidemocratic government of Portugal in 1974 and independence the following year. After a ten-year fight, European settlers in the British colony of Southern Rhodesia accepted African majority rule in 1980. The new government changed the country's name to Zimbabwe, the name of a great stone city built by Africans long before the arrival of European settlers.

South Africa and neighboring Namibia remained in the hands of European minorities. The large white settler population of South Africa achieved effective independence in 1961 but kept the black and mixed-race majority in colonial-era subjection, separating the races in a system they called *apartheid* (a-PART-hite). Descendents of Dutch and English settlers made up 13 percent of the population but controlled the productive land, the industrial, mining, and commercial enterprises, and the government. Meanwhile, discrimination and segregation in housing, education, and employment confined the lives of people of mixed parentage (10 percent of the population) and South Asians (less than 3 percent).

Indigenous Africans, 74 percent of the population, were subjected to even stricter limitations on housing, freedom of movement, and access to jobs and public facilities. The government created fictional African "homelands" as a way of denying the African majority citizenship and political rights. Not unlike Amerindian reservations, these "homelands" were located in poor regions far from the more dynamic and prosperous urban and industrial areas. Overcrowded and lacking investment, they were impoverished and lacking in services and opportunities.

e PRIMARY SOURCE:
The Rivonia Trial
Speech to the Court Read
how Nelson Mandela defended
himself against charges of treason before an all-white South
African court in 1964.

The African National Congress (ANC), formed in 1912, led opposition to apartheid (see Diversity and Dominance: Race and the Struggle for Justice in South Africa). After police fired on demonstrators in the African town of Sharpeville in 1960 and banned all peaceful political protest by Africans, a lawyer named Nelson Mandela (b. 1918) organized guerrilla resistance by the ANC. The government sentenced Mandela to life in prison in 1964 and persecuted the ANC, but it was unable to defeat the movement. Facing growing opposition internationally, South Africa freed Mandela from prison in 1990 and began the transition to majority rule (see Chapter 34).

The Quest for Economic Freedom in Latin America

Although Latin America had achieved independence from colonial rule more than a hundred years earlier, European and American economic domination of the region created a semicolonial order (see Chapters 28 and 31). Foreigners controlled Chile's copper, Cuba's sugar, Colombia's coffee, and Guatemala's bananas, leading by the 1930s to growing support for economic nationalism. During the 1930s and 1940s populist political leaders experimented with programs that would constrain foreign investors or, alternatively, promote local efforts to industrialize (see discussion of Getulio Vargas and Juan Perón in Chapter 31).

The Struggle for Economic Justice in Latin America

In Mexico the revolutionary constitution of 1917 began an era of economic nationalism that culminated in the expropriation of foreign oil interests in 1938. The Institutional Revolutionary Party, or PRI (the abbreviation of its name in Spanish), controlled Mexico until the 1990s and had overseen a period of economic expansion during the war years. But a yawning gulf between rich and poor persisted. Although the government dominated important industries like petroleum and restricted foreign investment, rapid population growth, uncontrolled migration to Mexico City and other urban areas, and political corruption undermined efforts to lift the nation's poor. Economic power was concentrated at the top of society, with two thousand elite families controlling much of the nation's wealth. At the other end of the economic scale were the millions of poor Mexicans struggling to survive.

Guatemala and the CIA

Guatemala's situation was more representative of Latin America in 1950. An American corporation, the United Fruit Company, was Guatemala's largest landowner; it also controlled much of the nation's infrastructure, including port facilities and railroads. To limit banana production and keep prices high, United Fruit kept much of its Guatemalan lands fallow. Jacobo Arbenz Guzmán, elected in 1951, advocated positions broadly similar to those of leaders like Perón of Argentina and Vargas of Brazil (see Chapter 31), who confronted powerful foreign interests. He advocated land reform, which would have transferred these fallow lands to the nation's rural poor. The threatened expropriation angered the United Fruit Company. Simultaneously, Arbenz tried to reduce U.S. political influence, raising fears in Washington that he sought closer ties to the Soviet Union. Reacting to the land reform efforts and to reports that Arbenz was becoming friendly to communism, the U.S. Central Intelligence Agency (CIA), in one of its first major overseas operations, sponsored a takeover by the Guatemalan military in 1954. CIA intervention removed Arbenz, but it also condemned Guatemala to decades of governmental instability and violence.

The Cuban Revolution

In the 1950s American companies dominated the Cuban economy. They controlled sugar production, the nation's most important industry, as well as banking, transportation, tourism, and public utilities. The United States was also the most important market for Cuba's exports and the most important source of Cuba's imports. Thus the needs of the U.S. economy largely determined the ebb and flow of Cuban foreign trade. By 1956 sugar accounted for 80 percent of Cuba's exports and 25 percent of Cuba's national income. But demand in the United States dictated keeping only 39 percent of the land owned by the sugar companies in production, while Cuba experienced chronic underemployment. Similarly, immense deposits of nickel in Cuba went untapped because the U.S. government, which owned them, considered them to be a reserve.

While high unemployment and slow growth afflicted the nation, profits went north to the United States or to a small class of wealthy Cubans. Cuba's government was also notoriously corrupt and subservient to the wishes of American interests. As reform-minded young Cubans organized for a national election, Fulgencio Batista, a former military leader and president, illegally seized power in a coup in 1953. Hostility to Batista and anger with the corruption, repression, and foreign economic domination of his government gave rise to the revolution led by Fidel Castro.

Fidel Castro (b. 1927) was a young lawyer who led a failed uprising in 1953. He returned to Cuba after his conviction and exile to establish a successful revolutionary movement in the countryside that included student groups, labor unions, and supporters of Cuba's traditional parties. When he and his youthful followers took power in 1959, they vowed not to suffer the fate of Arbenz and the Guatemalan reformers. Ernesto ("Che") Guevara (CHAY-guh-VAHR-uh), Castro's chief lieutenant who

Christopher Morris/Black Star

Cuban Poster of Ernesto ("Che") Guevara Che became a leading theorist of communist revolution in Latin America. He died in 1967 while leading an insurgency in Bolivia.

Race and the Struggle for Justice in South Africa

*One of South Africa's martyrs in the struggle against apart-
heid was the thinker and activist Steve Biko (1946–1977). Biko
was one of the founders of the Black Consciousness Movement,
which focused on the ways in which white settlers had stripped
Africans of their freedom. Between 1975 and 1977 police arrested
and interrogated him four times. After his arrest in August 1977,
the police severely beat him and denied him medical care. His
death in police custody caused worldwide outrage.*

[T]hese are not the people we are concerned with [those who
support apartheid]. We are concerned with that curious bunch
of nonconformists who explain their participation in negative
terms: that bunch of do-gooders that goes under all sorts of
names—liberals, leftists etc. These are the people who argue
that they are not responsible for white racism and the country's "inhumanity to the black man." These are the people who
claim that they too feel the oppression just as acutely as the
blacks and therefore should be jointly involved in the black
man's struggle for a place under the sun. In short, these are the
people who say that they have black souls wrapped up in white
skins.

The role of the white liberal in the black man's history in
South Africa is a curious one. Very few black organisations were
not under white direction. True to their image, the white liberals always knew what was good for the blacks and told them
so. The wonder of it all is that the black people have believed
in them for so long. It was only at the end of the 50s that the
blacks started demanding to be their own guardians.

Nowhere is the arrogance of the liberal ideology demonstrated so well as in their insistence that the problems of the
country can only be solved by a bilateral approach involving
both black and white. This has, by and large, come to be taken
in all seriousness as the modus operandi in South Africa by all
those who claim they would like a change in the status quo.
Hence the multiracial political organisations and parties and
the "nonracial" student organisations, all of which insist on
integration not only as an end goal but also as a means.

The integration they talk about is first of all artificial in that
it is a response to conscious manoeuvre rather than to the dictates of the inner soul. In other words the people forming the
integrated complex have been extracted from various segregated societies with their in built [sic] complexes of superiority and inferiority and these continue to manifest themselves

even in the "nonracial" setup of the integrated complex. As a
result the integration so achieved is a one-way course, with
the whites doing all the talking and the blacks the listening.
Let me hasten to say that I am not claiming that segregation is
necessarily the natural order; however, given the facts of the
situation where a group experiences privilege at the expense
of others, then it becomes obvious that a hastily arranged integration cannot be the solution to the problem. It is rather like
expecting the slave to work together with the slave-master's
son to remove all the conditions leading to [his] enslavement.

. . .

It will not sound anachronistic to anybody genuinely
interested in real integration to learn that blacks are asserting themselves in a society where they are being treated as
perpetual under-16s. One does not need to plan for or actively
encourage real integration. Once the various groups within a
given community have asserted themselves to the point that
mutual respect has to be shown then you have the ingredients
for a true and meaningful integration. At the heart of true integration is the provision for each man, each group to rise and
attain the envisioned self. Each group must be able to attain
its style of existence without encroaching on or being thwarted
by another. Out of this mutual respect for each other and complete freedom of self-determination there will obviously arise
a genuine fusion of the life-styles of the various groups. This is
true integration.

From this it becomes clear that as long as blacks are suffering from [an] inferiority complex—a result of 300 years of
deliberate oppression, denigration and derision—they will be
useless as co-architects of a normal society where man is nothing else but man for his own sake. Hence what is necessary as a
prelude to anything else that may come is a very strong grassroots build-up of black consciousness such that blacks can
learn to assert themselves and stake their rightful claim.

Thus in adopting the line of a nonracial approach, the liberals are playing their old game. They are claiming a "monopoly
on intelligence and moral judgement" and setting the pattern
and pace for the realisation of the black man's aspirations.
They want to remain in good books with both the black and
white worlds. They want to shy away from all forms of "extrem-
isms," condemning "white supremacy" as being just as bad
as "Black Power!" They vacillate between the two worlds,
verbalising all the complaints of the blacks beautifully while

became the main theorist of communist revolution in Latin America, had witnessed the CIA
coup in Guatemala firsthand. He and Castro believed that confrontation with the United States
was inevitable and moved quickly to remove the existing military leadership and begin revolutionary changes in the economy.

Within a year Castro's government seized and redistributed land, lowered urban rents, and
raised wages, effectively transferring 15 percent of the national income from the rich to the poor.

skillfully extracting what suits them from the exclusive pool of white privileges. But ask them for a moment to give a concrete meaningful programme that they intend adopting, then you will see on whose side they really are. Their protests are directed at and appeal to white conscience, everything they do is directed at finally convincing the white electorate that the black man is also a man and that at some future date he should be given a place at the white man's table.

In the following selection Anglican bishop Desmond Tutu (b. 1931) expressed his personal anguish at the death of Steve Biko, summarizing Biko's contributions to the struggle for justice in South Africa. Tutu won the Noble Peace Prize in 1984 and was named archbishop in 1988. From 1995 to 1998 he chaired the Truth and Reconciliation Commission, which investigated atrocities in South Africa during the years of apartheid. He stated that his objective was to create "a democratic and just society without racial divisions."

When we heard the news "Steve Biko is dead" we were struck numb with disbelief. No, it can't be true! No, it must be a horrible nightmare, and we will awake and find that really it is different—that Steve is alive even if it be in detention. But no, dear friends, he is dead and we are still numb with grief, and groan with anguish "Oh God, where are you? Oh God, do you really care—how can you let this happen to us?"

It all seems such a senseless waste of a wonderfully gifted person, struck down in the bloom of youth, a youthful bloom that some wanted to see blighted. What can be the purpose of such wanton destruction? God, do you really love us? What must we do which we have not done, what must we say which we have not said a thousand times over, oh, for so many years— that all we want is what belongs to all God's children, what belongs as an inalienable right—a place in the sun in our own beloved mother country. Oh God, how long can we go on? How long can we go on appealing for a more just ordering of society where we all, black and white together, count not because of some accident of birth or a biological irrelevance—where all of us black and white count because we are human persons, human persons created in your own image.

God called Steve Biko to be his servant in South Africa—to speak up on behalf of God, declaring what the will of this God must be in a situation such as ours, a situation of evil, injustice, oppression and exploitation. God called him to be the founder father of the Black Consciousness Movement against which we have had tirades and fulminations. It is a movement by which God, through Steve, sought to awaken in the Black person a sense of his intrinsic value and worth as a child of God, not needing to apologise for his existential condition as a black person, calling on blacks to glorify and praise God that he had created them black. Steve, with his brilliant mind that always saw to the heart of things, realised that until blacks asserted their humanity and their personhood, there was not the remotest chance for reconciliation in South Africa. For true reconciliation is a deeply personal matter. It can happen only between persons who assert their own personhood, and who acknowledge and respect that of others. You don't get reconciled to your dog, do you? Steve knew and believed fervently that being pro-black was not the same thing as being anti-white. The Black Consciousness Movement is not a "hate white movement," despite all you may have heard to the contrary. He had a far too profound respect for persons as persons, to want to deal with them under readymáde, shopsoiled [sic] categories.

All who met him had this tremendous sense of a warm-hearted man, and as a notable acquaintance of his told me, a man who was utterly indestructible, of massive intellect and yet reticent; quite unshakeable in his commitment to principle and to radical change in South Africa by peaceful means; a man of real reconciliation, truly an instrument of God's peace, unshakeable in his commitment to the liberation of all South Africans, black and white, striving for a more just and more open South Africa.

QUESTIONS FOR ANALYSIS

1. What are Steve Biko's charges against white liberals in South Africa?

2. What was the proper role for whites in the antiapartheid movement according to Biko?

3. How does Bishop Tutu's eulogy differ from the political spirit and point of view expressed in Biko's 1970 essay?

4. According to Bishop Tutu, what were Biko's strongest characteristics? Were these characteristics demonstrated in Biko's essay?

Source: First selection from Steve Biko, *I Write What I Like*, ed. by Aelred Stubbs C.R. Reprinted with the permission of Bowerdean Publishing Co., Ltd.; second selection from Bishop Desmond Tutu, *Crying in the Wilderness: The Struggle for Justice in South Africa*, ed. John Webster (William B. Eerdmans Publishing Co., 1982), pp. 61–63. Reprinted by permission of the Continuum International Publishing Group.

Within two years the Castro government had nationalized the property of almost all U.S. corporations in Cuba as well as the wealth of Cuba's elite. To achieve his revolutionary objectives, Castro sought economic support from the Soviet Union.

The United States responded by seeking to destabilize the Cuban economy and undermine the Castro government. U.S. punitive measures, the nationalization of so much of the economy, and the punishment of Batista supporters caused tens of thousands of Cubans to leave. Initially, most emigrants were from wealthy families and the middle class, but when the economic failures of the regime became clear, many poor Cubans fled to the United States or to other Latin American nations.

There is little evidence that Castro was committed to communism before the revolution, but his commitment to break the economic and political power of the United States in Cuba and undertake dramatic social reforms led inevitably to conflict with the United States and reliance on the Soviet Union. In April 1961, in an attempt to apply the strategy that had removed Arbenz from power in Guatemala, an army of Cuban exiles trained and armed by the CIA landed at the Bay of Pigs in an effort to overthrow Castro. The Cuban army defeated the attempted invasion in a matter of days. The Eisenhower administration had planned the invasion, but the new U.S. president, John F. Kennedy, agreed to carry it out and lived with the embarrassment. This failure helped precipitate the Cuban missile crisis. Fearful of a new invasion, Castro and Khrushchev placed nuclear weapons as well as missiles and bombers in Cuba to forestall the anticipated attack.

The failure of the Bay of Pigs tarnished the reputation of the United States and the CIA and gave heart to revolutionaries all over Latin America. But the armed revolutionary movements that imitated the tactics and objectives of Cuba's bearded revolutionaries experienced little success. Among the thousands to lose their lives was Che Guevara, captured and executed in 1967 by Bolivian troops trained by the United States. Nevertheless, Castro had demonstrated that revolutionaries could successfully challenge American power and put in place a radical program of economic and social reform in the Western Hemisphere.

SECTION REVIEW

- Independence in India and Pakistan led to war over Kashmir, which has continued to cause conflict.
- Algeria gained independence from France after a long and violent revolution.
- West African colonies eventually gained independence from Great Britain and France through negotiation, but the Belgian Congo fell under the power of a dictator.
- In southern African colonies large white settler populations resisted independence, and whites in South Africa instituted the system of segregation called apartheid.
- In Latin American nations economic nationalists sought to reduce or eliminate the economic influence of the United States.
- The CIA interfered forcefully in Guatemala, and its attempt to do the same in Cuba led to the Cuban missile crisis; meanwhile, Castro created a socialist economy.

BEYOND A BIPOLAR WORLD

Although no one doubted the dominating role of the East-West superpower rivalry in world affairs, newly independent nations had concerns that were primarily domestic and regional. Their challenge was to pursue their ends within the bipolar structure of the Cold War—and possibly to take advantage of the East-West rivalry. Where nationalist forces sought to assert political or economic independence, Cold War antagonists provided arms and political support even when the nationalist goals were quite different from those of the supporting superpower. For other nations, the ruinously expensive superpower arms race opened opportunities to expand industries and exports. In short, the superpowers dominated the world but did not control it.

The Third World

nonaligned nations
Developing countries that announced their neutrality in the Cold War.

Third World Term applied to a group of developing countries who professed nonalignment during the Cold War.

As a leader of the decolonization movement, Indonesia's President Sukarno was an appropriate figure to host a 1955 meeting of twenty-nine African and Asian countries at Bandung, Indonesia, that proclaimed solidarity among those fighting against colonial rule. This conference marked the beginning of an effort by the many new, poor, mostly non-European nations emerging from colonialism to gain more influence in world affairs. The terms **nonaligned nations** and **Third World**, which became commonplace in the following years, signaled these countries' collective stance toward the rival sides in the Cold War. If the West, led by the United States, and the East, led by the Soviet Union, represented two worlds locked in mortal struggle, the Third World consisted of everyone else.

Leaders of so-called Third World countries preferred the label *nonaligned*, which signaled their independence from Soviet or U.S. control. Leaders in the West noted that the Soviet Union

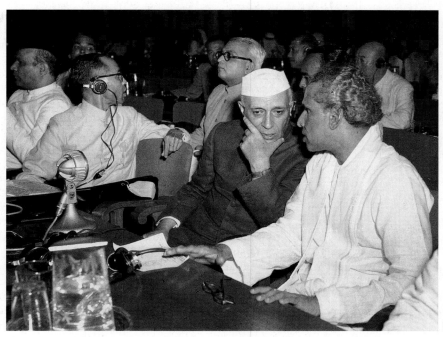

Bandung Conference, 1955 India's Jawa-harlal Nehru (in white hat) was a central figure at the conference held in Indonesia to promote solidarity among nonaligned developing nations.

The Nonaligned Movement

supported many national liberation movements and that the nonaligned movement included communist countries such as China and Yugoslavia. As a result, they refused to take the term *nonaligned* seriously. In a polarized world, they saw Sukarno, Nehru, Nkrumah, and Egypt's Gamal Abd al-Nasir (gah-MAHL AHB-d al–NAH-suhr) as stalking horses for a communist takeover of the world. This may have been the view of some Soviet leaders as well, since they were quick to offer military and financial aid to many nonaligned countries.

For the movement's leaders, however, nonalignment was primarily a way to extract money and support from one or both superpowers. By flirting with the Soviet Union or its ally, the People's Republic of China, a country could get weapons, training, and barter agreements that offered an alternative to selling agricultural or mineral products on Western-dominated world markets. The same flirtation might also prompt the United States and its allies to proffer grants and loans, cheap or free surplus grain, and investment for new industry or for infrastructure.

Nonaligned countries could sometimes play the Cold War rivals against each other. Nasir, who had led a military coup against the Egyptian monarchy in 1952, and his successor Anwar al-Sadat (al-seh-DAT) played this game skillfully. The United States offered to build a dam at Aswan (AS-wahn), on the Nile River, to increase Egypt's electrical generating and irrigation capacity, but it withdrew the offer when Egypt turned to the Warsaw Pact for arms in 1956. Wors-ened relations with the West then led Nasir to nationalize the Suez Canal and the Soviet Union to commit to building the dam. Later that same year Israel, Great Britain, and France allied to invade Egypt, aiming to overthrow Nasir, regain the Suez Canal, and secure Israel from any Egyptian threat. The invasion succeeded militarily, but the United States and the Soviet Union both pressured the invaders to withdraw, thus saving Nasir's government. In 1972 Sadat evicted Soviet military advisers, but a year later he used his Soviet weapons to attack Israel. After he lost that war, he improved relations with and sought increased aid from the United States.

Other nations adopted similar balancing strategies. In each case, local leaders sought to develop their nations' economies and assert or preserve their nations' interests. Manipulating the superpowers was a means toward those ends and implied very little about true ideological orientation.

Japan and China

No countries took more effective advantage of opportunities presented by the superpowers' pre-occupations than Japan and China. Japan signed a peace treaty with most of its former enemies in 1951 and regained independence from American occupation the following year. Renouncing militarism and its imperialist past (see Chapter 27), Japan remained on the sidelines throughout the Korean War. Its new constitution, written under American supervision in 1946, allowed only a limited self-defense force, banned the deployment of Japanese troops abroad, and gave the vote to women.

Japanese Economic Development

The Japanese focused their resources on rebuilding industries and expanding trade. Peace treaties with countries in Southeast Asia specified reparations payable in the form of goods and services, thus reintroducing Japan to that region as a force for economic development rather than as a military occupier. Japan was closely tied to the West by trade and able to benefit from the postwar recovery. At the same time, controls placed on Japan by peace conditions kept its military expenditures low during the Cold War, providing an exceptional environment to develop its economy.

Three industries that took advantage of government aid and new technologies were key to Japan's emergence as an economic superpower after 1975. Electricity was in short supply in 1950, and Tokyo suffered from chronic power outages. Japan responded by building projects that produced 60 million kilowatts of electricity between 1951 and 1970, most relying on hydroelectric power. Between 1960 and 1970 steel production and shipbuilding also developed rapidly, placing Japan among world leaders in both industries.

China and the Cold War

While Japan benefited from avoiding the heavy defense costs associated with the Cold War, China was at the center of Cold War politics. When Mao Zedong (maow dzuh-dong) and the communists defeated the nationalists in 1949 and established the People's Republic of China (PRC), their main ally and source of arms was the Soviet Union. By 1956, however, the PRC and the Soviet Union were beginning to diverge politically, partly in reaction to the Soviet rejection of Stalinism and partly because of China's reluctance to accept the role of subordinate. Mao had his own notions of communism that focused strongly on the peasantry, which the Soviets had ignored in favor of the industrial working class.

Cultural Revolution (China) Campaign in China ordered by Mao Zedong to purge the Communist Party of his opponents and instill revolutionary values in the younger generation.

Mao's Great Leap Forward in 1958 was intended to propel China into the ranks of world industrial powers by maximizing the output of small-scale, village-level industries and by instituting mass collectivization in agriculture. These untested policies demonstrated Mao's willingness to carry out massive economic and social projects of his own devising in the face of criticism by the Soviets and by traditional economists. By 1962 the revolutionary reforms had failed comprehensively, leading to an estimated 20 to 30 million deaths.

In 1966 Mao instituted another radical program, the **Cultural Revolution**, that ordered the mass mobilization of Chinese youth into Red Guard units. His goal was to kindle revolutionary fervor in a new generation to ward off the stagnation and bureaucratization he saw in the Soviet Union, as well as to increase his own power within the Communist Party. Red Guard units criticized and purged teachers, party officials, and intellectuals for "bourgeois values." Executions, beatings, and incarcerations were widespread, leading to a half-million deaths and 3 million purged by 1971. Finally, Mao admitted that attacks on individuals had gotten out of hand and intervened to reestablish order. Mao's wife Jiang Qing (jyahn ching) and radical allies dominated the last years of the Cultural Revolution, harshly restricting artistic and intellectual activity.

The rift between the PRC and the Soviet Union allowed U.S. President Richard Nixon (served 1969–1974) to revive relations with China. In 1971 the United States agreed to allow the PRC to join the United Nations and occupy China's permanent seat on the

AP Images

Chinese Red Guards During the Cultural Revolution, the Red Guards, young Chinese militants, sought to identify enemies of the Communist Party and Chairman Mao, sometimes labeling their own teachers, parents, and neighbors as enemies of the people. In this photo a victim wears a dunce cap on which his crimes are written.

**PRIMARY SOURCE:
One Hundred Items for
Destroying the Old and
Establishing the New** Read
this document of support for
Mao's socialist ideology and
commitment to destroy the old
ways of Chinese thinking by a
student group of Red Guards.

**The Beginnings
of the Israeli and
Palestinian Conflict**

**PRIMARY SOURCE:
The Palestinian
National Charter** Read how
attendees of the Fourth Palestine National Council defined
their homeland and pledged to
liberate it from Israel.

OPEC

**Organization of Petroleum
Exporting Countries (OPEC)**
Organization formed in 1960
by oil-producing states to
promote their collective
interest in generating revenue from oil.

Security Council. This decision necessitated the expulsion of the Chinese nationalist government based on the island of Taiwan, which had previously claimed to be the only legal Chinese
authority. The following year, Nixon visited Beijing, initiating a new era of enhanced cooperation between the People's Republic of China and the United States.

The Middle East

Independence came gradually to the Arab countries of the Middle East. Britain granted Syria
and Lebanon independence after World War II. Iraq, Egypt, and Jordan enjoyed nominal independence between the two world wars but remained under indirect British control until the
1950s. Military coups overthrew King Faruq (fuh-ROOK) of Egypt in 1952 and King Faisal (FIE-
suhl) II of Iraq in 1958. King Husayn (hoo-SANE) of Jordan dismissed his British military commander in 1956 in response to the Suez crisis, but his poor desert country remained dependent
on British and later American financial aid.

Overshadowing all Arab politics, however, was the struggle with Israel, a clear illustration
that the superpowers could not control all dangerous international disputes. British policy on
Palestine between the wars oscillated between favoring Zionist Jews—who emigrated to Palestine, encouraged by the Balfour Declaration—and support for the indigenous Palestinian Arabs,
who suspected that the Zionists were aiming at an independent state. As more and more Jews
sought a safe haven from persecution by the Nazis, Arabs felt more and more threatened. The
Arabs unleashed a guerrilla uprising against the British in 1936, and Jewish groups turned to
militant tactics a few years later. Occasionally, Arabs and Jews confronted each other in riots or
killings, making it clear that peaceful coexistence in Palestine would be difficult or impossible
to achieve.

After the war, under intense pressure to resettle European Jewish refugees, Britain turned
the Palestine problem over to the United Nations. In November 1947 the General Assembly
voted in favor of partitioning Palestine into two states, one Jewish and one Arab. The Jewish
community made plans to declare independence, while the Palestinians, who felt that the proposed land division was unfair, took up arms. When Israel declared its independence in May
1948, neighboring Arab countries sent armies to help the Palestinians crush the newborn state.

Israel prevailed and some 700,000 Palestinians became refugees, finding shelter in United
Nations refugee camps in Jordan, Syria, Lebanon, and the Gaza Strip (a bit of coastal land on
the Egyptian-Israeli border). The right of these refugees to return home remains a focal point of
Arab politics. In 1967 Israel responded to threatening military moves by Egypt's Nasir by pre-
emptively attacking Egyptian and Syrian air bases. In six days Israel won a smashing victory.
When Jordan entered the war, Israel took control of Jerusalem, which it had previously split with
Jordan, and the West Bank. Acquiring all of Jerusalem satisfied Jews' deep longing to return to
their holiest city, but Palestinians continued to regard Jerusalem as their destined capital, and
Muslims in many countries protested Israeli control of the Dome of the Rock, a revered Islamic
shrine located in the city. Israel also occupied the Gaza Strip, the strategic Golan Heights in
southern Syria, and the entire Sinai Peninsula (see Map 32.3). These acquisitions resulted in a
new wave of Palestinian refugees.

The rival claims to Palestine continued to plague Middle Eastern politics. The Palestine
Liberation Organization (PLO), headed by Yasir Arafat (AR-uh-fat), waged guerrilla war against
Israel, frequently engaging in acts of terrorism. The Israelis were able to blunt or absorb these
attacks and launch counterstrikes that likewise involved assassinations and bombings. Though
the United States was a firm friend to Israel and the Soviet Union armed the Arab states, neither
superpower saw the struggle between Zionism and Palestinian nationalism as a vital concern—
until oil became a political issue.

The phenomenal concentration of oil wealth in the Middle East—Saudi Arabia, Iran, Iraq,
Kuwait, Libya, Qatar, Bahrain, and the United Arab Emirates—was not fully realized until after
World War II, when demand for oil rose sharply as civilian economies recovered. In 1960, as
world demand rose, oil-producing states formed the **Organization of Petroleum Exporting
Countries (OPEC)** to promote their collective interest in higher revenues.

Oil politics and the Arab-Israeli conflict intersected in October 1973 during the Yom Kippur
War. Surprise attacks by Syria and Egypt threw the Israelis into temporary disarray, but Israel
won a clear military victory in the end. Supported by military supplies from the United States, it
drove back Syrian forces and trapped an Egyptian army at the Suez Canal's southern end. The

Black Sea

BULGARIA

RUSSIA

KAZAKHSTAN

UZBEKISTAN

CHINA

Caspian Sea

GEORGIA

ARMENIA

AZERBAIJAN

TURKMENISTAN

Ankara

TURKEY

Soviet occupation, 1979–1989
U.S. aid to rebels, 1980s
International and Northern Alliance
forces defeat Taliban, 2001

Mazar e
Sharif

Kabul

Islamabad

Euphrates R.

Tigris R.

Tehran

AFGHANISTAN

Herat

20°E

Crete

CYPRUS

U.S. troops, 1958, 1983–1984

Mediterranean Sea

SYRIA

Tikrit

Kirkuk

Damascus

LEBANON

Fallujah

Baghdad

IRAN

U.S. arms sales, 1955–1978:
$20.8 billion
Shah overthrown, 1979
American hostages taken,
1979–1981

Kandahar

Principal center of al-Qa
activity, 2004—

30°N

Quetta

ISRAEL

Tel Aviv

Amman

30°N

IRAQ

PAKISTAN

INDIA

Indus R.

JORDAN

Basra

Cairo

Kuwait

KUWAIT

U.S. and allies launch
First U.S.-Iraq War, 1991

LIBYA

EGYPT

U.S. arms sales, 1980s,
during Iran-Iraq War
Iraq invades Kuwait, 1990
Second U.S.-Iraq War, 2003

Persian Gulf

Karachi

Strait of Hormuz

Nile R.

Manama

QATAR

BAHRAIN

Doha

Dubayy

Abu Dhabi

Muscat

Tropic of Cancer

Aswan
Dam

Red Sea

Riyadh

UNITED ARAB
EMIRATES

30°E

SAUDI ARABIA

OMAN

Arabian Sea

Al-Qaeda headquarters,
1992–1996

SUDAN

Mecca

20°N

Oil embargo, 1973
Source of 17% of U.S. oil imports
in 1975
Largest buyer of U.S. arms, 1978

40°E

ERITREA

YEMEN

Sana

70°E

Mukalla

60°E

Aden

Gulf of Aden

50°E

*Socotra
(Yemen)*

DJIBOUTI

Djibouti

Bombing of USS *Cole*
by al-Qaeda, 2000

*INDIAN
OCEAN*

ETHIOPIA

SOMALIA

U.S. troops assist in relief of
famine, 1992–1993.
U.S. troops withdrawn, 1994.
U.S.-backed Ethiopian invasion
removes Islamist government,
2006

Members of the Organization of
Petroleum Exporting Countries
(OPEC)

Oil fields

Mogadishu

0   250   500 Km.

0   250   500 Mi.

0° Equator

N

© Cengage Learning

ARAB-ISRAELI CONFLICT inset:

Jewish state after UN partition
of Palestine, 1947

Israel after War of 1948–1949

Area controlled by Israel after
Six-Day War, 1967

Israeli-occupied area after
Yom Kippur War, 1973

By Egyptian-Israeli agreements of 1975 and
1979, Israel withdrew from the Sinai in 1982.
In 1981 Israel annexed the Golan Heights.
Through negotiations between Israel and
the PLO, Jericho and the Gaza Strip were
placed under Palestinian self-rule, and Israeli
troops were withdrawn in 1994. In 1994
Israel and Jordan signed an agreement
opening their borders and normalizing their
relations.

LEBANON

Beirut

Damascus

SYRIA

GOLAN
HEIGHTS

Haifa

*Sea
of Galilee*

Jordan R.

32°E

Tel Aviv

WEST
BANK

Amman

*Mediterranean
Sea*

ISRAEL

Jerusalem

Gaza

*Dead
Sea*

JORDAN

Port Said

*Suez
Canal*

EGYPT

Cairo

Suez

Nile R.

*SINAI
PENINSULA*

Elath

30°E

SAUDI
ARABIA

28°E

Sharm
el-Sheikh

Gulf of Suez

Gulf of Aqaba

Red Sea

32°E

36°E

MAP 32.3 **Middle East Oil and the Arab-Israeli Conflict, 1947–1973** Private European and American companies had long controlled oil resources. In the 1960s OPEC negotiated agreements for sharing control and eventually establishing national ownership. This set the stage for the use of oil as a weapon in the 1973 Arab-Israeli war as well as for subsequent price increases.

e Interactive Map

Shortage at the Pumps   As prices rose in the late 1970s, consumers tried to hoard supplies by filling gas cans at neighborhood stations. For the first time gas prices exceeded $1 a gallon.

James Pozarik/Getty Images

United States then arranged a ceasefire and the disengagement of forces. But before that could happen, the Arab oil-producing countries voted to embargo oil shipments to the United States and the Netherlands as punishment for their support of Israel.

The implications of using oil as an economic weapon profoundly disturbed the worldwide oil industry. Prices rose—along with feelings of insecurity. In 1974 OPEC responded to the turmoil in the oil market by quadrupling prices, setting the stage for massive transfers of wealth to the producing countries and provoking a feeling of crisis throughout the consuming countries.

The Emergence of Environmental Concerns

The Cold War and the massive investments made in postwar economic recovery focused public and governmental attention on technological innovations and enormous projects such as hydroelectric dams and nuclear power stations. Only a few people warned that untested technologies and industrial expansion were degrading the environment. The superpowers were particularly negligent of the environmental impact of pesticide and herbicide use, automobile exhaust, industrial waste disposal, and radiation.

The wave of student unrest that swept many parts of the world in 1968 and the early 1970s created a new awareness of environmental issues and a new constituency for environmental action. As youth activism grew, governments in the West began to pass new environmental regulations. Among them was the Clean Air Act of 1970. Earth Day, a benchmark of the new awareness, was also first celebrated in 1970, the year in which the United States also established its Environmental Protection Agency.

When oil prices skyrocketed, the problem of finite natural resources became more broadly recognized. Making gasoline engines and home

---

SECTION REVIEW

- After decolonization new nations organized the "Nonaligned Movement" to assert a middle ground between the Cold War rivals.

- After World War II Japan followed the capitalist industrial model while China under Mao tried and failed to industrialize using mass mobilizations and central planning.

- Israel's military victories over its Arab neighbors in 1967 and 1973 expanded the nation's borders, but initiated an enduring cycle of regional tensions and violence between Israelis and Palestinians.

- OPEC's 1973 embargo of oil shipments to nations that supported Israel soon led to steep price increases and a massive redistribution of wealth to oil-producing nations.

- During the 1970s young people provided crucial leadership to a worldwide movement to conserve natural resources and protect the environment.

heating systems more efficient and lowering highway speed limits to conserve fuel became matters of national debate in the United States, while poorer countries struggled to find the money
to import oil. A widely read 1972 study called *The Limits of Growth* forecast a need to cut back
on consumption of natural resources in the twenty-first century. Ecological and environmental problems now vied for public attention with superpower rivalry and Third World nation
building.

CONCLUSION

The alliance between the Soviet Union and the Western democracies led by the United States
did not survive into the post–World War II era. Shortly after the war, both sides began to prepare
for a new round of hostilities, establishing competing military alliances and attempting to influence the new governments of nations formerly occupied by the Axis. In the end this confrontation was projected into space, as each side sought to advertise its technological capacity through
satellite launches and finally a moon landing.

Each side portrayed this tension as a struggle between irreconcilably different social and
economic systems, and each side emphasized the corruption, injustice, and unfairness of its
opponent. When Winston Churchill spoke in 1946 of Soviet control in eastern Europe as an iron
curtain, he suggested that the Soviet system was, in effect, a prison.

Massive armies armed with increasingly sophisticated weapons, including nuclear weapons far more destructive than those dropped on Japan, defended the boundary that separated
the United States and its allies and the Soviet Union and its allies. This Cold War quickly became
global in character as distant civil wars, regional conflicts, and nationalist revolutions were
transformed by support provided by these rivals for global ascendancy.

The desire of colonized peoples to throw off imperial controls and establish independent
nations provided many of the era's flash points. The Western nations had defined World War II
as a war for freedom and self-determination. The Free French had promised greater autonomy
to African colonies, the United States had used nationalist forces to fight against the Japanese
in the Philippines and in Vietnam, and the British also had used forces recruited throughout its
empire to fight the war. Once organized and set in motion, these nationalist energies eventually
overwhelmed colonial rule. The most powerful force in the postwar era was nationalism, the
desire of peoples to control their own destinies.

In Africa, the Middle East, South Asia, and Latin America, this desire to throw off foreign
controls led to the creation of scores of new nations by the 1970s. Each nation's struggle had
its own character. While in India these passions led to independence, similar sentiments led in
China to the overthrow of a government seen as weak and subordinate to foreign powers and
the creation of a communist dictatorship. In much of Africa, the Middle East, and the Caribbean, nationalism overturned colonial rule. In the Middle East the desire for self-government
was complicated by the creation of the state of Israel. In Latin America, where most nations had
been independent for well over a century, nationalist passions focused on a desire for economic
independence and an end to foreign interventions.

The end of Japanese control in Korea and Vietnam led to territorial partitions that separated
Soviet-leaning and Western-allied polities. Civil war and foreign interventions soon followed.
In both cases the Soviet Union and China supported communist forces. The United States com-
mitted large military forces to protect the anticommunist governments, gaining a stalemate in
Korea and eventually losing in Vietnam. While these outcomes were mixed for the superpowers,
the wars were contained and managed so as to prevent direct engagement and nuclear conflict.

This period also witnessed the beginning of the International environmental movement.
Public attention increasingly focused on resource management, pollution, and the preservation
of endangered species. In response, the United States and governments in western Europe put in
place the first generation of environmental laws. The Clean Air Act in the United States and other
measures had an immediate impact, but both policymakers and the public grew aware of ever
more serious challenges. The gas crisis of the 1970s gave these efforts a sense of urgency.

KEY TERMS

iron curtain p. 848
Cold War p. 848
North Atlantic Treaty
 Organization
 (NATO) p. 848
Warsaw Pact p. 848
United Nations p. 848

World Bank p. 849
Marshall Plan p. 851
European Economic
 Community (Common
 Market) p. 851
Korean War p. 852
Vietnam War p. 853

Cuban missile
 crisis p. 855
Helsinki Accords p. 855
nonaligned nations p. 864
Third World p. 864
Cultural Revolution
 (China) p. 866

Organization
 of Petroleum
 Exporting Countries
 (OPEC) p. 867

EBOOK AND WEBSITE RESOURCES

Primary Sources

Comments on Algeria, April 11, 1961

The Rivonia Trial Speech to the Court

One Hundred Items for Destroying the Old and Establishing the New

The Palestinian National Charter

Interactive Maps

Map 32.1 Cold War Confrontation

Map 32.2 Decolonization, 1947–1990

Map 32.3 Middle East Oil and the Arab-Israeli Conflict, 1947–1973

Plus flashcards, practice quizzes, and more. Go to:
www.cengage.com/history/bullietearthpeople5e

SUGGESTED READING

Allison, Graham. *Essence of Decision: Explaining the Cuban Missile Crisis.* 1971. An influential study of decision making in a time of crisis.

Barraclough, Geoffrey. *An Introduction to Contemporary History.* 1964. A remarkable early effort at understanding the broad sweep of history.

Becker, Jasper. *Hungry Ghosts.* 1998. Explores the Great Leap Forward in China.

Chamberlain, M. E. *Decolonization: The Fall of the European Empires*, 2nd ed. 1999. A comprehensive overview.

De Witte, Ludo, trans. Ann Wright. *The Assassination of Lumumba.* 2003.

Dower, John. *Embracing Defeat: Japan in the Wake of World War II.* 1999. An excellent history of the American occupation of Japan.

Gelvin, James. *The Modern Middle East: A History.* 2007. A reliable introduction to the region.

Hitchcock, William. *The Struggle for Europe: The Turbulent History of a Divided Continent 1945–2002.* 2003. An excellent recent study of Cold War era Europe.

Karnow, Stanley. *Vietnam: A History*, 2nd ed. 1997. A detailed and balanced history.

Kyle, Keith. *Suez 1956.* 1991. Examines the international complications of a brief war.

Lapping, Brian. *End of Empire.* 1985. Covers the dissolution of the British Empire.

Leffler, Melvyn P., and David S. Painter, eds. *Origins of the Cold War: An International History.* 1994. Offers reconsiderations of earlier historical viewpoints.

Low, D. A. *The Egalitarian Moment: Asia and Africa, 1950–1980.* 1996. Explores the end of the colonial period.

MacDougall, Walter. *The Heavens and the Earth: A Political History of the Space Age.* 1985. Looks at the intersection of politics, technology, and international competition.

Mazower, Mark. *Dark Continent.* 1999. An outstanding reappraisal of Europe's twentieth-century history.

Meisner, Maurice. *Mao's China and After: A History of the People's Republic*, 3rd ed. 1999. A highly regarded survey.

Merrill, John. *Korea: The Peninsular Origins of the War.* 1989. Presents the Korean War as a civil and revolutionary conflict as well as part of the Cold War.

Nakamura, Takafusa. *A History of Showa Japan, 1926–1989.* 1998. A solid Japanese study of the reign of Emperor Hirohito.

Rabe, Stephen. *The Most Dangerous Area in the World: John F. Kennedy Confronts Communist Revolution in Latin America.* 1999. A useful exploration of the era.

Reynolds, David. *One World Divisible: A Global History Since 1945.* 2000. A very useful discussion of recent events.

Smith, Charles D. *Palestine and the Arab-Israeli Conflict*, 6th rev. ed. 2007. Comprehensive coverage of an ongoing crisis.

Walker, Martin. *The Cold War: A History.* 1993. A good general history.

Zubok, Vladislav, and Constantine Pleshakov. *Inside the Kremlin's Cold War: From Stalin to Khrushchev.* 1997. Among the best treatments of Cold War Soviet Union.

CHAPTER

33

CHAPTER OUTLINE

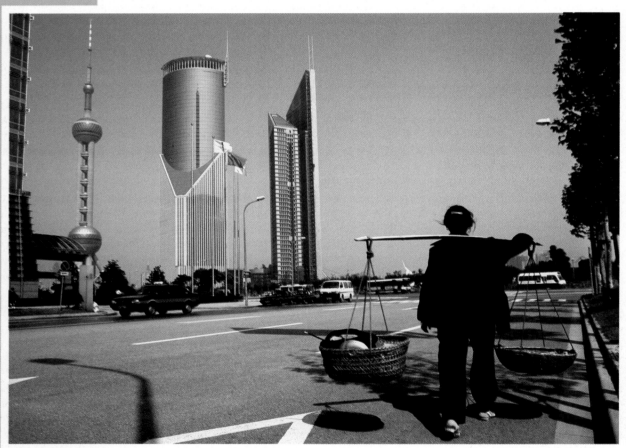

Dennis Cox/China Stock

Shanghai—Old Meets New The city of Shanghai is one of the great success stories in a rapidly growing Chinese economy, but its prosperity has left many behind. In this photo a poor woman walks past Shanghai's modern skyline carrying goods to market in baskets and a neck yoke, a technology thousands of years old.

Visit the website and ebook for additional study materials and interactive tools: www.cengage.com/history/bulletearthpeople5e

The End of the Cold War and the Challenge of Economic Development and Immigration, 1975–2000

At the end of the 1970s China began an ambitious program of economic reforms. Until then China, with the world's largest population, lagged far behind the mature industrialized nations of Europe and North America in economic performance, as well as behind neighboring nations like Japan and South Korea. Since the reforms, China has experienced rapid economic growth, becoming one of the few socialist nations to successfully make the transition to a market economy. Despite this remarkable expansion, over 100 million Chinese still lived in poverty in 2000. As is indicated in the opening illustration, ancient technology and poverty can exist in close proximity with modernity and affluence in China. These same problems of poverty and inequality exist across the globe. In an era of astounding technological change and, until 2008, spreading prosperity, 1.2 billion of the world's population lived on less than a dollar per day.

At the end of the twentieth century population growth continued to outstrip economic resources in many of the nations of the developing world. In wealthy industrialized nations as well, politicians and social reformers still worry about the effects of unemployment, family breakdown, substance abuse, and homelessness. In the last decades of the twentieth century, as in the Industrial Revolution (see Chapter 23), dramatic economic expansion, increased global economic integration, and rapid technological progress coincided with problems of social dislocation and inequality. Among the most important events of the period were the emergence of new industrial powers in Asia and the precipitous demise of the Soviet Union and its socialist allies.

- How did the Cold War affect politics in Latin America and the Middle East in the 1970s and 1980s?
- What forces led to the collapse of the Soviet Union?
- What explains differences in the rate of population growth among the world's cultural regions?
- How does wealth inequality among nations impact international migration patterns?
- How has technological change affected the global environment in the recent past?

POSTCOLONIAL CRISES AND ASIAN ECONOMIC EXPANSION

Between 1975 and the end of the century, wars and revolutions spread death and destruction through many of the world's least-developed regions. In most cases the origins of conflict were found in the experience of colonialism and foreign intervention, but each conflict also had a unique historical character. Throughout these decades of conflict the two superpowers sought to avoid direct military confrontation while working to gain strategic advantages. The United States and the Soviet Union each supplied arms and financial assistance to nations or insurgent forces hostile to the other. Once linked to superpower rivalries, local conflicts became deadlier. Conflicts where the rival superpowers financed and armed competing factions or parties are called **proxy wars**.

In Latin America superpower rivalry transformed limited conflicts over political rights, social justice, and economic policies into a violent cycle of revolution, military dictatorship, and foreign meddling. In Iran and Afghanistan resentment against foreign intrusion and a growing religious hostility to secular culture led to revolutionary transformations. Here again, superpower ambitions and regional political instability helped provoke war and economic decline. These experiences were not universal, however. During this period some Asian nations experienced rapid economic transformation. Japan emerged as one of the world's leading industrial powers, and a small number of other Asian economies entered the ranks of industrial and commercial powers, including socialist China, which initiated market-based economic reforms.

At the end of the 1980s the Cold War ended with the collapse of the Soviet system in eastern Europe, but the transition to democracy and market economy proved difficult. As both developing and former socialist nations opened their markets to foreign investment and competition, they experienced wrenching social change. Increased globalization coincided with increased inequality in many nations, but some developing nations also reaped substantial benefits from rapid technological change and world economic integration.

This period also witnessed a great increase in world population and international immigration. Population growth and increased levels of industrialization had a dramatic impact on the global environment, with every continent feeling the destructive effects of forest depletion, soil erosion, and pollution. Wealthy nations with slow population growth found it easier to respond to these environmental challenges than did poor nations experiencing rapid population growth.

Revolutions, Repression, and Democratic Reform in Latin America

In the 1970s Latin America entered a dark era of political violence. When revolutionary movements challenged the established order, militaries in many nations overturned democratic governments and instituted repressive measures. A region of weak democracy in 1960 became a region of military dictatorships with little patience for civil liberties and human rights fifteen years later.

The ongoing confrontation between Fidel Castro and the government of the United States (see Chapter 32) helped propel the region toward crisis. The fact that the Cuban communist government survived efforts by the United States to overthrow it energized the revolutionary left throughout Latin America. Fearful that revolution would spread across Latin America, the United States increased support for its political and military allies in that region, training many of the military leaders who led coups during this period.

The Brazilian Solution

Brazil was the first nation to experience the conservative reaction to the Cuban Revolution. Claiming that Brazil's civilian political leaders could not protect the nation from communist subversion, the army overthrew the constitutional government of President João Goulart (ju-wow go-LARHT) in 1964. The military suspended the constitution, outlawed all existing political parties, and exiled former presidents and opposition leaders. Death squads—illegal paramilitary organizations sanctioned by the government—detained, tortured, and executed thousands of citizens. The dictatorship also undertook an ambitious economic program that promoted industrialization through import substitution, using tax and tariff policies to compel foreign-owned companies to increase investment in manufacturing.

This combination of dictatorship, violent repression, and government promotion of industrialization came to be called the "Brazilian Solution." Elements of this "solution" were imposed across much of the region. In 1970 Chile's new president, **Salvador Allende** (sal-VAH-dor ah-YEHN-day), undertook an ambitious program of socialist reforms and nationalized Chile's heavy industry and mines, including the American-owned copper companies that dominated the economy. From the beginning of Allende's presidency the administration of President Richard Nixon (served 1969–1973) tried to subvert the Chilean government. Afflicted by inflation,

proxy wars During the Cold War, local or regional wars in which the superpowers armed, trained, and financed the combatants.

Salvador Allende Socialist politician elected president of Chile in 1970 and overthrown by the military in 1973. He died during the military attack.

CHRONOLOGY

	The Americas	Middle East/Africa	Asia	Eastern Europe
1970	1970 Salvador Allende elected president of Chile			
	1973 Allende overthrown		1975 Vietnam War ends	
	1976 Military takeover in Argentina			
	1979 Sandinistas overthrow Anastasio Somoza in Nicaragua	1979 Shah of Iran overthrown in Islamic Revolution	1979 China begins economic reforms	1978 USSR sends troops to Afghanistan
1980	1983–1990 Democracy returns in Argentina, Brazil, and Chile	1980–1988 Iran-Iraq War	1986 Average Japanese income overtakes income in United States	1985 Mikhail Gorbachev becomes Soviet head of state
	1989 United States invades Panama	1989 USSR withdraws from Afghanistan	1989 Tiananmen Square confrontation	1989 Berlin Wall falls
				1989–1991 Communism ends in eastern Europe
1990	1990 Sandinistas defeated in elections in Nicaragua	1990 Iraq invades Kuwait	1990s Japanese recession	1990 Reunification of Germany
		1991 Persian Gulf War		1992 Yugoslavia disintegrates; Croatia and Slovenia become independent nations
				1992–1995 Bosnia crisis
		1994 Nelson Mandela elected president of South Africa; Tutsi massacred in Rwanda	1997 Asian financial crisis begins	
	1998 Election of Hugo Chávez in Venezuela			

Dirty War War waged by the Argentine military (1976–1983) against leftist groups. Characterized by the use of illegal imprisonment, torture, and executions by the military.

Sandinistas Members of a leftist coalition that overthrew the Nicaraguan dictatorship of Anastasia Somoza in 1979 and attempted to install a socialist economy. The United States financed armed opposition by the Contras. The Sandinistas lost national elections in 1990.

Revolution and Counterrevolution in Central America

mass consumer protests, and declining foreign trade, a military uprising led by General Augusto Pinochet (ah-GOOS-toh pin-oh-CHET) and supported by the United States overthrew Allende in 1973. President Allende and thousands of Chileans died in the uprising, and thousands more were jailed, tortured, and imprisoned without trial. Once in power Pinochet rolled back Allende's reforms, dramatically reducing state participation in the economy and encouraging foreign investment.

In 1976 Argentina followed Brazil and Chile into dictatorship. Isabel Martínez de Perón (EES-ah-bell mar-TEEN-ehz deh pair-OWN) became president after the death of her husband Juan Perón in 1974 (see Chapter 31). Perón had been exiled in 1955, but returned and was elected president in 1973. Her administration faced a guerrilla insurgency, inflation, and labor protests. Impatient with the policies of the president, the military seized power and suspended the constitution. During the next seven years it fought what it called the **Dirty War** against terrorism. More than nine thousand Argentines lost their lives, and thousands of others endured arrest and torture.

While the left suffered these reverses in South America, a revolutionary movement came to power in Nicaragua in 1979, overthrowing the corrupt dictatorship of Anastasio Somoza. This broad alliance of revolutionaries and reformers called themselves **Sandinistas** (sahn-din-EES-tahs). They took their name from Augusto César Sandino, who had led Nicaraguan opposition to U.S. military intervention between 1927 and 1932. Once in power, the Sandinistas sought to imitate the command economies of Cuba and the Soviet Union, nationalizing properties owned by members of the Nicaraguan elite and U.S. companies.

Susan Meiselas/Magnum Photos, Inc.

The Nicaraguan Revolution Overturns Somoza A revolutionary coalition that included Marxists drove the dictator Anastasio Somoza from power in 1979. The Somoza family had ruled Nicaragua since the 1930s and maintained a close relationship with the United States.

U.S. president Jimmy Carter (served 1977–1980) championed human rights in the hemisphere and stopped the flow of U.S. arms to regimes with the worst records. Carter also agreed to the reestablishment of Panamanian sovereignty in the Canal Zone at the end of 1999, but his effort to find common ground with the Sandinistas failed.

He was defeated in the next election by Ronald Reagan, who was committed to reversing the results of the Nicaraguan Revolution and defeating a revolutionary movement in neighboring El Salvador. Because the U.S. Congress resisted any use of U.S. combat forces in Nicaragua and El Salvador and put strict limits on military aid, the Reagan administration tried to roll back the Nicaraguan Revolution through punitive economic measures and the recruitment and arming of a proxy force of anti-Sandinista Nicaraguans, called Contras (counterrevolutionaries).

Confident that they were supported by the majority of Nicaraguans and assured that the U.S. Congress was close to cutting off aid to the Contras, the Sandinistas called for free elections in 1990. But they had miscalculated politically. Exhausted by more than a decade of violence, a majority of Nicaraguan voters rejected the Sandinistas and elected a middle-of-the-road coalition led by Violeta Chamorro (vee-oh-LET-ah cha-MOR-roe).

In neighboring El Salvador another guerrilla movement, the FMLN (Farabundo Martí [fah-rah-BOON-doh mar-TEE] National Liberation Front), seemed on the verge of taking power. The Reagan administration responded by providing hundreds of millions of dollars in military assistance and by training units of the El Salvadoran army. The assassination of Archbishop Oscar Romero and other members of the Catholic clergy by death squads tied to the Salvadoran government as well as the murder of thousands of noncombatants by military units trained by the United States undermined this effort. However, the electoral defeat of the Sandinistas in Nicaragua and the collapse of the Soviet Union (see below) finally forced the FMLN rebels to negotiate peace, transforming themselves into a civilian political party.

During this same period, the violent political confrontation of right and left abated in South America as well. The right-wing military dictatorships established in Brazil, Chile, and Argentina all came to an end between 1983 and 1990, brought down by their own excesses and by popular desires for a return to constitutional government. By 2000, with the Cold War ended, 95 percent of Latin America's population lived under civilian rule.

U.S. Influence in Latin America

At the same time, the influence of the United States grew substantially. The United States had thwarted the left in Nicaragua and El Salvador by funding military proxies. It used its own military in a 1983 invasion of the tiny Caribbean nation of Grenada and again in 1989 to overthrow and arrest dictator General Manuel Noriega (MAN-wel no-ree-EGG-ah) of Panama. These actions were powerful reminders to Latin Americans of prior interventions (see Chapter 24), but they also served as reminders of American power at a time when socialism was discredited by the collapse of the Soviet bloc.

From this position of strength the United States pushed Latin American nations to reform their economies by removing limitations on foreign investment, eliminating many social welfare programs, and reducing public-sector employment. Latin American governments responded by selling public-sector industries, like national airlines, manufacturing facilities, and public utilities, to foreign corporations. But popular support for these policies, what Latin Americans called neo-liberalism, eroded quickly due to political scandals and a slowing world economy. A catastrophic economic and political meltdown in Argentina between 2001 and 2002 contributed to the appearance of a reinvigorated nationalist left in Latin America that sought to roll back neo-liberal reforms (see Diversity and Dominance: The Struggle for Women's Rights in an Era of Global Political and Economic Change). Among the most vocal critic of neo-liberalism and American influence was Hugo Chávez (HUGH-go SHAH-vez), elected president of Venezuela in 1998.

Islamic Revolutions in Iran and Afghanistan

Ayatollah Ruhollah Khomeini Shi'ite philosopher and cleric who led the overthrow of the shah of Iran in 1979 and created an Islamic republic.

Although the Arab-Israel conflict and the oil crisis (see Chapter 32) concerned both superpowers, the prospect of direct military involvement remained remote. When unexpected crises developed in Iran and Afghanistan, however, significant strategic issues came to the foreground. Both countries adjoined Soviet territory, making Soviet military intervention more likely. Exercising post–Vietnam War caution, the United States reacted with restraint. The Soviet Union chose a bolder and ultimately disastrous course.

Muhammad Reza Pahlavi (REH-zah PAH-lah-vee) succeeded his father as shah of Iran in 1941. In 1953 covert intervention by the U.S. Central Intelligence Agency (CIA) helped the shah retain his throne in the face of a movement to overturn royal power. Even when he finally nationalized the foreign-owned oil industry, the shah continued to enjoy American support. As oil revenues increased following the price increases of the 1970s, the United States encouraged the shah to spend his nation's growing wealth on equipping the Iranian army with American weaponry. By the 1970s popular resentment against the ballooning wealth of the elite families that supported the shah and the brutality, inefficiency, malfeasance, and corruption of his government led to mass opposition.

Ayatollah Ruhollah Khomeini (A-yat-ol-LAH ROOH-ol-LAH ko-MAY-nee), a Shi'ite (SHE-ite) philosopher-cleric who had spent most of his eighty-plus years in religious and academic pursuits, became the leader of the opposition. Massive protests forced the shah to flee Iran and ended the monarchy in 1979. In the Islamic Republic of Iran, which replaced the monarchy, Ayatollah Khomeini was supreme

Alexandra Avakian/Woodfin Camp & Associates

Muslim Women Mourning the Death of Ayatollah Khomeini in 1989 An Islamic revolution overthrew the shah of Iran in 1979. Ayatollah Khomeini sought to lead Iran away from the influences of Western culture and challenged the power of the United States in the Persian Gulf.

The Struggle for Women's Rights in an Era of Global Political and Economic Change

The struggle for women's rights has been one of the most important social movements of the twentieth and twenty-first centuries. Although we can identify fundamental similarities in objectives across cultural and political boundaries, women in less developed nations are forced to recognize that their objectives and strategies must take into account international inequalities in power and wealth. In this section Gladys Acosta, a militant Peruvian feminist, discusses the appropriate agenda for this struggle in the era after the fall of the Soviet Union and the rise of neo-liberalism.

Neo-liberalism *is the term used in Latin America to identify the free-market economic policies advocated by the United States. Among its chief characteristics are an end to the protection of local industries, a reduction in government social welfare policies, a reduction in public-sector employment, a commitment to paying debts to international creditors, and the removal of impediments to foreign investment. Many Latin Americans believe that neo-liberalism is a new form of imperialism.*

No one can abstain from the debate about the great historical systems of our time. Not even those of us who are trying to change the complex web of human relationships from a feminist perspective. Everywhere people are talking about the end of ideologies. But before we can grasp the significance of current events and their consequences, we need to pinpoint our various doubts and blank spots. Capitalism is the main pivot of our lives because we were born under its influence. It [has] hegemony. . . .

Gender, the main distinction between all people, is ignored in most philosophical, political or economic discussions. The reason for this lies partly in the low level of women's participation, but not entirely, because women are not always aware of the system of submission and repression to which we are subjected against our will. We need to find something which unites women in a gender-specific manner. That doesn't mean sweeping under the carpet all the differences between us, like social position, culture or age. . . .

Neo-Liberalism in Action

For those of us who live under the influence of the capitalist system, the situation is different. When I talk of neo-liberalism, I mean austerity measures, foreign debts, and increased liberties for all those who have the power of money at their disposal and the power of repression over those who make demands. We have now reached a new form of capitalist accumulation. The world's economic system is in a state of change and capital has become more concentrated and centralised. I would not go as far as to say countries don't exist anymore but national identities do certainly play a different role now. It is important to understand the dynamics because otherwise historical responsibilities are obscured and we no longer know whom we're fighting against. If we look at the bare face of neo-liberalism from a woman's point of view, we cannot fail to notice its murderous consequences. To create a more humane society we must continue to reject neo-liberalism here and now in the hope of being able to change the dead present into a living future. Under neo-liberalism there is a breathtaking circulation of commodities, but also an exchange of ideas, illusions and dreams. At the moment we're experiencing capitalism's greatest ideological offensive. It's all business: everything is bought and sold and everything has its price.

The Consequences of Neo-Liberal Politics

We women play an important role in this ever-more internationalized economy because we represent, as ever, a particularly exploitable workforce. A number of studies have revealed the existence of subcontractor chains who work for transna-

neo-liberalism The term used in Latin America and other developing regions to describe free-market policies that include reducing tariff protection for local industries; the sale of public-sector industries, like national airlines and public utilities, to private investors or foreign corporations; and the reduction of social welfare policies and public-sector employment.

arbiter of disputes and guarantor of religious legitimacy. He oversaw a parliamentary regime based on European models, but he imposed religious control over legislation and public behavior. The electoral process was not open to monarchists, communists, and other opposition groups. Shi'ite clerics with little training for government service held many of the highest posts, and stringent measures were taken to combat Western styles and culture. Universities were temporarily closed, and their faculties were purged of secularists and monarchists. Women were compelled to wear modest Islamic garments outside the house, and semiofficial vigilante committees policed public morals and cast a pall over entertainment and social life.

President Carter had criticized the shah's repressive regime, but the overthrow of a long-standing ally and the creation of the Islamic Republic were blows to American prestige. The new Iranian regime was anti-Israeli and anti-American. Seeing the United States as a "Great Satan" opposed to Islam, Khomeini fostered Islamic revolutionary movements that threatened the United States and Israel. In November 1979 Iranian radicals seized the U.S. embassy in Tehran tional companies "informally" and mainly employ women. Basically we are dealing with a kind of integration into the world market which often uses our own homes as its outlet. Obviously, this work is badly paid and completely unprotected and has to be done without any of those social rights which were formerly achieved by trade union struggles. The most important thing for us is to keep hold of just one thread of the enterprise so we can show how the commodities make their way to their final destination. As it advances worldwide, this capitalism also encourages the expansion of certain kinds of tourism. A visible increase in prostitution is part of this, whereby women from poor countries are smuggled into large, internationally operated rings which exploit them. The reports of Filipina women traded on the West German market send shivers down our spines. . . . What kind of freedom are you talking about there?

How the Adoption of Austerity Measures Affects Women's Lives

It is obvious that foreign debt is one of the most inhuman forms of exploitation in our countries when one considers the ratio between work necessary for workers' needs and work producing profit for employers. The experts have already explained how the prevailing exchange and investment structures have created international finance systems which keep whole populations in inhuman conditions. Although many people might think it crazy, the development model of the global economy has a marked relation to gender. As long as prices were slapped on some luxury consumer items there weren't any serious problems; but now the snares have been set around basic commodities. Women in every household are suffering every day as a result of impoverished economies and those who are most exposed to the effects of foreign debt are women.

When it comes to shopping, caring for sick children or the impossibility of meeting their schooling costs, the illusion of "leaving poverty behind" evaporates. Yet the problem is not only of an economic nature because under such circumstances the constant tension leads to grave, often lasting exhaustion. The psychosocial damage is alarming. The situation is ready to explode, so to speak. . . . The adoption of austerity measures

means a curtailment of the state's commitment to social services with a direct effect on women. Daily life becomes hell for them. The lack of even minimal state welfare presents women (and obviously children too) with crushing working days. There is a constant expenditure of human energy without any hope of rest! No relaxation, no breaks. . . . And if we consider what happens within the family, we notice that women keep the smallest portion of the meagre family income. They give everything to their children or those adults who bring home a pay packet. As a result malnutrition among women is increasing at an alarming rate and their frequent pregnancies represent a superhuman physical achievement.

We should not ignore the fact that violence of every form . . . goes hand-in-hand with the difficult situation I have described.[1] It's nothing new for women because the open wounds of sexual violence, abuse at home and the contempt of this *machista* culture, have always featured in our lives and our mothers' lives. The challenge is to prevent these from also affecting our future generations.

QUESTIONS FOR ANALYSIS

1. What is neo-liberalism?

2. According to Acosta, how does global economic integration fostered by neo-liberalism affect the lives of women as workers?

3. Acosta claims that indebtedness to foreign lenders leads to austerity measures. How does this impact families in poor countries?

Source: From Gladys Acosta, "The View of a Peruvian Militant," in *Compañeras. Voices from the Latin American Women's Movement*, edited by Gaby Küppers (London: Latin American Bureau, 1994). Reprinted with permission of the publisher.

1. In the last report of the Comisaria de mujeres in Lima (the only one in the country at present) 4,800 rapes were filed for 1990, of which 4,200 went to trial. The police commissioner, in reading the document, personally acknowledged the alarming social problem which is posed by the violence of men who are connected to their victims in some way and. which, indeed, persists throughout all levels of society.

---

and held fifty-two diplomats hostage for 444 days. Americans felt humiliated by their inability to rescue the hostages or negotiate their release.

In the fall of 1980, shortly after negotiations for the release of the hostages began, **Saddam Husain** (sah-DAHM hoo-SANE), the ruler of neighboring Iraq, invaded Iran to topple the Islamic Republic. His own dictatorial rule rested on a secular, Arab-nationalist philosophy and long-standing friendship with the Soviet Union, which had provided him with advanced weaponry. He feared that the fervor of Iran's revolutionary Shi'ite leaders would infect his own country's Shi'ite majority and threaten his power. The war pitted American weapons in the hands of the Iranians against Soviet weapons in the hands of the Iraqis, but the superpowers avoided overt involvement during eight years of bloodshed. Covertly, however, the United States used Israel to transfer arms to Iran, hoping to gain the release of other American hostages held by radical Islamic groups in Lebanon and to help finance the Contra war against the Sandinista government of Nicaragua. When this deal came to light in 1986, the resulting political scandal

Saddam Husain President of Iraq from 1979 until overthrown by an American-led invasion in 2003. Waged war on Iran from 1980 to 1988. His invasion of Kuwait in 1990 was repulsed in the Persian Gulf War in 1991.

intensified American hostility to Iran. Openly tilting toward Iraq, President Reagan sent the United States Navy to the Persian Gulf, ostensibly to protect nonbelligerent shipping. The move helped force Iran to accept a cease-fire in 1988.

While the United States dealt with Iran, the Soviet Union faced even more serious problems in neighboring Afghanistan. In 1978 a Marxist party with a secular agenda had seized power. Offended by these efforts to reform education and grant rights to women, traditional ethnic and religious leaders led a successful rebellion. The Soviet Union responded by sending its army into Afghanistan to install a communist regime. With the United States, Saudi Arabia, and Pakistan paying, equipping, and training Afghan rebels, the Soviet Union found itself in an unwinnable war like the one the United States had stumbled into in Vietnam. Facing growing economic problems and widespread domestic discontent over the war, Soviet leaders withdrew their troops in 1989. Three years later rebel groups took control of the entire country and then began to fight among themselves over who should rule.

Asian Transformation

Although Japan has few mineral resources and is dependent on oil imports, the Japanese economy weathered the oil price shocks of the 1970s much better than did the economies of Europe and the United States. In fact, Japan experienced a faster rate of economic growth in the 1970s and 1980s than did any other major developed economy, growing at about 10 percent a year. Average income also increased rapidly, overtaking that of the United States in 1986. But during the 1990s Japan entered a decade-long crisis that slowed GDP (gross domestic product) and average income growth dramatically.

There are some major differences between the Japanese and U.S. industrial models. During the American occupation, Japanese industrial conglomerates known as *zaibatsu* (see Chapter 29) were broken up. Although ownership of major industries became less concentrated as a result, new industrial alliances appeared. During the period of dramatic growth there were six major **keiretsu** (kay-REHT-soo), each of which included a major bank and firms in industry, commerce, and construction tied together in an interlocking ownership structure. There were also minor keiretsu dominated by a major corporation, like Toyota.

Tariffs and import regulations inhibiting foreign competition were crucial to the early stages of development of Japan's major industries. These restrictions and Japanese success at exporting manufactured goods through the 1970s and 1980s produced huge trade surpluses with other nations. Although the United States and the European Community engaged in tough negotiations to try to force open the Japanese market, these efforts had only limited success. In 1990 Japan's trade surplus with the rest of the world was double that of 1985. Many experts assumed that Japan's competitive advantages would propel it past the United States as the world's preeminent industrial economy, but its economy entered a deep recession in the 1990s and has not yet recovered. Before the crisis, housing and stock markets had become highly overvalued because large profits from trade fueled real estate and stock market speculation. The close relationship of government, banks, and industries also contributed to speculation and corruption. As the crisis deepened and prices collapsed, the close relationships between industry, government, and banks proved to be a liability, propping up inefficient companies. By the end of the 1990s Japan's GDP had suffered a loss greater than that suffered by the United States in the Great Depression and left the nation with a crushing debt burden.

Other Asian states imitated the Japanese model of development in the 1970s. These nations protected new industries from foreign competition while encouraging close alliances among industries and banks. The Republic of Korea, commonly called South Korea, was the most successful, using a combination of inexpensive labor, strong technical education, and substantial domestic capital reserves to support industrialization. It became a major global force in heavy industries such as steel and shipbuilding as well as in consumer industries such as automobiles and consumer electronics.

The small nations of Taiwan, Hong Kong, and Singapore also became industrial powerhouses. As a result of their rapid growth, these three nations and South Korea were called the **Asian Tigers**. While Taiwan suffered a number of political reverses, including the loss of its United Nations seat to the People's Republic of China in 1971 and the withdrawal of diplomatic recognition by the United States, it achieved remarkable economic progress, based in large part

### Sidebar (left column)

Soviet Invasion of Afghanistan

e **PRIMARY SOURCE: Islamic Government**
Learn why the future leader of Iran called for the establishment of new governments along conservative religious lines.

Japanese Economic Expansion and Crisis

keiretsu Alliances of corporations and banks that dominate the Japanese economy.

The Asian Tigers

Asian Tigers Collective name for South Korea, Taiwan, Hong Kong, and Singapore nations that became economic powers in the 1970s and 1980s.

on investment in the economy of the People's Republic of China. Hong Kong and Singapore—both former British colonies with extremely limited resources—also enjoyed rapid economic development. Both were historically important Asian ports and commercial centers that then developed manufacturing, banking, and commercial sectors.

newly industrialized economies (NIEs) Rapidly growing, new industrial nations of the late twentieth century, including the Asian Tigers.

These **newly industrialized economies (NIEs)** shared many characteristics that helped explain their rapid industrialization. All had disciplined and hardworking labor forces, and all invested heavily in education. For example, as early as 1980 Korea had as many engineering graduates as Germany, Britain, and Sweden combined. All had very high rates of personal saving, about 35 percent of GDP, that funded new technologies, and all emphasized outward-looking export strategies. And, like Japan, all benefited from government sponsorship and protection. Despite this momentum, the region was deeply shaken by a financial crisis that began in 1997. Like the recession that afflicted Japan, a combination of bad loans, weak banks, and the international effects of currency speculation led to a deep regional crisis that was stabilized only by the efforts of the United States, Japan, and international institutions like the International Monetary Fund.

China Rejoins the World Economy

Deng Xiaoping Communist Party leader who forced Chinese economic reforms after the death of Mao Zedong.

Tiananmen Square Site in Beijing where Chinese students and workers gathered to demand greater political openness in 1989. The demonstration was crushed by Chinese military with great loss of life.

After Mao Zedong's death in 1976, the Chinese communist leadership began economic reforms that relaxed state control, allowing more initiative and permitting individuals to accumulate wealth. The results were remarkable. Under China's leader **Deng Xiaoping** (dung shee-yao-ping) China permitted foreign investment for the first time since the communists came to power in 1949. Between 1979 and 2005 foreign direct investment in China grew to $618 billion as McDonald's, General Motors, Coca-Cola, Airbus, and many other foreign companies began doing business. As a result, China became a major industrial exporter and the world's sixth most important trading nation. Despite these changes, state-owned enterprises still employed more than 100 million workers, and most foreign-owned companies were limited to special economic zones. The result was a dual industrial sector—one modern, efficient, and connected to international markets, the other directed by political decisions. While the Chinese did not privatize land, they did permit farmers to sell what they produced. By 1984, 93 percent of China's agricultural land was in effect in private hands.

By 2009 China had become the world's third largest economy, passing Germany, but, despite great improvements, the Chinese people remained poor on average. Although per capita GDP in China reached $2,360 in 2009, it remained lower than that of Mexico. The combination of economic reforms, massive investments, and technology transfers from developed nations made China one of the world's major industrial powers in the early twenty-first century. The worldwide economic crisis that began in 2008 has affected Japan more powerfully than China. As a result, China is now poised to become the word's second largest economy.

Deng Xiaoping's strategy of balancing change and continuity avoided some of the social and political costs experienced by Russia and other socialist countries that abruptly embraced capitalism and democracy, but he faced a major challenge in 1989. Responding to inflation and to worldwide mass movements in favor of democracy, Chinese students and intellectuals led a series of protests demanding more democracy and an end to corruption. This movement culminated in **Tiananmen** (tee-yehn-ahn-men) **Square**, in the heart of Beijing, where hundreds of thousands of protesters gathered and refused to leave. After weeks of standoff, tanks pushed into the square, killing hundreds and arresting thousands.

SECTION REVIEW

- During the 1970s and 1980s, political violence grew in Latin America, sponsored in part by U.S. fears of communist subversion.

- The United States opposed revolutionary movements in Nicaragua and El Salvador.

- In the 1990s the United States pushed Latin American nations to introduce neo-liberal reforms that opened economies to greater foreign investment.

- A radical anti-American Islamic revolution led by Ayatollah Khomeini triumphed in Iran in 1979, and led to a ten-year war with Iraq.

- The Soviets intervened in Afghanistan in 1979 but failed to defeat local opponents backed by the United States and Pakistan.

- After three decades of rapid economic growth, Japan entered a deep recession in the 1990s.

- The four Asian Tigers experienced rapid economic growth as did China after Deng Xiaoping reformed and modernized its economy.

THE END OF THE BIPOLAR WORLD

After the end of World War II, competition between the alliances led by the United States and the Soviet Union created a bipolar world. Every conflict, no matter how local its origins, had the potential of engaging the attention of one or both of the superpowers. The Korean War, decolonization in Africa, the Vietnam War, the Cuban Revolution, and hostilities between Israel and its neighbors increased tension between the nuclear-armed superpowers. Given this succession of provocations, politics everywhere was dominated by arguments over the relative merits of the competing systems.

Few in 1980 predicted the startling collapse of the Soviet Union. Western observers tended to see communist nations as both more uniform in character and more subservient to the Soviet Union than was true. Long before the 1980s, deep divisions had appeared among communist states. Among the once-independent nations and ethnic groups brought within the Soviet Union, nationalism reappeared in the late 1980s and overwhelmed communism.

Crisis in the Soviet Union

**PRIMARY SOURCE:
The Last Heir of Lenin
Explains His Reform Plans:
Perestroika and Glasnost**
Read President Gorbachev's analysis of the Soviet Union's decline and his prescriptions for reform.

Mikhail Gorbachev Head of the Soviet Union from 1985 to 1991. His liberalization effort improved relations with the West, but he lost power after his reforms led to the collapse of communist governments in eastern Europe.

perestroika Policy of "restructuring" that was the centerpiece of Mikhail Gorbachev's efforts to liberalize communism in the Soviet Union.

Solidarity Polish trade union created in 1980 to protest working conditions and political repression. It began the nationalist opposition to communist rule that led in 1989 to the fall of communism in eastern Europe.

Communism Overthrown in Eastern Europe

Under U.S. president Ronald Reagan and the Soviet Union's general secretary Leonid Brezhnev (leh-oh-NEED BREZ-nef), Cold War rhetoric remained intense. Massive new U.S. investments in armaments placed heavy burdens on a Soviet economy already suffering from shortages that had become a part of Soviet life. Obsolete industrial plants and centralized planning that stifled initiative led to a declining standard of living relative to the West, while the arbitrariness of the bureaucracy, the manipulation of information, and deprivations created a crisis in morale.

Despite the unpopularity of the war in Afghanistan and growing discontent, Brezhnev refused to modify his unsuccessful policies, but he could not escape criticism. Self-published underground writings (*samizdat* [sah-meez-DAHT]) by critics of the regime circulated widely despite government efforts to suppress them. In a series of powerful books, the writer Alexander Solzhenitzyn (sol-zhuh-NEET-sin) castigated the Soviet system. Although he won a Nobel Prize in literature, authorities charged him with treason and expelled him in 1974.

By the time **Mikhail Gorbachev** (GORE-beh-CHOF) came to power in 1985, weariness with war in Afghanistan, economic decay, and vocal protest had reached critical levels. Casting aside Brezhnev's hard line, Gorbachev authorized major reforms in an attempt to stave off total collapse. His policy of political openness (*glasnost*) permitted criticism of the government and the Communist Party. His policy of **perestroika** (per-ih-STROY-kuh) ("restructuring") was an attempt to address long-suppressed economic problems by moving away from central state planning. In 1989 he ended the unpopular war in Afghanistan.

The Collapse of the Socialist Bloc

In 1980 protests by Polish shipyard workers in the city of Gdansk led to the formation of **Solidarity**, a labor union that grew to 9 million members. The Roman Catholic Church in Poland, strengthened by the elevation of a Pole, Karol Wojtyla (KAH-rol voy-TIL-ah), to the papacy as John Paul II in 1978, gave strong moral support to the protest movement.

The Polish government imposed martial law in 1981 in response to the growing power of Solidarity and its allies, giving the army effective political control. Seeing Solidarity under tight controls and many of its leaders in prison, the Soviet Union decided not to intervene. But Solidarity remained a potent force with a strong institutional structure and nationally recognized leaders. As Gorbachev loosened political controls in the Soviet Union after 1985, communist leaders elsewhere lost confidence in Soviet resolve, and critics and reformers in Poland and throughout eastern Europe were emboldened.

Beleaguered Warsaw Pact governments vacillated between relaxation of control and suppression of dissent. Just as the Catholic clergy in Poland had supported Solidarity, Protestant and Orthodox religious leaders aided the rise of opposition groups elsewhere. This combination of nationalism and religion provided a powerful base for opponents of the communist regimes. Communist governments sought to quiet the opposition by turning to the West for trade and financial assistance. They also opened their nations to travelers, ideas, styles, and money from Western countries, all of which accelerated the demand for change.

Bossu Regis/Corbis Sygma

The Fall of the Berlin Wall The Berlin Wall was the most important symbol of the Cold War. Constructed to keep residents of East Germany from fleeing to the West and defended by armed guards and barbed wire, it was the public face of communism. As the Soviet system fell apart, the residents of East and West Berlin broke down sections of the wall.

By the end of 1989 communist governments across eastern Europe had fallen. The dismantling of the Berlin Wall vividly represented this transformation. While communist leaders in Poland, Hungary, Czechoslovakia, and Bulgaria decided that change was inevitable, the dictator Nicolae Ceausescu (nehk-oh-LIE chow-SHES-koo) of Romania refused to surrender power and was overthrown and executed. The comprehensiveness of these changes became clear in 1990, when the Polish people elected Solidarity leader Lech Walesa (leck wah-LEN-sah) as president and the people of Czechoslovakia elected dissident playwright Vaclav Havel (vah-SLAV hah-VEL) as president.

Following the fall of the Berlin Wall, a tidal wave of patriotic enthusiasm swept aside the once-formidable communist government of East Germany. In the chaotic months that followed, East Germans crossed to West Germany in large numbers, and government services in the eastern sector nearly disappeared. The collapse of the East German government led quickly in 1990 to reunification.

The End of the Soviet Union

Soviet leaders knew that similarly powerful nationalist sentiments existed within the Soviet Union as well. The year 1990 brought declarations of independence by Lithuania, Estonia, and Latvia, three small states on the Baltic Sea that the Soviet Union had annexed in 1939. The end of the Soviet Union then came suddenly in 1991 (see Map 33.1). After communist hardliners botched a coup against Gorbachev, disgust with communism boiled over. Boris Yeltsin, the president of the Russian Republic, emerged as the most powerful leader in the country. Russia, the largest republic in the Soviet Union, was effectively taking the place of the disintegrating USSR. In September 1991 the Congress of People's Deputies—the central legislature of the USSR—voted to dissolve the union. In December a weak successor state with little central control, the Commonwealth of Independent States (CIS), was created and Gorbachev resigned.

The End of Yugoslavia

ethnic cleansing Effort to eradicate a people and its culture by means of mass killing and the destruction of historical buildings and cultural materials. Ethnic cleansing was used by both sides in the conflicts that accompanied the disintegration of Yugoslavia in the 1990s.

The ethnic and religious passions that fueled the breakup of the Soviet Union overwhelmed the Balkan nation of Yugoslavia. In 1991 it dissolved into a morass of separatism and warring ethnic and religious groups. Slovenia and Croatia, the most westerly provinces, both heavily Roman Catholic, became independent states in 1992. The population of Bosnia and Herzegovina was more mixed: 40 percent were Muslims, 30 percent Serbian Orthodox, and 18 percent Catholics. Following the declaration of Bosnian national independence in 1992, the Orthodox Serbs attempted to rid the state of Muslims in a process called **ethnic cleansing**. After extensive television coverage of atrocities and wanton destruction, the United States intervened and eventually brokered a settlement in 1995.

In 1999 new fighting and a new round of ethnic cleansing occurred in the southernmost Yugoslavian province of Kosovo. Seen by Serbs as their homeland, Kosovo had a predominantly Muslim and Albanian population. When Serbia refused to stop military action, the United

States, Britain, and France acted on behalf of NATO by launching an aerial war that forced the withdrawal of Serbian forces from Kosovo.

Progress and Conflict in Africa

Sub-Saharan Africa has experienced political instability, military coups, civil wars, and conflicts over resources since independence. It has also remained among the poorest regions in the world. Southern Africa, however, has seen democratic progress and a steady decline in armed conflicts since 1991. A key change came in South Africa in 1994, when long-time political prisoner Nelson Mandela and his African National Congress (ANC) won the first national elections in which the African majority could participate equally. Also hopeful has been the return to democracy of Nigeria, Africa's most populous state, after decades of military rulers. In 1999, after a succession of military governments, Nigerians elected President Olusegun Obasanjo (oh-LOO-she-gun oh-BAH-san-jo) (a former coup leader), and a 2003 vote renewed his term, despite serious voting irregularities. Similarly, in 2002 Kenyans voted out the party that had held power for thirty-nine years.

Genocide in Rwanda

Africa was also a scene of ethnic cleansing. In 1994 the political leaders of the Central African nation of Rwanda incited Hutu people to massacre their Tutsi neighbors. Since the major powers had promised to intervene in genocides, they avoided using the word *genocide* to describe the slaughter. Without foreign intervention, the carnage claimed 750,000 lives with millions more refugees. Finally, the United States and other powers intervened and the United Nations set up a tribunal to try those responsible for the genocide. In 1998 violence spread from Rwanda to neighboring Congo, where growing opposition and ill health had forced President Joseph Mobutu from office after over three decades of dictatorial misrule. Various peacemaking attempts failed to restore order and by mid-2003 more than 3 million Congolese had died from disease, malnutrition, and injuries related to the fighting.

The Persian Gulf War

The Persian Gulf War was the first significant conflict to occur after the breakup of the Soviet Union and the end of the Cold War. Iraq's ruler, Saddam Husain, had borrowed a great deal of money from neighboring Kuwait and failed to get Kuwait's royal family to reduce this debt. He was also eager to control Kuwait's oil fields. Husain believed that the smaller and militarily weaker nation could be quickly defeated, and he suspected that the United States would not react. The invasion occurred in August 1990.

The United States decided to react. Saudi Arabia, an important ally of the United States and a major oil producer, also supported intervention. With his intention to use force endorsed by the United Nations and with many Islamic nations supporting military action, President George H. W. Bush ordered an attack in early 1991. Iraq's military defeat was comprehensive, but Husain remained in power, crushing an uprising just months following his defeat. The United States imposed various conditions on Iraq that kept tensions high, helping create the conditions for a new war in 2003.

SECTION REVIEW

- The Cold War ended when growing unrest and criticism led to the collapse of the Soviet Union and allied socialist nations. Mikhail Gorbachev's reform policies accelerated this process.

- The rise of ethnic nationalism led to war and genocide in Yugoslavia.

- South Africa, Nigeria, and Kenya escaped from oppressive conditions, but hundreds of thousands lost their lives in ethnic violence in Rwanda and Congo.

- After Saddam Husain invaded Kuwait, the United States and its allies defeated Iraq in the first Gulf War of 1990.

THE CHALLENGE OF POPULATION GROWTH

For most of human history governments viewed population growth as beneficial, a source of national wealth and power. Since the late eighteenth century, however, growing numbers of experts and politicians have viewed population increases with alarm, fearing that food supplies could not keep up with population growth. Late in the nineteenth century some social critics expressed concern that growing populations would lead to class and ethnic struggle. By

MAP 33.1 **The End of the Soviet Union** When communist hardliners failed to overthrow Gorbachev in 1991, popular anti-communist sentiment swept the Soviet Union. Following Boris Yeltsin's lead in Russia, the republics that constituted the Soviet Union declared their independence.

© Cengage Learning

e Interactive Map

the second half of the twentieth century, fears of population growth were primarily attached to environmental concerns. Are urban sprawl, pollution, and soil erosion the inevitable results of population growth? The questions and debates continue today, but clearly population growth is both a cause and a result of increased global interdependency.

Demographic Transition

The population of Europe almost doubled between 1850 and 1914, putting enormous pressure on rural land and urban housing and overwhelming fragile public institutions that provided crisis assistance (see Chapter 27). This dramatic growth forced a large wave of immigration across the Atlantic, helping to develop the Western Hemisphere and invigorating the Atlantic economy (see Chapter 24). Population growth also contributed to Europe's Industrial Revolution by lowering labor costs and increasing consumer demand.

While some Europeans of the nineteenth century saw the rapid increase in human population as a blessing, others warned of disaster. The best-known pessimist was the English cleric **Thomas Malthus**, who in 1798 argued that unchecked population growth would outstrip food production. When Malthus looked at Europe's future, he used a prejudiced image of China to terrify his readers. A visitor to China, he claimed, "will not be surprised that mothers destroy or expose many of their children; that parents sell their daughters for a trifle; . . . and that there should be such a number of robbers. The surprise is that nothing still more dreadful should happen."[1]

The generation that came of age in the years after World War II lived in a world where Malthus seemed to have little relevance. Industrial and agricultural productivity had multiplied supplies of food and other necessities. At the same time, cultural changes associated with expanded female employment, older age at marriage, and more effective family planning had slowed the rate of population increase. By the 1960s Europe and other industrial societies had

Thomas Malthus

Thomas Malthus
Eighteenth-century English intellectual who warned that population growth threatened future generations because, in his view, population growth would always outstrip increases in agricultural production.

Chinese Family-Planning Campaign To slow population growth, the Chinese government have sought to limit parents to a single child. Billboards and other forms of mass advertising have been an essential part of the campaign.

demographic transition A change in the rates of population growth. Before the transition, both birthrates and death rates are high, resulting in a slowly growing population; then the death rate drops but the birthrate remains high, causing a population explosion; finally the birthrate drops and the population growth slows down.

The Politics of Population

Rhythms of World Population Change

made the **demographic transition** to lower fertility rates (average number of births per woman) and reduced mortality. In fact, the number of births in developed nations was barely adequate to maintain population levels.

By the late 1970s, the Third World had still not made the demographic transition and population growth became politicized. Leaders in some developing nations actively promoted large families, arguing that larger populations increased national power. When industrialized nations, mostly white, raised concerns about rapid population growth in Asia, Africa, and Latin America, populist political leaders in these regions responded by asking whether these concerns were racist.

This question exposed the influence of racism in the population debate and temporarily disarmed Western advocates of birth control. However, once the economic shocks of the 1970s and 1980s revealed the vulnerability of poor nations, governments in the developing world jettisoned policies that promoted population growth. Mexico is a good example. In the 1970s the government had encouraged high fertility, and population grew by 3 percent per year. In the 1980s Mexico rejected these policies and began to promote birth control, leading by the 1990s to an annual population growth of 1.7.

World population exploded in the twentieth century, more than doubling between 1950 and 1995 (see Table 33.1). Although the rate of growth has slowed since the 1980s, world population still increases by a number equal to the total population of the United States every three years. If fertility were to remain constant from today, with a world average of 2.5 children per woman, world population would reach nearly 30 billion in 2150, more than three times the 2050 projection found in Table 33.1. This is not likely because fertility is declining in many developing nations. As a result, most experts estimate a world population in 2150 of less than 10 billion.

Mortality rates have also increased in some areas as immigration, commercial expansion, and improved transportation have facilitated the transmission of disease. The rapid spread of HIV/AIDS is an example of this phenomenon. Less developed regions with poorly funded public health institutions and with few resources to invest in prevention and treatment experience the highest rates of infection and the greatest mortality. In Russia, for example, new HIV infections rose from under five thousand in 1997 to over ninety thousand in 2001. AIDS has spread most quickly and with the most devastating results in Africa, the home of 28 million of the world's 40 million infected people.

The Industrialized Nations

In the developed industrial nations of western Europe and in Japan, fertility levels are so low that population would fall without immigration. Japanese women have an average of 1.4 chil-

| **TABLE 33.1** | Population for World and Major Areas, 1750–2050 |

Population Size (Millions)

Major Area	1750	1800	1850	1900	1950	1995	2050*
World	791	978	1,262	1,650	2,521	5,666	8,909
Africa	106	107	111	133	221	697	1,766
Asia	502	635	809	947	1,402	3,437	5,268
Europe	163	203	276	408	547	728	628
Latin America and the Caribbean	16	24	38	74	167	480	809
North America	2	7	26	82	172	297	398
Oceania	2	2	2	6	13	28	46

Percentage Distribution

Major Area	1750	1800	1850	1900	1950	1995	2050*
World	100	100	100	100	100	100	100
Africa	13.4	10.9	8.8	8.1	8.8	12	23.7
Asia	63.5	64.9	64.1	57.4	55.6	61	57.1
Europe	20.6	20.8	21.9	24.7	21.7	13	5.3
Latin America and the Caribbean	2.0	2.5	3.0	4.5	6.6	8	9.4
North America	0.3	0.7	2.1	5.0	6.8	5	4.1
Oceania	0.3	0.2	0.2	0.4	0.5	1	0.5

* Estimated

Source: J. D. Durand, "Historical Estimates of World Population: An Evaluation" (Philadelphia: University of Pennsylvania, Population Studies Center, 1974, mimeographed); United Nations, *The Determinants and Consequences of Population Trends*, vol. 1 (New York: United Nations, 1973); United Nations, *World Population Prospects as Assessed in 1963* (New York: United Nations, 1966); United Nations, *World Population Prospects: The 1998 Revision* (New York: United Nations, forthcoming); United Nations Population Division, Department of Economic and Social Affairs, http://www.un.org/esa/population/publications/WPP2004/ 2004Highlights-finalrevised.pdf. The medium fertility estimate is used for the 2050 population projection.

dren and Italian women 1.2. Although Sweden tries to promote fertility with cash payments, tax incentives, and job leaves to families with children, the average number of births per woman is 1.4. By comparison, the average African woman has 5.1 children. Higher levels of female education and employment, the material values of consumer culture, and access to contraception and abortion explain the low fertility of mature industrial nations. An Italian woman in Bologna, the city with the lowest fertility in the world, put it this way: "I'm an only child and if I could, I'd have more than one child. But most couples I know wait until their 30's to have children. People want to have their own life, they want to have a successful career. When you see life in these terms, children are an impediment."[2]

The Aging Population of the Industrial World

In industrialized nations life expectancy improved as fertility declined. The combination of abundant food, improved hygiene, and more effective medicines and medical care has lengthened human lives. In 2000 about 20 percent of the population in developed nations was sixty-five or over. By 2050 this proportion should rise to one-third. Italy soon will have more than twenty adults fifty years old or over for each five-year-old child. Because of higher fertility and greater levels of immigration, the United States is moving in this direction more slowly than western Europe; by 2050 the median age in Europe will be fifty-two, while it will be thirty-five in the United States.

The combination of falling fertility and rising life expectancy in the industrialized nations presents a challenge very different from the one foreseen by Malthus. These nations generally offer a broad array of social services, including retirement income, medical services, and housing supplements for the elderly. As the number of retirees increases relative to the number of employed people, costs may become unsustainable. Economists track this problem by using the PSR (potential support ratio): the ratio of persons fifteen to sixty-four years old (likely workers) to persons sixty-five or older (likely retirees). Between 1950 and 2000 the world's PSR fell from twelve to nine. By 2050 it will fall to four.

In Russia and other former socialist nations, current birthrates are now actually lower than death rates. Birthrates were already low before the collapse of the socialist system and have contracted further with recent economic problems. Since 1975 fertility rates have fallen between 20 and 40 percent across the former Soviet bloc, and by the early 1980s abortions were as common as births in much of eastern Europe. Life expectancy has also fallen. Life expectancy for Russian men is now only fifty-seven years, down almost ten years since 1980. Much of the rest of eastern Europe has also experienced declining life expectancy caused by high unemployment, low incomes, food shortages, and the dismantling of the social welfare system of the communist era.

The Developing Nations

At current rates, 95 percent of all future population growth will be in developing nations (see Map 33.2 and Table 33.1). A comparison between Europe and Africa illustrates these changes. In 1950 Europe had twice the population of Africa. By 1985 Africa's population had drawn even with Europe, and, according to projections, its population will be three times larger than Europe's by 2050.

As the 1990s ended, other developing regions had rapid population growth as well. While all developing nations had an average birthrate of 33.6 per thousand inhabitants, Muslim countries had a rate of 42.1. This rate is more than 300 percent higher than the 13.1 births per thousand in the developed nations of the West. The populations of Latin America and Asia were also expanding, but at rates slower than sub-Saharan Africa and the Muslim nations. Latin America's population increased from 165 million in 1950 to 511 million in 1999 and is projected to reach 809 million in 2050, despite declining birthrates.

Despite efforts to reduce family size, the populations of India and China continue to grow. Today these two nations account for roughly one-third of the world's population. In China efforts to enforce a limit of one child per family led initially to female infanticide as rural families sought to produce male heirs. This is no longer the case. India's policies of forced sterilization created widespread outrage and led to the electoral defeat of the ruling Congress Party. Yet both countries achieved some successes. Between 1960 and 1982 India's birthrate fell from 48 to 34 per thousand, while China's rate declined even more sharply—from 39 to 19 per thousand. Still, by 2025 both China and India will each likely reach 1.5 billion.

Old and Young Populations

Population pyramids generated by demographers clearly illustrate the profound transformation in human reproductive patterns and life expectancy since World War II. Figure 33.1 shows

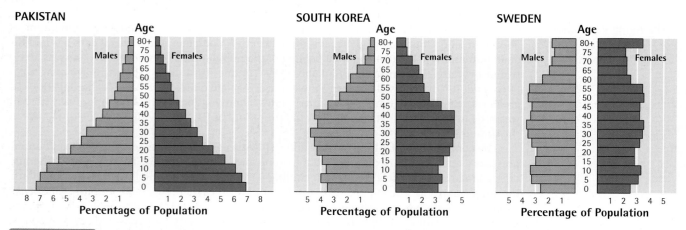

FIGURE 33.1 **Age Structure Comparison** Islamic Nation (Pakistan), Non-Islamic Developing Nation (South Korea), and Developed Nation (Sweden), 2001. *Source:* U.S. Bureau of the Census, *International Database,* 2001.

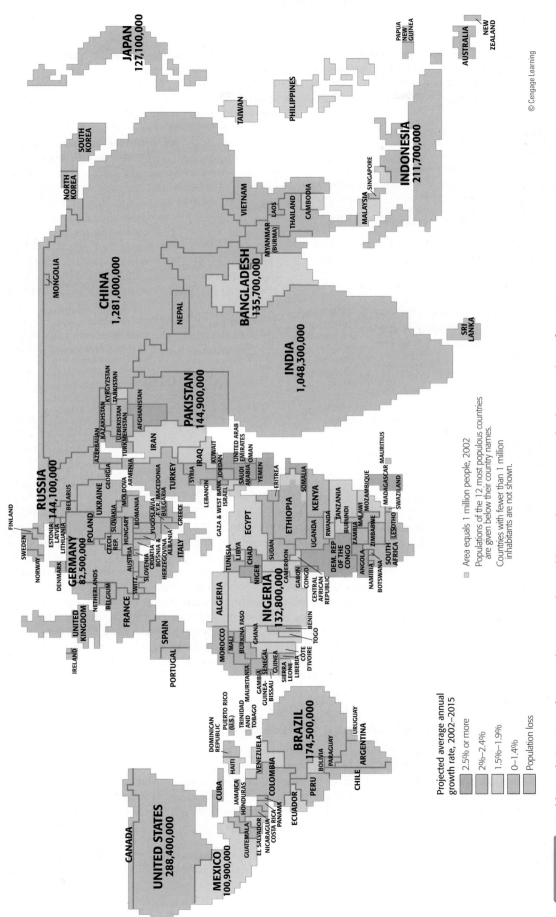

MAP 33.2 **World Population Growth** Every three years the world's population increases by the equivalent of a nation the size of the United States. Most of this population increase will be in some of the world's poorest nations. By 2050, for example, Pakistan, a nation of only 40 million in 1950, will have the world's third largest population. *Source:* Data from www.worldbank.org.

Projected average annual growth rate, 2002–2015

- 2.5% or more
- 2%–2.4%
- 1.5%–1.9%
- 0–1.4%
- Population loss

▪ Area equals 1 million people, 2002

Populations of the 12 most populous countries are given below their country names.

Countries with fewer than 1 million inhabitants are not shown.

© Cengage Learning

e Interactive Map

CANADA

UNITED STATES
288,400,000

MEXICO
100,900,000

GUATEMALA
EL SALVADOR
NICARAGUA
COSTA RICA
PANAMA

CUBA
JAMAICA
HAITI
HONDURAS
DOMINICAN REPUBLIC
PUERTO RICO (U.S.)
TRINIDAD AND TOBAGO

ECUADOR
COLOMBIA
VENEZUELA
PERU
BOLIVIA

BRAZIL
174,500,000

PARAGUAY
CHILE
ARGENTINA
URUGUAY

GUINEA-BISSAU
GAMBIA
GUINEA
SIERRA LEONE
LIBERIA
CÔTE D'IVOIRE

PORTUGAL
SPAIN
IRELAND
UNITED KINGDOM
FRANCE
NETHERLANDS
BELGIUM
SWITZ.
NORWAY
SWEDEN
DENMARK
GERMANY
82,500,000
FINLAND

MOROCCO
ALGERIA
MAURITANIA
MALI
SENEGAL
BURKINA FASO
GHANA
TOGO
BENIN
NIGER
NIGERIA
132,800,000
CAMEROON
GABON
CONGO
CENTRAL AFRICAN REPUBLIC

TUNISIA
LIBYA
CHAD
SUDAN
EGYPT
ETHIOPIA
UGANDA
RWANDA
BURUNDI
DEM. REP. OF THE CONGO
KENYA
TANZANIA
ANGOLA
ZAMBIA
MALAWI
ZIMBABWE
NAMIBIA
BOTSWANA
MOZAMBIQUE
SOUTH AFRICA
LESOTHO
SWAZILAND
MADAGASCAR
MAURITIUS
SOMALIA
ERITREA

ESTONIA
LATVIA
LITHUANIA
POLAND
CZECH. REP.
SLOVAKIA
AUSTRIA
HUNGARY
SLOVENIA
CROATIA
BOSNIA & HERZEGOVINA
ITALY
ALBANIA
F.Y.R. MACEDONIA
YUGOSLAVIA
ROMANIA
MOLDOVA
BULGARIA
GREECE
UKRAINE
BELARUS

RUSSIA
144,100,000

GEORGIA
AZERBAIJAN
ARMENIA
TURKEY
LEBANON
GAZA & WEST BANK
ISRAEL
SYRIA
IRAQ
JORDAN
KUWAIT
SAUDI ARABIA
YEMEN
UNITED ARAB EMIRATES
OMAN
IRAN

KAZAKHSTAN
KYRGYZSTAN
TAJIKISTAN
UZBEKISTAN
TURKMENISTAN
AFGHANISTAN

PAKISTAN
144,900,000

MONGOLIA

CHINA
1,281,000,000

NEPAL

INDIA
1,048,300,000

BANGLADESH
135,700,000

MYANMAR (BURMA)
LAOS
THAILAND
CAMBODIA
VIETNAM

SRI LANKA

NORTH KOREA
SOUTH KOREA

JAPAN
127,100,000

TAIWAN

PHILIPPINES

MALAYSIA
SINGAPORE

INDONESIA
211,700,000

PAPUA NEW GUINEA

AUSTRALIA

NEW ZEALAND

the 2001 age distributions in Pakistan, South Korea, and Sweden—nations at three different stages of economic development. Sweden is a mature industrial nation. South Korea is rapidly industrializing and has surpassed many European nations in both industrial output and per capita wealth. Pakistan is a poor, traditional Muslim nation with rudimentary industrialization, low educational levels, and little effective family planning.

In 2001 nearly 50 percent of Pakistan's population was under age sixteen. The resulting pressures on the economy have been extraordinary. Every year approximately 150,000 men reach age sixty-five—and another 1.2 million turn sixteen. Pakistan, therefore, has to create more than a million new jobs a year or face growing unemployment and declining wages. Sweden confronts a different problem. Sweden's aging population, growing demand for social welfare benefits, and declining labor pool means that its industries may become less competitive and living standards may decline. In South Korea, a decline in fertility dramatically altered the ratio of children to adults, creating an age distribution similar to that of western Europe.

SECTION REVIEW

- In the twentieth century the developed nations made the demographic transition to low birthrates, while the developing nations began by stressing higher birthrates.

- World population more than doubled between 1950 and 1995.

- In rich nations birth rates fell but longer life expectancy led to slow population growth; in the former Soviet Union the combination of low birth rates and declining life expectancy led to contracting population.

- Developing nations will contribute most of the world's future population growth, despite birth control efforts as in India and China.

UNEQUAL DEVELOPMENT AND THE MOVEMENT OF PEOPLES

The Economics of World Population Flows

Two characteristics of the postwar world should now be clear. First, despite decades of experimentation with state-directed economic development, most nations that were poor in 1960 were still poor in 2000. The only exceptions were a few rapidly developing Asian industrial nations and an equally small number of oil-exporting nations. Second, world population increased to startlingly high levels, and most of the increase was, and will continue to be, in the poorest nations.

The combination of intractable poverty and growing population generated a surge in international immigration. Few issues stirred more controversy. Even moderate voices sometimes framed the discussion of immigration as a competition among peoples. Large numbers of legal and illegal immigrants from poor nations with growing populations are entering the developed industrial nations, with the exception of Japan. Large-scale migrations within developing countries are a related phenomenon. The movement of impoverished rural residents to the cities of Asia, Africa, and Latin America (see Map 33.2 and Table 33.2) has increased steadily since the 1970s. This internal migration often serves as the first step toward migration abroad.

The Problem of Growing Inequality

Since 1945 the global economy has expanded more rapidly than at any time in the past. Faster, cheaper communications and transportation have combined with improvements in industrial and agricultural technologies to create material abundance that would have amazed those who experienced the first Industrial Revolution (see Chapter 23). Despite this remarkable economic expansion, the industrialized nations of the Northern Hemisphere enjoy an even larger share of the world's wealth than they did a century ago, accounting for a startling 74 percent of the world's economy in 1998.

Rich and Poor Nations

The gap between rich and poor nations has grown much wider since 1945. In 2001 Luxembourg and Switzerland had the highest per capita GNI (gross national income)—$39,840 and

TABLE 33.2 The World's Largest Cities (Population of 10 Million or More)

City	1950	City	1975	City	2000	City	2015
1 New York	12.3	1 Tokyo	19.8	1 Tokyo	26.4	1 Tokyo	35.5
		2 New York	15.9	2 Mexico City	18.1	2 Mumbai	21.9
		3 Shanghai	11.4	3 Bombay	18.1	3 Mexico City	21.6
		4 Mexico City	11.2	4 São Paulo	17.8	4 São Paulo	20.5
		5 São Paulo2	10.0	5 New York	16.6	5 New York	19.9
				6 Lagos	13.4	6 Delhi	18.6
				7 Los Angeles	13.1	7 Shanghai	17.2
				8 Calcutta	12.9	8 Calcutta (Kolkata)	17.0
				9 Shanghai	12.9	9 Dhaka	16.8
				10 Buenos Aires	12.6	10 Jakarta	16.8
				11 Dhaka	12.3	11 Lagos	16.1
				12 Karachi	11.8	12 Karachi	15.2
				13 Delhi	11.7	13 Buenos Aires	13.4
				14 Jakarta	11.0	14 Cairo	13.1
				15 Osaka	11.0	15 Los Angeles	13.1
				16 Metro Manila	10.9	16 Manila	12.9
				17 Beijing	10.8	17 Beijing	12.8
				18 Rio de Janeiro	10.6	18 Rio de Janeiro	12.7
				19 Cairo	10.6	19 Osaka-Kobe	11.3
						20 Istanbul	11.2
						21 Moscow	11.0

Source: From the International Migration Report 2002, United Nations, Department of Economic and Social Affairs, Population Division. © United Nations, 2003; the 2015 projection is from United Nations World Urbanization Prospects: The 2007 Revision. © United Nations, 2008. Reproduced with permission.

$35,630, respectively; the U.S. figure was $34,280; and Greece, the poorest nation in the European Union, had a per capita GNI of $11,430. The nations of the former Soviet Union and eastern Europe had per capita GNIs lower than some developing nations in the Third World. Russia's per capita GNI was $1,750 in 2001, less than Mexico's $5,530 or South Africa's $2,820, but higher than the Philippines' $1,030. Among other developing economies, Nigeria, India, and China had GNIs below $1,000.

Even in the industrialized world, there are haves and have-nots. Wealth inequality in the United States is now as great as on the eve of the 1929 stock market crash. Scholars estimate that the wealthiest 1 percent of households in the United States now control more than 30 percent of the nation's total wealth, while the poorest households have average incomes of under $5,000. Even in Europe, where tax and inheritance laws redistributed wealth, unemployment, homelessness, and substandard housing have become increasingly common.

Internal Migration: The Growth of Cities

In developing nations migration from rural areas to urban centers increased threefold between 1925 and 1950; the pace of migration then accelerated (see Table 33.2). While slums around the major cities of developing nations are seen as signs of social breakdown and economic failure, life in these urban slums was generally better than life in the countryside. A World Bank study

Garbage Dump in Manila, Philippines   In Third World nations thousands of poor families live by sorting and selling bottles, aluminum cans, plastic, and newspapers in urban landfills.

estimated that three out of four migrants to cities made economic gains. Residents of cities in sub-Saharan Africa, for example, were six times more likely than rural residents to have safe water. An unskilled migrant from the depressed northeast of Brazil could triple his or her income by moving to Rio de Janeiro.

As the scale of rural-to-urban migration grew, these benefits became more elusive. In the cities of the developing world basic services have been crumbling under the pressure of rapid population growth. In cities like Mexico City and Manila, which are among the world's largest cities, tens of thousands live in garbage dumps, scavenging for food. In Rio de Janeiro alone an estimated 350,000 abandoned children live in the streets and parks, begging, selling drugs, stealing, and engaging in prostitution to survive. Some nations have tried to relocate migrants back to the countryside. Indonesia, for example, has relocated more than a half-million urban residents since 1969.

Global Migration

Each year hundreds of thousands of men and women leave developing nations to go to industrialized nations. Dramatically rising numbers after 1960 led to increased ethnic and racial tensions. Political refugees and immigrants faced murderous violence in Germany; growing anti-immigrant sentiment strengthened right-wing political movements and led to riots in cities with large immigrant populations in France; and in the United States the government expanded its effort to control its southern border.

The Politics of Immigration

Immigrants from developing nations brought host nations many of the same benefits that the great migration of Europeans to the Americas provided a century earlier (see Chapter 24). The United States actively recruited Mexican workers during World War II and many European nations promoted guest worker programs and other inducements to immigration in the 1960s, when an expanding European economy experienced labor shortages. However, attitudes toward immigrants have changed as the size of immigrant populations grew, particularly during periods of economic contraction. Under pressure, native-born workers saw immigrants as competitors willing to work for lower wages and less likely to support labor unions. They demanded an end to immigration as a result.

High fertility among immigrants contributes to these tensions. Most immigrants are young adults who retain the positive attitudes toward early marriage and large families of their native cultures and have higher fertility rates than do host populations. In Germany in 1975, for example, immigrants made up only 7 percent of the population but accounted for nearly 15 percent of all births. Therefore, even without additional immigration, immigrant groups grow faster than longer-established populations. As immigrant populations increase in Europe and the United States in the twenty-first century, the resulting cultural conflicts will test definitions of citizenship and nationality.

SECTION REVIEW

- As the world economy expanded after World War II, the gap between rich and poor nations grew.

- In the fast-growing nations of the developing world urban populations have grown as a result of rural to urban migration.

- Most of the world's migration is the movement of young men and women from poor nations to rich nations.

TECHNOLOGICAL AND ENVIRONMENTAL CHANGE

Technological innovation powered the economic expansion that began after World War II. New technologies increased productivity and disseminated human creativity. They also altered the way people lived, worked, and played. Because most of the economic benefits were concentrated in the advanced industrialized nations, technology increased the power of those nations relative to the developing world. Even within developed nations, postwar technological innovations did not benefit all classes, industries, and regions equally. There were losers as well as winners.

Population growth and increased levels of migration and urbanization multiplied the numbers of acres farmed and factories, intensifying environmental threats. At the end of the twentieth century loss of rain forest, soil erosion, global warming, air and water pollution, and extinction of species threatened the quality of life and the survival of human societies. Environmental protection, like the acquisition of new technology, had progressed most in societies with the greatest economic resources.

New Technologies and the World Economy

Nuclear energy, jet engines, radar, and tape recording were among the many World War II developments that later had an impact on consumers' lives. New technology increased industrial productivity, reduced labor requirements, and improved the flow of information that made markets more efficient. The consumer electronics industry rapidly developed new products, changes seen in the music industry's movement from vinyl records to 8-track tapes, CDs, and then MP3 technologies.

Technology and Economic Growth

Improvements in existing technologies accounted for much of the developed world's productivity increases during the 1950s and 1960s, as faster, more efficient transportation and communication cut costs and expanded markets. But new technologies were important as well. Governments bore much of the cost of developing and constructing nuclear power plants and sponsored research into new technologies. None has proved more influential in the last three decades than the computer, which transformed both work and leisure (see Environment and Technology: The Computer Gets Personal). The first computers were expensive, large, and slow and only corporations, governments, and universities could afford them. Each new generation of computer was smaller, faster and less expensive. As a result, the serial utilization of desktops, laptops, and now hand-held devices transformed commerce, education, and government.

Computers also altered manufacturing. Small dedicated computers now control and monitor machinery in most industries. In the developed world factories forced by competition to

The Computer Gets Personal

The period since World War II witnessed wave after wave of technological innovations. None has had greater impact on the way people work, learn, and live than the computer. Until the 1970s most computing was done on large and expensive mainframe computers. These massive computers were primarily used for data storage and analysis, and the government agencies, universities, and large corporations that owned them controlled access.

Today most computers are in private hands, and most are devoted to communication and information searches, a transformation symbolized when the market value of the search engine Google surpassed that of IBM, developer of mainframe and PC computing. Few had anticipated the technological innovations that revolutionized the computer industry through miniaturization during the last three decades. The key development leading to smaller and cheaper computers was the microprocessor, a silicon chip that contained the computer's brains.

Initially developed to facilitate American defense research in the 1960s, the Internet was the second key to the commu-nication revolution. It allowed smaller, faster computers and related devices to become research portals that could access a vast international database of research, opinion, entertainment, and commerce. Small personal computers and the Web have had a revolutionary impact on modern culture, allowing individuals and groups—without the support of governments, corporations, or other powerful institutions—to collect and disseminate information more freely than at any time in the past (see Chapter 34).

In the last decade new technologies have permitted the integration of previously distinct devices. As a result, software and hardware providers now routinely blend the functions and uses of small laptop computers, cellular phones, and MP3 players to provide new business and professional applications and entertainment. Hand-held "convergence devices" evolving from the cellular telephone allow users to make phone calls, send e-mail, search the Internet, store and play music and videos, and store electronic texts. One result of this technological revolution is the appearance of plugged-in, self-identifying communities in venues like blogs, Facebook, and chat rooms that transcend or supplement older forms of community based on ethnic, regional, or economic identities.

Anthony West/Corbis

James Leynse/Corbis

From Mainframe to Laptops and PDAs   During the last forty years the computer revolution has changed the way we work.

improve efficiency and product quality depend on robots. Europe and the United States quickly followed Japan's lead in robotics, especially in automobile production and mining.

Globalization   The transnational corporation became the primary agent for these technological changes. By the twentieth century the growing economic power of corporations in industrialized nations allowed them to invest directly in the mines, plantations, and public utilities of less developed regions. In the post–World War II years many of these companies became truly transnational, having multinational ownership and management. International trade agreements and open markets furthered the process. Ford, Nissan, and other car companies not only produced and sold cars internationally, but their shareholders, workers, and managers also came from numerous nations.

The location of manufacturing plants overseas and the acquisition of corporate operations by foreign buyers rendered such global firms as transnational as the products they sold. In the 1970s and 1980s American brand names like Levi's, Coca-Cola, Marlboro, Gillette, McDonald's, and Kentucky Fried Chicken were global phenomena (see Material Culture: Fast Food). But in time Asian names—Hitachi, Sony, Sanyo, and Mitsubishi—were blazoned in neon and on giant video screens on the sides of skyscrapers, along with European brands such as Nestlé, Mercedes, Pirelli, and Benetton.

As transnational manufacturers, agricultural conglomerates, and financial giants became wealthier and more powerful, they increasingly escaped the controls imposed by national governments. If labor costs were too high in Japan, antipollution measures too intrusive in the United States, or taxes too high in Great Britain, transnational companies relocated—or threatened to do so. In 1945, for example, the U.S. textile industry was located in low-wage southern states, dominating the American market and exporting to the world. As wages in the South rose and global competition increased, producers began relocating plants to Puerto Rico in the 1980s and to Mexico after NAFTA went into effect in 1994 (see Chapter 34). Now China is the primary manufacturer of textiles.

Loss of Brazilian Rain Forest   The destruction of large portions of Brazil's virgin rain forest has come to symbolize the growing threat to the environment caused by population growth and economic development. In this photograph we see a tragic moonscape of tree stumps and fragile topsoil ripped open by settlers. The name given to this place is "Bom Futuro" ("Good Future" in English).

Claus Meyer/Peter Arnold, Inc.

Fast Food

Since early times empires and commercial enterprises have moved foods and beverages across national borders and cultural boundaries. The list of examples is very long. Sugar, coffee, tea, chocolate, corn, manioc, potatoes, wheat, wine, beer, distilled alcohols, tomatoes, and bananas are a small number of the foods and beverages carried from their origins to new continents and new peoples. In each case, host cultures accepted these additions to their cuisines while at the same time changing their preparation and altering their cultural meanings. Europeans sweetened chocolate, a bitter beverage consumed ritually by the Aztec elite, with sugar and it quickly became a beverage of mass consumption.

In modern industrialized nations fast food has come to cater to changing needs. Women and men in modern industrial societies marry later or not at all, and families have fewer meals together because of intense school and work schedules. As a result, fast food outlets have appeared everywhere to meet the needs of this busy, mobile population. In 2006 alone the world market for fast food grew by just under 7 percent, reaching sales of $155 billion.

Increased immigration and travel, as well as greater cultural connectivity promoted by films, television, and the Web, have combined to globalize ideas about food preparation and delivery. McDonald's now operates more than 31,000 restaurants in 119 countries. When a new franchise opened in Kuwait City, the drive-through line was over 10 kilometers long. Generally fast food meals cost the same in every cultural setting. In the United States, one of the richest countries in the world, McDonald's provides low-cost food to the masses, while in Pakistan, one of the poorest, these meals are luxuries. For many in the developing world, the fast food cuisines, restaurant designs, and styles of preparation represent the world of modernity and sophistication, not unlike the enthusiasm in the developed world for Mexican, Thai, or Ethiopian restaurants and cuisines.

Indeed, McDonald's is merely one of numerous examples of fast food globalization. KFC opened 1,500 outlets in China by the end of 2005, surpassing the McDonald's presence in this dynamic economy. Papa John's opened its fortieth outlet in Seoul and its twentieth outlet in Shanghai. Wendy's, Dominos, Cinnabon, and Subway have followed.

Many condemn this process as Yankee imperialism or as the unwanted homogenization of global culture. Tens of thousands have demonstrated, and some have gone to jail as a result of attacks on these symbols of foreign cultural penetration. Yet, as in earlier examples of unequal cultural exchange, local cultures have found ways to impose their tastes and values on these powerful international businesses. In Singapore McDonald's serves its signature hamburger on rice cakes instead of buns, and in Israel McDonald's established Kosher outlets. KFC, the most successful American chain in China,

Pizza Hut in India   The booming, cosmopolitan city of Mumbai hosts India's most modern industries and many of the country's strictest vegetarians, as seen by the vegetarian menu advertised by this Pizza Hut restaurant.

Ajaz Rahi/AP Images

serves a Beijing Duck Wrap with spring onions and rice gruel for breakfast. In India, with its large vegetarian population, McDonald's, Pizza Hut, and other successful franchises devote as much as 75 percent of their menu to vegetarian foods.

Every society produces a range of products that serve as class and culture markers and as forms of self-expression. In the modern world food helps mark consumers as "traditional" or "sophisticated" and as "rich" or "poor." Both the global success of fast food companies and the popular protests against them suggest the complexity of this form of cultural transmission.

Conserving and Sharing Resources

In the 1960s environmental activists and political leaders began warning about the devastating environmental consequences of population growth, industrialization, and the expansion of agriculture onto marginal lands. Assaults on rain forests, the disappearance of species, and the poisoning of streams and rivers raised public consciousness, as did the depletion and pollution of the world's oceans. Environmental damage occurred both in the advanced industrial economies and in developing nations. The former Soviet Union, where industrial and nuclear wastes were routinely dumped with little concern for environmental consequences, had the worst environmental record.

In the developed world industrial activity increased much more rapidly than population grew, and the consumption of energy (coal, electricity, and petroleum) rose proportionally. Indeed, the consumer-driven economic expansion of the post–World War II years became an obstacle to addressing environmental problems, since modern economies depend on a profligate consumption of goods and resources (see Map 33.3). When consumption slows, industrial nations enter a recession. How could the United States, Germany, or Japan change consumption patterns to protect the environment without endangering corporate profits, wages, and employment levels?

Since 1945 population growth has been most dramatic in the developing countries, where environmental pressures have also been extreme. In Brazil, India, and China, for example, the need to expand food production led to rapid deforestation and the extension of farming and grazing onto marginal lands. The results were predictable: erosion and water pollution. These and many other poor nations sought to stimulate industrialization because they believed that the transition from agriculture to manufacturing was the only way to provide for their rapidly growing populations. The argument was compelling: Why should Indians or Brazilians remain poor while Americans, Europeans, and Japanese grew rich?

Responding to Environmental Threats

Despite the gravity of environmental threats, there were many successful efforts to preserve and protect the environment. The Clean Air Act, the Clean Water Act, and the Endangered Species Act were passed in the United States in the 1970s as part of an environmental effort that included the nations of the European Community and Japan. Grassroots political movements and the media encouraged environmental awareness, and most nations in the developed world enforced strict antipollution laws and sponsored massive recycling efforts. Many also encouraged resource conservation by rewarding energy-efficient factories and manufacturers of fuel-efficient cars and by promoting the use of alternative energy sources such as solar and wind power.

Environmental Reforms in the Developed World

Environmental efforts produced significant results. In western Europe and the United States, air quality improved dramatically. Smog levels in the United States fell nearly a third from 1970 to 2000, even though the number of automobiles increased more than 80 percent. Emissions of lead and sulfur dioxide were down as well. The Great Lakes, Long Island Sound, and Chesapeake Bay were all much cleaner at the end of the century than they had been in 1970.

New technologies made much of the improvement possible; for example, pollution controls on automobiles, planes, and factory smokestacks reduced harmful emissions. At the same time, the desire to preserve the natural environment was growing around the world. In developed nations continued political organization and enhanced awareness of environmental issues seemed likely to lead to step-by-step improvements in environmental policy. In the developing world and most of the former Soviet bloc, however, population

SECTION REVIEW

- Improvements in existing technology and new technologies such as the computer have improved manufacturing efficiency and transformed leisure.

- Globalization created a more integrated world economy, connecting producers and consumers from different regions and nations and reducing the ability of a single nation to escape the effects of distant events.

- The environmental movement achieved some successes in developed nations, reducing pollution and improving resource management, but global progress was hindered by a lack of cooperation between developed and developing nations.

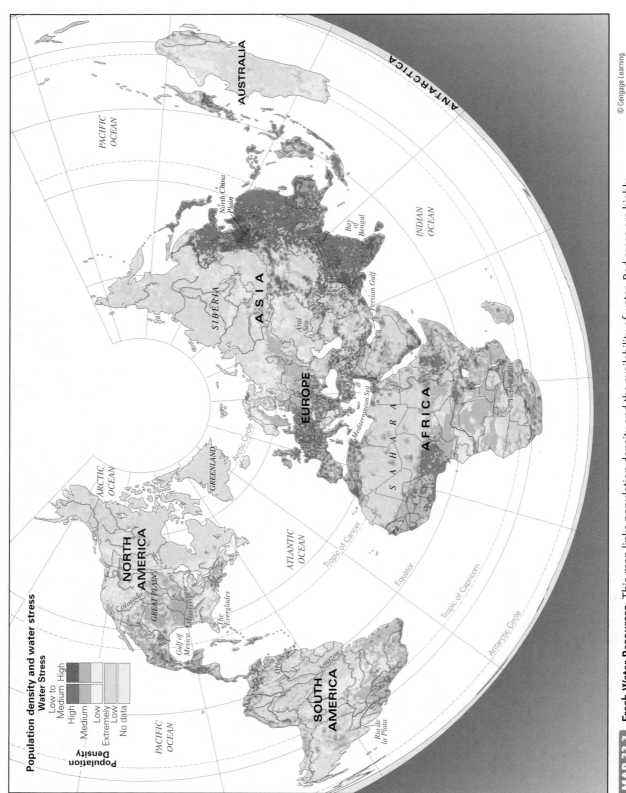

© Cengage Learning

MAP 33.3 **Fresh Water Resources** This map links population density and the availability of water. Red areas are highly stressed environments where populations use at least 40 percent or more of available water. Less stressed environments are blue. The deeper the shade of red or blue the greater the environmental stress. *Source:* From "Global Water Stress," *National Geographic,* September 2002, pp. 14–16. Reprinted by permission of the National Geographic Society.

pressures and weak governments were major obstacles to effective environmental policies. Since the 1990s the rapid expansion of China's industrial sector has put additional pressure on the environment.

It now seems likely that industrialized nations will have to fund global improvements and that the cost will be high. Nevertheless, growing evidence of environmental degradation has continued to propel popular reform efforts, as when the media drew attention to the precipitous shrinkage of Peru's Andean glaciers and to loss of rain forest in Brazil. Yet, without broad agreement among the rich nations, the economic and political power necessary for environmental protections on a global scale will be very difficult to institute. When representatives from around the world negotiated a far-reaching treaty to reduce greenhouse gases in Kyoto, Japan, in 1997, President George W. Bush refused American participation even though the treaty was affirmed by nearly all other industrial nations.

CONCLUSION

The world was profoundly altered between 1975 and 2000. Both the United States and the Soviet Union feared that every conflict and every regime change represented a potential threat to their strategic interests, and every conflict threatened to provoke confrontation between them. As a result, the superpowers inserted themselves into a succession of civil wars and revolutions. The costs in lives and property were terrible, the gains small. As defense costs escalated, the Soviet system crumbled. By 1991 the Soviet Union and the socialist Warsaw Pact had disappeared, transforming the international stage.

The world was also altered by economic growth and integration, by population growth and movement, and by technological and environmental change. Led by the postwar recovery of the industrial powers and the remarkable economic expansion of Japan, the Asian Tigers, and more recently China, the world economy grew dramatically. The development and application of new technology contributed significantly to this process. International markets were more open and integrated than at any other time. However, not all the nations of the world benefited from the new wealth and exciting technologies of the postwar era. The capitalist West and a handful of Asian nations grew richer and more powerful, while most of the world's nations remained poor.

Population growth in the developing world was one reason for this divided experience. Most of the world's population growth in recent decades is in developing nations with limited economic growth. Unable to find adequate employment or, in many cases, bare subsistence, people in developing nations have migrated across borders, hoping to improve their lives. These movements have often provided valuable labor in the factories and farms of the developed world, but they have also provoked cultural, racial, and ethnic tension. Problems of inequality, population growth, and international migration will continue to challenge the global community in the coming decades.

Growing population and the development process have forced marginal lands into production and stimulated the exploitation of new resources. The need to feed a rapidly growing world population has also pressured ocean resources. As the world's population reached 6 billion and the largest cities reached 20 million, the need to produce and deliver raw materials and finished goods has put tremendous stress on the environment. In the 1990s the rapid development of the Chinese and Indian economies compounded these pressures.

At the same time, new technologies and the wealth produced by economic expansion have allowed the world's richest nations to implement ambitious programs of environmental protection. As a result, pollution produced by automobiles and factories has actually declined in the richest nations. The question that remains is whether rapidly developing nations, such as China and India, will move more quickly than the mature industrial nations did to introduce these new technologies.

KEY TERMS

proxy wars p. 874
Salvador Allende p. 874
Dirty War p. 875
Sandinistas p. 875
Ayatollah Ruhollah
  Khomeini p. 877

neo-liberalism p. 878
Saddam Husain p. 879
keiretsu p. 880
Asian Tigers p. 880

newly industrialized
  economies
  (NIEs) p. 881
Deng Xiaoping p. 881
Tiananmen Square p. 881
Mikhail Gorbachev p. 882

perestroika p. 882
Solidarity p. 882
ethnic cleansing p. 883
Thomas Malthus p. 885
demographic
  transition p. 886

EBOOK AND WEBSITE RESOURCES

Primary Sources

Islamic Government

The Last Heir of Lenin Explains His Reform Plans: Perestroika and Glasnost

Interactive Maps

Map 33.1 The End of the Soviet Union

Map 33.2 World Population Growth

Plus flashcards, practice quizzes, and more. Go to:
www.cengage.com/history/bullietearthpeople5e

SUGGESTED READING

Adriaasen, W. L. M., and J. G. Waardensburg, eds. *A Dual World Economy: Forty Years of Development Experience.* 1989. A useful introduction to the complexity of development.

Bakhash, Shaul. *The Reign of the Ayatollahs: Iran and the Iranian Revolution.* 1990. An account of the Iranian Revolution and the early days of the Islamic Republic of Iran.

Berry, John A., and Carol Pott Berry, eds. *Genocide in Rwanda: A Collective Memory.* 1999. Covers a major calamity too readily forgotten.

Dyson, Tim, et al., eds. *Twenty-first Century India: Population, Economy, Human Development, and the Environment.* 2005. The culmination of a large research project.

Edgerton, Robert. *The Troubled Heart of Africa: A History of the Congo.* 2002. A convincing examination of this nation's history.

Foster, John Bellamy. *Economic History of the Environment.* 1994. An important synthesis.

Gaddis, John Lewis. *The Cold War: A New History.* 2005. A solid overview.

Kenez, Peter. *A History of the Soviet Union from the Beginning to the End.* 2006. Explains the demise of the USSR.

Kennedy, Paul M. *Preparing for the Twenty-first Century.* 1993. Asks whether world resources can cope with future population growth.

Krugman, Paul. *The Age of Diminished Expectations: U.S. Economic Policy in the 1990s.* 1997. An interesting criticism of American economic policy.

Lardy, Nicholas R. *China's Unfinished Economic Revolution.* 1998. A well-researched study of economic changes.

Maier, Charles. *Dissolution: The Crisis of Communism and the End of East Germany.* 1997. Covers the collapse of the Soviet empire in Europe.

McNeill, John R. *Something New Under the Sun: An Environmental History of the Twentieth Century World.* 2000. A survey coverage of a rising field of historical study.

Meredith, Martin. *The Fate of Africa: From the Hopes of Freedom to the Heart of Despair.* 2005. An overview of recent African history.

Rostow, W. W. *The Great Population Spike and After: Reflections on the 21st Century.* 1998. A challenging work that examines consequences of falling fertility in developed nations.

Rubin, Barnett. *The Fragmentation of Afghanistan.* 1995. Provides excellent coverage of the struggle between Soviet forces and the Muslim resistance.

Sampson, Anthony. *Mandela: The Authorized Biography.* 2000. A valuable introduction to the life and politics of the man.

Shenkar, Oded. *The Chinese Century: The Rising Chinese Economy and Its Impact on the Global Economy, the Balance of Power, and Your Job.* 2004. A business-oriented appraisal of the surging Chinese economy.

Skidmore, Thomas E., and Peter H. Smith. *Modern Latin America*, 6th ed. 2005. Provides an excellent general introduction to the period 1975 to 1991.

Stiglitz, Joseph E. *Globalization and Its Discontents.* 2003. An overview by a major economic thinker.

Thompson, Leonard. *A History of South Africa*, 3rd ed. 2005. Looks at a key African country.

Westad, Odd Arne. *The Global Cold War: Third World Interventions and the Making of Our Times.* 2005. A very useful discussion of the effects of Cold War rivalry on the developing world.

Wolf, M. *Revolution Postponed: Women in Contemporary China.* 1985.

NOTES

1. Quoted in Antony Flew, "Introduction," in Thomas Robert Malthus, *An Essay on the Principle of Population and a Summary View of the Principle of Population* (New York: Penguin Books, 1970), 30.

2. "Population Implosion Worries a Graying Europe," *New York Times*, July 10, 1998.

CHAPTER

34

CHAPTER OUTLINE

- Globalization and Economic Crisis
- The Question of Values
- Global Culture

ENVIRONMENT + TECHNOLOGY *Global Warming*

DIVERSITY + DOMINANCE *Conflict and Civilization*

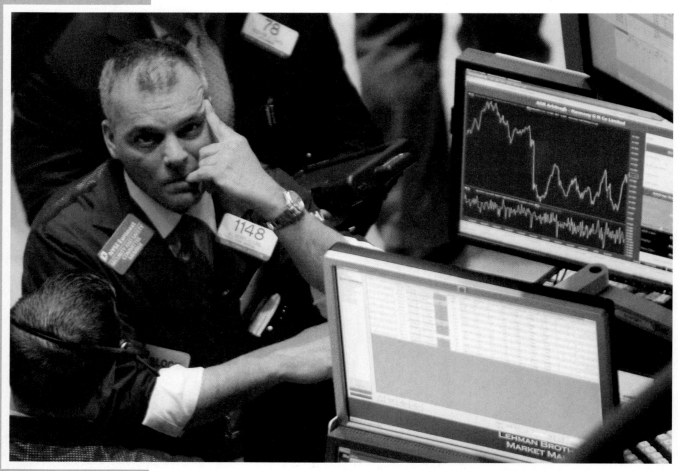

Watching Financial Markets Fall   After years of economic boom, much of it fueled by inflated housing prices in the United States and ingenious new financial instruments that concealed risk, the world's stock markets fell drastically in 2008–2009. American stocks lost approximately one-third of their value. The banking crisis and resulting unemployment reminded economists of the Great Depression of the 1930s. People in all walks of life, from heads of state, to retirees, to ordinary workers, were forced to reappraise their financial situations.

 Visit the website and ebook for additional study materials and interactive tools: www.cengage.com/history/bullietearthpeople5e

Justin Lane/epa/Corbis

902

New Challenges in a New Millennium

The workday began normally at the World Trade Center in lower Manhattan on the morning of September 11, 2001. The 50,000 people who worked there were making their way to the two 110-story towers. Suddenly, at 8:46 A.M., an American Airlines Boeing 767 with 92 people on board, traveling at a speed of 470 miles per hour (756 kilometers per hour), crashed into floors 94 to 98 of the north tower, igniting the 10,000 gallons (38,000 liters) of fuel in its tanks. Just before 9:03 A.M. a United Airlines flight with 65 people on board and a similar fuel load hit floors 78 to 84 of the south tower.

- What are the main benefits and dangers of growing political, economic, and cultural integration?
- What roles do religious beliefs and secular ideologies play in the contemporary world?
- How has technology contributed to the process of global interaction?

As the burning jet fuel engulfed the collision areas, the buildings' occupants struggled through smoke-filled corridors and down dozens of flights of stairs. Many of those trapped above the crash sites used cell phones to say good-bye to loved ones. Rather than endure the flames and fumes, a few jumped to their deaths.

Just before 10 o'clock, temperatures that had risen to 2,300° Fahrenheit (1,260° Celsius) caused the steel girders in the impacted area of the south tower to give way. The collapsing upper floors crushed the floors underneath one by one, engulfing lower Manhattan in a dense cloud of dust. Twenty-eight minutes later the north tower pancaked in a similar manner. Miraculously, most of the buildings' occupants had escaped before the towers collapsed. Besides the people on the planes, nearly 2,600 lost their lives, including some 400 police officers and firefighters helping in the evacuation.

That same morning another American Airlines jet crashed into the Pentagon, killing all 64 people on board and 125 others inside the military complex near Washington, D.C. Passengers on a fourth plane managed to overpower their hijackers, and the plane crashed in rural Pennsylvania, killing all 45 on board.

The four planes had been hijacked by teams of Middle Eastern men who slit the throats of service and flight personnel and seized control. Of the nineteen hijackers, fifteen were from Saudi Arabia. All had links to an extremist Islamic organization, al-Qaeda (ahl–KAW-eh-duh) (the base or foundation), commanded by a rich Saudi named Usama bin Laden (oo-SAH-mah bin LAH-din), who was incensed with American political, military, and cultural influence in the Middle East. The men were educated and well traveled, had lived in the United States, and spoke English. Some had trained as pilots so that they could fly the hijacked aircraft.

e **PRIMARY SOURCE:**
The Last Night Read a
list of instructions meant to be
reviewed on September 10,
2001, by the terrorists who
attacked the United States the
next morning.

The hijackers left few records of their motives, but the acts spoke for themselves. The World Trade Center was a focal point of international business, the Pentagon the headquarters of the American military. The fourth plane was probably meant to hit the Capitol or the White House, the legislative and executive centers of the world's only superpower.

The events of September 11, which became commonly referred to as 9/11, can be understood on many levels. The hijackers and those who sympathized with them saw themselves as engaged in a holy struggle against economic, political, and military institutions they believed to be evil. People directly affected, political leaders around the world, and most television watchers described the attacks as evil deeds against innocent victims.

To understand why the nineteen attackers were heroes to some and terrorists to others, one needs to explore the historical context of global changes at the turn of the millennium and the ideological tensions they have generated. The unique prominence of the United States in every major aspect of global integration, as well as its support for pro-American governments overseas, also elicits sharply divergent views.

GLOBALIZATION AND ECONOMIC CRISIS

globalization The economic, political, and cultural integration and interaction of all parts of the world brought about by increasing trade, travel, and technology.

The turn of the millennium saw the intensification of **globalization** trends that had been building since the 1970s. Growing trade and travel and new technologies were bringing all parts of the world into closer economic, political, and cultural integration and interaction (see Maps 34.1 and 34.2). The collapse of the Soviet Union had completed the dissolution of territorial empires that had been under way throughout the twentieth century. Autonomous national states (numbering about two hundred) became an almost universal norm, and a growing number of them had embraced democratic institutions. However, increasing interdependency would also facilitate a global economic crisis that exploded in 2008 when the massive accumulation of debt in American financial institutions became unsustainable.

An Interconnected Economy

Trade and 9/11

The expansion of trade, global interconnections, and privatization of government enterprises that gained momentum with the dismantling of Soviet-style socialist economies in the 1990s cooled abruptly in the wake of 9/11. The rate of growth in world trade fell from 13 percent in 2000 to only 1 percent in 2001.

Petroleum Prices

Growth in China and India resumed quickly, however, and the large populations of these two countries marked them as future world economic powers. Their growth increased pressure on world energy supplies, though the United States continued to consume a quarter of the world's petroleum production. OPEC's manipulation of world oil prices, combined with political instability in the Middle East, had caused crude oil prices to soar between 1973 and 1985. But aside from those years, the average price of oil remained consistently below $20 per barrel (adjusted for inflation) throughout the second half of the twentieth century. In the year 2000, however, oil prices began a new period of increase caused not by OPEC but by rising demand and confidence in the fevered pace of world economic expansion. By the middle of 2006, the price of a barrel of crude had crept past $70, and in 2008 it spiked to $145 a barrel. This increase fueled ambitious economic programs in producing countries like Russia, Saudi Arabia, and the small sheikhdoms of the Persian Gulf. Then, with the economic crisis of 2008, prices fell abruptly, causing disruption in those same countries.

Regional Trade Organizations

Regional trade associations came into being to promote growth, reduce the economic vulnerability of member states, and, less explicitly, balance American economic dominance. The twenty-seven member European Union (EU) was the most successful (see Map 34.2). The euro, a common currency inaugurated in 2002 and used in twelve member states, competed with the U.S. dollar for investment and banking. However, unequal levels of development among mem-

CHRONOLOGY

Politics	Economics and Society
2000 2000 Al-Qaeda attacks American destroyer USS *Cole* in Yemen	
2001 2001 George W. Bush becomes president of the United States	2001–2003 Terrorist attacks trigger global recession
2001 Terrorists destroy the World Trade Center and damage the Pentagon on September 11	2001 Shanghai Cooperation Organization formed
2001 United States armed forces overthrow Taliban regime in Afghanistan	
2002	2002 Euro currency adopted in twelve European countries
2003 2003 Unfounded fears of weapons of mass destruction lead United States and Britain to invade and occupy Iraq	
2004 2004 Terrorists bomb Spanish trains	2004 Ten new members admitted to European Union
2004–2009 Genocidal conflict ongoing in Darfur region of Sudan	
2005 2005 Terrorists bomb London transit system	
2005 Mahmoud Ahmedinejad elected president of Iran	
2006 2006 Iraqis elect a government under a new constitution	
2006 Hamas movement defeats PLO in Palestinian election	
2006 Israel attacks Hezbollah in Lebanon in response to its seizure of Israeli soldiers	
2007 2007 Assassination of Benazir Bhutto deepens political crisis in Pakistan	
2008 2008 Barack Obama elected president of the United States	2008 Collapse of mortgage debt bubble in United States triggers global recession

bers became a source of friction in 2009 as the world economic downturn devastated stock markets and increased rates of unemployment.

Despite the EU's expansion, the North American Free Trade Agreement (NAFTA), which eliminated tariffs among the United States, Canada, and Mexico in 1994, governed the world's largest free-trade zone. Yet heated debate in the United States over illegal immigration across

Palm Island, Dubai The seemingly unlimited wealth of the oil-producing states of the Persian Gulf spurred ambitious development plans like this one in Dubai, one of the United Arab Emirates. Its publicists proclaimed that "'Palm Island' would include 2,000 villas, up to 40 luxury hotels, shopping complexes, cinemas, and the Middle East's "first marine park" and would be "visible from the moon."

Jorge Ferrari/epa/Corbis Sygma

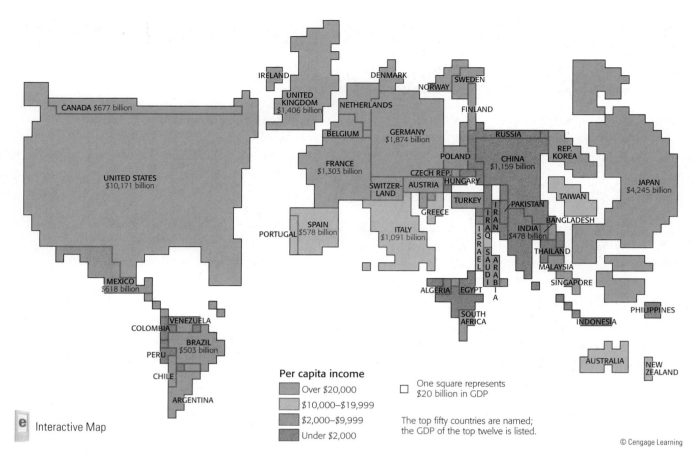

Per capita income
- Over $20,000
- $10,000–$19,999
- $2,000–$9,999
- Under $2,000

☐ One square represents
$20 billion in GDP

The top fifty countries are named;
the GDP of the top twelve is listed.

© Cengage Learning

e Interactive Map

MAP 34.1 **Global Distribution of Wealth** Early industrialization and efficient investment contributed to individual prosperity for the citizens of Japan and Western countries by the 1990s. However, economic dynamism in late-industrializing countries like China and India began to change the world balance of economic power in the early twenty-first century. In nearly all countries the distribution of wealth among individuals varies tremendously, with the gap between rich and poor generally increasing.

the Mexican border, as well anti-Hispanic prejudice, limited popular enthusiasm for the agreement. The third largest free-trade zone, Mercosur, created by Argentina, Brazil, Paraguay, and Uruguay in 1991 and subsequently expanded to include five associate members, planned to elect a parliament in 2010. Other free-trade associations operated in West Africa, southern Africa, Southeast Asia, Central America, the Pacific Basin, and the Caribbean.

The Shanghai Cooperation Organization (SCO), formed in 2001 with China, Russia, and four former Soviet Central Asian republics as members, originally pursued common security interests, such as combating separatist movements and terrorism. But its announced twenty-year plan for reducing barriers to trade and population movement took a step forward when Mahmoud Ahmedinejad, the president of Iran, one of five countries with observer status, formally applied for full membership in 2008. Bringing Iran's oil-rich economy into alignment with a rapidly developing China and a similarly oil-rich Russia promised to complicate the world economic and political picture even before the onset of the global fiscal crisis later that year.

World Trade Organization

World Trade Organization (WTO) An international body established in 1995 to foster and bring order to international trade.

In 1995 the world's major traders established the **World Trade Organization (WTO)** dedicated to reducing barriers and enforcing international agreements. Despite a membership of 153 nations, the WTO had many critics and regularly encountered street protests during its ministerial meetings. Some protesters feared that low-cost foreign manufacturers would shrink the job opportunities in richer states; others demanded continuing tariff protection for local farmers.

Efforts to rescue countries in economic trouble became a concern of the International Monetary Fund (IMF) and World Bank (see Chapter 32) and of wealthy countries that could afford to extend foreign aid. But few suspected that the globalized economy would turn into a source of anxiety for everyone.

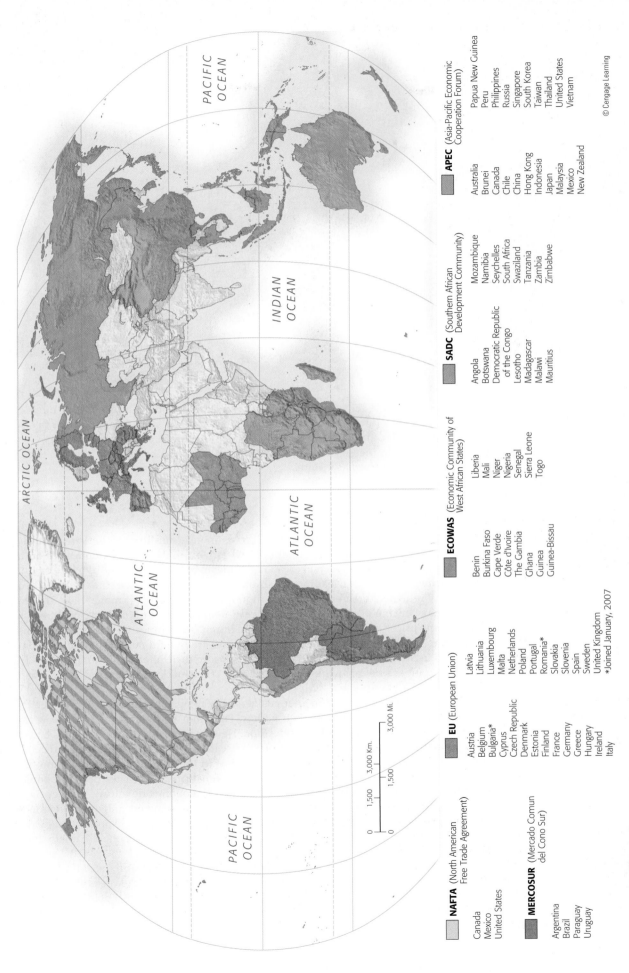

NAFTA (North American Free Trade Agreement)

Canada
Mexico
United States

MERCOSUR (Mercado Comun del Cono Sur)

Argentina
Brazil
Paraguay
Uruguay

EU (European Union)

Austria
Belgium
Bulgaria*
Cyprus
Czech Republic
Denmark
Estonia
Finland
France
Germany
Greece
Hungary
Ireland
Italy

Latvia
Lithuania
Luxembourg
Malta
Netherlands
Poland
Portugal
Romania*
Slovakia
Slovenia
Spain
Sweden
United Kingdom

*Joined January, 2007

ECOWAS (Economic Community of West African States)

Benin
Burkina Faso
Cape Verde
Côte d'Ivoire
The Gambia
Ghana
Guinea
Guinea-Bissau

Liberia
Mali
Niger
Nigeria
Senegal
Sierra Leone
Togo

SADC (Southern African Development Community)

Angola
Botswana
Democratic Republic
    of the Congo
Lesotho
Madagascar
Malawi
Mauritius

Mozambique
Namibia
Seychelles
South Africa
Swaziland
Tanzania
Zambia
Zimbabwe

APEC (Asia-Pacific Economic Cooperation Forum)

Australia
Brunei
Canada
Chile
China
Hong Kong
Indonesia
Japan
Malaysia
Mexico
New Zealand

Papua New Guinea
Peru
Philippines
Russia
Singapore
South Korea
Taiwan
Thailand
United States
Vietnam

© Cengage Learning

e Interactive Map

MAP 34.2 **Regional Trade Associations, 2004** International trade and development are major concerns of governments in developed and developing countries. NAFTA, Mercosur, and the EU are free-trade areas. The other associations promote trade and development.

President Barack Obama at Cairo's Sultan Hassan Mosque　Tensions between the United States and the Muslim world diminished somewhat after President Obama gave a speech in Cairo directed at Muslims. Speaking less than five months after taking office, he praised the positive elements of Islam and recognized the negative impact of American policies related to the Iraq War and the stringent anti-terrorist measures taken by the Bush administration. Iman Abdel Fateh, standing between the president and Secretary of State Hillary Rodham Clinton, served as a guide.

Global Financial Crisis

The global financial crisis that began in 2008 had roots in an Asian financial crisis a decade earlier. Vast amounts of European and American investment in Thailand, Indonesia, South Korea, and other East Asian countries had created an illusion of great economic dynamism; but in 1997 the investment boom burst, leading to a severe economic downturn in the region. When economic stability returned, greater investor caution reversed the flow of money. The United States in particular became a favorite place to invest, helping spur a rapid increase in stock market and housing prices and massive growth in the purchase of imported goods. Americans became wedded to borrowing money for houses, cars, and credit card purchases. Money from overseas invested in the U.S. treasury also made it possible for the United States to fight wars in Afghanistan and Iraq (see below) while lowering taxes. The American national debt climbed dramatically.

Collapse of the Housing Market

In 2008 the fevered boom in housing prices collapsed, leaving many homeowners so deeply in debt on their mortgages that they lost their homes. Their mortgage debts, however, were no longer being held by a bank in the traditional fashion. New and risky lending techniques based on an assumption that home prices would continue to rise indefinitely had caused the bad debts to be distributed throughout the banking system, not just in the United States but around the world. When Lehman Brothers, one of the country's foremost financial firms, declared bankruptcy in September, a recession turned into a catastrophic economic downturn. Stock prices fell, banks teetered on the brink of collapse, consumer demand plummeted, and unemployment climbed as employers laid off workers they could no longer afford. The effects spread worldwide. Knowledgeable political leaders and economists proclaimed it the worst economic crisis since the Great Depression of the 1930s.

Obama Financial Plans

The sense that Barack Obama had a firm understanding of the crisis and the ability to lead the country out of it contributed to his election as president. During the first weeks after he took office in January 2009, he proposed a series of steps, including massive increases in government spending, to jolt the economy back to health. Yet no one was sure that his plans would succeed, and no one expected the recovery to be swift. The trade expansion that had signaled the promise of globalization at the beginning of the century faded from memory, and the interdependence that had bound the world's economies in a cycle of growth became a dead weight that dragged many countries down.

Globalization and Democracy

The last decades of the twentieth century saw expansions of democratic institutions and personal freedom. People in many countries recognized that elections offered a peaceful way to settle differences among a country's social classes, cultural groups, and regions. Although majority votes could swing from one part of the political spectrum to another, democracies tended to encourage political moderation. Moreover, wars between fully democratic states were extremely rare.

Eastern Europe

The nations of eastern Europe embraced democracy after the fall of the Soviet Union, though some newly democratic states became subject to great mood swings among the electorate. The shift to private ownership of businesses after decades of rigid state control brought riches to a select few, and the removal of trade barriers characteristic of Cold War rivalry opened up new markets and fostered investment from the West.

By 2008, however, rising unemployment and falling export levels and stock prices threatened these experiments in free elections and free markets. Small countries like Iceland in the West and Latvia in the post-Soviet East saw governments fall, and fear of political instability spread widely. In Russia, the popular but somewhat authoritarian leader Vladimir Putin followed his country's constitution by stepping down in 2008 after two terms as president. However, he engineered the election of his protégé Dimitri Medvedev as his successor and assumed the office of prime minister himself. This move led some political thinkers to fear a possible return to Soviet era Russian domination.

Democracy in Asia

Asian democracies proved somewhat more stable. Beginning with free parliamentary elections in 1999, the populous state of Indonesia moved from years of authoritarian and corrupt rule toward more open political institutions. The following years saw a violent independence movement of the Acheh (ah-CHEH) district of northern Sumatra, the secession in 2002 of East Timor after years of brutal Indonesian military occupation, terrorist bombings on the island of Bali in 2004, and a devastating earthquake and tsunami in the same year. But democratic elections were regularly held. The losing candidates left office peacefully, and the populace at large accepted the results.

In India a major political shift seemed to be at hand in 1998 when the Bharatiya Janata Party (BJP) secured an electoral victory that interrupted four decades of Congress Party rule. The BJP success came through blatant appeals to Hindu nationalism, the condoning of violence against India's Muslims, and opposition to the social and economic progress of the Untouchables (those

Sectarian Strife in India   Hours after these Hindu youths clambered atop the sixteenth-century Babri Mosque in December 1992, hundreds of angry Hindu nationalists completely demolished the structure. The Hindus claimed that the Muslim place of worship in the northern Indian province of Uttar Pradesh had been erected upon the site of a temple commemorating the birthplace of Lord Ram, the incarnation of the Hindu god Vishnu. Thousands died in the riots that followed the razing of the temple. An Indian government archaeological team uncovered the foundation of an earlier temple-like structure.

Douglas E. Curran/Getty Images/Corbis

traditionally confined to the dirtiest jobs). In 2004, however, the Congress Party returned to power and governmental stability proved strong even in the face of sensational terrorist attacks in Mumbai by Pakistani gunmen in 2008.

Instability in Pakistan

Democracy in Pakistan itself proved more uncertain. President and former military commander Pervez Musharraf's (pair-VEZ moo-SHAH-ef) abrupt firing of the country's chief justice, combined with his unpopular support of the Bush administration's war policies, sparked protests and calls for impeachment. He resigned the presidency in 2008. Asif Ali Zardari (AH-sef AH-lee zar-DAH-ree), who succeeded him, had inherited the leadership of the majority Pakistan People's Party after the assassination the year before of his charismatic wife Benazir Bhutto, the daughter of a popular earlier prime minister. Zardari faced difficulties forming a strong government because of the growing movement of the Pakistani Taliban to impose their own governance and a rigid Muslim behavioral code in outlying districts, as well as popular opposition to American antiterrorist attacks launched from Afghanistan.

African Regimes

In sub-Saharan Africa, democracy had mixed results. Nelson Mandela, the leader of the African National Congress (ANC) who had become the first postapartheid president of South Africa in 1994 (see Chapter 33), left office in 1999 and was succeeded by the deputy president and ANC leader Thabo Mbeki (TAA-boh um-BEH-kee). Mbeki stepped down in 2008 amidst turmoil in the leadership of the ANC. But the democratic system did not seem threatened. Elsewhere some elected leaders, such as Robert Mugabe (moo-GAH-bay) in Zimbabwe, used violence and intimidation to hold on to power, and other states, such as Congo, were plagued with internal revolts and civil wars. Liberians emerged from fourteen years of civil war in 2003 and two years later chose Ellen Johnson-Sirleaf (SUHR-leef) to be Africa's first elected female head of state. In Sudan, the general who had led a military coup in 1989, Omar al-Bashir, became the first sitting head of state to be charged with genocide and crimes against humanity by the International Criminal Court in 2009. A festering conflict in Darfur in western Sudan, which had then cost hundreds of thousands of lives and displaced over 2 million people, was at the heart of the charges.

Regime Change in Iraq and Afghanistan

Weapons of Mass Destruction

The most closely watched experiments in democratization took place in Iraq and Afghanistan, countries that the United States invaded after the terrorist attacks of 9/11. Afghanistan's provision of a safe haven for Usama bin Laden and his al-Qaeda organization gave clear justification for the overthrow in December 2001 of the militantly religious Taliban regime. However, the rationale for invading Iraq was less clear. Leading up to the war the American government contended that Iraq was a clear and present danger to the United States because it possessed **weapons of mass destruction** (WMDs): nuclear, chemical, and biological weapons that it might supply to terrorists like bin Laden.

weapons of mass destruction Nuclear, chemical, and biological devices that are capable of injuring and killing large numbers of people.

When United Nations inspectors failed to find any banned weapons, a split widened between those nations wanting to continue inspections and those, led by the United States, wanting to intervene militarily. Deciding to go it alone, an American-led "coalition of the willing" opened the invasion of Iraq with a spectacular aerial bombardment of Baghdad on March 20, 2003. Twenty-five days later the United States declared that "major fighting" had ended, little realizing that guerrilla insurgency, sectarian violence, and economic devastation would continue for years.

e PRIMARY SOURCE: Declaration of Jihad Against Americans Occupying the Land of the Two Holy Mosques Read a speech given by Osama bin Laden to his followers in Afghanistan, and soon published worldwide.

Though Iraq fell into a state of turmoil because the coalition army was too small or otherwise unprepared to prevent the looting and destruction of government facilities and other lawlessness, a thorough search was launched for WMDs. The search came up empty, and intelligence analyses failed to uncover any evidence that Saddam Husain, Iraq's fallen dictator, had played a role in the 9/11 attacks.

North Korea and Iran

However, American concern for WMDs was not eliminated. North Korea had an open program to build nuclear weapons, and Iran was suspected of having a covert plan based in part on technological aid secretly given by the head of Pakistan's successful nuclear program. Iran's outspokenly anti-American and anti-Israeli president, Mahmoud Ahmedinejad, elected in 2005, and North Korea's dictator Kim Jong-il (kim jong-ill) presented the United States with difficult challenges. But the military invasion option chosen for Iraq, though favored by some Bush advisers, was held in abeyance in favor of diplomatic initiatives.

Iranian President Mahmoud Ahmedinejad After two terms under the comparatively liberal, but ineffective, government of President Mohammad Khatami, voters in the Islamic Republic of Iran elected a relatively unknown conservative in 2005. President Ahmedinejad has taken confrontational positions on international affairs, notably his denial of Israel's legitimacy as a state and his assertion of Iran's right to develop nuclear technology. This has enhanced his domestic popularity, while convincing many analysts that with the American defeat of Saddam Husain, Iran had become a major power in the Middle East and the Islamic world.

IRNA/Reuters/Corbis

The failure to find Iraqi WMDs having undermined his war scenario, President George W. Bush declared that the United States had actually invaded Iraq to liberate the Iraqi people and substitute democracy for oppression. An intense debate followed within the United States about whether the Bush administration had used deception in leading the nation into war. However, the question of whether the war would ultimately be deemed successful came to hinge on the establishment of democratic institutions in both Afghanistan and Iraq.

Return of the Taliban

Unfortunately, the power of a new Afghan government elected in 2004 did not extend over the entire country. By 2008 the Taliban were again a serious threat, and opium production, the key to the country's unrest, was higher than ever. Though the United States was able to enlist the participation of NATO forces in helping to police Afghanistan, the prospects for the country were so dim that President Barack Obama, succeeding George Bush in 2009, made intensification of efforts to bring peace and stability and suppress terrorism a key part of his foreign policy.

The "Surge" in Iraq

In Iraq, the United States time and again declared that the country was finally emerging from chaos and proceeding on the path to democratic rule. In actuality, despite the adoption of a constitution in 2006, lethal resistance to coalition troops and the newly organized Iraqi security forces remained strong until 2008, when the United States, under a policy called "the surge," began to organize and pay segments of the resistance movement to join the coalition side.

Before "the surge" the question had frequently been asked whether Iraq was on the verge of, or already engaged in, a civil war. But as the level of violence plummeted, it became possible to envision an orderly withdrawal of American forces that would give the country a reasonable chance for stability, reconstruction, and the soothing of still potent political and sectarian divisions. Soon after being elected, President Obama announced that American combat brigades would be withdrawn from Iraq by August 2010, though a sizable residual force would remain to train the Iraqi army and suppress terrorist activities.

Looking at the level of destruction visited on Afghanistan and Iraq in the name of democratization, other Middle Eastern countries hesitated to follow American urgings to liberalize their political systems. Though some small oil-producing countries in the Persian Gulf took cautious steps toward democratization and Kuwait for the first time allowed women to vote in 2006, large countries like Egypt and Syria continued to suppress most critics. Their governments feared that free elections would lead to Islamic political parties gaining a share of power as the religious Shi'ite parties had done in Iraq's first elections.

Hezbollah

The capture of 23 out of 128 seats in the Lebanese parliament by the Lebanese Shi'ite movement Hezbollah in 2005 and the absolute majority of seats won by the militantly anti-Israeli

Hamas movement in elections for the Palestine Governing Authority in 2006 seemed to confirm this fear, since both movements were strongly religious in their policies. Attacks launched by Israel against both Hamas and Hezbollah in response to kidnappings of Israeli soldiers in 2006 suggested that fear of domination by Islamic movements might in the future become more important than democratization in the Middle East, regardless of American preferences.

Hamas

In 2007 the elected Hamas government succeeded in driving its Palestinian rivals out of the Gaza Strip. During the following months, largely inaccurate rocket barrages launched from there against Israel became a major factor in Israeli politics. A security barrier built on the West Bank had almost eliminated attacks by Palestinian suicide bombers, but the rockets provoked public outrage even though the number of casualties was very small. During the final month of the manifestly pro-Israeli Bush administration, the Israel Defense Force undertook to deal once and for all with Hamas in the Gaza Strip. Aerial bombardments and ground force incursions left well over a thousand Palestinians dead. Israeli casualties were negligible. However, there was no sign that Hamas had been seriously harmed as a political organization. Worldwide reactions to the closely watched Gaza campaign engendered great criticism of Israel but no relaxation of the American determination to shun Hamas until it abandoned its opposition to Israel's existence. In democratic terms, neither the Israeli nor the Palestinian political systems seemed likely to produce governments capable of meaningful peace negotiations.

SECTION REVIEW

- Since the Cold War, global political relations have been defined largely by economic interconnections.

- To manage economic change, many nations have joined a variety of trade organizations, and free-trade policies have caused widespread controversy.

- Global interdependence and rapid economic expansion and speculation led to a global financial crisis in 2008 that plunged the world into the worst economic slowdown since the Great Depression of the 1930s.

- There has been a general worldwide trend toward democracy, especially in Asian countries.

- However, U.S. intervention in Iraq and Afghanistan has shown that the promotion of democracy by military force is very difficult, and in the Middle East the Israeli-Palestinian deadlock stands in the way of fundamental political change.

THE QUESTION OF VALUES

As people around the world first faced the opportunities of globalization and then the fear of global recession, they tried to make sense of these changes in terms of their own value systems. With 6 billion people, the world was big enough to include many different approaches, whether religious or secular, local or international, traditional or visionary. In some cases, however, conflicting visions fed violence.

Faith and Politics

Religious beliefs increasingly inspired political actions during the second half of the twentieth century, and the trend intensified as the new century began (see Map 34.3). Though for Americans this change reversed two centuries of growing secularism, Western analysts did not agree on the cause of the religious revival.

Fundamentalism

Evangelical Protestants became a powerful conservative political force in the United States, particularly during the Bush presidency. Around the world, Catholic conservatives led by Pope John Paul II, and Pope Benedict XVI, who succeeded him in 2005, forcefully reiterated politically sensitive teachings: opposition to abortion, homosexuality, marriage of priests, and admission of women to the priesthood. In Israel, hyperorthodox Jews known as *haredim* played a leading role in settling the Palestinian territories captured by Israel in 1967 and vehemently resisted both Israel's unilateral withdrawal from Gaza in 2005 and subsequent plans for withdrawal from the West Bank. And in India, Hindu zealots made the BJP party a powerful political force (see above).

Yet most discussions of faith and politics focused on Islam (see Diversity and Dominance: Conflict and Civilization). The birth of the Islamic Republic of Iran in the revolution of 1979

Darfur Refugees In 2003 a conflict broke out in the Darfur region of western Sudan. Marauding bands, largely from nomadic backgrounds, struck farming villages, killing ten of thousands. More than 100,000 people crossed the border into Chad as refugees. With both sides being of more or less the same ethnicity and religion, and with few great power interests at stake, the international community proved unable to take effective action.

Terrorism

terrorism Political belief that extreme and seemingly random violence will destabilize a government and permit the terrorists to gain political advantage. Though an old technique, terrorism gained prominence in the late twentieth century with the growth of worldwide mass media that, through their news coverage, amplified public fears of terrorist acts.

Usama bin Laden

Usama bin Laden Saudi-born Muslim extremist who funded the al-Qaeda organization that was responsible for several terrorist attacks, including those on the World Trade Center and the Pentagon in 2001.

made visible a current of Muslim political assertiveness that had been building for twenty years in several Muslim countries. But by the year 2000 acts of **terrorism** perpetrated by non-Iranian Muslim groups claiming to be acting for religious reasons were capturing the headlines.

Terrorism is a political tactic by which comparatively weak militants use grotesquely inhumane and lethal acts to convince a frightened public that danger is everywhere and their government is incapable of protecting them. Although terrorism has a long history, the instantaneous media links made possible by satellite communications, and the tradition in the news business of publicizing violence, increased its effectiveness from the 1980s onward.

Bombings, kidnappings, and assassinations made political sense to all sorts of political groups: secular Palestinians confronting Israel; national separatists like the Tamils in Sri Lanka, Basques in Spain, and Chechens in Russia; and Catholic and Protestant extremists in Northern Ireland, to name a few. But Muslim groups gained the lion's share of attention when they targeted the United States and Europe, recruited from Muslim populations all over the world, and made effective use of news coverage and audiovisual communications.

Their media star and ideological spokesman was **Usama bin Laden**. Born into a wealthy Saudi family and educated as an engineer, bin Laden fought against the Soviet Union in Afghanistan and there recruited and trained a core group of fighters called al-Qaeda. Though his family disowned him and Saudi Arabia stripped him of his citizenship, his calls for holy war (*jihad*) and his portrayal of the United States as a puppet-master manipulating both non-Muslim (e.g., Israel, India, Russia) and Muslim (e.g., Egypt, Algeria, Saudi Arabia) governments to murder and oppress innocent Muslims made sense to millions of Muslims, even if only a very few committed themselves to follow him into battle.

Al-Qaeda blew up American embassies in Kenya and Tanzania in 1998, crippled the U.S. Navy destroyer *Cole* during a port call in Yemen in 2000, and then capped everything by attacking the World Trade Center and the Pentagon on 9/11. When the "global war on terrorism" declared by President Bush failed to eliminate bin Laden, his mystique grew. Further terrorist attacks—by Indonesians on tourists on the island of Bali in 2002, by North Africans on commuter trains servicing Madrid in 2004, by English-born Muslims on the London transit system in 2005, and by Pakistanis on luxury hotels in Mumbai, India, in 2008—made it clear that the current of violence unleashed by al-Qaeda had become decentralized and that recruits and cells might no longer be taking orders from bin Laden. In the meantime, the primary center of terrorist activity had shifted to Iraq, where suicide bombings became commonplace. Most bombings there resulted in Muslim casualties as Sunni and Shi'ite groups squared off against one other, thus diminishing the image of the suicide bomber as a fanatic hater of the West.

DIVERSITY + DOMINANCE

Conflict and Civilization

In 1993 Samuel P. Huntington, a professor of government at Harvard University, published "The Clash of Civilizations?" in the journal Foreign Affairs. *This article provoked extraordinary debate, particularly after the 9/11 attacks on the World Trade Center and the Pentagon. Some readers deemed it an accurate description of a post–Cold War world in which Islamic countries were destined to conflict violently with the countries of Europe and North America. Others saw it as imprecise in its failure to clarify what a "civilization" is, imperialistic in its unquestioning assumption of Western superiority, and encouraging of anti-Muslim prejudice.*

Civilizational identity will be increasingly important in the future, and the world will be shaped in large measure by the interactions among seven or eight major civilizations. These include Western, Confucian, Japanese, Islamic, Hindu, Slavic-Orthodox, Latin American and possibly African civilization. The most important conflicts of the future will occur along the cultural fault lines separating these civilizations from one another.

Why will this be the case?

First, differences among civilizations are not only real; they are basic. Civilizations are differentiated from each other by history, language, culture, tradition and, most important, religion. The people of different civilizations have different views on the relations between God and man, the individual and the group, the citizen and the state, parents and children, husband and wife, as well as differing views of the relative importance of rights and responsibilities, liberty and authority, equality and hierarchy. These differences are the product of centuries. They will not soon disappear. They are far more fundamental than differences among political ideologies and political regimes. Differences do not necessarily mean conflict, and conflict does not necessarily mean violence. Over the centuries, however, differences among civilizations have generated the most prolonged and the most violent conflicts.

Second, the world is becoming a smaller place. The interactions between peoples of different civilizations are increasing; these increasing interactions intensify civilization consciousness and awareness of differences between civilizations and commonalities within civilizations. North African immigration to France generates hostility among Frenchmen and at the same time increased receptivity to immigration by "good" European Catholic Poles. Americans react far more negatively to Japanese investment than to larger investments from Canada and European countries. . . .

Third, the processes of economic modernization and social change throughout the world are separating people from longstanding local identities. They also weaken the nation state as a source of identity. In much of the world religion has moved in to fill this gap, often in the form of movements that are labeled "fundamentalist." Such movements are found in Western Christianity, Judaism, Buddhism and Hinduism, as well as in Islam. In most countries and most religions the people active in fundamentalist movements are young, college-educated, middle-class technicians, professionals and business persons. . . .

As people define their identity in ethnic and religious terms, they are likely to see an "us" versus "them" relation existing between themselves and people of different ethnicity or religion. The end of ideologically defined states in Eastern Europe and the former Soviet Union permits traditional ethnic identities and animosities to come to the fore. Differences in culture and religion create differences over policy issues, ranging from human rights to immigration to trade and commerce to the environment. . . . Most important, the efforts of the West to promote its values of democracy and liberalism to universal values, to maintain its military predominance and to advance its economic interests engender countering responses from other civilizations. . . .

The interactions between civilizations vary greatly in the extent to which they are likely to be characterized by violence. Economic competition clearly predominates between the American and European subcivilizations of the West and between both of them and Japan. On the Eurasian continent, however, the proliferation of ethnic conflict, epitomized at the extreme in "ethnic cleansing," has not been totally random. It has been most frequent and most violent between groups belonging to different civilizations. In Eurasia the great historic fault lines between civilizations are once more aflame. This is particularly true along the boundaries of the crescent-shaped Islamic bloc of nations from the bulge of Africa to central Asia. Violence also occurs between Muslims, on the one hand, and Orthodox Serbs in the Balkans, Jews in Israel, Hindus in India, Buddhists in Burma and Catholics in the Philippines. Islam has bloody borders.

Rejoinders to Huntington's thesis saw it as a cornerstone of the aggressive policies adopted by the Bush administration after 9/11. As an alternative, they stressed the common values held by peaceful societies and the need for intercultural understanding. Mohammed Khatami, the president of the Islamic Republic of Iran, found support for a more positive framing of the matter when the United Nations, following his proposal, declared 2001 the year of "Dialogue Among Civilizations." Almost simultaneously, the Organization of the Islamic Conference, a 57-member international body headquartered in Saudi Arabia and composed of states with large Muslim populations, elaborated upon this concept in the "Tehran Declaration on Dialogue Among Civilizations."

Tehran Declaration on Dialogue Among Civilizations

Praise be to Allah and peace and blessing be upon His prophet and kin and companion.

The representatives of Heads of State and Government of OIC member states . . . [recognizing] the United Nations General Assembly resolution 53/22, designating the year 2001 as the United Nations year of Dialogue among Civilizations;

Guided by the noble Islamic teachings and values [*each of the following principles is accompanied by reference to a verse in the Quran*] on human dignity and equality, tolerance, peace and justice for humankind, and promotion of virtues and proscription of vice and evil;

Drawing upon the Islamic principles of celebration of human diversity, recognition of diversified sources of knowledge, promotion of dialogue and mutual understanding, genuine mutual respect in human interchanges, and encouragement of courteous and civilized discourse based on reason and logic;

Reaffirming the commitment of their Governments to promote dialogue and understanding among various cultures and civilizations, aimed at reaching a global consensus to build a new order for the next millennium founded in faith as well as common moral and ethical values of contemporary civilizations;

Requests the Secretary-General of the OIC to submit this declaration for endorsement to the Chairman of the Eighth Islamic Summit and the 26th Islamic Conference of Foreign Ministers for appropriate action:

A) General principles of dialogue among civilizations

1. Respect for the dignity and equality of all human beings without distinctions of any kind and of nations large and small;
2. Genuine acceptance of cultural diversity as a permanent of human society and a cherished asset for the advancement and welfare of humanity at large;
3. Mutual respect and tolerance for the views and values of various cultures and civilizations, as well as the right of members of all civilizations to preserve their cultural heritage and values, and rejection of desecration of moral, religious or cultural values, sanctities and sanctuaries;
4. Recognition of diversified sources of knowledge throughout time and space, and the imperative of drawing upon the areas of strengths, richness and wisdom of each civilization in a genuine process of mutual enrichment;
5. Rejection of attempts for cultural domination and imposition as well as doctrines and practices promoting confrontation and clash between civilizations;
6. Search for common grounds between and within various civilizations in order to face common global challenges;

Acceptance of cooperation and search for understanding as the appropriate mechanism for the promotion of common universal values as well as for the suppression of global threats;
7. Commitment to participation of all peoples and nations, without any discrimination, in their own domestic as well as global decision-making and value distribution processes;
8. Compliance with principles of justice, equity, peace and solidarity as well as fundamental principles of international law and the United Nations Charter. . . .

A few years later, a joint proposal by the governments of Spain and Turkey received a similar endorsement by the United Nations. This led to the creation of the Alliance of Civilizations. The underlying principles of this organization were expressed in the 2006 report of its "High-Level Group," a body of eminent political, intellectual, and spiritual figures from around the world.

Alliance of CivilizationsReport of the High-Level Group

I. Bridging the World's Divides

1.1 Our world is alarmingly out of balance. For many, the last century brought unprecedented progress, prosperity, and freedom. For others, it marked an era of subjugation, humili-

ation and dispossession. Ours is a world of great inequalities and paradoxes: a world where the income of the planet's three richest people is greater than the combined income of the world's least developed countries; where modern medicine performs daily miracles and yet 3 million people die every year of preventable diseases; where we know more about distant universes than ever before, yet 130 million children have no access to education; where despite the existence of multilateral covenants and institutions, the international community often seems helpless in the face of conflict and genocide. For most of humanity, freedom from want and freedom from fear appear as elusive as ever.

1.2 We also live in an increasingly complex world, where polarized perceptions, fueled by injustice and inequality, often lead to violence and conflict, threatening international stability. Over the past few years, wars, occupation and acts of terror have exacerbated mutual suspicion and fear within and among societies. Some political leaders and sectors of the media, as well as radical groups have exploited this environment, painting mirror images of a world made up of mutually exclusive cultures, religions, or civilizations, historically distinct and destined for confrontation.

1.3 The anxiety and confusion caused by the "clash of civilizations" theory regrettably has distorted the terms of the discourse on the real nature of the predicament the world is facing. The history of relations between cultures is not only one of wars and confrontation. It is also based on centuries of constructive exchanges, cross-fertilization, and peaceful co-existence. Moreover, classifying internally fluid and diverse societies along hard-and-fast lines of civilizations interferes with more illuminating ways of understanding questions of identity, motivation and behavior. Rifts between the powerful and the powerless or the rich and the poor or between different political groups, classes, occupations and nationalities have greater explanatory power than such cultural categories. Indeed, the latter stereotypes only serve to entrench already polarized opinions. Worse, by promoting the misguided view that cultures are set on an unavoidable collision course, they help turn negotiable disputes into seemingly intractable identity-based conflicts that take hold of the popular imagination. It is essential, therefore, to counter the stereotypes and misconceptions that deepen patterns of hostility and mistrust among societies.

QUESTIONS FOR ANALYSIS

1. How important are culture and religion, as opposed to governing ideology or economic inequality, in explaining current world conflicts?

2. Do statements like these reflect the realities of international and intercommunal relations? Or do they merely serve the political interests of the authors?

3. Should general statements about culture play a role at the level of personal relations in the neighborhood, the workplace, or the classroom?

Sources: Samuel P. Huntington, "The Clash of Civilizations?," Reprinted by permission of *Foreign Affairs* 72, no. 3 (Summer 1993). Copyright 1993 by the Council on Foreign Relations, Inc. www.ForeignAffairs.com; "The Tehran Declaration on Dialogue Among Civilizations," Organization of the Islamic Conference, www.isesco.org.ma/english/publications/dig/CH11.php; "High-Level Group Report," Alliance of Civilizations, available online at www.unaoc .org/content/view/64/94/lang,english/.

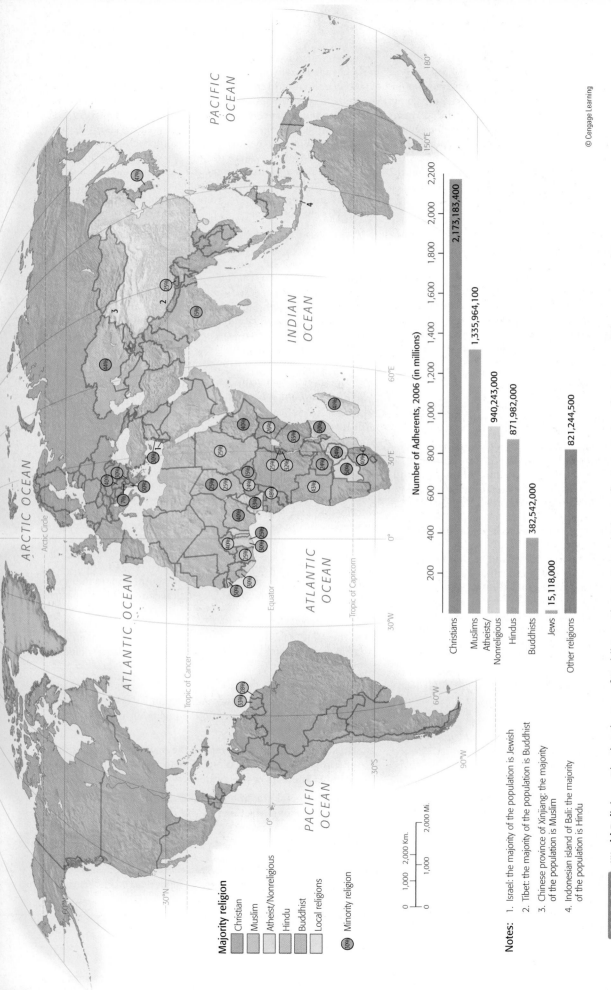

MAP 34.3 **World Religions** The distribution of Buddhism, Christianity, and Islam reflects centuries of missionary efforts. Hinduism and Judaism have expanded primarily through trade and migration. Chinese governments have actively curtailed religious practice. As religion revives as a source of social identity or a rationale for political assertion or mass mobilization, the possibility of religious activism across broad geographic regions becomes greater, as does the likelihood of domestic discord in multireligious states. (Data from *The New York Times 2003 Almanac*, ed. John W. Wright [New York: Penguin Books, 2002], 484–488. Copyright © The New York Times Company, 2002)

Majority religion

- Christian
- Muslim
- Atheist/Nonreligious
- Hindu
- Buddhist
- Local religions

50% Minority religion

Notes:
1. Israel: the majority of the population is Jewish
2. Tibet: the majority of the population is Buddhist
3. Chinese province of Xinjiang: the majority of the population is Muslim
4. Indonesian island of Bali: the majority of the population is Hindu

Number of Adherents, 2006 (in millions)

Religion	Adherents
Christians	2,173,183,400
Muslims	1,335,964,100
Atheists/Nonreligious	940,243,000
Hindus	871,982,000
Buddhists	382,542,000
Jews	15,118,000
Other religions	821,244,500

Interactive Map

Islam and Violence

In trying to explain a current of violence that could strike anywhere in the world but seemed to be centered on Muslims, some analysts argued that Islam itself encouraged violence against non-Muslims. The counterargument pointed out that terrorists came from many backgrounds and that the vast majority of Muslims saw their religion as one of peace. Others maintained that rigidly conservative Muslims like Usama bin Laden were blindly opposed to freedom and modernity. The counterargument pointed out that al-Qaeda used modern military and propaganda techniques and that many of its operatives, like bin Laden himself, graduated from modern technical programs. A third school of thought felt that the United States instigated al-Qaeda's wrath by supporting Israel and stationing troops in Saudi Arabia. The counterargument pointed out that the United States had also championed the Muslim cause in Bosnia and driven the secular dictator Saddam Husain out of Kuwait, an act that most Arab governments supported.

Universal Rights and Values

Universal Declaration of Human Rights A 1948 United Nations covenant binding signatory nations to the observance of specified rights.

Alongside the growing influence of religion on politics, efforts to promote adherence to universal human rights also expanded. The modern human rights movement grew out of secular statements like the French Declaration of the Rights of Man (1789) and the U.S. Constitution (1788) and Bill of Rights (1791). The **Universal Declaration of Human Rights**, passed by the United Nations General Assembly in 1948, culminated this movement by proclaiming itself "a common standard of achievement for all peoples and nations." Its thirty articles condemned slavery, torture, cruel and inhuman punishment, and arbitrary arrest, detention, and exile. The Declaration called for freedom of movement, assembly, and thought. It asserted rights to life, liberty, and security of person; to impartial public trials; and to education, employment, and leisure. The principle of equality was most fully articulated in Article 2:

> Everyone is entitled to all the rights and freedoms set forth in this Declaration, without distinction of any kind, such as race, color, sex, language, religion, or political or other opinion, national or social origin, property, birth or other status.[1]

This passage reflected an international consensus against racism and imperialism and a growing acceptance of the importance of social and economic equality. Most newly independent countries joining the United Nations willingly signed the Declaration because it implicitly condemned European colonial regimes.

NGOs

nongovernmental organizations (NGOs) Nonprofit international organizations devoted to investigating human rights abuses and providing humanitarian relief. Two NGOs won the Nobel Peace Prize in the 1990s: International Campaign to Ban Landmines (1997) and Doctors Without Borders (1999).

Besides the official actions of the United Nations and various national governments, individual human rights activists, often working through philanthropic bodies known as **nongovernmental organizations (NGOs)**, have been important forces promoting human rights. Amnesty International, founded in 1961, concentrates on gaining the freedom of people who have been tortured or imprisoned without trial and campaigns against summary execution by government death squads or other gross violations of rights. Arguing that no right is more fundamental than the right to life, other NGOs have devoted themselves to famine relief, refugee assistance, and health care around the world. Médecins Sans Frontières (Doctors Without Borders), founded in 1971, was awarded the Nobel Peace Prize in 1999 for offering medical assistance in scores of crises.

While NGOs often worked in specific countries, other universal goals became enshrined in international agreements. Such agreements made genocide a crime and promoted environmental protection of the seas, of Antarctica, and of the atmosphere (see Environment and Technology: Global Warming). The United States and a few other nations were greatly concerned that such treaties would limit their sovereignty or threaten their national interests. For this reason the U.S. Congress delayed ratifying the 1949 convention on genocide until 1986. More recently the United States drew widespread criticism for demanding exemption for Americans from the jurisdiction of the International Criminal Court, created in 2002 to try international criminals, and for declaring that "enemy combatants" taken prisoner during the "global war on terrorism" should not be treated in accordance with the Third Geneva Convention (1950) on humane treatment of prisoners of war.

Obama and Human Rights

The 2008 election of Barack Obama as the first African-American to hold the office of president of the United States was widely thought to signal a change in American attitudes on international rights issues. Not only was he the living embodiment of the ability of the Americans to see past skin color in selecting a leader, but on taking office he immediately announced the

Global Warming

Until the 1980s environmental alarms focused mainly on localized episodes of air and water pollution, exposure to toxic substances, waste management, and the disappearance of wilderness. The development of increasingly powerful computers and complex models of ecological interactions in the 1990s, however, made people aware of the global scope of certain environmental problems.

Many scientists and policymakers came to perceive global warming, the slow increase of the temperature of the earth's lower atmosphere, as an environmental threat requiring preventive action on an international scale. The warming is caused by a layer of atmospheric gases (carbon dioxide, methane, nitrous oxide, and ozone) that allow solar radiation to reach earth and warm it but that keep infrared energy (heat) from radiating from earth's surface back into space. Called the *greenhouse effect*, this process normally keeps the earth's temperature at a level suitable for life. However, increases in greenhouse-gas emissions—particularly from the burning of fossil fuels in industry and transportation—have added to this insulating atmospheric layer.

Recent events have confirmed predictions of global temperature increases and melting glaciers and icecaps. Greenland glaciers and Arctic Ocean sea ice are melting at record rates, and huge sections of the Antarctic ice shelf are breaking off and floating away. Andean glaciers are shrinking so fast they could disappear in a decade, imperiling water supplies for drinking, irrigation, and hydroelectric production. Drought has affected much of the United States in recent years, and Australia has experienced the "Big Dry," its worst drought in a century.

Despite this evidence, governments of the industrialized countries that produce the most greenhouse gasses have been slow to adopt measures stringent

enough to reduce emissions. They cite the negative effects they believe this could have on their economies. Because of these fears, many nations hesitated to sign the 1997 Kyoto Protocol, the first international agreement to impose penalties on countries that failed to cut greenhouse-gas emissions. It was a major environmental victory when Japan added its signature in March 2001, but to the consternation of many world leaders President George W. Bush rejected the agreement.

The American election of 2008 may have set the stage for changes that would finally make the climate control an area of action and not just worry. Shortly after being elected, Barack Obama announced to an audience of scientists and citizens concerned with climate matters: "You can be sure that the United States will once again engage vigorously in these negotiations, and help lead the world toward a new era of global cooperation on climate change."

D. Aubert/Corbis Sygma

Flooding in Bangladesh   Typhoon-driven floods submerge the low-lying farmlands of Bangladesh with tragic regularity. Any significant rise in the sea level will make parts of the country nearly uninhabitable.

closing of the widely condemned prison for "enemy combatants" at Guantanamo Bay, an American naval base in Cuba, and chose for his cabinet men and women strongly associated with the protection of rights and of the country's natural heritage.

Women's Rights

Women's Rights Conferences

The women's rights movement, which began on both sides of the North Atlantic in the nineteenth century, became an important human rights issue in the twentieth century. Rights for women

Beijing Women's Conference in 1995   This gathering of women from every part of the world, under United Nations auspices, illustrated the challenges posed by women's search for equality. The Chinese government, consistent with its policies of suppressing dissent and closely regulating social life, tried to limit press access to the conference. As in many other instances, these efforts to silence or control women's voices on issues like abortion and family planning proved ineffective.

Boulat/Sipa Press

became accepted in Western countries and were enshrined in the constitutions of many nations newly freed from colonial rule. In 1979 the United Nations General Assembly adopted the Convention on the Elimination of All Forms of Discrimination Against Women, and in 1985 the first international conference on the status of women, sponsored by the United Nations Division for the Advancement of Women, was held in Nairobi, Kenya. A second conference in Beijing ten years later added momentum to the movement. By 2007, 183 countries had endorsed the 1979 convention.

Besides highlighting the problems women face around the world, international conferences have also revealed great variety in the views and concerns of women. Feminists from the West, who had been accustomed to dictating the agenda and who had pushed for the liberation of women in other parts of the world, sometimes found themselves accused of having narrow concerns and condescending attitudes. Some non-Western women complained about Western feminists' endorsement of sexual liberation and about the deterioration of family life in the West. They found Western feminists' concern with matters such as comfortable clothing misplaced and trivial compared to the issues of poverty and disease.

Other cultures came in for their share of criticism. Western women and many secular leaders in Muslim countries protested Islam's requirement that a woman cover her head and wear loose-fitting garments to conceal the shape of her body, practices enforced by law in countries such as Iran and Saudi Arabia. Nevertheless, many outspoken Muslim women voluntarily donned concealing garments as expressions of personal belief, statements of resistance to secular dictatorship, or defense against coarse male behavior.

The conferences were more important for the attention they focused on women's issues than for the solutions they generated. Such efforts raised the prominence of human rights as a global concern and put pressure on governments to consider human rights when making foreign policy decisions. Skeptics observed, however, that a Western country might successfully prod a non-Western country to improve its human rights performance—for example, by granting

SECTION REVIEW

- The second half of the twentieth century has seen an increase in political action inspired by religious belief.

- Militant Islam has risen in response to authoritarian oppression in many Muslim countries and to the claim that the United States supports such authoritarianism.

- Universal standards of human rights have gained wider acceptance and underlie the work of the United Nations, individual states, and NGOs.

- Concepts of human rights have expanded to address genocide and environmental protection.

- Global debates on women's rights have addressed a variety of economic, political, and social problems but have also involved clashes over cultural values.

Debates over Rights

women better access to education and careers—but that reverse criticism of a Western country often fell on deaf ears—for example, condemnation of the death penalty in the United States. For such critics the human rights movement was seen not as an effort to make the world more humane but as another form of Western cultural imperialism.

GLOBAL CULTURE

Because of changes in electronic technology, today political and economic events have almost instantaneous impact in all parts of the world. A global language, a global educational system, and global forms of artistic expression have all come into being. Trade, travel, and migration have made a common popular culture unavoidable. These changes have delighted and enriched some but angered others.

The Media and the Message

Cultural Imperialism

cultural imperialism Domination of one culture over another by a deliberate policy or by economic or technological superiority.

The fact that the most pervasive elements of global culture have their origins in the West raised concerns in many quarters about **cultural imperialism**. Critics complained that entertainment conglomerates were flooding the world's movie theaters and television screens with Western images and that goods catering to Western tastes but manufactured in countries with low production costs, like China and Indonesia, were flooding world markets. In this view, global marketing was especially insidious in trying to shape a world with a single Western outlook based on capitalist ideology, and at the same time suppressing or devaluing traditional cultures and alternative ideologies. As the leader of the capitalist world, the United States was seen as the primary culprit.

The pace of cultural globalization began to quicken during the economic recovery after World War II. The Hollywood films and American jazz recordings that had become popular in Europe and parts of Asia continued to spread. But the birth of electronic technology opened contacts with large numbers of people who could never have afforded to go to a movie or buy a record.

Electronic Media

The first step was the development of cheap transistor radios that could run on a couple of small batteries. Perfected by American scientists at Bell Telephone Laboratories in 1948, solid-state electronic transistors replaced power-hungry and less reliable electron tubes in radios and other devices. Just as tube radios had spread in Europe and America in the decades before the war, small portable transistor radios spread rapidly in parts of the world where homes lacked electricity.

Television, made possible by the electron-scanning gun invented in 1928, became widely available to Western consumers in the 1950s. In poorer parts of the world TVs were not common until the 1980s and 1990s, after mass production and cheap transistors made sets more affordable. Outside the United States, television broadcasting was usually a government monopoly at first, following the pattern of telegraph and postal service and radio broadcasting. Governments expected news reports and other programming to disseminate a unified national viewpoint.

However, government monopolies eroded as the high cost of television production opened up global markets for rebroadcasts of American soap operas, adventure series, and situation comedies. By the 1990s a global network of satellites brought privately owned television broadcasting to even remote areas of the world, and the VCR (videocassette recorder) provided an even greater variety of programs. In the following decade DVD players continued the trend. As a result of wider circulation of programming, people often became familiar with different dialects of English and other languages. People in Portugal who in the 1960s had found it difficult to understand Brazilian Portuguese became avid fans of Brazilian soap operas. And immigrants from Albania and North Africa often arrived in Italy with a command of Italian learned from Italian stations whose signals they could pick up at home.

Global Communication

CNN (Cable News Network) expanded its international market after becoming the most-viewed and informative news source during the 1991 Persian Gulf War, when it broadcast live from Baghdad. Other 24-hour news broadcasters followed this lead. Like CNN, they offered fundamentally American viewpoints. In response, Al-Jazeera, based in the Persian Gulf emirate of

Qatar, broadcast statements by Usama bin Laden from 2001 onward and offered video footage and interpretation that differed greatly from American coverage of the war in Iraq in 2003.

The Internet

The Internet, a linkage of academic, government, and business computers developed by the American Department of Defense in the 1960s, began to transform world culture in the early years of the twenty-first century. Personal computers proliferated in the 1980s, and with the establishment of the easy-to-use graphic interface of the World Wide Web in 1994, the number of Internet users skyrocketed. Myriad new companies formed to exploit "e-commerce," the commercial dimension of the Internet, and students were soon spending less time studying conventional books and more exploring the Web for information and entertainment. Blogs, or weblogs, offered a vehicle for anyone in the world to place his or her opinions, experiences, and creative efforts before anyone with access to a computer.

As had happened so often throughout history, technological developments had unanticipated consequences. Although the new telecommunications and entertainment technologies derived disproportionately from American invention, industry, and cultural creativity, Japan and other East Asian nations took the lead in manufacturing and refining electronic devices. Cellular mobile phones became increasingly used for taking and transmitting pictures and connecting to the Internet. Non-Western countries that had adopted telephones late and had limited networks of copper wire benefited most from the improved communication. In 2007 the United States ranked seventy-second in per capita cellular phone use.

global pop culture Popular cultural practices and institutions that have been adopted internationally, such as music, the Internet, television, food, and fashion.

The Spread of Pop Culture

For most of history, popular culture consisted of folk tales and highly localized styles of dress, cooking, music, and visual expression. Only the literate few had full access to the riches of a broader "great tradition," such as Confucianism, Islam, or Buddhism. In modern times, government school systems increased literacy rates but also promoted specifically national values and cultural tastes. Prescribed languages of instruction eroded the use and memory of local languages and traditions. In their place there arose **global pop culture**.

Initially, the content was heavily American. Singer Michael Jackson was almost as well known to the youth of Dar-es-Salaam (Tanzania) and Bangkok (Thailand) as to American fans. Businesses sought out worldwide celebrities like basketball star Michael Jordan and championship golfer Tiger Woods to endorse their products. American television programs, following in the path of American movies, acquired immense followings and inspired local imitations.

But the United States had no monopoly on global pop culture. Latin American soap operas, *telenovelas*, had a vast following in the Americas, eastern Europe, and elsewhere. Mumbai, India, long the world's largest producer of films, made or inspired more films for international

Japanese Adult Male Comic Book After World War II comic magazines emerged as a major form of publication and a distinctive product of culture in Japan. Different series are directed to different age and gender groups. Issued weekly and running to some three hundred pages in black and white, the most popular magazines sell as many copies as do major newsmagazines in the United States.

audiences, like the 2009 Academy Award–winning *Slumdog Millionaire*. And the martial arts filmmakers of Hong Kong saw their style flourish in high-budget international spectaculars like director Ang Lee's *Crouching Tiger, Hidden Dragon* (2000) and the *Matrix* trilogy (1999–2003), which relied heavily on Hong Kong fight choreographers.

Emerging Global Elite Culture

global elite culture At the beginning of the twenty-first century, the attitudes and outlook of well-educated, prosperous, Western-oriented people around the world, largely expressed in European languages, especially English.

While the globalization of popular culture has been criticized, cultural links across national and ethnic boundaries at a more elite level have generated little controversy. The end of the Cold War reopened intellectual and cultural contacts between former adversaries, making possible such things as Russian-American collaboration on space missions and extensive business contacts among former rivals. The English language, modern science, and higher education became the key elements of this **global elite culture**.

Decolonization and Language

The emergence of English as the first global language began with the British Empire's introduction of the language to far-flung colonies. After achieving independence in the wake of World War II, most former colonies chose to continue using English as an official language because it provided national unity and a link to the outside world that local languages could not. Countries that chose instead to make a local language official often found the decision counterproductive. Indian nationalists had pushed for Hindi to be India's official language, but they found that students taught in Hindi were unable to compete internationally because of poor knowledge of English. Sri Lanka, which had made Sinhala its official language in 1956, reversed itself after local reporters revealed in 1989 that prominent officials were sending their children to English-medium private schools.

English as a Global Language

While similar postcolonial language developments extended the reach of French, Spanish, and other European tongues, the use of English as a second language was greatly stimulated by the importance of the United States in postwar world affairs. After the collapse of Soviet domination, students in eastern Europe flocked to study English instead of Russian. Ninety percent of students in Cambodia (a former French colony) chose to study English, even though a Canadian agency offered a sizable cash bonus if they would study French. In the 1990s China made the study of English as a second language nearly universal from junior high school onwards.

English has become the language of choice for most international academic conferences, business meetings, and diplomatic gatherings. International organizations that provide equal status to many languages, such as the United Nations and the European Union, often conduct informal committee meetings in English. In cities throughout the world, signs and notices are commonly posted in the local language and in English. Writers from Africa and India have received high honors for novels written in English, as have Arab and Caribbean authors for works written in French. Nevertheless, world literature remains highly diverse in form and language.

Global Science

By contrast, science and technology have become standardized components of global culture. Though imperialism helped spread the Western disciplines of biology, chemistry, and physics around the world, their importance expanded even further after decolonization as students from newly independent nations sought to compete at an international level. Standardization of scientific terms, weights and measures, and computer codes underlay the worldwide expansion of commerce.

Global University Education

The third pillar of global elite culture, along with science and globalized languages, is the university. The structure and curricula of modern universities are nearly indistinguishable around the world, making student experiences similar across national boundaries. Instruction in the pure sciences varies little from place to place. Some doctoral science programs in American universities now enroll mostly students from non-Western countries. Standardization is nearly as common in applied sciences such as engineering and medicine and only slightly less so in the social sciences. Although the humanities preserve greater diversity in subject matter and approach, professors and students around the world pay attention to the latest literary theories and topics of historical interest.

While university subjects are taught in many languages, instruction in English is spreading rapidly. Because discoveries are often first published in English, advanced students in science, business, and international relations need to know that language to keep up with the latest developments. Many courses in northern European countries have long been offered in English, and elsewhere in Europe courses taught in English have facilitated the EU's efforts to encourage students to study outside their home countries. The small Arab sheikhdoms of the Persian Gulf have led the way in persuading American universities to open up local branches and graduate programs.

Enduring Cultural Diversity

Although protesters regularly denounce the "Americanization" of the world, a closer look suggests that cultural globalization is more complex. Just as English has spread widely as a second language, so global culture is primarily a second culture that dominates some contexts but does not displace other traditions. From this perspective, American music, fast food, and fashions are more likely to add to a society's options than to displace local culture.

Japan and Cultural Diversity

Japan first demonstrated that a country with a non-Western culture could industrialize effectively. Individuality was less valued in Japan than the ability of each person to fit into a group, whether as an employee, a member of an athletic team, or a student in a class. Moreover, the Japanese considered it unmannerly to directly contradict, correct, or refuse the request of another person. From a Western point of view, these Japanese customs seemed to discourage individual initiative and personality development and to preserve traditional hierarchies. Japanese women, for example, even though they often worked outside the home, responded only slowly to the American and European feminist advocacy of equality in economic and social relations. However, the Japanese approach to social relations was well suited to an industrial economy. The efficiency, pride in workmanship, and group solidarity of Japanese workers played a major role in transforming Japan from a defeated nation with a demolished industrial base in 1945 to an economic power by the 1980s.

As awareness of the economic impact of Japanese culture and society began to spread, it became apparent that Taiwan and South Korea, along with Singapore and Hong Kong (a British colony before being reunited with China in 1997), were developing dynamic industrial economies of their own. Today India and the People's Republic of China are following the same path without forsaking their national tastes and heritages.

The Future of Diversity and Dominance

This does not mean that the world's cultural diversity is secure. Every decade a number of minority languages cease to be spoken. Televised national ceremonies or performances for tourists may prevent folk customs and costumes from dying out, but they also tend to devitalize rituals that once had many local variations. While a century ago it was possible to recognize the nationality of people from their clothing and grooming, today most urban men dress the same the world over, although women's clothing shows greater variety. As much as one may regret the disappearance or commercialization of some folkways, most anthropologists would agree that change is characteristic of all healthy cultures. What doesn't change risks extinction.

SECTION REVIEW

- The global pervasiveness of Western culture has provoked charges of U.S. cultural imperialism.
- Technology such as radio, television, and the Internet has played a major role in the spread of Western culture since World War II.
- Technology has also contributed to the emergence of a global pop culture that blends a variety of cultural elements from different countries.
- A global elite culture has also developed combining the English language, science, and higher education.
- Despite globalizing forces, cultural diversity remains strong, if not completely secure.

KEY TERMS

globalization p. 904
World Trade Organization (WTO) p. 906
weapons of mass destruction p. 910

terrorism p. 913
Usama bin Laden p. 913
Universal Declaration of Human Rights p. 917

nongovernmental organizations (NGOs) p. 917
cultural imperialism p. 920

global pop culture p. 921
global elite culture p. 922

EBOOK AND WEBSITE RESOURCES

e Primary Sources

The Last Night

Declaration of Jihad Against Americans Occupying the Land of the Two Holy Mosques

e Interactive Maps

Map 34.1 Global Distribution of Wealth

Map 34.2 Regional Trade Associations, 2004

Map 34.3 World Religions

Plus flashcards, practice quizzes, and more. Go to: www.cengage.com/history/bulletearthpeople5e

SUGGESTED READING

Appadurai, Arjun. *Modernity at Large: Cultural Dimensions of Globalization*. 1996. Treats the interrelationships between high culture and popular culture.

Barber, Benjamin R. *Jihad vs. McWorld: How Globalism and Tribalism Are Reshaping the World*. 1995. A widely read attempt to describe the world at the turn of the millennium.

Bulliet, Richard W. *The Case for Islamo-Christian Civilization*. 2004. Takes issue with Samuel Huntington's "clash of civilizations" theory.

Chua, Amy. *World on Fire: How Exporting Free Market Democracy Breeds Ethnic Hatred and Global Instability*. 2003. A pessimistic perspective on globalization and world trade.

Devine, Carol, and Carol Rae Hansen. *Human Rights: The Essential Reference*. 1999. A standard work on the subject.

Friedman, Thomas L. *The Lexus and the Olive Tree*. 1999. A readable and influential analysis of alternative pathways to the future.

Hoffman, Bruce. *Inside Terrorism*, 2nd ed. 2006. A well-regarded work on a complex topic.

Huntington, Samuel P. *The Clash of Civilizations and the Remaking of the World Order*. 1996. A controversial thesis that Islam and the West are destined for irresolvable conflict.

Kaplan, Robert. *Of Paradise and Power: America and Europe in the New World Order*. 2002. Examines the growing gulf between the United States and Europe.

Kupchan, Charles A. *The End of the American Era: U.S. Foreign Policy and the Geopolitics of the Twenty-first Century*. 2002. A realist perspective on the world balance of power.

Mamdani, Mahmood. *Good Muslim, Bad Muslim: America, the Cold War, and the Roots of Terror*. 2004. Explores the origins of Muslim militancy in opposition to the West.

Moore, Mike. *A World Without Walls: Freedom, Development, Free Trade and Global Governance*. 2003. A view of the global economy from a former director-general of the World Trade Organization.

Norris, Pippa. *Rising Tide: Gender Equality and Cultural Change Around the World*. 2003. Surveys the condition of women.

Pennycock, Alistaire. *The Cultural Politics of English as an International Language*. 1994. The rise of English as a global means of communication.

Priest, Dana. *Mission: Waging War and Keeping Peace with America's Military*. 2003. A critique of American military policies in the twenty-first century.

NOTES

1. "Universal Declaration of Human Rights," in *Twenty-five Human Rights Documents* (New York: Center for the Study of Human Rights, Columbia University, 1994), 6.

INDEX

Class struggle, Marx on, 723. *See also* Socialism
Clawson, Augusta, 817
Clean Air Act (United States, 1970), 869, 897
Clemenceau, Georges, 774, 775
Clergy (priests): *See also* Bishops; Religion; Protestant Reformation, 452; colonial Latin America, 484, 487; French monarchy and, 466; French Revolution and, 590, 592, 593, 594; Mexican independence and, 634, 636 *and illus.*; Suez Canal and, 739; El Salvadorean death squads and, 876; Shi'ite, in Iran, 877–878; collapse of Communism and, 882
Climate and weather (climate change). *See also* Drought; Monsoons; Rainfall; Chinese, 568(*map*); Little Ice Age, 424, 561, 576; population and, 444–445 *and fig.*; global warming, 918 *and illus.*
Clinton, Hillary Rodham, 908(*illus.*)
Clipper ships, 703
Clive, Robert, 693–694
Clothing (costume): Ottoman, 543, 544(*illus.*); Russian fur, 554(*illus.*); Turkish fez (cap), 665, 666(*illus.*), 782; Ottoman reforms, 667(*illus.*); Zulu, 686(*illus.*); cotton, 722 *and illus.*; Gandhi and, 825, 826 *and illus.*; Islamic women, 877(*illus.*), 878
Cloth manufacture. *See* Textile industry and trade
Clove plantations, 692. *See also* Spice trade
CNN (Cable News Network), 920
Coal, industrialization and, 611; in Britain, 462, 610(*map*); child labor and, 623; coal gas, 622 *and illus.*; coking of, 615, 620; steam engines and, 615(*illus.*), 616–617, 714; pollution from, 719–720
Cochin, pepper trade of, 437
Cocoa (cacao), 509, 701, 759, 761, 836. *See also* Chocolate; in Africa, 746, 828, 860, *and illus.*
Code-breaking, in World War II, 809, 815 *and illus.*
Coffee, 509, 537, 567, 701, 759, 761; in Mocha, 539; in Brazil, 500, 623, 647, 656; in Ceylon, 694; in Java, 551; in East Africa, 828, 859; in Colombia, 860
Coins (coinage): *See also* Currency; Portuguese gold, 429; Chinese copper, 562; Ottoman gold, 668
Coke-iron, 615, 620
Colbert, Jean Baptiste, 462, 472, 516
Cold War (Bipolar world; 1946–1991), 846–870. *See also* Superpowers, Cold War; Asian transformation, 880–881; capitalism and communism in, 849–852; China and, 866, 880, 881; chronology (1945–1975), 849; Cuba in, 846(*illus.*), 847, 855, 861–864; decolonization and nation-building, 847–848, 849, 856–860; eastern Europe and, 850–851, 852; Islamic Revolutions and, 877–880; Japan and, 865–866, 880; Korean War and, 852–853; Middle East, 867, 868(*map*); proxy wars in, 845; race for nuclear supremacy in, 855–856; Third World and, 864–865 *and illus.*; United Nations and, 848–849; Vietnam War and, 853 *and illus.*, 855; environmental concerns, 869–870; Latin America and, 860–864, 874–877; collapse of Soviet bloc, 882–883 *and illus.*; crisis in Soviet Union, 882; end of (1989–1991), 882–883

Collectivization of agriculture: in Soviet Union, 796–798 *and illus.*, 843; in China, 866
Colleges and universities: European, 463; in colonial Americas, 483, 484; conservative repression in, 602; Glasgow, 616; in Istanbul, 665; in Russia, 673; in India, 699; engineering, 715; in Middle East, 783; for women, 721; English language in, 922–923
Cologne, bombing of (1942), 814
Colombia, 641; independence of, 578(*map*), 634, 635(*map*), 640; Panama and, 759; coffee in, 860
Colonies (colonialism). *See also* British Empire; Decolonialization; Expansion; French colonies; Imperialism; New Imperialism; Plantations; *and specific colonies and colonial powers*; Viking, 424; of Madagascar, 422 *and map*; Brazil, 437; Pacific Islands, 420–421 *and illus.*, 422(*map*); Amerindian, in West Indies, 424; Philippines, 431; legitimacy of, 584; European, in Indian Ocean, 549(*map*), 702(*map*); European, in Africa, 745(*map*); Japanese, 730(*map*), 735, 736; European, in Asia, 754(*map*)
Columbian exchange, 478–480
Columbus, Christopher, 429–430, 431, 432, (*map*); in Caribbean region, 428(*map*), 430, 438
Comanche people, 480, 645
Commercial famines, 842
Committee of Public Safety (France), 594
Common Market (Europe), 851
Common Sense (Paine), 588
Commonwealth of Independent States, 883
Communication: *See also* Mass communication; Telegraph; in Japan, 730; cryptography and, 815 *and illus.*; radio, 788, 837, 920; computers and, 894, 921; global economy and, 893; television, 920–921
Communism (communist countries): appeasement of Nazi Germany and, 804; fascist fears of, 802, 803; in Indonesia, 857; in Vietnam, 830, 853; rivalry with capitalism, 849–852; in Cuba, 864; collapse of, 882–883, 885(*map*)
Communist Manifesto (Marx and Engels), 723, 724–725
Communist Party (China). *See also* China, People's Republic of; Mao Zedong; Guomindang and, 780, 805, 806, 807–808 *and map*; Long March (1934–1935) and, 805–806, 807(*map*); peasants and, 805–806, 813; victory of, 813–814; Red Guard purges and, 866 *and illus.*
Communist Party (Soviet Union), 778. *See also* Soviet Union; agricultural collectivization and, 843; Russian civil war and (1918), 775; purge trials and, 798; Stalin's industrialization and, 796; Gorbachev's reforms and, 822
Companies. *See also* Business; chartered, 506, 515, 516; in colonial North America, 492; insurance, 459, 516, 611, 668; joint-stock, 459, 494, 515, 547, 549(*map*), 611, 672; Japanese, 557–558, 731; shipping lines, 714; European, in Africa, 828; foreign owned, in Mexico, 832, 835; foreign-owned, in China, 881; e-commerce and, 921
Compass, 426
Computers, 894, 921

Comte, Auguste, 625
Concentration camps, 803, 816 *and illus.*
Concordat of 1801 (France), 598
Condition of the Working Class in England (Engels), 723
Condorcanqui, José Gabriel, 499
Condorcet, Marie-Jean-Antoine, 708
Confederate States of America, 642–643
Confederation of 1867 (Canada), 638
Conference on Security and Cooperation in Europe (CSCE), 855
Confucianism: in Korea, 556; in Qing China, 563, 566(*illus.*), 677, 681; ancestor worship in, 675
Congo, 847, 860, 884; palm oil in, 761
Congo Free State (Belgian Congo), 745, 745(*map*), 746; women in, 750–751
Congo River, 690, 692, 747(*illus.*)
Congress of People's Deputies (Soviet Union), 883
Congress of Vienna (1814–1815), 601–602
Congress Party (India), 888, 910. *See also* Indian National Congress
Congress (United States), 650; League of Nations and, 775; Central America and, 876; genocide convention ratified by, 917
Conquistadors, 438–441, 481, 487
Conscription (military draft): in Ottoman Empire, 665; in Japan, 730; in Nazi Germany, 803; in China, 807; in United States, 851
Consent of the governed, 584
Conservatism: Congress of Vienna and, 601–602; Napoleon's defeat and, 598, 601–602; nationalism and, 726; following World War I, 776; great powers and, 731, 732, 733; Christian, in United States, 912
Constantinople, 766, 781, 783. *See also* Istanbul; Ottoman conquest of (1453), 532, 569
Constitutionalists (Mexico), 833–834
Constitutional monarchy: in England, 465, 637; in France, 592, 602; in Brazil, 636–637; in Italy, 726; in Russia, 734
Constitutions, 632; French, 592, 595; Haitian, 581; Chilean, 637; Latin American, 638–640; Ottoman Empire, 670, 766; Prussian, 603; Mexico, 636, 834, 861; Venezuelan, 634, 637; Brazilian, 636, 837; Kenya, 859; Iraqi, 911
Constitution (United States), 589–590, 637; Convention (1787), 590; abolition of slavery and, 647; Amendments to, 647, 786; census in, 708; regional interests in, 641
Construction: *See also* Architecture; Engineering; in India under British rule, 824(*illus.*)
Consultative Group on International Agricultural Research, 850
Consumers (consumption), 897; cotton clothing, 722; European, 458, 566, 852
Continental Congress, 584, 588, 589
Contraceptives. *See* Birth control
Contracts of indenture, 705–706. *See also* Indentured labor
Contra War (Nicaragua), 876, 879
Cook, James, 703
Cooke, William, 618
Copernicus, Nicolas, 455–456
Copper, 558, 573, 616; Chilean, 656, 860, 874; in colonial Africa, 742, 747, 802
Copper coinage, in China, 562

Coral Sea, Battle of (1944), 811 *and map*
Le Corbusier (Charles-Edouard Jeanneret), 790
Córdoba (Argentina), 489
Corn. *See* Maize (corn)
Corn Laws (1815, Britain), 602, 626
Cornwallis, Charles, 588, 589*(map)*
Corporations. *See also* Business; Japanese *zaibatsu*, 731, 779, 880; American, in Cuba, 863; transnational, 652, 878–879, 894–895
Corruption: in Africa, 860; in China, 562, 568, 661, 674, 679, 735, 780, 808; in South Vietnam, 853; in Cuba, 861; in Japan, 880
Cortés, Hernán, 425*(map)*, 438–439
Cosmology, Amerindian, 484
Cosmopolitanism: in Indian Ocean trade, 436; Ottoman, 535; in Istanbul, 544, 665
Cossacks (Russia), 570, 572
Cotton clothing, 722 *and illus.*
Cotton (cotton industry). *See also* Spinning; Textiles; Caribbean, 438; Ottoman, 539; Chinese, 568; slave labor in, 647; Brazilian, 500; British, 606*(illus.)*, 611, 694, 697; Egyptian, 626, 668, 688, 745, 746, 759; Indian, 458, 516, 545, 548, 614, 626, 694, 696, 722, 759; in United States, 615, 623, 647, 759; mechanization of, 614–615, 626; African trade and, 746; Central Asian, 753
Cotton gin, 615
Council of Trent (1545–1563), 452
Counter Enlightenment, 584–585
Counter Reformation, 452, 455
Coureurs de bois, 496
Craftsmen (artisans): Portuguese ships, 430; Dutch, 458; Iranian guilds, 542; slave, in sugar plantations, 510; Ottoman, 538*(illus.)*, 543; Japanese, 557, 558 *and illus.*
Credit. *See* Loans (lending)
Creek peoples, 641, 644
Creoles, in Latin America, 487, 489, 500; independence and, 632
Crete, 536, 766
Crimean Turks, 569
Crimean War (1853–1856), 667–668, 672, 766; modernization of warfare in, 668, 671; nursing in, 669 *and illus.*
Croatia, 883
Crompton, Samuel, 614
Cromwell, Oliver, 465, 500
Crossbows, 423
Crouching Tiger, Hidden Dragon (film), 922
Crowther, Samuel Adjai, 691, 751
Crusades, Portuguese, 429
Cruzado (coin), 429
Cryptography, 814, 815 *and illus.*
Crystal Palace (London), 616
Cuba, 438, 860. *See also* Castro, Fidel; abolition of slavery in, 647, 648, 704; Chinese immigrants in, 649, 650; slave trade in, 507, 518, 690; Spain and, 507, 647, 648, 756, 758; sugar production in, 647, 656, 704, 758, 860, 861; United States and, 759, 861, 863, 864, 874; Guantanamo Bay prison, 918
Cuban missile crisis (1962), 847, 855, 864
Cuban Revolution (1959), 846*(illus.)*, 861–864, 874
Cudjoe (maroon leader), 514*(illus.)*
Cults: *See also* Religions; of domesticity, 624; of cleanliness, 788; of modernity, 787, 788; of Gandhi, 825
Cultural imperialism, 896, 920

Cultural relativism, 787
Cultural Revolution (China), 866 *and illus.*
Culture (cultural factors): *See also* Art and artists; Folk culture; Literature; Society; Westernization; *and specific cultures*; women and, 463; Latin American, 481, 484; Chinese, 568*(map)*; Japanese samurai and, 560; American, and immigrants, 651; New Imperialism and, 740–742, 751–752; Mexican, 833; global, 920–923; fast food, 896 *and illus.*; media and message, 920–921; pop, 921–922 *and illus.*; elite, and English language, 922–923; enduring diversity in, 923
Currency: *See also* Monetary system; paper, 562, 587, 593; Ottoman reform, 668; British pound, 717; German hyperinflation and, 777; in Guomindang (China), 813 *and illus.*; speculation in, and Asia crisis, 881; launch of Euro, 904
Curzon, Lord George, 695, 824
Custer, George Armstrong, 645
Cuzco (Inca), 439, 441
Cyrillic alphabet, 671
Czechoslovakia (Czechs), 775, 776*(map)*; breakup of, 885*(map)*; Nazi Germany and, 804; Soviet Union and, 852; fall of Communism in, 883

Dachau death camp, 816*(illus.)*
Da Gama, Christopher, 433
Da Gama, Vasco, 423*(illus.)*, 428*(map)*, 429, 433; in India, 434–435; ships of, 430 *and illus.*
Dagestan, 671
Dahomey, slave trade in, 521
Daimyo (Japanese warlord), 556, 558, 559, 728. *See also* Tokugawa shogunate
Dakar, Senegal, 832
Dalai Lama, 563
Damascus, 663, 783
Dams: hydroelectric, 716, 791, 865, 866; irrigation schemes and, 746, 791, 865
D'Annunzio, Gabriele, 795
Darby, Abraham, 615
Darby, Abraham, III, 615–616
Darfur, genocide in, 910, 913*(illus.)*
Darwin, Charles, 731–732
Darwin, Erasmus, 613
Date Masamune, 559
Davar, Cowasjee Nanabhoy, 626
D-day (World War II, 1944), 812
Death penalty: *seppuku* (ritual suicide), 561; guillotine, 594, 595 *and illus.*; ended, in France, 602; forced suicide, 661; in United States, 920
Death squads: in Brazil, 874; in El Salvador, 876
De Beers Consolidated, 748
Debt. *See* Foreign debt (international loans); War debt
Debt peonage, in Mexico, 833, 834
Deccan Plateau, drought and famine in, 842
Decembrist revolt (Russia, 1825), 672
Declaration of Independence (1776, United States), 584, 588, 593, 632, 647, 917
Declaration of the Rights of Man and the Citizen (1789, France), 592–593, 632, 917
Decolonization (1947–1990), 847–848. *See also* Independence; of Africa, 857, 858*(map)*, 859–860; chronology (1947–1971), 849; Latin

America and, 860–864; nation building and, 856–860; new nations in Southern Asia, 856–857, 858*(map)*; United Nations and, 849
Deforestation: in England and France, 461–462; in Americas, 484; for charcoal, 461–462, 484, 615; for sugar plantations, 510, 656; in China, 568; in British India, 696, 755, 761, 822; in Indonesia, 755; in Southeast Asia, 755; railroads and, 714, 761; World War II and, 818; food production and, 897; in Brazilian rainforest, 895*(illus.)*
De Gaulle, Charles, 859–860
Delhi, 545, 695, 891*(table)*; durbar pageants in, 696–697, 698*(illus.)*; as capital of India, 824
Democracy (democratic reforms): colonial North America, 493; in United States, 590; French Revolution and, 590, 595; socialism in India and, 657; in South Africa, 884; Chinese protests and, 881; globalization and, 909–910
Demographic transition, 885–886. *See also* Migrations; Population; Urbanization; (1960s–1990s), 886
Demonstrations. *See* Protests; Strikes
Deng Xiaoping (China), 881
Denmark, 851; astronomy in, 456 *and illus.*; Nazi invasion of, 808
De Porres, Saint Martin, 483*(illus.)*
Depression (economic): Ming China, 562; French Revolution and, 592; (1870s), 717; Great (1930s), 799–802, 838
Developing nations (Third World). *See also* Nonindustrial world; Cold War and, 864–865 *and illus.*; population growth in, 886, 888, 890; rural-to-urban migration in, 892; emigration from, 892–893; environmental degradation in, 893, 897, 899
Devil, witch-hunts and, 455
Devshirme system, 535, 539
De Witt Clinton locomotive, 617*(illus.)*
Dhaka, Bangladesh, 891*(table)*
Dhows (ships), 422, 434, 436
Diagne, Blaise, 832
Diallo, Ayuba Suleiman, 526–527 *and illus.*
Diamonds, 500, 742; mining, in Africa, *(illus.)*
Dias, Bartolomeu, 429
Díaz, Porfirio, 631
Dictatorship. *See also* Authoritarianism; populist, in France, 595, 598; in Venezuela, 641; in China (Guomindang), 780; in Soviet Union, 796 (*See also* Stalin, Joseph); in Latin America, 644, 802, 874; in Europe, 802 (*See also* Hitler, Adolph; Mussolini, Benito); in Indonesia, 857; populist, in Argentina, 838–839 *and illus.*; in Mexico, 835; in Iraq, 879; in Congo, 884
Diderot, Denis, 582
Diem, Ngo Dinh, 853
Diplomacy: *See also* Politics; and warfare, in Europe, 468–469; Chinese trade and, 567
Directory (France), 595
Dirty War against terrorism (Argentina), 875
Disease. *See also* Epidemics; Medicine; in colonial North America, 392; Amerindians and, 431, 438, 439, 447, 478–479; diphtheria, 478; influenza, 478, 774, 786; malaria, 478, 566, 755 *and illus.*; measles, 478; pulmonary plague, 478; dysentery, 505, 512, 520, 842; slaves and, 478, 505, 512–513, 520; smallpox, 438, 439, 478, 505, 520,